Introduction to Psychology
An Integrated Approach

The authors are lecturers in psychology at the University of
Manchester.

Peter Lloyd, MA (Dundee), PhD (Edinburgh), worked as a
research associate at the University of Edinburgh (1969–72) and
as lecturer in psychology at the University of Bradford before
joining the University of Manchester in 1974. He has published
articles on child language and communication and is the author
with M.C. Beveridge of *Information and Meaning in Child
Language* (1981).

Andrew Mayes, BA (Oxford), DPhil (Oxford), lectured in
psychology at the University of Leicester (1970–7) before going
to the University of Manchester. He has published articles on
memory and cognitive failure, edited and contributed to *Memory
in Animals and Humans* (1983) and *Sleep Mechanisms and
Functions in Humans and Animals* (1983), and is the editor with
S.G. Lee of *Dreams and Dreaming* (1973).

Antony Manstead, BSc (Bristol), DPhil (Sussex), lectured in social
psychology at the University of Sussex before joining the University
of Manchester in 1976. As well as articles on emotion and social
psychology, he is author with G.R. Semin of *The Accountability
of Conduct* (1983). Since 1983 he has been editor of the *British
Journal of Social Psychology*.

Peter Meudell, BSc (Hull), MSc (Manchester), PhD (Manchester),
has lectured at the University of Manchester since 1967. His
published articles are on the neuropsychology of memory and
related topics.

Hugh Wagner, BSc (Wales), PhD (Wales), has lectured in
psychology at the University of Manchester since 1969. He is the
author of published articles on perception and emotion.

Introduction to
Psychology

An Integrated Approach

Peter Lloyd, Andrew Mayes
A.S.R. Manstead, P.R. Meudell, H.L. Wagner

This edition published by Diamond Books 1998
Diamond Books is an imprint of HarperCollins*Publishers*
77-85 Fulham Palace Road
London W6 85B

First published in 1984 by Fontana Paperbacks
8 Grafton Street, London W1X 3LA
Second impression, with corrections, published by
Fontana Press in 1986
Third impression, 1987
Fourth impression, 1990

ISBN 0 261 67066 2

Figures by Illustra
Set in Linotron Times

Printed and bound in Great Britain by
Caledonian International Book Manufacturing, Glasgow

Contents

3. Perception

4. Consciousness and Attention

5. The Varieties of Learning and Memory: Their Simpler Forms

Boxes

Figures

Tables

Preface

What is the justification for bringing out another introductory text in a field that is already crowded? One reason is that enthusiasts for a subject like to share their enthusiasm with others, particularly those who are coming to the topic for the first time. But there is another and better reason. We believe the approach we have adopted is different and valuable and warrants an entry into the lists. The book's structure grew out of the belief that psychology should be seen as an integrated subject rather than a collection of disparate disciplines held together loosely by a common thread called mind. The collective view is perpetrated in most academic courses where the subject is taught under headings such as cognitive psychology, social psychology, physiological psychology, developmental psychology and clinical psychology. These purport to be the major branches of the subject, representing different interests and emphases.

It is not only that the subject is divided up in this way but also that the individuals who teach these courses get labelled (and label themselves) as one or other of the categories – A is a cognitive psychologist, B is a developmental psychologist, and so on. Hence the subject is taught in courses that run along parallel tracks with only occasional junctions or crossing points, and because assessment tends also to be on a course-by-course basis a pigeon-hole mentality is encouraged. And yet, judging by the advice offered to students by their academic mentors, this is not what is wanted. Students are exhorted not to see the subject as made up of independent, unrelated entities. They are told to make connections between the different parts and to try to see the essential unity in the subject. This seems to us admirable advice but how much help are students given to enable them to achieve this noble aim? In our experience, very little (and the authors of this book are all active

teachers and as culpable as anyone else), which leaves one won-
dering, is this out of indolence or is it actually too difficult?
Whatever the reason, we set out in this volume with the avowed
intent of making integration something more than a pious wish.

This target could have no chance of being met unless a group of
people were involved, since there no longer exist individuals who
are expert in all aspects of the discipline. However, if the result
were not to be a series of linked perspectives, the group would have
to work as a team, which almost certainly meant that they must be
colleagues in the same department, able to meet regularly to pool
their collective knowledge. Our model, therefore, was to take the
whole person and examine the properties and processes that
typically define such an entity. The list we finally drew up can be
found on the Contents pages. You will not find sections devoted to
traditional approaches like social, developmental, cognitive and
physiological psychology (although we separately subscribe to
these approaches). This is because we believe that these perspectives, along with others such as clinical, comparative and applied,
inform *all* aspects of human functioning. Nevertheless, subjects
which often appear in psychology syllabuses – such as 'perception'
and 'personality' – appear as chapter headings in this book. But we
have tried to eschew narrow approaches to any of these topics.
Thus, a central human property such as memory would traditionally receive a cognitive treatment. In our approach the contribution of cognitive psychology to our understanding of memory is
fully acknowledged but we also show that other branches of psychology have informed our understanding of this process. Memory
changes with age, it breaks down, it has a physiological basis, and it
is affected by the social situations in which it is used. A complete
picture of memory, therefore – one that draws on all the knowledge
that psychology is currently able to offer – should go beyond the
orthodox approach of cognitive or experimental psychology.

In taking on the task which academic psychologists usually avoid,
we have become aware of the enormity of the undertaking. It is easy
to say things like 'relate', 'integrate' and 'make connections' but it is
awesome in practice. One problem, for example, is the question of
where to place different pieces of knowledge. Person perception,
for instance, might be discussed in at least four chapters: Perception, Communication, Social Cognition or Interpersonal Processes.

Since many topics are like this, we have had to make decisions as to where to site the main treatment. But we have not been absolutist about this. In line with our integrative philosophy, we try to avoid the impression that a topic belongs exclusively in one place if it is evidently not the case. This means that a certain amount of repetition may be detected. We regard this as a virtue rather than a vice and an inevitable consequence of trying to break down the artificial divisions which usually characterize the subject. Nevertheless, we do not pretend that we have fully achieved the goal we set ourselves; we do, however, claim that we have come closer to bridging subject areas than is traditionally accomplished in psychology textbooks.

All teachers of a complex subject have to be aware of the potential amount of material from which they must abstract their simplified picture. The worry takes two forms. First, there is the concern that in trying to give an overview of the field one can simplify to the level of distortion. It is not just that every chapter in this book has been given full text treatment elsewhere in its own right but that most of the topics within the chapters have major works devoted uniquely to them. Perhaps it is enough to be aware of this danger, since it is inevitable that a relatively short introductory text will sometimes be inaccurate *in detail*, but we have striven never to simplify to the point of misleading the reader. Even if we do not always paint the whole picture, the portrait we offer is always recognizable as a proper likeness of the subject. The role of the guide to an academic discipline is to excite sufficient interest for the student to build on the foundations that are provided. To this end we have endeavoured to make the subject attractive and to give more thought than usual to the suggestions for Further Reading. We hope that teachers as well as readers will find these annotated bibliographies useful.

The second worry relates not to the material that is left on the cutting-room floor after editing but (to continue the cinematographic metaphor) to the film that is never even developed. With hundreds of new research studies being reported in journals, proceedings and books each month, it is impossible to keep apace even in fairly restricted research fields, let alone the wider discipline. So the really formidable worry is the amount of material that does not get considered in the first place. Again, it serves no purpose to allow such considerations to frighten one into a state of resigned impotence. We can at least comfort ourselves with the thought that with five minds and five different specialisms at work we have that much more chance of covering the huge terrain without letting major developments pass us by.

A book like this does not materialize without help and cooperation and I would like to conclude by acknowledging this. First, I would like to thank my fellow authors. Academics are busy people, and when I put the vision of this book to my colleagues I pointed out that it would not simply be a question of going away to write individual chapters: the success of the book would depend on getting outside one's specialism, on being receptive to the ideas of others and on a commitment to a series of discussions from which the shape of each chapter would emerge. Happily the approach was forthcoming and I am gratified. Others have also helped in a number of different ways: by reading and commenting on one or more chapters, by doing library searches, by checking references, typing and proofreading. We gratefully acknowledge the help of Margaret Barrow, Rachel Calam, John Churcher, Guy Csonka, John Edwards, Catherine FitzMaurice, Julie Hampson, Sylvia Lavalle, Virginia Lloyd, Lesley Meudell, Melissa Monty, Don O'Boyle, Brian Parkinson and Gun Semin.

P L
Manchester, 1983

1. The Nature of Psychology

1. The Nature of Psychology

Some aims and misapprehensions

What makes us laugh and why do people have different senses of humour? How can we improve our everyday memories? Why do we sometimes see and hear things that are not there? What makes some people leaders and others followers? How do people develop their political attitudes? Why do we often lose track of conversations at cocktail parties? What effect does alcohol have on sexual behaviour? Can intelligence be increased if children are brought up in particular ways? Why do people have 'nervous breakdowns'? Do animals have consciousness or are they qualitatively different from humans when it comes to mental powers? Do we inherit our personalities or are they the products of our unique experiences?

All of these questions are representative of the kinds that psychologists ask, and most people would agree that they are interesting. Yet many beginning students become disillusioned with psychology. Why does this happen? Part of the answer is illustrated by a common experience of professional psychologists. If such people should reveal at a party what they do, the response is almost invariably to the effect that the psychologist must know what his or her conversant is thinking and why. In fact, it is implied that they know more about what their conversants are thinking and why than the conversants themselves. Thus, some people become disillusioned with psychology because they start with a serious misapprehension of what the subject is about. Psychology is not just concerned with people's deeper and often unconscious motivations for thinking and acting in the way they do. This is only one of the subject's many topics – the one in which the great psychiatrist Freud made his major contributions. As the illustrative questions that open this chapter indicate, psychology is also concerned with many other phenomena. It studies the development of and the mechanisms which underlie how we perceive, attend, think, remember, learn, and use and understand language. It studies how our emotions and motivations develop and are controlled, and how we behave in social situations as well as how social situations control us. It also involves studying behaviour in other animals, both for its own sake and because of the light that may be thrown on human psychology.

Not all tyro psychologists are, however, misinformed about the nature of the subject and some of these still become disillusioned. There are other reasons why this may happen. First, the beginner may be aware of the kinds of phenomena that psychologists seek to explain, but have an unclear or narrow idea about what such an explanation should be like. This is because psychological phenomena can be described and explained at several different levels. The phenomenon of humour may illustrate this point. What causes people to experience humour? At the most obvious level, the answer to this question will require an analysis of the stimulating conditions that lead people to laugh or chortle. Thus, it is often said that the perception of an incongruity causes a humorous response ('I'm having friends for lunch.' 'Friends? How will you cook them?'). This explanation is likely to leave us unsatisfied, however, even if it is correct and completely specifies the conditions that elicit humorous responses. We are left with the more basic puzzle of what function such a response to incongruity can serve and, relatedly, why it ever came into existence. To answer these questions, we need to know what kinds of roles humour plays in social groups and whether anything like it exists among our near relations, the primates. It would also be helpful to know what brain mechanisms control humorous responses and how we respond physiologically when we find something funny. Finally, it would be valuable to see how humour develops (obviously the ability to perceive incongruities is increased through learning as we grow older, but perhaps the basic response is not learned) and what social and physiological factors modulate it. Only when we can explain humour in terms of its social and physiological functions, in terms of the brain mechanisms that control it, and in terms of its development history can we be said to have a full understanding of the phenomenon. This full understanding will require a comprehensive theory that links the different levels of explanation.

The nature of psychological explanations will be discussed in more detail later in this chapter. It is clear, however, that the descriptions of the eliciting antecedent conditions (such as incongruity in the case of humour) are not adequate explanations for psychological phenomena. This relates to the second reason for the tyro's potential disillusionment. Psychology is a young science which is still at the stage of trying to ask appropriate questions, and this can leave the student unsatisfied. With the example of humour, the task is to identify the source of our puzzlement and then to pose questions and answers which will resolve this puzzlement. The reason for the puzzlement with humour is fairly clear: it is because, unlike fear and anger, humour serves no perceptible function. This analysis leads to several clear questions. In the past, however, psychologists have asked certain very general questions that are now believed to be unanswerable or meaningless. One of these is illustrated by the last question in this chapter's first paragraph. It is not sensible to ask questions such as how much of my personality is determined by heredity and how much by experience. The reasons for this are discussed in the next chapter. In brief, heredity depends on genes in the fertilized egg, but the expression of these depends from the moment of conception on interactions with the environment. It is fruitful to ask how specific environmental factors interact with the genes, but not what the *relative* contributions of genes and environment are in one individual.

The youth of scientific psychology is not the sole reason why some psychologists, as well as novices, still ask the wrong questions. Part of the reason also lies in psychology's peculiarly fragmented and contentious history. From its inception, there have been fundamental disagreements about the subject matter that psychologists should be studying and how they should be carrying out their inquiries. Some researchers believed that the central subject matter of psychology is consciousness, its content and activities. This, they believed, could be studied directly by analysing reports of introspections. Others thought that consciousness comprises unreliable epiphenomena and that psychologists should pay attention only to external observable behaviour. The latter, behaviourist group was dominant in the West for many years in the middle of this century. As a result, psychology almost came to be the study of learning in the rat (as the representative of mammalian species), and such processes as attention (relevant to the cocktail-party problem) were eschewed because they were seen as subjective and unreliable. This meant that for a long time most scientific psychologists ignored questions that were of central importance to the understanding of mind. Instead, they addressed issues that are now seen as trivial or obvious. An outline of this polemical history is provided in the next section.

Youth and a contentious history have, then, led to inadequately formulated questions, but even when questions have been well formulated they have usually not been answered with any degree of completeness. This is a further source of disillusionment for the student. Many psychologists are told that their work extends little or not at all beyond the bounds of common sense knowledge. For example, psychologists have shown that mnemonic tricks, typically using visual imagery, can help improve everyday memory. But this knowledge has, in general form, been available since the time of the Greek poet-singer Simonides two and a half thousand years ago. These comments do not apply to the more biological aspects of psychology where knowledge is dependent on the use of very recently developed techniques. Even so, biological knowledge has not yet revolutionized our understanding of the workings of mind. Only when psychologists become able to explain thinking and remembering in terms of their underlying processes will knowledge proceed substantially beyond the common sense level. There are exciting signs that the subject is beginning to develop in just this way, going beyond the state of systematized common sense.

The diverse origins of psychology have led to an historical development in which the same psychological processes are analysed in somewhat different ways by different groups of people who have engaged in very little cross-talk with each other. Although this fragmentation of the subject has slightly decreased in recent years, it has been another source of disillusionment among tyro psychologists. For example, the nature of thought has been examined by several distinct groups of workers. Late in the nineteenth century, many psychologists tried to analyse how they solved problems by looking into the contents of their minds. Others have studied the way in which animals solved problems in the wild or in the laboratory. A third group is interested in how mental disorders, such as schizophrenia, disturb thinking. A fourth group concentrates on how thinking changes and becomes more effective in the course of development. A fifth group is most interested in finding out how thinking is affected by social influences. Finally, other people are concerned with how to measure thinking abilities and with finding ways to improve these measured abilities in applied situations. Very little integration of these groups' findings yet exists, and this lack of integration is reflected in standard textbook treatments. Such treatments tend to divide the subject into several branches, shown in Table 1.1 (their origins and nature are further described later in this chapter). The authors of this book believe that in order to understand psychological processes fully, each process must be considered from the multiple perspectives provided by the different branches of the subject. Only in this way can an integrated theory be developed. An integrated approach to the central psychological processes of perception, motivation, emotion, attention, learning, memory, thinking and verbal behaviour is therefore one of the aims of this book, and its rationale will be considered later in this chapter.

Historical origins

Psychology began as an institutionalized science in 1879, when Wilhelm Wundt founded the first psychological laboratory in Leipzig. His initiative was quickly followed by other German and American universities, and, somewhat more slowly, by Britain. These early laboratories used experiments mainly to explore the properties of sensory perception, feeling, thought and memory, all of which Wundt believed were closely dependent on physiological processes in the brain. Although the recognition of psychology as an experimental science may be dated from 1879, individual scientists, such as Wundt's great teacher Helmholtz, had earlier experimented on related problems in sensory perception. The whole movement had also been influenced by the philosophical tradition of the British Associationists, which began in the seventeenth century. This prescientific school of thought had tried to show that mental activity comprised simple components and that complex mental states were created by the association of these components. Its methods were not experimental.

Table 1.1 **The branches of psychology**

Branch	Cognitive	Physiological	Social	Developmental
Subject matter	The mind – processes such as perception, thinking and remembering.	How the brain controls the mind and behaviour.	How social factors and processes influence the mind and behaviour.	How the mind develops and changes with age – the factors that cause these changes.
Historical origins	Formally with the founding of Wundt's laboratory in 1879. Earlier the mind had been analysed philosophically by the British empiricists.	Late eighteenth-century with the ideas of the phrenologists – ideas that were tested on the brain in the nineteenth century.	Although the earliest experimental studies date back to the 1890s, the field began to develop its own identity in the 1930s and to flourish after the Second World War.	Developed in the twentieth century by the Swiss psychologist Piaget and the Americans Hall and Baldwin.
Influences	Since 1945, many ideas have been introduced from the information processing sciences of cybernetics and computing.	Genetics and evolutionary theory have played roles, but most ideas have come from basic brain sciences.	Diverse influences range from cognitive psychology through sociology to social anthropology. At present the influence of cognitive psychology is prominent.	Major influences are psychoanalytic theory and cognitive psychology. Ideas from social, comparative and physiological psychology are having increasing impact.
Comments	The central discipline of psychology, which draws heavily on the other branches. For many years it was inadequately valued because of the dominance of dogmatic behaviourism.	Expanding explosively because of the current very rapid growth of the brain sciences. Psychological theory, however, lags behind.	Interest has swung away from the study of groups and interpersonal processes towards the study of individual social cognition. The emphasis on information-processing is less marked in European social psychology.	The ideas of Piaget are still very important but have been exposed to much detailed criticism based on empirical research. There is renewed interest in the role of social and cultural factors.

Psychometrics	Comparative	Psychopathology	Applied
The measurement of individual differences both of mental abilities and personality.	Similarities between human and animal minds, with an emphasis on evolution.	The classification, analysis and treatment of mental disorders.	The application of psychological knowledge to practical problems.
Mental testing began in the late nineteenth century but developed rapidly in response to the manpower needs of two world wars.	In the ideas that came from Darwin's theory of evolution, published in 1859.	From nineteenth-century medical work on hypnosis or mesmerism and, later, the seminal influence of Freud.	In the twentieth century from the demands of industry, health, education and the armed forces.
Constructs like 'intelligence' and 'personality' are increasingly affected by ideas from mainstream psychology.	Evolution remains the guiding theory but there is a strong influence from physiological and cognitive psychology.	Both physiological and cognitive psychology have been and are very important.	Influences come from all the other disciplines but particularly from cognitive psychology.
More attention is now being paid to the analysis of mental abilities and personality. Without such analysis measurement is purposeless.	When behaviourism dominated few species were studied. From the 1930s the European ethologists have revived interest in observing many different species in their natural habitats.	The initial boost came from the 'depth' psychologies of Freud and Jung. In more recent years, there has been more stress on the role of brain dysfunction and maladaptive learning.	Applied contributions have as yet not been great and this may be a source of disillusionment. The prospects, however, are good. For example, treatments developed by clinical psychologists are improving and already are effective for some

The science that Wundt helped create aimed to explain the mechanisms of what would now be called cognitive activity and motivation – processes such as perception, memory, thinking, emotions and feelings. These processes constitute together what Hebb (1980) calls **mind**. Wundt and his followers believed that only the simpler activities of mind were open to experimental study because only they are largely conditioned by physiological changes. Although he wrote extensively on the social influences which affect our minds (in the ten volumes of his *Volkerpsychologie*), he did not believe that such influences were amenable to experimental investigation. In fact, social psychology did not come into existence as an independent experimental discipline until the 1930s. One reason for this was perhaps that social influences were regarded as too complex for experimental analysis. But it was also the case that the early psychologists were greatly affected by Victorian developments in biology and medicine, and so naturally directed their energies towards those mental phenomena most clearly related to the brain's physiology.

Not only did the first psychological laboratories serve to extend research on sensory physiology previously done by physiologists, but they did this in the context of the biological revolution created by Darwin's theory of evolution. Darwin's contribution to the development of psychology was twofold – general and specific. First, his theory stated that new species evolve because of the differential reproduction of hereditary characteristics, a process known as **natural selection**. The operation of natural selection meant that individuals, possessing inherited features which are well adapted to their environment, will survive and reproduce, whereas other individuals not possessing those features are less likely to survive so as to reproduce. The theory suggested that many species have evolved from common ancestors or have been exposed to similar environmental pressures and so will share many characteristics. Furthermore, some of these characteristics should be behavioural as Darwin believed that much behaviour is inherited. Such behaviour should also be well adapted to an individual species' environment as it has been selected for over aeons. Darwin's theory therefore encouraged the growth of comparative psychology – the comparison of human behaviour with that of other species. His second, more specific contribution to this embryonic discipline was his own work on the expression of emotion in humans and other animals. This work encouraged the belief that mental phenomena such as emotions are inherited and that their behavioural expression is very similar in humans and other mammalian species.

The Victorian era was also one of increasing humanitarian concern for the mentally handicapped and insane, and this concern was loosely associated with interest in hypnosis and its possible uses in treating mental and physical disorders. Experiments with hypnosis indicated the power of suggestion on the mind and showed also that mental phenomena are much more complex than had been previously supposed. They particularly highlighted the fact that there are many occasions when we do things for reasons which are not accessible to consciousness. Without this background knowledge, Freud probably could not have developed his psycho-analytic theories of normal and of neurotic behaviour, which stressed the role of **unconscious forces** in the control of our thinking and decisions. Freud had, however, also been a neurologist, and believed that the same rules of description and functioning apply to brain and mind. Indeed, there is evidence that his psychological theory can be mapped on to the theory of brain function which was prevalent in the late nineteenth century and that the psychological theory was derived from contemporary ideas about the brain (see McCarley, 1981). So, even medical psychology appeared within a biological framework.

Another early influence on psychology came from mathematics. Beloff (1973) has remarked that **statistics** can be called the charter of the inexact sciences, of which psychology is one. If so, a first draft of the charter was available late in the nineteenth century, even if it was not much used. Statistics involves the application of **probability theory** to empirical data. Its application to psychological data is essential if the science is to establish which effects are real rather than illusory, and if it is to test its theories successfully. Beloff suggested three roles for statistics in psychology. First, to estimate the value of mental processes that fluctuate continuously in a random way. Second, to state psychological laws which are always statistical tendencies rather than uniform relationships. Third, to see whether results confirm a prediction or are merely due to chance. Much of the relevant theory existed from early in the nineteenth century, but its growth was given a fillip by Francis Galton, Darwin's nephew. Galton was interested in quantifying individual differences of intellect for his study of the inheritance of genius. He showed that intelligence was distributed in the population, according to the bell-shaped **normal distribution**, which had been mathematically described by Gauss. He then went on to develop a means of measuring the degree to which two variables (such as intelligence and age) covaried or correlated. This correlation measure allowed an estimate of one variable's value to be made if the other's value was known. Statistical tests to enable psychologists to distinguish chance from real effects continue to be developed; however the British statistician R. A. Fisher created some of the most important earlier in this century.

Although the theory of psychology was influenced, from its inception, by its biological origins, its practice took very diverse forms. Psychologists in the Wundtian tradition, on the continent and in America, were primarily interested in understanding consciousness as it was manifested in emotions, thinking and perception. They pursued this interest by persuading trained subjects to report the contents of their own consciousness, i.e., to **introspect** as the physical environment was changed or while they solved problems. In contrast, the epigones of Darwin such as Romanes and Lloyd Morgan observed the **behaviour** of animals in order to discover how their minds worked. Both groups wanted to explain mental phenomena, but whereas the former group believed the task could be achieved directly by reporting the contents of consciousness, the latter group believed that mental processes could only be inferred indirectly, from consistent behaviour patterns. The nature of this dispute will be discussed later in the chapter, but historically, by around the time of the First World War there was sufficient dissatisfaction with the introspective method, because of its failure to yield unequivocal conclusions, for the American psychologist J. B. Watson to initiate the massively successful **behaviourist** revolution in human psychology.

In 1913, Watson proposed that introspection was not a valid method for understanding mind and argued instead that this could only be done through the analysis of behaviour. He was right to do this – as we shall show. But Watson also developed a theory of behaviour within his methodological framework to accord with the facts known in his time. Although, like other contemporary psychologists, Watson had earlier believed that many human tendencies are inherited instincts, he was gradually rejecting this view when he developed his behaviourist theory which proposed that human behaviour is learned as a complex set of **habits** through the **conditioning** process, discovered in the early years of the century by the great Russian physiologist Pavlov. Watson's specific behaviourist theory had three components. First, he held that complex behaviours were compounds of the atomic units, which were habits. Second, he emphasized that these behaviours were acquired. Third, he argued that activities like thought and feelings (such as hunger) took place peripherally, in the vocal cords and stomach respectively. These specific tenets are now known to be wrong.

Watson's behaviourist methods were particularly influential in America, and the 1940s and 1950s were dominated by the attempts of Hull to develop the specific theory, by studying learning in rats and explaining their behaviour in terms of intervening variables, which reflected brain activity. Tolman followed the same broad tradition, but believed that to explain learnt behaviour it is necessary to postulate **mental processes** (such as the ability to create maps of the outside world), which Watson and Hull were intent on denying. In the 1970s, B. F. Skinner kept alive a radical form of behaviourism which eschewed the postulation of any kind of hypothetical explanatory variables and simply concerned itself with describing the lawful relationships between stimuli and behavioural responses. Skinner's behaviourism is more like a technology, enabling one to predict behaviour, than a scientific system.

In the years following the Second World War a reaction against behaviourism gradually gained momentum. This reaction, which became dominant from the 1960s (perhaps marked by the publication of Miller, Galanter and Pribram's book *Plans and the Structure of Behavior* in 1960), was against what specific behaviourist theories denied, rather than against behaviourist methods. Modern psychology is still based on the objective analysis of behaviour, but it is directed towards explaining processes, such as attention, imagining and thinking, whose existence was effectively rejected by Watson and Hull. In this sense, Tolman's theory can be seen as a harbinger of modern psychology.

Interest in sensory and perceptual processes continued through the years dominated by Watsonian behaviourism, and was linked with the development of **Gestalt psychology**. The Gestaltists attacked the associationist philosophy, which still underlay the Wundtian approach to perception. They denied that percepts are built up from distinct atoms of sensation, which are somehow associated by the mind. Rather, they believed that we are directly aware of our percepts and that this **perceptual whole** is more than the sum of its parts. This is because the whole depends on the way the parts are organized. The Gestaltic school arose in Germany, led by men such as Koffka, Köhler and Wertheimer, and in the Wundtian tradition used introspective reports of conscious perceptual experience. Despite (and indeed because of) criticisms of introspection, the school has left a useful legacy. First, it clarified how the organization of sensory stimuli determines how they are perceived. Second, it inadvertently stressed that these perceptual processes are essentially unconscious and therefore inaccessible to introspection.

Since the Second World War there have been other changes which have further highlighted the swing away from the narrow confines of Watsonian behaviourism. After its promising beginnings, comparative psychology had become stultified as an approach in which one or two species, such as the rat, were selected as substitute humans and studied in a limited range of laboratory tasks. This approach declined with the emergence of ethology, a creation of European zoologists such as Lorenz, Von Frisch and Tinbergen. This discipline was concerned with studying animals' behaviour under natural conditions, in order to determine similarities and differences in different species' activities. It operated within a Darwinian framework, and, contrary to Watsonian behaviourism, reinstated instinct as a central explanatory concept. The ethologists studied many species in their **natural habitats** and argued that much of their observed behaviour comprised unlearnt **fixed action patterns** that were triggered (again without learning) by highly specific **releasing stimuli**. Only gradually was it appreciated that even these instinctive behaviours are subject to learnt modifications. Attempts to apply similar explanations to complex human behaviour (sociobiology) have been highly controversial.

Theorizing about human cognitive activities, like perception, remembering and thinking, has long been influenced by analogies with other information-processing systems. At one stage, it was popular to compare the human brain with a telephone exchange, but with the pullulating growth of **computer science** the analogies have become more sophisticated and probably more appropriate. For the past twenty or so years psychologists have been trying to understand those central mental processes, previously ignored by the behaviourists, as systems for interpreting, storing, accessing and reworking sensory information. In this task, they have been increasingly guided by analogies from computer science. The impact of this science has been threefold. First, the technology has made it possible to perform new and more difficult experiments. Second, it is possible to test the predictions of complex psychological theories by **simulating** them in appropriate computer programs. Third, it is possible to create perceiving, thinking or language-using machines, and this work on **artificial intelligence** may, in turn, suggest the ways in which these activities are performed by humans and animals. Unlike simulation, which uses computers to test ideas derived from studying humans, artificial intelligence often generates ideas from studying computers and applies them to living systems.

Scientific psychology: its subject matter

Definitions of a science are often misleading. Nevertheless, it is true to say that the central concern of psychology, since its beginning, has been the understanding of the mind in humans and (to a lesser extent) in animals. In this sense, 'mind' connotes the cognitive activities of perceiving, remembering and thinking, as well as the interaction of these with emotions and motivations. During the days of Watsonian behaviourism, it was more fashionable to say that psychology was the study of behaviour. As Hebb (1980) has argued, however, psychologists should try to explain the process of mind by studying behaviour. Although early behaviourists had an impoverished view of mental activities, this was not an inevitable result of their methodology, but rather of limitations in contemporary knowledge about brain and behaviour.

Mind has arisen through evolution because it enables animals to behave so as to increase their chances of surviving to reproduce. It has therefore been studied in a **biological context** as a product of brain activities that have been selected as species evolved. But in most vertebrates, mind develops and expresses itself in a **social environment**, so it is also important to study its activities as they are affected by social factors. The gulf between biological and social psychology often seems to be a very wide one. For example, biological psychologists may be interested in how thinking processes are generated by the brain or any equivalent information-processing system, whereas social psychologists are more likely to want to know how social factors influence *what* we think. To oversimplify, social psychologists assume the operation of those processes which other psychologists are seeking to explain. For them the components of mind are black boxes. They are not interested in the components within the black boxes, the interaction of which explains the function of each black box. Psychologists differ, therefore, in the **level of description** in which they couch their explanations. For example, if the effect of attitude on memory was being studied, social psychologists would want to discover the influence on memory of positive and negative attitudes towards the presented information. In contrast, cognitive psychologists would want to know how attitude affects attentional and perceptual processes so as to change memory. Finally, physiological psychologists aim to explain how brain processes generate these attentional and perceptual processes.

Several points arise from the fact that psychologists use different levels of explanation. First, different areas of psychology ask different questions and, because of this, use distinct **methodologies** and **technologies**: one may explore memory by recording the activity of single nerve cells or by examining the effects of advertising on relevant kinds of knowledge. This variety has prompted Beloff (1973) to propose that there are **psychological sciences** and that a single psychological science does not exist (see Box 1.1). Although he is, in one sense, right, his position is exaggerated because all these sciences are finally concerned with one thing – the understanding of mind. This relates to the second point, that a full understanding of a mental process means knowing about it at all levels of description. **Reductionist** accounts of the components in a mental black box do not tell us what the box produces, because for that we need to know what is being fed into the system from the social environment. Third, the levels of description are not independent, as they interact with one another. For example, it is well established that growing up in a rich social environment stimulates physiological, anatomical and neurochemical changes in the brain (Rosenzweig and Bennett, 1976).

A fourth point, related to those above, arises from a remark often made by psychologists who are interested in explaining mind in terms of quite low levels of description. These psychologists, much influenced by ideas drawn from computer science, argue that humans and animals are information-processing machines whose activities can be explained without reference to brain processes. In their view, many different kinds of **physical system** could process information in the same way as brains, and the central problem is to explain how information is processed, i.e., how sensory inputs are analysed, stored and retrieved. Although this argument is correct in essence, it is irrelevant to contemporary psychological research for two reasons. First, in our current state of ignorance one of the best means of discovering how living beings process information is to explore how the brain works. Knowledge of brain processes constrains theories about how information is being analysed. Second, as psychologists seek practical as well as theoretical knowledge, it is important for medical reasons to know how the brain controls mental activities. Only with this kind of knowledge is there a reasonable chance of alleviating many mental disorders.

Although, as we can see from Table 1.1 and Box 1.1, the detailed methods and techniques of the disciplines differ, all of them have in common the aim of understanding mental functions better and, perhaps, applying this knowledge. The best way to understand mental processes is by considering evidence taken from all of these disciplines rather than by treating them in isolation. This is one of the things we attempt to show in this book. For example, in order to obtain a clearer grasp of how visual perception of objects in the world is achieved, it is not enough to study how intact adult humans see things. We also get vital information by looking at how vision differs in various societies (Zulus

BOX 1.1
Theories and paradigms in psychology

It has been noted by Beloff (1973) that psychologists tend to fall into a number of compartmentalized groups. These groups are interested in somewhat different mental and behavioural phenomena, and their different interests are usually associated with the adoption of distinct theoretical assumptions, methods of research and technical languages. Such shared ideas are often referred to as paradigms, loosely following the usage of this term by the American philosopher of science Kuhn (1970). In this sense, paradigms offer a theoretical and practical framework for doing research in a given area. If it is appropriate, then the research will be productive of many new facts and ideas.

Since its beginning, scientific psychology has been influenced by a number of **research frameworks** that have differed in their subject matter and in the degree to which they have formally developed theories. Six examples may illustrate these features. First, **psychoanalysis** as developed by **Freud** (see Freud, 1954) was a dynamic theory of emotional development which, among other aims, sought to explain the causes of various kinds of psychopathology and offer treatments for their cure. Central to these aims was the process that brought unconscious motives, thoughts and feelings to consciousness, or which prevented this from happening. The highly complex theory was based largely on observations and interpretations of patient behaviour. It has been much criticized on the grounds that its hypotheses are impossible to disprove empirically. Second, the **developmental psychology of Piaget** (see Piaget, 1954) was a comprehensive attempt to explain the intellectual and moral growth of normal children. Like psychoanalysis, Piaget's theory was highly complex and involved a jargon which rendered it somewhat opaque to outsiders. It was initially built on fairly informal observations of children, but modern neo-

Piagetians have adopted a much more rigorous, controlled experimental approach. Third, **ethology** is concerned with cross-species comparisons of animal behaviour, based on observations made of animals in their natural habitat. Its central shared idea is therefore a methodological one and its general theory is less elaborate. Even so, early ethologists stressed the role of evolution and largely unlearned, or instinctive behaviour. Fourth, **psychometrics** is concerned with the measurement of individual differences in psychological characteristics, such as intelligence and personality. In the past, its methodology was very sophisticated but its theory rather impoverished. Psychometricians, just as much as Freudians, tended to operate in isolation from other psychological paradigms. Fifth, the notion of the mind as an **information-processing system** has been a very dominant research framework since the Second World War. Together with physiological psychology with which it cross-fertilizes research, it has constituted the mainstream of psychology in the past thirty years. Finally, **learning theory** represents an approach to research that has been in decline since the information-processing framework became dominant. Deriving their methods from strict Watsonian behaviourism, learning theorists studied conditioning in 'representative' animals in order to develop theories of learning that were universally applicable. In the heyday of the approach both theory and methods were highly sophisticated. Although the methods of modern learning theorists are similar, their theoretical aims are more modest, as they seek to explain specific learning effects rather than all learning.

There has been a strong historical tendency for psychologists to work within only one of the above research frameworks, and for there to be little cross-talk between these frameworks. It is the argument of this book that this tendency has been detrimental to the advancement of psychological knowledge. First, there is some **overlap** between the subject matter of the paradigms. For example, Piagetian and Freudian theory are both concerned with development, and psychometricians and information-processing theorists are both interested in thinking. These areas of overlap need to be specified and theoretical conflicts resolved. Second, many psychological problems can only be solved by **integrating** the approaches of several different frameworks even when these show little overlap with each other. If this integration is to be successful, it will be necessary to show how the different frameworks interrelate. Such a theoretical framework, linking the respective psychological disciplines, might be seen as a 'superparadigm', just as Newtonian physics was a 'superparadigm' linking more specific physical theories.

A striking example of postwar work that integrates work in many different frameworks is research on the genesis of **neuroses** and other **anxiety disorders**. The picture that emerges from this research is that individuals develop neuroses (such as excessive fear of animals) because their inherited personalities make them very susceptible to certain kinds of learning. The combination of appropriate personality and learning experience leads to the psychopathology. The inheritance of personality depends in turn on inheriting certain brain structures with varying degrees of sensitivity. These inherited physiological features cause the individual to interact differently with his social environment during development, and this progressive interaction determines the nature of the adult personality (see Gray, 1982). To be able to produce this picture, researchers have combined the approaches of psychometricians, learning theorists, developmental and social psychologists, behaviour geneticists, psychopathologists, information-processing theorists and physiological psychologists. The work provides a model for future psychological research. (See also pages 703–7.)

do not suffer from some visual illusions to which Western men are subject, and Eskimos are supreme at discriminating different kinds of snow), how it changes as we grow up (do we learn to see?), how it differs between individual adults (some of us are very good at recognizing faces), how animals see things (this knowledge is useful even when they see in a 'simpler' way), how brain damage disturbs how we see things (it is also possible to trace the course of visual information as it is processed by different brain regions), and finally how machines can be specified to mimic aspects of visual perception (artificial intelligence). To treat these sources of information in isolation would greatly reduce the chances of developing an appropriate theory about how humans see objects in the world.

The **conceptual unity** of psychology can also be appreciated when mental phenomena are viewed through the spectacles provided by evolutionary theory. This theory proposes that physical structures, mental abilities and behaviours only evolve because they are adaptive, i.e., they increase the odds that an individual will survive so as to reproduce. Mental abilities are therefore only likely to exist if they lead to adaptive behaviours. But these mental abilities have evolved in animals living in social groups. Social behaviour itself has been shaped by evolution, as an animal's chances of survival are closely dependent on how it behaves towards others in its social group. The selection of animals likely to show adaptive social behaviours may also lead to the selection of animals with mental abilities, whose other expressions may remain latent until the right circumstances arise to elicit them.

Precisely this has been argued with respect to **self-consciousness** and some other uniquely human abilities (see Humphrey, 1982). Humphrey has argued that 3 or 4 million years ago man's ancestors lived in social groups which, because of their lifestyle, developed unprecedented degrees of interdependency and trust – only in this way was it possible for them to survive by gathering and hunting. Such a society has its dark side since individual survival depended on the ability to outmanoeuvre others in the group. This ability itself partially depends on being able to predict what others are going to do. Although such prediction can be achieved by observing regularities of behaviour, this was unreliable with complex animals like our ancestors. Humphrey argues that better predictions are achieved by 'getting inside another's skin', i.e., by empathy. This can only be achieved if the actor has self-awareness and knows how he himself would feel in similar situations. Self-awareness therefore evolved because it increased our ancestors' social skills. Similarly, it has been speculated that long-latent abilities, such as doing higher mathematics, were mental 'spin-offs' from the need of our ancestors to develop sophisticated social skills.

There is, then, a close relationship between the evolution of mental abilities and social behaviour. Indeed, society itself is ultimately a product of biological evolution. This is not to say that there are not problems in applying evolutionary theory to social phenomena, but clarification of the problems illuminates both biological and social psychology. Natural selection operates on **individuals** and on **inherited** characteristics, but many social tendencies, such as **altruism**, seem to decrease an individual's chances of survival and so should not exist. But they do. Resolution of this paradox has increased understanding both of evolution and of some social behaviours. Some forms of altruism can be explained as kinship selection in that the self-sacrificing behaviour is primarily aimed at the individual's relatives. This is most apparent in parental behaviour, but there are many other examples, including the often self-destructive activities of worker bees. In such cases, the individual's survival chances decrease but those of his relatives increase. The relatives share many of the individual's inherited characteristics, including a tendency towards altruism, and it can be shown that this behaviour actually raises the probability that such features will be transmitted through the successful breeding of the relatives.

It is impossible to explain all cases of human altruism in this way, and there is persuasive evidence that porpoises and chimpanzees also show similar empathic behaviours. For example, porpoises have been seen to work in pairs, supporting an injured or unconscious fellow, so that his blow-hole remains above water and he does not drown (see Hebb, 1980). Porpoises have even been reported to aid humans in trouble at sea. Chimpanzees also come to the aid of their fellows who are under threat. It has been suggested by Hebb (1980) that these kinds of altruistic behaviours are not of adaptive value to the individual who displays them. Like mathematical ability they have evolved as a by-product of characteristics which are clearly adaptive, namely the capacity for sophisticated thinking. Such intelligence needs long periods of childhood for its adequate growth. Hebb argues that during infancy, intelligent animals, like humans, acquire the concept of 'self' by observing others, so that the concepts of 'self' and 'other' have a common core. Given this relationship, it is plausible that learning to act in a self-interested way may easily transfer into acting in an other-directed way. In other words, empathy may naturally (but not inevitably) lead to active sympathy.

One of Hebb's points is that empathic altruism is only inherited in the sense that certain cognitive abilities, which create its essential background, are inherited. The altruism itself is a tendency, learned by exposure to the society of one's own species. In human beings, altruism is acquired through exposure to particular cultures, some of which encourage it and others of which inhibit it. Human behaviours, more than those of any other species, are shaped by cultural factors. They are learnt activities, whose appearance requires the interaction of more strongly inherited features (such as thinking ability) with the cultural environment as the individual develops. At an abstract level, **culture** and **heredity** are independent means of transmitting information across generations. Hereditary information is held in the form of genes (as will be discussed in the next chapter) which partially determine an individual's physical structure and mental capacities. Cultural information is held in individuals' brains or in libraries, and determines the kind of skills which each generation can learn to develop. Without the appropriate cultural heritage, no human being would show higher mathematical skills. So, no account of mental activity would be complete without an explanation of how cultures emerge and interact with our biological inheritance.

The emergence of contemporary human minds is the result of epochs of subtle interplay between biological and social factors. The interplay is also apparent in the development of each individual human. To understand this interplay it is necessary to describe activities at several levels of description: the physiology and biochemistry of individual nerve cells, the activities of organized groups of nerve cells, the activities of individual 'information processors', and the activities of whole cultural groups. The inter-relationships between these different levels of description must then be revealed. This is the ambitious programme for the science of psychology. Some have argued that, either for philosophical or practical reasons, it cannot be fulfilled. It is to these criticisms that we now turn.

Scientific psychology: philosophical and methodological problems

Psychology has existed as an institutionalized science for over a hundred years. As a science, its basic aim must be the formulation and experimental testing of hypotheses about the mind. These hypotheses may be of two kinds. First, they may explain the relationship between different mental activities, or between mental activities and social events; i.e., all the concepts are at the same level of description. For example, 'Passive repetition improves subsequent recognition but not recall', and 'Awareness that an audience is present improves performance of simple tasks, but impairs performance of difficult tasks'. Second, in contrast to these explanations in 'breadth', reductionist hypotheses relate mental activities to a different and 'lower' conceptual level. For example, 'Some information is only transiently remembered because it is held in a short-term memory store and not transferred to a long-term store', and 'Activity in the midbrain reticular formation nonspecifically activates the cortex and so influences the efficiency with which easy and hard tasks are performed'. Critics of psychology have argued either that the programme of hypothesis formulation and testing can never advance far for reasons of principle or that methodological difficulties determine that its conclusions are bound always to be trivial.

Criticisms of the first kind are based on philosophical views about the nature of mind. Psychological hypotheses seek to identify either the **causal mechanisms** of, or the **causal links** between mental states. In this sense, psychology is **determinist,** and many philosophers have argued that determinism is inconsistent with the views that humans are **rational,** that their behaviour is goal-oriented (**purposive**) and that they have **free will.** In other words, if psychologists were successful in developing their determinist account of mind, then we would have to abandon the idea that humans are rational, purposive beings with free will. The philosophical critics believe that humans are like this and thus that psychology must be an ill-fated science.

There are several answers to such criticisms. First, it is clear that we are right to explain much human behaviour in terms of the goals to which it is directed, but such **teleological explanations** are not incompatible with causal ones. The thermostat is a machine which has the 'purpose' of maintaining its environment at a constant temperature, and at a more advanced level, a guided missile has the 'purpose' of homing in on a possibly elusive target. Yet both machines can be explained in terms of their causal mechanisms. Such explanations have been the particular concern of **cybernetics**, which is the science of control and communication. The concepts of this science, originally · developed to explain machine behaviour, have been effectively applied to human and animal behaviour. For example, the concept of **negative feedback** is central for the understanding of 'purposive' behaviour. Some devices, called servomechanisms, can control their own behaviour because the consequences of this behaviour are fed back into the system and then modify its subsequent behaviour. The device can compare the feedback information with some preset value. If it perceives negative feedback, it then acts to reduce the discrepancy between the two. Cybernetics carries two major implications for psychology. It shows that purposive behaviour can be explained in causal terms, and it shows that explanations of mind can be made in terms of what is done to information by devices that may take many different physical forms. Thus, information may be processed in the same way by human brains or by specially designed computing systems that operate on entirely different physical principles.

The second answer to the philosophical critics of psychology relates to rationality, and takes a form similar to the first point about teleological explanations. Human actions are rational when the actor understands what he is trying to do, can recognize when he has achieved it and can give reasons for his actions being the best means of achieving his ends. There is no doubt that some human actions are not rational. Freud and others highlighted situations in which the actor's proffered reasons for his behaviour were bogus (i.e., **rationalizations**) and the real driving force behind his behaviour lay elsewhere, inaccessible to his consciousness (see Chapter 13). But not all psychological explanations show that behaviour which is superficially rational is irrational at a deeper level. Indeed, the belief that they must always do this is known as the fallacy of psychologism. Just as they have provided causal models for purposive behaviour in general, cybernetics and the computer sciences are suggesting similar models that may explain rational behaviour without explaining it away.

The third counter to psychology's philosophical critics relates to **free will**. This is a trickier issue because the very concept of free will has been clouded in metaphysical confusion for over two millennia. Human beings are said to have free will when they are free to choose what they wish to do. The claim has metaphysical importance because most people believe that we are only justified in praising, blaming or even punishing people for their behaviour if they choose so to behave of their own free will. If psychology shows that all behaviour can be explained causally, then we would perhaps no longer be justified in doing these things. One prominent psychologist who believes this is Skinner (1971). In his view, the only reason for rewarding or punishing behaviour is to influence future behaviour in desired directions. Skinner may well be right about the implications of a deterministic psychology and he may also be right to reject the notion of free will. But, as with rationality and purposiveness in behaviour, free will may only be incompatible with some kinds of causal explanation. For example, if someone is a kleptomaniac or has been given a posthypnotic suggestion to steal, then we would want to argue that they are not free to choose what they will do in a shop. They are not free of certain overriding constraints. But it remains an open issue whether causal explanations of normal choice constrain in this way. If they do not then we can conclude that a view of man as predominantly purposive, rational and free (the view of the so-called humanistic psychologist) may be compatible with the determinist account of the scientific psychologist.

Another, and perhaps the major, problem for scientific psychology raised by its philosophical critics is the ancient **mind-body problem**. What is the relationship between mind and body, and how, if at all, do they interact? This, like the issue of free will, appears to be another intractable metaphysical problem despite the plethora of solutions which have been offered for it. Most thinkers have begun with the notion that mind is equivalent to consciousness and thinking, and have then sought to relate this to the physical activities of the brain and the body. In European thought from the time of the French philosopher Descartes, there has been a strong tendency to regard mind and brain as essentially different kinds of stuff – to be dualistic. Leibnitz believed that they were so different that they could not even interact; that they only appeared to do so because mental and physical events occurred in parallel in a synchronized fashion. If correct, this doctrine of dualistic parallelism would mean that physiological psychology is impossible because it would be based on the illusion that mind and body interact.

Many modern philosophers have, however, rejected dualism and adopted instead some form of **materialistic monism**, in which mind is seen as an aspect of the body and brain. In his doctrine of logical behaviourism, the Oxford philosopher Gilbert Ryle (1949) argued that all language describing states of mind can be shown on analysis to be about behaviour and possible occurrences of behaviour. This doctrine is probably false, and more recently another view, known as **identity theory**, has acquired currency. This view states that mental and brain events are identical in much the same way that lightning is identical with electrical discharges through the air. The analogy indicates that it is possible to imagine that the events concerned are not the same, that this must be discovered empirically and that the identified events are 'known' in different ways. Like scientific psychology, identity theory suggests a programme of research which will show how mental events depend on brain events, and vice versa. Both hold that, in general, there can be no mind without brain, although the details of the relationship remain to be found. *Whatever the details, however, identity theorists and most psychologists believe that brain events ultimately cause mental events.* This is because mental events are seen as a subclass of brain events and arise from other brain events. Mental events can only be said to cause physical events in a loose sense. For example, feeling frightened may be said to cause our hearts to beat faster. But the feelings of fear are associated with brain events (with which they may be identical) and these events are, in turn, caused by other brain events.

The materialist presumptions of many modern psychologists are inimical to many laymen who wish to believe in the survival of the mind after death and in the mind's ultimate independence from the body. Such independence is conceivable, given the way we use 'mental' language, but would be made much more plausible if the existence of phenomena such as telepathy and psychokinesis could be demonstrated. These hypothetical phenomena, studied by **para-psychologists**, are paranormal in the sense that they are apparently inconsistent with contemporary **physical theories**. Although some paranormal phenomena may become explicable as new physical discoveries are made, others, such as alleged communications from the dead and reincarnation experiences, are unlikely ever to be so explained. Parapsychological evidence is of two broad kinds: **anecdotal reports** of supposedly inexplicable phenomena and **laboratory studies** which try to study the phenomena under controlled conditions. Both kinds of evidence are very subject to fraud, largely because the stakes are so high. These frauds are often ingenious and hard to detect (see Hansel, 1966). Indeed, the ideal person to investigate many paranormal phenomena would be a magician, versed in disguising tricks, rather than a scientist. Anecdotal reports are also very subject to the distorting effects that strong preconceptions exert on perception and memory. As this book will show, what we see and later remember is often actively constructed from fragmentary evidence under the guidance of our beliefs (see Jahoda, 1969, for a discussion of examples of such distorted constructions in parapsychological research). If parapsychological phenomena were genuine, we would have to change radically, not only our physical theories, but also our view of mind. Given the problems with the evidence, however, the case is at best not proven, and, given the improbability of the putative phenomena, many psychologists are inclined to disregard it.

The dualist view of mind and body, shared by Descartes and by the British empiricist philosophers Locke and Hume, was associated with the belief that it is possible for the mind to be conscious of its own activities directly, through the process of introspection. Adoption of the introspective method by Wundt and his followers as the royal road to the understanding of the mind led to the first great methodological crisis in the history of scientific psychology, the full implications of which have still not been fully resolved. The heyday of introspective psychology was between 1880 and 1910. During this time all that trained introspectors could identify clearly were sensory contents such as the intensity of pain sensations. At the same time, others were showing that important mental activities were inaccessible to introspection. Freud was showing this with respect to a range of unconscious thoughts, emotions and motives.

Quite independently, Kulpe and his students in Würzburg were showing that all thought was what they called imageless – in effect, all thought was unconscious. They showed subjects pairs of numbers which they were asked to add, subtract or multiply. When the appropriate mental set was established, the subjects saw the numbers and produced the answer, but were not 'aware of any accompanying thinking. There was, for example, no imagery of the words 'add' or 'subtract'.

Taken to its logical conclusion, Kulpe's criticism means that our minds are never directly aware of their own activities. Rather, we are consciously aware of what we perceive and, by taking into account the context of our perceptions, we infer that we are engaged in a particular mental activity. For example, we infer that we are experiencing an afterimage caused by looking at a bright light. What we are directly aware of is seeing a light, but because it moves when our eyes move and does not disappear when we shut them, we infer we are experiencing a visual afterimage rather than seeing an outside object. According to this view, originally advanced in the nineteenth century by the American philosopher C. S. Peirce, all our knowledge of our sensations, emotions, thoughts and wishes, arises indirectly 'in connection with a judgement about external phenomena'. We are never directly aware of the activities of our minds and can only infer them to a very limited extent. For example, there is no way to infer, in Peirce's view, *how* we retrieve the fact that Paris is the capital of France.

If all that introspectionists could do was make crude inferences about their mental activities (crude because they often disagreed), then introspection could not provide an effective way of discovering how the mind worked. Either psychology was not a viable science or new methodologies would have to be found. The major new methodology, as already discussed, was Watsonian behaviourism, which was introduced in 1913. Watson's data base comprised observations of behaviourial regularities, occurring in a whole variety of situations, such as those that lead to the development of fear or laughter. In its modern form, these data are used to make inferences about how cognitive and motivational processes (i.e., the mind) work. Watsonian behaviourism led many psychologists to concentrate on collecting behavioural data from animals – such as rats, which were seen as representative of all mammals, humans included. These psychologists were little interested in what humans reported they perceived in different situations. In contrast, the approach of Gestaltic psychologists was to analyse systematically the stimulus conditions that gave rise to particular perceptions. From this knowledge it was hoped that it might be possible to infer how perception is performed. Modern psychologists use the methods of both Watson and the Gestaltists. The data collected – behavioural observations and reports of what is being perceived – are distinct from introspections and enable psychologists to infer the mental processes that give rise to them.

As already indicated, the full implications of these criticisms of introspectionism have not yet been fully resolved by psychologists. There is currently much debate about whether people are directly aware of some of their thoughts, feelings and emotions, or whether their nature is always inferred from what is being perceived and how they are behaving. The latter view proposes that we always attribute mental states to ourselves as an inference, in order to explain why we are behaving in a particular way. Critics of this **attributionist** account agree that in some uncertain situations we do identify our thoughts and feelings in this way, but that usually we know directly what we are perceiving, thinking or feeling, and this knowledge then influences how we behave. To summarize this view: it suggests that sometimes we are directly conscious of what we are perceiving, thinking or feeling, but sometimes we are not, and then we have to infer what we 'know' from the way we are behaving (see Chapter 4 for further discussion of unconscious cognition). Finally, holders of this view agree that we never have *direct* awareness of the *processes* of cognition. In other words, *what* we know may be conscious or unconscious, but *how* we come to know it is always unconscious, and psychologists must use behavioural and self-report data to infer the information-processing mechanisms that are involved.

One interesting corollary of these conclusions is that self-awareness (see Chapter 4) is not a direct awareness of self, but involves a complex inference. Hebb (1980), as already discussed, actually argues that the idea of 'self' and the idea of 'other' have a common core, which is the notion of person, and that this commonality helps explain phenomena like empathy, altruism and imitation. He points out that babies are likely to learn more about other people than about themselves initially since they themselves are only partially perceptible. Only gradually will the baby come to realize that he is a person like other people and that he has a special relationship to this person – his other. As an illustration of the close links between self and other, Hebb cited a personal experience. In young adulthood, an infection made it impossible for him to bend in the middle. This meant that he had to lower himself into chairs in an elaborate fashion. When he saw a friend sit down normally by bending in the middle, he had the feeling that he was watching an impossible action, so strong was the transfer of expectation from self to other. The view that the idea of self involves complex learning is supported by evidence that only humans and some of the great apes can acquire it (see Chapter 4). The view also implies that hallucinations, like the 'out-of-the-body' experience, in which the subject seems to be viewing his body from an external location, can only occur once the idea of self has been learned.

Even though most critics now accept that psychologists must try to explain mental processes by collecting behavioural and self-report data, there are some who argue that problems with this activity mean that psychological knowledge will remain trivial. It has not and will not advance significantly beyond the unsystematic, **common sense knowledge** that has accumulated over millennia. Several arguments lie behind this pessimism. First, it is very difficult to do experiments which test the hypothesis the experimenter wishes to test. This applies particularly to social situations and is associated with the phenomenon of the **self-fulfilling prophecy**. If a person thinks that he is a certain kind of person or that the experimenter expects him to perform certain kinds of action, then this will influence his behaviour, usually in the direction of the expectation. An amusing example of this is the claim that Freud's patients dreamed the kind of dreams that his theory led him to expect whereas Jung's patients dreamed the very different kinds of dream that his views required.

The effects of experimenter expectation were directly demonstrated by Rosenthal (1966). He asked undergraduate 'experimenters' to get a group of subjects to rate a series of photographed faces as successes or failures. One group of experimenters was told that the average rating would probably be one of relative success whereas another group was told that it would probably be one of relative failure. The results showed that the first experimenter group had subjects who gave relatively more successful ratings of the faces. The effects were subtle as the experimenters did not communicate verbally their expectations; these must therefore have been communicated nonverbally. Similar experimenter-expectation effects have even been shown with animal experiments where communication must be nonverbal. If experimenters think they are testing a stupid rat then it tends to behave stupidly. This phenomenon also has educational implications, for it has been argued, and evidence supports the claim, that if children are labelled as good or poor scholars then their academic performance tends to match expectation to some degree.

Experimenter-expectation effects do not, however, make psychology impossible, for two reasons. First, it has proved possible to study the effects and to gain some understanding of how they work. Indeed, this research has implications not only for methodology but in important applied areas, such as education and even medicine (so if you are labelled as an educational dimwit or as sick, that's what you tend to become). Second, it is usually possible to minimize the experimenter's influence on subjects, by automating the procedure or by keeping the experimenter 'blind'. For example, the experimenter in studies of the effect of drugs on behaviour should not know whether the drug or an inert **placebo** is being given. As the subjects' own expectations are known to influence their response to a drug, they also should not know whether they are receiving the drug or the placebo. This **double-blind** procedure enables experimenters to determine whether or not the drug is having any direct effect on behaviour. Actions of drugs, caused by expectations, are known as **placebo effects**. For example, about 30 per cent of recipients achieve pain relief after taking an inert placebo, but morphine is known to be a true analgesic because about 70 per cent of its recipients experience pain relief.

It may have occurred to the reader that **hypnosis** seems to be related to the phenomena of experimenter and placebo effects. In hypnosis, the hypnotist exposes his subject to an induction procedure which is supposed to heighten responsiveness to various suggestions, cause a trance-like appearance, alter body feelings and lead the subject to report that he has been hypnotized. On this view, hypnosis is a special state of enhanced suggestibility. For example, after undergoing hypnotic induction, subjects may be given the suggestion to forget all they have experienced in the past few minutes until a signal is given to release them from their amnesia. Some psychologists, however, are critical of the idea that there exists a special state of hypnosis. In their view, hypnotic amnesia may be produced simply by asking subjects to imagine they cannot remember, provided they are encouraged to develop positive attitudes, motivations and expectations towards the suggestion (see Barber and De Moor, 1972). The hypnotic state itself is, in their view, created by the subject's own expectations as to what the trance state is like. When given the induction procedure, the subject conforms to his own and the hypnotist's implicit expectations about the effect the procedure should have. Paradoxically, then, research on hypnosis has been hampered until recently by insufficient attention being paid to controlling the effects of suggestion. Better controlled, more recent research does, however, suggest two things. First, 'deep' hypnotic subjects are unaware that they are complying with the hypnotist's suggestions whereas 'lighter' subjects are aware that they are actively trying to fulfil the suggestions. Second, suggestions do seem to be *more* effective when subjects shift their style of thinking away from a verbal, detail-oriented strategy towards a more imaginal, nonanalytic, holistic-oriented strategy (Crawford, 1982).

The complex problems of research into hypnosis point to a second reason for pessimism advanced by critics of psychology's methodology. In psychological situations, many variables (i.e., measurable factors that can vary, like speed of reaction, time, and body temperature) interact to produce effects on mental function. It is extremely hard to tease apart how they cause their effects, particularly as the variables do not have simple additive effects. More commonly there is what is known technically as an interaction of variables. This is illustrated by the effect of different educational methods on pupils' scholastic performances. One cannot simply say that the direct instruction method is better than the discovery method, because the success of these methods depends also on the pupils' personalities. More extraverted children do better with the discovery method whereas more introverted children respond better to the direct instruction method (see Eysenck and Eysenck, 1981). Attempts to show the effectiveness of different methods that do not take personality (and probably other factors) into account would therefore be very misleading.

One particular interaction between the variable of time and many other variables, often referred to as the **Hawthorne effect**, reveals how easy it is to be deceived about what a given variable is actually doing. The Hawthorne experiments were a series of studies designed to identify those variables which would increase workers' industrial productivity. Initially, the experimenters found that many different changes seemed to increase productivity, but when eventually conditions returned to normal that too caused a productivity increase. In other words, novelty itself was causing the change. It is possible to control for novelty, however, as the Hawthorne experimenters eventually did themselves, and then see whether or not variables really are having a direct effect on psychological activity. These problems of situational complexity can therefore be overcome through the use of more sophisticated experimental designs.

The criticisms so far indicate that it is difficult for psychologists to test hypotheses properly with experiments; however such testing can be done with careful design of the tests. Critics may, however, advance a third argument, to the effect that because of ethical and legal prohibitions few important psychological hypotheses can be tested experimentally. It is not, for example, possible to do experimental brain surgery on humans, nor is it possible to do selective breeding experiments with human subjects, and nor, finally, is it possible to raise differently matched groups of humans under a range of impoverished and enriched environmental conditions. Without its experimental 'wolf children', so this argument goes, psychological knowledge will never significantly advance beyond what we already know from common sense. If science is 'the art of the possible', for psychologists not enough is possible for them to make the business worthwhile.

Perhaps the best answer to this criticism would be for the reader to examine the psychological knowledge described in this book, and then to judge whether psychologists have only reached trivial, common sense conclusions. But there are other points to be made, as we have overstated the critics' argument. First, although there are legal and ethical restrictions on brain surgery, selective breeding and selective rearing programmes in humans, accidents do happen, such as brain injury or a severely restricted upbringing, as in the case of Genie (see Chapter 9), and psychologists have taken the opportunity to examine their effects. Second, it is possible, to a limited extent, to test important hypotheses in humans, if less directly. For example, brain function can be studied in intact humans either by placing on their scalps electrodes that record electrical activity generated by their brains, or by injecting radioactive chemicals that enable researchers to calculate the activity of particular nerve cells when subjects are performing mental activities. Similarly, the inheritance of certain characteristics can be studied by examining those characteristics in fraternal and identical twins who have been brought up together or apart (see Chapter 2 for a further discussion).

Third, it is legally possible to do controlled neurosurgery on animals, and to implement animal programmes of selective breeding and rearing. To the extent that the chosen species are like humans, they may model the human psychological activities in which the researcher is interested. By this means, it may be possible to elucidate the brain mechanisms and the genetic and developmental processes that underlie the relevant activities.

There are, of course, limits to the human abilities that can be modelled in animals. For example, verbal behaviour is unique to humans. Even here, however, there is some evidence that the brains of the great apes have regions specialized for recognizing social communications that correspond to human brain regions specialized for language perception.

A climate of opinion has developed against vivisectionist research, so this doorway to psychological knowledge may, in future, be closed or partially closed. It is not within the scope of this book to assess the morality of doing cruel experiments on animals rather than humans. Two points are in order, however. First, vivisection and other cruel experiments represent the classic moral dilemma of deciding between two evils: on the one hand, cruelty to animals and, on the other, allowing suffering to continue that *might* have been alleviated if the experiments had been performed. Second, in weighing up this dilemma it is important to know how much pain is being inflicted. This is an empirically decidable issue, about which people are inclined to make unjustified assumptions. Studies can be done to see which of two or more conditions, already experienced, an animal will choose.

The answers to the last criticism, concerning psychology's viability as a science, suggest a strategy for doing research that is one of the themes of this book. In order to gain a better grasp of mental processes it is heuristically sound to draw data from many sources to see whether convergent implications can be derived. If they can, then the original hypotheses are confirmed, but if not, the underlying assumptions may need to be modified. For example, to develop powerful hypotheses about how we acquire and remember information about day-to-day events it is important not merely to study memory in intact adults under laboratory conditions. Memory abilities should also be looked at as they develop in children, as they change in relation to brain damage and activity, as they differ between individuals, as they are influenced by social factors, and also as they are expressed in animals. Such a diverse approach is more likely to lead to the development of novel and powerfully predictive hypotheses. Until quite recently, psychologists have shown a strong predilection to compartmentalize their study areas. An extreme form of this predilection leads to what has been described as the **functional autonomy of methods**. In this, methods once used to illuminate psychological phenomena eventually themselves become the objects of intense study (see Tulving and Madigan, 1970).

Conclusion

The science of psychology seeks to advance and test hypotheses about cognitive, motivational and emotional processes as these occur in social and nonsocial situations. It does this by using controlled experiments, to see how variables affect behaviour, and self-reports of what is perceived, thought, remembered and felt. These are supplemented by more informal observations, for example, surveys of opinion, and studies that look for correlations between mental attributes in different groups. In its one-hundred-year history as an institutionalized science, the subject has been enriched by ideas and methods drawn from biology (the brain sciences, genetics, evolutionary theory etc.), medicine, sociology and the computer sciences.

The diversity of influences is mirrored by the diversity of questions in which psychologists are interested. Whereas more biologically oriented psychologists are trying to explain mental processes in terms of 'lower' levels of description involving physiology and information-processing activity, social psychologists are trying to show how mental activities relate to one another, and how they influence and are influenced by, social factors. Nevertheless, the different levels interact and no reductionist view can be correct unless it takes account of social psychologists' findings. For this reason, each psychological process discussed in this book will be considered from several perspectives. The final chapter will review the debate that surrounds the application of psychological knowledge to practical problems in education, medicine, criminology, industry and other social situations. In the long run, the success of psychology, like that of physics, will be judged as much by its 'technological' impact on society as by the state of development of its theory.

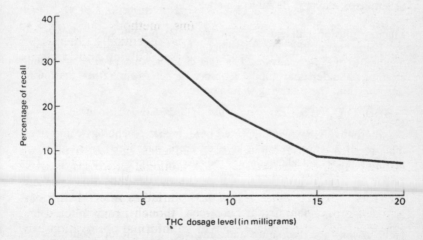

Figure 1.1 Marijuana and memory. An example of applying psychology to real-life problems. Subjects learned word lists under the influence of various doses of THC (marijuana's active ingredient) and then tried to recall the words a week later. Recall is poorer with higher doses.

The following chapter will briefly introduce ideas about behavioural genetics and the brain, which the reader will need to know if he is to understand the rest of the book. Students without a science background may find this chapter hard but should find their task eased if they read it with an accompanying primer of physiological psychology.

Further reading

Historical origins

For those interested in pursuing the intricate influences that have produced psychology in its modern form, a scholarly and readable history is:

THOMSON, R. (1968) *The Pelican History of Psychology*. Harmondsworth: Penguin.

Scientific psychology: its subject matter

Much confusion still exists about what the proper subject matter of psychology should be. For a fascinatingly written, stimulating and lucid defence of the view advanced in this chapter, that psychology should attempt to understand mind by observing behaviour rather than using introspection, the following should be read:

HEBB, D.O. (1980) *Essay on Mind*. Hillsdale, NJ: Erlbaum.

An alternative view, not supported here, is that psychology comprises a number of sciences, each asking different questions, using different methods and technical languages, and making different assumptions. This view is clearly developed in:

BELOFF, J. (1973) *Psychological Sciences: a Review of Modern Psychology*. London: Crosby Lockwood Staples.

Hebb's views on the nature and origins of altruism are controversial. Whether or not he is correct, it is very probable that much 'altruistic' behaviour is nepotistic, i.e., primarily directed towards biological relatives, or it is reciprocal, i.e., based on the likelihood of returned favours. These kinds of altruism may be directly selected for in evolution and be strongly inherited. They, and other aspects of altruism, are discussed from a sociobiological perspective in:

VINE, I. (1983) Sociobiology and social psychology – rivalry or symbiosis? The explanation of altruism. *British Journal of Social Psychology*, **22**, 1–11.

A more comprehensive and popular account of sociobiology and the problems it raises is provided in:

WILSON, E.O. (1978) *On Human Nature*. Cambridge, Mass.: Harvard University Press.

Scientific psychology: philosophical and methodological problems

A recent collection of essays that discuss philosophical questions relevant to psychology is provided by:

BOLTON, N., ed. (1979) *Philosophical Problems in Psychology*. London: Methuen.

For the reader who has a more general interest in the philosophy of science, a classic modern account, which advances the view that scientific hypotheses must be capable of experimental refutation, is found in:

POPPER, K.R. (1963) *Conjectures and Refutations*. London: Routledge and Kegan Paul.

Another prominent philosopher of science, Thomas Kuhn, has argued that science is essentially a more conservative activity than Popper suggests, in which during periods of *normal science* a consensus view of the science, characterized by shared theoretical assumptions, methods and language, and known as a paradigm, dominates the interpretation of experiments. Conflicting experimental results are reinterpreted so as to be consistent within the paradigm, and it is only when the conflicting evidence becomes overwhelming that the old paradigm is rejected and a new one introduced. Unfortunately the notion of a 'paradigm' is not easy to pin down. Some thinkers regard psychology as a science in which a number of different paradigms coexist. Thus, Freudian psychoanalysis and Piagetian developmental psychology are seen by some as different paradigms, and these are distinguished from the paradigms of physiological and comparative psychology. This view seems rather strange as these 'paradigms' are generally not concerned with interpreting the same experiments. If this criticism is correct then a psychological paradigm should provide a more general framework of assumptions, methods and language. Following this line of argument, others have argued that psychology is a preparadigmatic science and have used this conclusion to support their pessimistic belief that psychology is floundering and not developing new knowledge at the rate of the postparadigmatic physical sciences. If the reader wishes to be able to assess the acceptability of these proposals he is recommended to read:

KUHN, T.S. (1970) *The Structure of Scientific Revolutions*. Chicago: University of Chicago Press.

At a more mundane level, those interested in learning about elementary experimental design in psychology and in the use of statistics in psychological research, are recommended to begin with:

ROBSON, C. (1973) *Experiment, Design and Statistics*. Harmondsworth: Penguin.

It is worth emphasizing why statistics are so important in psychological research, whereas in physics their role is minor. If an experimenter wishes to show that a variable, such as the amount of alcohol consumed, is affecting a psychological variable in subjects, like skill in problem-solving or reaction time, he has to contend with the fact that these psychological variables are also being randomly influenced by many other factors. In order to show, therefore, that the variable is having a real effect, he needs to use statistical tests to determine the probability that his results could have occurred when there was *no* real effect. Only when this probability is low does he feel entitled to believe he has found a real effect.

If the reader is interested in the psychology of conscious experience, he will find that the following contains a useful collection of articles, including one by Sheehan on current thinking about the nature of hypnosis:

UNDERWOOD, G. and STEVENS, R., eds. (1979) *Aspects of Consciousness*, Volume 1, *Psychological Issues*. London: Academic Press.

A useful guide to the influence of the computer sciences on theorizing about cognitive process is given by:

BODEN, M. (1977) *Artificial Intelligence and Natural Man*. Brighton: Harvester Press.

2. The Biological Bases of Psychology

2. The Biological Bases of Psychology

General introduction

This chapter briefly and selectively reviews current biological knowledge that is relevant to a proper understanding of how minds, particularly human minds, work. It draws on contemporary thinking in the fields of evolutionary biology, genetics and the brain sciences. All of these fields are germane to explaining why human and animal behaviours take the form they do. Evolutionary biology explains that various human and animal behaviours exist because at critical times in evolution they were adaptive, i.e., they helped individuals by enabling them to survive and reproduce. Genetics is concerned with describing, *inter alia*, how genes interact with the environment, in determining how the brain develops, and hence ultimately what kinds of behaviour are shown. The brain sciences – for example, neurophysiology – try to elucidate the brain's micro-structure and its organization, and relate these to how it mediates behaviour and is responsible for mental phenomena. Although textbooks typically do not relate these sciences, in reality they are connected, and this chapter tries to highlight the more obvious links. Thus, evolution operates by the natural selection of inherited behaviours that are adaptive. This works by the selection of genes and these partially determine the form of brain structures that mediate the performance of adaptive behaviours. In the long term a biology of behaviour must make these and subtler associations explicit. At present, one can merely point out that each of the three disciplines provides techniques and knowledge that can help the others.

Evolution and genetics

BASIC GENETICS

The human brain and the behaviour it controls are products of evolution as are the brains and behaviour patterns of all other species. Each species produces more young than survive to reproduce, the survivors being naturally selected because they have inherited characteristics which are adaptive. It is, however, the units of heredity that are known as genes which are directly passed on to survivors' offspring, and these genes indirectly control the expression of the adaptive characteristics. Many characteristics are polygenic in that they are influenced by many genes, but some features, such as having curly rather than straight hair, are apparently largely determined by single genes. It is important to note that the form of all characteristics depends on a continuous interaction between genes and their environment from the moment of conception. No feature is solely determined by genes.

Parents transmit genes to their offspring in microscopic structures called **chromosomes**, contained within the nucleus of each body cell, including the fertilized egg. In humans, all body cells, except sperms and unfertilized eggs, contain twenty-three pairs of chromosomes. Sperms and eggs contain half sets which combine on fertilization to create twenty-three chromosome pairs. This means that each offspring receives half its genes from each parent. Human chromosomes contain thousands of genes so the probability of two individuals being genetically identical is negligible. In fact, this probably only occurs when two individuals develop from a single fertilized egg as happens with identical (monozygotic) twins. Nonidentical (dizygotic) twins develop from two fertilized eggs and are no more genetically similar than ordinary siblings.

Chromosomes are partly composed of long strands of the double helix molecule deoxyribonucleic acid (DNA). DNA can be likened to a string of beads in which there are four different kinds of bead, each kind of bead corresponding to a molecular group known as a nucleotide. Although genes cannot be isolated under the electron microscope, they consist of a stretch of DNA that controls the synthesis of a specific kind of protein. Proteins are composed of sequences of different amino acids, and their uniqueness of function is dependent on the specific sequence. It is the order of nucleotides on a gene that codes for this amino acid sequence. So each gene controls the production of unique proteins. In turn, proteins act either as structural molecules in cell membranes or as enzymes that catalyse specific chemical reactions in the cell. The progression which leads to the expression of a characteristic begins therefore with the synthesis of these important molecules. It is important to realize, however, that most genes in specialized tissues are 'switched off' and are not producing their unique proteins. Genes are 'switched on' by environmental stimuli impinging on their cells and influencing other 'regulator' genes, although this process is still poorly understood. So, in the growing individual, whether or not a characteristic appears depends partly on the environment being appropriate for 'switching on' its controlling genes.

Twenty-two of the twenty-three pairs of chromosomes found in humans are matched in the sense that for each pair there are corresponding gene loci where the matching genes are concerned with the control of the same characteristics. Different forms of the genes at matching loci are known as **alleles**, each allele coding the synthesis of slightly different proteins. If an allele is dominant then the characteristics it determines will be expressed even if the gene on its corresponding locus is different. When both genes must be of the same kind if a characteristic is to be expressed, they are called **recessive**. There are, in fact, degrees of recessiveness so that if there is a recessive, dominant gene combination the expressed characteristic will be slightly affected by the recessive gene, e.g., the eyes may be grey-blue rather than blue or brown. The terrible disorder of Huntington's chorea, in which involuntary movements and progressive loss of motor control are accompanied by a gathering dementia, is determined by a dominant gene. In contrast, the symptoms of the bleeding disease haemophilia are only apparent in individuals who have inherited two of the alleles that determine the disease. Like albinism and other diseases, it is transmitted by recessive genes. In considering alleles, it is worth indicating that most genes have some indirect influence on characteristics other than the one they predominantly control, and conversely that most characteristics are not solely influenced by genes at only one chromosomal locus.

Haemophilia, like colour-blindness, is more common in males, and both are carried by recessive genes. There are many such sex-linked characteristics and the reason for their existence is that the genes controlling them are borne on the twenty-third pair of chromosomes, known as the sex chromosomes. Human females inherit two large X sex chromosomes (carried by the egg and sperm cells) whereas males inherit a large X and a small Y chromosome. Recessive genes may be carried on the X chromosome to which there are no corresponding genes borne by the Y chromosome of males. In females, a haemophilia or colour-blindness (and possibly a dyslexia or reading difficulty) carrying gene may occur on one X chromosome, but not on the other. When this happens the characteristic is not fully expressed, but the female may act as a carrier, transmitting the disease to the next generation of male offspring.

Although most humans inherit twenty-three chromosome pairs, this inheritance can be disturbed so that where there is normally a related pair, one, three or four chromosomes are found. Such chromosomal abnormalities cause physical and mental disorders. This is particularly found with sex chromosome aberrations. Thus, women with Turner's syndrome only have one X chromosome and fail to develop sexually from puberty. It is also claimed that although aspects of their intelligence are normal, they have problems with arithmetic and various forms of spatial cognition. In Klinefelter's disease, which occurs in about one in four hundred births (some of the Pharaohs had it, as apparently do some Russian 'female' athletes), there is an XXY sex chromosome combination. Klinefelter cases have some intersexual features, in that their penis and testes are small, the testes non-sperm-producing and the breasts enlarged. Contrastingly, there are men with XYY sex chromosome combinations (about one in every thousand births). These individuals are above average height and, it has been claimed, very aggressive. Indeed, some XYY individuals in the USA and France were acquitted of criminal charges on the grounds that they were victims of their inheritance and not free to choose their behaviour. This again raises the point, made in the last chapter, about whether deterministic explanations are inconsistent with the ascription of responsibility. In this case the apparent conflict may be academic as recent evidence has failed to confirm that XYY men are more aggressive, although individuals with their genetic make-up are more likely to be found in prisons and mental hospitals. Not all chromosomal abnormalities are found on the sex chromosomes. For example, an extra chromosome on chromosome pair 21 is associated with Down's syndrome or mongolism, in which a characteristic physical appearance is associated with serious mental deficiency and a tendency to develop a very early dementia.

Genes, then, control the synthesis of specific proteins, and the emergence of characteristics depends on interactions between many genes as well as between genes and environment. In most cases, it is still difficult to see a clear link between the synthesized proteins and the characteristic that develops. An exception is found in the recessive hereditary complaint of phenylketonuria. This disease may be expressed as a mental deficiency with a tendency to convulsions early in life. It is caused by the inability to convert the amino acid phenylalanine into the amino acid tyrosine, so that the former substance accumulates and causes brain damage. Individuals with the disease have inherited a gene which fails to synthesize the normal protein that catalyses the conversion process. The disease can now be treated by putting identified individuals on a phenylalanine-reduced diet from a very early age (identification is based on a simple urine test). The efficacy of such treatment illustrates the important point that even if a characteristic is 'inherited' (as mental deficiency is in phenylketonuria), it may be changed radically by appropriate environmental manipulations. In general, to say that differences between individuals are largely caused by genetic factors does not mean that the differences cannot be abolished by changing the environment.

THE MODULAR VIEW OF THE BRAIN

The link between the activity of genes and the development of behavioural characteristics involves many intervening processes. One of these must be the growth of brain structures with specialized physiology and information-processing functions. Complex brains, like those of humans and other mammals, may be viewed as comprising many such specialized processing systems or modules. In evolution, new behavioural capacities emerge when a new module is created through natural selection. The new module must be integrated with those that already exist. If the brain was a highly interactive system in which each module was connected to a very large number of other modules, then the addition of a new module would require alterations in many other modules as well. Similarly, if one module was changed, a very large number of other modules would require compensating changes. For example, a change in language comprehension functions might affect motor skill performance. Highly interactive systems are difficult to improve without completely redesigning them. But evolutionary changes are small and each step needs to be adaptive, so it is likely that the brain is not, on the whole, highly interactive, but, as Dean (1982) has called it, 'modular', i.e., each module only directly influences a few other modules. One effect of this modularity is that damage to localized brain regions often disturbs highly specific functions, like colour vision or the ability to repeat spoken utterances. The fact that, unlike computers, mammalian brains have not been constructed at a single design stage, but in many small stages with each addition having to be integrated with structures already present, therefore provides important clues as to how such brains must be organized. They will be modular, and newer additions may often process similar information to older modules, but in more sophisticated ways.

EVOLUTIONARY THEORY

The evolutionary process of natural selection (differential reproduction of characteristics) only operates on characteristics that are inheritable in populations across long periods of time. Natural selection also requires that there is a struggle for survival in which only a proportion of individuals live to reproduce. These individuals will tend to possess the characteristics which are selected in evolution. Variability of characteristics is a further requirement of the process, and it depends on genetic variability. This variability has traditionally been thought to depend on point mutations in single genes – changes in the DNA code caused by radiation or chemical agents. This traditional view of the important source of genetic variability was associated with the modern synthesis of Darwinism according to which species are formed very gradually by the progressive accumulation of individual differences until two groups can no longer freely interbreed. Such gradual differentiation would occur when two initially identical populations become separated, typically by a geographical factor.

This gradualist view of evolution predicts that intermediate forms or 'missing links' should be found when species are formed from a common ancestor. The general difficulty of finding such intermediate forms has led to the recent formulation of an alternative account of how evolution occurs, which is known as the **punctuated equilibrium theory**. This explains the difficulty in finding missing links by proposing that species are usually very well adapted to their environments and remain constant for long periods of time, this constancy being assured by natural selection which eliminates harmful characteristics. These long periods of equilibrium are interrupted by brief periods of rapid evolutionary change, probably brought about by critical environmental alterations. In these periods of punctuated activity, new species may be formed in a few thousand years or even less – such a short time that intermediate forms are unlikely to be fossilized.

It is hard to see how the rapid changes postulated by the punctuated equilibrium theory could be based on single gene mutations. Rapid changes could, however, be based on chromosomal mutations which affect long stretches of DNA on chromosomes. A length of DNA may be removed and attached to another chromosome or it may be reinserted back-to-front in its original chromosome. The significance of chromosomal mutations can be appreciated if a distinction is made between structural and regulator genes. Most genes are structural in that they produce proteins, which are important for cell structure or for catalysing cellular chemical reactions. Some genes are, however, regulatory. They produce proteins that determine whether other genes are switched on or off. Chromosomal mutations may have the effect of bringing certain structural genes under the control of new regulators. This may radically affect the developmental plan because the structural genes may be active at different times or for longer periods. Relatively small genetic changes may therefore lead to dramatic alterations in brain structure and behaviour, that could not otherwise occur over a few thousand years.

The punctuated equilibrium theory of evolution has direct relevance to the view that humans, chimpanzees and gorillas evolved from a common ape ancestor, living about 5 to 8 million years ago (see Gribbin and Cherfas, 1982). The more traditional view, compatible with a gradualist account of evolution, and based on very limited fossil evidence plus much guesswork, is that the common ancestor for the ape and human lines lived about 15 to 20 million years ago, after which time the lineages diverged. Molecular anthropologists, who compare DNA and proteins across different species, have however shown that human genetic material is 99 per cent the same as that of chimpanzees and gorillas. By comparing genetic differences in species reliably known to have diverged from a common ancestor at a given time, it is possible to calculate the rate at which DNA differences accumulate in diverging species, and the rate turns out to be remarkably constant. Using this molecular clock, it has been possible to extrapolate that the evolutionary line of humans, chimpanzees and gorillas diverged about 5 to 8 million years ago. Further evidence suggests that the common ancestral line diverged from that of orang-utans at least 8 million years ago, and from that of gibbons rather more than 12 million years ago.

We are, then, genetically very similar to chimpanzees and gorillas, and yet our brains and behaviour have changed considerably. For example, the human brain is three times bigger than would be predicted for a primate of our size. This is shown by measuring the ratio of brain size to that of the spinal cord, which gives an indication of the brain's size relative to its inputs and outputs. Using this measure, the gap between humans and chimpanzees is *greater* than that between chimpanzees and hedgehogs (see Passingham, 1982). It seems probable that chromosomal mutations changed the controlling activity of certain regulator genes, so that the development plan for the brain was dramatically altered. This suggestion may be related to the further, well-supported claim that humans have evolved through **neoteny**. The notion of neoteny is illustrated by the assertion that humans are like sexually mature primate foetuses. Our developmental plan has been altered so that sexually mature humans have many of the characteristics of infant apes. For example, our upright gait, large brain housed in a domed skull, relatively hairless body and small jaws, are all characteristics of foetal apes and, therefore, neotenous features.

Neoteny appears to have played an important role in evolutionary history. There is, for example, evidence that the chordates (which include all vertebrates) evolved from a sea urchin which changed in a neotenous fashion (larval sea urchins are much more similar to chordates). Neoteny may well occur as a result of chromosomal mutations, which alter the developmental plan so that sexual maturation and other growth processes emerge at different rates. Under certain environmental conditions these neotenous changes confer an adaptive advantage on the individuals who show them. In the case of human ancestors, the nature of these conditions and the corresponding advantages is a matter for speculation. The view that humans developed as aggressive group hunters in the African savannah is now thought implausible because they could not have competed successfully against the predators that already existed. It seems more likely that humans emerged in the very harsh conditions that existed in Africa during the last few million years – conditions of drought associated with the Ice Age. Under these conditions, it might have paid to develop the versatility of a generalist so that ancestral humans would have hunted, gathered food or scavenged, depending on circumstances. Neoteny would have facilitated the growth of such generalist activities, which would have been further enhanced by the complex social groups that proto-humans would have developed. In contrast, chimpanzees and gorillas must have lived in more predictable habitats (for example, tropical forests), which encouraged the development of specialist adaptations.

The large brains of proto-humans that enabled them to become intelligent generalists also led to their developing more complex social interactions. In turn, their social environment may have acted as a powerful selective pressure for sophisticated cognitive skills, such as self-awareness (as suggested in Chapter 1). Social influences are important in other ways, too. Social stimulation seems essential for the development of many cognitive skills in mammals; without it, individual brains may be relatively atrophied. In the great apes and even more so in ancestral humans, societies become the means by which specific skills and knowledge are passed on – individuals acquire such things by imitating others who already possess them. This is the beginning of culture. Most distinctively human characteristics are acquired within cultures. These cultures, relative to those of nonhumans, store vast amounts of knowledge, which are transmitted by *teaching* as well as the less certain and more informal processes of imitation. Behaviour may differ enormously across cultures even though the individuals constituting the differing cultures may be genetically very similar. It is possible to argue that whereas selection of genetic characteristics must operate on individuals, the selection of cultural characteristics may operate on social groups: those with certain knowledge, skills and values may not be able to compete against others and consequently they suffer destruction or are absorbed by the dominant cultures. Even so, it must be remembered that the ability to create cultures, and the form those cultures take, depend on individuals in a society inheriting appropriate brain mechanisms – both generalist mechanisms and mechanisms which enable them to acquire human language.

The extent to which behaviours are determined by cultural background or by genetic make-up is a popularly disputed issue. It has raged particularly over whether sex differences in aggressiveness and verbal and visuospatial abilities are genetic in origin and whether human predilections for fighting wars are similarly determined. To resolve these disputes one can assess the variability of behaviour across cultures, and, assuming that cross-cultural genetic differences are minimal, ascribe most of the discovered variability to cultural factors. In contrast, features found in all (or nearly all) cultures may be less influenced by cultural than genetic factors. For example, men are found to be more physically and verbally aggressive than women in nearly all cultures. The fact that certain kinds of culture do not exist may indicate that our inheritance constrains the range of cultures we are likely to develop. Most culturally linked behaviours are social – e.g., aggressiveness, sexuality, altruism, ambitiousness, religiousness – and it has been argued by some **sociobiologists** (who apply evolutionary and ethological ideas to human social behaviour so as to argue that it is strongly genetically constrained) that these kinds of tendency are strongly inherited. Theorists like Edward Wilson (1978) have claimed that the kinds of society and culture created by humans are constrained by the influence of genes, selected during the past few million years when our ancestors were hunter-gatherers. For example, he asserts that we are genetically predisposed to classify people dichotomously into friends and aliens, to suspect and fear the actions of strangers, and to resolve conflicts with them aggressively. Even if sociobiologists are right about the heritability of socially motivated behaviours, they have not shown *how* genetic factors exert their control. But, furthermore, the measurement of heritability is itself very tricky. Scientific treatment of such issues is the business of behaviour genetics, which is discussed next.

Behavioural genetics

Behavioural and brain genetics is concerned with three basic problems. First, what genes are involved in the development of each relevant characteristic? Second, how do these genes interact with their environment from the moment of conception so as to produce the relevant characteristic? Third, to what extent is each relevant characteristic determined by genetic factors? Very little is known in relation to the first two problems. Nevertheless, recent research suggests it is becoming possible to map the relationship between specific genes and behavioural characteristics. This is done by showing that the characteristics occur in individuals and families in association with specific 'genetic markers'. These genetic markers may be other characteristics, such as red-headedness, or they may be the ability or inability to manufacture specific proteins. In either case, it is often known on which chromosomes the responsible genes occur, and hence it is inferred that the gene(s) responsible for the behavioural characteristic occur on the same chromosome. For example, following an analysis of this kind in nine affected families, it has been claimed that a form of developmental dyslexia (in which individuals who are otherwise cognitively normal have a problem in learning to read and spell) is strongly determined by a dominant allele on chromosome 15 in humans (see Smith *et al.*, 1983). The gene probably influences the growth of those parts of the left hemisphere of the brain that are responsible for aspects of verbal ability.

There has, however, also been a considerable amount of research on the effects of single gene mutations in paramecia, nematode worms, fruitflies and mice on the behaviour and brain functions of these species (see Quinn and Gould, 1979, for a review). This research has shown that changes in single genes affect the proteins that control the physiological functions in single nerve cells. One such change affects the nerve-like single cell of the paramecium, so that instead of retreating when it comes up against a resistant surface the mutant strain continues to try to move forward. This pawn mutant has suffered a change in one kind of protein and that has altered one aspect of its physiological reactivity and, finally, behaviour. Single gene mutations (known as point mutations) also affect the way in which nerve cells link up to form complex circuits. This may sometimes be achieved by altering the development plan for brain differentiation. In a mutant strain of mice, called reelers, the cortical surface of the brain is formed inside out, so that nerve cells that normally lie in the deepest level are on the outside. In nonmutant mice the outside level develops last at the deepest level and then migrates through the older levels to the outside. In reeler mice this migration does not occur because a vital signal is absent. Although the brains of reeler mice show compensatory changes so that their cortexes seem functionally indistinguishable from those of normal mice, Siamese cats, which possess the gene for temperature-dependent albinism, show many functional abnormalities of vision because the relevant parts of their brains develop aberrantly. Single genes, then, may have dramatic effects both on the brain's structure and on its functioning.

The complexity of the processes which lead from gene expression to behaviour is emphasized by the occurrence of situations where a given environment has different effects on different **genotypes** (these are complete sets of genes, whereas the term **phenotype** refers to the complete set of an individual's observable characteristics). For example, glutamic acid intake makes dull children more intelligent, but has no effect on average or bright children (see Eysenck and Kamin, 1981). Such interactions must be considered when psychologists approach the third kind of genetic problem: the extent to which behavioural characteristics are genetically determined. This kind of issue has exercised psychologists to a much greater degree. In resolving it, one must be aware that it is not meaningful to speak of the extent to which a particular characteristic is inherited *in an individual* (although this has often been claimed). This is because genetic and environmental factors are inextricably intertwined. Thus one cannot ask what proportion of an individual's intelligence is caused by his or her genotype. We can, however, consider how the characteristic varies *in a given population* and estimate what proportion of this variation is owing to genetic differences between individuals, to differences in the environments to which they are exposed, and to interactions between these differences (as mentioned at the beginning of the paragraph). The proportion of the variability in a given characteristic caused by genetic differences between individuals is called **heritability**. For example, in Western societies the heritability of intelligence has been estimated as 80 per cent. But in a different environment this value might be radically different.

Psychologists have been concerned to show that not only does intelligence have a high heritability, but that personality characteristics such as introversion, neuroticism and psychoticism are also inherited. Many believe that susceptibility to serious depression or to schizophrenia is also inherited, and there is also evidence that homosexuality has an appreciable heritability. These conclusions about polygenically determined characteristics are based on a variety of sources although there are drastic limits on the extent to which one can manipulate humans genetically or environmentally. All the sources involve comparisons of averages (for the relevant characteristic), or correlations for individuals showing known degrees of genetic difference and varying degrees of difference in the environment to which they are exposed. Thus, behaviour geneticists have relied, first, on comparisons between monozygotic and dizygotic twins reared together or reared apart. Second, they have examined family resemblances between individuals who vary in the closeness of their kinship. Third, they have studied adoptive children and compared them with their foster parents' biological children. Fourth, and more controversially, some psychologists have estimated heritability from the degree to which a characteristic shows regression to the mean. (Regression to the mean is the tendency of children with parents who are extreme in a given characteristic to show scores on that characteristic that are closer to the average.) Eysenck has argued that the extent of regression shown by intelligence gives a measure of its heritability.

The use of all four of the above sources has been criticized, but some confidence may be placed in heritability estimates if all four sources yield similar values. The criticisms can be illustrated by considering the controversy about the heritability of intelligence (see Eysenck and Kamin, 1981). First, there are several studies that show high correlations for the intelligence of monozygotic twins brought up apart. These correlations are higher than those for dizygotic twins or ordinary siblings who are brought up *together*. In the former case there is, of course, genetic identity whereas in the latter there are marked differences in genotypes. It has been argued, however, that even when they are brought up apart monozygotic twins have been exposed to very similar environments. The same point has been made with respect to comparisons between monozygotic and dizygotic twins who are reared together. There is evidence that identical twins are treated in a more similar way than are ordinary siblings or dizygotic twins. Even monozygotic twins vary in physical likeness and this seems to be a factor in deciding how alike they will be treated. Kamin has claimed that monozygotic twins who are physically more alike are also more similar in intelligence. He also claims, in support of the same argument, that dizygotic twins of the same sex are treated more alike than opposite sex twins, and both are treated more alike than ordinary siblings. Although the genetic differences between these groups are about the same, single sex dizygotic twins are most alike in intelligence.

Comparisons of intelligence between adoptive and biological children are intended to examine the effects of genetic differences when environment is held constant. Early comparisons, which were between *different* families with adoptive and biological children, found a very low correlation between the intelligence of adoptive children and their foster parents. This appears to be an artefact because adoptive parents, unlike biological ones, tend to be drawn from a restricted group in society – typically, those people with high intelligence. It is because their intelligence shows so little variability relative to that of biological parents that the correlation with their adoptive children's intelligence is so low. A more appropriate design requires families to be selected, so that each has an adoptive and matching biological child. When this has been done, the parent-child correlation for intelligence has been found to be very similar for adoptive and biological children. Kamin has also claimed that the average intelligence of adoptive children tends to be closer to that of their adoptive than of their biological parents.

The interpretation of correlations between the level of intelligence of individuals with differing degrees of kinship presents severe problems because, in these cases, as the degree of genetic dissimilarity increases, so does the kind of environment to which individuals are exposed tend to become more dissimilar. Galton

(1869) studied intellectual eminence in three hundred families and found that whereas for every hundred eminent men he identified, thirty-one had eminent fathers, he could find only three eminent grandsons per hundred eminent men. Although Galton concluded from such observations that genius was hereditary, his conclusion was dependent on the implicit use of a model about the role of genes and environmental differences in family relationships which enabled him to discount the influence of environmental factors. Kamin has argued that all available models of kinship relations depend upon false assumptions (see Eysenck and Kamin, 1981) and if he is right, one cannot use the kinds of data cited by Galton to estimate the heritability of intelligence.

Finally, it has been argued contrary to Eysenck (see Bodmer, 1972) that regression to the mean occurs whenever parents with an extreme value of a characteristic are selected, if that characteristic is determined by many causes. Some of these causes will tend to increase a characteristic, such as intelligence, whereas others will tend to decrease it. Although most commonly the causal factors balance out to give average intelligence, in rare cases they will act largely in one direction so as to produce very high or very low intelligence. This is what has happened with high- or low-intelligence parents. The causal factors are likely to be less biased with their children, who will show less extreme intelligences. It follows from this that parents will also show regression to the mean. If a group of very bright and very dull children are chosen, then it will be found that their parents show regression to the mean. The multiple causes will be both genetic and environmental, so without further assumptions nothing can be inferred about heritability. Indeed, regression would occur for characteristics entirely determined by the environment.

Several conclusions may be tentatively drawn from these criticisms. First, methods of calculating heritability in humans cannot be used to give accurate estimates. Typically, the methods fail to tap the environmental variability to which the relevant population is exposed. Second, despite the criticisms, it is intuitively likely that characteristics such as intelligence, personality and susceptibility to psychoses have heritabilities appreciably greater than zero. This amounts to saying that there is relevant genetic variability in modern societies. Third, it is unclear that precise measures of heritability have much practical or theoretical value. Appreciable heritability means that a characteristic may have been selected for in evolution or could be bred for by a eugenicist dictator. Level of heritability simply gives a measure of the ease with which such selective processes can operate. It seems much more fundamental to determine which genetic and environmental factors determine characteristics, such as intelligence, and how they do so. This suggestion is supported by two further observations. First, regression to the mean could only be used to estimate the heritability of intelligence if more was known about intelligence's genetic and environmental causes. For example, Eysenck assumes that very bright parents will provide ideal environments for fostering brilliance (and conversely for dull parents). But this is unproven and, more important, there are many unknown environmental factors that may act less favourably for the children of bright parents than they did for the parents. These factors must be identified. Second, even if heritability could be accurately calculated for a given population at a given time, its value might dramatically change if it was discovered that certain previously unexperienced environmental factors greatly influenced the growth of a characteristic. For example, with certain genotypes, exposure as a foetus to certain drugs or hormones might greatly increase adult intelligence. If such treatment was only available to some, the heritability of intelligence must be reduced.

Above all, focusing on calculations of heritability detracts attention from the processes intervening between gene expression and behavioural characteristic. As briefly described in Chapter 1, preliminary work on such processes is interesting. Thus, genotype and environment may interact to produce a nervous system which is very difficult to arouse. Individuals with such nervous systems will be hard to condition and so may develop weak consciences and find social interactions more rewarding than punishing. They become extraverts unless exposed to undue amounts of social conditioning. If they are neurotic, they may also under some circumstances become criminals (see Eysenck, 1977). Such models point the way that future behaviour genetics in humans should move; but nevertheless, they are polemical and hard to test. The human approach may be complemented by animal research where there is more possibility of identifying the stages intervening between genotype and phenotype.

SELECTIVE BREEDING

Research on the effects of single gene mutations on brain development was described earlier in this section. Work has also been done on the selective breeding of behavioural characteristics in animals. Two examples of selective breeding in rats are particularly famous. Tryon (1940) tested rats on maze-learning, and then mated quick learners together and slow learners together. Over several generations he was able to get clear separation of quick and slow learners. Later research showed one problem with this kind of programme: it is difficult to control exactly for what you breed. Thus, the animals were not generally 'bright' or 'dull'. The 'bright' rats were good at maze-learning but not at learning other tasks, and they also showed higher levels of motivation and emotion. The Tryon rats have, however, illuminated gene-environment interactions. For example, Cooper and Zubek (1958) found that 'bright' offspring suffered when brought up in an impoverished environment whereas 'dull' offspring did not. Conversely, 'bright' offspring did not particularly benefit from early exposure to an enriched environment whereas 'dull' ones did. These results have been speculatively related to the levels of cholinesterase in the cortex (see pages 93, 276). Levels of this chemical seem important in maze-learning and its level is known to depend on the nature of the early (and perhaps later) environment. This influence would then also seem to depend on genotype. Although interesting, these results would be more relevant if Tryon 'bright' rats modelled similar processes to those found in intelligent human behaviour. This is highly improbable.

A similar problem arises with the Maudsley reactive and nonreactive strains of rats. These were previously thought of as fearful and unfearful strains because the 'fearful' rats showed a high rate of defecation and little ambulation when placed in a noisy, bright and supposedly frightening open space. There is doubt, however, whether these measures tap the processes of fear as they operate in humans. The breeding schedule used also led to considerable inbreeding of the strains. The reactive rats were found to be heavier, and have lower metabolic rates and higher blood cholesterol levels. Whether these characteristics are related to the behavioural ones remains a moot issue. Broadhurst (1960) was able nevertheless to show that the behavioural differences persisted even when he controlled for the influence of the mother and the foetal environment. The former was controlled by cross-fostering reactive offspring with nonreactive mothers from birth, and vice versa with nonreactive offspring. The foetal environment was controlled by crossbreeding reactive males with nonreactive females, and nonreactive males with reactive females (the offspring did not differ significantly, which is perhaps surprising). Levine and Broadhurst (1963) also found some evidence that early handling had more effect on emotionality in reactive than nonreactive rats – another example of an interaction between genes and environment.

Human and animal work on behaviour genetics suggests that many behavioural characteristics are inherited. Therefore, they probably arose through the processes of natural selection in evolution. These processes operated more directly to select brain structures and cellular activities. The history of evolution from simple invertebrates to the complex brains of primates can be considered at two levels. First, it involves the development of the atomic unit of nervous systems – the neuron, or nerve cell. Little is known about how this unit has evolved over the past 400 million years, but we can say that its mechanisms seem to be fairly similar in simple invertebrates and mammals. Second, evolution involves changes in the organization and size of nervous systems or brains, i.e., in the way neurons are linked together and the number of more complex processing units into which they are incorporated. The next section will consider the physiology and chemistry of the neural units, the broad activities of which are common to so many species. It will then be possible to review the larger scale structure of brains, and particularly those of mammals.

Neurons, neurotransmitters and hormones

The human brain contains about ten thousand million neurons together with ten times as many glia cells, that seem to serve a variety of nutritive and other largely unknown supportive roles. In contrast, the nervous systems of invertebrates such as the sea snail Aplysia may contain only a thousand or so neurons. Although no two neurons are identical in form, most share simple structural and

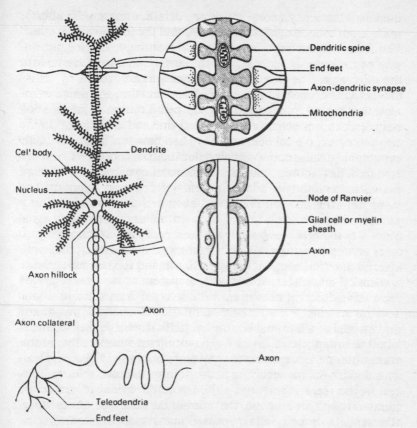

Figure 2.1 A typical neuron showing some of its major physical features. (After Kolb and Whishaw, 1980, p. 33)

functional features whether they are found in humans or Aplysia. They contain a cell body, dendrites and one or more axons. The cell body contains the nucleus in which lies most of the cell's DNA. This is the neuron's powerhouse. The dendrites form a delicate, bushy tree around the cell body. They are the main structure through which the neuron receives incoming signals. The axon projects away from the cell body and carries the signals, received by the dendrites, to other parts of the brain. Unlike dendrites, axons only branch at their ends where they communicate with other neurons. In the human brain many axons are covered in a white **myelin sheath**, made from specialized Schwann cells, that speeds the rate at which signals are conducted. The sheath is discontinuous, being punctuated by the nodes of Ranvier, and the signals jump from one node to the next, a process called **saltatory conduction**.

Nervous systems are networks of neurons through which information is passed from one cell to another. Transfer of information between neurons occurs at specialized sites called **synapses**. In the human cortex, typical neurons may have between 1000 and 10,000 synapses and may receive signals from 1000 other neurons. Modern research has shown that although most synapses are formed between axons and dendrites, they also occur between dendrite and dendrite, axon and cell body, and axon and axon. Information is passed along the axon in the form of an electrochemical signal known as the **action potential**. At their synapses, axons enlarge to form **terminal boutons**, which contain many tiny sacks called **vesicles**. Each vesicle contains between 10,000 and 100,000 molecules of a chemical messenger, known as a **neurotransmitter**. There are, in fact, many different neurotransmitters found in human and animal nervous systems. When action potentials have passed down an axon and arrived at a terminal bouton, vesicles discharge their contents into the synaptic cleft. At an axon-dendritic synapse, the neurotransmitter molecules cross the gap and combine with receptor sites on a dendrite of the receiving neuron. Information is thus transferred to the receiving neuron although its 'decision' to fire action potentials will depend on the combined effect of hundreds or thousands of its receiving synapses. Some of these inputs are excitatory and make it more likely to fire whereas others are inhibitory and make it less likely to fire. Recent research, however, makes very clear that incoming signals are not describable simply as excitatory or inhibitory. The action of neurotransmitters on receptor sites has many effects, some of which last for around a millisecond and others of which are much longer lasting (see Iversen, 1979).

The ability of neurons to transmit and receive signals depends on specialized properties of their surrounding membrane. Further membrane properties enable neurons in the embryo to recognize each other and form structural contacts. In the membrane, a protein layer is sandwiched between two layers of fat, or lipid. It is membrane proteins that determine its properties. There are five kinds.

First, **protein pumps** use metabolic energy to move charged molecules (**ions**) against concentration gradients to maintain their levels on either side of the membrane. Second, **channel proteins** offer selective pathways for specific ions to diffuse through the neuron's membrane. Third, **receptor proteins** provide sites with which specific neurotransmitters can combine to pass on their information. Fourth, **enzyme proteins** catalyse specific chemical reactions around the membrane surface. Fifth, **structural proteins**, among other functions, help maintain the integrity of subcellular components. Clearly, all these proteins are under close genetic control.

In its resting state the inside of a neuron is about 70 millivolts negative relative to its outside. The outside is ten times richer in positively charged sodium ions whereas the inside is ten times richer in the less common, positively charged potassium ions. This imbalance is maintained by a protein sodium-pump that pumps sodium ions out of the neuron in exchange for potassium ions. There are also channels that allow potassium ions near the membrane to seep out continuously, with the result that the cell's interior is negatively charged. When an input activates the neuron, sodium channels on the axon membrane by the cell body are opened by a voltage change, and sodium ions flow into the cell for about one millisecond before the channels shut again. The flow of sodium ions changes the charge of the neuron's inside from negative to positive and begins the self-reinforcing process of the action potential, that carries on down the axon until it reaches the terminal boutons, where it causes neurotransmitter molecules to be released. The resting state is restored by potassium channels opening and allowing positively charged potassium ions to flow out of the cell and return it to negativity. The membrane is briefly refractory so the action potential only moves away from the cell body, like a flame moving down a fuse.

Action potentials are of the same amplitude, so information in the neuron is represented by the frequency of such impulses (and possibly by their temporal patterning). This information is decoded at the neuron's synapses where the combination of neurotransmitter molecules with receptor proteins causes channels to be opened and ions to flow in or out of the cell. This causes the generation of a train of action potentials, the number of which is a function of stimulus

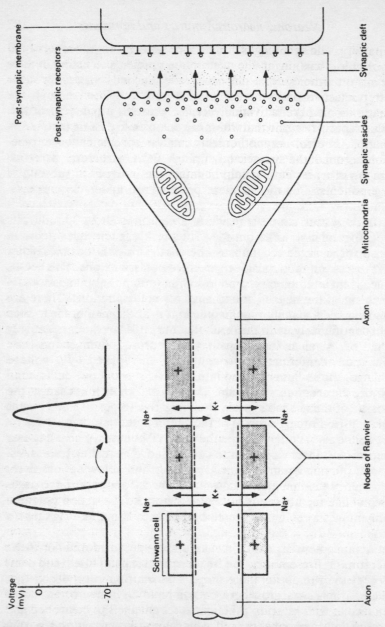

Figure 2.2 Action potentials approaching a synapse by saltatory conduction, a process in which impulses leap from one node of Ranvier to the next and which speeds conduction greatly.

intensity. The decoding of stimulus intensity involves **temporal** and **spatial** summation at the neuron's synapses. The more neurotransmitter molecules a synapse receives in a given time, the more temporal summation there will be. Spatial summation involves the integration of the activations at all a neuron's synapses. For this reason, it is often said that whereas axons transmit information from one brain region to another, information-processing and integration occurs at the synaptic boundaries between neurons. To stress the point again: both action potentials and synaptic integration of signals depend on the function of specialized membrane proteins. These proteins are very unevenly distributed across the cell's surface so as to concentrate where they are needed.

In human and animal brains many different neurotransmitters are found (the suspected number is in excess of thirty and rising). Furthermore, even a single neurotransmitter, such as **acetylcholine**, is excitatory at some synapses and inhibitory at others, depending on the nature of the protein receptors. Even the view that one neuron releases only one kind of neurotransmitter has now been challenged. Indeed, some evidence suggests that more than one kind of chemical messenger may be released from one synapse depending on the pattern of action potentials reaching the terminal bouton. As well as acetylcholine, there appear to be several groups of neurotransmitters in mammalian brains. First, there are simple amino acid molecules, such as **GABA** and glycine. GABA is the brain's commonest inhibitory transmitter, appearing in up to a third of the brain's synapses. The movement disorder of Huntington's chorea has been linked with a fairly specific deficit of GABA in certain brain regions (the corpus striatum). Second, there is the group of monoamine transmitters, including **noradrenaline**, **dopamine**, **serotonin** and **histamine**. The importance of these messengers in psychological function is illustrated by the fact that the hallucinogenic drug mescaline is similar in structure to noradrenaline and dopamine, whereas **psilocybin** and **LSD** resemble serotonin. Presumably, the drug molecules influence the same receptor sites as do the naturally occurring neurotransmitters. Third, there is a growing group of neuropeptides, consisting of chains of amino acids (like small proteins). The neuropeptides include the **enkephalins** and **endorphins**, known as the **opioids** because functionally they resemble the opium drugs, morphine and heroin. In fact, it was the search for naturally occurring substances that bound to the same neuronal receptor sites as morphine which led to the discovery of the opioids. They appear to be released during acupuncture and following hypnotic suggestions for pain relief, and one of their actions does reduce perceived pain.

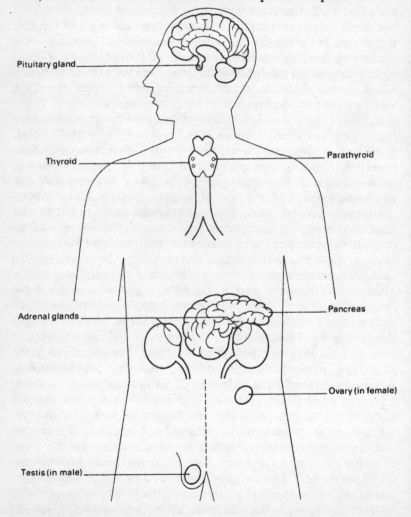

Figure 2.3 The endocrine system.

Many of the neuropeptide transmitters have been found not only in synaptic vesicles but also in other parts of the body where they act as **hormones**. Hormones are also chemical messengers, but they are released by specialized endocrine glands directly into the bloodstream. They are carried in the bloodstream to many parts of the body and brain, where they act on specialized cellular receptor sites in a variety of target areas. Endocrine glands are, in turn, controlled directly or indirectly by the brain. For example, hormone production of the pineal gland and the posterior part of the pituitary is directly controlled by signals arriving from adjacent brain systems. Many endocrine glands are indirectly controlled, however, via the anterior pituitary, which itself is indirectly controlled by the **hypothalamus** which overlies it. For example, the pituitary releases the hormone **adrenocorticotrophic hormone (ACTH)**, which stimulates the adrenal cortex gland to release **corticosteroid** hormones. These serve important functions in adapting to stress and emotional arousal. An example of a substance which acts both as a neurotransmitter and a hormone is **vasopressin**. Vasopressin is released by the posterior pituitary and acts antidiuretically on the kidney as a hormone, to concentrate urine and conserve water in the body. It is also found at synaptic vesicles in certain brain sites where, among other poorly identified functions, it seems to strengthen memory for a variety of tasks in animals and humans. The occurrence of molecules acting as both neurotransmitters and hormones indicates that quite small genetic changes arising in evolutionary history may enable natural selection to adapt an already existent substance for other functions.

The close relationship of hormones and neurotransmitters is emphasized by the fact that many hormones influence behaviour by acting on brain structures. Thus the 'stress' hormones, known as corticosteroids (as well as ACTH), act directly on neurons in those parts of the brain that play a role in mediating emotional behaviour. Similarly, the predominantly male sex hormones, known as androgens, that are released by the testes and the adrenal cortex, act on neuronal receptors in the brain so as to increase sex drive in both males *and* females. The androgens also play a different, longer-term role in brain development. They appear to act on the foetal brain (and perhaps again on the pubertal brain) so as to make it differentiate in a male fashion (see Stevens and Goldstein, 1983). The early action of these hormones therefore influences adult sexual and sex-linked behaviours by changing the brain's microstructure and physiology.

Whereas hormones act on their targets from a distance, classical neurotransmitters act very locally at synapses. There is, however, evidence that some messengers, like noradrenaline, are sometimes released from neurons at nonsynaptic sites. They diffuse across the space between neurons and act on a rather more distributed set of neuronal receptors. Noradrenaline is believed to stimulate many cortical neurons (those covering the massive hemispheres of the mammalian brain like a crust) in this way, so as to make them better able to discriminate background noise from meaningful signals. The effect may be described as modulatory. Some researchers have distinguished between neurotransmitters and neuromodulators – only the former have a major effect on receiving neurons whereas the latter 'tune' neurons so that they will respond differently to later neurotransmitter stimulation. Many substances modulate neuronal sensitivity in this way. **Prostaglandins** provide a clear example of such substances. They cause long-term shifts in neuronal sensitivity.

Mammalian brains may be seen as comprising a collection of linked, special-purpose neuronal processing or computer systems. Each of these will contain neurons that release specific neurotransmitters. If the metabolism of these neurotransmitters becomes disturbed for any reason, then the special-purpose computer systems will cease to work properly, and the victim will show specific psychological deficits. Similarly, drugs that affect the functioning of the particular neurotransmitters may affect specific psychological processes (although the effects may be *less* specific as particular transmitters are often used by several independent neuronal-processing systems). For these reasons, it is very important to identify where in the brain particular neurotransmitters are distributed. New methods of selectively staining some transmitters has enabled researchers to find where in the brain dopamine, noradrenaline and serotonin are distributed. Remarkably, although less than 1 per cent of the brain's neurons release these neurotransmitters, they act on a much higher proportion of neurons. Furthermore, disorders of certain of the monoamine neurons cause behavioural problems. First, Parkinsonism, in which the patient suffers from rigidity, resting tremor and difficulty in initiating movements, is caused by atrophy of dopamine-releasing neurons, which link the midbrain to the corpus striatum. Second, schizophrenia, which is typically characterized by thought disorder, inappropriate emotions, auditory hallucinations and delusions of persecution, is possibly caused by a functional overactivity of dopamine in brain regions that mediate emotion and thought (see Chapters 8 and 13). These regions have been shown to contain abnormally high numbers of dopamine receptors at post mortem in some schizophrenics. Third, some forms of recurrent depression are believed to be caused by there being very low levels of noradrenaline at similarly placed neuronal sites. Mania may be caused by noradrenaline overactivity at these same sites. It is easy to see how susceptibility to schizophrenia or depression might be genetically transmitted. Presumably, an individual's genotype may cause his dopamine or noradrenaline 'control system' to be unstable, and hence easily disrupted by adverse environmental conditions such as the presence of a virus or of high levels of stress.

In order to understand how psychoactive drugs work, it is necessary to know about the metabolism of the neurotransmitters on which they act. Conversely, study of drug action has helped illuminate neurotransmitter function. Many neurotransmitters, like the monoamines dopamine and noradrenaline, are synthesized from precursor molecules usually in the cell body. In neurons using noradrenaline as a transmitter, the amino acid tyrosine is converted to L-DOPA, which is converted to dopamine, which is converted to noradrenaline. Each conversion stage is catalysed by a specific proteinous enzyme, in the cell body at present, and transported down the axon at a rate of ten to twenty centimetres a day. Precursors, like tyrosine, have to be supplied from food, so it is interesting to note the growing evidence that diet can influence psychological states (see Kolata, 1982). For example, high-protein meals may raise blood tyrosine and ultimately brain noradrenaline levels, and seem to improve mood in depressives and in normal people. Similarly, high-carbohydrate meals may raise blood tryptophan levels (tryptophan is the precursor of serotonin), and make people more sleepy and tolerant to pain. Once synthesized, transmitters are stored in vesicles, which may release their contents into the synaptic cleft when action potentials reach the terminal bouton. Transmitter molecules pass on their chemical message by combining with one or two kinds of receptor site – in both cases one effect is the flow of ions into or out of the receiving neuron. The first kind of receptor is associated with a specific ion channel that opens briefly when the receptor is bound to a transmitter molecule. When a transmitter molecule combines with the second kind of receptor, a second messenger (cyclic AMP or cyclic GMP) is released inside the receiving neuron in large numbers. This second messenger amplifies the effect of the transmitter and sets in train a series of chemical events. One result of these is the opening of specific ion channels, but there may also be longer lasting changes on the neuron's membrane and in its nucleus, and these may underlie long-term memory. Finally, transmitter molecules must be removed from the receptor sites so as to keep transmission open. They are either degraded in the synaptic cleft by specific enzymes, as happens with acetylcholine, or there is an active re-uptake mechanism that returns them to the transmitting neuron, as happens with the monoamines. Released noradrenaline is either returned to refill emptied vesicles or it is destroyed in the terminal bouton.

Drugs may act on transmitter synthesis, storage, release, on receptor mechanisms or on the enzyme degradation process. For example, **amphetamine** particularly stimulates the release of dopamine and has the effect of increasing alertness. High doses, however, lead to symptoms identical with paranoid schizophrenia, a finding compatible with the view that this disease is caused by over-activity of dopamine neurons in brain systems mediating emotional and thinking behaviours. This view is also supported by the discovery that **antischizophrenics** have the ability of binding to dopamine receptors and preventing the normal effect of dopamine – they are dopamine antagonists. Further support derives from the observation that Parkinsonism patients, who are treated with large oral doses of the dopamine precursor L-DOPA, sometimes develop schizophrenic symptoms. Presumably, their dopamine-dependent thinking and emotional brain systems are becoming overactive. In contrast to these drug effects, depressives seem to be helped either by **monoamine oxidase inhibitors**, which prevent noradrenaline (and other amines) from being degraded in the terminal bouton, or by **tricyclic drugs**, which block the re-uptake of noradrenaline (and serotonin) from the synapse. In both cases, the drugs increase the effective activity level of noradrenaline. Mood and alertness are also mildly increased by the **methylxanthines**, found in tea and coffee. These drugs prevent cyclic AMP from being broken down and therefore potentiate the action of this second messenger at receptor sites binding noradrenaline and dopamine.

As already mentioned, work on morphine led to the discovery of the opioid neuropeptide transmitters. The minor tranquillizers reduce anxiety and alertness and are known to bind to receptors in the brain with high affinity. This has led to the search for naturally occurring substances that also bind to these sites. Recently, a substance has been isolated from human urine, that binds strongly to these receptors, but has the opposite effect to **benzodiazepine** tranquillizers, such as Valium, in that it seems to increase alertness, and even perhaps anxiety (see Gilling and Brightwell, 1982). It might be, therefore, that the benzodiazepines are antagonists to a neurotransmitter that is involved in brain systems, controlling alertness and anxiety.

Neurotransmitters are key components of the system that passes information between neurons. Drugs affect behaviour because they influence neurotransmitter function and hence disrupt or stimulate neuronal-processing systems. A single neurotransmitter may be a part of many such systems. For example, acetylcholine is probably involved in distinct systems that mediate aspects of alertness, perception, mood and memory. It is known to be widely distributed in the brain, and drugs that impair its action are believed to ameliorate Parkinsonism and depression, but worsen schizophrenic and chorea symptoms as well as impairing memory, whereas drugs that increase the effective level of acetylcholine's action have the opposite effect (see Pincus and Tucker, 1974). Among other things, these findings imply that some psychological functions depend on a balance between the influences of certain acetylcholine-using versus dopamine-using or noradrenaline-using neurons.

To summarize: mammalian brains comprise up to billions of neurons, organized into many networks, each with specific information-processing roles. Information is passed from system to system down the linking axons in the form of patterns of action potentials. At the synaptic junctions between neurons the message is encoded in chemical agents, and at these sites information is integrated, i.e., processing occurs at the receiving surface of neurons. An understanding of how the brain controls behaviour depends, therefore, on knowing how its neurons are organized and interrelated.

The human brain, its evolution and principles of organization

The nervous system of humans and other mammals can be divided hierarchically into several different levels. At the highest level is the division of central and peripheral nervous systems (CNS and PNS). The former is encased within bony tissue and comprises the brain, within the cranium, and the spinal cord within its vertebral casing. These structures contain the vast majority of neurons. The PNS lies outside the bony casing, connects the CNS to sensory receptors, muscles, internal organs and glands, and comprises thirty-one pairs of spinal nerves together with twelve pairs of cranial nerves. It is divided into the somatic and autonomic nervous systems (ANS). The former receives sensory information from the external world and sends signals to the striated muscles, involved in voluntary movements; and the latter innervates internal organs, such as the heart, stomach, intestines and some glands. The peripheral ANS, which receives signals from as well as sending signals to these 'viscera', is itself divided into sympathetic and parasympathetic components. Activity of the former is generally supposed to prepare the internal organs so that the body will be capable of responding to an emergency by rapid and sustained exertion, whereas activity of the latter generally creates a quiescent and relaxed state in which bodily resources are conserved and restored.

BOX 2.1
A note on the peripheral autonomic nervous system

Psychologists have lavished what is probably a disproportionate amount of attention on the peripheral ANS because they have been interested in changes in visceral activity. There are several good reasons for concentrating on physiological changes occurring in the viscera. First, such changes are closely associated with the development of motivational and emotional states. Second, and relatedly, psychosomatic diseases are caused by prolonged disturbances of visceral function that are, in turn, caused by the mode of ANS control. As there are distinct forms of psychosomatic disease, it is vital to discover how emotion and stress can activate the ANS in different ways in different individuals and circumstances. For example, ulceration is associated with high levels of parasympathetic activity and this is often found in stressed individuals, who feel helpless because there is nothing they can do to cope with the stress. Conversely, cardiac disease is associated with prolonged, high levels of sympathetic activity in stressed individuals, who are actively trying to cope with uncertain situations (see Mayes, 1979). Third, and again relatedly, visceral activity has been used as a measure of arousal and attentiveness. The discipline of **psychophysiology**, which measures the physiological correlates of different psychological and behavioural states, has in the past been greatly concerned with levels of visceral activity. Among its discoveries one can include the identification of **autonomic response specificity** in individuals. For example, with the same stress, some individuals may show a reliable decrease in the blood supply to their hands whereas others may show changes in their heart rates (see Mayes, 1979).

Unfortunately, although there are good reasons for assessing visceral changes, psychologists have tended to write as if they believed that these changes are generated by the peripheral ANS acting on its own. The reality is that the peripheral ANS acts mainly as a link between the viscera and the CNS, and that its activities are coordinated and controlled particularly by the limbic system and the hypothalamus. This tendency to view the peripheral ANS as somehow autonomous from CNS control is perhaps connected to the fact that the structure of its motor output side is different from that of the peripheral somatic nervous system, which innervates striated, skeletal muscles rather than the smooth muscles and glands that the ANS innervates. Whereas the cell bodies of the neurons that innervate skeletal muscles lie within the ventral horns of the spinal cord, the cell bodies of neurons

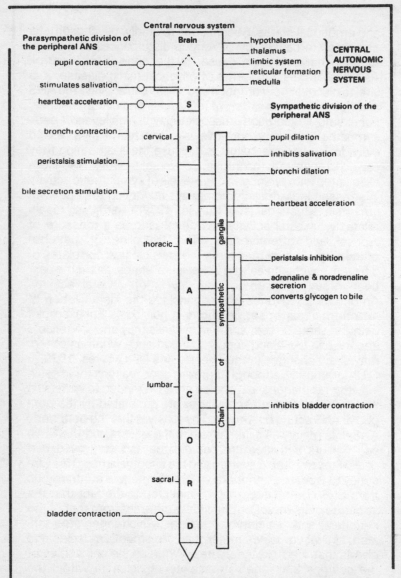

Figure 2.4 The central and peripheral autonomic nervous system.

innervating smooth muscles either lie in a connected chain of twenty-two **ganglia** (the PNS equivalent to nuclei in the CNS [see page 102]) on either side of the spinal cord (this applies to the sympathetic arm of the ANS) or in a collection of ganglia near to the site of the target organs (this applies to the parasympathetic arm of the ANS).

It is unclear to what extent this difference in the structural organization of the peripheral ANS and somatic systems reflects differences in mode of function. Several points are, however, worth making. First, smooth muscles, unlike striated ones, are usually innervated by the complementary and generally antagonistic sympathetic and parasympathetic systems. Second, any peripheral differences are likely to have a central counterpart. Thus, the hypothalamus seems to be organized so that its posterior nuclei activate and integrate sympathetic responses (those associated with arousal and emergency reactions) whereas the more anterior nuclei activate and integrate parasympathetic responses (more associated with energy conservation). Third, it is the controlling functions of the hypothalamus and limbic system that explains why visceral activity is so closely linked to mood and motivational state. Similarly, it is these CNS systems that relate moods and motivational states to various kinds of hormonal activity (ultimately mediated by endocrinal glands). The hypothalamus can either exert this control through the anterior or posterior pituitary, or it can do it through its control of the sympathetic branch of the peripheral ANS. This branch of the peripheral ANS innervates the **adrenal medulla**, an endocrine gland lying close to the kidneys. In stressful or arousing contexts, this gland releases adrenaline and noradrenaline. Release of these hormones causes a nonspecific amplification of sympathetic effects because they activate most of the target organs innervated by the sympathetic ANS. This occurs because noradrenaline also happens to be the neurotransmitter released by the post-ganglionic neurons of the sympathetic ANS to activate the target organs.

Finally, it is generally supposed that whereas the somatic

PNS (controlled by basal ganglia, motor cortex, cerebellum) is concerned with voluntary movements, the ANS (central and peripheral) controls involuntary movements. This distinction is clearly of basic interest to psychologists. Its reality is supported by the known differences in organization of the neural systems that respectively control striated and smooth muscles. Although it has been argued that smooth muscles can be voluntarily controlled (see Chapter 5), it is likely that this can only be done indirectly by acting on the striated-muscle system or by imaginatively changing one's mood. Indeed, it is this link between mood and smooth-muscle activity that argues most strongly for the involuntary nature of visceral control.

The vertebrate brain is standardly divided into forebrain, midbrain and hindbrain. Within this division the forebrain is subdivided into telencephalon and diencephalon, and the hindbrain is subdivided into metencephalon and myelencephalon. In the human, these five linked substructures weigh about 1440 grams. Although this is only 2 per cent of body weight, the brain uses 20 per cent of the body's oxygen supply to maintain its function. It is therefore richly supplied with blood as well as protected by a **blood-brain barrier** that prevents harmful substances from damaging neurons. The brain and spinal cord are also bathed in **cerebrospinal fluid** that fills spaces called **ventricles** within the brain and occupies the region between the inner two of the three membranes, or **meninges**, that surround the CNS. The functions of this fluid are only partially understood but probably include nutritive and protective roles.

The whole brain is divided into left and right halves that are mirror images of each other. The two halves are linked at different levels by connecting fibre tracts or commissures. In humans, the telencephalon is massively developed and more or less the only visible brain region. It is divided into left and right **cerebral hemispheres** linked by the 200 million myelinated (and therefore fast-conducting) fibres of the corpus callosum. This is the largest commissure in the human brain although others, such as the **anterior** and **posterior commissures**, connect structures beneath the surface of

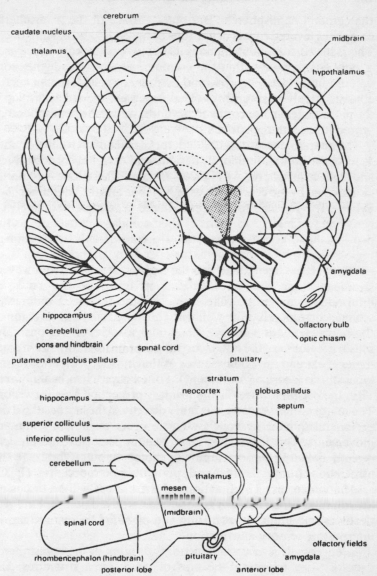

Figure 2.5 The human brain and spinal cord: a 'transparent' and a schematic view.

the cerebral hemispheres. The outer surface of the hemispheres comprises layered sheets of neurons between 1.5 and 4.5 mm thick. This is the cortex, and in humans its 2 square metres of surface area is only containable within the cranium, because it is highly convoluted into ridges, or **gyri**, and fissures, or **sulci**. Human cortex consists largely of recently evolved **neocortex** which has displaced the more ancient paleocortex to the underside of the hemispheres or buried it beneath the surface.

The human neocortex is divided, for reasons of convenience, into four lobes: frontal, temporal, parietal and occipital cortices of left and right hemisphere. As Figure 2.6 shows, these lobes are partly demarcated by the central sulcus of Rolanda and the lateral sulcus of Sylvius. It is possible to differentiate the neocortex more finely by classifying its regions in terms of their cellular architecture, as the depth of the six neocortical layers varies considerably from region to region (each layer being characterized by particular kinds of neurons). It has been found that the regions identified in this way by Brodmann can also be identified in terms of the kinds of information-processing that they perform. Thus, Brodmann's scheme corresponds quite well with the more functional division of the neocortex into sensory, motor and association regions. The sensory regions are the initial cortical receivers of information from the eye, ear and the bodily senses of touch, pain, temperature and kinaesthesis (sense of movement). For example, Brodmann's area 17 in the occipital cortex is the primary projection area for vision. The motor cortex sends signals fairly directly to the motor side of the peripheral somatic nervous system in order to initiate voluntary movements. This leaves two large regions of cortex that are less directly linked to sensory inputs or motor outputs. These are the association frontal cortex and parietotempero-occipital (PTO) association cortex. The functions of these areas will be discussed later in this chapter, but, in general, it is believed that they are respectively important in organizing and planning behaviour, and in interpreting sensory information.

Telencephalic structures beneath the cortex of the hemispheres comprise two important systems of interrelated structures: the limbic system and the basal ganglia. The structures of the limbic system, such as the hippocampus, amygdala, septum and cingulate, form a circle on the inner surface of each hemisphere, surrounding

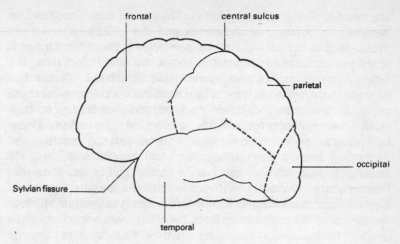

frontal **central sulcus**

parietal

occipital

Sylvian fissure

temporal

(a) Principal lobes of the left cerebral hemisphere

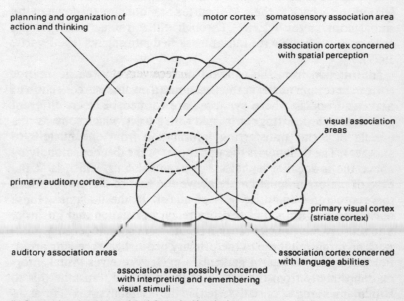

planning and organization of action and thinking **motor cortex** **somatosensory association area**

association cortex concerned with spatial perception

visual association areas

primary auditory cortex

primary visual cortex (striate cortex)

auditory association areas

association cortex concerned with language abilities

association areas possibly concerned with interpreting and remembering visual stimuli

(b) General functional areas of the left cerebral hemisphere

Figure 2.6 Main divisions of the human neocortex and some of its major functions.

the junction with the diencephalon. The system acts as an interface between the association neocortex and the older regions of the brain, such as the hypothalamus (see below). From the former it receives interpreted information about the world, and from the latter, information about the internal state of the body. Whatever its functions turn out to be, it must be concerned with integrating these information sources for certain purposes and then feeding its conclusion back to neocortex and older subcortical brain regions. Popularly, it is supposed to be involved with modulating emotion and memory processes. In contrast, the basal ganglia, which include structures such as the caudate nucleus, globus pallidus and putamen, are believed to be important in initiating complex voluntary movements. Like the limbic structures, the caudate nucleus receives massive projections from the PTO association neocortex and also from midbrain structures like the substantia nigra (atrophy of which is associated with the motor disorder of Parkinsonism). The received information must be processed further and is funnelled indirectly back to the motor cortex or more directly down to the spinal cord motor system. Through either route, basal ganglia activity is responsible for initiating skilled movements (see Evarts, 1979).

Information from the caudate nucleus actually reaches motor cortex via certain nuclei in the **thalamus** (a **nucleus** is a collection of nerve-cell bodies where synapses are formed between different groups of neurons. It is contrasted with a **tract**, which consists of a bundle of axons transferring information from one nucleus to another). The thalamus is the upper part of the diencephalon, lying above the lower diencephalon, or **hypothalamus**, which is at the base of the brain immediately above the roof of the mouth. Both these structures comprise sets of nuclei. In the thalamus, these nuclei can be grouped as sensory relay, association and intrinsic. The sensory relay nuclei receive inputs from specific sensory pathways and transmit these to the primary neocortical receiving areas. For example, the **lateral geniculate nucleus** receives visual information directly from the retina of the eye, and transmits this to Brodmann's area 17 (visual cortex) in the occipital cortex. The association nuclei do not receive such *direct* sensory inputs and project to the association neocortex. Thus, the **dorsomedial thalamic nucleus** projects to frontal association cortex, and the **pulvinar** at

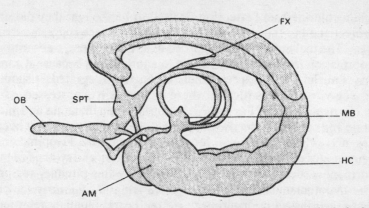

Figure 2.7 Model of the human limbic system. Major structures include the hippocampus (HC), amygdala (AM), septum (SPT), mammillary bodies (MB), olfactory bulbs (OB) and fornix (FX). (After L.W. Hamilton, *Basic Limbic System Anatomy of the Rat*, New York: Plenum, 1976)

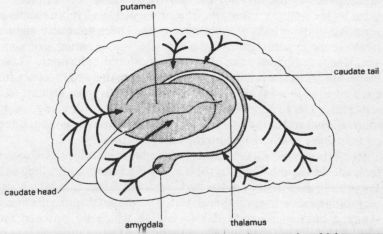

Figure 2.8 Relation between basal ganglia and cortex, in which arrows indicate projections of neocortex on to basal ganglia structures.

the posterior of the thalamus projects to PTO association cortex. The intrinsic nuclei comprise the **midline** and **intralaminar** nuclei and have connections with other thalamic nuclei, the limbic system and the reticular formation (see below). Sometimes called the 'diffuse thalamic system', they are believed to play a role in maintaining alertness and attention. It used to be thought they did not project at all to the neocortex, but recent evidence suggests otherwise. The thalamus may be regarded as a relay system, transmitting information from one brain region to another, but because it comprises nuclei with synapses, where inputs are integrated, it should also be viewed as a structure where information is processed.

The hypothalamus lies at the junction between thalamus and midbrain and connects directly with parts of the pituitary, which it overlies and whose hormonal functions it controls. Hypothalamic neurons directly innervate the posterior pituitary and synthesize the hormones, such as vasopressin, released by this pituitary region. The hypothalamus also produces releasing and inhibitory factors that reach the anterior pituitary via the portal blood system, and influence this pituitary region's ability to synthesize and release its characteristic hormones. This hypothalamic activity is itself partly controlled by feedback from hormones released by endocrine glands, such as the thyroid, the activity of which is controlled, in turn, by the anterior pituitary. The activity of the hypothalamus is sensitive to the effects of these hormones. There are many minute nuclei in the hypothalamus that play a vital role in eating, drinking, sex, sleep, temperature control and emotional behaviour. These nuclei are interconnected, but they are also strongly connected with parts of the limbic system, such as the hippocampus, septum and amygdala. The hypothalamus plays a role, therefore, in mediating motivational and emotional behaviour, and its activity is modulated by influences reaching it from the limbic system.

Its motivational and emotional functions are closely related to the fact that the hypothalamus is the major CNS system controlling and integrating the activities of the peripheral ANS (see Box 2.1). Most of its influence on the peripheral ANS is mediated through the many synaptic links in the **reticular formation** which lie between the hypothalamus and the peripheral neurons which control the internal organs and glands. These synapses allow further influences to be brought to bear on viscera, such as heart and stomach. If the hypothalamus is suddenly destroyed, the result is death because the internal milieu, controlled by factors like blood pressure, heart rate and respiration rate, is drastically disrupted. More gradual destruction in the form of a slow-growing tumour does not have this effect, however, because it gives a chance for brain regions below the hypothalamus to exert their influence in maintaining the internal milieu. This they achieve by sending their signals to the synapses on the pathways between the hypothalamus and peripheral ANS. Even so, midbrain and hindbrain systems can only keep the internal milieu stable under a narrow range of conditions. They lack the integrative power of the hypothalamus, whose flexible control of ANS functions is increased by the modulatory influences reaching it from the limbic system, particularly the complementary influences of the amygdala and hippocampus.

The midbrain and hindbrain (except for the cerebellum) are often referred to collectively as the **brainstem**. In the human brain, the central part of the brainstem is occupied by the reticular formation that runs for about 5 cm from the top of the spinal cord to just beyond the midbrain into the thalamus. The reticular formation contains a mixture of criss-crossing fibre tracts and over ninety nuclei which give it the appearance of an amorphous network (hence its name, as 'reticulum' means a 'net'). One of the major components of the reticular formation carries motor commands from many brain regions over many synaptic relays, down to the striated and smooth muscles (as it does, for example, with signals originating in the hypothalamus). There is also an ascending reticular formation which influences cortical activity, in an apparently nonspecific way. Evidence shows that there is an ascending reticular activating system, located in the tegmentum (floor) of the midbrain, activity of which maintains behavioural wakefulness by electrophysiologically activating neocortical neurons. These effects on the neocortex are achieved indirectly via synaptic relays in the intrinsic thalamic nuclei. Many neocortical neurons receive these arousing influences, but the thalamic projection on to the neocortex is point-to-point and not diffuse as was previously believed (Steriade, 1983), i.e., each thalamic neuron projects to one or a few neocortical neurons rather than many, widely distributed ones. Some reticular formation influences do involve diffuse projections, however. For example, axons from neurons in the gigantocellular field of the midbrain tegmentum divide and project to neurons through the brain. It has been estimated that 300 of these cells can influence 9 million cells in the brainstem reticular formation alone (see Carlson, 1977).

As well as containing reticular formation nuclei the midbrain tegmentum also contains the substantia nigra and the red nucleus that connect to the basal ganglia and the cerebellum, and are involved in controlling skilled voluntary movements. The roof, or tectum, of the midbrain contains the inferior and superior colliculi. The former acts as a relay nucleus for auditory information en route from the cochlea of the ear to the **medial geniculate** nucleus and thence to the primary auditory cortex. The superior colliculi receive visual information directly from the retina, but they are also interconnected to the visual areas of the neocortex. Although they do not seem important in interpreting visual stimuli, they do control several visual reflexes and play a role in orienting towards peripherally placed stimuli so that these can be better analysed by cortical mechanisms.

Beneath the midbrain lie the pons and cerebellum of the metencephalon and the **medulla oblongata** of the myelencephalon. The pons and medulla are brainstem structures and contain many reticular formation nuclei. The medulla, in particular, contains nuclei that are important in regulating cardiovascular and respiratory functions, as well as maintaining skeletal muscle tone. The pons is a large bulge in the brainstem, lying **ventral** (on the stomach side of) the cerebellum. In addition to containing reticular formation and other nuclei, such as the **raphe** and **locus coeruleus** (that may play a role in the control of waking, sleeping and attention), it contains tracts linking forebrain and brainstem to the cerebellum. Like the cortex, the cerebellum comprises two highly convoluted hemispheres, but unlike cortex, the cerebellum shows a high degree of cellular organization with *very little variation from region to region*. More than with most brain systems, it is easy to see the cerebellum as a computing system with highly specialized functions. It receives inputs from visual and auditory systems, parts of the neocortex and the reticular formation, and sends outputs to those systems believed to be involved in motor control. These connections are consistent with its hypothesized role in mediating and acquiring skilled movements and with the fact that its removal causes a condition characterized by jerky, ill-coordinated motion.

The brainstem structures of the medulla, pons and midbrain developed early in evolution and changed little in organization from fish to humans. Varations between species in the size of specific regions reflect the rule that size and complexity index the importance of the functions, controlled by a region, for the species in question. For example, bats employ a system like sonar and show unusual enlargement of the inferior colliculi that are involved in this function. Similarly, the cerebellum, which is also a phylogenetically old structure, is particularly large in the great apes and humans. These species probably had **brachiating** ancestors, and complex, skilled movements, whether of the arms or the other limbs, still play a central role in their lifestyles.

Although the principle that 'ontogeny recapitulates phylogeny' (i.e., development repeats the course of evolution) is a crude generalization, it is clear that in the early stages of embryonic development all vertebrates that have cerebral hemispheres appear quite similar. In vertebrates the CNS first appears in the embryo as a straight tube of neural tissue which then differentiates into the three enlargements of forebrain, midbrain and hindbrain. Then the forebrain divides into telencephalon and diencephalon, and the cerebellum appears. Differentiation continues until the cerebral hemispheres expand and overlay the diencephalon and the cerebellum grows further to cover the midbrain. It is this expansion of the cerebral hemispheres (and also the cerebellum) that most characterizes vertebrate evolution over 400 million years. This change is hard to specify in relation to general adaptability or intelligence because the human brain is greatly surpassed in size by the brains of whales and elephants. A more appropriate measure is the *ratio of brain size to the cross-sectional size of the brainstem* immediately above the spinal cord. As most of the brain's inputs and outputs pass through the medulla in this region, the ratio gives an index of the amount of brain tissue available for processing equivalent numbers of inputs and outputs, in different species. Using this ratio, it has been found that the superiority of humans over chimpanzees is greater than the superiority of chimpanzees over hedgehogs (see Passingham, 1982).

This expansion of the human brain does not reflect a uniform increase in the size of all brain structures. Rather it is due to the massive evolutionary growth of the neocortex and its underlying, connecting white matter (comprising myelinated axons). Whereas in the hedgehog these structures constitute under 20 per cent of the whole brain's volume, in the bush baby they constitute 47.4 per cent, in the chimpanzee they constitute 76.3 per cent, and in humans they constitute 80.4 per cent. In primates, this relative expansion of neocortex follows a single mathematical rule relating neocortex to overall brain size – a rule to which the human brain conforms. Similarly, the proportion of association neocortex tô overall cortex increases progressively in rats, cats, monkeys and humans. Within the primate family, however, the size of association neocortex can be predicted from the size of the whole brain. The predictive laws are not general evolutionary ones because they are specific to primates. For example, Passingham (1982) has calculated that if humans were insectivores, as hedgehogs are, the neocortex should only constitute 33.2 per cent of their total brain volume.

THE SIGNIFICANCE OF TWO BRAINS

Although the human brain, in terms of total neocortex and association neocortex, is a large, but otherwise typical example of a primate brain, it has been argued that it is unique with respect to the lateralization of function of the cerebral hemispheres. In most people, it seems that the left hemisphere is specialized in processing complex sequences of information and in controlling complex sequences of movement. These abilities probably explain why the left hemisphere is so important in controlling verbal behaviour. Conversely, the right hemisphere in most people is superior at simultaneously processing information from a variety of sources, which may explain its pre-eminent role in visuospatial processing, aspects of emotional behaviour and the perception of certain musical forms. These functional lateralizations are associated with structural asymmetries between the cerebral hemispheres. Most strikingly, the neocortical region, known as the **planum temporale**, which lies in the posterior and superior temporal lobe and forms part of a cortical area vital for verbal comprehension, is larger on the left hemisphere in the great majority of people. This difference is apparent in the later stages of embryonic growth and may be very large: the left planum temporale can have a volume at least seven times greater than that of the right. Although anatomical and functional asymmetries have been found in other mammals and birds, the functional differences are much more apparent in humans than in other primates. This lateralization of function may prove very significant. Thus, it has been shown that the macaque monkey's brain contains a region like the planum temporale, the neurons of which respond to sounds. As in humans, this region sends projections to Brodmann's area 44 in the frontal association neocortex. In humans, this latter area is involved with speech production. Macaques do not possess language in the human sense so lateralization of function in the left hemisphere probably enables the neocortex to increase its processing abilities dramatically.

The evolutionary changes epitomized by the mammals and especially the primates have, then, involved a great expansion of the neocortex and, to a lesser extent, other telencephalic systems. This expansion has increased the brain's power to process its inputs and outputs. There are two major ways of characterizing how this has occurred. The first is the doctrine of **encephalization** which states that as the forebrain grew in evolution it took over the functions previously performed by the evolutionary older structures of the brainstem. Acceptance of this doctrine depends on the use of a crude conception of function. For example, if vision is regarded as a simple, undifferentiated function, then it makes sense to say that as the neocortex expanded it became more important for seeing as the superior colliculus became less important. Vision is achieved, however, by the performance of many distinct subprocesses. As the forebrain expanded, the superior colliculus did not lose the visual functions it had possessed in earlier vertebrates. Rather, visually based skills and flexibility increased as new processing capacities were added with the expansion of the forebrain.

This second characterization of evolution in terms of the addition of new modular units is consistent with the views of the great English neurologist Hughlings Jackson. Jackson believed that the nervous system was hierarchically arranged so that more recently evolved structures controlled and integrated the activities of older and simpler processing structures. For example, with movement control the lowest level is that of the isolated reflex organized in the spinal cord. At the next highest level in the brainstem the same movement would be represented in a different way so that it can be coordinated with movements of other parts of the body. At the neocortical level, the movement would be represented yet again so that it is placed in context in a model of the physical world. This enables the movement not only to be coordinated with the other movements, but also to be produced in a planned fashion dependent on what is happening in the environment. The hierarchical model therefore proposes that new modes of processing emerge in evolution enabling the various categories of behaviour to be generated in more sophisticated ways. These newer systems control the older, lower-level ones to some degree and may exert some of their behavioural effects through them. Destruction of the higher systems leaves the lower-level systems to control behaviour in their simpler fashion (as illustrated in the example of ANS control used earlier in this chapter). When new modular units evolve they carry out novel processes, the effects of which may therefore control and coordinate the activities of older structures concerned with the same behavioural categories.

The techniques of physiological psychology: discovering what the brain does

How do we know that encephalization does not represent an important evolutionary trend, and that the mammalian brain is organized to some degree hierarchically into functional modules? These and other insights into the brain's functioning have been gained through the use of four major kinds of approach. The first approach involves identifying those behavioural functions which are lost when different brain regions are destroyed or temporarily put out of action. The second approach involves identifying the behavioural effects of influencing the activity of different brain regions either by electrical or pharmacological means. The third approach is correlational. It involves relating behavioural and psychological activities to the electrical, biochemical and metabolic activities of different brain regions. The fourth approach is essential for the interpretation of the other three. It involves tracing the connections between different nuclei in the brain and identifying the detailed structure of particular brain regions, such as the hippocampus and specific parts of the neocortex. Ideally, all four approaches should be used in determining the functions of brain regions because there are so many interpretive problems associated with each approach. If the implications of all approaches are convergent then confidence in their truth is justifiably increased. This section will briefly describe how technical advances have increased the power of the four approaches. In addition their interpretive problems and instances where their implications seem or do not seem to be convergent will also be discussed.

Brain damage can be accidental, as it usually is in humans, or it can be the result of experimentally placed and induced lesions. For ethical reasons, experimental lesions are performed only on animals, with the exception of humans who are given neurosurgery in order to remove tumours, for example, or for psychosurgical reasons (i.e., when the brain is thought to be 'normal' but the surgeon believes that destroying part of it will alleviate certain psychiatric symptoms, such as aggressiveness or obsessionalism). Brain scientists must therefore rely on finding appropriate 'animal models' of human behaviour. For example, the control of eating and other motivated behaviours has been explored by lesioning parts of the hypothalamus in rats and other nonhuman mammals. The assumption is that these behaviours are mediated in humans by the hypothalamus in much the same way. Lesion research involves three stages: (1) locating the lesion accurately in an appropriate region, (2) isolating precisely what psychological functions are disturbed, and (3) checking precisely where the brain damage has been made. The first stage is not often feasible in studies of human brain lesions because the damage is usually accidental. In animals it is also difficult and depends partly on the identification of anatomically homogeneous regions (approach four is necessary for this). Three-dimensional maps, known as stereotaxic atlases, of the brains of various species have been produced so that experimenters can place lesions in the structures they intend. Lesions deep in the brain are usually made by passing electric currents through the target region. Cortical lesions, however, may be produced by aspirating tissue, and techniques are now being developed that will make use of the chemical specificity of brain regions to use drugs in order to destroy carefully selected systems.

At post mortem analysis it is possible to identify very precisely the extent of brain damage in animals and humans. In humans, however, it is often necessary for practical reasons to locate lesions in living patients. The invention of Computerized Axial Tomography (CAT) has made this procedure more accurate. The CAT scan involves taking X-ray pictures in different positions around the head so that a computer can convert the signals into 'brain slices'. These cross-sectional slices are patchworks of light and dark regions where the shade indicates the density of the corresponding brain tissue. As damaged regions have densities different from those of healthy tissue they show up on some of the CAT scan slices. The technique is noninvasive and safe, which is a boon, but it is not perfect because certain kinds of damage are not picked up well by it. For example, regions where there has been slow atrophy are hard to locate. Identification is better with the more recently developed Positron Emission Tomography (PET). This technique measures the extent to which different brain regions are metabolically active – lesioned structures show up because they have abnormally low metabolic levels. Typically, the technique involves injecting a radioactive form of glucose which is not metabolized and so accumulates in active neurons. The half-life of the radioactive glucose is a few hours, and it breaks down by emitting positrons which are picked up by detectors around the head. Brain slices are computed, the colouring or shading of which relates to the level of metabolism of their component regions. Location is very precise, but unfortunately PET scanners require 'dedicated' cyclotrons to produce their positron-emitting radioactive tracers. Fortunately, newer techniques are becoming available without this kind of limitation.

If lesions have been accurately placed and located, it is still necessary to decide what functions have been lost. When this is done the usual argument is that the lost function(s) was mediated by the destroyed region. This argument is wide open to criticism. First, the lost functions may be secondary to a nonspecific effect of the lesion. For example, the subject may feel ill and therefore not want to eat or be unable to solve tricky learning tasks. Second, removal of a structure may have upset the activity of other intact regions and this may be causing the functional disturbance. For example, posterior cortical lesions on one side of the brain cause permanent blindness in the opposite half of visual space (i.e., left lesions cause blindness in the right half of space). A second lesion to the superior colliculus on the other side of the brain restores vision. The interpretation is that the first **unilateral** lesion has disturbed the dynamic balance of excitation and inhibition between the two halves of the superior colliculus, so the inhibited part can no longer mediate vision. The second lesion improves vision by restoring the balance. Third, functions may recover to some extent after a lesion so that it is difficult to decide what exactly is lost. None of these criticisms can be answered .

conclusively except by considering the implications of the other three approaches mentioned earlier in this section.

RECOVERY FROM BRAIN DAMAGE

Recovery of function following brain damage is an important issue in its own right. First of all, it is known that some functions are less disturbed when damage is sustained at an early age, or is the cumulation of several smaller lesions spread out over time (*serial lesions*). For example, severe lesions to the left neocortex, or even hemispherectomy in children under the age of five, has little effect on verbal ability, so that as adults special tests are needed to show that they have subtle problems with the syntactic aspects of language. In contrast, similar lesions in adults will leave them with permanently devastated verbal abilities, often nearly mute and incapable of understanding common words. Even so, twenty-year-olds are less affected than forty-year-olds. Tumours that are slow growing often leave functions unaffected whereas equivalent vascular lesions (or *strokes*) have drastic effects. Similarly, in rats it has been shown that serial lesions of the lateral hypothalamus leave motivated eating and drinking intact whereas a single large lesion has dramatic effects on these functions. These effects have implications for the way in which the brain is organized and for how it responds to injury.

There are several explanations of why functional recovery occurs after brain damage and why it is less complete under some circumstances. First, in 1914, Von Monakow suggested that lesioning causes a state of shock (diaschisis) in structures connected with the damaged one. Recovery from this shock leads to the return of some functions. Although there is little direct evidence for such effects in the brain, severing the spinal cord leads to a state of *spinal shock*, which persists for weeks and is associated with the loss of spinal reflexes. These return with recovery from spinal shock. Second, it has been speculated that other tissue, particularly that surrounding the lesion, may take over the initially lost function. It is, however, very difficult to show that if an ability returns it is being performed in the same way as it was in the prelesion state. For example, rats with single-stage lateral hypothalamic lesions initially show a loss of motivational eating and drinking. If, however, they are force fed and watered and so prevented from dying, they eventually are able to show apparently regulatory eating and drinking. Even so, their motivated behaviour is not the same as before. They only drink with meals and, unlike intact rats, do not eat after being given insulin injections that lower their blood sugar (see Teitelbaum, 1971).

Recovery of the same functions as were present pretraumatically might nevertheless be associated with the regrowth of neural tissue posttraumatically. Neurons are not replaced in the adult mammalian brain because they do not divide after the completion of embryonic development and, unlike in the PNS, when axons are destroyed they do not regrow. On the other hand, if a region is 'denervated' by destruction of a nucleus that projected to it, other neurons may sprout axons and form synapses with the denervated region. This kind of neural regrowth is much more prominent in the neonatal than in the adult brain. Its functional value, however, is dubious. Regrowth may be linked with the emergence of posttraumatic epilepsy and has been associated with abnormal visual behaviour in hamsters given unilateral neonatal lesions of the superior colliculus (Schneider, 1979). Recent research has been directed at finding ways of encouraging damaged axons to grow and reconnect with their disconnected targets. Growth may be facilitated by 'bridges' of embryonic neural tissue. There is even evidence that embryonic neural tissue grows and forms connections in adult brains. Transplanting foetal basal ganglia tissue (dopamine-containing neurons) alleviates the symptoms of experimental Parkinsonism in rats (the motor disturbance is reduced) or so it has been claimed (Perlow *et al.*, 1979). There is also interest in the use of pharmacological factors that may increase functional recovery by stimulating regrowth – **nerve growth factors** (chemicals that maintain neuronal integrity) – and the endorphins have been considered in this connection.

A third explanation of functional recovery is that the ability to show a behaviour has returned because the victim has learned to perform it in a different way. This kind of phenomenon is particularly prominent in human split-brain patients. These patients have had their left and right hemispheres disconnected from each other by severing the corpus callosum and possibly other linking commissures, so as to alleviate the symptoms of very severe epilepsy (the fits are propagated across the corpus callosum). It is possible to present sensory information to one hemisphere or the other in isolation with such patients and therefore to assess the abilities of each hemisphere as they are disconnected from each other. Using appropriate techniques, it has been possible to show that the right hemispheres of these patients may have quite sophisticated verbal comprehension abilities. Testing is difficult, however, because the patients learn to cross-cue information from one hemisphere to the other. For example, one patient was able to name visually presented numerals flashed briefly to his right hemisphere. His left hemisphere was the only one controlling speech and it did not receive the information. The right hemisphere knew the number but could not speak (it could pick the right numeral from a display, though). To transfer the information the patient's left hemisphere nodded his head until it reached the number shown the right hemisphere, at which point the right hemisphere stopped the nodding, so the left knew the correct numeral. This communication was possible because nodding, unlike fine movements, is equally controlled by both hemispheres. If an experimenter failed to spot that cross-cueing was occurring, he might erroneously believe that interhemisphere communication was occurring via a new subcortical route and that the right hemisphere's number-counting ability was not being tapped (see Gazzaniga, 1978).

The problems of interpreting brain lesions may be reduced if it is also possible to examine the effects of stimulating the target region. For example, if parts of the hypothalamus are stimulated electrically or by application of the neurotransmitter **angiotensin**, previously water-sated rats can be made to drink within seconds. These findings are congruent with the notion that activity in certain hypothalamic neurons leads to motivated drinking, and that destroying these neurons inhibits motivated drinking. Results of the two approaches are not always so obviously convergent. Thus, in most right-handed people neocortical lesions only cause language disturbances that are not secondary to motor or sensory deficits, if they occur within a limited region in frontal and PTO association cortex of the left hemisphere. Electrical stimulation of neocortex outside this region also has the effect of disturbing verbal behaviour, and the effects of stimulating within this region are not those which the lesion studies would suggest (such stimulation blocks natural function whereas in the hypothalamic example it appeared to mimic it). The language regions defined by the two sets of results therefore seem to differ both in extent and internal organization.

Research using the PET scanner, i.e., a correlational approach, supports the implication of findings with electrical stimulation that neocortical regions, beyond those indicated by lesion studies, mediate verbal functions. Use of the PET scanner shows that when subjects engage in silent verbal activities, parts of their right neocortex, as well as parts of their left, become very active metabolically. The conflict is capable of resolution because, although lesions usually cause language problems only when they are on the left neocortex, evidence from split-brain patients shows that the right hemisphere *is capable* of performing some language functions. Although the PET scanner findings suggest that these capabilities are used in normal verbal activities, it would seem that their loss through lesions may be compensated by other regions. This problem might be better pursued by correlational techniques other than the PET scanner. Despite its ability to locate with pinpoint accuracy regions of differing metabolic activity, the PET scanner has very poor temporal resolution. In order to gain appropriate measures of those brain structures which became active during a task, it is necessary to perform that task for some minutes. Electrophysiological techniques, in contrast, can measure neural changes that occur over milliseconds.

There are two broad kinds of electrophysiological techniques. The first is used primarily in humans and involves recording brain activity picked up from the scalp – the EEG. This activity is affected in characteristic ways when particular kinds of stimuli are perceived, but the 'signal' is often hidden in random neural noise. To amplify the signal-to-noise ratio, psychologists often average the EEG to many events of the same kind so that only the time-locked activity is preserved in the **average evoked potential** (AEP). The EEG differs dramatically in sleeping and waking and may sometimes reveal the presence of, for example, epilepsy. Similarly, components of the AEP are affected by the way in which subjects attend to stimuli. There is, however, uncertainty about which brain regions produce scalp-recorded EEG and AEPs. Recently, it was possible to show by directly recording from the limbic system of conscious patients that the hippocampus and amygdala may help generate the scalp-recorded AEP components associated with attention (Halgren *et al.*, 1980).

The second electrophysiological technique involves recording the action potentials generated by individual neurons – **single-unit recording**. Researchers hope to use the technique to identify the kinds of informational input that activate neurons in different brain regions. It has been most effective so far in plotting how information is processed in the brain's sensory systems. For example, in Brodmann's area 17 (primary visual cortex) the neurons respond best to simple visual stimuli such as bars of light in specific orientations in particular small parts oi the visual field. Area 17 neurons send information through several further relays (or processing stages) to parts of the temporal neocortex. Here, most neurons still respond best to simple stimuli but their orientation and spatial position matter far less. Furthermore, in rhesus monkeys there are temporal cortex neurons that respond most to complex stimuli, such as monkey paws or even monkey faces (Perrett *et al.*, 1982). This last observation suggests that one of the temporal cortex regions plays a special role in facial recognition. If so, lesions to this region should impair this ability selectively. Similarly, as there are neurons in the anterior intrinsic thalamic nuclei that respond selectively to visually presented objects only if they are *familiar*, one would predict that lesions to this region should impair recognition memory selectively, on the assumption that the neurons mediate this form of memory (see Mayes, 1983).

Interpretation of findings with single-unit recordings is particularly dependent on discoveries made using the fourth approach to understanding the brain's functions: plotting the flow of information through the brain's subsystems by determining their anatomical connections. The potential of this approach has been greatly enhanced by the introduction of tracer substances, for example *horseradish peroxidase*, which can be used to identify pathways which eluded earlier techniques. The modern techniques have enabled researchers, for example, to plot the projections of the retina into the neocortical and midbrain systems and to show that the two are interconnected. This work has not only shown that primary visual cortex projects to 'visual' regions of the temporal neocortex, it has shown that these latter regions then send projections down into the hippocampus and amygdala of the limbic system and perhaps, after more relays, the anterior thalamic intrinsic nuclei. It also suggests that these links are reciprocated. One interpretation of this picture is that visual information is progressively analysed as it passes through neurons of the 'visual' neocortex, until by the time it has reached temporal association cortex the brain has contructed a representation of the visual world. This interpreted visual information has to be further processed by the limbic and thalamic systems if it is to achieve stable storage in the association neocortex (see Chapter 6). Similar research has also shown that projections from the primary cortices of the 'spatial' senses of vision, hearing and touch eventually converge on the parietal cortex and the frontal cortex. These regions appear to use the received information differently: lesion studies suggest that the parietal cortex plays a key role in spatial orientation and constructing spatial images whereas the frontal cortex plans actions, which it must do on the basis of available information about spatial factors.

Anatomical knowledge, then, helps guide thinking about functions of different brain regions because one can use it to infer the kind of information that is reaching a region and where that region is sending that information after further processing. Recently, it has become possible to gain related insights even in living humans. For example, Gur *et al.* (1980) used a modified CAT scan technique to determine what brain regions absorbed radioactive Xenon (inhaled and hence transferred into the blood) more rapidly in a group of right-handed males. It is known that grey matter (cell bodies and small unmyelinated axons) absorb and clear blood-borne Xenon four times more quickly than white matter (myelinated, long axons). So the technique was used to calculate the proportion of grey to white matter in the left and right hemisphere neocortices. It was found that the proportion of grey matter was greater on the left side, particularly in the more frontal regions. This suggested that the left neocortex is specialized more for processing and transferring information within localized regions whereas the right neocortex is specialized more for transferring information between widely separated regions. It is the existence of these distinct operating modes that may explain why the left hemisphere became specialized for language and the right for more visuospatial functions.

The brain's functions: a brief outline, illustrated by specific cases

In evolutionary terms, the brain can be seen as a system for producing adaptive behaviour. In humans and other complex mammals this means that the system must be able to do several kinds of thing. First, it must be able to control and coordinate skilled sequences of movements. Second, it must have perceptual systems enabling it to represent what is going on in the physical and social environment. Third, it must be able to monitor its internal states so as to be able to select behaviours that will maintain these in a balanced condition. Fourth, it must store information about past encounters with rewarding or punishing aspects of the environment. This will allow it to create representations of what *will* happen in order to plan its behaviour, although simpler systems will also exist at a level of the brainstem and diencephalon for directing motivated behaviour in a more automatic, 'stimulus-bound' fashion.

Two comments are warranted about this general picture. First, it suggests a distinction between voluntary, planned behaviours and more automatically controlled and sometimes involuntary behaviours. The former require considerable forebrain, particularly neocortical, mediation whereas the latter are mediated more by diencephalic, brainstem and cerebellar mechanisms. This is especially interesting with acquired skills. As these are learned, they become 'automated' and control passes to some degree from neocortical to brainstem etc. mechanisms. When this happens, whether the skill is car-driving, typing or even reading, the demands on *attention* are reduced (see Chapter 4). Complex representations of reality are created in the neocortex and their creation uses a great deal of neocortical processing capacity. Selective attention is necessary because the neocortex only has limited capacity for creating such representations. When skills become automatic they are probably represented differently by a different 'brainstem' system. Selective attention is associated with the phenomenon of arousal. When we attend to something we become more aroused and, within limits, this leads to improved performance. But what is arousal and why does it exist?

The answer to both questions is that we do not really know. Feelings of increased arousal are associated with a characteristic EEG pattern – one in which the waves of fluctuating electrical potentials are small and irregular. Both these features seem to be basically neocortical properties induced particularly by activity of the mid-brain and thalamic reticular formation. These systems seem to tune neocortical neurons so that they process information more effectively (high arousal levels are, however, disruptive). The tuning may be of the whole neocortex or of selected regions, and may arise automatically as part of the sleep-wake cycle or in response to powerful stimuli, or it may be produced 'at will'. Selective attention itself seems to be related to a voluntary increase in arousal so forebrain regions probably cause the reticular formation to tune up specific neocortical regions. The attentional-arousal system may have evolved as a 'spin-off' from the more primitive sleep-wake arousal system. This latter system is of great evolutionary age and it has been conjectured that it arose because sleep provided a means of keeping animals safe and immobile when not engaged in vital biological functions (see Chapter 7).

The second comment relates to the fact that brains are not only concerned with sensory analysis and generating behaviour; they are 'preset' to satisfy certain motivational requirements. This is an evolutionary imperative which means that the brain will find some classes of stimuli rewarding and others punishing. In turn, this suggests that activation of particular neurons should be rewarding whereas activation of others should be punishing, not just because their activation causes pain, but also because it causes other kinds of unpleasantness. Such neuronal reward and punishment systems were identified thirty years ago by Olds and Milner (see Chapter 7). They found that rats would work to be given electrical stimulation to some brain regions and to avoid or escape stimulation in other regions. Subsequent research has shown that reward-system neurons are found particularly in the limbic system and hypothalamus, and closely connect to other neurons in the midbrain and the frontal cortex. It has also shown that the stimulation produces the effects of the different natural rewards such as sex, food and water. Whether the more subtle and complex human rewards can be explained in these terms remains to be seen.

To return to the four major functions of the mammalian brain: in considering which regions mediate them, it is useful to remember Jackson's hierarchical view of brain organization. Thus, reflex and automatic motor sequences are coordinated at spinal cord and brainstem levels, whereas the initiation and control of voluntary movements involves the influence of neocortex, basal ganglia and cerebellum directly on motor neurons and on spinal and brainstem mechanisms. The forebrain systems are particularly important in planned actions. The frontal association cortex plays a central role in goal-directed behaviour. When it is damaged, patients may persevere in actions that are no longer appropriate, and fail to solve problems that depend on the construction of an overall plan and the flexible use of substrategies (see Shallice, 1982). The frontal cortex needs to control attention and arousal voluntarily, and to this end it has projections down to the reticular formation. To perform its function it also needs information about the body's internal state (relative to rewards and punishments), which it receives from the limbic system and hypothalamus, and interpreted information about the outside world, which it receives from the PTO cortex. It must also draw on cortically stored memories to predict future events and help to set appropriate goals.

The high-level plans generated in the prefrontal association cortex are effected by signals sent directly or indirectly to the motor cortex, which directly influences motor neurons. The plans may be effected by signals that do not reach motor cortex (Brodmann's area 4). In both cases skilled movements are the result. It is interesting to note that disorders of skilled movements, known as **apraxias**, are found after parietal and, to a lesser extent, frontal lesions. Apraxics cannot perform skilled movements like those involved in dressing or hammering a nail despite good intelligence and basically normal sensory and *motor* functions. They seem to have lost access to learned movement programmes. Other kinds of movement disorder are caused by basal ganglia lesions. The basal ganglia receive projections from the frontal and PTO association cortices and act on brainstem mechanisms either directly or indirectly via the motor cortex and other cortical regions. Single-unit recordings show that basal ganglia neurons and also neurons in the **cerebellum** become active before those in the motor cortex and well before movement itself. It is not therefore surprising that Parkinsonism patients (who have atrophy of the substantia nigra in the midbrain, a structure projecting to the forebrain basal ganglia) have problems initiating movements, and that Huntington's choreics with basal ganglia cannot inhibit involuntary movements. These lesions do not produce paralysis, however, unlike those of the spinal cord, brainstem and, to some extent, the motor cortex.

Perceptual systems are also organized at neocortical and brainstem levels. For example, visual inputs are analysed and interpreted within the PTO association cortex. Damage within this region can cause visual **agnosias** (see Chapter 3), which are deficits in extracting meaning from inputs despite the presence of intact basic sensory functions. For example, **prosopagnosics** cannot recognize previously familiar faces although it is unknown whether their lesions lie in the temporal cortex region where neurons respond selectively to faces. In contrast, brainstem visual systems such as that of the superior colliculus seem to analyse visual stimuli just sufficiently to control the switching of attention (and hence the processing powers of the visual cortex) to important and previously unattended occurrences. The retina also projects directly to the suprachiasmatic nucleus in the hypothalamus. This nucleus ensures that the sleep-wake cycle is entrained to the rhythm of night and day, and severing its retinal connection causes the sleep-wake cycle to run 'free'.

The goal of sensory (or perceptual) analysis is a representation of objects as they exist and move in space. In the case of vision, one begins at the retina with an uninterpreted image. Information about this image is processed by many synaptic relays before the goal is achieved. Much of this processing occurs in parallel. Not only are visual inputs sent in parallel to the midbrain, neocortex and other systems, but even within the neocortex beyond area 17, separate regions exist that selectively process colour, movement, orientation etc. at the same time. At a later stage, of course, many of these parallel informational streams converge as they are combined in the formation of representations, or in the limitation of planned actions.

Meaningful actions depend on integrating such interpreted sensory data with information about internal and motivational states. Some of this integration occurs in the limbic system which is an interface receiving both processed sensory data from the cortex and motivational data from the hypothalamus and brainstem. It has already been suggested that the limbic system is necessary for reliable recognition memory. This role is fulfilled when limbic influences stimulate neocortical storage and remembering – a kind of stimulation that probably depends on the rewarding or punishing associations of the to-be-stored events. Activity of the **amygdala** seems to be necessary for appreciating and learning about the reward or punishment associations of events. If it is damaged, animals and humans show aspects of the **Kluver-Bucy syndrome**. They will make sexual advances towards very inappropriate targets, eat and orally explore unsuitable objects, and show very little fear and anger, probably because they can no longer choose apt targets for these emotions. The amygdala is, then, very important in selecting motivationally appropriate objects. Consequently, it has a strong influence on the planning system of the frontal association cortex. This and other limbic system influences enable the planning system to draw on past experiences.

The evidence just cited makes it clear that the limbic system, particularly the amygdala, plays a key role in emotional behaviour. The system mediates the appraisal of situations as pleasant or unpleasant, thereby giving them emotional 'colour'. It is also likely to be important in learning whether situations have pleasant or unpleasant associations, and thus determining which emotions those situations will elicit in the future. There is some evidence that limbic appraisal mechanisms are 'automatic' and, in humans, may sometimes be overridden by neocortical processes that are concerned with more elaborative interpretations of situations (see Mayes, 1979). Such processes may be operating when soldiers in action show minimal signs of stress because they are able to reinterpret the battle situation as relatively unthreatening. When limbic mechanisms appraise a situation as 'emotional', they activate hypothalamic and brainstem processes that result in the fairly stereotyped hormonal, ANS and voluntary motor responses associated with strong emotion (see Chapter 8).

Thinking involves the manipulation of internal representations to achieve goals (e.g., solving problems). It therefore involves retrieval of selected parts of previously stored representations. This process is likely to require the frontal planning system. It is also likely to be helped by the creation of a language system, in which the learned symbols arbitrarily correspond to aspects of the internal representations and hence to features of outside reality (see Chapter 9). Thinking ability is pre-eminent in humans and verbal ability is unique to them. Both depend strongly on activity within PTO and frontal association cortex. There is no doubt that many thinking activities are closely dependent on the intactness of verbal (particularly verbal comprehension) abilities. Some types of thinking may, however, depend on other kinds of representational processes. This question is tractable in principle, because in most people verbal functions are mainly controlled by the left hemisphere. Left-hemisphere lesions should therefore leave certain thinking abilities unaffected, particularly the ability to think about relationships in space. In practice the question is much fuzzier, although there is good evidence that such abilities are less disturbed than those which obviously depend on verbal comprehension. Aphasias, or language disorders, caused by brain damage, which are not due to sensory or motor loss, are not losses of all symbolic skills. Even patients with **global aphasia** (loss of all verbal skills) can still recognize the meaning of road signs and other arbitrary symbols, and can learn the meanings of plastic symbols.

Thinking abilities are, then, multifarious, and consequently lesions in many cortical association regions may disturb them. Thus, the capacity to think about visuospatial relations (e.g., do geometry) is particularly disrupted by right temperoparietal lesions, whereas thinking about verbal analogies is most disrupted by left temperoparietal lesions. It is striking that lesions of frontal association cortex have remarkably little effect on performance in conventional intelligence tests which tap both verbal and visuospatial thinking skills. Performance on these tests is badly affected by lesions of left and right temperoparietal cortex. It would seem that thinking depends on a number of specific processing capacities mediated by these regions, and that intelligence tests do not require the orchestrating skills of the prefrontal cortex because they can be solved by using fairly automatic, stereotyped algorithmic procedures. On the other hand, there are problems for which no obvious solution procedure exists (the Tower of Hanoi puzzle is an example for those who know it) and which require a flexible strategic approach (drawing on many of the temperoparietal cortex specialisms). Frontal lesions cause deficits in solving these problems. To use a simile: PTO association cortex is like a set of specialized scientists or technicians whereas frontal association cortex is like the general manager who coordinates their activities.

Much has already been said about verbal abilities and more will be said in Chapter 9. A number of general points will, however, be made here about the brain's role in language. First, in most people the left hemisphere is dominant in controlling verbal behaviour. Second, even so, some verbal capacities reside in the right hemisphere, as split-brain studies show. The right hemisphere seems to have poor syntactic and phonetic abilities, is more or less mute, and is best at comprehending concrete words that are associated with images. Third, recovery from aphasia, induced by left-hemisphere strokes, probably depends, in part, on the extent to which the right-hemisphere mechanisms are able to take over. Recovery is always incomplete because the right hemisphere mediates verbal abilities in a different and somewhat inferior way. Fourth, verbal processing is not only performed by parts of the left neocortex, but also by the left hemisphere's basal ganglia and by the left thalamus. Lesions or stimulation of these latter structures also disrupt verbal behaviour. Fifth, verbal abilities are differentially organized within the left hemisphere. This claim is best supported by lesion studies which show that posterior association cortex lesions tend to cause selective reading and writing problems (**alexias** and **agraphias**); lesions in the region of the posterior temporal cortex (which include the planum temporale) cause verbal comprehension problems (**Wernicke's aphasia**); and more anterior lesions cause speech and writing (i.e., language production) problems (**Broca's aphasia**). Language functions are, however, learned, and individuals probably differ in precisely how and where these functions are organized within the left hemisphere. Much still needs to be discovered about how the brain mediates different aspects of language.

Sixth, and related to this last point, the search may be constrained by knowledge of anatomical structure and neuronal interconnections. It has already been pointed out that the planum temporale (within a region that may analyse verbal stimuli) is larger on the left hemisphere, and that the left anterior regions contain relatively more grey matter. These differences are less apparent in left-handers who organize verbal processing more bilaterally. Not only do these data suggest that the left hemisphere is dominant in verbal behaviour because it evolved earlier so as to specialize in processing sequential stimuli and generating sequential responses (verbal processes are supremely sequential), but also they begin to indicate how information is transmitted through the left hemisphere so as to produce verbal behaviour. Ultimately such knowledge may enable machines to be constructed with verbal abilities comparable to those of humans.

Verbal behaviour is a kind of psychological function unique to humans. Like other psychological processes it can only be fully understood against its biological and social backgrounds. The social and cultural environment determines the forms that language takes and how it develops. This environment interacts with the biological factors that have been the subject matter of this chapter. Thus verbal abilities are functions of particular brain structures. The development of these brain structures is, to a considerable extent, under genetic control, and the controlling genes have been selected in evolution, because three or four million years ago their expression in the ancestral human phenotype was associated with kinds of behaviour that conferred an advantage for survival. One can therefore see how verbal and other behaviours are biologically based, and how behaviour, the organization of brain structures, the expression of genes and the forces of evolution interact as a complex system. One should also remember, however, that the types of behaviours that emerge and the way in which they develop depend on the environment, particularly the social environment. These influences are considered more fully in the rest of this book.

BOX 2.2
Problems with homunculi, or little men in the brain

Attempts to explain how the human mind works have long been bedevilled by the ubiquity of a particular form of circularity. This circularity is equally apparent in traditional explanations of how the brain mediates mental phenomena. The problem can be illustrated by considering accounts of how perception and intentional actions are achieved. If an individual correctly reports seeing a chair then the theorist postulates a series of events, starting in the retina of the eye. Basically, signals, coded as patterns of neuronal action potentials, are transmitted to the posterior neocortex (as well as other brain regions). There, the signals are interpreted as indicating, say, the presence of a chair near the speaker. But what, or perhaps who, interprets the signals – a little man in the head? The danger lies in regarding visual perception as a process in which signals are transmitted into the neocortex on to the internal equivalent of a television screen, where they are made sense of by a being with *all* our cognitive abilities. The trouble is that to get the little man to work, one has to postulate another, littler man in his head to interpret the signals there, and so on *ad infinitum*. This problem can be put another way to fit the modern idiom. Human beings are supposed to create **representations** of the visual world (like maps, which represent the landscape) in their brains. But unless these representations are interpreted and are somehow able to activate behaviour, they are as useless as a map under the bonnet of a car. Such a map is ineffective in directing the car until it is made sense of by the driver. To gain these powers for representations in the brain it is tempting to introduce little men, or homunculi.

The homunculus problem reappears when one tries to explain how we choose and perform voluntary actions. Voluntary actions are thought to be chosen consciously and freely, and we are aware of their more global aspects while performing them. This traditional association with consciousness and freedom of choice produces an almost ineluctable tendency to imagine that there is a little man in the brain directing voluntary operations. Clearly, it is essential to explain the operations that make possible perception and voluntary action without recourse to a notion like the homunculus, which constitutes in concealed form the very thing that needs to be illuminated by analysis. This has not proved easy: It is apparent even in some famous theories. For example, William James postulated that voluntary acts differ from involuntary ones in that they always begin with a mental representation or image of the muscular movements to be performed. The actor may have no image of the desired end of the action (which may comprise the sensory feedback caused by carrying it out successfully) and for this reason voluntary behaviour requires learning. This theory has heuristic value and captures part of the truth, but leaves two basic difficulties unsolved. First, how does the image or motor plan lead to the action? To be fair, James thought of the relationship as analogous to the stimulus and response in a reflex, but this lacks plausibility and leaves open the temptation to reintroduce the homunculus. Second, just like muscle movements, images or motor plans can be voluntarily produced, so one is left with the puzzle as to how they are generated, and this, once again, makes tempting recourse to the homunculus.

Insight into how fundamental psychological phenomena can be explained without circularity has been derived in recent years from work on artificial intelligence (AI). Although research on creating machines that can perceive and think like humans is still in the early stages, it has made clearer the broad lines that must be followed to achieve progress. For example, the brain must be regarded as a collection of special-purpose processors, each one much more stupid than the person as a whole, none of which requires a 'self' to interpret their outputs. Ideas about the brain's processor may be stimulated by AI and rigorously tested by artificial simulation. As far as perception is concerned, this approach makes plain that the sensory signal is successively transformed as it passes through the brain. It is nonsense to talk of an image *like* that of a perceived object residing in the neocortex. At the level of AI-inspired componential analysis, there is even doubt as to whether anything exists corresponding to a conscious self that directs many voluntary operations. We introspectively feel that such a general director exists. But this is dangerously close to the homunculus returning, to initiate voluntary behaviour, and AI thinking suggests that behaviour can be rationally generated without such a being. There is no need to postulate an 'action-generating' processor which is conscious and which has cognitive powers equivalent to those of the whole person. (See also Box 5.1.)

Further reading

General

Readers who find this chapter particularly difficult may find their path cleared if they study it in conjunction with the following introductory text:

TEYLER, T.J. (1978) *A Primer of Psychobiology*. Oxford: Freeman.

The following is an excellent, up-to-date treatment of physiological psychology that covers many of the topics in this book from a physiological point of view:

CARLSON, N.R. (1985) *Physiology of Behaviour*. Third edition. Boston: Allyn and Bacon.

For a lively collection of essays on current issues in genetics and evolution, the following is recommended:

GOULD, S.J. (1978) *Ever Since Darwin: Reflections in Natural History*. London: Burnett Books.

Evolution and genetics

A very readable account of human evolutionary origins, based on palaeontological evidence and with informed sociobiological speculations, is:

LEAKEY, R. and LEWIN, R. (1978) *People of the Lake*. Harmondsworth: Penguin.

The conclusions of the last book are in apparent conflict with the implications of 'molecular anthropology'. This material is clearly presented in the following book, which also contains much useful material about molecular genetics, evolutionary theory and human origins:

GRIBBIN, J. and CHERFAS, J. (1982) *The Monkey Puzzle*. London: Bodley Head.

Given our genetic closeness to chimpanzees, the next book gives a lucid review of the behavioural and brain factors that most clearly differentiate our species from chimpanzees:

PASSINGHAM, R.E. (1983) *The Human Primate*. Oxford: Freeman.

Natural selection is generally supposed to operate in individuals, hence the problem of explaining why such behaviours as altruism and homosexuality exist (assuming they are heritable), because their very nature prevents them from being passed on to the next generation. The first book below gives an account from a sociobiological viewpoint of how many such complex human behaviours emerged as inherited characteristics. The second book is a collection of papers that show why sociobiology remains so controversial. The last considers the possibility that genes in one animal can exert phenotypic effects on other animals and tries to work out the implications of this for the transmission of inherited characteristics.

WILSON, E.O. (1978) *On Human Nature*. Cambridge, Mass.: Harvard University Press.

CAPLAN, A.L., ed. (1978) *The Sociobiology Debate: Readings on the Ethical and Scientific Issues Concerning Sociobiology*. New York: Harper and Row.

DAWKINS, R. (1982) *The Extended Phenotype*. Oxford: Freeman.

Behavioural genetics

The idea that behaviour results from a continuous interaction between genes and their immediate and distant environment – the theme of this section – is well illustrated in:

VALE, J.R. (1980) *Genes, Environment and Behavior: an Interactionist Approach*. New York: Harper and Row.

The following contains a very readable collection of articles on the problems of assessing the degree to which a complex characteristic, such as intelligence, is inherited:

RICHARDSON, K. and SPEARS, D., eds. (1972) *Race, Culture and Intelligence*. Harmondsworth: Penguin.

The same topic is interestingly pursued in debate form in the next book, which succeeds in identifying a number of key issues in this area:

EYSENCK, H.J. and KAMIN, L. (1981) *Intelligence and the Battle for Mind*. London: Pan.

This chapter has argued that research estimating heritability of behavioural characteristics is much less important in the long run than the development of ideas about how genes control brain maturation and hence, ultimately, behaviour. Such ideas are dependent on the use of models in very simple animals. Thinking and research in this field is well reviewed in the following paper:

STENT, G.S. (1981) Strength and weaknesses of the genetic approach to the development of the nervous system. *Annual Review of Neurosciences*, **4**, 163–94.

Neurons, neurotransmitters and hormones

For an excellent introductory review of neurotransmitter functions, see:

IVERSEN, L.L. (1979) The chemistry of the brain. *Scientific American*, **341**, 118–29.

The next two books provide reviews of the relationships between neurotransmitters, drugs and behaviour.

WARBURTON, D.M. (1975) *Brain, Behaviour and Drugs*. London: Wiley.
IVERSEN, S.D. and IVERSEN, L.L. (1975) *Behavioural Pharmacology*. Oxford: Oxford University Press.

For an account of how drugs affect psychoses and motor disorders in interactive ways, and of how this relates to the metabolic bases of such diseases, the following is well worth reading:

PINCUS, J.H. and TUCKER, G.J. (1974) *Behavioural Neurology*. Oxford: Oxford University Press.

Carlson's textbook (noted above) provides a good review of neuron physiology, but the following volume (which also includes Iversen's article) contains complementary coverage of the topic by Stevens:

The Brain: a Scientific American Book (1979) Oxford: Freeman.

The human brain, its evolution and principles of organization

Good treatment of these topics is available in Carlson's textbook and in the article by Nauta and Feirtag in *The Brain* (noted above), which also contains a review of brain development by Cowan. Passingham's book (mentioned above) is also highly relevant, as to a lesser extent is Gribbin and Cherfas's *Monkey Puzzle*.

The next book makes a well-argued case for the importance of guiding thinking about the brain's functions by using ideas derived from artificial intelligence, and in doing so gives a lucid description of theories of brain organization, including Descartes's reflexology, encephalization and Jackson's hierarchical levels of control view:

OATLEY, K. (1978) *Perceptions and Representations*. London: Methuen.

The techniques of physiological psychology

Once again, the impact and nature of techniques used to explore brain function is clearly described by Carlson and in *The Brain*. In contrast,

Oatley argues that it is very difficult to make inferences about brain function from the findings of the standard techniques of lesioning and stimulation. In this chapter it has been argued that a convergent operations approach is essential if clear interpretations are to be achieved, and that it is vital to know how brain structures are organized and interconnected. A well-illustrated account of the recently developed correlational techniques (CAT and PET scans) is provided by:

GILLING, D. and BRIGHTWELL, R. (1982) *The Human Brain*. London: Orbis.

.

The brain's functions

Good reviews of the brain's functional roles are provided by Carlson and by Gilling and Brightwell (see above). For an excellent and much more detailed account of how the human brain mediates complex functions such as memory, perception, planning and verbal behaviour the reader is recommended to study the following textbook:

KOLB, B. and WHISHAW, I.Q. (1985) *Fundamentals of Human Neuropsychology*. Second edition. Oxford: Freeman.

There have been many reviews of the functional differences between the left and right hemispheres, but a comprehensive treatment which includes discussion of laterality of functions in relation to sex differences, learning problems, psychiatric disorders and consciousness is provided by:

SPRINGER, S.P. and DEUTSCH, G. (19871) *Left Brain, Right Brain*. Oxford: Freeman.

The final two references are to more advanced discussions of functional lateralization. The first examines the evidence for such asymmetries in birds and mammals, and assesses the role of experience in their development. The second argues that the dichotomy of verbal and nonverbal functions in humans (dealt with by left and right hemispheres) is based on more fundamental differences in the way in which the two hemispheres process information. Both reviews are accompanied by peer discussions.

DENENBERG, V.H. (1981) Hemispheric laterality in animals and the effects of early experience. *Behavioral and Brain Sciences*, **4**, 1–49.
BRADSHAW, J.L. and NETTLETON, N.C. (1981) The nature of hemisphere specialization in man. *Behavioral and Brain Sciences*, **4**, 51–91.

3. Perception

Figures

3. Perception

Introduction

Everything that we do, and everything that we are, is influenced by, even depends on, information which the CNS (central nervous system) obtains from the environment. This information is obtained through the senses. We shall regard perception as the process of acquisition of information from the environment. It is a central theme of this chapter that we cannot reduce the study of perception to the study of the senses. An explanation of why this is so will serve to introduce the chapter.

Perception is an active process, and it is active in three distinct ways. First, the CNS is not passively at the mercy of the innumerable sources of energy capable of stimulating the sensory receptors. The organism seeks stimulation, and this search depends on motivation, attitudes, personality and the need to communicate with others. We should speak of *feeling*, *looking* and *listening* rather than of touch, vision and audition. For practical and for theoretical reasons, however, most investigators of perception have treated the individual as a passive recipient of stimulation. This has been achieved by restricting the experimental subject's freedom for environmental exploration, using a variety of means (for example, instructions to fixate visually a single point, headphones, bite-bars to restrict head movements). The result is that much perceptual psychology is about this artificially restricted mode of perceiving, and this must be reflected in this chapter.

Secondly, perception is selective. The same processes that promote the environmental search lead the individual to attend selectively to particular sensory channels, or even to particular aspects of the information in one channel. These selective processes in perception will be considered in detail in the following chapter.

Thirdly, perception is interpretive. Just as an individual's motivation, attitudes and so on determine the search for stimulation, so
they influence the way in which objects and events are perceived.
Ambiguous stimuli, for example, may be perceived differently,
depending on the observer's expectation of the type of stimulus
that will be presented, or on the observer's motivational state.

As well as being active, perception often does not bear a one-to-
one relation with the physical world. Indeed, hallucinations and
dreams provide examples of perception-like occurrences that need
have no immediate sensory basis. In making such a statement
about the relation between the perceptual and physical worlds we
are, intentionally, sidestepping the ancient philosophical discussion of the existence of a physical world, and how we can have
knowledge of it except through our senses. We here adopt the
pragmatic approach that perception is veridical if it accords with
the nature of objects or events as revealed by physical instruments,
even though the use of these instruments requires the intervention
of the senses. Certainly, people behave, generally, as if we share a
common, real, physical environment, and this must guide our study
of perception.

Perception is not reducible to sensations. We perceive objects
and events in the real world, we do not construct them from
sensations. When we handle and look at an orange, we do not
impose a sensation of orange colour in the eyes on to the sensations
of roundness, pitted smoothness, resilience, coldness, weight and
so on from the receptors in the skin, muscles and joints of the hand
and arm, and on to the fragrance originating in the nose. Rather,
we perceive the orange as an object in the hand (since many of the
hand's receptors require physical contact with the object), and
most of the other sensations are inextricably bound in with the
object.

The final reason why we cannot reduce perception to the study of
the senses is that, within limits, we can perceive objects in an
equivalent way with different senses. 'It matters little through
which sense I realize that I have blundered into a pigsty', as
Hornbostel (1927) put it. The limits, however, are important. The
senses do not have equal capacities for detecting and differentiating among objects. They are specialized to respond primarily to
particular forms of energy. Most of us are able at least to com-

prehend metaphorical relations between sensory modalities:

> Heard melodies are sweet, but those unheard
> Are sweeter; therefore, ye soft pipes, play on;
> (Keats, 'Ode on a Grecian Urn')

Some people, indeed, report **synaesthetic** experiences, in which, for example, musical notes are actually experienced as particular colours. Despite this, certain sensory qualities must be considered **unique** to particular modalities – red is a visual property, middle C is auditory, and the fragrance of a rose is olfactory. Other properties are **common** to more than one sense – size, texture, shape, duration and distance. Some philosophers have drawn a similar distinction between **primary qualities**, which resemble the physical properties of the objects and are inseparable from them (what we here call common properties), and **secondary qualities**, which do not resemble objects but seem to be properties of a particular sense (what we call unique properties). Aristotle wrote of a 'common sense', the function of which is to apprehend the primary qualities by integrating the senses. This is akin to our definition of perception, the use of the senses to gain information about the environment, most importantly of the common properties, but integrated with the properties unique to each sensory system.

In this chapter we shall concentrate on a discussion of the perception of the human environment rather than on the individual senses and the qualities unique to them. However, for historical reasons, and also because an understanding of higher perceptual processes depends on knowledge of sensory systems and processes, the next sections will deal briefly with these matters as they relate to what are probably the most important of the sensory systems in the human, vision and audition.

Sensory systems

THE SENSES AND THEIR CLASSIFICATION

The sensory receptors through which we obtain information about the internal and external environment all function as transducers. converting energy in a particular form (the adequate stimulus) into action potentials in neurons. A number of attempts have been made to classify the senses. The traditional classification is into the **special senses** (vision, audition, olfaction, gustation), the **cutaneous senses** (touch/pressure, cold, warmth), and the **visceral senses** (pain, muscle tension, joint position etc.). A more functional classification, proposed by Sherrington in 1906, is into **exteroceptors** (concerned with external events), **interoceptors** (the internal environment), and **proprioceptors** (the position of the body in, and its movement through, space). Gibson (1966) took issue with this classification partly on the ground that it is fallacious to ascribe proprioception to a separate sensory system. Vision, for example, is of paramount importance as a source of proprioceptive information, as we shall see on pages 189–90. Gibson's alternative classification is into five 'perceptual systems' (visual, auditory, haptic, taste-smell and basic orienting system), each of which is based on a distinct set of receptors and receptor organs.

It should be clear by now that any classification of the senses – indeed, any attempt to list them – is of very little value in the study of perception. Even Gibson's scheme, involving as it does distinct receptors and receptor organs, fails to take full account of the extent to which the senses are used to extract equivalent information from the environment. The senses are, of course, the basis of our contact with the environment, and the qualities unique to them are an essential component of perception. We therefore turn now to a brief account of these matters, concentrating on those modalities that we use to explore the environment: vision and audition.

THE VISUAL SYSTEM

The organ of vision is the eye, the gross structure of which functions to focus light on to a mosaic of receptors. The receptors form the rear layer of the **retina**, which is composed of several types of neuron and other cells. The receptors fall into two classes, the **rods** and the **cones**. Cones are found over the whole of the retina, their density falling off away from its centre. Conversely, rods have their greatest density in the peripheral parts of the retina, decreasing in frequency towards the centre, where there is a depressed region, the **fovea**, which has only cones. When we look at objects we orient the head and eyes, and accommodate, to bring light reflected from the object to a focus on the fovea.

When light strikes a receptor it initiates a chemical change in a photopigment contained in the receptor. This change produces a graded electrical response, the **receptor potential**, which may activate successive neurons in the visual pathway. Information is passed from the receptors by way of the **bipolar cells** to the **ganglion cells**, the axons of which form the **optic nerve**. This transfer of information is not, however, simple. Except in the fovea, each bipolar cell synapses with a number of receptors, and with a number of ganglion cells. Furthermore, two additional types of cell, **horizontal** and **amacrine** cells, connect numbers of other cells together, providing a high degree of information-processing in the retina itself.

The optic nerves converge at the **optic chiasma**, in which fibres from the nasal halves of the two retinas cross to the other side, while those from the temporal halves remain on the same side. Thus, each of the **optic tracts**, behind the chiasma, carries information from both eyes about one side of the visual field; left visual field to the right side of the brain, right visual field to the left. It is likely that the fovea projects to both sides of the brain, since unilateral lesions higher in the visual pathway produce regions of blindness that do not include the foveal region. The ganglion cell axons in the optic tract synapse in the **lateral geniculate nucleus** (LGN), axons from which pass to the visual cortex in the occipital lobe. Visual pathways also travel to subcortical centres, including the **superior colliculus**. The importance of these pathways is discussed on pages 191–2.

The rods and cones differ in their overall sensitivity and in the wavelength of light to which they respond maximally. Rods are far more sensitive than cones, so that at low levels of illumination they alone are stimulated. This is known as **scotopic** vision. There is only one class of rod, and for this reason scotopic vision is achromatic. Changes in receptor potential are the same no matter what the wavelength of the stimulating light, provided that light is sufficiently intense. At higher levels of illumination vision is subserved by the cones, and is known as **photopic** vision. Unlike scotopic vision, photopic vision is chromatic.

The basis of colour vision is the existence of three types of cone possessing different photopigments, maximally sensitive to light in the short-, medium- or long-wavelength regions of the spectrum (called, respectively, S, M and L cones). When light of a given wavelength composition falls on the retina it produces different graded potentials in the cones, depending on their relative sensitivity to those wavelengths. Interactions in the retina convert differences between the potentials of pairs of cone types into differential firing rates in the ganglion cells. Most ganglion cells carry chromatic information, and they code it in a spectrally opponent manner, decreasing their rate of firing to one range of wavelengths and increasing it to others. Thus, for example, there are cells that increase their firing rate to long-wavelength stimuli and decrease it to short wavelengths (denoted $+R-G$ cells), and others that do the reverse ($-R+G$). Little additional processing of chromatic information seems to occur in the LGN, but the visual cortex further modifies this type of information. We have as yet, however, a very incomplete picture of cortical processing.

The colour of a surface is not solely dependent on the wavelength composition of the light reflected from that surface, but is influenced by the prior stimulation of the retina, and by the simultaneous stimulation of adjacent areas. Successive effects are shown by the **negative afterimages** that appear after inspection of a bright stimulus for a short time. The afterimage has a hue that is **complementary** to that of the original stimulus. (Two hues are complementary if, when mixed in equal proportions, the result is achromatic. Red and bluish-green are complementary, as are blue and reddish-yellow.)

Negative afterimages are a consequence of two types of adaptation (see Box 3.1). **Photopigment bleaching**, rendering the stimulated area of the retina less sensitive to the stimulating wavelengths, and **neural rebound**, which is the tendency for an opponent cell to change its rate of firing beyond its resting level on cessation of a stimulus, thereby signalling, in effect, the presence of the opposite stimulus.

Just as the perception of a surface is affected by prior stimulation, so it is influenced by the nature of its surroundings. The effect of adjacent areas is normally such as to increase the contrast between them, and is known as **simultaneous contrast**, or **chromatic induc-**

Figure 3.1 Simultaneous contrast.

Figure 3.2 Simultaneous contrast depending on contour.

tion. The effect is best seen when one area is larger than, and surrounds, the other, and appears as the addition to the smaller area of the hue complementary to that of the surround. Thus a grey patch in a red surround appears a desaturated blue-green. As is also the case with afterimages, simultaneous contrast is not limited to chromatic stimuli. Figure 3.1 shows simultaneous contrast between the two grey areas and the black and white surrounds. No certain neural basis for simultaneous contrast can be described, although the effects can be made to depend on contour and structure, suggesting a cortical mechanism.

Figure 3.2 shows little contrast until a thread, or something similar, is placed across the whole figure along the black-white border. This provides a contour, allowing the contrast mechanisms to operate. Note further that if the thread is moved slowly to one side the induced lightness/darkness within the ring 'follows' it, to a certain extent, maintaining the uniformity of the areas bounded by the contours.

As we shall see, contrast is a pervasive feature of perception. Mechanisms that cause objects to stand out against the background clearly have adaptive significance, since they increase the organism's ability to respond to objects in the environment (see Box 3.1).

BOX 3.1
Adaptation: its effects and uses

Sensory adaptation is the decrease in sensitivity of an organism to continued or repeated stimulation. As such it is an essential and ubiquitous aspect of sensory function, serving to remove from the information reaching the brain that which concerns unchanging environmental features, thereby rendering the information-processing system maximally sensitive to changing features. The organism that best detects environmental change has an adaptive advantage. Adaptation can probably take place at any stage in the transmission of information within the nervous system. We have seen, for example, that adaptation of the visual receptors, by way of photopigment bleaching, may be observed by a decrease in sensitivity to the stimulating wavelengths and a complementary afterimage. These two observations are typical of the consequences of continued stimulation: **adaptation with negative aftereffect**. Such effects may be elicited by continued stimulation of any sensory modality.

Adaptation and its consequences are well illustrated in the case of thermal sensitivity, using a demonstration first formally reported by Weber over a hundred years ago. Fill three containers with water, one of them (large enough to accommodate both hands) at a temperature that feels only slightly warm, one hotter, and one colder than this. With both hands initially in the first container the water temperature feels the same to both. Now put one hand into each of the other containers for a few minutes. During this immersion a gradual lessening of the initial sensations of hot and cold occurs. This is adaptation. Next, the hands are both replaced into the first container, and it will be noticed that the same water now feels warm to the hand that has adapted to cold, and cool to the hand that has adapted to hot water.

There are alternative ways of describing this result. Following Gibson we can say that adaptation is followed by a negative aftereffect, so that the perception of subsequent stimuli is distorted, shifted in a direction *away* from the direction of adaptation. Alternatively, we can say that adaptation is followed by **contrast**, so that the difference between stimuli on the adapted dimension is accentuated, as the sensory system shifts to a new **adaptation level** (see Helson, 1964). This view of the effects of adaptation emphasizes its biological function. The decrease in absolute sensitivity that is adaptation is accompanied by an increase in sensitivity to **change** in the region of the adapting stimulus. That is, the nearer stimuli are to the adapting stimulus the more easily are they discriminated from one another.

The changes that accompany and follow adaptation provide powerful methods for investigating perceptual processing. If, for example, adaptation to one stimulus has no effect on the perception of another, its detectability for instance, then it may be inferred that the two stimuli do not share a common mechanism in the perceptual process. Using this technique of **selective adaptation** the properties of the mechanisms underlying perception may be investigated. It is generally found that the perceptual mechanisms respond to (and adapt to) a range of stimulus values with maximal response at some central value. The shape of the curve relating degree of elevation of detection threshold following adaptation to the difference between the interacting stimuli is taken to reflect the **tuning characteristic** of the mechanism.

However, such techniques involve the use of stimuli at or near the detection threshold, and it is possible that different mechanisms underlie suprathreshold perception. **Aftereffects** provide a way of examining the properties of such mechanisms. Measurement of the extent to which prolonged viewing of one stimulus affects the perception of subsequently presented stimuli allows inferences to be made about the properties of the mechanisms underlying their perception in a way entirely analogous to selective adaptation. We will see a number of applications of these methods in this chapter.

THE AUDITORY SYSTEM

The human ear has evolved partly to collect and transduce sound waves into action potentials in the auditory nerve. Sound waves travel along the **external auditory meatus**, the outer channel open to the air, to the eardrum, or **tympanic membrane**, which passes the vibrations via three articulated bones, the **ossicles**, to the **fenestra ovalis**, a membrane-covered opening in the bone surrounding the inner ear. The sounds are transmitted by this to a liquid-filled structure, the **cochlea**, which is a coiled, tapering tube. Along the length of the cochlea is the **organ of Corti**, which bears the auditory receptors, hair cells attached between two membranes. Vibrations in the cochlea cause these membranes to move relative to one another, with a consequential shearing action on the hair cells. This produces receptor potentials which can lead to action potentials in the auditory nerve. It is not necessary for us to describe the complex neural pathways of the auditory system here. We note simply that both cochleas send information to both sides of the brain. Indeed removal of the entire auditory cortex (in the temporal lobe) from one hemisphere causes hardly any reduction in auditory acuity. Certain subcortical centres, the **superior olivary nuclei**, receive input from both ears, and seem to be involved in the location of sounds.

The coding of auditory information is less well understood than that of visual information. The chief auditory quality that we need to consider is **pitch**. Pitch is primarily dependent on the frequency of vibration of the sound wave, higher frequencies producing sensations of higher pitch. In our present state of knowledge, it seems that pitch is coded by three distinct means, depending on the frequency of the stimulus. At frequencies from the lowest audible (about 20 Hz) to about 400 Hz, the firing rate of individual neurons is the same as the stimulus frequency. At frequencies above this, up to about 5000 Hz, the auditory nerve as a whole fires at the stimulating frequency, but *individual* fibres fire once every two or more cycles, a mechanism known as **neural volleying**. At frequencies above about 5000 Hz, frequency coding of pitch breaks down, and it appears that 'place' coding takes over; pitch is indicated by *which* neurons are firing, not by firing rate. **Loudness**, the intensive aspect of auditory experience, which depends primarily on the amplitude of vibration of the sound wave, seems to be coded by the number of neurons firing in the auditory nerve, and this applies throughout the range of audible frequencies. While the pitch of a pure tone is primarily dependent on the frequency of the stimulus, it varies also with intensity. For tones below about 1000 Hz, pitch decreases with increasing intensity. For tones above about 3000 Hz pitch increases with increasing intensity.

Pure tones, however, are a laboratory artifice. The sounds that we encounter normally are of varying types, and degrees, of complexity. Complex sounds that are composed of mixtures of frequencies that are not multiples of one, fundamental frequency (**aperiodic sounds**) may be called noises. More often we reserve the term for sounds that are unwanted or obtrusive. The annoyance that a sound causes is clearly related to its intensity, but even fairly low levels of sound can be annoying, especially if we do not have control over them, or if we are engaged in a task requiring auditory attention (conversation, listening to music). Exposure to loud sounds, such as attendance at a rock concert, will cause a **temporary threshold shift**, making the subsequent detection of low-intensity sounds more difficult. Prolonged or repeated exposure to loud sound can be a serious industrial danger ('boilermakers' deafness') unless precautions are taken to protect the hearing of persons working in noisy environments. This deafness is most extreme in the frequency range most strongly represented in the noise, and is due to damage to the hair cells in the organ of Corti. The effects of noise on performance will be considered in Chapter 4.

. The notes produced by musical instruments are frequently referred to as **periodic**, that is, they are composed of a fundamental, lowest frequency, defining the pitch of the note, and a number of overtones, or **harmonics**, which are multiples of the fundamental. However, when strictly periodic notes are produced electronically they sound dull and 'unmusical'. **Timbre**, the quality that differentiates the same note produced by different instruments, depends primarily on the characteristic pattern of harmonics of which the note is composed. But timbre is also influenced by the temporal characteristics of the note, a fact most simply evidenced by the difficulty even experienced musicians can have when trying to identify the instrument on which a very brief note is produced. The **sound spectrogram**, a device used for showing graphically the frequency composition of a sound, shows that this composition changes during the playing of a note, a process that is modified by the instrumentalist. When groups of instruments or voices are producing the same note, differences in tuning and harmonic structure of each source produce a highly complex sound form (the 'chorus effect'). Add to this the fundamentals and harmonics from other groups of instruments, and the musical stimulus can be seen to be an extremely complex one.

The relationship between pitch and frequency in music is of particular interest. Certain **intervals** (frequency differences) are generally considered **consonant** (pleasing), while others are **dissonant**. Consonant intervals involve simple ratios of frequencies (the octave is 2:1, the major fifth is 3:2), while the tones forming a dissonant interval are in less simple ratios. These simple numerical intervals, however, are not quite as precise as this suggests. The subjective octave is actually produced by an interval slightly greater than doubling, and the size of the ratio increases as we ascend the musical scale.

While a number of theories have been proposed to explain consonance and dissonance in music, these have usually referred to relatively simple physical features of musical tones (for example, the brain has been said to 'dislike large numbers'). It is clear that these phenomena cannot be reduced to such simple explanations – a statement that is true also of much else in the perception of music. Agreement on what are consonant scales has never been universal, although there is enough agreement to suggest some common basis (the octave, fifth and fourth are common intervals in many non-Western scales). Repeated exposure to dissonant intervals, either experimentally or through a new musical idiom, can lead them to be experienced with increasing consonance. The appreciation of relative pitch, then, is not fixed. Furthermore, it appears that it has to be learned in infancy and, of course, each child learns the musical scale of his or her own culture.

ASPECTS OF SENSORY FUNCTION

In general, changes in stimulus values produce changes in perception; increasing the intensity of light, for example, leads to an increase in brightness. The study of the relationships between stimuli and the sensations to which they give rise is known as **psychophysics**, a term coined by Fechner (1860) who pioneered this area. Psychophysics is of enormous historical importance in the development of psychology.

One of its branches, dealing with the nature and measurement of the **psychophysical function** relating stimulus and sensation, gave a great impetus to measurement theory in general, and provided the basic methods on which many of the methods used in all areas of psychology are based. The other branch of psychophysics is concerned with **sensory thresholds**, which while chiefly of historical interest, has provided methods and concepts that are still useful today.

We shall distinguish two types of sensory threshold. The **absolute threshold** is the lowest intensity of stimulus that can be detected. The **differential threshold** is the smallest detectable change in a stimulus. As Fechner discovered, however, attempts to measure these thresholds fail to produce a single value at which a change from no detection to detection occurs. Rather, the result is a range of values over which the probability of detection changes from 0 per cent to 100 per cent. Fechner attributed this to the action of random error, but it subsequently led to the re-examination of the concept of threshold. Why must we assume that sensory systems operate with such fixed limitations? One alternative view is that the threshold varies continuously, so that a particular stimulus might at one moment be above the threshold, and at the next below it. Detection of such a stimulus would then follow the sort of probability function found in practice.

An alternative approach, **signal detection theory**, rejects the notion of threshold altogether. Each sensory channel always carries **noise** (in the sense of any activity that interferes with the detection of a signal). The amount of noise varies randomly about some average value. When a stimulus is presented, the activity to which it gives rise in the sensory system adds to the noise existing at that moment. The task of the person is to determine whether the level of activity in the system at any time is the result of noise alone, or a stimulus added to noise. If the stimulus is very strong (the signal-to-noise ratio is high) the task is easy; the resulting high level of activity could not result from noise alone. The weaker is the stimulus, the greater is the probability that the activity in the sensory system could result from noise alone, so that the person would detect the stimulus (that is, correctly decide a stimulus is present) less frequently. From this analysis, it can be seen that the detection of a stimulus is a statistical matter, and the observed gradual change from 0 per cent to 100 per cent detection found in the measurement of thresholds is exactly what would be expected.

In connection with this brief discussion of the concept of threshold we turn now to the notion of **subliminal perception**. This topic has a long and controversial history. At first sight the very term seems to be self-contradictory; subliminal means below threshold. Yet there are cases in which the influence of a stimulus, or aspects of a stimulus, of which the person claims to be unaware can be demonstrated. Some of the earliest of such demonstrations involved asking people to guess which of two weights is the heavier, when that person claimed not to be able to detect any difference (that is, the difference was subliminal). Subjects guessed correctly more often than would be expected if they were guessing on a purely chance basis. This phenomenon has been demonstrated in various modalities, and it has been established that the larger the stimulus or stimulus difference, the better are the guesses. Such results need not cause us to revise our ideas about sensory function. If one adopts the view that there is a real, but variable, threshold, the explanation is that on some occasions the stimulus (or stimulus difference) is above the momentary threshold, and the greater the intensity of the stimulus (or difference), the more often this is true, resulting in more correct 'guesses'. To signal detection theory, any stimulus adds activity to the noise in the system, so increasing the probability that the brain will conclude that a stimulus is present. Increasing the stimulus intensity increases the activity further, and increases the probability that a 'guess' will be correct.

BOX 3.2
Visual masking

Masking occurs when two stimuli are presented in such a way that one causes a decrement in the perception of the other, usually shown by an increase in the detection threshold of the masked stimulus.

The simplest form of visual masking (**luminance masking**) occurs when a target stimulus is followed by a masking stimulus that is a light flash. The effect is to decrease the probability of detection of the target. Masking is maximal when the stimuli are presented simultaneously, and falls off more or less symmetrically with increasing temporal separation of target and mask, so that masking occurs when the mask precedes the target (**forward masking**) and when it follows the target by up to about 100 msec (**backward masking**). In the simultaneous condition masking can be attributed simply to the greatly reduced signal-to-noise ratio that the superimposition of the more intense and often longer lasting mask produces. To explain forward and backward masking a mechanism to bridge the temporal gap is required, and this is provided by the more rapid rise of and more prolonged neural effects of more intense stimuli. That luminance masking occurs in a peripheral location is shown by presenting target and mask to the two eyes separately (**dichoptic presentation**), when masking is almost completely absent.

A mask composed of a random pattern of lines (**visual noise**) has a greater effect on a patterned target than does a luminance mask, indicating that some additional process is involved. The additional mechanism is central since visual noise masking is not markedly reduced by dichoptic presentation. Visual noise masking is maximal when mask and target are presented simultaneously. Sperling (1963) demonstrated that when an array of letters was masked by visual noise, and the mask delay was varied, each 10 msec (approximately) additional delay allowed an additional letter to be identified from the array. He argued that the mask interrupted the processing of target information. Breitmeyer and Ganz (1976) have argued that mask information becomes **integrated** with that of the target. Visual noise masking is used in studies of visual information processing to limit the time for which information is available for processing.

A third type of visual masking occurs when target and masking stimuli are presented with their contours in closely adjacent locations. If the mask follows the target the phenomenon is known as **metacontrast**. The target may be a disc and the mask an annulus surrounding the position of the disc. In more recent work letters have been used as targets. The distinctive features of metacontrast seem to depend on proximity and paralleleity of contours. The effect is usually found to be maximal when an interval of about 75 msec separates target and mask, with little or none when the two are presented simultaneously. Breitmeyer and Ganz (1976) have argued that metacontrast results from the inhibition of the **sustained channels** in the visual pathway (which have a longer latency, fire throughout stimulus presentation, and are thought to underlie pattern vision) by the **transient channels** (which have shorter latency, fire only at onset and offset of a stimulus, and which underlie the detection of change and movement).

A fourth type of masking may be called **feature masking**. This is the increase in detection threshold for a feature that occurs maximally when that feature is followed by a masking stimulus with the same feature (for example, a grating stimulus of particular spatial frequency and orientation). This has similar properties to metacontrast, and is used like selective adaptation in the investigation of channels in visual processing.

Pattern and object perception

FEATURE ANALYSIS AND CHANNELS

In 1959, Hubel and Wiesel reported the first results of experiments in which they recorded the electrical activity of single neurons in the primary visual cortex of cats. In these experiments, and those reported subsequently, using both cats and monkeys, they and other workers demonstrated that each cell has a receptive field, but not the simple concentric excitatory-inhibitory fields that are found for ganglion cells. Exploring the receptive field of a typical cortical neuron with a small spot of light might reveal an elongated excitatory region, flanked by inhibitory regions. Using an adjustable bar of light reveals that such a cell produces a maximal response when stimulated with a bar that has the same width as the excitatory region, without overlapping into the inhibitory regions.

An elongated excitatory region clearly has an orientation with respect to the vertical, and a cell such as that described could act as a detector of lines or bars of a particular range of widths and of orientations, with a central, optimal width (or size) and orientation. A second class of cell is found to respond maximally to a stimulus consisting of an edge separating bright and dark areas. These two types of cell are known as **simple cells**. Other cells are found that respond to bars or edges in particular orientations, but not limited to a single retinal location, as is the case with simple cells. Rather, these **complex cells** respond to such stimuli anywhere within a fairly large area of the retina. Still other cells, known as **hypercomplex cells**, also respond maximally to bars of particular widths in particular orientations, but have inhibitory regions completely surrounding the elongated central excitatory region, and so respond maximally to bars of a particular length. Others have been found that respond to corners (intersecting edges).

The discovery that the visual cortex of cats and primates contains large numbers of cells that respond to relatively simple features of stimuli resulted in the re-emergence of theories that assume that perception proceeds by a process of analysis. Complex stimuli are assumed to be analysed into distinctive features (at the simple-cell level), and complex and hypercomplex cells show early stages of the subsequent reconstruction of the environment from these features. There are, however, numerous difficulties with this type of explanation. Unless one is very wary, it is easy to be carried along with this hierarchical process to assume that at cortical levels beyond the primary visual projection areas are to be found neurons selective for more and more complex and unique features of the visual environment. The logical limit of this is to suppose that there exists a neuron selective for every distinguishable feature of the world (e.g., 'grandmother cells', sensitive only to the visual image of one's grandmother). It is true that a very few cells have been found that seem to be selective to very complex stimuli, and the example usually cited is the finding by Gross *et al.* (1972), in the cortex of a monkey, a neuron that was selectively triggered by the shadow of a monkey's hand, held vertically. The apparent significance of this finding is reduced by further cells recorded by Gross *et al.* that were maximally responsive to such items as a haemostat, forceps and a bottle brush! Gross himself pointed out that it is impossible to be sure that the stimuli used to investigate the specificity of a cell include the best possible stimulus.

The feature analysis theorist need not, of course, extend the process to these extremes, and there are other grounds for doubting this hierarchical view of the perceptual process. The most compelling of these are that both simple and complex cells receive inputs directly from the LGN, and complex cells respond more rapidly than simple cells and cannot therefore represent a later processing stage. Furthermore, as we shall see in later sections, perceptual theories have to take account of 'top-down' influences on perception; the ways in which, for example, memory, context and meaning influence what is perceived.

An alternative approach to sensory information processing is one that considers the system to work like an arrangement of parallel filters, analysing, say, a visual scene by decomposing it into component **spatial frequencies** (light and dark alternations), much as Fourier analysis is used to analyse a complex wave-form, such as a sound or an EEG wave, into component simple waves (sine waves). There are grounds other than those already given for preferring a spatial filter description. The cells in area 17, originally described as feature analysers for bars, turn out to be rather more responsive to a grating of optimal frequency than to a bar of optimal width, and are much more selective for spatial frequency than for bar width. Mechanisms such as these are referred to as **channels**. This term has particular advantages in the psychophysical sphere as the techniques used cannot give any direct information about processing at the neuronal level. A channel is taken to be an independent functional element of the system. Nevertheless, parallel human psychophysical and primate physiological research frequently produce very similar results, suggesting that the neural basis for the channels discovered in human work is similar to that in the monkey. Microelectrode studies with cats indicate that although some 'feature analyser' cells are detectable shortly after birth, these only develop fully if the animal is allowed appropriate visual experience. Cats reared from birth to five months of age with exposure only to either horizontal or vertical stripes not only appear, behaviourally, to be blind to the other orientation, but seem not to possess the cortical units responsive to them.

SPATIAL FREQUENCY AND ORIENTATION

One of the earliest and most convincing pieces of evidence for the existence of multiple channels for spatial frequency came from a

selective adaptation experiment (see Box 3.1) of Blakemore and Campbell (1969). The subject viewed a high-contrast sine grating for one minute, after which the contrast threshold (the lowest contrast at which the subject reported a grating rather than a uniform field) was measured for a grating of the same or a different spatial frequency. The maximal rise in threshold was for the test grating with the same frequency as the adapting grating, decreasing with gratings of higher and lower frequencies.

Similar results have been obtained with other methods, such as **subthreshold summation**, which is based on the assumption that if two stimuli presented together have a lower combined detection threshold than they have individually they are being processed by the same channel(s). Campbell and Kulikowski (1966) investigated orientation channels, showing that a **masking** stimulus raised the threshold of a test stimulus maximally when the two had the same orientation, the effect reducing to half for vertical or horizontal stimuli when the gratings differed by 12 degrees. Orientation tuning was less fine for oblique gratings, the effect decreasing to a half with a 15-degree difference. This result is consistent with a variety of evidence showing that visual performance is superior for vertical and horizontal stimuli than for obliques, that has been called the **oblique effect** (see Appelle, 1972).

Aftereffect studies have generally shown that the channels underlying suprathreshold orientation and spatial frequency processing have similar properties to those found with threshold techniques. In the spatial frequency domain, Blakemore and Sutton (1969) showed that viewing a grating caused distortion of subsequently viewed gratings such that higher frequency gratings appeared to have even higher, and lower frequency gratings even lower, frequency. Since the spatial frequency channels have a large degree of overlap a single stimulus will affect, and cause adaptation in, a number of channels to the extent that each is sensitive to that stimulus. The perceived frequency of the grating must represent some combined output of the stimulated channels. A subsequent grating of slightly different spatial frequency is processed by an overlapping set of channels, but channels further away from the adapting stimulus frequency will be less adapted. The peak response, and hence the percept, will therefore be shifted to a spatial frequency further from the adapting stimulus.

Channels for the processing of other types of information can also be investigated by these techniques. Chromatic channels have already been discussed, and channels for luminance, temporal frequency and motion have all been studied. Later in this section we shall see the application of similar techniques to aspects of auditory perception. It is also possible to investigate interactions between channels, and the best-known example is that between orientation and chromatic channels first demonstrated by McCollough (1965). She demonstrated an effect, since dubbed the **McCollough effect**, that is a chromatic aftereffect contingent upon the orientation of a grating pattern. This is induced by alternately viewing (for example) a red/black vertical grating and a green/black horizontal grating for a relatively long period. On subsequent viewing of achromatic gratings, the majority of observers report that a vertical grating appears faintly blue-green, and a horizontal one pink-violet. This effect is an example of a class of phenomena known as **contingent aftereffects**, in which the appearance of an aftereffect in one dimension is made to be contingent on another dimension. Contingent aftereffects have been demonstrated between most pairs of channels, and can be made contingent on more than one dimension. More generally, selective adaptation and masking can be shown to be dependent on combinations of features.

It is usually argued that since these techniques reveal the existence of independent channels for these features, contingent effects demonstrate the existence of channels for combinations of features. The fact that contingent effects like the McCollough effect are relatively weak implies that only a proportion of the orientation or other channels are involved in their production, these being the ones processing the combination of features involved.

SPEECH PERCEPTION

For human beings the most important application of auditory pattern recognition is in the perception of speech. The speech stimulus is an extremely complex one but may, for certain purposes, be considered to be composed of basic sound units, **phonemes**. Each language uses a limited set of phonemes which can each be thought of as composed of sets of **distinctive features** which may, acoustically, be defined by physical characteristics of the speech sound pattern. A distinctive feature provides the distinction between two phonemes. The words *bin* and *pin*, for example, differ because of one feature of the initial consonant; the *b* sound is **voiced** while the *p* is **voiceless**. This distinction may be demonstrated by saying out loud the syllables *ba* and *pa*, when the vibrations of the vocal folds will be heard, and felt, to be delayed in the case of *pa*. Acoustically the voicing difference is described as a difference in **voice onset time** (VOT). In the case of *ba* VOT is about 10 msec, for *pa* it is about 100 msec. VOT is only one of a number of acoustic features that define phonetic differences in speech.

A type of theory of speech perception that has considerable currency bases the process on hypothesized feature analysers or detectors in the auditory system, selectively responsive to characteristics of the speech stimulus. The best developed feature detector theory is that of Eimas (see Eimas and Tartter, 1979), and in this view the basis of speech perception is the existence of feature detectors responsive to distinctive features of speech. Eimas's theory has been most fully described for the voiced-voiceless dimension, although in principle it applies equally to other distinctive features.

It is hypothesized that two types of detector exist for this dimension, one maximally responsive at short VOTs, the other at longer VOTs (see Figure 3.3). A stimulus with a VOT within the range of the first detector will be perceived as voiced; one within the range of the second detector will be perceived as voiceless. The boundary between voiced and voiceless speech sounds occurs where the sensitivity curves of the two detectors overlap. The location of this can be determined experimentally with the use of artificial speech sounds (produced by a speech synthesizer), with varying VOTs. Subjects can be asked to identify a stimulus as, for example, *ba* or *pa*. The boundary is the VOT of that stimulus that is equally likely to be assigned to either category, since each type of detector is equally stimulated.

Since 1973 considerable evidence has accumulated that is usually interpreted as supporting the feature detector approach. Much of this evidence has come from the use of aftereffect methods (called **selective adaptation** in this literature, see Box 3.1). In one example of this, Eimas and Corbit (1973) had subjects identify a series of

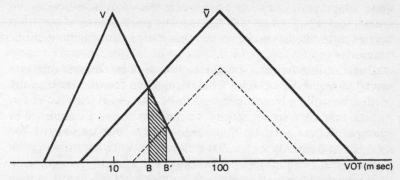

Figure 3.3 Hypothesized mechanism underlying perception of voiced and voiceless speech sounds. V and V̂ represent diagrammatically the sensitivity of two feature detector cells sensitive maximally to short and long VOT respectively. B is the VOT of the boundary between perception of voiced and voiceless sounds. The dashed line represents the sensitivity of V̂ after adaptation to a voiceless syllable. B' is the postadaptation boundary.

speech sounds on the dimensions *ba* to *pa*, and *da* to *ta*, with VOTs varying in 5 msec steps, before and after listening to repeated presentations of either a voiced (*ba* or *da*) or voiceless (*pa* or *ta*) syllable. Repeated presentation caused the voiced-voiceless boundary to be shifted towards the type of stimulus used as the adapting stimulus. Thus, for example, after adapting to a voiceless syllable, some stimuli that had previously been classed as voiceless were classed as voiced. Furthermore, this effect occurred regardless of the other feature of the adapting syllable, that is, whether its place of articulation (*bilabial*, as in *ba* and *pa*, or *alveolar*, as in *da* and *ta*) was the same as the stimulus being tested. This latter result is consistent with the view that adaptation has taken place to a distinctive feature rather than to a phoneme or some other higher order characteristic of the stimuli. Eimas's theory explains these results by suggesting that repeated presentation of, say, a voiceless syllable selectively adapts the long VOT detector, so that it is rendered, temporarily, less sensitive. As can be seen in Figure 3.3, the effect of this is to shift the point of intersection of the sensitivity curves, and hence the boundary between short and long VOT, towards the adapting stimulus. Stimuli in the shaded region will, after adaptation, show an aftereffect; they will be perceived as voiced instead of voiceless. Subsequent studies have shown that similar aftereffects occur after adaptation to other phonetic dimensions.

Certain other types of evidence also support a feature analyser model of speech perception. The existence has been demonstrated of discontinuities in the perception of speech sounds by young infants that correspond to the boundaries found in adults. For example, Eimas *et al.* (1971) demonstrated that one-month-old infants can differentiate sounds differing in VOT by 20 msec, but only when the difference crossed the (adult) feature boundary. In this, and similar experiments, use was made of the fact that high rates of **non-nutritive sucking** occur in infants exposed to novel stimuli. Repeated presentation of a stimulus is accompanied by a decrease in sucking rate, which can be increased again by presenting a discriminably different stimulus. For speech sounds differing by 20 msec in VOT, this occurred only when the second stimulus was in a different phonetic category to the first, to which adaptation had occurred. Such evidence suggests that speech perception proceeds by feature extraction, and is not dependent on higher level functions, such as the ability to produce speech.

A number of criticisms may be made of the feature detector approach to speech perception (see Diehl, 1981). It has been demonstrated, for example, that boundary shifts can be obtained with nonspeech stimuli, suggesting that the mechanisms involved are not part of a specialized speech-processing system, as Eimas assumes. However, it is not essential for a feature analysis model to separate an acoustic analysis stage of perception from the general auditory processing system.

The most telling criticism of the approach, however, is that it seems unable to cope with the context effects that produce the enormous range of variation in real spoken language, as opposed to isolated syllables. These include the facts that speech sounds vary according to semantic context, that we can rapidly become accustomed to language spoken in a different accent (a different phonemic structure), and that the perceived phonemic structure of speech depends on context. (Compare, for example, the samples *a whole Dover sole* and *a hold over me*. The last word changes the perceived nature of what has preceded it.) In short, isolated phonemes are not a feature of spoken language, and speech perception cannot be reduced to either phoneme or distinctive feature detection.

There are other theories of speech perception that attempt to account for these **top-down** influences. The **motor theory**, for example (Liberman, Cooper, Shankweiler and Studdert-Kennedy, 1967), holds that speech perception is accomplished by the same neural mechanisms that underlie speech production. The auditory stimulus produces motor commands to the muscles involved in speech production, the phonemic structure of which is then recognized. This does not, however, circumvent the problem of the complexity and variability of the relation between phonemic and acoustic structures. Additionally, it has been shown that phonemes differ according to the context in which they are *produced*.

The **analysis-by-synthesis** approach (Stevens and Halle, 1967) suggests that the listener constructs a neural representation of the utterance that is based on its immediate acoustic features and on other information such as context, using the generative rules of speech production. If the representation is sufficiently similar to the input, the input is recognized, otherwise the representation is modified until it is. However, for such a process to arrive with any speed at an adequate match of the input, it is necessary for considerable analysis of the signal to be performed. It seems likely that a more satisfactory account of speech perception will combine an acoustic feature analysis stage, part of the general auditory processing system, with a subsequent stage that takes account of other sources of information.

READING

Just as speech perception may be viewed as the recognition of complex auditory patterns, so reading is a complex visual pattern recognition task. In the past fifteen years or so, research and theory on reading have attracted considerable attention among experimental psychologists. This upsurge of interest parallels the growth of computer technology, allowing the simulation of complex models of higher mental processes, and the growth of the information-processing models that are at the core of cognitive psychology.

Earlier information-processing models of reading were serial-stage in nature, with the visual input being transmitted stage-by-stage to a semantic system, each stage providing the data base for the next. However, there is ample evidence that reading is an activity in which processing is influenced in a variety of ways by the context in which the processed stimulus occurs (see Levy, 1981). One such context effect is known as **semantic priming**, which is the shortening of the time taken to make the judgement of whether a stimulus is a word or a nonword, that occurs when the stimulus is preceded by a semantically related word. For example, the target word *butter* will be recognized as a word more quickly when it is preceded by the associated word *bread* than when preceded by *nurse*. This effect clearly depends on the extraction of meaning from the cueing word.

More recent models have taken an interactive view of the processes involved in reading. McClelland and Rumelhart (1981), for example, started from the results of early experiments in letter perception showing that words can be recognized under conditions when accurate recognition of all the letters is impossible. Further, individual letters are more easily perceived in letter strings, the more closely the letter strings approximate to real words. One possible explanation for this is that word shape is perceived directly. However, word shape alone is not sufficiently distinctive to specify a particular word, and it has been shown that the effect is obtained when word shape is changed by mixing upper- and lower-case type of widely differing size (Adams, 1979).

In their **interactive-activation** model of reading, McClelland and Rumelhart postulate that presentation of a display activates **feature nodes**, which in turn activate **letter nodes** with which the features are consistent, and inhibit letter nodes with which they are inconsistent. The most strongly activated letter nodes activate **word nodes** with which they are consistent, which, in turn, feed back to the letter nodes, reinforcing the activation of letters consistent with the word. Nodes at the same level are mutually inhibitory, since only one letter and word may occupy each location. One possibly contradictory result is the finding that the advantage of words over single letters in letter recognition occurs for pronounceable nonwords as well as for real words. Thus, it might be argued that the level above the letter node level should be a more general **ortho-graphic** one, rather than the specific word level proposed. However, there is evidence (Glushko, 1981) that the time taken in, and the accuracy of, pronouncing words and nonwords is influenced by knowledge of the pronunciation of specific words similar to the target word. For example, we know how to pronounce *reat* because it is similar to *real*, but it might take us longer to vocalize the nonword than the word. In the model, feedback from activation of specific words, following their activation by a partial set of letter nodes, would reinforce activation of letter nodes in strings that are similar to the specific word.

An alternative approach is to view reading as a problem-solving or hypothesis-testing process. Hochberg (1976) has suggested that the reader uses a portion of text to establish a **speech plan** which predicts the next parts of the text. The eyes then jump to a new portion of text which may or may not confirm the prediction and hence the plan. If the plan is confirmed, it is extended; if not, it is modified. Only words imaged on the fovea can be subjected to feature analysis, but words later in the text can, by their outline shape, confirm the plan. The next fixation is thus likely to jump beyond such a word if its shape conforms to that of the expected word. In this way details like substituted letters may be missed. Similarly, words or phrases can be skipped over by the eyes in their movement from one fixation to the next.

Such an analysis fits with the known nature of eye movements during reading (see Rayner, 1981). These are irregular, and seem at first haphazard. Faster readers make fewer fixations, and fewer are made when reading text with a familiar grammatical structure and with familiar concepts and words. Fixations tend to jump over often-used words and phrases. Furthermore, fixations are often made on earlier parts of the text, as if a new piece of information suggests that an important, plan-modifying word has been missed (like a *not*) or misread (*content* for *context*, for example).

Speech perception and reading are both ways of receiving linguistic communication. Some models propose a central process shared by reading and speech perception, and the interactive-activation model considers phonological influences in reading. It is clear that the two processes of speech perception and reading have much in common (see Nickerson, 1981). It is very unlikely, for example, that the knowledge of the world and of linguistic rules that enables us to understand the same sentence in spoken and printed form are stored twice. It is also unlikely that both listening and reading tap different processes in the application of such knowledge. It has frequently been suggested that reading as a process is dependent on speech and/or speech perception, that is, that at some stage in processing printed material a translation from a visual to a phonological code takes place. Reading ability is usually acquired much later in childhood than is speech recognition, and seems to require specific instruction that is not, apparently, necessary for speech recognition. Furthermore, methods of reading instruction typically involve the use of symbol-sound correspondences, and many readers do **subvocalize** when reading silently (as is typical of the beginning reader). Alternatively, phonological codes might not serve an essential role in the perceptual process of reading, but might do so in the representation of speech. (See Chapter 10 for a discussion of reading disorders.)

OBJECT PERCEPTION

The basic problems in object perception are to understand the processes that enable us first to determine that certain parts of the sensory input represent objects and second to recognize the objects. The separation of these two does not imply that they are independent, nor even that they necessarily occur in that order. The Gestalt psychologists long ago discussed the features that determine the separation of parts of the visual field into objects, and the **principles of organization** that determine the grouping of elements into patterns or objects. The former include size and enclosure (areas tend to be seen as objects if they are small and are surrounded by a contour), and convexity (*a* in Figure 3.4 looks like an object on a surface, *b* like a hole in a surface). The principles of organization include proximity (the circles in *c* are seen as rows, not columns), similarity (*d* appears as a cross on a background), good continuation (*e* is seen as composed of the parts in *f*, not those in *g*). Perhaps the most important principle is that of **common fate**. When we move our sense organs relative to objects in the environment,

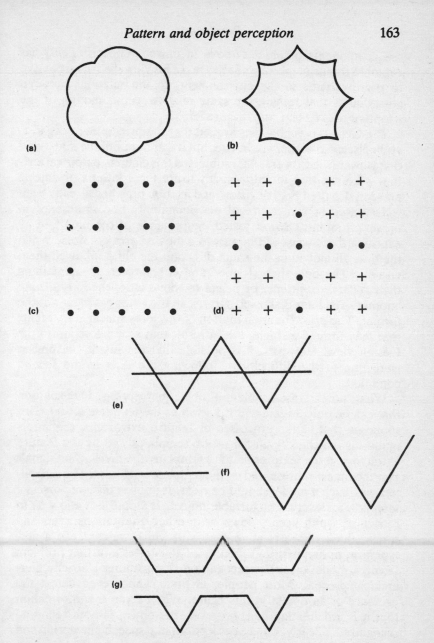

Figure 3.4 Gestalt principles of organization.

the components of objects move in unison. Gibson (1979) has explored this principle in some depth. In his view we are responsive to the invariants in the environment, to the relations between components that remain the same relative to our motion or the adoption of different angles of regard.

The Gestalt psychologists argued that the principles of organization discussed earlier are innate, but it was not until the mid-1960s that Bower (see Bower, 1982) subjected this claim to empirical test. It was known that infants visually fixate the contours of objects presented in their field of vision, and fixation time had already been widely used as a measure of discriminability and preference in preverbal infants. Bower tested the principle of common fate by exposing three-week-old infants to a moving array of dots. When the dots all moved in the same direction the child followed them visually. The dots then stopped and either rotated, maintaining their relative positions, or began to move independently of one another. The infants showed surprise in the latter case, but not the former. The prior common motion of the spots specified to infants that they formed a single unit, a result that seems to confirm the Gestalt view. However, it is possible that the infants' responses were due to the difficulty of following the dots in the second condition.

What, now, of the problem of object perception? One solution that can be quickly rejected is known as the **template model**. This supposes that, after processes of feature extraction, the information is matched against a set of 'templates' fed by the feature extractors. If the features match a template, the mechanism signals that the object represented by the template is present. The difficulties with such a model should be clear. It implies that we possess a template for every recognizable object. It would not allow us to recognize sᴈuıɥʇ upside down or in other orientations, sizes and forms (think of the relative ease with which we can read a new typeface, or handwriting). Figure 3.5 illustrates a further problem facing a model of object recognition that assumes a strictly hierarchical process. Most people, at first, cannot even detect the presence of an object in this figure. When given the information that it is a dalmatian dog, however, the object is both seen and recognized. Clearly, object perception, like speech perception and reading, involves 'top-down' processing.

Figure 3.5 Limitations of the template model of object recognition: the object is difficult to see until its identity is known. (Courtesy of R. C. James, photographer)

Many recent models of object perception have adopted a **computational approach**. Essentially, this approach distinguishes three levels in the understanding of any information-handling system: **function** (what the end result of the system is, in the present case the recognition of an object from its image on the retina), **mechanism** (the 'hardware' by which this is performed, here the anatomical structures and physiological processes), and **algorithm** (how the mechanism performs the function, the computational steps in the process of transforming the image to object recognition). The computational approach aims to understand the algorithm, and it generally attempts to do this by modelling the system with computer simulations.

Early computational models (see McArthur, 1982) were limited in a number of ways. For instance, their input was restricted to a very small class of 'objects', such as line-drawings of simple polyhedra, or they used a search process that looked for the presence of regions that were meaningful as specific objects, then looked for confirmation in other regions. This would not only require just the right pieces of specialized knowledge to be available from a vast cerebral library at the very earliest stages of processing, but also assumes that one particular part of the image can be chosen as the starting point. A recent model developed over a number of years by Marr and his colleagues (see Marr, 1982) avoids such difficulties by attempting to handle *real* three-dimensional scenes, and by delaying the necessity for specialized knowledge to the last stages. It is also unusual in that it attempts to make use of the information available from object motion which, as we have seen, is a most important source.

The process of visual perception is regarded as starting with the image on the retina as a mosaic of elements varying in lightness (the **grey-level array**). The end-point is the production of a **meaningful description** of the image (for example, 'this is an animal', or 'this is my grandmother'). At most stages of processing only **general world knowledge** is assumed, such as that the world is constituted mainly of solid, nondeformable objects which can only occupy one place at a time. Such knowledge is taken to be a part of the 'design' of the visual system, and does not 'descend' from higher levels. The first stage in the process is the transformation of the grey-level array to a **primal sketch**. The simple cells described earlier in this section, functioning not as feature detectors but as spatial filters or bar masks, signal the places in the grey-level array at which light-dark transitions occur. This parallel filtering of the whole array results in a nearly complete description of the pattern of spatial variations in light intensity (edges and contours).

The next stage is the separation of figure and ground; which light-dark transitions represent outlines and which changes in the orientation of a surface? Various visual processes can contribute to this, including stereopsis, object motion, shading, texture gradients and perspective. Algorithms have been developed for devising structure from the first two, showing that specialized knowledge of objects is not required. Using these processes the viewer produces a **2½-dimensional sketch** which specifies contours and orientations of surfaces. The sketch is a **viewer-centred** description of the scene, and for full object recognition has to be replaced by a fully three-dimensional **object-centred** description. That is, the description must allow the recognition of the object from different viewpoints.

This step is accomplished by obtaining from the 2½-dimensional sketch a description in terms of a set of linked **generalized cones**, three-dimensional bodies of constant cross-sectional shape and varying size, with a major axis. (Stick figures can be recognized because they represent the axes of such generalized cones.) Thus, for example, a standing human figure may be represented first by an overall body axis (vertical), which may be refined into trunk and attached head and limbs. One of the latter, say an arm, can be represented as two cones (upper and lower arm), the lower arm as arm and hand, and so on. Thus, each axis becomes the reference for the description of the subdivisions of that part. It is only after this that specific knowledge of objects is required, in the form of a catalogue of **three-dimensional models**, indexed in various ways, most importantly by degree of specificity. Objects are assumed to be arranged hierarchically, so that objects may be recognized at various levels from the most general (e.g., upright object) through broad categories (e.g., biped) to the most specific (e.g., granny).

Marr and his colleagues have demonstrated mathematically for most stages that high-level information is not required, and algorithms for many of the processes have been devised. However, the fact that a step is mathematically possible and may even be simulated with a computer program does not demonstrate that such a step takes place in human perception. By itself, the computational approach might tell us nothing about perception (that is, the algorithm has to be related to function and mechanism), and might perhaps best be used as a way of testing the practicability of processes suggested by psychological and neurophysiological research. Nevertheless, Marr's model does map on to what is known of the visual process at a few points, for example, the functions of the cortical simple cells. An example of a link with visual function is seen in the difficulty we have in recognizing objects from different views. It may be that more computation is required if the view presents a foreshortened axis, or that the axes identified do not readily allow access to the catalogue of models in the final stage. Certain types of agnosia (see Box 3.3) might represent disruption of particular stages in the model, although they do not support that view rather than others.

Although this model is the best developed of the computational approaches, it is admitted that the last stages, at least, are little more than conjecture. The notion of a catalogue of three-dimensional models is rather simplistic, and it is likely that semantic processes contribute to the last stages of object perception (see Warrington, 1982). Certainly, we should expect that those who are continuing Marr's work will continue to improve the model.

BOX 3.3
Effects of brain damage on vision and the mechanisms of form and object perception

Successful visual perception leads to the identification of meaningful objects located in space. Brain damage may affect this process in several ways. First, destruction of the striate cortex (the cortical region which receives visual information first and most directly from the retina) causes the patient to have no conscious awareness of light. Recent evidence suggests, however, that this is not total blindness as patients can locate lights and even discriminate poorly between shapes, although they usually deny seeing anything. This unconscious vision has been dubbed **blind sight** (see Weiskrantz, 1980). Its existence, which has not gone unchallenged (see Campion, Latto and Smith, 1983), implies that other structures (possibly the superior colliculus of the midbrain) can perform basic visual analyses but cannot transmit the results of their activities to the brain regions which subserve consciousness.

Second, selective damage to cortical regions which receive visual information from the striate cortex can, in rare cases, cause highly specific forms of sensory loss, which affect discrimination of colour, movement, position or depth. For example, in **cerebral achromatopsia** the ability to name, sort and match colours is lost and the world appears grey, drained of colour even though retinal sensitivity to light wavelengths is normal, as is discrimination of movement, position and depth. The existence of these selective sensory disorders suggests that different 'extrastriate' cortical structures work in parallel to analyse separate kinds of basic visual features from the information they receive from the striate cortex. This suggestion receives support from studies of monkeys, which show that their 'extrastriate' cortex is subdivided into regions, each of which contains neurons which respond optimally to specific kinds of sensory features, like colour, stereoscopic depth and movement (see Cowley, 1982, for an excellent review).

Third, damage to structures in the posterior cortex, which receive visual information from the 'extrastriate' areas can, in rare cases, cause a loss of the ability to recognize objects via vision. These **agnosias** are losses of recognition, which are not due to intellectual deterioration, language impairment or disturbances in discriminating basic sensory qualities, like position or movement. Agnosics may make such discriminations well which suggests that the relevant extrastriate regions can still transmit information to undamaged cortical areas that mediate conscious discriminations. Selective agnosias exist, which implies that separate cortical regions work in parallel to identify different kinds of object. For example, in **prosopagnosia** patients have difficulty in recognizing even highly familiar faces although basic sensory functions and the ability to identify objects may be well-preserved.

Two classical object agnosias, **apperceptive** and **associative agnosia**, seem to affect different stages in the identification of objects from visual stimuli. In apperceptive agnosia a patient cannot identify visually presented objects by naming or miming. He or she cannot copy drawings of objects or shapes, or match objects. Despite this, basic discriminations of light intensity, size and colour are good; furthermore, palpated objects can be readily identified. Clearly, a fairly early stage in creating a representation of the visual stimulus has been disrupted. Damage to the posterior cortex of the right hemisphere seems to be particularly linked with disruption of a slightly later stage in deriving a representation of visually presented objects. Affected patients have great difficulty in making sense of pictures, degraded in various ways. For example, they are poor at identifying objects photographed from unusual angles, or at recognizing drawn shapes which are overlapping or incomplete. Warrington (1982) has argued that they cannot categorize objects properly according to their perceptual similarities. Associative agnosia probably involves a disturbance of a still later stage in perception. Patients with this disorder are poor at recognizing objects even though they can accurately copy drawings of them. It has been speculated that such patients either cannot access their semantic systems (which contains their knowledge about perceived objects) via visual inputs, or that the semantic system itself is damaged. Both possibilities may obtain. Some patients can identify objects by touch but not vision, whereas others have difficulty with touch and vision and may be poor at defining objects' properties. The former may have lost visual access to the semantic system whereas the latter may have damage to the system itself.

The model we have just described assumes general world knowledge as part of the design of the visual system. The pioneering work of Piaget (e.g., 1937) apparently demonstrated that infants do not develop a full **object concept** (that is, an understanding of the nature and permanence of objects and their positions in space) until about fifteen to eighteen months of age. Observations made of infants' responses to the hiding or passing out of sight of objects demonstrated a gradual sequence of change from (up to two months) no response to hiding, through looking after the object (two to four months), reaching for a partly hidden, but not a fully hidden, object (four to six months), reaching for a hidden object, but looking in its usual hiding place rather than a new place (six to twelve months), and finally (twelve to fifteen months), when the object is hidden under a cloth and the cloth then is changed in position with another cloth, looking for the object in its original position. Only after this will the child make use of the information that is apparently available to it about objects' hiding places. (All these ages are subject to variability.)

This timetable of development, however, probably owes more to the methods used than to the object concept. At the earliest stages, for example, infants may simply not have the motor skill to pick up a cloth covering an object. Alternative approaches to this problem are described by Bower (1982). Using heart rate as an index of surprise, Bower has shown that infants evidence more surprise when an object fails to reappear after being hidden than when it does reappear. Similarly, infants as young as eight weeks showed anticipatory head and eye movements when an object passed behind a screen; that is, they looked to the point at which it should reappear just as, or just before, it did so. This seems to be strong evidence that these infants 'believed' in the continued existence of hidden objects, except that it is possible that it results merely from an inability to arrest ongoing head movements. However, testing with objects that stopped showed that the head movement paused at that point for a few hundred milliseconds, before continuing on the original path of the object.

Further research has indicated that at ages below about five months infants will look towards the place where previous repeated movement has taken an object, rather than to where the object has, just for once, actually moved. It is as if the young infant does not identify an object as the same one when it begins to move. Michotte (1962) showed that adults will judge an object to be the same but changing in appearance, when it changes only one of its features (shape, colour or size), and are likely to say that it has been replaced when two or three features change. Similar results hold with an object passing behind a screen. Parallel studies showed that three- to four-month-old infants tracked a completely changed object in exactly the same way as they did an unchanged object. Infants beyond about five months, however, looked back to the point of disappearance when a changed object appeared. Thus, it seems that, for younger infants, the continued identity of an object is determined primarily by continued movement, while older children take account of other features. Similar, but less clear-cut, evidence supports the view that an object that stays in one place is deemed by younger infants to remain the same object, while a single object seen in different places becomes different objects.

It would appear that at around the age of five months coordination of place and movement is achieved, the infant becoming aware that a single object can move from place to place and retain its identity. Yet an infant at this age still cannot find an object that has been hidden in front of him or her. Further investigation has shown that the fact of passing out of sight is not the key factor in this failure. An infant will reach for an object after the room has been darkened, even at an age when he or she will fail the hidden object test. Surprisingly, infants also fail the test when objects are covered with a transparent cup, apparently leaving the object entirely visible. This result is reminiscent of Piaget's early observation that a small object placed on top of a larger one effectively becomes invisible for the infant. Presumably, the two objects in each of these cases are perceived as one object. Thus, the target object and the transparent cup must be a single object if the infant is using the rule that two objects cannot simultaneously occupy the same space. The young infant seems to be using only the most general of world knowledge, failing to separate objects with shared boundaries and shared space. From the age of five months onwards the infant is learning to modify and extend this general world knowledge.

Spatial perception

Objects have characteristics apart from those already discussed; they have size and shape, and are located in space in particular directions and orientations, and at particular distances. In the sections that follow we shall distinguish between two broad classes of information that we can obtain from the environment about objects, **static** and **dynamic**. Most investigation has been of static information, and we shall consider that first.

STATIC INFORMATION

Classically, a number of **cues** to the relative distance of objects has been listed. **Interposition** results when one object partially hides another from view; the latter must be further from the observer. **Size** acts as a cue to distance. When, for example, two objects of the same size are at different distances, the farther one has a smaller retinal image. Size and distance, however, are reciprocally related, so that distance can be a cue to perceived size. (We return to this on pages 180–1.)

The next two cues can be considered special cases of size. Parallel lines and edges receding from the observer appear to converge into the distance. This is **linear perspective**. Any surface receding from the observer demonstrates a **texture gradient**. The elements making up the texture of the surface subtend a decreasing angle at the retina as the surface recedes from the observer. **Shadows** may give the same sort of information as interposition, depending on the direction of light; and **shading** similarly, but more importantly, gives information about distances of parts of a surface from a light source, and emphasizes the texture of surfaces. Since lighting is normally from above, convex surfaces show a different pattern of shading from concave surfaces. That this shading acts as a cue for three-dimensional surface shape can be demonstrated by inverting a picture of lunar craters, which turns them into platforms. Two final cues of this type are **aerial perspective** (objects at a great distance are less distinct than close objects) and **vertical position** (to an observer standing on a surface, objects further away on the surface appear higher in the visual field). The group of cues just discussed are sometimes called **pictorial cues**.

One further static monocular cue is **accommodation**, the action of changing the shape of the eye's lens in order to focus, on the retina, objects at different distances. The information this provides is

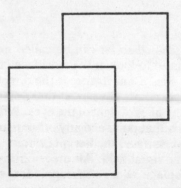

Figure 3.6 Representation of relative distance by the cue of interposition.

relatively weak, as can be seen by the fact that pitting it against almost any of the pictorial cues by means of simple two-dimensional drawings leads to an appearance of relative distance, despite the fact that accommodation is not different for the two parts of the figure. Figure 3.6 illustrates this with the cue of interposition.

The fact that we can identify these as potential sources of information about the relative distances of objects from an observer does not of itself demonstrate that we can or do use them. It is, however, a simple matter to set up laboratory tests in which one or other of the cues is varied independently of the others. Such experiments show that each of the cues can be used in isolation to determine relative distance. It is also possible so to arrange stimuli that the visual system is misled into misperceiving the relative distances of objects, so that the size of even familiar objects is distorted. Perhaps the most famous such demonstration is the **Ames room**. This is a room shaped as shown in the plan view in Figure 3.7. The vertical dimensions of the room, however, and the shapes and sizes of objects on the rear, sloping wall are carefully calculated so that to a person viewing through a small aperture in the front wall it appears to have a conventional, rectangular floor plan. Two adults stand at the positions marked, so that one is twice as far from the observer as the other. The cues informing the observer that the room is rectangular are so powerful that the farther person looks the same distance as, but about half the size of, the nearer person.

STEREOPSIS

The cues we have discussed so far can be called **monocular cues**. When both eyes are used to look at the world we can identify two additional, **binocular cues**. **Convergence** is the directing of the two eyes to fixate on a single point. The nearer that point is, the greater is the angle between the lines of sight of the eyes. When the eyes are fixated on a point, only that point and any other features falling on an imaginary, concave surface, the **horopter**, form a single, fused image in the binocular visual field. All other objects form double images, and this **diplopia** provides a stimulus for the act of convergence on a new point.

Like accommodation, however, convergence is a weak cue, and

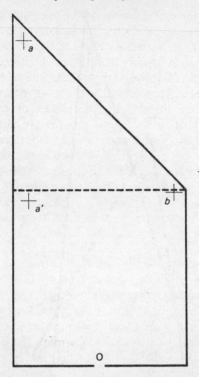

Figure 3.7 Plan view of Ames's room. To an observer at O, the person at *a* appears to be at *a'*, the same distance as *b*, and appears smaller than *b*.

the two are probably only used when no other information is available. Yet binocular vision adds a particular experience of depth to vision, and gives, at least for vision near to the eyes, an enormous advantage over one eye alone (try threading a needle with one eye closed!). This is the result of stereopsis. Since the eyes view the world from slightly different positions, objects at different distances form images on the two retinas that have different separations. This **relative retinal disparity** is illustrated in Figure 3.8. If a pair of stimuli are constructed to match the two views of the object and are presented separately to the eyes, they are seen in depth.

The investigation of stereopsis is accomplished largely by the use of **random dot stereograms**. These were introduced by Julesz (see

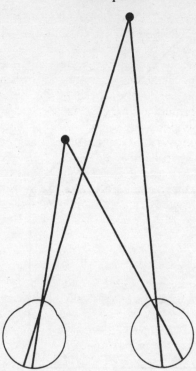

Figure 3.8 Relative retinal disparity.

Julesz, 1971), and are usually generated by computer. In its simplest form a stereogram consists of a pair of figures that can be presented separately to the two eyes, one consisting essentially of a random arrangement of small squares, the other being the same except that in one area of the figure the squares are shifted slightly horizontally. When the two halves are fused by the visual system, the area in which the dots are shifted appears to be in a different plane to the rest of the figure. Whether it appears to be in front or behind depends on the direction of shift. If the dots in the right eye are shifted to the left the area is seen nearer than the background and the reverse direction of shift gives the reverse impression of depth. This follows directly from the geometry of the arrangement.

The advantage of the random dot stereogram for the study of

stereopsis is that it provides a way of excluding all other sources of depth information. Each half of a stereogram looks like a random array of dots, with no depth information of its own. The fact that viewing such a pair stereoscopically gives rise to the appearance of surfaces in three dimensions demonstrates that it is not necessary for information processing to proceed to the stage of pattern recognition before forming a three-dimensional view of the world, a notion that had previously been widely held. A basic problem in understanding stereopsis is made apparent by this conclusion. If the fusion of left and right eye inputs is made before recognition, on what basis is the fusion made? How does the visual system 'decide' which elements of the view in the left eye to match with which in the right? This problem of **global stereopsis** is more severe in complex scenes, involving, for example, surfaces curved in the third dimension. Observers take longer to form a fused, three-dimensional image of more complex stereograms, indicating that some time-consuming process is involved.

Microelectrode studies have shown that cats and monkeys, which have stereopsis, have in their visual cortexes large numbers of cells which, while having orientation specificity, respond selectively to stimuli that are imaged with particular amounts of retinal disparity. These presumably form the physiological basis of stereopsis, and it has been supposed that the problem of global stereopsis is solved by detectors with the same disparity having mutually excitatory connections, but inhibitory connections with those selective to disparities representing a different depth. In this way, an element fusing with another not in its plane would receive more inhibitory influence, and a fused pair surrounded by similarly fused elements more excitatory influence. While neurophysiological evidence for such a system is sparse, computer simulation has shown that such a network would produce global fusion.

DYNAMIC INFORMATION

Dynamic information about relative distance arises from the **motion gradients** that are the different relative motions across the retina of the images of objects at different distances, resulting as we move. The images of objects nearer than the point of fixation move in such a way as to appear to move in the direction opposite to head movement, while farther objects appear to move in the same direction. The notion of a gradient arises because the further from the fixation point an object is, the faster does its motion appear. The term **motion parallax** should be confined to circumstances when only two objects provide relative apparent motion, which is how motion information has usually been investigated. The importance of motion as a source of spatial information is shown by the fact that demonstrations such as Ames's room only work fully when viewed without movement.

Motion gradients are the chief determinants of perceived relative distance in ambient perception. However, when isolated, motion parallax is an ambiguous cue. Gibson and his associates (1959) placed two paint-spattered transparent sheets at different distances between a light source and a translucent screen. When the sheets were motionless, observers saw a single flat surface. If the sheets were moved in the same direction and at the same speed, the shadows of the blobs on the sheet nearer the screen moved more slowly than the others. Observers reported two surfaces, but there was disagreement about which was nearer. Some reported spontaneous reversals of apparent depth. In the absence of other cues, then, motion parallax not resulting from the observer's own movement cannot specify relative distance (see Ittelson, 1960).

Objects that move towards an observer **loom** in the field of view, that is, the size of the retinal image increases with the approach of the object. Looming tells us that an object is approaching and the end result of that continued process, of course, is collision. It is accompanied by **optical expansion**, and has been used as a stimulus in studies of infant perception of distance. An early, classic attempt to study this was the use by Gibson and Walk (1960) of the **visual cliff**. This consisted of a strong glass platform, immediately below one half of which was a chequered surface. Below the other half the patterned surface was about one metre below the glass. Infants would not crawl from the first half on to the second, even with their mothers calling them. Clearly, these infants could perceive the distance (depth) of the pattern. Unfortunately, of course, this method can only work with children who are old enough to crawl, by which time they have had considerable experience of manipulating objects in space.

In one of the earliest studies of infants' response to looming objects, White in 1963 (see Bower, 1982) dropped objects on to a transparent screen placed over the faces of babies lying on their backs. Electrodes attached to the babies' temples allowed the recording of blinking. From the age of eight weeks onwards, an object falling towards the face elicited blinking, which did not occur on withdrawal of the object from close to the face. Blinking was not observed in younger infants, although it can be produced by puffing air into the eyes of much younger babies.

Bower (1982) took issue with this sort of experiment. First, he claimed that there is no evidence that adults blink on the approach of objects towards their faces (a claim that can easily be shown to be erroneous by any reader, using his or her hand and a cooperative friend!), so that it is not an appropriate response to use as an index of perceived looming. Furthermore, infants lying on their backs cannot move their heads further back as an object approaches (as will an adult), neither can they put their hands in front of their faces, since their arms are used for support. It has also been argued that infants lying on their backs never fully awaken. To overcome these difficulties Bower and his colleagues (1970) seated infants in a semi-upright position and filmed their behaviour while large objects were swung towards their faces. Under these conditions infants as young as six days showed a defensive pattern consisting of eye-widening, head-retraction, and interposition of their hands between the objects and their faces. Further experimentation showed that infants made a different type of response (including blinking) when only the air movement that accompanied the object was presented. But when only two-dimensional optical expansion was used, the defensive pattern occurred, albeit in reduced strength. Whether this reduction was due to the absence of air movement or of other distance cues is not clear.

There are, however, still alternative explanations. Infants might have been responding to the expansion as such, rather than to the approach this suggests to an adult. To test this, Bower and his colleagues used two stimuli that presented equivalent optical expansion: a large cube that approached to within 20 cm of the infant, and a small cube that approached to within 8 cm. Only the smaller, closely approaching object produced the defensive pattern of response, indicating that the infants were responding to the approach, not the optical expansion of the stimulus. However, it is possible that backward head movement might reflect the infants' visual following of the upward-moving contour of the stimulus, rather than an attempt to avoid an apparently approaching object. Experiments using simpler stimuli have, indeed, shown such a response to upward-moving contours. There is currently dispute about whether or not these movements occur when approaching objects have *no* upward-moving contours, Yonas's group finding that they do not (Yonas *et al.*, 1979), Bower's that they do (Dunkeld and Bower, 1980).

The picture remains confused. Blinking is, at best, an unreliable indicator of perceived approach in infants. Backward head movement alone might reflect visual pursuit of upward-moving contours, although it is difficult to explain the hand interposition reported by Bower on such a basis, and critics of this work seem not to have paid any attention to this aspect of the defensive response.

SIZE AND DISTANCE

We have mentioned that the size of a familiar object can provide a cue to its distance from the observer, but that misperceiving its distance can, conversely, cause a misperception of its size. The retinal image size of an object is inversely proportional to its distance. Perceived size, however, is readily shown not to be simply related to retinal image size; a person walking away from us does not appear to shrink appreciably. Our ability to perceive the real sizes of objects at different distances is known as **size constancy**. Parallel constancies hold in the perception of shape, brightness, colour and velocity. In general we can define constancy as the tendency for our perceptual experience to be relatively constant despite changing viewing conditions. Objects look more like their 'real' selves than like the retinal stimulation they provide. Much of what we have to say about size constancy applies equally to the other constancies. Constancy provides one of the main ways in which we maintain the perceptual stability of the world.

Size constancy does not work only with familiar objects, a fact that rules out explanations based on memory for the 'real' nature of objects. Gilinsky (1955) placed triangles at distances ranging from

100 to 4000 feet from observers, who matched them for real size with an adjustable, nearby triangle. Except for the farthest triangles, observers showed almost perfect constancy, the near triangle being adjusted to very nearly the same real size as the distant ones. Triangles, of course, have no standard or familiar size.

Another classic study (Holway and Boring, 1941) demonstrated that size constancy, at least for unfamiliar objects, depends on the perception of distance. Observers viewed a disc at distances up to 120 feet, and attempted to match its size with a variable disc at 10 feet. With full lighting and binocular vision there was a slight tendency to overconstancy. Monocular viewing under the same illumination produced near perfect constancy, and progressively reducing distance information gradually reduced the extent of constancy. Even with minimal distance information, however (viewing in darkened surroundings, monocularly through a tiny aperture that reduced accommodation cues), observers did not completely match the stimuli by their retinal image size.

If we may conclude that distance perception is an ability that does not depend on learning, may we draw the same conclusion about constancy, or does the infant have to learn to combine distance information with retinal image size to construct a perception of object constancy? **Shape constancy** (the relative invariance of perceived shape with variations in slant of the surface) may be considered a special case of size constancy, since a change of retinal shape with changing slant is actually a change in the size of elements (e.g., distance between contours) of a surface (compare perspective and texture gradients, page 173). Experiments have indicated that infants as young as twelve weeks will discriminate shapes on the basis of their real shape, but are unable to do so on the basis of either projected retinal shape or slant alone (see, e.g., Caron, Caron and Carlson, 1978).

This result may be interpreted as indicating that infants respond directly to what might be called **higher-order variables** in the stimulus information, and is reminiscent of the inability of infants to cope with the hidden object tasks we considered on pages 170–2. The infant seems to be responding to the common properties of the environment, not to unique properties of proximal stimulation (see pages 195–6). This suggests a reversal of the long-dominant view that perceptual development procedes by the gradual association of inputs through the different senses, as described in the classic view that 'touch educates vision', that we learn to see the environment by exploring it with the more primitive and direct sense of touch, and associating what we feel with the visual input. The alternative view (see Gibson, 1969, and Bower, 1982) is that the infant starts with an **amodal** perceptual experience, and this is gradually **differentiated** with development. Thus, for example, an infant will turn his or her eyes in the direction of a sound not because he or she has an auditory experience and expects a visual one, but because some environmental event has occurred in that direction. Blind children, and sighted children in darkness, will also make this response, both to the age of about four months.

One very interesting example that fits well with this view of perceptual development comes from the use of a **sonic guide** with young infants. This is a device that may be worn on the head, and provides the wearer with auditory information about the environment through modulation of an emitted tone. Nearer objects produce higher pitched tones, smaller objects quieter tones, and rough objects 'fuzzier' tones. Blind adults can rarely learn to use such a device to a full extent. However, congenitally blind infants rapidly come to make appropriate responses when given the device for the first time. For example, in the very first session with a sixteen-week-old blind boy, an object was slowly moved towards his face, close enough to touch him. After only three trials convergence movements of the eyes occurred and, on the seventh, he interposed his hands between the object and his face. He was then able to track moving objects with his head, and to reach and touch an object as small as a 1-cm cube. He also played a version of 'peekaboo' with his mother, turning his head from side to side to remove her from the sound field and then bring her into it again. Similar observations have been made with a number of other blind infants (see Bower, 1982), and with sighted infants in darkness.

Together, these observations suggest that there is some inborn ability that is lost with development. Clearly, however, there cannot be an innate ability to use the completely artificial relation between acoustic and spatial features provided by the sonic guide. Bower points out that the pitch and intensity increases that the sonic guide provides as an object approaches, parallel the pattern of optical expansion that is its visual accompaniment for sighted infants. Thus, although the stimulation is different at a sensory level, there is a common higher-order variable that could underlie the perception of an approaching object if directly perceived in amodal perception.

Development consists of the differentiation of modalities and the calibration and specification of information provided through them. Instead of passing from 'sensing' to perceiving, perceptual development could even be described as passing from perceiving to sensing. This change could be observed in attempts to get a thirteen-month-old congenitally blind girl to use the guide. After resistance she eventually was able to reach for objects. However, having once grasped an object she héld it to her ear. Since the object itself was silent, this caused the sound to disappear. To her, presumably, sound was firmly established as a property of objects, not a medium for locating them.

Motion perception

In preceding sections we have seen instances of the importance of motion as a source of information about the environment. We now turn to the perception of motion itself.

MOTION OF OBJECTS IN THE ENVIRONMENT

We can identify three potential sources of information about the motion of objects. The most obvious is the progressive displacement of the image of an object across the stationary retina, **image displacement**. Secondly, the eyes may track a moving object, so that its image remains in the same place on the retina, **ocular pursuit**. Finally, when an object moves relative to other objects in the environment its retinal image is displaced relative to those of the other objects, **configuration change**. In the perception of the real world it is probable that all three normally play a role, but laboratory investigations have attempted to unravel their relative importance.

Ocular pursuit. This is readily demonstrated to be an effective source of motion information. If an observer is seated in complete darkness, and a small spot of light is then caused to move slowly, the observer can track it with a smooth pursuit eye movement, and will report the light to be moving. Since the only information available to the observer is the motion of the eyes in the head, the perception of motion must be due to some aspect of this motion. But it is not necessary to conclude that it is the afferent input from the extraocular muscles that provides this information (**inflow theory**). An alternative possibility is that the motor command to move the eyes provides the information (**outflow theory**).

The same alternatives arise when we consider the fundamental question of why the world does not appear to move when we scan it with our eyes. Eye movement in the stationary environment causes retinal image displacement which, we have already intimated, is a potential source of motion information. Does the world remain stable because of afferent feedback from the extraocular muscles, or because of the motor command (earlier psychologists would have said the *intention*) to move the eyes? The issue can be decided by two simple demonstrations. First, close one eye and move the other by pushing it, through its lid, with a finger. The resulting image displacement is perceived as movement of the environment in the reverse direction to the eye movement. Since the extraocular muscles are stretched in the same way as with normal eye movement the perceived motion must be due to the absence of the usual efferent command.

The second demonstration, although equally simple, is not equally recommended. Mach in 1885 inserted putty into the orbit of one of his eyes to prevent it moving. Attempts to produce normal eye movement caused the world to apparently sway, this time in the same direction as the intended movement. This demonstration has been repeated with the use of curare to paralyse the eye muscles.

The most widely accepted explanation of these demonstrations, of the stability of the world with normal eye movements, and of the perception of motion with ocular pursuit, follows an approach introduced by von Holst and Mittelstaedt (1950). It is proposed that there is a central comparator that compares an **efference copy** of the motor command with the resulting afferent signal, the **reafference**. In the case of the eyes moving normally in the stationary visual field the image displacement provides a reafferent signal that exactly matches the efference copy of the motor command to move the eyes. The result of the matching signals is the perception of an unmoving environment. When the eyeball is passively moved, the reafference does not match an efference copy, since no motor command has been sent to the extraocular muscles. The result is motion perceived according to the direction of image displacement.

In Mach's demonstration there is an efference copy but no change in the reafference. The eye has been 'told' to move, but the retinal image has not been displaced. The consequence is that the world is perceived as moving in the same direction as the eye movement, and to the same extent. Finally, motion is perceived in ocular pursuit for the same reason. The efference copy is compared with an unchanging reafference, and the tracked object is seen to move in the direction of eye movement.

Image displacement. It might seem that we could demonstrate the role of image displacement in motion perception as readily as we can that of ocular pursuit. However, if we move a small light about in an otherwise dark room the observer will track it. We cannot maintain fixation unless we have a point to fixate and, of course, as soon as we provide an additional stationary fixation point we have produced conditions under which configuration change information is available.

It is generally assumed that the basis for the perception of motion through image displacement is the successive stimulation of retinal elements that form the 'receptive fields' of cortical motion detectors. These, and parallel motion channels in the human visual system, have been investigated by the same types of technique that we discussed in connection with channels for spatial frequency and orientation, including aftereffects. A **motion aftereffect** (MAE) occurs after prolonged viewing of a moving display. It can, for example, be seen after watching the credits 'rolling up' on a television screen, when a stationary picture appearing immediately afterwards is seen to move in the opposite direction. MAEs require the additional property of channels, or selective tuning, for velocity.

The maximal strength of the aftereffect occurs when fixation is maintained on a stationary point. Accurate ocular tracking of the motion prevents the occurrence of an aftereffect. These facts demonstrate that the MAE is due to a process in the image displacement system, since the tracking condition, which excludes only that source of information, does not produce an MAE. This also provides clear evidence that image displacement can, and does, operate as a motion stimulus.

The normal and sufficient stimulus for the perception of motion via the image displacement system seems to be the progressive stimulation of adjacent retinal locations. The phenomenon of **apparent movement** might be taken as indicating that, while sufficient, successive stimulation is not necessary. When two spatially separated stimuli are presented in succession, a certain combination of distance and temporal intervals leads observers to report that a single stimulus has moved between the two positions. Apparent movement is not an abstruse laboratory phenomenon, but forms the basis of the dominant forms of entertainment in industrialized societies – cinema and television. There is no real movement of images on the screen during the showing of a 'movie'. What is projected is a series of scenes showing successive and separate positions during movement, separated by a blank screen. The changing positions, and the temporal separation of the successive frames, provide the conditions for **beta movement**.

Can we conclude from the occurrence of apparent movement that the image displacement system does not need progressive stimulation of retinal elements? There are a number of reasons why such a conclusion would be erroneous. First, the stimulus conditions for the occurrence of apparent movement are rather critical. Korte, in 1915, formulated a series of laws showing how apparent movement depends on restricted spatial and temporal relations, and on luminance. If the same mechanisms underlie the perception of real motion the same restrictions would apply, which they do not. Secondly, Kolers (1963) has shown that only a limited range of apparent movement speeds can be obtained (about 15 to 25 degrees per second), while real motion can be seen over a much wider range (1 to 125 degrees per second). Thirdly, real movement appears faster than apparent movement with the same start and end positions and times. Finally, Rock and Ebenholtz (1962) demonstrated that apparent movement is still produced when the successive stimuli are fixated through small apertures, so that they stimulate the same retinal elements, indicating that the image displacement system need play no role in its perception.

Configuration change. Conditions in which ocular pursuit and image displacement may be studied in isolation are, of course, highly artificial. Usually, objects moving in the environment do so against a background of stationary or differently moving objects, providing configuration change. One could argue that under almost all conditions, even the most simplified, the nose and other anatomical borders to the visual field provide a stationary reference with which a moving object produces configuration change.

Clearly, the visual system is presented with something of a problem in interpreting configuration change which is, by its very nature, relative. The displacement of an object relative to its background is, alone, an ambiguous source of information; which has moved, the object or the background? Since we do not suppose that the other motion detection systems are 'switched off' during configuration change, we might assume that ocular pursuit or image displacement would solve the problem. But if these other systems tell us what part of the environment is moving, what need is there for a configuration change mechanism? Indeed, what evidence is there for motion detection via such a mechanism?

Incontrovertible evidence that configuration change is a powerful source of information concerning object motion comes from the phenomenon of **induced movement**. The most familiar example of this is the appearance of the moon through broken cloud on a windy night. Instead of seeing the clouds moving past the stationary moon, we see the moon scudding through the clouds. The only information we have for the perception of motion in the moon is the configuration change actually caused by the cloud motion. Frequently, the transference of perceived motion from clouds to moon is complete, so that the clouds appear stationary, despite the fact that they must be providing motion information through the ocular pursuit and/or image displacement systems. Similarly, the moon provides information through these systems that it is actually stationary.

PERCEPTION OF SELF-MOTION

The nonauditory parts of the inner ear (the **vestibular system**) contain **semicircular canals** which provide information about rotary

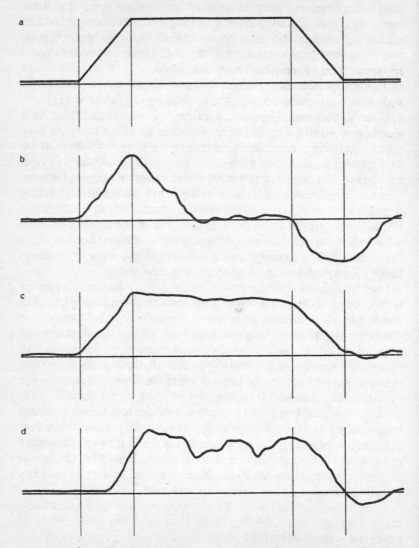

Figure 3.9 Perceived self-motion resulting from rotation applied to body or surround in (a) horizontal line indicates stationary; (b) rotation in darkness; (c) rotation in light; (d) rotation of surround only.

motion, and a **utricle** which provides information about head tilt and linear motion. When acting as self-motion detectors, these structures depend on the inertia of the liquid they contain, which causes deformation of sensory structures (the **crista** in the canals and the **macula** in the utricle). Mechanically, such a system can only respond during **accelerated** motion.

This feature of the vestibular system implies that some other source of information is available about self-motion (or **vection**), and the experiment illustrated in Figure 3.9 illustrates this. As is shown in Figure 3.9(b), the sensation of rotation (**circular vection**) that results when a person is rotated in darkness about a vertical axis gradually decreases during motion at a constant speed. However, the same motion with illuminated surroundings is experienced as continued rotation, with only a slight adaptation (see Figure 3.9(c)). Clearly, visual information acts as a source of vection information. A stationary sound source instead of the visible environment would also provide this information.

If, instead of rotating the observer inside a stationary environment we rotate a vertical cylinder around the observer, the person at first perceives veridically. Gradually, however, self-motion is perceived, and this vection increases until the surroundings appear to be stationary, and all the applied motion is perceived as vection (Figure 3.9(d)). Thus, as well as supplementing vestibular information, visual input can be made to dominate self-perception. An everyday example of this demonstration is the feeling we sometimes have that our train is in motion when in fact it is an adjacent one that is moving, and we are still motionless in a station.

Just as visual motion provides important information about self-motion, so it is important in the maintenance of **posture**. Classically, posture, as a proprioceptive function, was considered to be controlled by 'proprioceptors'. It is, however, easy to demonstrate that vision has a proprioceptive function, simply by observing that body sway increases when the eyes are closed.

Rather more complex methods are required to demonstrate the **dominance** of vision over the traditional proprioceptive senses. If we expose an observer to a large stimulus field rotating clockwise about the line of sight we find that, after a latent period that is characteristic of visual-vestibular interactions, the observer starts to lean to the right, even to the extent of falling over. Similarly, a large stimulus field moving downwards in front of an observer causes the person to lean forward; if it moves upwards, the person leans backwards. Clearly, moving visual stimuli are effective in causing changes in posture. Lee and Aronson (1974) have used a large suspended room that can be made to swing to and fro. As the room swings towards an observer standing inside it the person sways backwards, and conversely as the room swings away from the observer. If the amount of sway of the room is not too great, the observer may be unaware that the room is moving. Toddlers can be made to fall over in this room, suggesting that balance is even more firmly under visual control early in starting to walk. This can be recreated in adults by standing them on a narrow beam. It should be apparent from these examples that it is visually given **motion** that is the important information in maintenance of posture.

SELF-MOTION OR OBJECT MOTION

The most important question outstanding from our discussion of motion is what circumstances determine whether we see object motion or experience vection? A consideration of the examples given in the preceding sections suggests that the difference is in the size (or retinal extent) of the moving images, and this makes functional sense. Movement of the body causes image motion across the whole retina, with the exception of fixated objects and any that happen to be moving in the same direction and angular speed as the observer. Thus, although self-motion causes motion **gradients**, whole-field moving stimuli of the types used in the studies just mentioned will be adequate stimuli to suggest vection. Object motion would then be attributed to the movement of smaller parts of the visual field, especially when accompanied by configuration change.

In support of this suggestion is the finding that adding stationary elements to a large stimulus rotating about the line of sight decreases the effects of such stimuli, presumably by providing contradictory whole-field information. We can, however, readily demonstrate that it is retinal **location**, rather than image size, that is the important differentiating characteristic. Large, centred stimuli extend further into the retinal periphery than do small ones. If we take stimuli of constant area, but present them in different retinal locations, centrally as a disc, and with increasing retinal eccentricity as a narrowing annulus, we find that the vection or postural effects increase with retinal eccentricity. Small, centrally fixated rotating stimuli are seen as moving objects and produce MAEs, whereas small, peripherally moving stimuli produce vection and postural effects and no MAE. The object motion–self-motion distinction, then, is central–peripheral, not small–large. This distinction is not, of course, an absolute one. As an annular stimulus is expanded the object motion effects are gradually replaced by vection effects, and a wide range of stimuli produce both.

Current thinking about the distinction we have just outlined sees it as part of a general distinction that can be made between **focal vision** and **ambient vision**. This distinction has its origin in neurophysiological studies in the 1960s, when it was shown, for example, that lesions in the visual cortex of hamsters led to impairment of object recognition, while those in the superior colliculus led to impairment of spatial orientation. On the basis of similar work with monkeys Trevarthen (1968), among others, suggested that the subcortical system subserves general locomotor behaviour, and can be thought of as an ambient visual system. The phylogenetically more recent cortical visual system can be thought of as a focal system, being largely concerned with objects in the central field of vision. Although the functional distinction between the two is not complete, we can crudely characterize them as concerned with orientation and locomotion, and with visual attention and object recognition respectively. Although the focal system is primarily a visual one, the ambient visual system forms part of a relatively undifferentiated suprasensory ambient system, as has been made clear by our discussions of visual-vestibular interactions (see also Box 3.3).

Some of the characteristics of these **two modes of visual processing** can be distinguished, although we must stress that these are not absolute. First, focal vision primarily concerns the central parts of the visual field, whereas ambient vision involves, primarily, the peripheral parts. Secondly, focal vision is usually accompanied by awareness of processing, while ambient vision functions well in the absence, or near absence, of awareness. Thirdly, most focal functions are dependent on luminance, whereas ambient functions are relatively independent of luminance. Fourthly, ambient functions are unaffected by alterations in the sharpness of the visual image, whereas refractive errors interfere with focal functions. Consideration of the characteristics of the two types of vision described in these last two paragraphs leads us to suggest that perceptual development as we have described it in this chapter is largely the development of focal vision, ambient vision being an aspect of 'amodal' perception we described on pages 182–3.

Person perception

The most important objects in the human environment are people. People produce spoken and written language, and we have examined the perception of these in this chapter. Now we wish to turn to the perception of persons themselves. At one level, person perception may be considered an example of the problem of object perception: how do we recognize that an object in the environment is a person, and how do we recognize the particular person (indeed, we used the perception of a person as an example on page 167). At a second level, person perception is concerned with the perception of attributes, motives and emotions in others. We shall call these **face recognition** and **social perception** respectively.

FACE RECOGNITION

Work on the development of the recognition of faces was reviewed by Gibson (1969). Typically, the research to that date involved the observation of the infant's response (fixation or smiling) to stimuli ranging from a homogeneous disc to the infant's own mother, moving and speaking. In summary, this work showed that newborn infants demonstrate no preference for static patterns that resemble a face, over other patterns of similar complexity. Moving real faces will elicit more fixation very early, and smiling by four or five weeks. At about six weeks the infant is more likely to smile at black dots within an oval or round contour than at a realistic drawing of a face, and various other visual stimuli also elicit smiling as readily as does a face. By three months infants fixate a schematic drawing of a face more readily than one with the features scrambled, and by three to four months will smile more at a real face than a realistic or schematic portrayal. By five to six months differential smiling to the mother and an experimenter are shown, and the infant for the first time responds differently to different facial expressions, and may respond with more vocalization to a female than to a male face.

Gibson took facial recognition as an example of the perception of complex objects. The pattern of results just outlined was interpreted as showing a course of development that starts with the response to high-contrast borders in the stimulus field. The infant gradually becomes able to extract spatial (but not yet facial) features. Invariant relations among features (for example, the position of the eyes) are then processed and, eventually, the invariant spatial characteristics of a human face become distinguished. The infant is then (at about five to six months) able to perceive individual patterns as deviations from the general structure of faces, and is in a position to start to recognize individuals (although the face of the primary caregiver may be recognized earlier). The final stage is the recognition of facial resemblances, reflecting the perception of relations among feature sets.

One indication that this view of development might be inaccurate comes from studies of imitation. It has been reported that newborn infants will imitate such facial acts as mouth-opening, eye-widening and tongue-protrusion (see, e.g., Meltzoff and Moore, 1977). Field and her colleagues (1982) have shown that infants as young as thirty-six hours will imitate a model's facial expression of happiness, sadness or surprise under conditions than seem to rule out alternative explanations such as the model imitating the baby, or shaping the baby's expression. These results seem to demonstrate that infants possess an innate capacity to compare sensory information obtained visually with that obtained proprioceptively from their own facial movements.

There is other evidence that demonstrates more explicitly that the newborn infant, in this area as in others, has far greater perceptual abilities than had previously been thought. Carpenter (1975), for example, showed that a two-week-old infant looked longer at his or her mother talking than at the mother's silent face, and more at that than at a speaking stranger. Moreover, when the faces and voices of the two adults were mixed, the infants showed distress, looking away from the face and occasionally crying. Infants, then, seem at this age to be able to recognize and differentiate particular faces and voices. It seems that young infants can detect and perceive more information than they normally require (or than is required by many laboratory studies).

Many studies of the recognition of faces by adults have been interpreted from the point of view of memory processes. For a discussion of these and other approaches see the volume by Davies *et al*. in the Further Reading to this chapter.

SOCIAL PERCEPTION

Social perception has a number of similarities with the other types of perception we have considered in this chapter. By definition it is concerned with the obtaining of information about our social environment. As in perceiving the physical environment, social perception is active and selective; we interact with other people but we can, if we choose, ignore information (or people). Information about the social environment comes through all the senses, but we are concerned with higher-order variables rather than with patterns of stimulation, getting our information from an analysis of the **appearance-behaviour-context array** presented to us. Our perception is influenced by expectations and motivation, and these may be influenced by what we read or what is said to us about other people. Social perception proceeds, in part at least, by processes of **categorization**, during which we place people and their actions and motives into categories on the basis of initial information, revising and refining the categories as we obtain further information.

In all these cases, the differences between object and social perception are quantitative rather than qualitative. There are ways, however, in which the two processes are rather different (Gelman and Spelke, 1981). We interact with people in a way that we do not with objects. Their actions and appearances are likely to be influenced by our presence in a way that objects are not. If we pick up an object we know why it is moving and changing its appearance. We can only infer the reasons for changes in the behaviour of another person. Our perception of others is greatly affected by comparing them with ourselves. We infer that a person feels sad not only because of nonverbal cues (see Chapters 8 and 10), but because we know that we would feel sad in similar circumstances. Conversely, we might evaluate our own state by a process of **social comparison**, observing how others behave in similar circumstances (see Chapter 11).

For these reasons, and because social perception is an integral part of communication, interpersonal processes, and emotion, we shall consider it further in the appropriate chapters as it contributes to and reflects these processes.

Concluding remarks: theory and experiment in perception

A chapter as brief as this cannot pretend to be a complete survey of the area of perception. We have tried to give an impression of the scope of the subject, and to use the topics we have included as illustrations of the wide range of empirical and theoretical approaches that contribute to our understanding. It should not be thought that these approaches are limited to the topics in relation to which we have discussed them. Computational methods are by no means only applied to object perception, and information-processing approaches are ubiquitous.

The theories we have considered may all be categorized as **constructivist** theories. All propose that there is insufficient information in the proximal stimulus to specify unambiguously the properties of objects or events in the environment, and that perception is constructed with the aid of knowledge, expectations, and inference. An opposing view is J. J. Gibson's (1979) theory of **direct perception**, which represents an evolution of his ideas to which we alluded in the first part of the chapter. A modified theory of direct perception is that of Shaw and Turvey (see Michaels and Carello, 1981).

The key notions of these theories are as follows. They are essentially **ecological** theories, emphasizing that animals have evolved within a particular environment which therefore constrains perception. Since the perceiving person has such a close relationship with the environment, there is no reason to suppose that it is necessary to perform any computations on the input. Rather, perception of the environment is direct in the sense that it is the pick-up of **invariants** in the sensory information. An invariant is a property of the stimulus array that specifies a property of the environment. We can refer to two classes of invariant, **transformational**, which specify the nature of a change (e.g., rotating, approaching, ageing), and **structural**, which specify the constant properties of objects (e.g., roundness, blueness, granny's face). The invariants are perceived as to what objects 'afford' the organism, that is, what an object may be used for (how it is, in a sense, 'designed' for the animal that has evolved in relation to it). To perceive an **affordance** is to perceive **meaning**. Hence, meaning is not assigned during the process of perception, but is perceived directly.

It is impossible to do this approach justice here. Its main contribution to date has been to stimulate discussion by challenging the premises of other theoretical approaches. It has been criticized widely, partly because of data that seem to contradict it (see, for example, Gyr, Willey and Henry, 1979), and partly through misunderstandings of what the theory actually says. Thus, Ullman (1980) attacked what he said is the basic premise that no processing intervenes between stimulus and perception. Yet Gibson did not claim that there was no processing, a view that would clearly be absurd, but that it is irrelevant to the psychological process of perception. What he proposed was the study of the invariants in the environment and what they afford the organism.

One problem with the ecological approach is that it has generated relatively little experimental work, a criticism that cannot be applied to the various constructivist approaches. The direct perception theories are stimulating, and have drawn attention to invariants in perception. Whether or not they stimulate research as well as argument remains to be seen.

Further reading

General

Two good, recent texts on perception are:

BRUCE, V. and GREEN, P. (1985) *Visual Perception: Physiology, Psychology and Ecology*. London: Erlbaum.

SEKULER, R. and BLAKE, R. (1985) *Perception*. New York: Knopf.

The next two books provide thorough treatments of perception (the second one mentioned has a somewhat more physiological viewpoint), and both constitute further reading for many of the sections in this chapter.

CARTERETTE, E.C. and FRIEDMAN, M.P., eds. (1973–8) *Handbook of Perception*. Ten volumes. New York: Academic Press.
HELD, R. *et al.*, eds. (1978) *Handbook of Sensory Physiology*, Volume VIII, *Perception*. Berlin: Springer Verlag.

A highly readable account of perceptual development, concentrating on Bower's own work and theoretical approach, is:

BOWER, T.G.R. (1982) *Development in Infancy*. Second edition. Oxford: Freeman.

See also the chapter by Haith in Held, *op. cit.* And for the philosophical and theoretical basis of perception, see Volume I of *Handbook of Perception*.

Sensory systems

A thorough survey of the structure and function of the senses is:

GELDARD, F.A. (1972) *The Human Senses*. Second edition. New York: Wiley.

Relevant volumes of the *Handbook of Perception* include chapters on sensory function. See in particular the chapters by DeValois and DeValois, and by Boynton on colour vision, in Volume V, *Seeing*. Noise and its effects are discussed in section VI of Volume IV, *Hearing*, and music in the chapter by Risset in that volume and by Deutsch in Volume X, *Perceptual Ecology*. For a fuller discussion of psychophysics and signal detection theory, see:

CORSO, J.F. (1967) *The Experimental Psychology of Sensory Behavior*. New York: Holt, Rinehart and Winston.

Pattern and object perception

The chapters by Robson in Volume V of the *Handbook of Perception*, and by Braddick, Campbell and Atkinson in Held, *op. cit.*, provide discussion of the feature analysis/visual channel nature of perception processing. The information-processing approach is presented by:

SPOEHR, K.T. and LEHMKUHLE, S.W. (1982) *Visual Information Processing*. San Francisco: Freeman.

Speech perception is reviewed by Darwin in the *Handbook of Perception*, Volume VII, *Language and Speech*, and its development is discussed in:

EIMAS, P.D. and TARTTER, V.C. (1979) The development of speech perception. In H.W. Reese and L.P. Lipsitt, eds., *Advances in Child Development and Behavior*, Volume 13. New York: Academic Press.

A critical discussion of the feature detector approach to reading is presented by:

DIEHL, R.L. (1981) Feature detectors for speech: a critical appraisal. *Psychological Bulletin*, **89**, 1–18.

For reviews of recent reading research see:

TZENG, J.L. and SINGER, H., eds. (1981) *Perception of Print: Reading Research in Experimental Psychology*. Hillsdale, NJ: Erlbaum.

LESGOLD, A.M. and PERFETTI, C.A., eds. (1981) *Interactive Processes in Reading*. Hillsdale, NJ: Erlbaum.

PIROZZOLO, F.J. and WHITROCK, M.C., eds. (1981) *Neuropsychological and Cognitive Processes in Reading*. New York: Academic Press.

Spatial perception

For a discussion of stereopsis, see:

JULESZ, B. (1971) *Foundations of Cyclopian Perception*. Chicago: University of Chicago Press.

Constancy and the size-distance and shape-slant invariance hypothesis are discussed in the following two books (see especially the chapter by Carlson in Epstein's volume):

EPSTEIN, W., ed. (1977) *Stability and Constancy in Visual Perception*. New York: Wiley.

MASSARO, D.W. (1975) *Experimental Psychology and Information Processing*. Chicago: Rand McNally.

Motion perception

For reviews of motion perception see the chapter by Sekuler in Volume V of the *Handbook of Perception* and that by Sekuler, Pantle and Levinson in

Held, *op. cit.* The chapter by Anstis in the latter volume provides a discussion of apparent movement, and that by Dichgans and Brandt in the same volume is a good overview of visual-vestibular interaction.

Person perception

Two readable reviews of face recognition are:

BENTON, A.L. (1980) The neuropsychology of facial recognition. *American Psychologist*, **35**, 176–86.

SERGENT, J. and BINDRA, D. (1981) The differential hemispheric processing of faces: methodological considerations and interpretation. *Psychological Bulletin*, **89**, 541–54.

The following volume is a useful compendium of research and theory on face recognition:

DAVIES, G.M., ELLIS, H.D. and SHEPHERD, J.W., eds. (1981) *Perceiving and Remembering Faces*. London: Academic Press.

A thorough coverage of the many aspects of social perception is provided in:

SCHEIDER, D.J., HASTORF, A.H. and ELLSWORTH, P.C. (1979) *Person Perception*. Reading, Mass.: Addison-Wesley.

4. Consciousness and Attention

4. Consciousness and Attention

Introduction

Most people would say that during their waking life they are conscious individuals. As William James has written, 'The first and foremost fact which everyone will affirm to belong to his inner experience is the fact that consciousness of some sort goes on' (James, 1890). In other words people are **aware** of their own thoughts, they are able to plan what they might do hours, days or even years ahead, they are aware of what other people are saying and what is meant by what is being said, and they can see and interpret what is happening in the world. This list of course is practically endless since one cannot exhaust all the different aspects of mental life which any individual might be conscious of at any moment. What one can do, however, is to assert with some confidence that, as individuals, we are conscious of ourselves, of others and of things around us in the world.

The incontrovertible existence of our own consciousness does not, however, tell us whether other people are conscious in the same way or even if they are conscious at all, since we have no direct access to their experiences. It is fairly safe to infer from the behaviour of other people, however, that their actions stem from a consciousness not dissimilar to our own. More importantly, personal knowledge we have of our own consciousness, or our belief in the consciousness of others, does not tell us whether consciousness need play a necessary role in the explanation of human behaviour. Consciousness might be, for example, an irrelevant by-product of collective neuronal activity in the same way that heat is an irrelevant but unavoidable consequence of the workings of the internal combustion engine. This view that consciousness might play no causal role in people's behaviour but may be a secondary, irrelevant consequence of brain action has been termed **epiphenomenalism** and such a view has occasionally found adherents within psychology, most notably among proponents of a purely behaviourist approach to the study of man.

On the other hand, many modern cognitive psychologists would not accept the view that consciousness is merely an epiphenomenon. Rather they would subscribe (even if covertly and implicitly) to what has been termed an **interactionist** view of the relationship between brain and mind. Proponents of this position assert, like those espousing epiphenomenalist ideas, that consciousness is in some quite unknown way **generated** by brain activity but, in contrast to the epiphenomenalist view, interactionists would argue that conscious activity can influence brain mechanisms and thus, in turn, direct behaviour. In other words our consciousness might not be an irrelevant concomitant of cortical and subcortical activity (merely the 'glow' of neuronal operation) but might play a major causal role in our perceptions, thoughts and actions.

How conscious mental activity might modify neural activity is, of course, as totally baffling as the question of how, in the first place, consciousness could be a property of the interaction of millions of cells within the nervous system.

ATTENTION AND CONSCIOUSNESS

Since this chapter is entitled 'Consciousness and Attention' the reader might be forgiven for asking why consciousness should be linked with attention rather than with all, or at least some, other cognitive activities. After all, are we not conscious when we are engaged in other mental operations such as holding a conversation, committing something to memory, watching a football match or enjoying an orange? The answer is, of course, that we are conscious during all of these diverse activities, but many psychologists have equated the most prominent current contents of a person's consciousness (whatever these contents might be) with what necessarily the individual is attending to. Accordingly attention and consciousness are intimately linked: what is in the forefront of our consciousness is that to which we are **paying attention**. As one psychologist put it recently, 'Attention is the experimental psychologist's code name for consciousness' (Allport, 1980a).

As we shall see, our level of consciousness or our ability to pay attention – our degree of alertness – varies as a function of several quite different factors. However, it is important to note that the linking of consciousness with attention implies that attention is not some cognitive skill or process additional to other aspects of cognition, such as perceiving, memorizing or thinking: rather it is the act of engaging in these mental processes. We do not, for example, decide to remember something and then 'add' various amounts of attention to our mnemonic processes, the size of the addition being related to the quality of our memory. Rather we engage in conscious mental activities which are relevant for good memory with varying degrees of effectiveness so that, for example, if we are thinking about what to say at a meeting in a strange town while asking someone for directions, our memory for the directions may be less good than if our mind had been free of other conflicting or irrelevant activities. Our degree of alertness seems not to affect how much attention we 'have' but how effectively we **distribute** it.

Of course we are usually conscious of more features of our environment or different aspects of our thought processes than those that at any moment happen to be most prominent in the centre of our attention. We are **peripherally aware**, for example, of the room in which we are sitting even while concentrating on reading a book or enjoying a favourite TV programme. Intuitively, therefore, we can split the contents of our consciousness at any one time into those things of which we are **focally aware** (i.e., those parts of our environment to which we are currently paying deliberate attention and which are thus in the centre of our awareness) and those of which we are only peripherally or marginally aware (e.g., those parts of the environment which are picked up or processed without the need for **focal attention** and which are thus on the fringes of our awareness). The limits of focal attention and the extent of our awareness of things in peripheral consciousness will form a major part of this chapter. A further major aim will be to examine the conditions under which conscious focal attention is always necessary for efficient mental operations and, relatedly, the conditions under which **unconscious processing** can guide behaviour and thought.

Since this last aim invokes a distinction between conscious and unconscious information-processing, we shall now briefly consider what these two terms mean in the present context.

CONSCIOUS AND UNCONSCIOUS PROCESSING

One of the major failings of introspection as a technique in psychology is that we can introspect only about our conscious experiences. Some of the contents of adult consciousness are, however, the end-products of a series of processes of which we are not consciously aware and which are not therefore available for introspective analysis. No amount of detailed thought, for example, if not supported by other evidence, will tell us how we are able to see different colours or lines in different orientations. We are aware of colour and lines as 'outputs' from some other systems or as 'inputs' to consciousness, but we are not aware of the processes which extract colour and orientation from the environment. Such processes, at least in adults, appear to occur **automatically** in the sense that they can be executed efficiently with little or no conscious monitoring or focal attention. In short, they can be carried out unconsciously.

Many early psychologists denied the interest of such unconscious processes to the psychologist, arguing that these processes were largely the province of physiologists and that the subject matter of psychology was exclusively conscious mental life, its method being introspection. However it seems that most skills which require conscious focal attention during their acquisition need it less and less as the skill becomes mastered. Unconscious processes therefore appear to be the 'precipitates' of earlier conscious processes, and for this reason alone they are of considerable interest to psychologists. These issues will be developed later in this chapter.

While we might not be too unwilling to accept the idea that some primitive processes occur without our having direct conscious knowledge of them, we may feel some resistance to the suggestion that *all* our psychological activities, including even our social behaviour, are governed by processes of which we remain quite unaware. Nevertheless, this suggestion has been made (Nisbett and Wilson, 1977). Nisbett and Wilson argue that if people are asked about what they think governed their behaviour after they have taken part in an experiment in social psychology, their verbal descriptions do not correspond very well with the theoretical analyses given by psychologists about the processes which (according to the psychologists) *actually* mediated their behaviour. Accordingly, Nisbett and Wilson suggest that the awareness people feel they have about what guides their behaviour is illusory and what really does guide their actions is unavailable to them.

This is a controversial area, but three comments seem appropriate. First, asking people what they feel went on in an experiment after it has finished may tell us merely that the subjects concerned forget rather rapidly what conscious processes they went through during the course of the test. Second, if the descriptions given by these people of what they thought was going through their minds during an experiment do not correspond with the theories of social psychologists, this may simply mean, even if the subjects have good memory, that the psychologists' hypotheses are not entirely appropriate. If they were more apposite, perhaps people's introspections and psychologists' descriptions would tend to coincide. Third, under some conditions (Joynson, 1974) individuals are actually very good at describing the factors which might affect their social behaviour (i.e., lay and academic views sometimes *do* coincide), and even quite young children can give good descriptions of the properties of their memory processes which are not so dissimilar from those of expert psychologists! The point where the dividing line lies between processes which operate without awareness and processes which principally involve conscious knowledge is by no means clear, but there is no evidence as yet which unequivocally relegates aspects of our conscious awareness to epiphenomena.

VARIETIES OF UNAWARENESS

Of course unconscious processes which occur automatically, over which we have little control, whose outputs, but not whose workings we are aware of, and which typically involve perceptual processes, are not the only kind of unconscious process which could be envisaged.

A second type of unconscious process quintessentially involves memory. While many mnemonic processes occur unconsciously in the sense described above, the products of such processes are themselves preserved at an unconscious level (i.e., in a **store**) but at a level which, subsequently, can more or less readily be made conscious (i.e., when we remember). In other words, while we have no direct access to the workings of our memory systems – no amount of introspection will tell us whether, for example, we forget because the passage of time **degrades** our memories or because newer memories in some way **interfere** with older ones – we can make conscious (**retrieve**) the earlier products of our mnemonic processes which, in the meantime, have been out of conscious awareness. Freud termed such unconscious processes **preconscious** and he described them as being **latent** since, given appropriate conditions, they could more or less readily be brought into conscious awareness merely by a wish on the part of the individual.

In contrast to the first type of unconscious process whose outputs are automatically signalled to consciousness (usually without error) and the second type of process whose outputs are frequently signalled to consciousness under the control of the individual (but which are notoriously error-prone), a third type of unconscious process does *not* signal its products readily to consciousness. The description of this type of unconscious process is also attributable to Freud, who believed that this was the **unconscious proper**. He argued that many of our experiences stored in memory would be so painful to us if they were made conscious that we actively prevent them from gaining access to awareness: we repress them. Even though these factors are not available to consciousness they nevertheless exert powerful indirect influences on our consciousness and behaviour, and, according to Freud, they can be made conscious again only through special therapeutic techniques such as hypnosis, word-association analysis or the interpretation of people's dreams.

Since mnemonic processes are considered in the next chapter and since Freudian views on the structure of the mind and personality are discussed in Chapter 13, we will consider only the first type of unconscious (automatic) processing, and in particular those processes involved in visual and auditory perception.

Alertness and consciousness

INTRODUCTION

Much of experimental psychology is concerned with how people deal with various types of environmental information, for example how they remember stories, how they can discriminate tables from chairs and how they solve problems. Psychologists have investigated such skills by varying aspects of the task which they give to people: by manipulating, for example, the difficulty of the story, discrimination or puzzle.

An organism is not merely externally driven, however, and the cognitive activities initiated by environmental stimulation occur against the background of the internal state of the individual – in other words, against his level of arousal, alertness or attentiveness. Accordingly, we might expect that performance at most cognitive tasks is systematically related as much to this state as to the properties of the information to be processed. (Indeed, Kahneman [1973], has actually implied that our cognitive capacity is directly related to the current state of arousal. In other words, within limits, Kahneman believes the more aroused we are, the more conscious resources we can draw on; arousal may thus determine how much attention we are able to pay in particular situations.)

Of course it is obvious that an individual's performance at any task when he is fully awake will be vastly different from his performance when he is almost asleep; but there are also smaller, albeit no less interesting, differences in alertness during normal wakefulness. These changes in alertness are of two types and are mediated by different systems within the brain. First, there are **tonic** differences which reflect intrinsic, slow changes of the basal level of arousal within an individual throughout a twenty-four-hour day, or even across a lifetime. Second, there is a **phasic** change in attentiveness which reflects short-lived variation in an organism's arousal over a period of seconds and which is initiated by novel or important environmental events.

TONIC ALERTNESS

It was originally thought that a structure in the brainstem, the reticular formation, was solely responsible for arousing and maintaining consciousness. Complete sectioning of the brainstem below the reticular formation left an animal paralysed (since the sensory and motor nerves were severed) but the animal remained fully alert when awake and had normal sleep-wake EEG patterns (i.e., it showed high-frequency, low-amplitude electrical activity during waking and high-amplitude, low-frequency activity during sleep). However, if the brainstem was sectioned above the reticular formation, not only was the animal paralysed but it also appeared to be in a state of continuous slow-wave sleep. Relatedly, direct stimulation of the intact reticular formation awoke a sleeping animal, while destruction of it produced somnolence. Subsequently, however, it has been shown that other structures, in the thalamus and hypothalamus, are also involved in the sleep-wake cycle and that coordinated activity of all these systems is necessary for the initiation and maintenance of conscious awareness (see Chapter 7).

During normal wakefulness our degree of alertness is not constant; there is **diurnal variation** in our psychological performance (reflecting changes in alertness) just as there are diurnal variations in physiological measures such as body temperature, respiration and blood pressure. In other words, we do not simply oscillate between two states of sleeping and waking; rather, physiological and psychological variation is continuous throughout waking, and, indeed, throughout sleeping.

Physiological measures like body temperature increase from early morning to reach a maximum in the evening and, on the whole, human performance follows this pattern; people are better at doing reaction-time tasks, letter-cancelling tasks and arithmetical tasks later in the day than they are shortly after waking. These results are readily interpretable in terms of a variation in our degree of alertness under control of the reticular formation and associated structures, throughout our daily waking life. Of course there are individual differences in when people feel at their optimum for work, and it seems that introverted individuals reach their peak level of performance earlier in the day than do extraverts (Blake, 1971). In addition, it has been suggested that **extraverts** are chronically less aroused than **introverts** and consequently engage in more stimulus seeking in order to 'drive' their indolent arousal system. However, while extraverts do tend to perform less well at later periods of monotonous vigilance tasks which require sustained attention (i.e., extraverts do less well at times when the stimuli, or the task, are no longer novel or interesting and are consequently no longer arousing), the relationship between physiological measures of alertness (such as EEG) and the extraversion-introversion dimension is unclear (Gale, 1973).

Of course, **endogenous factors** like diurnal rhythms are not the only factors which might influence our performance. **Exogenous factors** like noise, high temperatures, sleeplessness, drugs, anxiety and nervousness may also affect how well we carry out cognitive or other tasks. Although these factors are obviously quite different from each other it is frequently argued (e.g., Broadbent, 1971) that their effects on behaviour can be most easily understood if they are all assumed to influence a common underlying state, that state being our overall level of arousal. Some of these factors (like loss of sleep) serve to lower arousal, while others (such as drugs like amphetamine) tend to increase it. Are the effects of arousal induced by these various factors additive? In other words, as we become more and more aroused, does our performance correspondingly improve? The answer to this question, across a wide range of experiments, has reliably been found to be negative. As people's arousal is increased (for example by drugs, by systematically varying the voltage of electric shocks or by varying the intensity of auditory noise) performance improves only up to a certain point; beyond that point, however, increases in arousal cause performance to deteriorate. It is also found that the optimum level of arousal for a given task depends upon its difficulty: the more difficult an individual finds the task, the less the externally induced arousal is needed in order to achieve maximum performance.

At an intuitive level we have only to consider 'stage fright' to see an obvious example of how **overarousal** can lead to impaired performance. But why should over- (or under-) arousal lead to less efficient performance? Easterbrook (1959) has suggested that changes in our alertness change the effectiveness with which we sample the range of cues that we use to guide our activities. In other words, our focal attention becomes *narrower* the more aroused we become. If we are underaroused, for example, our attention will be too broad and we might select information from the environment uncritically and thus our performance might be rather poor because our actions are guided by many pieces of irrelevant information. As we become more aroused our focal attention becomes more efficient since irrelevant information is likely to be rejected, leaving only that which is critical for the execution of the task concerned. As arousal further increases, however, we tend to focus on fewer and fewer aspects of the task and, since some of those we neglect may be critical, our performance suffers. A change in our arousal therefore appears to affect how we allocate our attentional resources, and it seems unlikely that it affects how *much* attention we give to a task.

What evidence is there that heightened arousal makes us respond to relevant sources of information almost to the exclusion of other, less critical ones? Hockey (1978) asked people to concentrate on carrying out a visual tracking task while at the same time doing a subsidiary task which involved responding whenever one of six lamps, arranged in an arc around the subjects, came on. Hockey found that under arousing conditions (induced by very high levels of white noise) people performed less well on the secondary task (light detection) but maintained or, in other experiments, improved on their performance in the primary task compared to ordinary quiet conditions involving less arousal. Under the conditions of this type of experiment, therefore, as people's arousal increases, they tend to bias their attentional resources towards the dominant sources of information at the expense of the less important ones.

It is of some relevance to mention that some acute schizophrenic patients frequently describe attentional problems as part of their difficulties, saying, for example, that they cannot concentrate, are unable to cope with all the stimuli that they receive and cannot 'shut things out'. Venables (1977) has in fact argued that these patients have a relatively low level of arousal and consequently cannot restrict the range of their attention to critical aspects of situations; they are thus flooded with information from all quarters. There seems little doubt that these patients do have **attentional deficits,** but whether these are the cause of the patients' problems or are merely a consequence of it remains unknown.

Interestingly, while many indicants of alertness suggest that as we grow older our basal, tonic level of arousal decreases, there appears to be little change across age in the briefer phasic variations in arousal that occur in response to environmental signals. It is to these transitory changes in alertness that we now turn our attention.

PHASIC ALERTNESS

If an animal is confronted by a new, threatening or unusual stimulus, several transitory changes in its behaviour occur. The animal pricks its ears, moves its head towards the source of the stimulus, its pupils dilate, its heart rate decreases, respiration is inhibited, its muscles become tense and the EEG is desynchronized. If the stimulus is particularly threatening, the animal may adopt a defensive reaction involving hissing and snarling and, of course, may run away. Although humans do not prick their ears, they too show this **orienting response** when exposed to arousing stimuli. These changes in behaviour are characterized by two factors. First, they are **transitory**, and second, they **habituate** with repetition – repeated presentations of the same stimulus usually ensure that the orienting response progressively fails to be initiated.

A little thought will tell us that this orienting response might serve two psychological functions. On the one hand, detection of a significant environmental event may alert the organism so as to enable more efficient subsequent stimulus-processing to occur (we might thus need less information to categorize the event or take less time to achieve more extensive analyses of it). On the other hand, this alertness may enable the preparation of responses to deal with (or even escape from) the source of stimulation. Indeed, Pribram and McGuinness (1975) have claimed that there are two different structures in the limbic system, one centred on the amygdala and one centred on the hippocampus, which mediate these two aspects of orientation to important stimuli.

One way of investigating the processes that occur over the period of the phasic alerting response is to study the electrical responses of the brain. If we record the EEG continually, we obtain a good general picture of the state of an individual (whether he is drowsy or fully alert etc.) at any one period of time. On the other hand, while the EEG is a fairly good indicant of the general state of alertness, there are more subtle transitory changes in the electrical activity of the brain which are superimposed upon the general background activity and which are made in response to specific environmental events. On any one occasion that an external stimulus is processed by an individual, however, the specific response is somewhat obscured by the normal background electrical activity. Accordingly, in order to demonstrate and investigate the specific responses of the brain to particular stimuli, the **average** of many such individual responses must be taken; irrelevant background activity is then averaged out since it is different from trial to trial, but the specific response is highlighted since this is identical from trial to trial. The procedure is illustrated in Figure 4.1 and the average electrical response to a stimulus so obtained is called the **evoked potential** because it is the specific electrical response of the brain evoked by an external signal.

Such an evoked response is recordable from the scalp within 10 msec of the presentation of a stimulus and usually lasts for no more than about 500 msec. The evoked potential is not a single response, however, but, as Figure 4.1 shows, is made up of several components (that is, there is a series of positive and negative peaks). The **early components** of the evoked potential occur whatever a subject is instructed to do in response to a stimulus and occur even if the subject is asleep: these components thus appear to reflect **automatic stimulus-processing** which does not require conscious attention on the part of the subject. The presence or magnitude of the **later components**, however, can be influenced by the instructions given to the individual about what he must do with a stimulus which is presented in a particular task, and thus these later components appear to reflect **voluntary conscious attentional processes**. For example, if a person is presented with a sequence of letters and digits and is then required to count the letters, the later components of the evoked potential to the letters will be enhanced relative to those of the evoked potential to digits. The early components will, however, be similar for both letters and digits. The late components will occur even when a subject expects a stimulus which does not

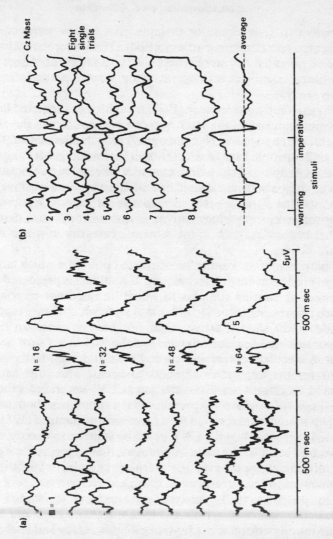

Figure 4.1 (a) shows, on the left-hand side, eight individual evoked responses to a stimulus. The right-hand side shows the average of 16 to 64 such individual evoked responses. (b) shows eight individual CNVs (see page 216) after presentation of a warning signal (along with evoked responses to the warning and imperative stimuli) and the average of these eight trials (bottom tracing). The latter shows a clear drift in potential between the warning and imperative stimuli. (After Hassett, 1978)

actually occur, as when, for example, in a regular series of words presented one at a time, one is omitted. The late components of the evoked potential therefore reflect electrical indicants of high-level, transitory cognitive activity involving conscious attention and expectancy.

Hillyard and his associates (1973) have further suggested that the magnitude of one of the later negative components of the evoked potential (the so-called N_1 component) reflects **stimulus set**, that is, the ability people have to select stimuli for further processing on the basis of simple physical characteristics like colour or position in space; they also suggest that one of the very late positive components (the P_3 wave) reflects **response set**, that is, a subsequent stage of processing which assigns a sensory input to a particular higher order class such as the semantic category to which a word might belong.

There is another kind of event-related potential which has been discovered by averaging techniques. If a subject is presented with a warning or alerting stimulus to which he need not respond and which primes him that a second stimulus, to which some response is needed, will shortly arrive, then not only is there an evoked response to the warning stimulus but there is also a slow negative drift in electrical potential recorded from the scalp as the subject waits for the imperative stimulus to occur. This drift has been termed **contingent negative variation** (CNV) and reflects the electrical signs of a person's expectancy that a stimulus is about to occur and his readiness to respond to it. Loveless and Sanford (1974) have indeed suggested that the CNV might be split into two components separated in time. The early component, they argue, reflects part of the orienting response to the warning stimulus while the later component reflects preparation to make a response.

Do people actually analyse and respond to stimuli more efficiently when they are alerted by a warning signal, and is their behavioural performance (as assessed by accuracy and latency, for example) related to the magnitude of their CNV (as indicated by the maximum negative drift, for example)? The first part of this question has been explored by varying the interval between a warning stimulus and an imperative stimulus (the **foreperiod**) and investigating how accuracy and latency of response vary as a function of foreperiod. The relationship between performance and foreperiod is U-shaped: if the imperative stimulus immediately follows the warning stimulus, performance is relatively poor; as the interval between the two increases, however, performance becomes better (reaching an optimum about 500 msec after the warning stimulus); further increases in the foreperiod, however, make performance deteriorate. In other words, it takes time for an optimal level of phasic arousal to build up and, once reached, this optimum cannot be long maintained before it returns to a basal level. While there are correlations between behavioural indicants of performance and measures of the magnitude of the CNV, these correlations are usually quite small and this probably reflects the fact that the CNV is only one of many indicants of a person's transitory state of alertness.

CONSCIOUSNESS AND THE CORTEX

The fact that damage to some subcortical structures can produce total losses of consciousness does not mean that consciousness is a property of cells in these regions. Rather, these systems are involved in the more subservient role of initiating waking, maintaining alertness, and orienting: they activate and modulate cortical activity, but it is this latter which in some way originates and controls conscious experience.

Lesions or electrical stimulation of the cortex never produce complete loss of consciousness as such; rather, they produce more or less specific defects in our ability to process information (to read, to recognize objects, etc.). If complete loss of consciousness is not a characteristic of cortical damage, then what kinds of changes in consciousness are observed after damage to the cortex in humans? If we assume that consciousness involves at least an awareness of our own body, an awareness of our own skills and knowledge and an awareness of the external environment, then certain kinds of cortically damaged patients show a partial loss of these types of awareness. For example, disorders of the awareness of **body image** have occasionally been reported after cortical damage. These usually involve a unilateral loss of body consciousness in that the patient behaves as if one half of his body were nonexistent. Thus this kind of patient may show no anxiety about the affected half, he may omit to shave one half of his face, he might not cover his limbs on that side with bedclothes and may even leave them suspended out of bed in an uncomfortable, careless manner. Often this disorder of consciousness of parts of the patient's own body is associated with a neglect of one half of visual space: such a patient might draw only one half of a figure that he was given to copy and, more significantly, would not be aware that he had neglected the other half of the visual stimulus. In a similar vein, some other patients can identify stimuli presented in isolation to either ear, hand or visual half-field, but, if both ears, hands or half-fields receive simultaneous stimulation, then the patients report experiencing only one of the signals and remain quite unaware that the other occurred (the other signal being 'extinguished').

While damage to the brainstem systems might produce a more or less permanent and total loss of consciousness, losses of conscious awareness after restricted cortical damage can thus be rather selective, affecting the person's consciousness of quite specific aspects of himself and of his environment. There is no one part of the cortex, however, which is 'responsible' for conscious awareness. The loss of visual location awareness is attributable to occipital lesions, the loss of body image awareness to parietal lobe lesions, the 'extinction' of an ear with double stimulation is associated with temporal lobe damage, and, as we shall see in the next section, the ability to coordinate these different aspects of awareness is critically dependent upon the integrity of the frontal lobes. The ability to reflect on ourselves and on our environment is therefore likely to be a property of most, and probably all, of the cortex and is not confined to just one region.

Focal attention: the capacity of consciousness

INTRODUCTION

Wright and Vlietstra (1975) have argued that there is a major developmental shift in the nature of the stimuli that control our attention, and, accordingly, that as children grow older a shift takes place in the mode of obtaining information from the environment. Wright and Vlietstra distinguish between **exploratory** and **search**

behaviours. Exploratory behaviour is characteristic of the young child and is 'more spontaneous and less systematic than search behaviour . . . [and it] occurs in shorter sequences; shows less continuity from one sequence to another; and is more directed by external stimuli'. Search behaviour, which is frequently a characteristic of adult attention, is, in contrast to exploratory behaviour, more **organized**, more **convergent**, and is **goal-oriented** since it is directed by a high-level intention or **plan**. Thus while exploratory behaviour might be said to be motivated by **curiosity** and is often guided by any attention-capturing stimulus (a bright or a new toy, for example), search behaviour is directed from a plan reflecting an adult's needs, interests or aspirations, and stimuli are analysed or ideas pursued only if they are relevant and possibly informative for the task at hand. As adults, we both explore and search depending upon circumstances; the young child can only explore. As an example, consider an experiment by Mackworth and Bruner (1970). They examined the eye movements that adults and six-year-old children made to various pictures. The contours, bright and dark features, and points of high contrast were fixated by the youngsters; in contrast the adults fixated the informative areas of the pictures which, of course, did not always coincide with those parts which had immediate visual impact and which the children scanned.

Whether, as adults or as children, our attention is **captured** by external events or whether, as mature individuals, we **direct** our attention in some goal-directed way, in both cases we are **selective**: in choosing to pay focal attention to one thing, we must neglect others. While this seems self-evidently true, it does raise an important question: namely, why should we be so selective?

THE NEED FOR SELECTIVE ATTENTION

It seems obvious that living organisms need, among other systems, perceptual processes in order to negotiate the world in which they live, memory processes in order to profit from experience and, especially in the case of humans, linguistic processes in order to communicate thoughts to others. But why should such organisms need an attentional system which allows only certain aspects of

BOX 4.1
Eye movements

There are four types of eye movements (see Alpern, 1972, for a review). First there is a **constant tremor** of the eye of relatively high frequency (30–100 Hz) and very low amplitude (17 secs/arc). Although small in amplitude, this tremor is not merely a form of 'noise', since abolishing it by various means makes visually presented information disappear in systematic ways (e.g., Alpern, 1972). Second, there are **vergence** movements which converge or diverge the eyes in a coordinated way as we focus on near or distant objects. Third, there are **pursuit** movements which we make when tracking moving objects. The fourth type of eye movements is of particular interest since the movements are 'driven' by the internal plans of a person when scanning stationary displays such as pictures or text. These movements are called **saccadic** movements, and typically we make about three such movements per second when examining visual scenes: in between these movements the eye is stationary for about 300 msec and this period is called a **fixation**. Since vision is suppressed during a saccadic movement, the fixational pause of the eye is effectively the only time that we can take in and process visual information. Saccadic movements are necessary since the retina is not uniform in its sensitivity and acuity: to examine any stimulus in detail we must bring its image on to the **fovea**. Accordingly, patterns of eye movements reflect patterns of attention and interest.

Figure 4.2 shows the patterns of eye movements made by normal people when examining the same picture after being given several different instructions about the kinds of information to extract. Obviously the scanning patterns across the picture are planned rather than disorganized and reflect the intentions of the subject. Some people with damaged frontal lobes, however, show chaotic eye movements across visual scenes: they can no longer form effective plans for action in general nor for sequencing their

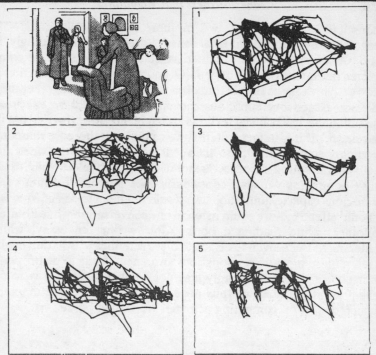

Figure 4.2 Eye movements while examining a picture under various instructions. (1) Free observation. (2) 'Is the family rich or poor?' (3) 'How old are the people in the picture?' (4) 'What were they doing before the man entered the room?'. (5) 'Can you recall how the people were dressed?' (After Luria, 1973)

patterns of saccadic eye movements in particular (see Luria, 1973). Interestingly, young children are also rather poor at systematically scanning pictures for information (Vurpillot, 1976): this behaviour, too, probably reflects the young child's inability to generate good search plans and might also reflect the immaturity of their frontal cortex systems, if these actually mediate planned, organized behaviour.

the environment or their thought processes into central awareness? One reason might be that our consciousness is **limited in capacity** – we can monitor only one complex activity in consciousness at any one time. In other words, we may not be able consciously to carry out two or more tasks simultaneously if, together, they exceed our total conscious resources; accordingly, if the two tasks are to be executed satisfactorily one must be completed before the other is begun. (Of course one might expect that if two activities are so simple that even when carried out together they do not exceed our conscious capacity, both should be executed simultaneously as satisfactorily as each might be when carried out in isolation.) If it is in fact true that we cannot sustain more than one complex activity at a time then it is apparent that the need for selective attention is a consequence of the need to select which idea, task or process we shall consciously take part in. Without such conscious capacity limitations we would not need to select what we should attend to – we could listen to one conversation while holding another, while reading a book, while writing an essay, while listening to Beethoven . . . Each of these activities in isolation might well require most of our conscious awareness if it is to be properly pursued, and thus we simply may not be able satisfactorily to do them all in **parallel**: we thus need to decide at any one moment which of several competing activities we should pursue.

CONCEPTIONS OF LIMITED CAPACITY

Most psychologists would accept that there are limits on our abilities to take part in two or more simultaneous activities. However, they have disagreed in recent years over the form that our limited resources take.

At one extreme it has been argued that we have limited but very general purpose resources which can be 'programmed' to take part in any task. The same general purpose resources are said to be involved in all our activities from singing and dancing to doing mental arithmetic. With a finite pool of common resources this view should predict that the allocation of resources to one task must necessarily take them away from another, if, together, the two tasks exceed our total conscious capacity; further, this must occur whether the two tasks are similar or dissimilar to each other since in both cases the tasks merely compete for the same limited resource (Broadbent, 1958).

At another extreme it has been suggested that we have several independent, specific processing resources each of which is concerned only with the execution of a particular kind of activity: in other words, the brain might be regarded as a series of independent processors operating in parallel. Thus we might have arithmetical resources which are quite separate from our musical skills, and accordingly, on this hypothesis, we might expect that if two tasks could be carried out by two different processing systems then they should be capable of being carried out as well together as they could be in isolation; i.e., dissimilar tasks might be performed in parallel. Two similar tasks, however, might compete for the same resource and thus performance on either or both might suffer (Allport, 1980a,b).

In between these two extremes we can envisage that there might be specific resources for arithmetic or whatever, but, in addition, that the outputs of these specific resources are monitored by a **general purpose executive controller**. This would not control individual responses or activities (these being the province of the specific resources concerned) but would control higher level operations such as time-sharing between two or more tasks. Since, putatively, we have specific resources available to us, the performance of tasks which require different resources (i.e., those involving two quite dissimilar tasks) should be rather better than the performance of two tasks which compete for the same specific resource (i.e., two tasks which are very similar to each other). However, since executive monitoring of two tasks will be more difficult than the monitoring of one, dual tasks, however dissimilar they might be, should be executed together rather less well than in isolation. In short, this hypothesis suggests that we have both high-level general resources which are involved in most tasks and lower level specific resources which are involved only in particular activities (Broadbent, 1977).

GENERAL AND SPECIFIC RESOURCES

Behavioural evidence
There are two ways, through experiment, in which we can investigate these three hypotheses. First, we can study whether two tasks which have similar processing requirements cause greater disrup-

tion of performance than two tasks which have dissimilar processing demands. If the first view of our limited capacity is correct, then, so long as the difficulty of the two similar and the two dissimilar tasks is held constant, two similar tasks should cause no greater disruption of joint performance than two dissimilar tasks. Brooks (1968) asked people to make judgements about aspects of a mental image of a letter Ⅿ (whether, when moving in imagination around the periphery of the letter from a given starting point, a right angle that one 'came across' was an internal or an external one). These judgements were carried out most effectively by saying the required responses ('yes' it was external or 'no' it was internal) rather than by pointing to them in a visual display. Conversely, making judgements about aspects of a remembered sentence (whether each word in the sentence was, in turn, a noun or not) was best carried out by the pointing response and not by the spoken response. It therefore appears that while looking and pointing conflicts more with visual imagining than does speaking, speaking on the other hand conflicts more with sentence analysis than does looking and pointing. These task-specific effects have been called **structural interference** by Kahneman (1973) and obviously indicate the existence of some **dedicated** cognitive structures – in the case of the Brooks experiment a system involved in the storage, manipulation and production of linguistic units on the one hand, and, on the other, a system involved in the processing of visuospatial information, whether this is driven by 'real' visual input or by imagined visual input.

These types of data strongly suggest that we cannot conceive of our limited capacity simply as resulting from the fact that tasks of any type compete for the same limited pool of general purpose resources. Is it therefore better to consider man as consisting of a set of parallel independent process-specific functions? A second, related type of experiment suggests not. If we have only process-specific resources then, if we combine two quite dissimilar tasks (which therefore engage two different processing systems) these two tasks should be performed as well together as they are in isolation. However, it is invariably the case that when the two dissimilar tasks are performed together, there is some decrement in one or the other task relative to performance when carried out separately. Thus, for example, McLeod (1977) asked people to do a tracking task (keeping a visually presented, constantly moving dot in line with a marker) either on its own or in conjunction with an arithmetic task (adding 2 or subtracting 7 from a number heard over headphones). It is difficult to imagine that doing mental arithmetic has a great deal in common with visual tracking but, compared to tracking performance in isolation, tracking performance when the subjects had to do the arithmetic task was impaired. Thus, while we do appear to possess process-specific systems, their outputs are monitored by some higher level process and this central system finds monitoring two quite separate and specific domains of processing more difficult than monitoring one.

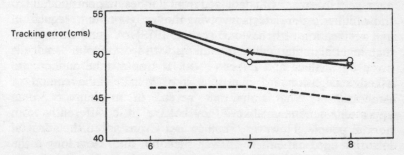

Figure 4.3 Tracking error scores across the last three days of McLeod's experiment. −−−−− tracking alone, 0——0 tracking and adding 2, X——X tracking and subtracting 7. (After McLeod, 1977)

Neuropsychological evidence

Regions of the brain are not equivalent in the types of processing that they carry out. Rather the brain appears to be organized into **functionally distinct components** and brain damage can selectively destroy or disconnect a given subsystem. The varieties of selective disorders of cognition after brain damage are manifold but two examples should give the flavour of the types of deficits that can be observed and thus, by implication, of the specific kinds of processing that appear to take place. First, patients can show gross disturbances of language production and comprehension while their musical skills remain relatively intact. Conversely, a person's musical skill may be impaired after a stroke but his language abilities may remain quite intact. Second, some patients are able to read but cannot write while others can write but cannot read. Such **double dissociation** of function suggests that we have more or less specialized domains of processing which deal, in the examples just given, with linguistic as opposed to musical abilities, or with writing as opposed to reading. (See Chapter 2 for a discussion on modularity.)

Specific disorders of cognition such as these tend to occur particularly after damage to the posterior regions of the brain, especially the parietal and temporal lobes. Damage to the frontal lobes, on the other hand, does not usually produce dramatic impairments in any particular cognitive function: execution of routine cognitive abilities is often barely affected after such damage. However, with damaged frontal lobes, patients do tend to show higher order defects involving the 'programming, regulation and verification of behaviour' (Luria, 1973). A good example of high-level planning failure in patients with frontal lobe damage is given by Shallice and Evans (1978). If frontal lobe patients are asked straightforward questions like 'What is the capital of America?' or 'What is nine times seven?' or 'In what way are an apple and a banana alike?' they behave little differently from normal people. However, Shallice and Evans asked their frontal lobe damaged patients to answer questions like 'How long is the average man's spine?' This type of question is not one that can be answered immediately on the basis of 'routine' knowledge but requires a systematic sequence of operations for its solution. There are many possible sequences, but one might be: (a) retrieve information about the average man's height, (b) generate a visual image of a man, (c) estimate the length of his legs and his head, (d) subtract the answer to (c) from the answer to (a) to obtain the solution.

Shallice and Evans's frontal lobe patients performed very poorly on these tasks, answering questions like the one illustrated in bizarre ways (one patient replied that the length of a spine was five feet even though he knew the average height of a man to be not much more than this). They therefore argue that these patients could probably perform each of the stages or processes involved in a plan satisfactorily but that they are deficient in generating it in the first place or using it to guide action in the second. It is interesting to note that this inability to *use* information, which is in fact available, is not only a characteristic of frontal lobe patients; it is also a feature of the elderly. Rabbitt (1979), for example, has shown that the normal old-aged can describe differences in the probabilities that 'signals' will be presented in particular locations, but, unlike the young, they do not employ this information to guide their search of possible target positions.

EXECUTIVE AND MONITORING FUNCTIONS OF CONSCIOUSNESS

One approach to the study of the capacity of conscious awareness has been through the study of short-term memory. People can hold accurately only a rather small amount of information in their minds at any one time and the capacity of this 'primary memory' system has been related by some psychologists to the capacity of conscious awareness. However, even if there were unequivocal evidence for the existence of a short-term memory process (see Chapter 6 for details), it seems unlikely that conscious processing can merely be equated with a storage system: we are limited in our capacity for holding several items simultaneously in awareness, but our limited conscious resources are also involved in the executive control of task-related activities in addition to the storage of currently relevant information.

Other psychologists have frequently argued that human action is organized at and controlled by many different **levels of processing**. Writing in the 1940s, Craik likened the highest level of conscious control to the activities of a wartime commander: '. . . the C in C Fighter Command presumably says: "we want a sweep carried out over such and such an area"; he does not have to add: "this means Spitfire number so and so must have so many gallons of petrol in its tanks and care must be taken that its plugs are clean and guns are loaded" ' (Craik, 1966). This analogy is meant to bring out several ideas. First, that action can be organized and programmed at different levels: the initiation and monitoring of a high-level plan is of concern to the central executive while the minutiae of its execution are left to subordinates. Of course the subordinates also will have appropriate plans, at their level, and they too will delegate where necessary. Second, the central organization is probably relatively unaware of the precise details involved in the execution of the plan but will be kept informed of the outcomes at important stages in its operation.

While we might have an inkling of the role an air vice marshal might play in an air battle, we might not be quite so clear about what functions a **high-level planning and regulating** system would have in human activity, or, to pose the question differently, what are the functions of consciousness? What does consciousness do? It is easy to become metaphysical in asking questions about the role of conscious processes in human activity but provided we restrict our considerations to the functions which consciousness might subserve in cognition we might avoid the worst excesses of sheer speculation. Sternberg (1980) has recently described several types of conscious planning and decision-making processes and his description of what he terms **metacomponents** of mind helps to put flesh on the notion of the 'high-level processes' discussed above. Sternberg argues that when faced with a task, or a combination of tasks, the decisions people must make and the plans they must employ include the following: (1) understanding exactly what the task or problem is that needs to be carried out or solved, (2) selection of lower order specific skills or processes which are relevant to the execution or solution of the task, (3) selection of a strategy or organizing the sequence in which the lower order skills (which may be many and various in a given task) are to be employed, (4) balancing the amount of time allotted to an aspect of the task against how much the given time restriction will affect the overall quality of performance, (5) keeping track of what has already been done, what is currently being done and what still needs to be done during the course of an activity, and then, finally, (6) when the results from lower order specific processes are available, evaluating them and ultimately combining them into a solution or response.

These functions thus ascribe to conscious activity both an **executive** role involving the nature, order and timing of various activities (i.e., an intentional or a planning function) and a **monitoring** role involving scanning and evaluating whether performance has matched intention (i.e., an attentional function). We may have different plans at different times and we may monitor the success or failure of the operation of different skills that we possess, but it is the same limited-resource conscious part of us which initiates and scrutinizes action. (See Chapter 7.)

There are several issues raised by this description of a central, high-order regulating system, but an obvious one is the implication that, in the same way that an air vice marshal can implicitly call upon ground crews, so conscious processes can draw upon, set in motion and monitor the operation of many subsystems of rather specialized abilities ('lower order skills'). Further, these specific skills are at any one time available but latent (i.e., they are 'there' but not in operation), and may be activated according to the particular demands of a task and the plans that have been formulated to cope with it. Finally, since the subsystems are 'stored' out of consciousness, they may also be able to operate with some degree of **autonomy** (i.e., without conscious monitoring) when they have been activated.

ATTENTION AND INTELLECTUAL COMPONENTS OF MIND

The traditional approach to the study of intellectual abilities has been to present people with a range of cognitive tasks and to find out how well each individual does on each of the separate tasks. The tasks might include verbal fluency, arithmetical abilities, picture interpretation and constructional skills. An invariable finding from such studies is that someone who does well on one type of test will also do well on another, different type of test and, similarly, someone who performs poorly on the tests will tend to do so 'across the board'. In short, performances at tasks which are apparently quite dissimilar are correlated. As Spearman and Jones (1950) concluded on the basis of such correlational studies,

> The earliest fundamental observation made was that the intertest correlations, although widely varying in magnitude, were at least regularly positive in sign. On behalf of the old and charitable view, that a person's inferiority in one kind of performance is likely to be compensated by superiority in another, there was found no support whatsoever. On the contrary, it appeared that failure in anything is rather a bad than a good augury for all other things.

Positive correlations between all types of mental tests have led, not unnaturally, to the conclusion that the tests must have some factor in their execution in common, and in addition, since the correlations are often quite small, it has also been concluded there must be factors which are unique to the particular tasks concerned (over and above the common factor). The common factor (usually called 'g') has been equated with general intellectual ability (**general intelligence**) and the more unique factors with narrower, more specfic types of abilities. Clearly this conclusion from correlational studies parallels that from the more experimental ones discussed above, and it is tempting to identify the 'general purpose pool of cognitive resources' inferred from the experimental dualtask studies with the notion of 'general intelligence' as derived from the correlational mental-testing studies.

If 'g' involves the same processes as those involved in the executive and monitoring functions of attention, there should be a high positive correlation, across individuals, between measures of general intelligence and performance at attention-requiring tasks. Such correlations are invariably small and no single informationprocessing measure of task performance ever accounts for more than about 10 per cent of the variance of tests which purport to measure general intelligence (Hunt, 1980). This probably reflects the facts that the attention-demanding tasks involve many specific subskills as well as executive and monitoring abilities while the performance of people on general intelligence tests is influenced not only by 'g' but by other social, cultural and educational factors. In addition, it is likely that other factors such as chronic anxiety or stress, which are at least as potent as intellectual ones, might influence the effectiveness with which we deploy our attentional resources. Individual differences in performance are thus an intriguing and important area of investigation but, involving as they do conative, cognitive and affective factors, it is an exceedingly difficult field in which to design elegant experiments. (See also pages 544–7.)

Efficient processing without focal attention

INTRODUCTION

Much of the regulation of our body goes on without our being aware of it. Our respiration, circulation, digestion and excretion, for example, occur without our constantly having to monitor them. Indeed these processes can occur automatically in states of coma where there are no signs of consciousness remaining. Of course, under normal circumstances, although we are not aware of the processes themselves, we are made aware of their operation when they reach critical points (e.g., we feel hungry). Similarly we can consciously influence some parts of these systems should we choose to do so (e.g., we can hold our breath, within limits, at will). In short, some automatic processes, under control of the nervous system, operate efficiently without conscious monitoring but give signals of their state at critical points and can, more or less, be subject to conscious control.

Are there any 'higher' functions which could also be said to operate in this fashion, i.e., are there any cognitive processes that can operate automatically, without the need for focal attention? Posner and Snyder (1975) have recently listed three criteria for evaluating whether any particular cognitive activity involves automatic processing. First, by definition, since such tasks do not require the intervention of conscious focal attention, the efficient execution of automatic tasks should be largely unaffected by the presence of other tasks or mental activities which do require focal attention. Thus the extremely complicated skill of walking can be carried out without our having to 'think' consciously how to do it, and as a result we can hold sensible conversations while fell-walking. On the other hand, holding a conversation and simultaneously trying to read a technical book are both tasks which might be expected to require conscious focal attention; consequently one or both of these activities might suffer in ways which they would not if one were performed unconsciously. Second, automatic processes may be initiated consciously but they may also operate effectively without intention as when, for example, with our eyes open, we invariably see objects in visual space whether we consciously choose to or not. In other words, unconscious processes might operate passively insofar as little can be done to prevent their efficient operation, whereas conscious processes may be active in the sense that they reflect deliberate choices or strategies on the part of the individual. Third, however initiated, skills which can be carried out automatically need not give rise to conscious awareness, as when, for example, we discover during the course of a car journey that, with our mind on other things, we have been driving for several miles yet cannot recall any part of the route or our actions.

AUTOMATIC PROCESSING

The role of practice

Physiological processes like respiration are **hard-wired** or **pre-programmmed** into us; for obvious reasons we do not have to learn how to do them, and they usually remain outside consciousness since they have never been there in the first place. In contrast, most higher psychological processes require full conscious involvement during their acquisition although they progressively do not as the skill or process becomes mastered. As William James (1890) has summarized,

> A strictly voluntary act has to be guided by idea, perception and volition, throughout its whole course. In an habitual action, mere sensation is a sufficient guide, and the upper regions of brain and mind are set comparatively free.

The need for focal attention might thus decrease as we become practised: automatic processes, in the first sense of Posner and Snyder, may occur as a result of learning. Consider driving a car. To begin with the learner driver has to decide whether to depress the clutch, shift the gear lever, press the accelerator, signal, look in the mirror, etc. All these different activities, in the novice, do not yet have an organized sequence imposed on them nor any priorities assigned to them, and therefore the learner constantly has to evaluate options and decide upon appropriate actions. In other words, the tyro is engaged in those planning and decision-making activities which are characteristic of focal attention. Not surprisingly, novice drivers do not have spare capacity for even casual conversation. Contrast this with the skilled driver who could probably plan a lecture while driving himself to deliver it.

If we turn from observations of the real world to the controlled environment of the laboratory, then here too these suggestions tend to be confirmed. Skilled pianists can repeat prose heard over headphones while at the same time sight-reading music at the piano; professional typists can recite nursery rhymes from memory while typing from copy; and, after several weeks' training in the laboratory, two subjects were able to read short stories for comprehension while at the same time writing words to dictation (see Neisser, 1976a, for discussion and references).

The benefits of automation, consequent upon a task becoming practised, are clear: given some degree of proficiency, **conscious control** is **freed** from menial activity and can **monitor** (the now) more important or relevant activities. Thus the skilled concert pianist can think about the interpretation of the music rather than struggle to find the correct chords; the tournament tennis player can think about strategy rather than how to stand in order to make an efficient backhand shot.

While normal people can carry out two complex tasks simultaneously only after they have had extensive practice, patients with split brains (whose left hemisphere is disconnected from the right hemisphere) can do so shortly after their operations, even if unpractised.

If normal blindfolded people are asked to sort spheres into an upper compartment and cylinders into a lower one with the left hand (**right-hemisphere-controlled**), and simultaneously to sort the opposite way round with the right hand (**left-hemisphere-controlled**), they perform very poorly relative to a condition in which both hands sort the objects in an identical way (i.e., when both hands simultaneously put spheres into the upper compartment and cylinders into the lower compartment). Patients with **split brains**, however, perform as well with 'opposite' instructions for the two hands as they do with both hands operating under identical instructions. In other words '. . . commissurotomy patients show no performance decrement when required to perform different or even opposite tasks with left and right hands, whereas normal subjects have great difficulty in making independent decisions for two simultaneously operating hands, displaying severe impairment in performance when required to do so' (Ellenberg and Sperry, 1980).

Interestingly, however, while the commissurotomy patients were better than controls at sorting when the hands sorted in opposite fashion, they were worse than normal people when both hands sorted in an identical way. In the latter condition normal subjects synchronized their hand movements (their hands moved in phase with each other) in order to achieve efficient performance; in contrast, the patients with split brains sorted with their hands in such a way that there was little relationship between what the right and left hands were doing. It therefore appears that in normal people the intact corpus callosum keeps the left and right hemispheres working together in a single attentional system. This ensures, for example, synchronous activity of both hands where it is efficient to do so (because the two tasks have similar demands) but prevents the efficient execution of two conflicting tasks simultaneously. In the absence of the corpus callosum, and thus of the unified or integrated attentional system that it somehow brings about, the commissurotomy patients are on the one hand able to maintain independent attentional systems, one within each hemisphere, but on the other they are unable to organize synchronous activity.

BOX 4.2
The cerebral hemispheres and dual-task performance

In a seminal report Kinsbourne and Cook (1971) showed that after practice people could balance a dowel rod in their right hand for longer if they were silent compared to when they were talking. The original explanation for this effect was that the manual acitivity of each hand is programmed largely by the contralateral hemisphere of the brain, that in right-handed people speaking is controlled by the left hemisphere and that, therefore, the two apparently quite dissimilar tasks (speaking and right-handed dowel-balancing) interfered with each other because they both involved activation of the same cerebral hemisphere. Support for this view also comes from the observations that speaking interferes less with *left*-handed dowel-balancing than it does with right (since, putatively, the two activities are controlled by different hemispheres) and that manual ability of the left hand is impeded more by a visuo-constructive task thought to involve the right hemisphere than is the right hand (Hellige and Longstreth, 1981).

Although the hemispheres may appear to function to some extent as independent systems, this does not necessarily mean that the involvement of a *single* hemisphere in the mediation of two tasks will automatically lead to poor simultaneous performance. Even within a hemisphere there may be relatively independent functional systems and if two tasks involve different resources within one half of the brain, little mutual interference may occur. Thus speaking and right-handed dowel-balancing (for example) interfere with each other, not just because they involve the left hemisphere *per se*. but because they both compete for the same control system (possibly fine motor coordination) and this happens to be localized in the left hemisphere. However, when large right-handed movements are made (requiring vision to assess their outcome) simultaneous speaking does *not* affect their accuracy or speed (Lomas, 1980): gross motor control under the guidance of visual feedback uses a control system within the left hemisphere that is not involved in talking, and consequently little mutual interference occurs.

Of course, after years of practice, skilled concert pianists can exercise the kind of independent functioning of the hands (and thus of the two hemispheres) that the commissurotomy patients show immediately after the sectioning of the corpus callosum. Such performance in practised normal people, however, is, as already noted, probably attributable to an increase in the degree of automation of the skill concerned so that it no longer requires conscious monitoring for its efficient execution. The similar behaviour of some practised normal people and split brain patients may therefore be due to quite different factors: in the one case high-level monitoring of the execution of multiple tasks is no longer necessary, while in the other it is no longer possible.

It is, of course, one thing to say that **practice** enables a task to **bypass** focal attention and quite another to say what exactly has changed following extensive experience. Clearly, as a result of learning, something significant does happen to the coding of inputs to outputs or to the kinds of plans necessary for a task's execution, but precisely what is still largely a mystery.

Without intention

When we look at something, or when we listen to someone speaking, how far does perceptual analysis occur without focal attention? Or, to pose the same question in a slightly different way, to what level can stimuli be automatically analysed in the absence of a conscious intention?

One way in which this question can be investigated is to present people with a word which is the name of a colour, but which is actually printed in another, different colour. Thus the word 'RED', printed in green ink, might be shown to an individual, the task being to ignore the word as such and simply to name the colour of the ink in which it is printed as rapidly as possible. Compared to a control condition, where a word which does not name a colour is presented (e.g., 'DOG'), the reaction time to name the colour of the print is much longer when the stimulus word is, itself, a colour name. An obvious interpretation of this **Stroop effect** (as it has become known, after the person who discovered it) is that even though people do not intend to process the word, since it is irrelevant for the particular task, nevertheless they cannot help but do so. Consequently, at some stage in the execution of the task they have two conflicting colour names available to them, one of the actual, physical colour of the word and the other of the colour that the word itself represents. In separating these two available responses, subjects take longer than in the condition where the representation that the word signifies (in the example, an animal) does not conflict with the colour-naming response (Dyer, 1973).

A related effect occurs in **lexical decision tasks**. In these situations people are shown a mixture of proper English words and pronounceable but nonsensical words and they have to indicate as quickly as they can whether the word they see is an English word or not. Compared to nonsense words like 'dake', nonsense words like 'blud' take longer to reject as proper words, probably because we cannot help but covertly say words when we see them. Since neither 'dake' nor 'blud' is visually a proper word but acoustically 'blud' is, the latter word provides conflicting evidence about which decision to make and so it takes us a little longer to arrive at the appropriate response (Rubenstein, Lewis and Rubenstein, 1971).

It seems reasonable to argue, therefore, that in both these situations people did not need to make a particular kind of analysis of the stimulus (and probably consciously never thought of so doing) but nevertheless, even without volition or intention, these analyses were carried out and their results were signalled to consciousness for evaluation.

How extensive is this automatic processing of inputs? We have seen, for example, that the 'sound equivalent' of a visually presented word can be generated without focal attention, but can a word's meaning also be analysed without necessarily involving full conscious capacity? A major method of investigating how far, or to what level, stimuli are analysed without the need for high-level conscious involvement, is to employ the **dual-task paradigm**. If we give people two tasks to carry out, one of which demands their full conscious involvement, we can then examine what they know about the other task and how it might affect performance on the primary task.

Such studies have typically involved the **shadowing** task where the subject is required to repeat back one message played through headphones to one ear while simultaneously a second, different message is played to his other ear. Listening to one message and repeating it as one hears it is a very demanding task and is assumed to 'lock' all the conscious resources of the individual. Accordingly, whatever people know about the other message, or however it influences the attended message, must be a consequence of analyses which took place without the need for focal attention. This 'dichotic-listening' paradigm was originally employed by Cherry (1953), who found that if people were asked after the experiment about the content of the unattended message (the message which was not shadowed), they could give only fairly crude descriptions of this information. Thus they knew whether the message was speech or not and they knew whether it was a man or a woman speaking but they could not report any of the words that had been played nor what language the speaker was using and, therefore, not surprisingly, they also knew nothing about the gist of the unattended speech. Partly on the basis of these data Broadbent (1958) and

Treisman (1960) have argued that only 'simple' features such as frequency, colour and position can be analysed without focal attention. And furthermore, in a recent series of experiments Treisman (Treisman and Gelade, 1980; Treisman and Schmidt, 1982) has argued that while the extraction of features (like colour) is an automatic process, the combination of features into whole percepts is an activity which requires conscious intervention. The evidence for such a view comes from two kinds of experiments. First, Treisman and Gelade showed that the speed of searching for disjunctive features embedded in other irrelevant features (e.g., searching for any blue letter or any S of whatever colour among green Xs and brown Ts) is unaffected by how many irrelevant letters are present: such data, Treisman argues, reflects automatic, nonconscious, parallel processing. In contrast, the time taken to search for a target specified by the conjunction of two features (e.g., blue and T) depends systematically upon how many irrelevant items (blue Xs and green Ts) people have to examine in their search. That is, conjunctive features appear to be processed in a qualitatively different way to disjunctive ones and this is because, Treisman argues, conjunctions of features (which define a whole percept) require conscious, serial analysis. Second, Treisman and Schmidt showed that under difficult perceptual conditions (involving brief exposure) people sometimes report illusory perceptions (e.g., they report seeing green Xs when in reality they were shown green Zs and blue Xs). It is argued that this reflects the fact that while elementary features have been analysed, the temporal constraints have prohibited proper serial, conscious 'glueing' of the extracted features, and illusory combinations of features are thus occasionally the result. (It is interesting to note that some brain-damaged patients suffer these illusory perceptions or distorted perceptions – metamorphopsias as they are called – much of their waking life: see Critchley, 1953, pp. 298–306. Since these illusions appear to be modality-specific, however, it is difficult to see how they could arise from a disorder of conscious processing.)

In spite of this recent attempt by Treisman to preserve the idea that only low-level features of stimuli are analysed automatically (and also to maintain the associated view that perception requires attention), we now know, however, that while people cannot remember (or are never aware of) the meaning of messages to which they are not paying attention, the semantic aspects of such stimuli nevertheless are analysed and do influence their behaviour. Using the dichotic listening paradigm, McKay (1973) has investigated how a word presented on the nonshadowed ear (and therefore, by definition, the unattended channel) affected the interpretation of an ambiguous sentence presented and shadowed on the other ear. For example, subjects might have heard, and repeated as they heard it, the sentence: 'They threw stones at the bank yesterday.' When either the word 'money' or the word 'river' was presented on the unattended ear at the moment that the ambiguous word 'bank' occurred, McKay found that the ambiguity of the word in the attended ear was resolved, the interpretation of the shadowed sentence having been biased towards the meaning indicated by the unattended word. This effect occurred in spite of the fact that the individuals in the experiment could not say, when asked, what the unattended word was. In related types of experiment Lewis (1970) has shown that the delay in shadowing an attended word is increased if a word of similar meaning is presented on the nonshadowed ear and Corteen and Wood (1972) have shown that previously conditioned autonomic responses to words (achieved by pairing some words with electric shocks) are elicited to an equal extent when, subsequently, the words are presented to an attended or to an unattended ear.

Granted these behavioural effects of the meaning of individual words, does the semantic interpretation of unattended messages proceed further and, specifically, are individual words integrated into phrases or even sentences to form more complex meaningful units which can influence behaviour? The answer appears to be negative since McKay (1973) found that unattended phrases which should have helped to make an ambiguous sentence clear did not, in fact, do so. McKay asked people to shadow ambiguous sentences like 'they are flying planes', which could mean 'planes that are flying' or 'someone is flying planes'. Presenting a disambiguating phrase on the unattended ear (e.g., 'growling lions', which can suggest only the interpretation 'lions that are growling' and thus might bias the interpretation of the attended sentence to 'planes that are flying') had no effect upon the interpretation of the sentence shadowed on the attended ear.

Taken as a whole, therefore, these results suggest that while direct, simple or routine aspects of a word's meaning might be extracted without focal attention (since such information which has not been given the benefit of focal analysis still biases the responses to information which has), complex aspects of the relationships between words are not signalled automatically (since unattended stimuli which provide this information and which would reduce the ambiguity of attended sentences do not do so). That only a limited analysis of meaning can take place without conscious attention is, of course, rather obvious if we think of any sophisticated piece of writing. Consider this verse of Ted Hughes:

> Days are chucked out at night.
> The huge labour of leaf is simply thrown away.
> Great yesterdays are left lying.
>   ('Lumb Chimneys', 1979)

It is obvious that the understanding and interpretation of this cannot be 'automatic' since the words and phrases are used in a highly original way to convey meaning, and we have to think about what is meant. Only when stimuli follow well-trodden paths can focal attention be bypassed.

PROCESSING WITHOUT AWARENESS?

Why can we not report overtly stimuli which do not receive full focal attention but whose meaning is analysed (at least to a limited extent) and which can influence our behaviour? There are three possibilities. First, in dichotic listening experiments, since people are asked about the nature of the unattended stimuli *after* the task is finished they may well have been aware of the stimuli at the time but, when tested, they had merely forgotten about the details of the message. Second, limited aspects of an unattended word's meaning may be available to the subjects but, because the word did not receive focal analysis, people find it rather difficult to put into words what they experienced: tested in some other way than verbal report (through recognition, for example) they may well indicate their knowledge. Third, the subjects may not be able to report what they experienced, even though the stimuli actually affected their behaviour, because they were never aware of them in the first place.

There is no doubt that memory is important in dichotic listening experiments since, if people's recognition memory for unattended information is systematically assessed, then they show extremely *good* recognition of nonattended stimuli occurring at the moment shadowing stops but they perform at chance level (i.e., they have no memory) for items presented a few seconds *before* they stop shadowing (Norman, 1969). This certainly reflects a memory failure, but whether this failure is attributable to extremely rapid forgetting of relatively poorly analysed semantic information or whether it is due to other mnemonic factors is unclear (see Chapter 6).

Obviously there are experimental situations where the role of memory can be minimized. In **backward masking paradigms**, for example, a single word (followed by a masking stimulus) might be presented, the subject being required immediately to report the word he was shown. Clearly there are minimum demands upon memory in this experiment, and, with a suitable choice of stimulus and temporal parameters, it can be shown that although people might not be able to say what the word was, it could nevertheless subsequently bias the interpretation given to other words (Marcel and Patterson, 1978; Marcel, 1983). Does this mean that the semantic aspects of the word were analysed and stored without awareness? Although this interpretation is frequently given, it seems an unnecessary one since in other similar experiments where people were unable to *report* words, they could however select, in a kind of recognition experiment, the taxonomic category to which a word belonged (Allport, 1977). This rather suggests that in backward masking experiments people can extract only a limited semantic description of the stimulus word, and while this description is not adequate for identifying it (and therefore for saying the item) it is adequate for discriminating one class of words from another.

In other words, in these experiments the subjects probably did have the semantic information available to them (they were aware of it) but they could indicate their awareness only through more sensitive tests of what they knew, rather than through overt verbal report.

If some failures to indicate knowledge are due to secondary factors such as mnemonic failures or test insensitivity, are there any genuine or unambiguous instances of processing without

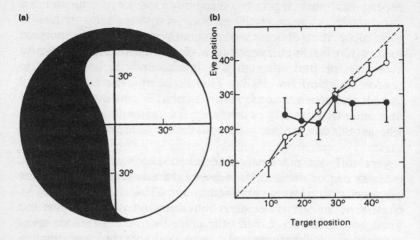

Figure 4.4 (a) shows the visual field of a cortically blind patient: the black areas indicate the part of the visual field in which he reports no vision; (b) shows the patient's eye movements to a signal in the blind field as a function of the target's actual position. Initially, he makes rather random eye movements to the target, ●——●, but after some practice he moves his eyes to exactly where the stimulus is, O——O, but still reports that he fails to see anything. (After Zihl, 1980)

awareness? Although Dixon and Henle (1980) have recently reviewed experiments which they believe indicate clear evidence that unconscious processing of information can occur, many of the experiments that they cite can be criticized as reflecting mnemonic failure on the one hand or the use of inappropriate or insensitive measures of people's knowledge on the other. However, just because many experiments can be criticized on methodological grounds, it does not necessarily follow that the distinction between conscious and unconscious processing is not a valid one. Indeed, some clinical, experimental data, without obvious methodological flaws, provide quite strong evidence for the distinction. Some cortically blind patients consistently report that they see absolutely nothing in particular parts of their visual field. Yet these very patients, when asked to point to where something is in the same (blind) field can do so with above chance accuracy in spite of their feeling that the task is a rather silly one since they are not consciously aware of anything being present in that part of their visual field. What appears to be happening therefore is that position information is being effectively signalled by the patients' remaining visual system and although this information can gain access to response systems (so that the patient can point with his finger) it cannot gain access to conscious awareness. What the patient can do and what he is conscious of being able to do thus appear to be **dissociated**. While in normal people the ability to specify an object's position in visual space probably depends upon the integrity of several different processes, the behaviour of these brain-damaged patients suggests that at least one of these processes can operate independently of conscious involvement (Weiskrantz *et al.*, 1974). The phenomenon is called **blind sight** and illustrative data, based on eye movements, are shown in Figure 4.4. (See Box 3.3 for more discussion of blind sight and page 335 for further discussion of unconscious processing.)

THE PRICE OF AUTOMIZATION: ERRORS

When individuals are unskilled at an activity they tend to make errors. In the absence of the appropriate knowledge, without the right type of training or with insufficient practice, people's performance will be flawed even though they might be fully attending to the task with all their resources. In the jargon of cognitive psychologists, such performance is **data-limited** because the subjects concerned do not yet have the relevant information to accomplish the task fluently and, accordingly, increasing the amount of attention applied to the task can hardly improve performance until they acquire the requisite knowledge (Norman and Bobrow, 1975).

As a skill becomes **routinized**, however, errors due to ignorance begin to decrease and eventually, as we have already noted, a highly **overlearned** activity can be performed without continuous conscious monitoring. On the other hand, this automization is not itself free from error although the errors that we make as a result of knowing how to do something, not surprisingly, are unlike those that we make when in the process of learning how to do it. Let us consider the errors that we make in our daily lives when we are engaged in highly overlearned activities. Reason (1979) has recently asked people to keep a diary of the kinds of **mental lapses** or **absent-minded errors** made over a long period. The following are typical of his subjects' reports: 'I put shaving cream on my toothbrush', 'When I got up on Monday morning, I found myself putting on Sunday's sweater and jeans instead of working clothes', 'I unwrapped the sweet, put the paper in my mouth and threw the sweet into the waste bucket', and, finally, 'I intended to drive to place X, but then I "woke up" to find I was on the road to place Y'.

It is easy to recognize the genre! These errors typically occurred in the morning (8 am to 12 am), round about tea-time (4 pm to 6 pm) and after dinner (8 pm to 10 pm) but more importantly, Reason was able to classify the errors into several types. The most frequent of these (40 per cent) were memory failures ('I started to walk home and had covered most of the distance when I remembered I had set out by car') and the next most frequent (20 per cent) were 'test' failures where the error appeared to stem from a failure to verify the progress of an activity at various critical decision-points and, consequently, the person's actions proceeded towards a goal other than that specified by his original intention (e.g., 'I brought the milk from the front step to make myself a cup of tea. I had put the cup out previously. But instead of putting the milk into the cup, I put the bottle in the fridge'). These latter errors are particularly interesting since they suggest that once a skill is practised, we can delegate its execution to a lower order system, not necessarily involving conscious awareness, and that occasionally a critical decision-point is reached which might be shared by other activities; if, at this moment, our focal attention is elsewhere and we are not monitoring the outcomes of our actions, another plan, system or subroutine which is in some way 'stronger' than the one we have set in motion might be automatically initiated and we then proceed to a different, unintended, outcome.

Thus we cannot run on **automatic pilot** if we wish to avoid errors. In performing highly overlearned tasks we must periodically check what we are doing at certain key points since, if we do not, although our mind will be totally free of mundane concerns, we will sometimes unconsciously carry out bizarre sequences of actions as intended actions overlap with other, unintended sequences of behaviour.

In acquiring a skill we must pay full conscious attention to it in order to learn what we have to do; we then make errors because we do not know exactly what is required. Having learned the skill we make errors because, although we know what to do, we fail to make conscious notes of our actions at appropriate times.

Consciousness and self-consciousness

INTRODUCTION

We made earlier a distinction between conscious and unconscious processing of information but this is not the only one that can be made: we can also distinguish between the running continuous span of consciousness on the one hand and the awareness of that consciousness on the other. In other words, we can distinguish between having an experience and being aware of having an experience. The latter involves **self-awareness** or **self-consciousness** and our sense of knowledge of ourselves as individuals. The sources of our self-awareness have proved of interest to people of quite varied intellectual backgrounds, from social anthropologists to neuropsychologists, and we shall now examine some of their work on the origins of self-consciousness.

THE PHYLOGENY AND ONTOGENY OF SELF-RECOGNITION

In recent years many cherished notions about the uniqueness of man among other animals have become increasingly suspect. This is a consequence especially of our growing understanding of the abilities of the great apes, and in particular of our greater knowledge of the mentality of the chimpanzee.

It was originally speculated that man was the only **tool-user** or -fashioner and that this distinguished him from lower animals; we now know, however, that many animals apart from man make and use their own tools. Cooperative hunting, deemed by many to be a precursor of shared linguistic activity in men, is also done by male chimpanzees. Further, chimps not only have a rudimentary linguistic system of their own, they can also be taught more sophisticated human languages. These issues will be developed in Chapter 9 but for the moment it should be noted merely that tool use and fabrication, cooperative hunting and communication abilities are not necessarily uniquely human characteristics.

As an ultimate criterion of human uniqueness the ability to reflect on one's experiences – to be aware that one is experiencing rather than 'merely' experiencing – has been held out as the final bastion. In other words, although the behaviour of quite lowly animals often appears to stem from a complex, internal modelling of the environment rather than being merely a stereotypical response to it, and we might not therefore shy away from describing the animals' behaviour as resulting from some form of consciousness in the same way that we would for humans (Griffin, 1976), nevertheless, the argument might go, man is surely the only animal who is self-consciously aware and who can thus reflect on his own experiences. However, in a series of ingenious studies, Gallup (1977) has shown, at least in a preliminary way, that this is not, in fact, the case.

Gallup put chimps in front of a mirror and observed their reactions. Initially they made social responses to their reflection, treating the image as another animal of their species. After a few days' exposure to the mirror, however, the chimps began to change their responses and, rather than responding to the mirror as such, they began to *use* the image in the mirror in order to groom themselves. At this stage the animals were anaesthetized and a red-coloured dye was painted on parts of their faces. On recovering from the anaesthetic, and when confronted with the mirror, the chimps immediately began to touch the parts of their actual faces (i.e., not the image in the mirror) where the rouge had been applied. The fact that the chimps used the mirror for grooming and for examining their body suggests that they must have been aware that the image they saw in the mirror was of themselves. To the extent that self-recognition implies a rudimentary concept of self, man is therefore clearly not the only animal with self-awareness. However, the self concept as indicated by mirror self-recognition appears to be confined to the great apes since various monkeys, macaques, baboons and gibbons fail to demonstrate any indication of self-recognition. As Gallup has put it, 'Without an identity of your own it would be impossible to recognize yourself. And therein may lie the basic differences between monkeys and great apes. The monkey's inability to recognize himself may be due to the absence of a sufficiently well-integrated self concept.'

When does the awareness of self arise in children? There are several clues available from observations of the development of the child's use of language to refer to itself and to other people. Lewis and Brooks (1975) have examined one-year-old children's ability to name appropriately pictures of familiar individuals. Children learn the name of their father first, and some months later the name of their mother. With pictures of themselves they tend to say 'baby' (or, at least, something like it!). Children learn their own names at about two years old and begin using personal pronouns about six months later. By the age of three, nearly all toddlers can name pictures of themselves and use the appropriate pronouns in describing them.

This rather suggests that children find it easier to name (and thus conceptualize) people who are at some psychological distance from themselves. The father, usually less involved in the life of the child, is thus a clearer, more separate individual from the infant than is the mother who, because of her greater closeness, is far less easy for the young child to separate from itself. The ability to name oneself and talk about oneself comes rather late in relation to other names, presumably because it requires the child to be able to take a different perspective; i.e., figuratively, it requires the ability to see ourselves as others see us.

Purely linguistic analyses of self-consciousness are not entirely satisfactory, however, since the child may well be self-aware but this awareness may not be reflected in its use of language. In addition, therefore, developmental psychologists have also employed Gallup's technique by confronting children with a mirror after the discrete application of rouge to the face. At about one year old, babies do not touch the rouge but tend to search the mirror for the image as they would any new object. By two years old, however, between 63 per cent and 73 per cent of children touch the rouge on their own face and frequently display vanity in front of the mirror!

The linguistic data and the mirror-confrontation evidence both therefore suggest that self-awareness begins to emerge at around two years of age and it seems likely that during these first twenty-four months of life the child has to go through various cognitive stages in order for the self concept to arise. For example, since we know that very young children do not realize that objects are permanent features of the environment (when objects are covered, for example, the baby will show no signs of searching for them nor manifest distress at their disappearance and will behave as if the objects no longer exist), the development of the concept of object or people permanence seems an essential precursor for the development of the sense of self. Without it, a child could hardly think of itself as a distinct, lasting entity since it could not conceive of any object existing outside its immediate present.

Self-consciousness is not, however, something that happens in a preprogrammed way once certain stages of cognitive development have unwound. Rather the conception we have of ourselves depends upon social interaction: self-awareness can be achieved only by seeing oneself from differing points of view, namely those of other people. In this connection it is worth noting that chimpanzees reared in social isolation failed to recognize themselves in a mirror. The 'extent' and 'form' of our self-consciousness will thus depend upon the circumstances of our youth as much as it will upon an unfolding biology. (See Chapter 1, on the evolution of consciousness.)

SELF-RECOGNITION AND THE TWO HEMISPHERES OF THE BRAIN

The severing of the corpus callosum in man has led to numerous thought-provoking issues about brain-behaviour relationships but none more so than the question of the presence or otherwise of consciousness and self-consciousness in each of the two disconnected hemispheres. No one would doubt the consciousness and self-awareness of the left hemisphere: there is no question about it being a 'person'. All spoken language of the commissurotomized patient is initiated and executed by the left hemisphere and the patient talks freely about 'I', 'me', 'myself' and so on: there is thus nothing in casual conversation, at least, that could make anyone doubt the existence of an aware, self-conscious individual 'in' the left hemisphere. Although the right hemisphere, unlike the left, cannot initiate speech, it does possess an equally complex set of abilities, and in the same way that we might speak of an animal being conscious when it demonstrates behaviour which appears to be not merely an unvarying and mechanical response to a situation, so we may be equally confident that the right hemisphere is conscious.

Can the right hemisphere reflect on itself and so be termed self-conscious? Some recent work shows that this also appears to be the case. Sperry, Zaidel and Zaidel (1979) showed photographs of various persons exclusively to the right hemisphere of commissurotomized patients. Because the right hemisphere cannot speak, Sperry *et al.* asked the patients to give nonverbal gestures, thumbs up or down with the right-hemisphere-controlled left hand, to indicate approval or otherwise of the photographed people. To illustrate the patients' behaviour, and to indicate the kind of evidence which Sperry *et al.* believe indicates that the right hemisphere has a self-consciousness not unlike that of the left hemisphere, we cannot do better than quote directly their description of one of their patients, LB:

> Towards the end of this testing session, LB was presented with a choice array containing four portrait photos of adult males, three strangers and one of himself in the lower left position. When asked if he recognized any of these LB pointed promptly to the photo of himself. Asked for a thumb sign evaluation, he gave a decisive 'thumbs-down' response but unlike other 'thumbs-down' signals, this one was accompanied by a wide, sheepish and (to all appearances) self-conscious grin. When we then asked if he knew who it was, LB after only a short hesitation guessed correctly 'myself'. Interpretation: LB recognized himself readily with the right hemisphere. The tongue-in-cheek 'thumbs down' response to his own photo accompanied by a broad grin indicates not only self-recognition in the minor hemisphere but also a subtle sense of humor and self-conscious perspective befitting the total situation. The emotional effect was transferred centrally and also peripherally and was sufficiently distinctive, combined with other cues, that the left hemisphere soon guessed the correct identification.

It is difficult to escape the conclusion that the right hemisphere at least shows some characteristics of self-awareness. (The verbal, left-hemisphere response, even though the photograph was shown only to the right hemisphere, Sperry and his group attribute in part to relatively nonspecific signalling between the hemispheres via intact brainstem connections.)

SELF-AWARENESS OF OUR ABILITIES: METACOGNITION

The recognition of ourselves as unique, separate individuals appears to occur at a relatively early age in children, but a child's abilities to reflect upon other aspects of his developing skills come somewhat later. The ability to reflect upon the characteristics of our perceptual, attentional, mnemonic and other cognitive processes has been termed **metacognition** since it involves some superordinate ability to think about the nature of our cognitive processes rather than merely to use them.

As adults we are aware of the likely factors which might govern our cognition. Thus, even before reading the next chapter on memory the reader might be able to answer the following questions. How many unrelated words could you repeat back accurately after you had heard them spoken (in other words, what is your **immediate memory span**)? Would it be more difficult if you were required to repeat the words back in the reverse order? Would the number of words that you could repeat be affected if the words were of a similar sound, if they were of a similar meaning or if they formed a sentence? You will, doubtless, after some reflection, be able to give sensible answers to each of these questions (and others like them) since mature individuals can not only use their cognitive processes but they also have good insights into their characteristics.

Can young children show this kind of reflective behaviour? As far as the questions about memory are concerned (and, indeed, other aspects of cognition) it appears that they cannot. Take children's estimates of their immediate memory span, for example. As children get older their actual memory span increases from about three items correct at about age five, to about five or six items correct at age ten, but, if asked before doing the test about the likely size of their short-term memory five-year-olds grossly overestimate their span (they think they could get about seven items correct!) while ten-year-olds are quite accurate in their estimates. In other words, the five-year-old does 'have' a span (albeit rather small) but is not aware of his limitations; by ten years of age, however, reality and children's intuitions begin to coincide – they are aware of their limitations (Yussen and Levy, 1975).

Another example of this lack of reflective awareness comes from studies of visual search. Miller and Bigi (1977) gave seven- and eight-year-old children many pieces of coloured paper differing in colour, shape and size in addition to two 'target' red triangles. The youngsters were asked to make a game for others to play which involved finding the target triangles among other shapes; one game was to be easy (the targets were to be capable of being found quickly) and another was to be difficult. A little reflection, without the need for experiment, will tell us that the *more* items there are in the search game and the more *similar* the items to be searched are to the targets, the more difficult the task will be. Nearly 70 per cent of seven-year-olds and about 80 per cent of eight-year-olds realized (as indicated by the games that they devised) that the *number* of items in the search game would be important for search speed; i.e., the two age groups differed little in this respect. However, while over 60 per cent of eight-year-old children realized that item similarity would be an important determiner of search performance, only about 35 per cent of the seven-year-olds were aware of this. The relative unawareness of seven-year-olds of similarity as a factor in visual search means that in some situations they may not search very efficiently since they do not realize the determinants of effective looking. Thus, for example, in searching for a familiar face among a crowd of all-too-similar adults, the younger child may not direct his search to a salient, discriminating feature like hair colour, spectacles or whatever.

Cognitive and metacognitive development probably occur in a parallel and interacting way. On the one hand, the more our cognitive apparatus is used, the more knowledge we have to reflect upon; on the other hand, the more knowledge about ourselves that we acquire through thinking about our skills, the more it can direct our behaviour in realistic and appropriate ways.

Whether the great apes, or the right hemisphere of split-brain patients can show this kind of self-awareness is an open question.

Further reading

Introduction

There is a vast literature on the mind/body problem, but a good introduction, written from the point of view of a psychologist (and including useful suggestions for further reading) is:

FODOR, J.A. (1981) The mind-body problem. *Scientific American*, **244**, 124–32.

Also of value, especially the Introduction and Chapter 1, is:

JAYNES, J. (1976) *The Origin of Consciousness in the Breakdown of the Bicameral Mind*. London: Allen Lane.

The history and use of introspection as a technique is described in the following (see especially Chapter 2):

MILLER, G.A. (1962) *Psychology, the Science of Mental Life*. Harmondsworth: Penguin.

A latter-day variant of introspection is discussed by:

ERICSSON, K.A. and SIMON, H.A. (1980) Verbal reports as data. *Psychological Review*, **87**, 215–51.

Freud's descriptions of the relationship between the different types of conscious and unconscious processes are given in many of his works, but a good introduction is Chapter 1 of:

FREUD, S. (1935) *The Ego and the Id*. London: Hogarth Press.

The history and other conceptions of the unconscious can be found in:

WHYTE, L.L. (1967) *The Unconscious before Freud*. London: Associated Book Publishers.

Alertness and consciousness

The arousal theory of the effects of various stresses is discussed in detail in the following book (see especially Chapter 9):

BROADBENT, D.E. (1971) *Decision and Stress*. London: Academic Press.

The same author has also reviewed the effects of noise on behaviour:

BROADBENT, D.E. (1978) The current state of noise research: reply to Poulton. *Psychological Bulletin*, **85**, 417–29.

Various ideas about 'broad' and 'narrow' attention and their relation to psychopathology are well discussed in:

WACHTEL, P.L. (1967) Conceptions of broad and narrow attention. *Psychological Bulletin*, **68**, 417–29.

There are several excellent chapters on attention and schizophrenia in:

MAHER, B.A., ed. (1977) *Contributions to the Psychopathology of Schizophrenia*. London: Academic Press.

A detailed commentary on the evoked potential and the CNV is given by:

PICTON, T.W., CAMPBELL, K.B., BARIBOU-BRAUN, J. and PROUIX, G.B. (1978) The neurophysiology of human attention: a tutorial review. In J. Requin, ed., *Attention and Performance*, Volume VII. New York: LEA.

Speed accuracy factors in performance are discussed in the following (especially Chapters 4 and 5):

POSNER, M. (1978) *Chronometric Explorations of Mind*. New York: LEA.

The kinds of cognitive impairment that can occur after brain damage are given extensive clinical and experimental discussion in:

WALSH, K.W. (1978) *Neuropsychology*. London: Churchill Livingstone.

Another good source for clinical descriptions is:

HEILMAN, K.M. and VALENSTEIN, E. (1979) *Clinical Neuropsychology*. Oxford: Oxford University Press.

Focal attention: the capacity of consciousness

The development of attention is discussed in:

HALE, G.A. and LEWIS, M., eds. (1979) *Attention and Cognitive Development*. New York: Plenum.

Also worth examining is:

MACKWORTH, J.F. (1976) The development of attention. In V. Hamilton and M.D. Vernon, eds., *The Development of Cognitive Processes*. New York: Academic Press.

A book which gives a good description of notions of limited capacity (see especially Chapters 1, 2, 7, 8 and 9) is:

KAHNEMAN, D. (1973) *Attention and Effort*. Englewood Cliffs, NJ: Prentice-Hall.

Another good source (especially Chapters 1, 2 and 3) is:

PARASURAMAN, R. and DAVIES, D.R. eds. (1984) *Varieties of Attention*. London: Academic Press.

A relevant paper, focusing on some methodological issues, is:

DUNCAN, J. (1980) The demonstration of capacity limitation. *Cognitive Psychology*, **12**, 75–96.

A good source of material for studies of dual task performance is:

ALLPORT, D.A. (1980) Attention and performance. In G. Claxton, ed., *Cognitive Psychology: New Directions*. London: Routledge and Kegan Paul.
BROADBENT, D.E. (1982) Task combination and selective intake of information. *Acta Psychologica*, **50**, 253–90.

The earlier work is given in Kahneman, *op.cit*.

An excellent description of the functions of the frontal lobes is given in Walsh, *op. cit.*, especially Chapter 4.

There is a lucid account (see especially Chapter 11) of the executive and monitoring functions of consciousness that are summarized in this section in:

HILGARD, E.R. (1977) *Divided Consciousness: Multiple Controls in Human Thought and Action*. New York: Wiley.

The summary in this section is also related to:

SHALLICE, T. (1972) Dual functions of consciousness. *Psychological Review*, **79**, 383–93.

For dual task studies seen from a neuropsychological perspective see:

KINSBOURNE, M. and HISCOCK, M. (1983) Asymmetries of dual task performance. In J.B. Hellige, ed., *Cerebral Hemisphere Asymmetries*. New York: Praeger Press.

Efficient processing without focal attention

Posner, *op. cit.* (especially Chapter 4) is a primary source for views on automatic processing. A good review of the effects of practice on skills of divided attention is in the following book (especially Chapter 5):

NEISSER, U. (1976) *Cognition and Reality*. San Francisco: Freeman.

A stimulating discussion of the cognitive psychology of practice with special reference to ageing is:

RABBITT, P. (1980) Cognitive psychology needs models for changes in performance with old age. In A.D. Baddeley and J. Long, eds., *Attention and Performance*, Volume IX. New York: LEA.

The literature on the shadowing paradigm is extensive, but a reasonable source (especially Chapters 4 and 5) is:

UNDERWOOD, G. (1976) *Attention and Memory*. Oxford: Pergamon.

The best source of reference for research into processing without awareness, a methodologically problematic area, is:

DIXON, N.F. and HENLE, S.H.A. (1980) Without awareness. In M. Jeeves, ed., *Psychological Survey 2*. London: Allen and Unwin.

Also relevant is:

CARR, T.H. and BACHARACH, V.R. (1976) Perceptual tuning and conscious attention: systems of input regulation in visual information processing. *Cognition*, **4**, 281–302.

A prime source for recent work on slips of attention is:

REASON, J. and MYCIELSKA, K. (1982) *Absent-Minded Errors*. Englewood Cliffs, NJ: Prentice-Hall.

Consciousness and self-consciousness

Epstein, Lanza and Skinner, in the article mentioned below, have shown that with appropriate training pigeons can be made to peck at mirror-reflected marks on their own bodies. This implies three possibilities: (a) self-awareness must be attributed to quite lowly animals, or (b), since we might not wish to ascribe self-consciousness to birds, we must not, as the authors actually argue, attribute it to man either, or, and perhaps most likely, (c) pigeons and infants show similar mirror behaviour under appropriate conditions for quite different reasons. This debate will doubtless continue, as a similar one has in the area of nonhuman language usage (see Chapter 9 above):

EPSTEIN, R., LANZA, R.P. and SKINNER, B.F. (1981) Self-awareness in the pigeon. *Science*, **212**, 695–6.

An excellent source for the development of self-recognition is:

LEWIS, M. and BROOKS-GUNN, J. (1979) *Social Cognition and the Acquisition of Self*. New York: Plenum.

The following book gives an idiosyncratic account of the split-brain studies and their contribution to our understanding of conscious and self-conscious processes, but Eccles does also present alternative views and he gives extensive references for further reading (see especially Chapters 1 and 2):

ECCLES, J.C. (1980) *The Human Psyche*. Berlin: Springer-Verlag.

Metacognition is discussed in detail in:

FLAVELL, J.H. (1977) *Cognitive Development*. Englewood Cliffs, NJ: Prentice-Hall.

The development of metamemory is considered in detail in:

FLAVELL, J.H. and WELLMAN, H.M. (1976) Metamemory. In R.V. Kail and J.W. Hagan, eds., *Perspectives on the Development of Memory and Cognition*. Hillsdale, NJ: LEA.

The development of various types of conscious awareness is discussed in:

LUNZER, E.A. (1979) The development of consciousness. In Underwood and Stevens, *op. cit.*

General

The history of the role played by consciousness in experimental psychology is traced in:

HILGARD, E.R. (1980) Consciousness in contemporary psychology. *Annual Review of Psychology*, **31**, 1–26.

There are several useful chapters in:

POPE, K.S. and SINGER, S.L., eds. (1978) *The Stream of Consciousness*. New York: Plenum.

A book which covers exactly what its title suggests is:

CROOKS, J.H. (1980) *The Evolution of Human Consciousness*. Oxford: Clarendon Press.

Stimulating discussions can be found in:

HUMPHREY, N. (1983) *Consciousness Regained: Chapters in the Development of Mind*. Oxford: Oxford University Press.

5. The Varieties of Learning and Memory: Their Simpler Forms

5. The Varieties of Learning and Memory: Their Simpler Forms

Introduction

Learning and memory lie at the centre of the web of psychological processes. Without them perception, speech and thinking could not occur, and conversely these activities determine the fabric of memory. We infer that a memory has been acquired whenever experience gives rise to relatively lasting changes in behaviour. Learning is linked to remembering because it is the process whereby experience modifies behaviour. Its effects are apparent when memories are retrieved. Even so, memories are normally 'behaviourally silent', only influencing behaviour when they are retrieved. The range of memory phenomena is great; including such complex capacities as the retention of detailed knowledge about language and the world (**semantic memory**) and about our personal histories (**episodic memory**), as well as much simpler capacities found even in primitive animals, such as learning to ignore unimportant events which are repeated (**habituation**).

There is no clear dividing line between the acquisition of memory and other causes of behavioural change. For example, **perceptual aftereffects** (see Chapter 3) may persist for some time but are not usually regarded as involving a form of memory. This view depends on the largely unsupported claim that aftereffects depend on radically different processes from genuine memories. Even brain damage, which no one regards as a form of learning, may alter subsequent behaviour because the damage causes a reorganization of nervous connections. For example, damage to one side of the midbrain in newborn hamsters leads to an abnormal growth of connections between nerve cells with the result that these animals look away from, rather than towards, suddenly presented visual stimuli (Schneider, 1979). Such neural changes may interestingly resemble the changes underlying the function of memories.

It has also been suggested that the changes in the brain which lead to the development of epilepsy may be similar to those which underlie some kinds of memory (see Goddard and Douglas, 1975). The uncontrolled spasms of neural activity which constitute epilepsy can be triggered by daily electrical stimulation of sites within the temporal lobe of rats. In this process, known as kindling, the rats become gradually more susceptible to convulsions until they occur spontaneously. The **sensitization**, which is long-lasting, depends on microscopic changes in the hippocampus and amygdala, two temporal lobe structures believed to be important in complex human memory. Furthermore, these structures become more sensitive to the neurotransmitter acetylcholine as a result of kindling. Sensitivity to this substance has also been related to memory in animals and humans. Thus, although the development of epilepsy cannot be regarded as a form of learning, the changes which mediate it may interestingly resemble, and therefore model, the changes which underlie memory formation.

Although this chapter focuses on simple learning processes, and the next one on complex learning processes, this is a division of convenience and may obscure certain points. First, even though there are different specific issues which arise in the study of simple and complex learning, there are nevertheless general problems which apply to all kinds of learning and memory. These are discussed in the next section. Second, the processes of simple and complex learning interact although we remain largely ignorant of the nature of this interaction. Third, the general picture of the learner, based on simple learning tasks, has influenced our thinking about what occurs when complex information is acquired. More recently, theoretical ideas derived from studying complex human learning have been applied to simple learning tasks (see Dickinson, 1980).

The third point warrants expansion. In the middle years of the century, the prevalent view of the learner, associated with famous names such as those of Thorndike, Watson and Hull, was that of an **automaton** – a being driven by automatic links between stimuli and responses. These links were either present at birth through the offices of heredity, or were acquired later as habits, which were

stamped in inflexibly through the satisfaction of biological needs. This picture was supposed to apply not only to the simpler kinds of animal learning from which it was originally drawn, but also to the activities of the complex human learner. The influence of this automaton metaphor has waned (but is not yet dead) and a **cognitive view** of the learner has waxed in popularity. According to this view, the learner produces a **representation** of the world in his brain and this representation is modified by experience. This formulation proposes that learning leads to the creation of a representation of reality which can be expressed in behaviour more flexibly than the automaton view implies. Although it is generally agreed that some version of the cognitive view must apply to complex learning, it is more polemical to what extent the view can be applied to simpler forms of learning (see Dickinson, 1980). The major challenge is to make the cognitive view sufficiently explicit so as to be able to identify those varieties of animal and human memory where sophisticated representations are involved.

The main issues in memory research

In the century since Ebbinghaus initiated the modern era of experimental research into memory, many psychologists have been exercised by the question of how many kinds of memory there are. It is perhaps more useful to determine how similar different kinds of memory are in terms of the answers to four basic questions. First, what information is **registered** by the brain and what processes are necessary for this registration to occur? Second, how does the brain **store** the acquired information? Third, what changes in the brain occur over time which are responsible for **forgetting**? Fourth, how is the information, previously latent, made manifest in the process of retrieval?

These four general questions are implicit within the framework provided by the hallowed division of memory into the stages of registration, storage and retrieval. This trichotomy was indeed discussed by the Greeks, which indicates how little our conception of memory has changed in 2000 years. Thus, Plato likened memory to the storage of impressions in wax, and also to keeping birds in an aviary, and later Aristotle combined these images by comparing memory to a library in which representations like wax tablets were kept according to an organized plan necessary in such a large storehouse (see Marshall and Fryer, 1978, for a history of thinking about memory models). The library metaphor can be used to elucidate the traditional division of memory. What is registered in memory corresponds to the contents of a book, its initial entry into the library and the manner of its indexing. Storage and forgetting correspond to what happens to a book once it has been entered into the library. It may be vandalized or stolen, or remain intact in its assigned position. When a reader wants to find a particular book, a random search would probably fail so he is likely to institute an ordered search using the index. The metaphor makes clear the vital point that forgetting (i.e., unsuccessful retrieval) may occur for two main reasons. Either a book (or a memory) is in the library store but cannot be found (it is inaccessible but available) or it is no longer in the store although it was once (it is unavailable). Everyone has experienced the first kind of forgetting, which is signalled by the unprompted remembering of a previously lost memory.

The classical memory models contain two noticeable features. First, they implicitly depend on a cognitive view of the learner, so that some may challenge their application to the simpler and apparently more 'automatic' kinds of learning seen in primitive animals. Even if cognitive models are inappropriate to these kinds of simple learning, however, they still require the processes of registration, storage and retrieval, and suffer forgetting. Second, the wax tablet and library are metaphors for what happens in the brain, about which we knew very little until the twentieth century (which is why our thinking advanced little in two millennia). This ignorance is illustrated by the difficulty in deciding whether forgetting is caused by memory becoming lost within the store or through its being completely erased from the store. Although some forgotten memories may be recovered spontaneously, many never are, so to determine this issue it is necessary to know whether the changes in brain organization, which underlie storage, have decayed away, been modified, or remained unaltered. Without such physiological knowledge it is not only hard to distinguish effects of storage from effects of retrieval, but also the effects of registration from those of storage (see Watkins, 1978). Fortunately, the brain processes underlying memory are beginning to be disentangled.

When learning takes place memory is only formed if certain physiological changes occur in the brain. These so-called **consolidation processes** can be considered at two levels, the **microscopic** and the **macroscopic**. The microscopic changes involve activities within neurons and between them, probably at the synaptic junctions. If successful learning causes 'rewiring' of the brain we should ultimately be able to detect changes within and between neurons. Many believe, for example, that learning initiates a sequence of processes which causes proteins to be manufactured and transmitted to synapses where they produce long-lasting structural and functional alterations (see Mayes, 1981, for a discussion). Furthermore, as these processes may take some time to complete, memory must be mediated in the interim by a separate short-term storage system which rapidly comes into play at the start of learning. In primitive invertebrates, such as the sea snail Aplysia, it is already becoming possible to identify the neurons and neuronal changes that underlie the form of memory known as habituation. The gradual loss of habituation may be associated with the slow reversal of these critical physiological changes (Kandel, 1976). When these changes become precisely measurable it will be possible to decide whether particular forms of forgetting are caused by storage loss or by loss within the memory store.

The macroscopic brain changes which underlie memory are far more difficult to identify. First, it must be shown which brain regions suffer microscopic changes specifically related to the kind of memory in question. For example, knowledge of language appears to involve changes in the cerebral cortex whereas other, simpler kinds of memory, such as that for habituation, can be mediated by changes at the level of the spinal cord. How small a volume of brain tissue may be necessary for various forms of memory storage is still a matter of great controversy. Even if the tissue mediating storage can be identified, a second and far harder issue must be resolved. *How is the stored information, produced by the brain changes, represented?* An awareness of this issue is apparent in the writings of the British empiricist philosophers for whom ideas (sensory and other memories) were pale copies of impressions (perceptions). Their view has a modern echo. Memories are probably stored in regions where the relevant information is processed, so to understand how complex information is represented in storage we need

BOX 5.1
The forms of representations. Are images different kinds of representations from descriptions?

Although people feel they know what is meant by some memories involving representations of the world, or representations of rules, they may be deceiving themselves. No doubt the view of the learner of complex material as an automaton is wrong, but what exactly are the properties of the representations of knowledge constructed by the brain? Models of the world tend to be regarded as pictures in the head. The rememberer is felt to have a kind of internal TV screen which can show scenes now past. The trouble is that the picture has to be interpreted. This cannot be done by having a picture created in another part of the brain – a suggestion that leads to an infinite regress. The picture imaged in memory has to be interpreted by the brain, and this means that the information present in it has to be represented in a different way by the brain.

It is the form of such representations which is nebulous, as is the manner in which they are encoded and later decoded so that memory can be expressed in appropriate behaviour. This uncertainty is illustrated in the current controversy about whether remembered mental images of things in the world involve different kinds of representations from remembered verbal descriptions of outside reality. Those who believe that imaging and remembering in words both involve the same kind of abstract descriptive representations (descriptionalists) are not denying that mental images occur. Although there is great individual variability in the intensity and manipulability of visual images, they certainly occur. Indeed, it is known they are generated preferentially by the right hemisphere whereas the left hemisphere is more concerned with remembering in words (see Paivio and Linde, 1982). Nor do most descriptionalists want to say that images are epiphenomena, i.e., mental smoke thrown off by the operation of the brain, but themselves doing no cognitive work.

More plausibly, it might be thought that descriptionalists are denying that visual images involve similar representations to visual perception. But many do not deny this as there is evidence that imaging is similar to visual perception. Perky (1910) found that people confuse imaging with perceiving. More recently, Finke and Schmidt (1978) have shown that the negative visual aftereffect, known as the McCollough effect, can also be produced by imagining horizontal and vertical black stripes in the target figures. It has also been found that subjects are more sensitive to imagined vertical lines than oblique ones, just as is found when such lines are seen in the real world (see Kosslyn, 1981). Finally, a woman who could voluntarily produce intense visual hallucinations showed suppression of the electrophysiological response of her visual cortex when she looked at a moving checker pattern (Schatzman, 1980). These findings suggest that perception and imaging use similar brain systems and

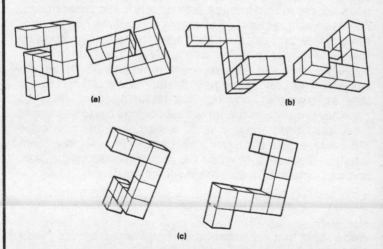

(a)

(b)

(c)

Fig. 5.1 Pairs of patterns used for shape comparisons. (a) A 'same' pair that differs by an 80° rotation in the picture plane; (b) a 'same' pair that differs by an 80° rotation in depth; (c) a 'different' pair that cannot be matched by any rotation (see Shepard and Metzler, 1971).

may be subjectively similar. It therefore seems likely that they involve similar kinds of representation. Hence, a descriptionalist has to argue that both our perceptions and our images involve the same kind of representational code as our verbally coded memories.

Although in none of the three cases can reality be represented as an uninterpreted picture, it is still possible that imagery uses a code radically different from that used by verbal memory. Imagery may somehow map more directly on to the things it represents. For example, Shepard and Metzler (1971) asked subjects to decide whether or not two perspective drawings were identical, and found that time to respond accurately increased as a function of how much the figures needed to be rotated so as to correspond (see Figure 5.1). A similar relationship would have been expected if subjects had made judgements about real three-dimensional objects by rotating them. There was then a similarity between the manipulability of real and imagined objects. This does not prove that images are not coded like descriptions, however, as it is possible to create a set of descriptions for real objects, and rules for their transformation, which yield the same results (see Anderson, 1978). The issue is therefore still unresolved, as is apparent from Block (1981). Selective effects of brain damage indicate that we can accurately 'see' a cup without knowing what it is for, and conversely we can know what cups are for without being able to see them. Descriptionalists argue that these two sorts of knowledge are represented by the same code. We will only learn whether they are right when we know more about the brain and can simulate its activities with computers.

to know how that information is represented by the brain in perception and thinking.

The processes of retrieval are likely to depend intimately on how information is represented by the brain. It is clear that retrieval of complex memories in humans must be highly organized as it occurs so quickly. Our ability to retrieve specific items rapidly from our vast store of knowledge is indeed remarkable. Unfortunately, the detailed mechanisms of this ability are not open to introspection as retrieval processes are essentially unconscious. Indeed, we often retrieve certain kinds of memory when attending to something else. This is illustrated when we perform an overlearnt motor skill, such as driving, while talking to someone. Even so, most researchers believe that with complex human memory, retrieval can be divided into a fallible **search process**, which is helped by cues related to the object search, and a usually less fallible **identification** or **discrimination process**, which underlies **recognition**. Everyone is familiar with the experience of failing to recall a person's name but immediately recognizing it when it is mentioned by someone else.

In Chapter 2, it was suggested that the brain comprises many relatively independent functional subsystems or modules, each of which processes certain kinds of information in characteristic ways. These processing operations correspond to the registration of particular kinds of information, which it seems likely are stored in the modules responsible for processing them. Retrieval and forgetting are also likely to reflect the particular module's manner of operation. If two modular units are formed from similarly organized brain tissue then it seems likely that the memory systems they serve are also similar, whereas units based on differentially organized brain tissue are likely to serve memory systems more radically distinct in terms of the principles of registration, storage (at micro- and macroscopic levels), retrieval and forgetting. For example, the memory systems for language and motor skills may be very different as verbal behaviour is primarily controlled by the neocortex whereas motor skills depend greatly on activity in the cerebellum, and these structures are organized in different ways. In contrast, the memory systems for imagery and words are probably much more similar. Although visual imagery seems to be primarily controlled by the posterior regions of the right neocortex (see Paivio and Linde, 1982) and language by the left neocortex, the organization of these regions is very similar. Indeed, it has been argued that whether we remember a scene in visual images or in words, what we store is the same kind of thing, namely **propositions** or **meanings**. The left hemisphere decodes these stored meanings into verbal descriptions and the right hemisphere decodes them into visual images (see Anderson, 1978, and Box 5.1 above for a discussion of this issue).

It has been shown that elucidation of the principles of registration, storage, retrieval and forgetting depends critically on our knowledge of brain processes. It also requires a precise description of the factors which affect the different forms of memory. This has been the main concern of psychologists studying memory. In the future our understanding will no doubt be greatly enhanced by the approaches of artificial intelligence. These offer a means of rigorously testing complex memory models by computer simulation. They also provide an alternative source of ideas about such vexed matters as how retrieval can be organized so as to find items (which can be described in so many ways) rapidly in our vast memory stores.

Evolution and the forms of memory

In evolution, natural selection leads to the emergence of individuals and species sufficiently well adapted to their environments that their chances of surviving and reproducing are good. Appropriate behaviours constitute an important subset of the adaptations a species must show. In an environment which is relatively invariant over time, these behaviours can be transmitted from one generation to the next under the direct control of genes. These innate or instinctive behaviours will emerge at some stage in development, under a wide range of environmental conditions, provided that the individual possesses the relevant genes. In other words, the behaviour's appearance is relatively insensitive to the conditions prevalent during upbringing. Even so, the degree of insensitivity has its limits. For example, neonatal rats need tactile stimulation of the genital region if they are to initiate their bladder-emptying reflex. Without this trigger the genetic programme does not switch on the reflex (Manning, 1967).

Ethologists, studying animal behaviour under natural conditions, have highlighted the importance of instinctive or unlearnt behaviours. Their work has shown that rigid, stereotyped behavioural sequences are initiated by **innate releasing mechanisms** when specific features of stimuli are perceived. For example, in the breeding season male sticklebacks will attack rival males on the edge of their territory, in a stereotyped fashion. This behaviour is elicited equally well by appropriately positioned but crude models, provided these have a red underbelly (Tinbergen, 1969). These instinctive behaviours emerge even when there is no possibility of specific learning experiences. Nevertheless, experience can modify and refine instinctive behaviours. For example, although cuttlefish without experience will attack and eat shrimps, the latency to launch such an attack reduces considerably with age (Wells, 1958). Similarly, the accuracy with which a newly hatched laughing-gull chick pecks at its parent's red beak to elicit regurgitated food improves with time, partly as a result of learning. One-week-old chicks have also learned to distinguish the shape of their parents' beaks so that they peck selectively at these (Hailman, 1969).

Although instinctive behaviours which are the direct expression of certain genes may be useful adaptations in constant and predictable environments, they rapidly become maladaptive when the environment changes. When this happens the species will become extinct unless its genetic make-up changes fast enough. Some species, like the shellfish Lingula, have avoided this problem by living in the same, unchanging niche for up to 600 million years. Other species, living in more changeable environments, have adapted by developing the ability to learn new behaviours. What can be learnt is still under genetic control although the range of behaviours, which can be acquired, is enormously increased. Oakley (1983) has recently suggested a classification system for these forms of learning and memory. First, he identifies behaviours for which the developmental programme is only open for a limited period of time. If, during this period, the environment experienced is of one kind then the animal will develop certain behaviours. Beyond this **critical period** for learning the animal will have great difficulty in reversing the consequences of that learning. For example, neurons in the visual cortex of cats become preferentially sensitive to bars which are oriented either horizontally or vertically, depending on whether the cats were brought up, during the critical period for their visual development, in environments with stimuli predominantly oriented horizontally or vertically. The cats, brought up in these selective environments, are visually insensitive to the stimuli oriented in ways which they have not previously experienced (Blakemore and Cooper, 1970). Later selective experience does not have these effects nor can it reverse the effects of early experience.

Oakley calls these kinds of early learning **variable epigenesis**, as experience can only influence future behaviour in a limited number of directions and the effects, which tend to be irreversible, are only achievable during a brief period. This kind of learning system is most useful when environmental variability is limited, and when changes occur they tend to be long-lasting. But many species live in ecological niches where things like the source of food vary on a day-to-day basis. These species must have both **flexible** and **lifelong learning systems**. The range of behaviours which can be acquired or dispensed with by this second kind of learning system is very much greater. Oakley points out, however, that even these learning systems are not entirely generalized in terms of what they can readily learn. They are specialized to register and store those kinds of information, which previously have been of particular advantage to the species. There are, then, constraints on what a species can learn to do. Nevertheless, this kind of learning is lifelong, covers a wide range of behaviours and is reversible.

Psychologists have been mainly interested in these lifelong learning capacities of which there are probably several kinds. The number and their classification remains polemical, but Oakley proposes a scheme which distinguishes broadly between **event**, **reference** and **working memory systems**. In his view, working memory systems retain certain kinds of information for brief periods in order to support the performance of some current task. They have been postulated particularly for verbal materials in the context of speech production and verbal comprehension, as will be discussed in the next chapter. Event memory is seen as a simple kind of system which keeps a record of sensory or motor events. Oakley cites as examples the ability of humans to remember simple visual events and the ability of many species to remember the taste and odour of foods. Reference memory involves longer-term storage and more elaborate kinds of information. He subdivides it into **association memory**, **representational memory** and **abstract memory**. Association memory is concerned with the detection and storage of likely causal relationships between sensory and motor events. It includes classical and instrumental conditioning which are discussed later in this chapter. It may also include habituation, in which an animal learns that an event does not predict reliably any other event of significance. Oakley also suggests that aspects of skilled performance may involve association memory. More complex multi-event storage systems are referred to as representational memory. They enable the animal to create spatiotemporal models of the physical and social environments, and in humans the power of this modelling is enhanced by the use of language. Human memory for life episodes (**episodic memory**) is an example of representational memory. Oakley's final system – abstract memory – is concerned with the extraction and storage of rules, particularly those which can be derived from representational systems. Unlike representational memory, abstract memories are not tied to particular spatial and temporal contexts. For example, our understanding of the concept 'quantity' has been abstracted from many experiences of its use and is context-free.

Oakley points out that both lifelong and early learning may be acquired by the individual in a social or nonsocial context. If the context is social then the individual may directly acquire the knowledge that others have already attained rather than solve the necessary problems in isolation, i.e., the learning is culturally transferred. Many species show cultural learning through their evolved ability to learn by observation and imitation. For example, when a female monkey in a group of Japanese monkeys picked up the knack of removing sand from sweet potatoes by washing them in the sea, the habit was soon acquired by the rest of the colony (Miyadi, 1964). Special kinds of learning ability may emerge in evolution to facilitate cultural transmission of this kind. In this respect, recognition of individual members of one's species might be very useful (so face recognition should be very good in species that culturally transmit knowledge), but undoubtedly the supreme cultural adaptation is the appearance of human language (see Passingham, 1982). This allows us to teach the young far more than they could ever learn otherwise and it also allows us to store knowledge in facilities such as libraries rather than in our brains.

If Oakley is right and event memory, the varieties of reference memory, and working memory are distinct forms of memory, then they should depend on distinct modular brain systems which should have evolved separately. As more complex systems evolved, animals were endowed with more flexible strategies for coping with their environments. This view suggests that the evolution of learning is a progressive affair in which originally simple 'learning adaptations' to kinds of environmental change, common to many species, have built upon them more complex memory systems, allowing subtler responses to environmental variability. An adaptation will appear in a distant ancestor and then be transmitted, albeit in modified forms, to its diversifying lineage. It is apparent, however, that even animals with simple brains may show sophisticated learning adaptations if they occupy an ecological niche which demands these. For example, goby fish usually live between the low and high tide marks. When disturbed in a rock pool after the tide has gone out, they can accurately leap from pool to pool back to the sea. Experiments have shown that twelve hours of 'high tide' in an artificial situation are sufficient for the fish to learn the pools' locations. This striking ability seems to involve a kind of representational memory, which many believe to be limited to 'advanced' animals like mammals. It is therefore even more impressive that invertebrates, with very small brains, such as many wasp and bee species, show a similar ability to learn about the spatial relations between food and their nests (see Tinbergen, 1969).

These remarkable special-learning adaptations suggest another way in which apparently universal learning abilities, such as conditionability, may have evolved. This is **convergent evolution**, in which properties emerge independently, at different times in different species facing similar environmental pressures. It contrasts with the situation in which a property emerges only once in an ancestral form. Even though flatworms, bees, sharks and humans can all learn that sensory events, which they cannot control, are associated (i.e., they show classical conditioning), the ability may have evolved separately in each case so that its detailed characteristics and nervous mechanisms may also differ. This view implies that the modular brain systems controlling a particular memory system evolved separately, employ distinct neural processes, and hence achieve the same memory ability in radically different ways. The alternative is that the memory system can be mediated by the same kinds of simple neural processes in all species in which it is present, but that advanced species may have acquired further adaptations which make behavioural control more flexible – adaptations which depend on more complex neural structures.

In the 1960s, Bitterman (1965) conducted a series of studies which seemed to support the second alternative. He tried to relate ability at difficult learning tasks to the degree of development of the neocortex in mammals, birds, reptiles, amphibia and fish. One task he used was **probability learning**, in which one alternative is randomly rewarded 70 per cent of the time and the other alternative is rewarded on the remaining 30 per cent of the trials. Monkeys and rats learn to select the most rewarded alternative on nearly all trials. In contrast, fish and turtles match, i.e., without ordering their responses, they choose each alternative at a level corresponding to its frequency of reward. Similarly, when an animal is presented with a long series of problems in which it must learn which of two stimuli is associated with reward, early research suggested that only higher animals such as monkeys developed **learning sets**, i.e., they learnt to solve each problem in one or two trials, perhaps by using a rule such as 'win-stay, lose-shift'. A related type of task involves **reversal learning sets** in which at first A is rewarded and not B, and then B is rewarded and not A, and so on in a continuous cycle. Bitterman found that mammals, like rats, became very fast at learning the later stages of this task, whereas fish such as goldfish were just as slow to learn after 150 reversals. He also found that removing most of a rat's neocortex made it behave as poorly as a fish.

Bitterman's conclusions about the relationship between neocortical development and the learning abilities he measured are no longer viewed with much confidence. First, these abilities seem to depend much less on species' differences than they do on procedural factors such as whether stimuli are two- or three-dimensional, and the amount and type of reward used. Second, subsequent studies have shown that birds and reptiles, which lack a neocortex, can develop reversal learning sets. Some fish also have this ability, and much more dramatically, so has the invertebrate woodlouse, whose brain is organized in a manner radically different from that of the vertebrates (see Oakley, 1978). It seems probable that abilities such as forming learning sets may have emerged independently in the course of evolution and that the likelihood of their being displayed will depend on the evocation of appropriate sensory and motivational conditions. For example, some of the learning abilities, served in mammals by the neocortex, may, in birds, be mediated by the independently evolved and differently structured hyperstriatum.

Even so, recently evolved structures, such as neocortex and hyperstriatum, with their intricate organizations, probably do mediate forms of learning and memory too complex for simpler neural structures. It is difficult to determine this because in each species, performance on a given learning task interacts with a unique combination of sensory, motivational and motor factors. It is clear, however, that those forms of representational and abstract memory which are expressed through language critically depend on the neocortex. The neocortex may also mediate **cross-modal integration**, which may be a necessary precursor of human language. Cross-modal integration is displayed when objects are recognized as being the same when experienced through different senses. For example, monkeys fed in the dark on lab. chow, the geometric form of which indicated whether it tasted pleasant or foul, were subsequently able to pick out the tasty chow by sight alone, thus revealing shape matching between sight and touch (Cowey and Weiskrantz, 1975). This ability probably depends on those neocortical regions where information from the different senses converges. In contrast to mammals, reptiles, which lack a neocortex, show relative isolation of the senses from each other.

The neocortex seems to be involved in the creation of complex representations of the environment, the manipulation of these representations and the abstraction of rules from them. In other words, it controls complex thought and stores the products of such thought. The **insightful learning** of Köhler's (1925) chimpanzees provides a clear example of complex thought and memory for its products. In one of Köhler's tasks, the chimpanzees had to reach a piece of fruit. To do this they were given a short stick with which to pull in a longer one, which was at the far side of some bars. The longer stick was necessary to reach a piece of fruit. The solution came to some animals in one go after a period of experimental activity and appraisal of the situation, rather than as a result of semi-random trial-and-error activity. This insight learning suggests that the animals could represent and manipulate a representation of the spatial environment in their heads so as to extract appropriate rules of conduct. They retained the rules and could apply them in new situations. A similar ability was shown recently by another chimpanzee, Sarah, who was able to learn the mathematical concept of proportionality in one context and then apply it in a new one (see Passingham, 1982). In Oakley's terms these animals are showing representational and abstract memory as well as skill at manipulating their representations. Their abilities reveal the intimate link between thinking and complex memory.

Learning and memory may be described as falling on a dimension which runs from simple, automatic processes to complex, cognitive (i.e., representational) ones. The former are viewed as inflexible links between stimuli and responses, which are stamped in automatically through the satisfaction of biological needs. In the course of evolution more complex kinds of learning and memory have been added to the more ancient, simple forms. This was achieved by the creation of new brain systems. According to the great Victorian neurologist Hughlings Jackson (1932), there is a **hierarchy of levels of control** in the brain. For example, with movement control the lowest level of integration is provided by spinal cord reflexes, these isolated components are orchestrated into coherent postural or locomotor movements by brainstem mechanisms, and finally the forebrain offers a range of controls which integrate the behaviours into a wider context. Although the lower levels retain some autonomy, the higher levels of the hierarchy normally coordinate the target behaviours and allow control to be much more flexible. Applied to learning, Jackson's view suggests that specific adaptations may be achieved by both primitive and sophisticated brain systems, but that the latter will normally modulate the former. His view contrasts with the unsupported **encephalization theory** which postulates that functions such as learning are transferred from older to newer brain regions in the course of evolution.

The remainder of this chapter considers some of the simpler forms of memory proposed by Oakley, and their physiological basis. To summarize this section: there seem to be many kinds of learning and memory, controlled by different brain systems. Many believe that certain forms of memory arose independently in different animal groups, but if this is so, their brain mechanisms and detailed features are unlikely to be identical. For example, reversal learning sets in the woodlouse are not mediated by the neocortex although they probably are in mammals. Complex learning abilities have also been added to simpler ones, modulating their expression and giving greater flexibility in the face of environmental change. Finally, there is a dimension, applicable to learning and memory, ranging from automatic processes to complex, representational (or cognitive) ones. The extent to which relatively simple forms of learning, such as conditioning, are representational is a matter of controversy.

Early learning

FORMS OF EARLY LEARNING

Experiential influences on development vary along three major dimensions. The influences vary in terms of their apparent **specificity**, they vary in the degree to which they only operate during a critical period of development, and they vary in the extent to which they are **reversible**. The first dimension is illustrated by studies which compare the effects of various kinds of **deprivation** with those of a normal upbringing in order to determine which aspects of early experience promote normal development. Thus, puppies raised under socially isolated conditions are very poor as adults at problem-solving, behave oddly in novel situations and show little response to painful stimuli (Scott, 1958). The implication is that early social experience provides a backcloth against which a wide variety of behaviours can emerge – the effects seem to be nonspecific. A possible mechanism for this kind of general effect of experience is revealed in comparisons of rats brought up in **enriched** or **impoverished environments** (which vary with respect to sensory as well as social stimulation). Enriched environment rats have heavier and thicker cortices, and, in particular, those regions responsible for vision contain neurons which are richer in chemicals such as proteins and form more synaptic connections (Rosenzweig and Bennett, 1976). The improved learning skills shown by these rats, and the skills of Scott's normally reared dogs may, in part, be results of their greater neural resources, which arise from the nonspecific stimulatory effect of experience.

Such apparently nonspecific effects of experience are legion. For example, early handling and even aversive experiences in many species make them less fearful in later life (Levine, 1960). Early visual experience is essential for normal visual development – total light deprivation causes severe problems although not blindness. In humans, activities in preschool years seem vital for the later achievement of initiative (as opposed to learned helplessness), trust, compassion and curiosity. Our feeling that these effects are results of the general stimulation of early experiences may, however, be more a reflection of ignorance than of reality. The effects of many individual cases of specific learning may be mistaken for a homogeneous stimulating effect. We have already described how upbringing in a specific visual environment leads kittens to develop specific sensitivities to lines or bars in previously experienced orientations. Early visual experience involves many similar kinds of specific sensitizations, which, acting together, may give the impression of being a nonspecific phenomenon.

Rats, given unpleasant treatments when about thirty days old, instead of becoming placid adults, actually develop a whole range of fears. Between twenty and thirty days of age there is an intermediate stage during which such treatments paradoxically lead to less general fear but more specific fears. There seems to be a critical period beyond which experience is either ineffective or has different effects. Similarly, many types of visual sensitization must take place early or they will never occur. In humans who do not have a squint treated before they are aged seven or eight, the previously lazy eye remains partially blind even though the muscular fault has been corrected. The deficiency lies in the brain and cannot be compensated by later experiences. Although early experiences are sometimes necessary for maintaining functions present at birth, they also stimulate other specific abilities which develop later.

Recent evidence suggests that the critical period **plasticity** of cortical neurons in the visual system depends on their being bathed by the neurotransmitter noradrenaline (Pettigrew, 1978). Noradrenaline seems to increase the ability of neurons to tell signals from background noise, and is mainly manufactured by a small cluster of bluish neurons, called the locus coeruleus, which lies in the brainstem. This nonspecific system influences much of the cortex and may play a special role in early learning effects, which are irreversible. Another kind of irreversible effect is seen in lambs, isolated from their natural mothers and raised by humans. These never fully reintegrate with the flock. The critical period varies across different behaviours and species, as does the reversibility of behaviours acquired during it. In higher species, the period is less critical in that acquired behaviours are more readily reversible. It is merely a time during which certain kinds of learning are relatively easier. The development of human language is an interesting intermediate case (see Chapter 9). Studies suggest that language is acquired differently and more readily up to the age of five or thereabouts, and that those rare individuals who are not exposed to it until a later age learn to a reasonable level of proficiency. The famous case of Genie supports these generalizations: she acquired speech but has trouble with grammar, and also, atypically, has right-hemisphere control of speech (see Kolb and Whishaw, 1980; and also Chapter 9).

IMPRINTING, BIRD SONG AND MIGRATION

Early learning influences the development of perception, general learning ability, socialization, motivation and language. There are large cross-species differences in the range of behaviours which can be affected by such learning. Many of the experiential influences have critical periods during which learning is typically very rapid and often seems to be based on mere **observation**. Furthermore, the kinds of thing which can be learned during this period seem, in many cases, to be constrained, and once they have been acquired it may be difficult or impossible to unlearn them. These phenomena are well illustrated in the development of three kinds of bird behaviour: song, migration and social attachment.

The functions of bird song include the attraction of females (song is mainly a male prerogative) and the repulsion of rival males from an individual's territory. It may also help retain a female after pairing and stimulate her reproductive physiology. In some species, the full adult song develops normally in birds which have been raised as nestlings in acoustic isolation from conspecifics. Many birds, however, including those of the sparrow family, need to hear song of their own species while young if their singing ability is to develop normally. In his pioneering research Thorpe (1972) showed that chaffinches raised in acoustic isolation from five days after hatching developed a song which was normal in length but not properly differentiated into elements or phrases. Chaffinches, deafened at an early age and thus prevented from hearing their own vocalizations, developed an even more abnormal song consisting of a more or less continuous screech. Similar effects have been observed in deafened white-crowned sparrows, which as adults sing only a series of disconnected notes (see Marler, 1981). It has been postulated that young birds have a **genetically transmitted template** of their species-specific but *simplified* adult song, but deafened birds are unable to match their own output to the model so do not attain even a simplified adult song. If young white-crowned sparrows are exposed in their first three months to adult singing, then, when they begin to sing months later, they produce close copies of what they have heard. These are fully adult songs which are elaborations of the simpler template song. A young swamp sparrow can retain this elaborated template song for up to 240 days without rehearsing it, then, provided the sparrow can hear its own output, it can accurately reproduce the song (see Marler, 1981).

Once the template is modified by hearing adult song during the critical period the learning is permanent and irreversible, even if the bird is later deafened. In the white-crowned sparrow and many other sparrows, exposure to the songs of other species does not affect the stored template, so young birds exposed in this way will grow up to sing the unelaborated template song. This selectivity can be remarkably specific. For example, young swamp sparrows will reject syllables produced by song sparrows in a song-salad, drawing syllables from the adult song of both species. Such selectivity contrasts with the catholicism of the marsh warbler, of which individuals have been reported to imitate the songs of up to seventy-six other species. Even the white-crowned sparrow may, however, introduce novel elements into its adult song. Inventions are created individually and retained within the whistled section of the song, whereas the fixed components of the elaborated template occur in the trilled section (Marler, 1981). In the case of the marsh warbler, the ability to incorporate bird song components from nearly a hundred European species enables an elaborate song to be rapidly acquired, the distinctiveness of which is determined by the patterning of alien elements. In some respects, mynah birds and some species of parrot are even less constrained with respect to what they can learn: they can mimic a very wide range of sounds and their learning is not apparently confined to an early critical period. Mynahs, however, never imitate the sounds of other species in the wild although they learn to mimic the spoken words of their human captors.

What can be learned and when it can be learned is, then, a very variable phenomenon across bird species. Even if a critical period exists, in some species it seems to be extendable for late-born young which have received minimal exposure to adult song (see Marler, 1981). The timing of the period is probably controlled by sex hormone activity. Thus, if young male chaffinches are castrated before they come into song, they continue to be able to learn from exposure to adult song. An implant of the male sex hormone testosterone will then enable them to learn to sing the full adult song a year later than normal birds (see Thorpe, 1972). Levels of testosterone must determine for how long the inherited song template can be modified by exposure to a genetically constrained range of adult singing.

Canaries, unlike sparrows and chaffinches, do not seem to have a critical period for learning adult song. They learn a new song each year. There are several interesting features of this ability. Only male canaries sing, and their singing is related to the greater size of certain structures in their forebrains. These structures control singing, are larger in males than in females, and are largest in males with complex songs. Each autumn the structures shrink in size as the old song is forgotten and enlarge the following spring when the new song is learned. Growth is probably controlled by release of the male sex hormone testosterone, which is known to increase the size of these forebrain regions in males and in females without ovaries. It is probably because these song-controlling regions can regress, then regrow annually, that canaries do not show a single critical period, i.e., the ability to learn a new song depends on the ability of certain key brain regions to regress, then regrow. It may also explain another fact. Canaries, like chaffinches, control singing with the forebrain regions of their left hemisphere even though the sides of the brain are symmetrical. If these structures are destroyed in the left hemisphere (but not the right), song is lost. Seven months later, however, it is learned anew, this time being controlled by the right hemisphere. A similar phenomenon is seen in humans. Language is controlled by structures in the left hemisphere and is particularly vulnerable to lesions of this hemisphere. Unlike canaries, though, adult humans do not possess right hemispheres that are good at taking over the lost functions. Infant humans show much greater transfer to the right hemisphere. Perhaps if, like the canary, adult humans showed regression and regrowth in their forebrains they also could recover lost language abilities through the right hemisphere's auspices (see Nottebohm, 1982).

Although inherited constraints operate in the cross-generational transmission of bird song, the process does represent a form of **cultural transmission**. Study of an island population of saddlebacks has shown that a new dialect can rapidly emerge when there is a cultural mutation, as opposed to a genetic one. In this process, one individual makes an error in the dialect-learning process, and this error is then learned by others and spread through the population as a new dialect. Similar kinds of culturally transmitted change probably account for the milk-bottle-opening behaviour of tits and the nesting habits of swallows. In the space of less than one hundred years Californian swallows changed from being cave-nesting birds to nesting almost entirely in barns and other human constructions. Fledged male swallows probably learnt about suitable nest sites during exploratory migrations carried out during the first months of life. Such knowledge may, then, be culturally acquired and transmitted, especially as the young seem to follow the nesting practices of their adult conspecifics. What determines cultural change for this behaviour remains a mystery.

The ability of young birds and other animals to undertake seasonal migrations, in which they locate their goal accurately and return precisely to their starting point, is equally poorly understood, especially as the young of many species do not migrate with adults. There is, however, evidence that they develop these capacities in somewhat the same fashion as birds acquire song. That is to say, the basic ability of a young bird to orient towards the goal site of its first migration develops with minimum specific experience (as also may its 'knowledge' of how far to fly), but the fine tuning of such knowledge may require a variety of kinds of learning, which are still poorly understood. The extent of this learned contribution probably differs markedly across species. For example, swallows are likely to learn more from adult conspecifics than will parasite cuckoos who lack such an opportunity. Very little relevant research has been done, but it has been shown that hand-reared indigo buntings only select the normal southerly migration direction if they have been exposed as juveniles, prior to their autumn migration, to a normal rotating planetarium night sky. Their initial orientation can be biased when the stars rotate about a fictitious axis (Orion rather than the Pole Star) and is random when they have no early exposure to celestial movements (Emlen, 1972). In this species, polar north is set by early experience even though their initial migratory orientation 180° away from this direction cannot be.

The notion of a critical period in learning owed its original popularity to the study of **imprinting** by ethologists such as Konrad Lorenz (1937). It was noticed that various early-maturing bird species, when newly hatched, rapidly learn to follow any of a range of animate or inanimate moving things to which they are exposed. In nature, they would normally imprint on their own mothers. Mere exposure is sufficient for the acquisition of this following behaviour and young chicks, ducklings or goslings so imprinted, usually become socially and sexually attached to targets similar to the imprinted one. Subsequent work has shown that the acquired attachments are difficult to reverse, and that after the critical period the young are more likely to flee from, than to follow, moving objects. Unlike many other kinds of early learning, however, the range of stimuli which can be imprinted is large. Apart from a preference for moving objects, chicks, ducklings and geese learn to follow visual stimuli rather indiscriminately – even objects such as moving balloons, or the waddling Konrad Lorenz. In relative contrast, newly hatched chicks and ducklings show a tendency to follow models emitting the calls of their own species much more readily than models emitting calls of related ones (Gottlieb, 1965).

Attachment and **familiarity** develop from the following response, and once this has happened other stimuli are perceived as unfamiliar, which tends to lead to fear and flight. Consistent with this is the finding that isolated chicks can be imprinted over a longer time than can group-reared chicks, which imprint on each other (Guiton, 1959). However, formation of abnormal imprinted responses is not always associated with the later appearance of inappropriate sexual attachments. For example, in bullfinches sexual imprinting during adolescence can override early experience in deciding mate selection (Nicolai, 1956, cited by Hinde, 1970). The duration of the critical period for imprinting is therefore subject to environmental influences, and not all of the consequences of imprinting are immutable. Scott (1963) has suggested that the formation of initial social attachments in mammals is like imprinting in birds, but the extent to which such primary socialization in mammals is confined to a critical period remains uncertain. For example, current research no longer supports the view that early **maternal deprivation** has irreversible effects and contradicts the view that there is a critical period for the formation of the mother-infant bond (Herbert *et al.*, 1982).

It remains controversial to what extent early learning effects are confined to critical periods and what determines the confinement. Each type of learning must be assessed on its own merits. For example, even the detrimental effects of rearing rats in 'impoverished' environments can be partially compensated by subsequent exposure to an 'enriched' environment (see Rosenzweig and Bennett, 1976). Whether or not imprinting in chicks is rigidly confined to a critical period, there does seem to be some evidence that this discriminating visual following response is somewhat distinct from apparently similar discriminations which may be acquired throughout adult life. Imprinting in chicks is prevented or lost by lesions in a brain region known as the hyperstriatum ventrale, whereas this lesion does not impair chicks' ability to learn a visual discrimination in which they run to a stimulus associated with a rewarding blast of warm air (see McCabe *et al.*, 1982).

Associative learning processes

HABITUATION

All species, from primitive invertebrates to humans, show a decrease in their response to a stimulus if it is repeatedly presented without being systematically associated with rewards or punishments. This decline in reactivity is known as **habituation** and it may persist for days or even longer if the unreinforced stimulus (i.e., an

unrewarded or unpunished one) is repeated many times. Habituation of reflexes is found in disconnected spinal cords and may be
produced in the sea snail Aplysia by repeated electrical stimulation
of single sensory neurons (see Kandel, 1976). In vertebrates, novel
stimuli may at first elicit a combination of orienting and defensive
reflexes, in which the animal prepares to attend to the novelty, or to
defend itself against the possible threat. The novelty wears off with
repetition so that the habituated animal ignores the previously
novel stimuli, and can therefore attend to others more important
for its survival. Habituation is, then, a useful adaptation which is
present throughout life. It emerges very early in human infants,
who readily show habituation to novelty. Indeed, their ability to
habituate has been used to show that four-day-old babies can learn
to recognize and remember visual shapes for at least a few minutes
(Slater *et al.*, 1982).

In humans and other mammals, habituation is very selective.
Thus, if subjects have come to ignore a particular tone, a slight
change in its pitch or loudness is sufficient to make them pay
attention to it again. This is **dishabituation**. If babies are shown a
particular cube repeatedly at various depths, they soon lose interest
in it, but immediately pay attention again when shown a different-
sized cube which projects the same solid angle on the retina. This
process of dishabituation is nicely illustrated by the Bowery El
Phenomenon. Residents of the Bowery, New York, became so
used to the regular night-time passage of the neighbourhood
overhead railway (the 'El') that they slept relatively undisturbed.
When the railway was axed, however, they complained of being
woken from their sleep by the 'deafening' silence, which occurred
at the times when the trains used to pass.

It used to seem strange to regard habituation as a form of
associative learning, but some theorists would argue that a habituated animal has learned that a particular event is not causally
related to any biologically significant events (see Dickinson, 1980).
A representation is formed that the event does not predict any
significant further event. Alternatively, habituation has been interpreted as involving the learning of an association between an event
and the context in which it occurs, so that the context eventually
predicts the stimulus reliably and the stimulus then elicits no
response (Tighe and Leaton, 1976). Cognitive theorists would

certainly argue that habituation requires the creation of an event representation, as Slater *et al.*'s (1982) four-day-old babies seem to show; i.e., it involves a form of event memory. The problem is that although representations are probably involved in the habituation to novelty shown by higher vertebrates, it is less plausible that representations are a prerequisite for habituation in Aplysia. The issue is important because the physiology and biochemistry of habituation are now well understood in Aplysia, but we are unsure how good a model it provides of vertebrate habituation. We still need to know *what* is learned in habituation.

The nervous system of the Aplysia is small and simple. It comprises identifiable neurons, the connections of which can be precisely plotted, which means that the 'wiring plan' for simple behaviours may be fully specified. The neurons which control the gill withdrawal reflex are known. This reflex is a response to the touching of the end of the breathing chamber (or gill) and involves withdrawing the gill into a protective mantle. Repeated touching of the gill, or repetitive stimulation of the appropriate sensory neuron, causes habituation. In both cases, ten to fifteen stimulations lead to habituation of at least one hour's duration, and prolonged repetition may extend this period to three weeks or more. The behavioural depression is believed to be caused by a reduced release of neurotransmitter by the sensory neurons at their synaptic junctions with motor neurons. This effect is caused, in turn, by less calcium entering the sensory cells at critical moments. The result is that the motor neurons are less activated even though the sensory neurons are still being stimulated by the gill touches to the same degree. Further changes occur in the sensory neurons when the habituation is made to last for weeks (see Kandel and Schwartz, 1982).

In Aplysia, dishabituation of gill withdrawal is produced by the presentation of a strong and probably unpleasant stimulus to the animal's head or tail – a process known as **sensitization**. Sensitization is a form of learning, independent of habituation, in which a strong stimulus strengthens a wide range of reflex behaviours. If the stimulus is repeatedly given, the sensitization may last for weeks. When this happens the terminal regions of the sensory neurons, which are part of the gill withdrawal reflex circuit, increase in size so that more neurotransmitter is released. Sensitization occurs at the same sites as habituation but involves a change in the opposite direction; i.e., more neurot. release from sensory neurons. The change is produced by action of the neuron activated by the unpleasant tail stimulus. This neuron releases serotonin which stimulates a chain of events in the sensory neuron, enabling it to release more neurotransmitter when activated. Central to the chain of events is the manufacture of a very important kind of molecule called cyclic-AMP. The availability of this molecule in the sensory neuron matches the duration of short-lasting sensitization, and if sensitization is prolonged cyclic-AMP sets in train the underlying structural changes (see Kandel and Schwartz, 1982).

Habituation and sensitization in Aplysia seem, then, to be very mechanistic processes. It is difficult to see that either of them require stored representations, let alone stored representations of causal relationships or their absence (Kandel and Schwartz do suggest, however, that the mechanisms of sensitization in Aplysia are very similar to those of classical conditioning, which is at least associative learning). Perhaps habituation in vertebrates sometimes involves a different and more flexible kind of learning, although Kandel and Schwartz would disagree. The possibility is supported by two kinds of evidence. First, habituation in Aplysia is local to the habituated system. In mammals like rats, however, damage to certain parts of the brain, such as the limbic system, leaves unimpaired the basic response (for example, alerting to a novel stimulus) but prevents the animal from habituating this response. This would not happen in Aplysia. Second, Sokolov (1977) and others have argued that habituating to novel stimuli requires a setting up by the brain of a representation of past experience against which current stimuli can be matched. When there is a match, alerting to the stimulus will no longer occur. The neocortex and limbic system play a central role in this kind of habituation and have been shown to contain three kinds of neuron. The first, afferent neurons, respond whenever a given event occurs. The second, extrapolatory neurons, only begin responding when the event has occurred several times. The third, comparator neurons, respond to input from afferent or extrapolatory neurons, but not to input from both. Their output is such that they allow an alerting (or orienting) response to occur either to novel events or the omission of expected events.

It remains unclear whether habituation and dishabituation of reflex responses in invertebrates and spinal-cord preparations are forms of mechanistic learning in which automatic stimulus-response links are weakened or restored, whereas habituation to novel stimuli in vertebrates is a more cognitive kind of learning. Certainly the latter kind of habituation requires complex representation of events (indeed, humans can habituate to verbal stimuli with particular meanings). But the actual weakening of the link between the neurons representing the stimulus and those producing the response may still be mediated by the same kind of cellular mechanisms in both Aplysia and humans.

CONDITIONING

In the 1940s and 1950s the study of classical and instrumental conditioning in animals played a central role in psychology. Researchers, using the framework provided by the behaviourist tradition, saw themselves as trying to unravel laws of learning universal to all species, and theorists such as Hull, Mowrer and Guthrie aimed to discover the laws underlying the learning of stimulus-response associations. This kind of research is no longer regarded as so important, for two reasons. First, psychologists are more sceptical about the existence of **universal laws of learning**. Not only are there kinds of learning other than conditioning, but it is even unproven that the mechanisms of conditioning are the same in vertebrates and invertebrates. Second, the behaviourist account of what is learnt in conditioning, viz. **automatic stimulus-response links,** is under challenge. Even in the halcyon days of Hullianism, Tolman argued that animals form cognitive representations of environmental events which mediate the behaviour produced by a stimulus. His voice in the wilderness has now become a compelling chant (see Dickinson, 1980).

Although they use different terminologies, both cognitivists and behaviourists agree that conditioning involves the formation of an association between events, which must be related systematically in time so that the first predicts the second. For this reason, sensitization is not conditioning because there is no systematic relationship between the strong sensitizing stimulus and the reflexes it sensitizes. Behaviourists have distinguished operationally between two forms of conditioning. **Classical** or **Pavlovian conditioning** (after the Russian physiologist Pavlov who pioneered research into conditioning in the 1920s) occurs when a stimulus (the **conditioned stimulus**, or CS) and another stimulus (the **unconditioned stimulus**, or UCS), which typically causes a reflex response, are presented in a specified relationship to each other which does not depend on how the subject responds to the CS. For example, in Pavlov's famous studies with dogs, the animals learned to salivate at the sound of a bell (CS), which regularly preceded the arrival of food (UCS). The food's presentation was not, however, *contingent* on the dog's salivating, i.e., it was not a reward. Pavlov believed that the dogs showed their anticipation of the UCS when the CS was presented, by responding to the CS in a way similar to that in which they responded reflexly to the UCS. This is Pavlov's principle of **response substitution** and, although it has exceptions, it correctly indicated that the classically conditioned response does bear a close relationship to the response made reflexly to the UCS (see Eikelboom and Stewart, 1982). For example, male rats repeatedly gratified by females in a given context begin after a while to release the sex hormone testosterone when merely exposed to the context. They do this rather than anything else because release of this hormone is *part* of the process of excitement shown in sexual activity.

The second kind of associative learning traditionally identified is **instrumental conditioning** in which the presentation of a **reinforcing stimulus** (i.e., a UCS which is either a reward or a punishment) is made contingent on the subject's performing an act specified by the experimenter. This type of learning has been dubbed **operant conditioning** by Skinner to emphasize that the response is produced in a different way from the response in classical conditioning, which he terms 'respondent' to indicate its quasi-reflex nature. Whatever the status of this claim, instrumental conditioning involves producing particular responses (CRs) when certain stimuli are present (CSs) in order to obtain a reward or avoid punishment (UCSs). Thorndike and, later, Hull, believed that giving UCSs shortly after a response was made, was necessary for the automatic strengthening of the link between the response (CR) and the circumstances in which it was produced (the CS). Unlike Pavlov, they believed this **law of effect** applied also to classical conditioning. Hull, in particular, believed that the UCS provided reinforcement essential for learning and that the reinforcement consisted in the **reduction of drive states** such as hunger, thirst and fear. Their automaton view of the learner influenced thinking about learning and memory through the middle years of this century.

The behaviourist view of conditioning and its central role in learning never achieved complete dominance: even in the 1940s and 1950s cognitivists such as Tolman disputed its main tenets. The debate revolved around several issues. First, what is learned and stored in conditioning? Second, what are the mechanisms underlying conditioning? In the Hull-Tolman debate this question was particularly concerned with the role of **reinforcement**: was it necessary for learning? Third, and related to these two major issues, was the question as to whether there were forms of learning other than conditioning, and indeed whether instrumental and classical conditioning were distinct forms of learning. This third question was critically connected with the possibility that there may be universal laws of learning.

Modern cognitivists such as Dickinson (1980) argue that conditioning involves the formation of central representations of causal relationships (or at least predictive relationships) between events. Classical conditioning usually involves learning that stimulus event A predicts stimulus event B. But it can involve learning that stimulus event A predicts that stimulus event B will not occur – **conditioned suppression**. It may even involve learning that stimulus event A is not systematically related one way or the other to stimulus event B – **learned irrelevance**, which is similar to habituation. In instrumental conditioning, subjects may learn that behavioural event A predicts stimulus event B, or that it predicts that B will not occur. Subjects may also learn that no behavioural event has any effect on the occurrence or nonoccurrence of stimulus event B. This is called **learned helplessness** and has been used as a model for depression in humans. Depressed individuals are supposed to learn that there is nothing they can do in order to cope with unpleasant reality and they consequently stop trying, i.e., become depressed (see Maier and Seligman, 1976).

The central representations of causal relationships between events formed in conditioning somehow mediate the new responses which an animal may show. The new learning may, however, be behaviourally silent. This occurs in **latent learning**. If two events of no motivational significance, such as a light and a tone, are paired together, there will be no behavioural change. But something has been learnt because if the later stimulus is later predictive of food, the subject will subsequently salivate to either stimulus event. This suggests that reinforcement is not necessary for associative learning, although it may be for behavioural change. Dickinson argues that subjects learn that event A predicts event B when the occurrence of event B is *surprising* because it is not predicted by any other events other than A. If A occurs in conjunction with a more powerful event C, then the subject tends to learn that C predicts B, but not that A predicts B. This is **overshadowing**. Similarly, if A has previously been found to predict B, and D is subsequently paired with A, the subject may fail to learn that D also predicts B. This effect of **blocking** is held to occur because the occurrence of event B is no longer surprising. If event B is modified so that it once more is surprising then the subject does learn that D also predicts it.

Why does the second event have to be surprising rather than reinforcing for associative learning to occur? Modern cognitivists argue that surprise is necessary if the two events are to be processed together in a limited-capacity learning system. This view compares the conditioning animal to humans, processing and storing complex information within constraints set by limited-capacity attentional and short-term memory systems. If the capacity of the conditioning system is limited then the capacity devoted to particular events must be adaptively determined by features such as their surprisingness. Some information is maintained longer in short-term memory. Even among cognitivists there is disagreement about precisely which features determine the amount of cognitive processing applied to events A and B, although there has been a recent attempt to integrate their approaches in a mathematico-physiological model (Grossberg, 1982). There has, for example, been disagreement about how to interpret the phenomenon of **latent inhibition**, in which pre-exposure only to event A impairs the ability to learn later that event A predicts event B (the effect seems very like habituation). This phenomenon is somewhat similar to the effect in which prior exposure to two stimulus events (together) makes it more difficult later to discriminate between them in conditioning (Bateson and Chantrey, 1972). All these researchers agree that the likelihood of a subject's learning that event A predicts event B will depend on their previous experience.

If conditioning involves cognitive processes similar to those employed in complex human learning, then what is stored as a result of such processing? Dickinson considers two different forms of representation, known as procedural and declarative. When a subject learns that tone predicts food, he might store the equivalent of either 'When the tone is on, approach the food magazine' (a **procedural representation**, which is like an instruction), or 'The tone causes food' (a **declarative representation**, which is like a description). There must be rules for translating the declarative representation into an action, otherwise the conditioned subject would remain frozen in thought. Declarative representations, however, are able to 'integrate chains of association'. In other words, when A predicts B, and B predicts C, A will be seen to predict C if the representations are declarative. Such integrations are harder to conceive with procedural representations and they are found with both classical and instrumental conditioning, although not under all conditions. Dickinson concludes that current evidence slightly favours the view that conditioning involves declarative representations.

The major problem facing the cognitive theorist is how the memory of association is converted to action. Dickinson explains classical conditioning in terms of an **excitatory link model** according to which excitation of event A excites the representation of event B, which automatically elicits a response like the unconditioned one. This is similar to Pavlov's principle of stimulus substitution, which requires that the CR be like the UCR. Deviations from strict stimulus substitution may occur because only some aspects of event B are represented. A potentially more serious exception is found with the conditioning effect associated with drug-taking. It is well known that continued taking of drugs such as morphine and alcohol leads to **tolerance** so that the addict has to take increased doses to achieve the same effect. Although tolerance is partially due to physiological factors, it has been shown that it is also partially due to a response which is classically conditioned to the distinctive environmental cues associated with drug-taking. This response is opposite in direction to the physiological response produced by the drug and so counteracts its effect. For example, alcohol lowers body temperature whereas the conditioned tolerance response increases body temperature (see Eikelboom and Stewart, 1982). Overdosing may even be an inadvertent consequence when the drug is taken in unusual surroundings so that the counteracting conditioned effects are minimized. Not all conditioned drug effects are counteracting ones, however, and Eikelboom and Stewart argue that Pavlov's stimulus substitution principle is not violated when one takes into account what the UCS really is. In conditioned tolerance it can be argued that the drug itself elicits some reactive response.

Dickinson goes on to suggest that an excitatory link model cannot explain instrumental conditioning. The model would require a 'backward' excitatory link from the representation of stimulus event B to the representation of behavioural event A, and such links are known to be very weak. He therefore argues that the two forms of conditioning must involve storage of qualitatively different kinds of information. Even so, he believes that the mechanisms of learning are probably the same in the two forms of conditioning. There are many parallels between the two. Both show **generalization**: i.e., the likelihood of the CR declines as the CS becomes increasingly different from that used in original training (see Figure 5.2). In both cases, the steepness of this generalization gradient increases if subjects are punished for responding to a stimulus differing from the original CS. Similarly, in both cases the CR shows **extinction**, i.e., it becomes less likely if the UCS no longer follows the CS. One possible exception to these parallels is the **partial reinforcement extinction effect**. In instrumental conditioning it is found that resistance to extinction (of the CR) increases if, during training, the UCS only followed the CS some of the time. This effect is rarely found in classical conditioning. Nevertheless, the similarities between the two forms of conditioning are impressive and point to a considerable overlap of learning mechanisms.

The similarities between classical and instrumental conditioning may, however, be exaggerated because, despite the experimenter's best intentions, instrumental tasks involve classical reinforcement contingencies, and many classical tasks involve instrumental responses (see Mackintosh, 1978). In the first case, the problem is that even when a task is defined operationally as instrumental con-

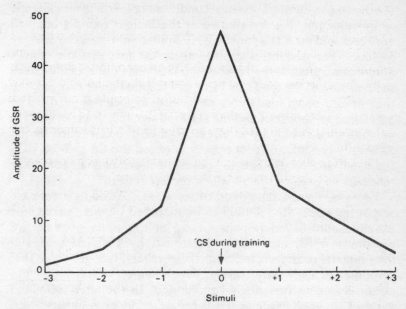

Figure 5.2 Generalization gradient. Stimulus O indicates the tone to which a galvanic skin response was originally conditioned. Stimuli +1, +2 and +3 indicate increasingly higher tones and stimuli −1, −2 and −3 indicate increasingly lower tones. Generalization decreases as the difference between originally conditioned and test tone increases.

ditioning such that the subject's CR predicts the UCS, there is also an implicit relationship between the CS (in the presence of which the CR is produced) and the UCS, which is of a classical sort. Similarly, in a classical conditioning task, the CR may change the effect of the UCS (making this more or less rewarding) so that it becomes like an instrumental response. For example, when Pavlov's dogs salivated to the sound of the bell just before food was presented, the salivation made the dry food more palatable.

In the above example, however, it has been found that dogs continue to salivate to a bell (CS) even when this response actually prevents the provision of food. This classically conditioned response is not suppressed via an instrumentally acquired inhibition. A similar effect may be illustrated dramatically by the phenomenon of **autoshaping** in which classical conditioning seems to masquerade as instrumental. Pigeons trained in the famous Skinner box will approach and peck at a panel if its illumination signals the delivery of food. The pecking is controlled by the fact that the panel's illumination predicts food even when the behaviour actually causes the *omission* of the food (the birds still respond more than half the time if the panel-food links have already been formed). The autoshaped response of pecking at a food signaller does not seem to be controlled readily by its effect. Rather it is controlled by the classically conditioned contingency between the CS and the UCS (lit panel and food). This is because it represents an automatic tendency to explore stimuli which predict reward.

There is, then, a dimension of responses. At one extreme are responses which do not seem to be modified by their effects, for example autoshaped responses, and at the other extreme are responses which are readily controlled by both classical and instrumental contingencies. Some researchers, though, argue that responses actually differ subtly, depending on whether they are classically or instrumentally conditioned. In the later 1960s and early 1970s, great excitement was generated by experiments which seemed to show that humans and animals could modify autonomic responses such as heart rate, blood pressure and gut activity – responses which had previously been considered involuntary and only amenable to classical conditioning. The new research suggested that the responses could be instrumentally conditioned even in animals whose voluntary muscles were paralysed by curare. Rats, it was claimed, could increase or decrease their heart rate depending on which response led to reward, and this control was not mediated by, for example, fast or slow breathing or jumping up and down. Subsequently, doubt has been cast on the reliability of the animal studies (see Miller and Dworkin, 1974). Nevertheless, it would be foolish to prejudge the issue of which responses can be instrumentally as well as classically conditioned. In humans, very fine-grained instrumental control of heart rate and blood pressure has been demonstrated. We are still unsure whether this control is direct, mediated indirectly via the voluntary muscle system (by holding one's breath, for example), or even indirectly through the medium of imagination. Sensory feedback does, however, seem to be critical for voluntary control of responses – if one cannot feel what one is doing, control is impossible. As autonomic responses normally produce little sensory information, experimenters have tried to help subjects use this minimal sensory information. They have used both hypnosis, to focus subjects' attention on their autonomic responses, and **biofeedback**, in which an external signal shows the subject which way a particular autonomic response, e.g., blood pressure, is changing. We can only learn that an autonomic response predicts reward if we can detect it, and biofeedback and hypnosis enable us to do this by indicating when the response occurs. If biofeedback and hypnosis enable us to control the responses then the medical benefits may be immense.

If modern cognitivists are right, conditioning involves storing representations of causal relationships between events. Their general view is supported by the forms of latent learning, in which new memories are made that can be 'behaviourally silent'. The view is also consistent with the occurrence of **contrast effects**, in which the effect of a specific reward or punishment is influenced by the learner's exposure to other rewards and punishments. For example, rats trained to do a task for a large reward, then shifted to a small reward, temporarily drop their level of responding below that of rats given the smaller reward throughout. It is as if their cognitive expectations have been disappointed. If Dickinson (1980) is correct then the form of representation stored differs in classical and instrumental conditioning although their learning mechanisms may be very similar. The kinds of response shown in the two forms of conditioning may be relevant both to the problem of representation and to mechanisms. Dickinson also argues that the conditioning subject has a cognitive system with experientially derived expectations and a limited capacity to process event information.

According to this last claim, the ease of forming associations should depend mainly on previous experience, and otherwise the choice of CS and UCS should not matter too much. This claim, known as the **equipotentiality principle**, may be too extreme. There seems to be a dimension of **preparedness** in the formation of associations. At one extreme, learning is very rapid (often occurring in one trial), and at the other, it may be almost impossible. For example, in his famous fear-conditioning experiment with 'Little Albert', Watson made the child frightened of a rat which he previously liked, by pairing its presence with a loud, disturbing noise. Attempts to repeat this study using familiar objects, such as a wooden duck, as CSs were unsuccessful. Fear-conditioning to small furry animals is prepared whereas that to wooden ducks is not. It has been suggested by Eysenck (1979) that prepared conditioning of this kind may 'incubate' rather than show extinction, i.e., presentation of the CS alone after conditioning may strengthen the CR whereas it normally weakens it. Oakley (1983) argues that preparedness in conditioning is an inherited characteristic. If, in a species' history, individuals are often exposed to certain biologically significant kinds of association, then the ability to learn rapidly about these associations comes to be genetically transmitted. These genetic constraints apply to both classical and instrumental conditioning.

BOX 5.2
Conditioning, phobias, conscience, crime and personality

If Eysenck (1979) is correct, conditioning (particularly of the classical variety) is important in several areas of human mental life. It has long been argued that fear may be conditioned as a response to a previously neutral stimulus when this is paired with a painful or unpleasant UCS. The conditioned fear is a drive which motivates the defensive and avoidance behaviours and has properties which differ radically from the reflex response to pain (Bolles and Fanselow, 1980). This form of classical conditioning therefore presents problems for Pavlov's principle of stimulus substitution. Watson, Eysenck and others have proposed that the disruptively strong and irrational fears, known as **phobias**, are caused by the classical conditioning of fear to CSs such as spiders, closed spaces, snakes and rats. To become objects of phobia, these stimuli must be paired with unpleasant or painful events.

There are problems with the conditioning theory of

phobias. First, some phobias are much more common than others. For example, irrational fear of spiders is much more common than fear of snakes. Eysenck (1979) has suggested that this is because we are biologically prepared to associate some stimuli with fear much more readily than others – a proposal which has been accused of circularity. Second, phobias often get worse even though the patient has only been exposed to one pairing of the CS with an unpleasant UCS. Thus phobias differ from most classical CRs in the rapidity of their learning and the fact that they do not show extinction when the CS is presented without the UCS. Eysenck (1979) cites evidence that, under some circumstances, classical CRs show incubation rather than extinction, i.e., the CR gets stronger even when the CS is presented alone. Incubation, he claims, tends to occur when the CR is a drive such as fear, when the fear association is biologically prepared, and when the CS is present only briefly (which is normally the case). He also claims that people with introvert and neurotic personalities are more aroused by unpleasant stimuli and hence show stronger conditioning of fear, and more incubation.

Eysenck's claims (1979) are polemical, and many believe that phobias are also acquired indirectly through observation learning and being taught that some things are threatening (see Rachman, 1974). It does seem, however, that the conditioning techniques of behaviour therapy are effective in treating some phobias. The techniques are intended to induce fear to extinguish rather than incubate. For example, in **systematic desensitization** the therapist gets the patient to relax in the presence of the feared stimulus. To achieve this end the patient is taught how to relax and then told to imagine a series of increasingly fear-provoking stimuli. Only when he can relax while imagining the threat is the patient advanced to yet more threatening stimuli. In the end he is relaxed in the presence of the most frightening stimulus in the series. **Flooding** achieves the same end by giving the subject *prolonged* exposure to a strong fear CS by itself.

If emotional states such as fear can be classically conditioned, it is plausible to suggest that this form of learning may strongly influence the frequency of certain social behaviours, and perhaps the development of personality and conscience. This is precisely what Eysenck has proposed (see Eysenck and Eysenck, 1981; and Eysenck, 1982). In this view, introverts have inherited highly aroused and arousable nervous systems, which enable them to form conditioned associations to aversive UCSs very rapidly. Neurotics also form such associations rapidly because they inherit very active autonomic nervous systems. Introverts and neurotics rapidly acquire associations between negative emotional states and antisocial intentions and behaviours (which have been punished). This has two effects. First, introverts particularly become less socially outgoing than extroverts. Second, they tend to develop stronger consciences about immoral and illegal acts. Conscience is here viewed as a **conditioned emotional response** which controls much moral behaviour.

Eysenck argues that many criminals have poorly developed consciences either because of their upbringing or because they have inherited nervous systems insensitive to conditioning aversive emotions. This is compatible with the view that some forms of criminal behaviour have a strong inherited component – a view supported by evidence that criminal tendencies in adopted children are related more closely to their natural than to their adoptive parents. It needs to be proved that one of the inherited characteristics is poor ability to show aversive conditioning. If correct, one might argue that rehabilitation of criminals would benefit from intensive reconditioning, particularly at a time when the 'permissive' society has reduced the opportunities for conscience-forming conditioning. An early example of such a programme was the attempt by Maconochie to introduce a 'token economy' on the penal colony of Norfolk Island over a century ago. Maconochie awarded points (tokens) for pro-social behaviour and took them away for offences; i.e., he made sure there was a close temporal association between behaviour and reward or punishment. The system was very successful although his efforts were opposed by the British Establishment, which eventually had him relieved of his post.

Eysenck's view that conditioning plays a central role in the areas discussed is disputed by others who believe that cognitive factors are important even if their role is only vaguely specified. Eysenck's riposte is that verbal learning may, for example, be involved in specifying the kind of thing which we fear, but that this kind of verbal learning is itself an example of classical conditioning. It certainly appears possible to increase certain kinds of verbal response (such as saying plural nouns) by 'rewarding' subjects for producing them – even when they are unaware of what is going on (see Honig, 1966). The fact that this argument can be made indicates that we have not yet specified precisely enough the characteristics of complex representational learning and how these differ from classical conditioning.

A famous example of prepared classical conditioning is learnt **taste aversion** to certain foods and drinks. Many animals that become sick after eating food with a distinctive taste and smell will later selectively avoid the food (Garcia et al., 1955). Human subjects are nauseated by the food's smell and taste. The association may be acquired in one trial even when several hours separate the eating from the nausea. This form of conditioning is very persistent, is resistant to physiological disruptions of the brain, is resistant to extinction, and appears very early in development. Garcia and Koelling (1966) also showed that although rats readily learned to avoid saccharin-flavoured water, the drinking of which led to sickness, they did not learn to avoid 'bright-noisy' water, i.e., water associated with lights and clicks. Only the taste-sickness association was prepared. In contrast, quails, whose food selection is initially controlled by vision, do associate the colour of drinking water with later sickness (Wilcoxon, Dragoin and Kral, 1971). Most examples of classical conditioning only occur if there is close spatiotemporal contiguity between CS and UCS, and for this reason, among others, it has been argued that aversion shows there are no universal principles of classical conditioning (see Seligman and Hager, 1972). Not everyone accepts this argument, however (see Dickinson, 1980, for an opposing view).

Instrumental conditioning is also affected by inherited biological constraints. For example, rats learn to avoid unpleasant events much more quickly if the avoidance response is a species-specific defence response (SSDR), such as fleeing or freezing (staying immobile). If the required response is something like lever-pressing, which is not compatible with fleeing or freezing, rats have great difficulty in learning to make the response to avoid electric shocks. Under appropriate conditions, rats will even return to the source of an electric shock to 'bury' it – this is another SSDR for the rat (see Terlecki, Pinel and Treit, 1979). Similar kinds of 'mis-behaviour' have been described by Breland and Breland (1972). They found that their attempts to train animals for TV commercials were sometimes thwarted by the appearance of instinctive behaviours. For example, they trained pigs to pick up large wooden coins and drop them into a piggy-bank. Although the pigs soon learned the task and were actually dropping several coins for each food reward, their behaviour gradually showed a strange trans-formation. Instead of depositing the coins, they began to drop them and root for them, repeating this sequence several times so that the coins ceased to reach the piggy-bank. In similar circumstances, raccoons are equally unwilling to release the coins – they dip them repeatedly in and out of the bank's slot while rubbing them in a miserly way. In both species, the association of coin and food activates largely innate food-related behaviours.

The ease with which conditioned associations are formed is, then, probably a function both of previous experience and of inherited constraints on what can be learned. Conditioning may also occur, however, in conjunction with other, more complex forms of learning which enable causal relationships to be repre-sented. The two forms of learning may interact and may not always reach the same conclusion about which events are causally connec-ted. For example, Seligman (in Seligman and Hager, 1972) des-cribed how he acquired a conditioned nausea to the taste and smell of sauce Béarnaise having once been sick after eating some. He knew perfectly well, however, that the sickness was caused by gastric 'flu and not the sauce. In other words, his conscious expect-ations, acquired through complex representational learning processes, contradicted the event association implied by his conditioning. This decoupling is more likely with prepared forms of conditioning, but suggests that mechanisms of learning for conditioning and complex cognitive learning differ. The development of conscious expectations about events should not be equated with conditioned 'expectations', which may occur without the subject's awareness and even develop in states such as sleep. As humans show so much complex learning, comparisons of conditioning in them and other animals can be problematic. For example, classically conditioned responses extinguish faster in humans, and it has been suggested that this is because the CRs are modulated by more complex human memories (Weiskrantz, 1982). Similarly, animals and humans are not alike when instrumental responding is controlled by particular patterns of reward or punishment. For example, on a **fixed-interval reinforcement schedule**, when reward is only given after a fixed delay following the previously rewarded response, animals learn to pause after a reward and then respond at an accelerating rate until the next reward is delivered. In contrast, humans either respond at a high rate throughout the interval, or at a very low rate just before the reward is due (Lowe *et al.*, 1978). The evidence is that human subjects either acquire the verbal memory that the task requires a given number of responses (leading to intense activity) or, correctly, that rewards are only given at fixed intervals after responding (leading to a few, pre-reward responses). Rats and pigeons learn by instrumental conditioning that their behaviour leads to reward, whereas humans are either learning by complex processes or are using these to modulate their instrumental conditioning (see Honig, 1966, for a general view). This 'cognitive overlay', shown by humans, is probably mediated by the neocortex.

Like habituation, conditionability seems to be an almost universal property of nervous systems. It is found in animals ranging from humans to invertebrates such as the sea snail, the flatworm and the fruitfly, Drosophila. Invertebrates, for example the land snail, show blocking and latent learning of event associations, which has led Kandel and Schwartz (1982) to argue that they are appropriate physiological models for vertebrate conditioning. It is polemical, however, whether vertebrate neuronal processes and the macroscopic interneuronal organizational changes differ radically.

Their apparent similarity may arise from convergent evolution. If this is not so, however, we have much to learn from invertebrate models of conditioning. For example, single gene mutants of the fruitfly known as Dunce, Amnesiac and Turnip have different selective failures of associative learning (Dudai and Quinn, 1980). These genetic failures are caused by the absence of specific enzymes in their nervous systems. Similar problems may be found in species with more complex brains.

The physiological and biochemical bases of memory

THE CONSOLIDATION OF MEMORY

The brain's role in learning and retention has mainly been pursued by examining conditioning in subhuman mammals and birds. More recently, researchers have begun to analyse memory physiology in invertebrates such as the sea snail whose neural sites, where memory is stored, can be located. The problem with such studies is that they may not be relevant to complex memory in humans. At the macroscopic level of neural reorganization this is almost certainly the case – neural activity related to conditioning may indicate how such memories are structured, but will tell us little about complex human memory. On the other hand, microscopic changes within and between neurons may be similar in many kinds of memory and across many species.

One view, advanced in the last century and many times in this, is that the neural changes which mediate stable memory are initiated by learning but then take some time to complete. During this consolidation period an interlinked sequence of biochemical and structural changes takes place within plastic neurons, the end result of which is a change in the synaptic connections between the information-storing neurons, i.e., the brain is 'rewired'. These changes can be blocked and amnesia produced if appropriate biochemical or physiological treatments are given in a limited period following learning. During this period, it has also been suggested, memory depends on one or more short-term stores. Short-term storage may be at the same neural and synaptic sites, but involves physiological processes with rapid onset and fairly rapid decay (see Hebb, 1949). In some theories, as in Hebb's, the short-term storage processes are also consolidation processes, which initiate further changes so that eventually neural structures are altered on a long-term basis. Kandel and Schwartz's (1982) account of short- and long-term sensitization in the Aplysia fits this account well. The short-term changes initiate local increases in neural cyclic-AMP and this both mediates short-term memory and, if it continues to be present in large amounts, eventually causes structural changes, which subserve long-term memory.

Most attempts to test the consolidation hypothesis have tried to disrupt memory by giving various disruptive treatments shortly after learning, i.e., they involve **experimental retrograde amnesia**. It is well known that severe concussion usually causes forgetting of the events which occurred immediately before the accident. Experimenters have tried to produce similar amnesias in animals for conditioned tasks in order to determine the time course of consolidation, the processes that are involved in it, and whether there are also short-term storage processes for conditioning. This approach is illustrated by the research of Gibbs and Ng (1977) and Mark (1979) on learning and memory for a simple conditioned response in the chick. The chicks learned (in one trial) to avoid coloured pellets flavoured with quinine. After training, they gave the chicks one of three kinds of agent – potassium chloride, which disturbs neuronal electrophysiological activity; sodium pump blockers such as ouabain, which disturb the chemical milieu of neurons; and protein synthesis blockers, which prevent neurons from making proteins, vital for their structure and for maintaining chemical processes. Agents like potassium chloride only caused amnesia if given within five minutes of training, and then caused an amnesia which developed very quickly. Sodium pump blockers caused amnesia when given up to ten or fifteen minutes after training, but this amnesia was only complete about ninety minutes later. Finally, protein synthesis blockers caused amnesia when given up to thirty minutes after training, with the amnesia taking some time before it was complete.

Mark (1979) interpreted these findings as showing that the chicks' long-term memory for conditioning depends on a sequence of consolidation processes, which continue for about thirty minutes after training. These changes are initiated by learning causing high levels of neural activity, which changes the balance of charged atoms inside and outside the affected neurons, and ends with structural changes dependent on protein synthesis. He also believes that the memory is held earlier by two short-term stores. One is a very short-lasting store and is related to the activity of potassium chloride, and the other is a more delayed and longer lasting store, which depends somehow on sodium pump activity (this pump maintains the chemical balance inside and outside neurons). Memory for the avoidance response is seen as depending first on the very brief store, and finally on the long-term structural store, although the lifetimes of the stores will overlap.

Unfortunately, the picture obtained from Mark's interpretation is deceptively simple, and many researchers who have used the approach of experimental retrograde amnesia in mammals now believe either that it does not support the idea of protracted consolidation or that it is irrelevant to this idea. There are several basic problems (see Mayes, 1983). First, estimates of the duration of consolidation vary wildly across different tasks and species, and do not relate clearly to the disrupting agent. Estimates vary from less than a second to days, months or even years. Second, the onset of amnesia after the disruption can vary from almost immediate to weeks. Third, the loss of memory is not irreversible since it can frequently be reversed by 'reminder' treatments. Reminders only work if an animal has learnt the task earlier, but may consist of being returned to the learning situation, having the same motivational state aroused which was aroused in the learning situation, or being injected with hormones, such as noradrenaline,which were also produced by training.

These results may mean several things. First, treatments may be disrupting consolidation processes only partially. Second, Gold and McGaugh (1975) have suggested that memories will be only transient unless stimulated by **nonspecific physiological activation**, which occurs in the period following learning. They believed that disruptive processes disturbed the nonspecific processes, which included increased activity of the reticular activating system and release of hormones such as vasopressin, adrenalin and adrenocorticotropic hormone. If these nonspecific activities were artificially generated in the period after learning then the effects of amnesic agents could be counteracted, or even nullified. Third, amnesic agents may be disturbing retrieval processes and not consolidation *per se*, i.e., memories will be formed but be irretrievable. One controversial set of results supports this possibility and suggests that the unique vulnerability of memory in the immediate period after learning may be an illusion. It is claimed that if an animal is re-exposed to the learning situation (or some aspect of it) just before the disruptive treatment, then amnesia will occur even though the memory is days old and presumably well consolidated. If this claim is correct, it implies that any recently retrieved memory is vulnerable to physiological disruption, presumably because its retrievability is reduced. These effects with reactivated memories have, however, only been found with animals, so it is possible that they do not involve memory, but merely how the animal interprets the task (see Mayes, 1983, for a discussion).

The problem of consolidation as it applies to complex memory will be considered again in the next chapter, but it is clear that currently there is no generally agreed interpretation of retrograde amnesia effects in animals. If simple memories do take an appreciable time to consolidate, this is as yet unproven. We need to know more about where the relevant memory changes occur in the brain and what structural modifications of neurons are involved. This has been achieved in the Aplysia, but not properly in vertebrates. There have been some exciting developments, however. In the rabbit, it has recently been found that small lesions in the cerebellum disrupt the learning and retention of a classically conditioned eye-blink response without affecting the production of the UCR (see Lavond *et al.*, 1981). Examination of this cerebellar region after conditioning may well reveal microscopic changes, perhaps at synapses, which represent the storage system for the task. If this is so, the time course of these changes after conditioning may be plotted. It is already known that temporarily blocking the activity of the neurotransmitter GABA in this region causes a reversible amnesia for the task.

The biochemical and physiological changes which underlie the ability of chicks to imprint to a flashing light have also been studied (see Rose, Hambley and Heywood, 1976). Lesions of a small region of the chick forebrain – the hyperstriatum ventrale – prevent imprinting or its retention without affecting the performance of apparently similar visual tasks (McCabe *et al.*, 1982). Electron microscope studies show that after imprinting there are increases in what are known as synaptic apposition zones, which probably means that certain circuitry pathways are strengthened (Bradley, Horn and Bateson, 1981). Earlier work had suggested that imprinting initiated a sequence of biochemical changes specific to neurons in the hyperstriatum. It seemed that first the enzyme RNA polymerase was synthesized, then RNA was produced, and finally new protein was synthesized. This biochemical sequence may produce the synaptic changes which probably store memory of the imprinted stimulus.

Despite these relative successes, it is extremely hard to locate where memories are stored in vertebrate brains, and without this knowledge the time course and nature of the microscopic changes mediating memory are unlikely to be identified. It still remains plausible to argue, however, that learning initiates increased neural activity (probably including nonspecific processes), which set in train a series of further processes, ending with structural changes at the synaptic links between neurons. There are many ways in which synapses may change in learning. For example, sensitization in Aplysia and imprinting in chicks depend on distinct kinds of synaptic change. Even at this level of analysis, therefore, different kinds of memory in different species can be related to separate structural changes. The possibilities for synaptic 'rewiring' are myriad, however, and may form the basis of enormous amounts of information storage. For example, most cortical neurons form thousands of synapses with their neighbours and many of these synapses may be modifiable.

THE PHYSIOLOGICAL PROCESSES WHICH REPRESENT MEMORY

To understand how the brain represents the information which it stores one first needs to know where this information is stored. Despite the encouraging examples cited above, this issue is still surrounded by uncertainty. Part of this uncertainty arises from the work of Karl Lashley (1929). Lashley destroyed various parts of the neocortex in rats, before or after they learned to solve complex mazes. He summarized his conclusions in two principles. The **principle of mass action** stated that it is the amount of cortical tissue removed, not its location, which determines the degree of memory loss. The related **principle of equipotentiality** states that cortical regions are interchangeable with respect to memory, probably because in addition to their specific functions they serve a general computing function. This interpretation of equipotentiality is supported by recent research, which suggests that the occipital cortex has a general role in spatial learning as well as a specific role in vision (Thompson, 1982). Thompson's lesion studies have also led him to modify and extend Lashley's thinking in other ways. He finds that different kinds of conditioned task are disturbed by lesions in separable cortical and subcortical regions. He does find, however, that all these specific memory systems are affected by lesions in a common, nonspecific set of structures, including parts of the thalamus, midbrain and pons. These structures comprise the reticular formation and probably mediate some of Gold and McGaugh's nonspecific processes, which help memory consolidation (and perhaps retrieval). If Thompson is correct, then memories for different tasks are stored in different brain regions, in a more localized fashion than Lashley believed, although there may be a widely distributed nonspecific memory system which modulates many kinds of memory.

The organization and location of conditioned memories has also been explored by recording the brain's electrical activity during and following learning. Olds and his group (see, for example, Olds *et al.*, 1972) recorded activity in single nerve cells and argued that learning causes rerouting of impulses, so, following classical conditioning, the CS's presentation should have effects at sites not previously affected by it. When neurons showed changed activity very early in conditioning or very soon after the CS's onset, Olds and his colleagues inferred that the changes mediated memory. They did record such changes at several subcortical sites in the limbic system, thalamus, midbrain and pons. Unfortunately, this kind of work has great technical and interpretive problems, which have led to its virtual discontinuance. It also presupposes that the brain is like a telephone exchange in which a new memory is represented by a new route through the exchange.

The telephone-exchange view of information representation is radically different from the position adopted by John (1972). He believes that information (about conditioning, but presumably other things as well) is represented in a statistical fashion by the average behaviour of widely distributed neural networks, rather than in the specific behaviour of individual neurons. But whether memory information is represented in a deterministic or statistical fashion, the existence of new memories still depends on discrete changes at synapses. John found support for this position in studies which recorded brain activity during retrieval of conditioned responses. He found that successful retrieval was associated with distinct patterns of neural activity in many different brain regions. These patterns depended on what was being retrieved rather than on the physical properties of CSs. His studies have not been replicated and are very controversial. It is doubtful, for example, whether lesions in all the brain regions showing the retrieval patterns would cause memory problems for the critical task.

The contrast between determinist and statistical views of information representation is perhaps clarified by considering how an ideal observer would determine which memory an animal was retrieving. On the **determinist view**, the observer would be able confidently to specify the activity representing the memory in an individual neuron (or a few) after one retrieval. On the **statistical view**, he would either have to average the activity of the neuron over many retrievals, or look at the pattern of activity of thousands of neurons during a retrieval. These views are distinct, but current technology is possibly not adequate to differentiate them. Furthermore, although it is easy to imagine constructing a memory system on determinist lines, it is much more difficult to see how a statistical system would work. This does not, of course, prove that the brain is a determinist system, but it does indicate that we still have no clear conception of how the brain represents simple memories (such as mediate CRs), let alone more complex memories. Information is probably stored in those brain regions which represent it during learning, but how this representation is coded and how it is later retrieved remain among the major problems of science. The next chapter considers them further, in the context of more complex representational and abstract memory.

Further reading

Introduction and the main issues in memory research

Some basic issues in memory research, including the trichotomy of registration, storage and retrieval, and its problems, are clearly discussed in the following two books:

BADDELEY, A.D. (1976) *The Psychology of Memory*. New York: Harper and Row.

GRUNEBERG, M.M. and MORRIS, P., eds. (1978) *Aspects of Memory*. London: Methuen.

Evolution and the forms of memory

Oakley has provided two excellent, if controversial, accounts of the evolution of learning and cognitive processes:

OAKLEY, D.A. (1979) Cerebral cortex and adaptive behaviour. In D.A. Oakley and H.C. Plotkin, eds., *Brain, Behaviour and Evolution*. London: Methuen.

OAKLEY, D.A. (1983) The varieties of memory: a phylogenetic approach. In A.R. Mayes, ed., *Memory in Humans and Animals*. Wokingham: Van Nostrand.

All the issues connected with how information is represented in animal memory are reviewed and discussed in the following paper:

ROITBLAT, H.L. (1982) The meaning of representation in animal memory. *Behavioral and Brain Sciences*, 5, 353–406.

Differences in animal abilities are related to thinking and intelligence in the following book:

L. WEISKRANTZ, ed. (1985) *Animal Intelligence*. Oxford: Oxford University Press.

Early learning

For a comprehensive review of our knowledge about imprinting see:

HESS, E.H. (1973) *Imprinting: Early Experience and the Psychobiology of Attachment*. Wokingham: Van Nostrand.

For an excellent collection of papers on imprinting, migration and bird song, presented in the context of the notion of prepared learning, see:

SELIGMAN, M.E.P. and HAGER, J.L., eds. (1972) *Biological Boundaries of Learning*. New York: Appleton-Century-Crofts.

For a review of the physiology and biochemistry of perceptual learning and conditioning see:

SOKOLOV, E.N. (1977) Brain functions: neuronal mechanisms of learning and memory. *Annual Review of Psychology*, **28**, 85–112.

The following books set animal learning in its wider ecological and evolutionary context:

HINDE, R.A. (1970) *Animal Behaviour: a Synthesis of Ethology and Comparative Psychology*. Second edition. New York: McGraw-Hill.
HINDE, R.A. (1982) *Ethology*. London: Fontana Paperbacks.

Associative learning processes

The following book provides a wide-ranging discussion of habituation and its development:

TIGHE, T.J. and LEATON, R.N. (1976) *Habituation: Perspectives from Child Development, Animal Behavior and Neurophysiology*. Hillsdale, NJ: Erlbaum.

For another comprehensive review of habituation see:

PEEKE, H.V.S. and HERZ, M.J. (1973) *Habituation*, Volume 1, *Behavioural Studies*, and Volume 2, *Physiological Substrates*. London: Academic Press.

Conditioning is exhaustively and excellently reviewed in the following book:

MACKINTOSH, N.J. (1974) *The Psychology of Animal Learning*. London: Academic Press.

The following volumes give an impression of the impact which thinking about cognitive processes has had on the study of 'simple' animal learning:

HULSE, S.H., FOWLER, H. and HONIG, W.K. (1978) *Cognitive Processes in Animal Behavior*. Hillsdale, NJ: Erlbaum.
SPEAR, N.E. and MILLER, R.R., eds. (1981) *Information Processing in Animals: Memory Mechanisms*. Hillsdale, NJ: Erlbaum.

For a review of the effects of biofeedback on the instrumental conditioning of autonomic nervous system responses see:

MILLER, N.E. (1978) Biofeedback and visceral learning. *Annual Review of Psychology*, **29**, 372–404.

Pavlov's work and its relevance to brain function, personality and psychopathology are considered at an accessible level in this book:

GRAY, J.A. (1979) *Pavlov*. London: Fontana Paperbacks.

The following book comprises a set of papers on the uses of conditioning in psychopathology and other areas of human behaviour:

DAVEY, G., ed. (1981) *Applications of Conditioning Theory*. London: Methuen.

The physiological and biochemical bases of memory

The following chapter gives a comprehensive review of recent theorizing about memory consolidation and the microscopic processes mediating memory:

MAYES, A.R. (1983) The development and course of long-term memory. In Mayes, *op. cit.*

For a more detailed description of the view that stored information is represented by the statistical tendency of the brain to display specific spatiotemporal patterns of activity, and the evidence for this view, see:

JOHN, E.R. (1976) A model of consciousness. In G.E. Schwartz and D. Shapiro, eds., *Consciousness and Self-Regulation*. London: Wiley.

This reference discusses 'cognitive overlay', i.e., how simple forms of learning such as conditioning are modulated by more complex processes that involve neocortical function:

OAKLEY, D.A. (1983) Learning capacity outside neocortex in animals and man. Implications for therapy after brain-injury. In G.C.L. Davey, ed., *Animal Models of Human Behaviour*. London: Wiley.

A clear review of recent thinking about long-term potentiation (LTP) is given in the last reference. LTP is found in the hippocampus (itself in the limbic system) and involves a change in neuronal connectivity that may underlie more complex forms of representational memory.

LYNCH, G. and BAUDRY, M. (1984) The biochemistry of memory: a new and specific hypothesis. *Science*, **224**, 1057–63.

6. Complex Human Memory

Tables

6. Complex Human Memory

A brief history

This chapter is primarily concerned with those forms of complex memory which, as mentioned in Chapter 5, Oakley referred to as representational, abstract and working memory. They are most prominent in humans and have been most studied in our species. Research has tended to concentrate on representational memory, or memory for episodes (episodic memory), although in recent years the balance has been partially redressed. The extent to which these three kinds of memory are distinct remains controversial, however.

In 1885, Hermann Ebbinghaus published a monograph which marked the beginning of modern research into complex human memory and also initiated a highly influential approach to such research. Ebbinghaus sought to make the problems of memory tractable by simplifying the learning task and learning activity. Acting as his own subject, he achieved this by learning in a **rote** fashion, eschewing the use of meaningful associations, and by learning **nonsense syllables** (for example BYM), which had little intrinsic meaning. This enabled him to reach several general conclusions about learning and memory. For example, he concluded that we forget at a rate which decreases with time, and that the amount learnt is proportional to the time spent learning (the **total time hypothesis**).

Although most of his generalizations have held up well, it is now known that the total time hypothesis only applies when subjects try to learn material in the same way. This reveals a weakness in Ebbinghaus's approach as he deliberately ignored different ways of learning. The significance of this factor was emphasized by Bartlett (1932) who initiated another major approach to memory research, by indicating how important **effort after meaning** is for good memory. Bartlett believed that effort after meaning was central to learning and retrieval, so that research which used impoverished materials and limited subjects' learning and retrieval strategies was doomed to failure. Instead, he studied memory for meaningful material, such as stories, under more natural conditions. This last aspect of his work has recently been revived in the current emphasis on memory in everyday life (see Gruneberg, Morris and Sykes, 1978).

The two approaches not only used different methodologies, but also inspired conflicting models of complex memory. Ebbinghaus's epigones tended to regard the human learner as a passive automaton, who associates sensory inputs automatically. This model is, of course, similar to the one which has been applied to simpler forms of memory in animals. In contrast, the Bartlettian tradition is associated with a view of the human learner as an active and flexible processor of information, who tries to interpret new inputs meaningfully and reconstructs the past from its fragmentary remains by using his current knowledge of the way the world normally is.

The Bartlettian model has much in common with the **information-processing framework** within which most memory research has been conducted since the Second World War. A progenitor of this kind of theorizing was William James, who suggested in 1890 that transient conscious memories were held in a store known as primary memory, which was distinct from the large-capacity store of long-term memories that he called secondary memory. Primary memory was an early conceptualization of working memory. The information-processing framework likens the human brain to a computer in that it receives information, which it operates on and transforms in various ways, while transferring the progressively transformed input from one kind of store to another. This modern framework also implicitly incorporates the division of memory into registration, storage and retrieval. Registration and retrieval are analysed in terms of their constituent subprocesses, which include the way the input is represented, whereas storage is analysed in terms of its mediating physiological states.

Information-processing theorists therefore try and explain

memory phenomena in terms of two broad notions: the existence of different kinds of memory store, and the variety of operations which can be performed on inputs before and after storage (for example, see Atkinson and Shiffrin, 1968). Unfortunately, the evidence used to discriminate the effects of differences in storage and differences of processing has usually been grossly inadequate. It is often unclear whether theorists wish to make a distinction concerning stores or processes. Nevertheless, many theorists have wished to distinguish between long- and short-term memory (Oakley's working memory). This distinction is discussed in the next section. Many have also wished to distinguish between semantic (abstract) and episodic (representational) long-term memory. This distinction derives from Tulving (1972). According to it, **semantic memory** is for context-free information of the kind which is found in dictionaries and encyclopedias. It is abstracted from the flux of experience. For example, my remembering that Delhi is India's capital is semantic memory. In contrast, **episodic memory** is for autobiographical information and events, defined by their context of occurrence. Memory for a list of recently shown words is episodic because their appropriateness is defined by their learning context. It remains uncertain whether the differences between episodic and semantic memory are any greater than those between different forms of episodic memory. How these forms of memory are registered, stored and retrieved will be considered later in this chapter, in order to throw light on this problem.

The distinction between short- and long-term memory

SHORT-TERM SENSORY STORES

Probably less than one-hundredth of the sensory information that impinges every second on the human senses reaches consciousness, and of this one-hundredth, only one-twentieth achieves anything approaching stable storage. An influential view of what happens after information reaches the sense organs is illustrated in simplified form by Figure 6.1. This model includes **preattentional sensory stores** from which some information is successfully passed to a **limited-capacity, short-term store**. Some information that

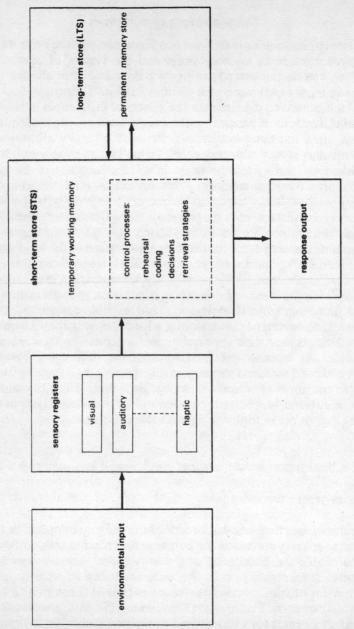

Figure 6.1 How information is sequentially processed and stored according to the modal model of Atkinson and Shiffrin. (Copyright 1971, Scientific American, Inc. All rights reserved. Reprinted by permission)

reaches this stage passes into a more **permanent long-term store**, usually through the process of **rehearsal** (see page 331). The boxes in the model represent specialized stores and the arrows represent processes that transform the information into new forms. This picture of memory, known as the **modal model** (see Atkinson and Shiffrin, 1968), has been heavily criticized (for example, see Wickelgren, 1974, and Crowder, 1982a) although it is still influential. This section considers the evidence for preattentional short-term sensory stores.

Brief sensory stores are generally claimed to have several features. First, they hold 'raw', or unprocessed sensory information, i.e., like a photograph for vision, or an echo for audition. Second, the stored information has not been consciously processed. Third, the stores are more capacious than postattentional short-term memory. Fourth, the information is only stored for between one and a few seconds. Most research has been performed on the postulated preattentive visual store, known as the **icon**. Sperling (1960) developed a technique to show that more information is available immediately after visual stimulation than can be recalled a few seconds later. He showed subjects arrays comprising three rows of four letters each for a total of 50 milliseconds. Then, by presenting a high-, medium- or low-pitched tone, he indicated that they should recall the top, middle or bottom rows. Although subjects could not predict which tone would be sounded, they succeeded in recalling three-quarters of the letters from each row. Sperling inferred that about ten of the twelve letters were available immediately after presentation. When asked to recall all the letters, however, subjects could only recall four or five letters, so the information must have been lost rapidly. This conclusion was supported by the finding that the advantage of **partial reports** was lost if the auditory signal was delayed for a second or so. The 'visual' nature of the store was suggested by the finding that brighter stimuli lead to more persistent icons and also that successively presented patterns merge if they are presented close together in time (see Keele, 1973).

Similar effects have been reported, supporting the existence of an **echoic store**. For example, Treisman (1964) played the same spoken message to both ears, but with one message lagging behind the other. Her subjects shadowed one message to prevent them

BOX 6.1
Eidetic and other forms of sensory memory

If sensory memory exists, then it should represent information in a way similar to that which is found in perception. Evidence that there is such a similarity between visual perception and imagery was cited in Chapter 5. Perhaps the most dramatic form of visual memory is the ability to form **eidetic images**. This ability is rare, although it has been claimed to be commoner in children and nonliterate cultures. 'Eidetikers' can look at a picture for a few seconds, then when it is removed report seeing its image as if it were located in front of their eyes. They can scan the image and describe details from it as long as they can maintain it, which is usually several minutes. The eidetiker describes details from his image as if he is seeing rather than remembering them, and the image can be projected on to outside surfaces. Even so, the image is not an exact photographic reproduction of the original as eidetic children usually make omissions and distortions, and retain most exactly the parts of the original picture which they found most interesting (Haber, 1969).

Eidetic imagery does not usually persist very long and does not usually store great amounts of information. One striking exception was a woman studied by Stroymeyer and Psotka (1970) who could retain very detailed images for long periods. She was able to merge the remembered images of two random-dot stereograms, shown a day apart, so as to form a three-dimensional image. Each stereogram contained thousands of dots. Some have wished to argue that eidetic imagery is a unique form of visual memory, but Gray and Gummerman (1975) have concluded that it is more plausibly seen as lying at one extreme of an intensity dimension for visual images.

Evidence for **auditory sensory memory** is less dramatic. It is perhaps apparent in our ability to recall the particular accents in which acquaintances speak. A few words are usually sufficient to identify the owner of a particular voice.

Diana Deutsch (1970) has studied similar phenomena with music, and has shown that a sensory memory is probably involved. She found that retention of individual tones is impaired when the interval, interpolated before memory-testing, is filled with other tones, but not so much by spoken words. The interference is greater with more similar tones. Memory for individual tones is very poor, however, so the retention of tunes clearly requires additional processes.

Despite the prevalent belief that smells often evoke memories, little research has been done on **olfactory memory** itself. Engen and Ross (1973) exposed subjects to forty-eight different smells and then tested recognition after various delays. Initial recognition was poorer than it would have been for similar visual and auditory stimuli, but there was effectively no forgetting over a three-month retention interval. Although subjects preferred familiar odours, they did not remember them better than novel ones, which suggests that verbal coding is not an important mediator of olfactory memory. There was evidence, however, that similar smells interfere with each other in memory.

There are more esoteric examples of sensory memory which are most unlikely to require verbal coding. For example, following the amputation of a limb, not only does the patient feel that the limb is still there, but also may experience pain in a form, and at the position, in which it had been some time before the severance. These **phantom pains** may persist for years, and indicate that some record of intense pain may be durably stored by the brain (Melzack and Wall, 1982). Sensory memories, then, may be transitory or durable, and may or may not be bolstered by further verbalized interpretations. In some sense they are stored copies of original perceptions, but both original perceptions and memories are themselves meaningful interpretations of reality.

from attending to the other. When the message in the 'rejected' ear was ahead of that in the 'attended' ear, subjects noticed that the messages were identical if the lag was just over a second long. When the attended message led, however, the identity of the messages was noticed with a much greater lag. One interpretation of these findings is that the unattended message is held briefly in an unanalysed form like an echo. Sperling's partial report technique has also been modified to demonstrate both echoic memory and short-term tactile memory. In the latter case, subjects' hands were stimulated with air puffs, and tones then cued subjects to describe the stimulation received in particular parts of their hands. Once again, more information was available initially than a second or so later (Bliss *et al.*, 1966).

The need to postulate brief, large-capacity, preattentional sensory stores has been challenged (see Holding, 1979). The methods used for calculating the amount of information that is initially available have been criticized, and Holding believes that little more information is available immediately than a second or so later. Estimates of the stores' durations vary from a fraction of a second to many seconds, for reasons which the store model cannot easily explain. There is also evidence that estimates of duration and processing demands (as reflected by what is being recalled) are not independent (Erwin, 1976). The icon persists longer when subjects are required to recall stimuli with a higher information content. There is even some doubt as to whether the input is held in a raw, unanalysed form. For example, Treisman (1964) found that her bilingual subjects could spot when unsynchronized French and English messages were the same, even though the messages were not sensorily identical. How can one distinguish between what is held in the store and what can be read out from it? At present there seems to be no answer to this question.

Brief persistence of sensory impressions may be useful in some situations. For example, a rising intonation pattern identifies 'John went home?' as a question. Such a pattern can only be detected if people can briefly retain sound segments longer than a word. Sensory memory seems to exist but its duration may be a function of the time which has been spent processing the sensory input. As Holding (1979) argues, if very brief sensory memory needs a separate store, then many further stores will be required for sensory memories that last for seconds, minutes or hours. More plausibly, the same storage system is involved in all cases but is activated to a greater degree in the different cases. On the other hand, it may be a basic property of neurons that, once activated, they take time to return to a neutral state, and Sakitt (1976) has even proposed that the icon may be a result of persistent retinal activity. Whatever the mechanism, however, only a fraction of incoming sensory information ever reaches consciousness.

THE SHORT-TERM STORE OR WORKING MEMORY

The original form of the notion that attended information is held briefly in a short-term store has been heavily criticized (Wickelgren, 1974; Crowder, 1982a) and modified (see Baddeley and Hitch, 1974). The original modal model tried to explain why so much information is only fleetingly available by postulating the existence of a single store with limited capacity from which information was rapidly lost by displacement unless consciously maintained. The store was supposed to contain *verbal* information, coded in terms either of **acoustic features** or the **articulatory (motor) activities** necessary for producing it, i.e., words were stored as sounds or articulatory movements, rather than as meanings. Sensory information, particularly from the visual and auditory modalities, was appropriately processed and passed into the store in this form, when attention was paid to it. Information could only achieve stable, long-term storage by being passed from the short-term store via rehearsal activities. In their version of the modal model, Atkinson and Shiffrin (1971) argued that the fate of incoming information is a function of structural constraints, like the short-term store with its limited capacity, and of control processes, which determine what information is further processed and in what ways. What is the evidence for this kind of short-term store?

In the past, much emphasis was placed on a phenomenon known as the **serial position effect**. To produce this effect, subjects are shown twelve to sixteen words in succession. They are then asked immediately to recall the words in any order they like. Typical results are illustrated in Figure 6.2. The recall graph is U-shaped, with good recall of the first few words (the primacy effect) and of the last few words (the recency effect). If the subjects can only recall after a delay filled with activity, the last few items are no

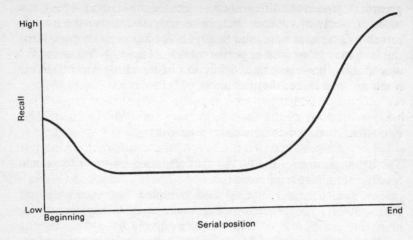

Figure 6.2 Typical serial position curve in which item-recall is a function of list position.

longer well recalled whereas the first few still are. Other variables influence the two effects differently as well (see Wickelgren, 1973). For example, slowing the rate of word-presentation only increases the **primacy effect**. These results have been interpreted as showing that the **recency effect** is caused by words being retrieved from the short-term store whereas the primacy effect arises from retrieval of words in long-term storage. Basically, the evidence indicates that without much processing words are rapidly forgotten, and subjects process words more at the beginning of the list. The last items are only remembered, if they are recalled first and immediately tested.

Do transiently remembered items differ from those more stably remembered, as the modal model predicts? Early work did find evidence for acoustic coding of items. For example, Conrad (1964) found that subjects made the same kind of acoustic errors when they tried to remember *visually* presented consonant sequences in order as they did when trying to detect similar spoken consonants against a noisy background. Similarly, Baddeley (1966a) found that immediate recall of the order of short lists of words was seriously impeded if the words were acoustically similar (e.g., caught, short, taut, nought), but not if they were semantically similar (e.g., huge, big, great, gigantic). After a delay, precisely the opposite effect was found (Baddeley, 1966b). There is no doubt, however, that acoustic and other nonsemantic features often achieve long-term storage, and there is also evidence that transiently remembered information may be semantically encoded (Shulman, 1972). It could be, therefore, that the mode of information-coding reflects the processing which has occurred in a given context rather than being a property of the short-term store (see Wickelgren, 1973). Acoustically coded information may be transient or enduring. What determines the difference may be the *nature* of the store, but equally it may be simply the strength with which storage has occurred in a single kind of store.

Most adults can repeat back in the correct order between five and nine spoken digits. The relative constancy of this **digit span** stimulated the view that the short-term store has a fixed capacity of 7±2 slots into which new information can be put, and from which it is lost by displacement unless voluntarily rehearsed (held in consciousness). If the magic number 7∓2 is exceeded for an individual then the early items in the series are likely to be displaced by the later items, and therefore lost (Miller, 1956). Digit span, however, probably depends on an interaction between strategies of information-processing and structural constraints. Improved strategies enhance the digit span. Thus, one subject from the USA has learned to increase his digit span to eighty digits after one and a half years of practice, by organizing the spoken digits into hierarchies of meaningful **chunks** (Ericsson *et al.*, 1980). For example, 1815 might be perceived by him as a date – a single chunk – rather than as four separate numbers – four chunks. There is still a limitation, and this is really one of *attention*. We can consciously process information only at a certain rate, and basically one chunk at a time, and while we are doing this other information is being forgotten. It is interesting to note that Ericsson and his colleagues' subject still had an average *letter* span of only five to seven letters after hundreds of hours practising with digits.

Digit span increases as children get older probably because they develop more efficient strategies for processing information and organizing it into larger chunks (Dempster, 1981). The number of chunks that can be briefly retained does not seem to change greatly with age, nor does it differ much between adults with spans around seven and the American who managed to increase his span to over seventy digits. If a chunk is what a person perceives and can retrieve as a unit, however encoded, then the number of chunks which can be briefly remembered is limited to something like 7±2. Once again, this limitation is one of attentional processing, and of either the capacity of a short-term store or the strength with which storage has occurred in a single store.

If short-term storage is distinct from longer-term storage, then there should be some kind of brain damage which impairs the latter but leaves immediately tested memory untouched. This dissociation is seen in organic amnesia, in which damage to parts of the limbic system, such as the hippocampus, causes patients to be unable to learn and remember things properly. Severe cases will forget everything they were told and saw just a minute or two previously, and have no day-to-day memory at all. But their digit spans are often normal and they will also display a normal recency effect. This disorder can be interpreted in several ways. First, in support of the modal model, amnesics may have a normal short-term store, but fail to transfer information properly into a separate long-term store. Second, they may encode acoustic features, but fail to encode semantic or meaningful features, and forget things very rapidly as a result. There is evidence, however, that amnesics do encode meaningful information normally (Mayes *et al.*, 1978). Third, there may be a single storage process and amnesics may only store information very poorly, so that they forget very rapidly.

A few brain-damaged patients have also been described, in whom damage to the left parietal cortex is associated with a selective problem of short-term memory (see Shallice and Warrington, 1977). These rare patients have digit spans which are reduced to one or two items, and do not show recency effects with orally presented word-lists. These deficits are memory failures rather than problems with repeating speech, as they may also be apparent in recognition tests, which minimize any speech demands. The deficit is remarkably specific. It only affects the short-term retention of spoken language – short-term memory for nonspeech sounds (such as the roar of a vacuum cleaner) is normal. Short-term retention of visually presented verbal stimuli is also effectively normal. Finally, Shallice and Warrington have claimed that these patients have normal long-term memory even for spoken verbal stimuli (although the claim has been challenged by Glanzer and Clark, 1979). If correct, these claims imply that the modal model is wrong in detail. Either information does not pass into long-term storage via a short-term store, or there may be a number of such stores, which can hold different kinds of information for short periods. The disorder can also be interpreted in terms of a single-store view of memory. The patients may have a subtle problem with perceiving phonemes in speech, such that listening to speech is like listening to a foreign language – it is forgotten almost immediately. If they can get to *understand* what is said, however, they will remember normally and for long periods.

Baddeley and Hitch (1974) formulated the influential working memory hypothesis, which considerably revises the modal model treatment of short-term memory. They proposed that short-term memory comprises a number of **independent subsystems**, each of which is involved in mediating different aspects of cognition, i.e., is doing work. The subsystems do not have to be regarded as distinct stores, but merely as independent capacities. Working memory may be likened to a number of jugglers, most of whom juggle with only one *kind* of ball. How many they can keep in the air will depend on their juggling skills (processing ability) and on gravity (the constraint provided by storage). In their early work, Baddeley and Hitch found that if subjects were simultaneously required to remember the order of six digits (just within their digit spans) and perform tasks involving comprehension, problem-solving, reading and speech production, then performance on the latter tasks was impaired. This suggested that aspects of short-term memory are involved in mediating these cognitive tasks.

Hitch (1980) suggests that working memory may be divided into an **output system**, or **articulatory loop**, which retains speech output; an **input system**, which retains recently spoken language; a **nonverbal system** which briefly retains visuospatial information; and a **general purpose central executive**, which can 'juggle' with most kinds of information. If subjects are required to perform a digit-span task (holding six digits in memory) while simultaneously being presented with a list of words, to be recalled in any order (one task is visual, the other auditory), they show a normal recency effect although their primacy effect is reduced. This implies that the system responsible for digit span is largely independent of the one which mediates the recency effect. The implication is further supported by the lack of correlation between the two in adults, and by a study which showed that poor beginning readers had a lower digit span than good beginning readers, but showed the same-sized recency effects (Byrne and Arnold, 1981). (See pages 590–2.)

Hitch argued that the recency effect depends on the input system whereas digit span depends primarily on the articulatory loop. Suppressing the ability of subjects to articulate the words in a list, by getting them to repeat an irrelevant sound like 'the', does not affect the recency effect, but it does reduce the number of words that can be repeated in order (digit span). Irrelevant articulation therefore uses the articulatory loop, but not the capacity of the input system. Interestingly, the capacity of the articulatory loop seems to be equivalent to the number of words which can be spoken in two seconds. The loop's capacity is also reduced by **phonemic similarity** between words, and its breakdown is related to the commission of errors, phonemically related to correct items. The loop maintains the *order* of verbal items, and in conjunction with the central executive is responsible for digit-span performance in most cases.

Less is known about visual short-term memory, although there is good evidence for such an independent system. The central executive is very similar to the limited-capacity attentional system, considered in Chapter 4. The working memory hypothesis postulates that this general-purpose processor is associated with a number of special-purpose **slave systems**. What work do these systems perform? The input system may aid the comprehension of complex sentences by briefly retaining partially analysed versions of earlier parts of such sentences until the central executive can analyse them further. Thus, the patients of Shallice and Warrington, whose input systems are probably deficient, have difficulty in understanding complex sentences. The articulatory loop (as well as the central executive) seems to be involved in reasoning and mental arithmetic tasks, and its involvement in speech production is suggested by the form taken by Spooneristic errors (for example, saying 'Tasted the whole worm' instead of 'Wasted the whole term'). The existence of these phonemic exchanges suggests that several words are activated together, and the fact that they rarely occur with words more than six words apart accords well with the postulated capacity of the loop (about six words can be spoken in two seconds). Less research has been done on the visuospatial system, but if it exists then it is most likely to be involved in nonverbal and spatial kinds of thinking.

Current thinking about short-term memory is therefore couched in different terms from the original modal model. Brief retention abilities are now believed to depend on the activities of several relatively independent systems, which do not only retain verbally encoded information. These systems are conceived of as performing distinct cognitive functions. Whether the systems depend on distinct *stores* or *kinds of processing* is not specified, but the old emphasis on specialized stores is reduced. Wickelgren (1974) has indeed argued that all available results can be explained in terms of a **single-store model**. According to him, acoustic, semantic and visuospatial information can all be held in the same store, and how quickly they are forgotten will depend on their strength of storage and the number of similar competing items in memory. In his view, if short- and long-term storage are distinct then the mathematical laws which describe how information is forgotten from them over time must be different, and they are not.

This section began with the assertion that very little sensory information achieves stable storage. We live under conditions of continuous information-overload. Information is lost rapidly because its durability depends on how we process it and for how long, and, because there is a drastic limit on how fast we can process information, much information can only be briefly retained. Short-term memory is unlikely to depend on the kind of specialized store considered by Wickelgren, nor is it likely that different physiological storage processes underlie it relative to information that is retained for minutes rather than seconds.

The registration of information

HOW DOES THE WAY INFORMATION IS ENCODED AFFECT REMEMBERING?

Episodic and semantic memory is often for complex information, comprising many different kinds of features. Psychologists in the Bartlettian tradition have long held the view that how well this information is remembered depends on *what* is encoded. In particular, they have argued that 'effort after meaning', leading to the encoding of semantic features, gives rise to better memory. Craik and Lockhart (1972) developed an influential modern version of this viewpoint which is known as the **level or depth of information approach**. They proposed that the more deeply information was processed (and therefore encoded), the more slowly it was forgotten. With words, deep features tended to correspond with meaningful aspects, and shallow features with physical features, such as letter structure or word sound.

Typical evidence for the depth of processing hypothesis is provided by a study of Craik and Tulving (1975). They required subjects to answer questions about a series of words, then gave them an unexpected recognition test for the words. In one experiment there were four kinds of question. Subjects were asked whether words were in capital letters (visual); whether the words rhymed with selected target words (phonemic); whether they belonged in a particular semantic category; and whether they would fit in selected sentences (sentence). Table 6.1 illustrates some typical questions. The surprise recognition test involved presentation of the words they had seen, intermingled with the same number of novel words. Subjects had to indicate which words they had seen before. It was found that recognition improved as depth of encoding increased, i.e., in the order visual, phonemic, category then sentence processing. Also, if the answer to a question was 'Yes', then recognition was better than if the answer was 'No'. Further experiments showed that these effects also applied to recall.

The depth of processing approach has stimulated many studies like that of Craik and Tulving, in which **incidental learning**, i.e. subjects do not know their memory is to be tested, is combined with an **orienting task**, i.e. questions are asked, which are devised to get subjects to encode some features and not others in the target material. Depth effects apply to memory for nonverbal as well as verbal stimuli. For example, later recognition of pictures can be improved if subjects are asked to interpret what they mean (Meudell, Mayes and Neary, 1980), and recognition of faces can be improved above the levels produced by spontaneous learning if subjects are required to make general judgements about the owners

Table 6.1 **Examples of questions in Craik and Tulving's 1975 experiment**

Depth of encoding	Question	Answer	
		Yes	*No*
Visual	Is the word in capital letters?	TABLE	table
Phonemic	Does the word rhyme with WAIT?	Hate	Chicken
Category	Is the word a type of food?	Cheese	Steel
Sentence	Would the word fit the sentence:		
	'He kicked the —— into the tree'?	Ball	Rain

of the faces (for example, are they honest, friendly or attractive?). Judgements about specific facial features (for example, nose size) leads to much poorer recognition (see Bower and Karlin, 1974). In general, emphasis on the interpretation of stimuli – i.e., finding meaning in them – leads to better recall and recognition.

Craik and Lockhart's original formulation claimed that deeper processing corresponded to more semantic encoding of stimuli, and that this led to better memory because semantic features are forgotten more slowly. They also claimed that there are two kinds of rehearsal. **Rehearsal** is the continuance of information-processing when the stimulus may no longer be present, and it may either elaborate on the processing already performed (**elaborative rehearsal**) or merely repeat or maintain the processing already performed (**maintenance rehearsal**). According to Craik and Lockhart, only elaborative rehearsal improves memory. In an ingenious experiment, Craik and Watkins (1973) found that if subjects continued to process words *in the same way*, then the duration of this rehearsal was unrelated to delayed recall; that is to say, 'rote' rehearsal does not improve recall. Finally, Craik and Lockhart criticized the modal model. For them, memory was a product of how information is perceived, and transience or durability of memories depends on what is encoded. Short-term memory therefore involves superficially encoded information and what is held in consciousness.

The original depth of processing formulation has been criticized and altered (see Cermak and Craik, 1979). An initial difficulty was the notion of depth. The presupposition behind this notion was that information is processed *sequentially* after it arrives at the sense organs. Features that are processed later are encoded more deeply. In Craik and Tulving's (1975) study, however, it was found that the reaction time to some questions about word structure was slower than that to questions involving word meaning, and yet the former questions led to much poorer memory. There was therefore a danger than 'depth' might be treated in a circular fashion, i.e., deeper encoding is defined as that which leads to better memory. As a result, less stress is now placed on the notion of 'depth' than on the **qualitative features of encoding**, which features lead to good memory, and why they do so. Although the encoding of semantic features is believed to lead to good memory, contrary to the view of Craik and Lockhart, there is no conclusive evidence that semantic features are forgotten more slowly than physical features. Thus, physical and semantic features are forgotten at the same rate provided they were learnt to the same degree initially (Nelson and Vining, 1978). Also, 'low'-level features of words are obviously well retained, as words with odd spellings (for example, 'phlegm') are better remembered than words with common spellings, such as 'primate' (Hunt and Elliott, 1980). If semantic features are not forgotten more slowly, why does their encoding lead to better memory?

The most influential answer to the above question is that semantic encoding makes a memory more distinct from other competing memories. This explains why negative answers to semantic orienting questions do not help memory much. For example, to encode that 'dog' is not a form of food does not distinguish the word from most competitors, whereas encoding that it *is* a domestic animal does. **Semantic encodings** of a stimulus tend to distinguish it from other items in memory far more successfully than **phonemic** or **structural encodings**. There are exceptions, however. If subjects are asked to pronounce words in atypical ways then their later remembering is helped considerably (Eysenck, 1979). In such cases, the physical encoding has been made distinctive. Eysenck (1979) argued that whereas encoding distinctive features particularly helps recognition, **elaborative encoding** may be more helpful to later recall. Elaborative encoding basically involves the encoding of *more* features, and particularly more meaningful features. It has been reported several times that when orienting tasks encourage the encoding of several relatively unrelated semantic features, then memory is greatly enhanced (see Eysenck, 1979). Although increased elaboration of encoding tends to mean increased distinctiveness of encoding, the two can be dissociated from each other.

It is interesting to note that orienting tasks that encourage subjects to encode material in relation to themselves give rise to even better memory than nonpersonal semantic orienting tasks (see Greenwald, 1981). Information encoded in relation to the self is being related to a very rich construct system and so is likely to be highly distinctive. If Lord (1980) is right, then the encoding is most effective if it takes the form of verbal descriptions rather than visual images. He found that such descriptions were the best means of remembering things about ourselves, whereas information about other people is better remembered in terms of visual images. He argued that this is because we learn about other people mainly by seeing them whereas we learn about ourselves in a more abstract fashion.

The **distinctiveness hypothesis** is itself open to criticism. Apart from the difficulty of predicting in advance what will make a memory distinctive, it has been argued that memory distinctiveness depends on the conditions of retrieval (see Bransford, 1979) as well as those of learning. The emphasis is on **transfer-appropriate encoding** to ensure that the memory will be distinctive at retrieval. Even semantic encoding may be inappropriate relative to structural encoding. For example, if a subject is asked to remember a word's *size*, then performance will be best after a 'structural' orienting task. Although semantic encodings usually lead to more distinctive memories, different kinds of semantic encoding are appropriate to different retrieval tasks. For example, Barclay and his colleagues (1974) asked subjects to remember unambiguous words like 'piano'. During learning, the words were embedded in sentences which encouraged the encoding of different features. Thus, a piano was processed as a heavy object or a musical instrument. Subjects' memory was tested by cues such as 'You can play it' or 'It's difficult to move'. Their recall was much better when the cue matched the conditions of learning. The notion of transfer-appropriate encoding is closely related to Tulving's (1979) hypothesis of **encoding specificity**, which will be further discussed later in this chapter. According to this hypothesis, cues are only effective at retrieval insofar as they have been encoded during initial learning.

Encoding something in a distinctive way (perhaps partly because it often requires elaborative encoding of extra features) tends to involve attentional effort. Hasher and Zacks (1979) have argued that much encoding is not like this. It is automatic and uses very little attentional capacity. Typically, such encoding can be performed with only minimal disturbance of other cognitive activities and can occur without intentional direction. Hasher and Zacks claim that information about event frequency, recency and location is automatically encoded, and that memory for this information changes little with practice or increasing age. Aspects of word meaning may also be encoded automatically, but this clearly is an acquired skill which has reached the stage of automatization. Some aspects of the encoding of faces also seem to make minimal attentional demands. Thus, Kellogg (1980) found that faces are remembered even when they have not been attended to properly. He showed a series of faces to subjects while simultaneously requiring them to do complex multiplications. Although subjects recognized the faces at an above-chance level, their encoding had not disturbed their mental arithmetic. Also there was no relationship between their memory and their self-reported degree of attention to the faces.

Whereas it is difficult to influence **automatic encoding, effortful encoding** can be controlled to some degree by the learner, or by an experimenter through the use of orienting tasks. This kind of encoding increases with practice and age, and is impaired by disorders that affect motivation and attentional capacity. For example, the poor memory of depressives can probably be traced to the fact that they do not elaboratively encode what they experience (see Hasher and Zacks, 1979). Also, Rabinowitz and his colleagues (1982) reported that part of the memory failure shown by old people arises because of their reduced attentional capacity. It was found that the old people's failure to encode specific semantic features properly could be simulated in young subjects by making them learn while simultaneously performing a demanding task, which effectively reduced their attentional capacity.

The relationship between attention and encoding raises an important question about what is meant by encoding. Whether a feature is encoded automatically or with considerable effort, the learner is, at that time, able to indicate directly his knowledge of the encoded feature. For example, if he saw a blue postbox and encoded its blueness then he would, at that time, be able to say the box was blue rather than red. If encoding entails this kind of ability then it must involve the processing of information which reaches consciousness or attention. There is evidence, however, that even if information is processed *unconsciously* it has an *indirect* impact on subsequent memory (see Dixon, 1981). Two experiments illustrate this assertion. In the first, Eagle and his colleagues (1966) briefly showed subjects a picture of a tree in which was embedded the shape of a duck. The picture was shown too briefly for the subjects to identify that there was a duck embedded in it, i.e., there was no conscious encoding. Nevertheless, when asked to generate stories about a country scene, viewing the picture significantly increased their tendency to introduce ducks into their stories. Dixon (1981) cites other experiments in which aspects of **subliminally** viewed pictures get incorporated into subsequent dreams. In the second experiment, Kunst-Wilson and Zajonc (1979) showed subjects drawings of irregular polygons for a thousandth of a second. Subsequent recognition of these shapes did not exceed the level expected by chance, but the subjects had an *aesthetic preference* for the polygons they had seen, relative to similar but novel polygons.

It seems, therefore, that encoding must be accessible to consciousness (and use at least minimal attentional capacity), if later recognition and recall are to be possible. Subliminal processing may generate lasting memories but these can only be expressed indirectly. When a complex event is perceived, attentional resources are deployed so that some of its features are encoded in preference to others. Generally, encoding more meaningful features leads to a more distinctive memory – and hence a better one. This kind of encoding also often involves more effort. It is associated with greater dilation of the pupils (a measure of attentional effort) and is more disruptive of a concurrently performed task, which suggests that it uses more capacity (see Eysenck and Eysenck, 1979). Structural encoding may, however, be more demanding than semantic encoding, when the structural information is atypical. For example, reading inverted and reversed sentences places much heavier demands on graphemic than semantic analysis. It also seems to lead to better memory for the graphemic features as Kolers (1979) has found that subjects can read such sentences faster when they are re-presented after a year, even though their semantic contents are not recognized.

In Kolers's experiments, structural encodings of sentences lead to very good memories; they are also very effortful. It is also plausible to argue that the encodings are distinctive because the sentence structures are atypical. There is, however, some evidence that more effortful encoding leads to better memory independently of *what* kinds of features are being encoded. For example, Tyler and his colleagues (1979) found that the more effortful of two semantic orienting tasks was associated with better memory. It is likely that the **storage** of a feature will be superior if more effort is expended in its encoding. This suggests a further modification of the distinctiveness hypothesis. Complex information is encoded in terms of multiple features or attributes. Subsequent memory is a function of the **distinctiveness** of the encoded features *and* the *strength* with which they are *stored*; i.e., what is encoded and how strongly it is stored. This depends partly on the deployment of attention and the effort devoted to encoding. Orienting tasks will not only affect what is encoded, they will also affect storage strength. For example, a structural orienting task may not prevent semantic encoding, but it will weaken the storage of semantic features. This hypothesis also explains why, contrary to Craik and Watkins's (1973) claim, continued maintenance rehearsal of structural features does improve long-term recognition (see Nelson and Vining, 1978). Also, contrary to Craik and Lockhart's (1972) view, short-term memory phenomena are consequences both of *what* is encoded and how inadequately this information is stored. These consequences arise because in short-term memory tasks attentional resources are overstretched.

It should not be forgotten, however, that most people perceive complex events and materials with a mental set directed towards comprehension through the extraction of meaning. Indeed, the operation of this set may result in their acquiring things that were not present in the original material. Thus, in studying a series of sentences, subjects tend to make **inferences** which are hard to distinguish from the original sentences. For example, shown a sentence such as 'Three turtles sat on a log and a fish swam beneath *it*', subjects have great difficulty later in distinguishing it from its natural inference: 'Three turtles sat on a log and a fish swam beneath *them*'. This kind of **constructive encoding process** is particularly important in the perception of complex, sequential material, such as stories or real-life events, where it sometimes causes distortions. Similarly, interitem organizational processes are prominent in learning lists of items (for example, words). The learner typically groups items according to a personally meaningful scheme, so as to aid subsequent recall. Although recognition is possible without this kind of organization, it is found that rote repetition leads to very poor recall. Clearly, organizing items into groups means they can be retrieved in groups, provided the groupings are remembered. The encoding involved is elaborative, but it probably does not increase the distinctiveness of memory for individual items.

ENCODING AND THE DEVELOPMENT AND DEMISE OF MEMORY

Young children (about five years old) do not use the range of rehearsal and encoding strategies employed by older children and adults. As a result their memory for complex information also tends to be less good, although their storage and retrieval processes may also be underdeveloped and contribute to the inadequacy of their memories. They tend not to **plan** their learning despite the fact that even five-year-olds possess many of the basic encoding skills. This deficiency in **self-programming** is associated with another in **metamemory** – knowledge about their own memory and memory in general. Relative to older children, young children cannot judge well when it is necessary to learn something *actively* rather than rely on its automatic acquisition. They are less good at predicting how other people will remember on the basis of what they did during learning, and do not understand that properties of materials such as familiarity and categorizability can be used in the learning process (see Belmont, 1978). Young children are also less accurate at predicting whether they will be able to recognize items which they have failed to recall; i.e., they do not have a 'feeling-of-knowing' to the same extent as older children (see Gruneberg, 1983).

The poor memory of young children therefore partly arises because they do not self-programme themselves to use the appropriate encoding skills that they possess. This failure may be caused by their lack of knowledge of their own memories. Thus, young children's failure to rehearse results in poor memory, but although they can rehearse when instructed to do so, they cease to do so when instructions are no longer given even though their memory deteriorates again. In other words, they can rehearse elaboratively but fail to do so spontaneously (see Gruneberg, 1983). Turnure and his colleagues (1976) illustrated this phenomenon further in a study in which they showed to five-year-old children twenty-one pairs of pictures of common objects and gave different groups separate instructions. Children were told to label the pictures (which they do spontaneously); to generate a sentence about each pair; to repeat an experimenter-selected sentence; and to construct fantasies about the paired objects. Later, the children were shown one object in each pair and asked to say what the other was. They recalled one, three, eight and sixteen objects in each respective test. Despite this, they failed to use the successful strategies spontaneously.

There is an interesting similarity between adult patients who have sustained damage to the frontal lobes of the brain and young children. Both groups have problems in planning their learning and retrieving activities although many of the basic skills exist to be called upon. Thus, frontally lesioned patients show very poor spontaneous learning of unrelated word-pairs, such as 'monkey-house'. But if they are instructed to form visual images which link the pairs, their memory improves to normal levels. They do not continue to use this strategy, however, unless explicitly instructed to do so. As the frontal lobes continue to develop long after birth, it is possible that five-year-old children do not yet have fully functional frontal lobes, so that their self-programming in many cognitive areas is inadequate. In addition to this kind of deficiency, the encoding abilities of young children will also be deficient because they lack the rich range of knowledge upon which adults can draw to make their encodings more distinct.

Memory declines with age, but the rate of decline is extremely variable. Short-term memory, except under conditions of divided attention, holds up better than longer-term memory. The ability to acquire episodic and semantic memories declines, and memory for long-past episodes and, to a lesser extent, well-established semantic memories also may deteriorate. The causes of these age-related deficits are likely to be manifold, but some old people at least seem to show encoding problems that are similar to those found in young children and frontal-lobe patients. They use less elaborative encoding than younger adults with better memory. For example, they have been found to show less semantic grouping or **clustering** when learning lists of words, and Nebes (1976) found that his elderly subjects were less likely to use visual imagery in learning paired-associate words. These deficits were failures to use appropriate encoding skills spontaneously, as the elderly subjects could still be encouraged to use the skills that were intact. Part of the memory problem of ageing may therefore be associated with the atrophy of the frontal lobes. Not all elderly people with poor memory, however, show this kind of problem. Other encoding failures are associated with declining intelligence, which is aggravated in the diseases of dementia. Elderly patients with the movement control disorder known as Parkinsonism may experience dramatic thought-slowing so that they encode less and suffer consequently from poor memory (Wilson *et al.*, 1980). It should be stressed that the old are likely to suffer retrieval problems, which spring from the same source as their encoding problems. Finally, as will be discussed on pages 357–8, a major problem in old people's memory, particularly in those suffering from the form of premature dementia called Alzheimer's disease, involves an ill-understood storage deficit.

INDIVIDUAL DIFFERENCES IN ENCODING, AND SUPERNORMAL MEMORY

There are enormous individual differences in people's episodic and semantic memories. These differences are not merely general as they may also apply to specific kinds of material. In other words, a person may have good or bad memory generally or he may have good or bad memory for colours or faces or words. Herrmann and Neisser (1978) gave students a memory questionnaire, the results of which indicated that, as well as a general factor, there were a number of specific memory factors including memory for conversations, names, errands, people and things learnt by rote. Similar memory abilities have been identified by giving large groups of people batteries of memory tests (Guilford, 1982). Although the causes of these individual differences in memory are poorly understood, an important factor is likely to be the effectiveness of encoding.

Individual differences are probably of two kinds. First, much processing of complex information is performed by various parts of the neocortex – these regions are also likely to store the information. The physiological efficiency of these regions is probably inherited and determines the effectiveness with which distinct kinds of information are encoded. For example, the physiological efficiency of one region may control the encoding of colour whereas that of another region will control the encoding of faces. Memory for faces and colours seems to be distinct. Second, the effectiveness with which particular kinds of materials are encoded and remembered depends on the richness of the knowledge store upon which the learner can call in encoding. If you know a lot about something you can rapidly elaborate distinctive encoding of related, new material. For example, expert chessplayers can retain meaningful chess positions after very brief exposures. Their ability to do this is markedly superior to that of average players although their memory in general and that for meaningless chess positions is not superior. Unlike the average players, experts have a vast pool of chess lore which enables them to interpret new 'games' very rapidly. Another striking illustration of this effect is the finding of a correlation between knowledge of football and memory for an arbitrary TV collection of football scores. Football fans were presumably able to encode even this low-grade material in a rich and elaborative way (Morris *et al.*, 1981).

As elaborative encoding based on meaningful interpretation of material predicts good memory, it is not surprising that high intelligence shows some association with excellent memory. For example, high verbal ability predicts that subjects' verbal memory will be superior, but their memory for other kinds of material will not necessarily be so (see Hunt, 1978). There is evidence that subjects with high verbal ability are faster at retrieving very well established semantic memories. It is likely that such fast *retrieval* of semantic information is a key factor in enabling them to encode rapidly and distinctively. As high verbal ability subjects continue to show superior digit spans even when the rate of presentation is too fast for elaborative encoding, it has also been suggested that their attentional capacities are greater and that this facilitates their memory (see Eysenck, 1983). It should be noted, however, that tests of visuospatial ability have been less successful in predicting spatial memory (see Eysenck, 1983, for a discussion of this problem). **Cognitive style** may sometimes be more important than ability in generating effective encodings of material.

Although intelligence and background knowledge determine the effectiveness of encoding, the encoding of specific information may be regarded as a trainable skill. For example, the French artist Boisbaudran (1911) developed a training system which enabled his students to study paintings so that they could later reproduce them with great accuracy. The knowledge and skills acquired by the students were specifically intended to provide a rich framework for encoding the paintings. Training markedly developed their abilities to paint reproductions.

Temperament and **psychopathology** may also influence what and how much is encoded during learning, but current evidence is somewhat confused (see Eysenck, 1983). For example, although it has been claimed that anxious individuals engage in less semantic processing, most studies show equivalent effects on the encoding of structural and semantic features. Either **anxiety** generally reduces the amount of elaborative processing or it reduces the strength with which information is stored. It may do both by decreasing effective attentional capacity. It has already been stated that **depression** reduces elaborative encoding, perhaps by its effect on motivation. **Schizophrenia** has also been reported to impair verbal memory, and although some of this impairment is a result of a decline in cognitive efficiency, some of it persists even when the cognitive losses are taken into account (Calev *et al.*, 1983). Storage, as well as encoding and retrieval, may therefore be deficient in some schizophrenics.

The explanation of **exceptional memories** has always been a challenge to psychologists and several 'mnemonists' have been studied in depth. One of the most remarkable was the Russian journalist Shereshevskii, who has been described by Luria (see Baddeley, 1976). This man could repeat back a list of seventy

BOX 6.2
Mnemonics and the use of imagery

We sometimes wish to remember materials which are difficult to interpret in a very meaningful fashion. **Mnemonics** may help in achieving this end as they are devices for making things memorable by increasing the distinctiveness of structural rather than semantic features. Many mnemonics, however, are intended to improve recall more than recognition, and do this by artificially creating cues for retrieval and artificial links between list items that are not meaningfully related. These kinds of mnemonic probably only have a small effect on memory distinctiveness. Traditionally, there has been a distinction between reduction coding and elaboration coding in mnemonics. A **reduction code** reduces the amount that needs to be remembered, by, for example, offering a cue, such as a knotted handkerchief, that something, unspecified by the cue, needs to be remembered. **Elaboration coding** is more important because it requires the encoding of extra information, either to increase memory distinctiveness or to provide linking retrieval cues to improve recall.

It is difficult to remember the colours of the rainbow and their order. The task is made easier by learning the mnemonic sentence, 'Richard of York gained battles in vain', the first letters of which begin the names of the colours of the rainbow: red, orange, yellow, green, blue, indigo and violet. The sentence is meaningful and therefore quickly learned, and it provides cues both for the colours and their order. This example of a **special-purpose mnemonic** also illustrates the fact that we have particular difficulty in remembering the order of unrelated items. An example of a **general-purpose mnemonic** which overcomes this difficulty for any kind of list of up to ten items is the peg mnemonic system. A short poem has to be learned, for example: 'One is a bun, two is a shoe, three is a tree, four is a door, five is a hive, six is for sticks, seven is for heaven, eight is a gate, nine is for wine, ten is a hen.' The learner then forms an image of item one in the list interacting with the bun. For example, if the first item is a knife then it could be imagined sticking into the bun. The procedure is continued through the list, and recall is achieved by reproducing the rhyme and regenerating the images in turn. It is extremely effective for remembering short, ordered lists.

Like many mnemonics, the peg system makes use of visual imagery, and it has been argued that this kind of elaborative encoding may lead to especially strong memories. Paivio (1969) showed that how well a word can be remembered is best predicted from the ease with which it evokes an image, i.e., from its imageability. Similarly, sentences comprising more imageable words are better remembered than abstract sentences, even though they are no more easily understood. Paivio argued that imageable words and sentences are better remembered because they can be encoded in terms of a **dual coding**: a verbal and an imagery one. Verbal encodings seem to be performed mainly by the left hemisphere whereas visual imagery is generated more within the right hemisphere (see Paivio and Linde, 1982). The processing of language and images therefore seems to involve distinct mechanisms even if the nature of the codes does not differ fundamentally (see Box 5.1). Even so, the dual encoding hypothesis has been criticized for other reasons. For example, although people differ markedly in their reported intensity of imagery and in their ability to manipulate imagery, these individual differences do not clearly predict differences in any kind of memory. This predictive failure either indicates the irrelevance to memory of imagery, or, more likely, the difficulty we have in rating so subjective a process. The question of the importance of imagery for mnemonics, and for memory in general, remains open.

words, numbers or letters without reaching his limit. Lists like these, or of more complex materials, he retained with great fidelity for decades. He used rich, multisensory images to encode materials, which he developed into a mnemonic system when he became a professional mnemonist. Two things were noticeable about his performance. First, he could reorganize and elaborate materials, which for him were meaningless, with great rapidity. Second, this facility notwithstanding, he showed a remarkable ability to retain memories for very long periods. Shereshevskii showed the phenomenon of **synaesthesia**, in which stimulation in one sensory modality evokes imagery in another, and this may have made his memories even more distinctive, although it is doubtful that this is a sufficient explanation of their durability.

Whereas Shereshevskii's encoding involved imagery and did not rely strongly on the meaning of the material he learned, other mnemonists encode in different ways. An exceptional subject, V.P., studied by the American psychologists Love and Hunt, relied on linguistic associations, which, in polyglot fashion, he used with great speed to organize previously meaningless material into an intricate network of meaningful associations. A third case – that of the calculation and memory prodigy Professor Aitken, who was studied by Hunter – used imagery as did Shereshevskii, and the verbal associations typical of V.P. Most of Aitken's great body of associations were arithmetical. For example, he could reorganize '1961' as the equivalent of '37×53' or '44^2+5^2' or '40^2+19^2' almost instantly. Like Shereshevskii and V.P., he accumulated this knowledge over many years and used it in performing very complex mental arithmetic problems in his head, as well as displaying feats of memory (see Baddeley, 1976).

Part of the remarkable ability of mnemonists can, then, be explained by their rapid formation of highly distinctive and elaborate codes for new information. This no doubt depends on unusual knowledge, the acquisition of special encoding skills and probably also on their possession of neocortexes which are 'physiologically' very efficient. It also seems likely that this is not the whole story. Extremely effective storage may also be involved in some, if not all, cases. For example, a subject studied by Coltheart and Glick and dubbed Sue d'Onim (see Baddeley, 1976), had an exceptional ability to repeat spoken words backwards. Her ability to manipulate spatial images was only average, but she had an outstanding iconic memory and could also visually encode letters at four times the normal rate. The unusual durability of her memory for visually presented material seems to be a result of powerful storage rather than facile encoding.

Retrieval

RELATIONSHIP OF RETRIEVAL CUES TO REGISTRATION

William James and many psychologists since have believed that recall is never truly 'free' or spontaneous. It only occurs as a consequence of **cueing**. Whether explicitly or implicitly presented, cues determine the direction of the retrieval process, and its success depends on the appropriateness of the available cues. Such cues may be of two kinds. First, the cue may have been encoded in original learning so that it forms part of the information to be recalled. Second, the cue may not have been encoded during original learning, but it still enables the subject to infer what the information to be recalled is likely to be. Jones (1979) characterizes these cues as depending on **intrinsic** and **extrinsic knowledge** respectively, and believes that they both aid recall although probably in different ways. This belief is denied by the encoding specificity principle (see Tulving, 1979), which claims that cues only help retrieval if they have been encoded during learning. In some ingenious studies with colleagues, Tulving found that when words like 'black' were encoded with weak associates like 'train', then later presentations of such weak associates aided recall. In contrast, presentation of a strong associate such as 'white' did not improve recall above the level found without explicit cues. Tulving (1979) argued that the normal superiority of semantic encoding arises largely because our predominantly semantic 'set' means that similar semantic features will be available as cues at retrieval.

There is a danger of treating the encoding specificity principle in a circular fashion and to argue that if a cue helps memory then the corresponding feature has been encoded, but if it does not then the feature could not have been encoded. A reasonable hypothesis might be that cues dependent on intrinsic knowledge are particularly effective in helping retrieval of complex information, but that cues dependent on extrinsic knowledge are also effective, albeit less so and in different ways. This may be because intrinsic knowledge cues are more likely to bear a unique relationship to the to-be-remembered information. Extrinsic knowledge cues may sometimes cause reconstructive distortions at retrieval because they only permit inferences from general knowledge and do not bear such a unique relationship to the to-be-remembered information, as will be further discussed on pages 350–4. Retrieval of information involves reconstruction of the way in which it was originally encoded through processes initiated by the perception of intrinsic and extrinsic knowledge cues. These processes are unconscious and are still poorly understood.

RECALL AND RECOGNITION

Retrieval is usually assessed by determining whether subjects can recall target information or whether they can recognize it. Recall may be unaided by explicitly presented cues (**free recall**) or aided by explicit hints (**cued recall**). Recognition of a series of target items may be tested by showing a mixture of **target** and **distractor** items one at a time and requiring the subject to identify which items he has learned (**Yes/No recognition**). It may also be tested by presenting each target item with one or more distractors and requiring the subject to identify the target (**forced-choice recognition**). More targets are usually identified in recognition tests than in recall tests, and in this sense recognition tests may be said to be easier. This fact is compatible with **two-stage** views of remembering, which posit that remembering involves a search or generation process followed by one of identification (see Zechmeister and Nyberg, 1982, for a discussion). It is usually proposed that recall tests require both processes whereas recognition tests only require identification processes. Two things follow from this claim. First, there should be variables which influence recall and recognition in different ways. Second, recognition should never be worse than recall.

Several variables do influence recall and recognition differently. Thus, it is easier to recall common words than rare ones. Subjects presented with lists of common or rare words will recall more of the common ones. In contrast, they will later recognize more of the *rare* words. This is known as the **word-frequency effect** and is usually interpreted in terms of the two-stage retrieval view by arguing that it is easier to elaborate linking codes between common words (helpful for search and therefore recall), whereas rare words are more distinctive (helpful for identification and therefore recognition). There is, however, little independent evidence for these claims (see Zechmeister and Nyberg, 1982). A second variable which influences recall and recognition differently is **intention** to learn. For example, casual inspection of a word-list will cause little impairment in recognition relative to that following intentional learning whereas it will drastically affect recall. Recognition is little disturbed, at least partly because maintenance rehearsal increases familiarity but has little or no effect on recall. As familiarity increases so does recognition (see Mandler, 1980). A third differentially significant variable is learning **strategy**, as people seem to learn material differently depending on whether they expect a recall or recognition test. Tversky (1973) showed pictures to subjects, half of whom expected to be tested by recall and half by recognition. Performance was better when they received the expected test than when they were surprised by the other kind of test. If there are recognition and recall appropriate encoding strategies, then how someone performs at one kind of test may not predict how they will do at the other. It is therefore interesting that recognition and recall levels sometimes correlate poorly (see Brown and Monk, 1978).

Although recognition and recall may be facilitated by somewhat distinct encoding patterns, this does not prove that recognition only involves an identification process. If this were so, recognition should never be poorer than recall. Recognition is not the most sensitive measure of memory. Relearning can show that memory is still present because there are savings relative to first learning even when there is no recognition (see Zechmeister and Nyberg, 1982). More importantly, it is now also known that under certain conditions recall is superior to recognition. For example, if target words such as 'dog' are presented for study with weak associates such as 'bone', then later recognition of target words produced as free responses to strong associates like 'cat', which were not presented during initial study, is very poor. In fact, such recognition is worse than recall, cued by the weak associates that were present during initial study (see Tulving, 1979; and Zechmeister and

Nyberg, 1982, for a discussion). In other words, recognition failure of recallable words may occur when recognition is cued inappropriately, i.e., by cues that were not encoded during initial learning.

The generality of such recognition failure has been questioned. The superiority of recall is most easily shown with common words with many shades of meaning, where the wrong shade of meaning may be cued for the recognition test (see Zechmeister and Nyberg, 1982). Even if this is so, it is likely that both recognition and recall tests usually involve both search and identification processes. The search process may differ as the kind of cue differs in recognition and recall tests. Recognition tests require a search for background or contextual features of the target information whereas recall tests require a search for the target itself from the contextual features. For example, to *recognize* a face we may need to retrieve where and when we have seen it before, whereas to recall the person to whom we lent a book we begin with the context of giving in order to help remember their face or name.

Mandler (1980) has argued that recognition may only involve retrieval when memory has become poor. He asked subjects to sort out sets of unrelated words into categories and then gave a surprise memory test. At short intervals there was a good correlation between the number of words recalled and the number of categories used in sorting. This suggested that recall is improved by organization at registration. Although at the short interval there was little relationship between the number of categories used and recognition, this relationship became very strong when the interval was increased to five weeks. This suggested to Mandler that when memory is poor, recognition depends on organizational processes at encoding because it involves a search process. Recognition, when memory is strong, does not require this kind of search process. It remains unproven whether this kind of recognition involves a different kind of search not dependent on category organization, or whether, as Mandler argued, it involves a detection of familiarity, independent of any process that searches for a meaningful context.

Although the processes of retrieval search are largely mysterious, some light is thrown on them by two effects which may occur when retrieval is only partly successful. In the first, it has been reported that even when subjects fail to recall target information they may be able to predict accurately whether they will be able to recognize this information (see Gruneberg, 1983). This **feeling-of-knowing** is a form of what is known as metamemory, i.e., knowledge about the accuracy of one's memory or the qualities of memory more generally. Its existence suggests that retrieval of complex information may be partial and that recalled features form the basis for an estimate of the likelihood of recognition. This interpretation receives support from the second, 'partial retrieval' effect, which is known as the **tip-of-the-tongue** phenomenon. Subjects, given the definitions of rare words, may be unable to retrieve the defined word, but nevertheless identify certain of its features, such as its first letter, number of syllables, and phonetic structure (Brown and McNeill, 1966). This ability does not depend solely on inferences based on general knowledge of the kinds of words involved, but also on retrieval of some of the features of the word encoded when it was learned. When subjects can retrieve a number of target features, they know they are close to success and would recognize the target if it was shown. It remains unexplained, however, how they know they are retrieving target features.

CONTEXT- AND STATE-DEPENDENT FORGETTING AND RETRIEVAL

Further evidence relevant to Mandler's (1980) argument that recognition sometimes only involves familiarity detection without a search process is found in the effects on remembering of shifts of background context or internal state. It has been reported several times that if the background context is altered between learning and memory-testing, recall is impaired. For example Godden and Baddeley (1975) had divers learn lists of words either on land or fifteen feet under water. Recall was tested later in either the same context or a different one. In the changed context there was a 30 per cent decrement in recall, which was not an artefact of the greater movement involved in the change conditions. When Godden and Baddeley (1980) looked at the influence of context change on recognition, however, they found no effect. **Context-dependent forgetting** seemed only to apply to recall.

A similar pattern of results is seen with **state-dependent forgetting** (see Baddeley, 1982). If a subject's internal state is changed between learning and remembering, either by the selective administration of a drug at one stage only or by giving a hypnotic suggestion to influence mood selectively at each stage, recall will be impaired but not recognition (see Zechmeister and Nyberg, 1982). A well-known example of this phenomenon is the alcoholic's inability when sober to recall where he hid the bottles secreted while he was intoxicated, but remembering this vital information next time he is in a drunken state. State-dependent effects are most readily produced by drugs or mood manipulations that have clear sensory effects. There is also a suggestion that the drug effects may occur even when the drug is administered immediately after learning.

It has already been shown that when 'context' influences the way in which an item is encoded, then a change in context between learning and memory test is detrimental for both recall and recognition. Thus, if a cue is presented only during learning then recall and recognition are worse than when it is also presented for the memory test. The kind of context that affects encoding of the target material is referred to by Baddeley (1982) as **interactive context**. Background environment and internal state are encoded at the time of learning but do not affect the target's encoding and so are referred to as **independent context**. The presence of the independent context at both learning and retrieval helps the retrieval process essential for recall, but has no effect on recognition. Recognition therefore must either involve a different kind of search or only a familiarity identification process. If Mandler is right, then when memory is very poor, recognition may involve a search process similar to that of recall. This view must mean that recognition will be impaired by changes in independent context or state cues when memory becomes very poor. The prediction awaits test.

RETRIEVAL AND RECONSTRUCTION

Like other psychological processes, retrieval can be seen as a hierarchical system on the upper levels of which reside consciously formulated plans and on whose lower levels rapid, automatic and unconscious search processes operate. It is, for example, possible to decrease context-dependent forgetting by making subjects imaginatively recreate the conditions of learning (see Zechmeister and Nyberg, 1982). At the top of their control hierarchy, subjects consciously formulate their search plan, but how it is mediated at lower levels and why this facilitates target recall is unknown. Interaction between levels of the control hierarchy may be apparent in studies which show that in free recall and tests of verbal fluency people tend to recall a burst of a few related items and then pause before their next burst.

Examination of the variables that influence the speed of automatic retrieval processes has most commonly involved short-term memory tasks, using the **Sternberg paradigm**. In this paradigm, a sequence of items is presented, followed by a **probe** which subjects have to identify either as a member of the list or otherwise. Decision time increases in linear fashion by about forty milliseconds for each extra item in the list (if they are numbers). The paradigm has been extensively explored and its interpretation is most unclear. Results may be interpreted as showing that subjects engage in a sequential search, or, equally plausibly, in a parallel search that is slower for longer sequences. Furthermore, when items are better learned so as to be more durably stored, there is less evidence that decision time increases as a function of set size. Indeed, decision time is little longer in well-learned sets with seventy-two members than it is with sets comprising seven members.

Sentis and Burnstein (1979) have indeed claimed that when subjects studied stories that fitted consistently with their expectations, then their recognition judgement times actually *decreased* as the proportion of the relevant story they needed to retrieve *increased*. If the stories contained inconsistent components, then recognition times increased as the proportion of the story they needed to retrieve also increased. Sentis and Burnstein suggested that the consistent stories were stored as unified wholes or Gestalts, for which the whole is easier to retrieve than individual parts. This may be a common feature of meaningful material in enduring memory. It is apparent that information organization affects the speed and accuracy of automatic retrieval processes.

Retrieval of complex information is a problem-solving process, in which the rememberer must consciously plan to select cues that effectively trigger automatic search processes. For example, what were you doing on 3 January 1981? To help retrieval you might think first what you were doing in general around the end of 1980 and beginning of 1981, so that you can gradually focus on the appropriate area of memory. It might be supposed that the above process results, with luck, in the accurate reproduction of something stored in memory. This view of remembering was not shared by Bartlett (1932) who believed that we reconstruct the past with the help of our general world knowledge or schemata. For him, remembering the past is analogous to the activity of a detective who infers what has happened from footprints in the ground and his general knowledge of the ways of the world and what causes footprints. In the same way we remember the past, reconstructing it from our vestigial specific memory in accordance with our general-knowledge expectations. We do not, however, feel we are guessing or inferring. Rather, we feel we are remembering (Spiro, 1980).

Bartlett's reconstructive hypothesis is a way of emphasizing the importance of extrinsic knowledge cues in retrieval. These cues are generated from our general knowledge and usually enable us to reproduce the past more accurately. Evidence for their operation is drawn, however, from situations where inappropriate expectations cause reconstructive distortions. It is necessary to show that reconstruction occurs at the time of retrieval. This is because **constructive distortions** are sometimes known to occur when new information is interpreted using inapt schemata – such interpretations may be unconscious. Spiro (1980) has shown that distortions may occur after the time of learning. He read subjects a short story about a couple, and a few minutes later added incidentally whether or not they had married, an addition that either confirmed or conflicted with the story's theme. Recall of the story was tested two days, two weeks or six weeks later. At the longer intervals, subjects made 'reconciling errors', in which the story was made consistent with the later conflicting item of information. They were confident about these errors and felt they were remembering them. Interestingly, the reconciling distortions did not occur when subjects knew from the beginning that they were engaged in a memory study. This suggests that memory distortions are more common in everyday life than under the 'immunizing' conditions of laboratory research.

Importantly, Spiro found that distortions did not occur after two days, which indicates that they were not made at the time of hearing the conflicting information, but only at delayed retrieval when memory for the original story was weaker. Reconstructive distortions may, then, only become significant once the original specific memory has faded. After they have occurred, however, they, rather than the original· memory, will probably be remembered. If remembering involves reconstruction on the basis of world knowledge or schemata, it should get better over time when the schemata change and become more appropriate. Piaget and Inhelder (1973) found exactly this when they tested the memory of three- to eight-year-old children for ordered arrays. Ten sticks, in order of length, were shown to the children. A week later they were asked to draw the sticks from memory. Children under four or five years old drew very inaccurately, with the sticks more-or-less equal in length. Six to eight months later, 90 per cent of the five- to eight-year-olds drew the lines more accurately. It was argued that in the interval their knowledge of serial order had developed. Similar effects were demonstrated for memory which relies on the notions of horizontality and verticality. Special training in these schemata further enhanced the improvement of children's memory for appropriate material.

The reconstruction hypothesis has been criticized because of the vagueness with which it describes the general-knowledge structures that form its basis. These structures may be anything which can lead to an expectation about what happened in the past. Some researchers refer to **scripts** (Schank and Abelson, 1977) which contain our knowledge of what goes on in everyday events such as visits to a restaurant or cinema. But, clearly, reconstruction is also affected by more general knowledge, better identified with the vaguer Bartlettian notion of **schemata**. Many experiments have further shown that memory is affected by our **stereotypes** of people. There has been some controversy about the effects of listening to or reading material which agrees or disagrees with one's stereotypical attitudes. George (1979) has suggested, however, that people who have heard speeches inconsistent with their attitudes remember as much of these as they do of consistent speeches, but that they weaken the effects of inconsistent speeches by distortion and a tendency to recall less important features. Our social attitudes may be relatively self-perpetuating as we interpret and reconstruct new information in terms of them. In contrast, the formation of attitudes on new issues is disproportionately affected by the vividness and the consistency or inconsistency of the new information (as Reyes, Thompson and Bower, 1980, show).

Reconstructive distortions are also relevant to practical affairs, such as **eye-witness testimony**. Thus, Loftus and Palmer (1974) showed subjects a film of a traffic accident. Shortly after seeing the film, subjects were asked about the speed of the vehicles before the crash. For some subjects the phrase 'smashed into each other' was used, whereas the more neutral 'hit each other' was used for the others. A week later the former group was much more likely to remember mistakenly that there had been broken glass at the scene of the accident. They had inferred that the word 'smash' meant that the crash had been severe, and used this inference in actively reconstructing details of the event. There is evidence that this problem of distortion is aggravated when subjects are hypnotized to remember more of a witnessed crime or accident (Putnam, 1979). Such subjects are particularly susceptible to leading questions. It is important once again to note that subjects believe they are remembering rather than inventing.

The mode of operation of intrinsic-knowledge cues (which were encoded during learning) and extrinsic-knowledge cues (schemata, scripts, stereotypes) may differ, but people normally seem unable to recognize whether a retrieved memory is cued intrinsically or extrinsically. If Tulving is right, well-learned strong memories are mainly cued intrinsically, but when complex memories are faint, extrinsic cues probably play a significant role. As memories age, they may break into isolated fragments which can only be linked by the reconstructive processes associated with extrinsic cueing (see Jones, 1979).

Storage

STORAGE AND ACTIVATION

Although storage precedes retrieval we discuss it later because of the extreme difficulty of showing that a memory phenomenon is caused by a change in storage rather than one of encoding and/or retrieval. Thus, if a treatment given during learning improves later memory, it may have enriched encoding and/or it may have strengthened the storage of what would have been encoded anyway. Similarly, an agent may increase forgetting by causing a disturbance of storage and/or disrupting retrieval. Methodologically the alternatives are hard to disentangle but there seems to be a bias against explanations in terms of storage changes. This was shown by Loftus and Loftus (1980) who found, in a large survey, that a big majority of both professional psychologists and lay people believe that once things are learnt they are permanently stored, and that forgetting is always caused by lapses of retrieval. The view seems to be mainly based on the fact that once-forgotten information can sometimes be later remembered, either spontaneously or through the influences of hypnosis, brain stimulation or drugs. As Loftus and Loftus point out, this is often shaky evidence and certainly inadequate for the conclusion, but it nevertheless reveals a strong bias in people's theoretical outlooks.

Two broad kinds of **storage change**, however, have been postulated. First, it has been proposed that storage processes must be consolidated in the period during and perhaps after learning. The discussion of this proposal in Chapter 5 showed that we are still uncertain whether these changes occur very rapidly or relatively slowly. It also remains contentious whether or not treatments given around the time of learning affect memory because of their influence on the strength of consolidation. Second, it has been proposed that forgetting over time or because of some treatment is partially or wholly caused by the **decay** of what has been stored. This issue is discussed further on pages 360–5.

The problem of confidently identifying a variable, the effect on memory of which is at least partially caused by its influence on storage, is illustrated by memory improvement found usually when arousal is high during acquisition. Events of great emotional significance are well remembered; more strikingly, even the peripheral details of these **flashbulb memories** are well remembered. For example, one can recall precisely what one was doing at the time of the significant event. As emotion causes nonspecific physiological arousal, the activation may be the source of the strong memory. Other manipulations of arousal improve delayed memory (and may impair immediate memory). Thus delayed memory is better in the afternoon when arousal is higher; it is better if the learning material is arousing; and it may be better in introverts (although extraverts have better immediate memory). It has been claimed that introverts have more aroused or arousable nervous systems (see Eysenck, 1977, for a review).

Even if arousal influences storage, there is rather confused evidence that it also affects the encoding of complex information. High arousal may narrow attention and focus it upon dominant sources of information. During retrieval it may speed the search for dominant items (an animal whose name begins with 'm') but slow it for obscure items (a member of the cat family whose name begins with 'o'). It is difficult to control these effects on encoding and retrieval in order to prove that arousal also influences storage.

ORGANIC AMNESIA, INFANTILE AMNESIA, AGEING AND STORAGE

Organic amnesia was mentioned earlier in this chapter (page 326). Patients with this disorder learn new information very poorly and even if they do eventually learn it, they forget it abnormally fast. It has been suggested that the lesions of the medial temporal lobe, which cause this disorder, disturb the consolidation and maintenance of memory strorage (Squire *et al.*, in press). This view has been denied by those who believe amnesics show deficiencies in their encoding and/or retrieval processes. It has been suggested, for example, that amnesics do not encode elaboratively and hence do not create distinctive memories. It has also been suggested that amnesics do not encode background contextual information, which causes great difficulty in retrieving complex memories. Finally, it has been suggested that amnesics are excessively sensitive at retrieval to competitive interference from other items in memory.

There is evidence, however, that the two encoding hypotheses only apply to patients who also have incidental damage to the frontal cortex. It is known that lesions of the frontal cortex alone do not cause severe memory deficits, but may prevent patients from spontaneously using elaborative encoding, although they can do so if given guidance; such lesions may also cause them to be very poor at judgements of item recency – judgements which depend on the use of context. Furthermore, there is reason to believe that excessive sensitivity to interference in amnesics is a consequence of their poor memory and not its cause (see Mayes, 1984, for a discussion). Therefore, by process of elimination, the view that temporal-lobe amnesics have a consolidation deficit gains plausibility. If so, two comments should be made. First, the amnesic not only fails to learn and remember new episodic and semantic information, but also fails to remember such information acquired up to several years before his brain damage (see Squire *et al.*, in press). The affected consolidation process may therefore be one which continues for a very long time – much longer than usually imagined. Second, there are many tasks that amnesics can learn to do and retain normally. For example, they are able to show classical conditioning, learn motor and perceptual skills, and even acquire cognitive skills such as reading mirror-reversed words or generating numerical series. Some of these skills may involve cortical processing and storage. It therefore seems that activity in the medial temporal lobes is necessary for some kinds of cortical storage and not for others. The activity is necessary for memories that can be consciously recalled and recognized.

If the medial temporal lobes are necessary for consolidation of storage then poor consolidation may be partly responsible for the poor memory associated with infancy and old age. It is known that rats under fifteen days old can learn new tasks but not retain them as adults can. A similar phenomenon of **infantile amnesia** is known in humans. Adults can typically remember nothing from the first two or three years of life. The average age from which first memories are recalled is between three and four. Douglas (1975) has argued that in both cases the poor memory is a result of the functional immaturity of the hippocampus, lying within the medial temporal lobe. Animals such as guinea pigs, in which the hippocampus is much more mature at birth, do not show infantile amnesia. Although Douglas's hypothesis is very attractive, it should be viewed cautiously since many mammalian brain systems are immature at birth. Also, poor adult memory for early infancy may be related to the very different ways in which adults and infants encode the world – the adults may no longer generate the cues appropriate for retrieving very early memories.

Memory also deteriorates in the elderly, although the extent to which this happens is controversial. In the pathological condition of

presenile dementia, however, the first symptom is often a selective and severe memory disturbance. Presenile dementia and normal ageing are both associated with a loss of neurons from the hippocampus, so it is reasonable to suppose that both are partially caused by a failure of consolidation. Elderly people, however, suffer from a multiplicity of ills. We have already suggested that they have reduced attentional capacity, and Eysenck (1977) has argued that they are worse than younger people at the elaborative processing of complex information. As elaborative encoding in the elderly can sometimes be improved by giving them instructional guidance, it is likely that some of their memory deficit is caused by atrophy of the frontal cortex. The elderly also typically show much worse recall than recognition of distant events (relative to the young), which suggests that they also have less efficient search processes operating during retrieval.

Forgetting

REPRESSION AS A CAUSE OF FORGETTING

Theories of forgetting must explain two broad classes of phenomena. First, why forgetting increases at a rate which steadily declines with the lengthening of the retention interval. Second, how specific causes of forgetting, such as context change between learning and retrieval, or the experience of severe trauma, operate. The explanations may, of course, overlap, because some specific causes of forgetting may operate more intensely as time passes. There is a division between theories which propose that forgetting arises because of the gradual loss of what is stored, and those theories which argue that it is a result of cognitive or emotional factors acting during retrieval. The latter theories draw their support from observations showing that forgotten memories are recovered spontaneously, particularly when the causes of forgetting are removed, as when a person shifts back to the same internal state that he was in during learning.

Like many others, Freud believed that information, once acquired, is permanently stored and that much forgetting is caused by **repression** acting during retrieval. He proposed that if a memory is emotionally painful then at retrieval we are motivated to focus our attention in other directions, so as not to reactivate the pain. We may sometimes be aware of this process and sometimes not. Whatever its status, the theory is clearly not comprehensive because it cannot explain why forgetting increases with time or why we forget pleasant events. In fact, its truth should suggest that we remember pleasant experiences more than unpleasant ones. Precisely this was reported in one study which found that 50 per cent of subjects' memories were of pleasant events, 30 per cent were of unpleasant events and 20 per cent were of neutral events (Waldfogel, cited by Hunter, 1957). It is not known, however, what proportion of our experiences is pleasant or unpleasant, so the finding may be unrelated to memory. Even so, the remembered intensity of the pain of childbirth has been shown to decline with time (see Hunter *et al.*, 1979). This memory effect, however, may not be caused by repression. Indeed this is unlikely as the effect increases with time.

Identifying repression in the laboratory has proved so difficult that no convincing experimental demonstrations of it exist. For example, Glucksberg and King (1967) taught subjects associates like 'dox-memory'. Some of the remote associations of the response terms such as 'memory' (for which 'brain' is a remote associate because it is linked to 'mind' which, in turn, is linked to 'memory') were then paired with shock. When subjects' recall of the original pairs was tested, they recalled fewer of the responses that had been remotely associated with shock. Although this poor recall could be caused by the emotional links of the responses activating repression, another explanation is possible. Recall was tested immediately after learning, and the emotional disturbance could have caused arousal, which impairs immediate and improves delayed recall. In a similar study, it has been shown that the subject-produced associates of emotional words (e.g., 'angry') are recalled worse immediately, but better after twenty-eight days than are associates of neutral words, such as 'cow' (Bradley and Morris, 1976). Patients show similar momentary blocks of memory particularly at emotionally significant points during psychotherapy. These also may be consequences of arousal rather than repression. Repression may be more important in memory pathology. **Hysterical amnesias** (or **fugues**) have been described in which the victim completely forgets the events of a circumscribed period of time, which had been linked with emotional trauma. For example, a woman who was mischievously told that her husband had been killed suffered extreme emotional turmoil for two days, and then emerged oblivious of the traumatic events. Although the events were inaccessible to conscious recall, they did manifest themselves in nightmares and under hypnosis. In severe fugue states, the individual may forget about his past life and lose his personal identity, and assume a new life with apparent lack of concern. The switch is triggered by an emotional crisis which is avoided by the fugue state. Although the memories eventually become consciously accessible again they may be repressed for months or longer. These strange dissociations of memory are also apparent in the disorder of multiple personality, of which well over a hundred cases have been reported. **Multiple personality** is an extreme form of fugue state, in which several, often very different personalities, coexist in one body. One personality may have no memory of the actions of another, who is 'in control' at a different time. In the famous case of Eve, this ignorance was one-way since Eve Black knew all about Eve White but not vice versa (see Kihlstrom and Evans, 1979, for a discussion of hysterical amnesia).

In the above cases repression probably operates unconsciously. Sometimes, however, an individual may consciously try to repress memories. Hypnotic amnesia is an interesting intermediate example. Lightly hypnotized subjects, instructed to forget what they have been told, may consciously try to repress their memories until the suggestion is lifted. Deeply hypnotized subjects, in contrast, are not aware that they are repressing appropriate retrieval activity. This is the phenomenon of **dissociation**, in which conscious activities coexist with unconscious ones to which they have no access.

WHY DOES FORGETTING INCREASE OVER TIME?

Gestalt psychologists stand alone in proposing that memories change qualitatively and autonomously with the passage of time. They argue that complex memories change so as to become more internally consistent and in the direction of good Gestaltic form.

For example, irregular shapes will increasingly be remembered as more regular and symmetrical. There are no convincing demonstrations that such spontaneous changes in shape memory occur (see Baddeley, 1976). As already discussed, however, there is some evidence for reconstructive distortions of memory for stories, in the direction of greater simplicity and consistency. This kind of change is not spontaneous. Rather, it occurs when we try to remember feeble memories which conflict with our general expectations or other knowledge. After a distorted and simplified version has been recalled, it is this that is more readily remembered. No evidence exists for qualitative changes occurring without active retrieval. If a remembered story is later reconstructed wrongly, the wrong version tends to be recalled even after the subject has reread the original – so strong is the impact of the distorted recall.

Although memories may not spontaneously change in a qualitative way with the passage of time, many theorists hold that their stored representations do decay spontaneously. This view has been denied by extreme **interference theorists**, who believe that forgetting increases with time solely because of increasing interference between competing memories. The more one learns, the more competition operates at retrieval, but storage does not deteriorate. The retrieval problem may be compared to trying to find a particular green marble in a big bag of coloured marbles – the larger the number of marbles and the more similar they are to the critical one, the harder is the task.

If the extreme interference theory was correct, then there should be no increase in forgetting with time when interference is abolished. Unfortunately, all attempts to reduce interference tend to have other confounding effects that may disturb storage processes directly. Thus, anaesthetizing an animal, or cooling its brain, will probably reduce interference and consolidation. Early observations showing that human memory was improved if subjects were allowed to sleep after learning were the cause of some excitement. It is now known, however, that sleep is a time of great mental activity during which interference may not be reduced. Furthermore, postlearning sleep does not benefit memory if it occurs during the day. The effects of sleep on memory are small, and there is evidence that 'quiet sleep' and 'active sleep' may play different roles. For example, deprivation of active sleep (see Chapter 7) may slightly disturb memory but only for complex and unfamiliar material (see Baddeley, 1976). In summary, attempts to abolish interference selectively and so demonstrate that it is the only cause of increased forgetting with time have not succeeded and many researchers are now willing to concede that memory may also decay with time.

The studies failed for another reason. Interference theorists now argue that forgetting occurs, not only because of interference from new information experienced after learning – **retroactive interference** (RI) – but also because of interference from older memories – **proactive interference** (PI). Associative interference theorists traditionally analysed PI and RI using paired-associate lists, containing items like 'dog-mountain' or 'XUF-24'. To examine PI, the effects of learning a first list (A-B) on the learning of and memory for a second list (A-C), learned later, were tested. The two lists contained the same stimulus terms, e.g., 'dog', which were associated with different response terms, e.g., 'mountain' or 'carpet'. RI was investigated by examining the effects of learning A-C on memory for A-B.

Experiments with the A-B, A-C paradigm or variants of it suggested three generalizations. First, interference is greater when learning of the competing material is increased, so that recall of the target material is worsened. Conversely, overlearning the target material protects it from interference. It is probably also true that the more competing associations that are learnt, the worse is target recall. Second, interference is greater when the competing memories are more similar. Although these effects are similar for PI and RI, a third effect points to a difference. It is claimed that PI increases with time whereas RI decreases. In both cases, degree of interference was compared with a control condition D-E, A-C or A-B, D-E, in which the other learnt responses were unrelated to the target associations.

When McGeoch developed **associative interference theory** in the 1930s, he only postulated an RI process, which, he argued, caused forgetting by creating competition between target and competing items that were associated with the same stimulus. This view might be generalized so as to state that retrieval cues that once uniquely led to a target memory cease to do so after interference, leading instead to a number of competing memories. The cues will only uniquely lead to the target, then, if they are linked to the appropriate contextual markers, e.g., the A cue learnt in this room yesterday. A simple interpretation of the competition view would suggest that as interference increases, so will the number of **intrusion errors** from the competing material. In a classic study, Melton and Irwin (described in Baddeley, 1976) showed that this prediction is not met. They varied the number of second-list learning trials between 0 and 40, before testing the relearning of the first list. They found very few intrusion errors, but also they found that the total interference level increased up to ten second-list trials and then levelled out, whereas the number of intrusions increased at first and then declined almost to zero. They therefore argued that RI is caused, not only by response competition, but also by another factor.

Melton and Irwin suggested that first-list responses were extinguished because they were not reinforced during second-list learning. Underwood subsequently developed this concept (see Baddeley, 1976) which he called **unlearning**. Unlearning was likened to extinction in conditioning because both are supposed to recover spontaneously with time. RI diminishes with time because the first list spontaneously recovers from its unlearning. In contrast, PI increases with time for the same reason – the first list is increasingly able to exert response competition on the second. According to Underwood, RI involves both unlearning and response competition, whereas PI involves only response competition. The major evidence for this view is derived from the use of **modified free recall** (MMFR). This procedure is used with A-B, A-C tasks and allows the subject to try and recall both B and C responses to the A stimulus without any time pressure. It is therefore supposed to be free of response competition. Despite this, RI causes interference using the MMFR procedure.

The postulation of unlearning is probably wrong, however. MMFR is unlikely to remove response competition because retrieval of a competing item makes its subsequent retrieval *more* and not less likely, i.e., the competition may actually get fiercer after each retrieval. If the assumption was right, it would have embarrassing consequences because PI also causes interference using the MMFR procedure. The data are more easily explained by supposing that PI and RI act similarly and on two stages of memory. First, interference may cause a block of retrieval (as in the tip-of-the-tongue effect) even though subjects would recognize the target if it was presented. Second, subjects may be able to retrieve target and competing items but confuse them at the recognition stage. This proposal explains Melton and Irwin's results. Most of the interference in their study was caused by retrieval block. Their subjects only made intrusion errors when they confused items at the recognition stage. But there was little confusion and it soon began to decline anyway with further learning of the second list. This also suggests that retrieval block and recognition confusion are differently affected by the amount of learning of competing material. If so, they must be independent processes. Furthermore, if the interpretation of Melton and Irwin's study can be generalized, most interference may be caused by retrieval block. Certainly, studies which use A-B, A-C recognition tests support this view.

It remains to be explained why PI increases and RI decreases with time. First, the empirical validity of this claim has been challenged. It has been claimed in contrast that, for example, PI only slows down subsequent learning by making distinctive encoding less likely. If learning is allowed to proceed to the same level as that of control groups, there is no tendency of the PI-exposed group to forget faster (see Crowder, 1982b). Even if such criticisms turn out to be invalid, Baddeley (1976) has suggested an explanation for the original claim. He compared the remembering of two competing memories with the discrimination of superimposed visual stimuli (see Figure 6.3). When one stimulus is very strong it will be easy to discriminate, but the other, weaker stimulus may not be discriminable. Similarly, the stronger of two competing memories will be easier to remember and will block the other more strongly. Baddeley suggests that memories decay with time in the same way that forgetting occurs. Consequently, the first learnt memory will be much weaker at first, but as time passes the strengths of the two competing memories will become very similar. Hence PI should increase with time and RI diminish.

One significant feature of Baddeley's explanation is its emphasis on **memory decay** as the main cause of forgetting. Interference is seen only as a minor, contributory factor. This probably reflects the true state of affairs. It has indeed been very difficult to demonstrate significant PI in situations outside the usual laboratory tasks (see Baddeley, 1976, for a discussion). One reason for this seems to be

Figure 6.3 A visual analogy of how competition between memory items may work. (a) shows no competition, (b) shows competition between equally strong memories, (c) shows competition between a strong and a weak memory. The analogy shows that response competition affects memory discriminability or recognition.

that when learning of competing materials is spaced out over time, interference is greatly reduced. Interference seems to depend mainly on degrading the uniqueness of cues to memory, but if these cues are associated with distinctive temporal or other contexts then this degradation is likely to be minimal. If this conclusion is correct then we know little about the main cause of forgetting, because we are ignorant of storage processes, let alone how they deteriorate over time.

Semantic memory

Most of this chapter has been concerned with memory for specific events (episodic memory). Some psychologists believe, however, that memory for general knowledge (semantic memory) is basically different. One can ask several related fundamental questions about semantic memory. First, how does it differ from episodic memory? Second, how are semantic memories such as concepts acquired? Third, how are semantic memories organized to facilitate retrieval?

The initial basis for the semantic/episodic distinction is that semantic memories are abstract, involving concepts and general rules, and do not involve knowledge of individual instances. This suggests that they do not require the storage of contextual information, which helps define individual instances. In contrast, episodic memory must involve such contextual information. Even this position has been challenged by Jacoby and Witherspoon (1982), who argue that memory for a concept depends on memory for individual instances of the concept, that act as sources for generalization and analogy. If this was correct, then contextual information would be important for both semantic and episodic memory. Most psychologists seem to accept, however, that the retrieval of overlearnt general knowledge does not involve retrieval of particular instances and therefore of context.

It has been shown that certain forms of cortical atrophy cause the loss of specific forms of general knowledge without affecting the ability to acquire new episodic memories, provided these do not depend on the lost general knowledge. Conversely, organic amnesics retain their overlearnt pretraumatic general knowledge but cannot acquire new episodic memories. Similarly, hypnotic subjects, given amnesia instructions, forget specific episodes of the trance state but remember general knowledge acquired during it, such as the odd fact that amethysts turn yellow when heated (see Kihlstrom and Evans, 1979). These last facts should be viewed cautiously as organic amnesics are poor at acquiring new semantic as well as episodic memories and remember distant episodic memories normally, and hypnotic subjects are 'acting out the role given by the hypnotist' and probably do not count factual knowledge as memory, and so do not try to repress their memory for it.

A plausible interpretation of the above data is that general knowledge is stored in the cortex in a highly differentiated and organized way. Cortical lesions may, for example, selectively disrupt arithmetical knowledge, or knowledge of concrete versus abstract words and vice versa. The limbic system regions, damaged in organic amnesia, are important in the acquisition of new episodic *and* semantic memories and may be involved in their initial retrieval. Like semantic memories, episodic memories are also stored cortically. This view implies that the two memory systems are very similar, even if semantic memories do eventually become context-free. The view is supported by evidence showing that variables affect both forms of memory in the same way. For example, information that has recently been in episodic memory is more rapidly retrieved from semantic memory (see Anderson and Ross, 1980).

There are two major views about the acquisition of general knowledge, such as concepts. One, consistent with what has just been said, states that it depends on learning about specific instances and generalizing from them, i.e., it depends initially on episodic memory although it will probably cease to be so dependent when the instances are forgotten. Second, it is claimed that individual experiences trigger an abstraction process, leading to the extraction of concepts and rules, and this process is completely independent of episodic memory and, therefore, of the limbic system. It is the former view which is supported here. Whatever are the precise mechanisms of generalization, which underlie concept formation, the process is clearly helped by the use of examples of the concept, drawn from a wide variety of contexts (see Baddeley, 1983, for a discussion; also Chapter 9).

Our semantic memory systems are impressive both because they are vast and because we can retrieve information so rapidly from them. For example, we know almost instantly that 'Dogs bark' is true, whereas 'Cats fly' is false. This indicates that semantic information is stored in a highly organized way. A popular account of this organization is the proposal that knowledge is stored as a **hierarchical network** of interrelated concepts, with more abstract concepts (e.g., bird) higher up the hierarchy than more concrete ones (i.e., robin). Stored with each concept is a set of **attributes**. In order to economize on storage the attributes apply only to the relevant concept rather than those linked to it higher in the hierarchy (Collins and Quillian, 1972). For example, 'has a red breast' would be stored with the concept 'robin', but 'can fly' would be stored with the concept 'bird'. In their model, Collins and Quillian predict how quickly people can assess the truth of simple sentences. They argue that the further one has to move through the network, the greater will be one's reaction time. Thus, 'Robins can fly' should

Table 6.2 **An example of a hierarchical semantic system (according to Collins and Quillian)**

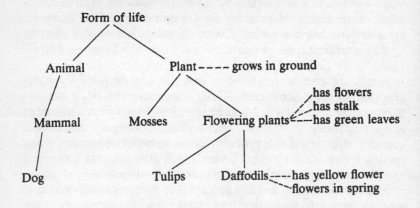

take longer to verify than 'Robins have red breasts'. On the whole, this kind of prediction is fulfilled.

The results may, however, be explained by arguing that judgements are faster when the claimed property is more typical, or representative, of the concept. For example, 'A mammal is an animal' takes longer to verify than 'A dog is an animal' because for most people dogs are more typical animals. The **network search model** predicts the opposite results. Judgements of falsity are also made too rapidly from the viewpoint of the network model, and furthermore they are faster when the hypothetical nodes are further apart. For example, it takes longer to decide that a bat is not a reptile than that it is not a colour (see Morris, 1978, for a discussion). It could be that the latter judgement is more rapid because one can rapidly decide that reptiles do not share any properties with colours. It is only when there is overlap that further checking is necessary to see if they are really distinct. Although this explanation is possible, it seems implausible that we really compare the concepts in this way.

The view that retrieval time depends on typicality of the property, rather than distance moved through a hypothetical network, suggests that concepts are much fuzzier things than the network model requires. As the philosopher Wittgenstein argued, concepts do not have precise defining features, but have members that bear a loose **family resemblance** to one another. Accordingly, some members can be more typical than others. Typicality can be determined empirically by asking people to rate instances of it, and more typical instances can be shown to be more quickly identified.

No satisfactory theory of semantic memory organization yet exists as no current theory can embrace all the phenomena. For example, the cortical atrophy that impairs semantic memory affects the ability to make subordinate judgements, such as 'A wren is a bird', more severely than superordinate ones, like 'A wren is an animal'. This is not what the network model suggests, and other theories only explain it in a *post hoc* manner. More basically, no model shows how the appropriate part of the semantic system is initially accessed. The question therefore remains open as to whether we retrieve our general knowledge in a radically different manner from that which we use to retrieve specific instances. Only future work can show whether the acquisition, storage and retrieval of semantic and episodic memories differ in important ways. The retrieval of both will, however, involve many parallel operations.

Further reading

A brief history and general

There are now many good general texts on memory. We recommend the following:

BADDELEY, A.D. (1983) *Your Memory: a User's Guide*. Harmondsworth: Penguin.

This provides a comprehensive, clear and popular introduction, whereas the author's earlier volume gives a more advanced treatment, particularly of tricky topics such as associative interference theory. It is also good on the subject's history:

BADDELEY, A.D. (1976) *The Psychology of Memory*. New York: Harper and Row.

The above two books are well complemented by the following one, which gives a detailed account of accommodative reconstruction in recall, levels of processing, metamemory, mnemonics and individual differences in memory:

ZECHMEISTER, E.B. and NYBERG, S.E. (1982) *Human Memory*. Monterey, Calif.: Brooks/Cole.

Memory in everyday life is currently a popular research area. The following volume gives many examples (e.g., eye-witness testimony, education) of investigations into memory that have practical implications:

GRUNEBERG, M.M., MORRIS, P.E. and SYKES, R.N., eds. (1978) *Practical Aspects of Memory*. New York: Academic Press.

The distinction between short- and long-term memory

There is an excellent chapter in Baddeley, *op. cit.* (1983) on working memory. The topic is given a more technical and complementary treatment in the following:

HITCH, G.J. (1980) Developing the concept of working memory. In G. Claxton, ed., *Cognitive Psychology: New Directions*. London: Routledge and Kegan Paul.

For a critical look at the notion of echoic memory see:

HOLDING, D.H. (1979) Echoic storage. In N.S. Sutherland, ed., *Tutorial Essays in Psychology*, Volume 2. Hillsdale, NJ: Erlbaum.

For a comprehensive critique reinterpreting the notion of iconic storage see:

COLTHEART, M. (1980) Visual information processing. In P.C. Dodwell, ed., *New Horizons in Psychology*. Second edition. Harmondsworth: Penguin.

Finally, for a defence of the single-trace theory of short-term memory phenomena, see:

WICKELGREN, W.A. (1974) Single trace fragility theory of memory dynamics. *Memory and Cognition*, **2**, 775–80.

The registration of information

There are useful discussions of the relationship between encoding and retrieval in the following book, which also has chapters on the history of memory theorizing, the development of memory and its physiology, and the organization of semantic memory:

GRUNEBERG, M.M. and MORRIS, P., eds. (1978) *Aspects of Memory*. London: Methuen.

The following collection of edited chapters shows how the 'depth of processing' theory has been developed and modified since Craik and Lockhart's (1972) formulation:

CERMAK, L.S. and CRAIK, F.I.M., eds. (1979) *Levels of Processing in Human Memory*. Hillsdale, NJ: Erlbaum.

For a detailed account of the development of children's memory see:

KAIL, R. (1980) *The Development of Memory in Children*. San Francisco: Freeman.

Individual differences in memory are comprehensively treated in:

EYSENCK, M.W. (1977) *Human Memory: Theory, Research and Individual Differences*. Oxford: Pergamon.

Baddeley, *op. cit.* (1976) also gives an interesting account of a series of people with supernormal memory.

Retrieval

Eysenck's book, cited above, also considers retrieval mechanisms in episodic and semantic memory. The two-stage (search then recognize) theory of retrieval and the relationship between recall and recognition tests is very clearly discussed by Zechmeister and Nyberg, *op. cit.* For an account of context- and state-dependent forgetting, together with a discussion of a range of memory phenomena and a theoretical argument, see:

BADDELEY, A.D. (1982) Domains of recollection. *Psychological Review*, **89**, 708–29.

In the following book, a number of pathological and other forms of forgetting are described and explained predominantly as retrieval failures:

KIHLSTROM, J.G. and EVANS, F.J. (1979) *Functional Disorders of Memory*. Hillsdale, NJ: Erlbaum.

For a different slant on the notion of reconstruction in memory see:

JONES, G.V. (1979) Analysing memory by cuing: intrinsic and extrinsic knowledge. In N.S. Sutherland, ed., *Tutorial Essays in Psychology*, Volume 2. Hillsdale, NJ: Erlbaum.

For a recent collation of factors related to the recollection of people in social situations see:

HASTIE, R. *et al.*, eds. (1980) *Person Memory: the Cognitive Basis of Person Perception*. Hillsdale, NJ: Erlbaum.

Finally, the following paper shows that young children make reconstructive distortions at delayed testing when stories about popular characters, for example James Bond, do not conform to stereotype. Interestingly, when the clash with stereotype is made more prominent older children show *less* reconstructive distortion, unlike younger children. This suggests that reconstruction is fairly automatic and that older children have developed a form of metamemory which allows control of it under some circumstances:

CECI, S.J., CAVES, R.D. and HOWE, M.J.A. (1981) Children's long-term memory for information that is incongruous with their prior knowledge. *British Journal of Psychology*, 72, 443–50.

Storage

Activation and memory are reviewed by Eysenck, *op. cit.*, who also considers the literature about ageing and memory. There is a detailed discussion of infantile amnesia in Kihlstrom and Evans, *op. cit.*, and they also discuss memory and ageing. Organic amnesia is comprehensively discussed in the following volume:

CERMAK, L.S., ed. (1982) *Human Memory and Amnesia*. Hillsdale, NJ: Erlbaum.

The argument that amnesia may be a storage failure because encoding and retrieval deficits have not been demonstrated is developed in:

MEUDELL, P. and MAYES, A. (1982) Normal and abnormal forgetting: some comments on the human amnesic syndrome. In A. Ellis, ed., *Normality and Pathology in Cognitive Function*. London: Academic Press.

For those who wish to pursue further the subject of the physiological bases of storage of complex memories, the state of the art is clearly shown by the following edited volume. Although the many contributors to this volume agree on certain points there are still many basic areas of disagreement:

SQUIRE, L.R. and BUTTERS, N., eds. (1984) *Neuropsychology of Memory*. New York: Guilford Press.

Forgetting

Kihlstrom and Evans, *op. cit.*, review current thinking about repression as it occurs in psychopathology, and Baddeley, *op. cit.* (1976), is very good on associative interference theory. An unusual defence of the Gestaltic theory of forgetting is presented in the following monograph:

GOLDMEIER, E. (1982) *The Memory Trace: its Formation and Fate.* Hillside, NJ: Erlbaum.

Since Ebbinghaus it has been believed that we forget information over time at a negatively accelerated rate. Recently, however, Bahrick has shown that with overlearnt semantic information, although forgetting occurs in the first 5 years, none may occur over the next 25 years:

BAHRICK, H. P. (1984) Semantic memory content in permastore; fifty years of memory for Spanish learned in school. *Journal of Experimental Psychology*, General, **113**, 1–29.

Semantic memory

Useful reviews of semantic memory can be found in Morris's chapter in Gruneberg and Morris, *op. cit.*, and also, for a popular, complementary treatment, in Baddeley, *op. cit.* (1983).

Some of the neurological evidence is considered in the following edited volume, which also illustrates the approach of this and the previous chapter – that hypothetical memory processes should be examined from many perspectives in many species to see if one's predictions hold reliably:

MAYES, A.R., ed. (1983) *Memory in Animals and Humans.* Wokingham: Van Nostrand.

7. Motivation

7. Motivation

Introduction and historical background

Most laymen expect to learn from psychology why people behave as they do. In particular, they expect to be told why people sometimes behave oddly and abnormally, or that the reasons given for more normal behaviour may cloak more subtle, hidden (and usually sexual) ones. This popular conception corresponds roughly with the central aim of psychologists to explain how goals (or motives) control human and animal behaviour. The psychology of motivation seeks solutions to a number of interlinked questions. It must explain not only why different individuals are affected so variously by goals such as food, sex or glory, but also why one individual sometimes intensely strives for a goal to which on another occasion he is indifferent. More formally, psychologists try to discover how the various motives gain control over behaviour. This requires the identification of inherited and learning components. They must also explain how competition between goals is resolved so that one motive gains control of behaviour. As competition between goals is often inadequately resolved, it is also important to understand the consequences of conflict. Finally, psychologists have studied how dominance by a given motive may make behaviour more intense as well as influencing the direction of perception and thinking.

The common sense account of how behaviour is directed relates closely to the philosophical doctrine of **rationalism** according to which people freely choose certain goals which they then pursue. Their decisions are based on reasons for and against various goals and once decided they reason about the best means to their ends. The doctrine postulates a hierarchy of goals in which specific actions are justified in terms of more general goals, which are seen as desirable. It does not explain why these more general goals are desirable, but tries to consider how competition between goals is resolved. The rationalist view is **teleological** in that behaviour is explained in terms of its ends rather than its causes. Motivated behaviour is future-directed whereas psychologists seek to explain behaviour in terms of causal mechanisms. There need, however, be no conflict. The behaviour of **servomechanisms**, such as guided missiles or thermostats, can be explained in terms of their aims, but there is also a good mechanistic account of their actions.

Unfortunately, it has not always been clear whether psychologists have been trying to provide the causal mechanisms which underlie the common sense teleological description of rationalism. Rather, the mechanistic accounts sometimes appear to deny that behaviour is directed towards goals in the way claimed by common sense. The suggestion is that the conscious reasonings associated with motivated behaviour are puppet plays and that the driving mechanisms of behaviour must be sought elsewhere. Precursors of this suggestion are apparent in the tradition of British empirical philosophy. Hobbes, for example, believed all behaviour was directed by the avoidance of pain and the search for pleasure, regardless of the conscious reasons given for acting. Later, the emergence of Darwinian evolutionary theory stimulated attempts to explain human and animal behaviour in terms of a set of inherited instincts. The acme of **instinct theorizing** was reached by McDougall (1908), who listed eighteen instincts including pugnacity, reproduction, self-assertion, gregariousness and others related to basic bodily needs. For McDougall an instinct was 'an inherited or innate psychological disposition which determines its possessor to perceive, and pay attention to, objects of a certain class, to experience an emotional excitement of a particular quality upon perceiving such an object, and to act in regard to it in a particular manner, or, at least, to experience an impulse to such action'. Despite his emphasis on their innateness, McDougall did concede, however, that instincts can be modified by experience.

The tendency to interpret McDougall's theory as saying that instincts rather than conscious reason direct behaviour was probably enhanced by the almost simultaneous emergence of Freud's psychoanalytic account of motivation. Freud (1975a) postulated that human behaviour was controlled by two innate systems of energy – the libido, or **life instinct**, which was released in sexual and pleasure-related behaviours, and the **death instinct**, which was released in aggressive acts. These instincts largely operated beyond the range of the individual's awareness so that his consciously proffered reasons for action were frequently misleading and self-deluding rationalizations. For Freud, therefore, and, to a lesser extent, for McDougall, it is often the case that what someone believes to be the goal of their actions as well as their reasons for selecting it are unrelated to the true goal and causes of their behaviour. Motivational theories have, then, not only tried to provide the causal mechanisms underlying goal-seeking behaviour, but also have denied some of the common sense account of how goals are selected and direct action.

In this century, apart from psychoanalysis, there have been two major approaches to the psychology of motivation. One derives from the instinct theory of McDougall and is represented by the thinking of postwar **ethologists**, trying to explain the behaviour of animals in their natural habitats. The other derives from the behaviourist tradition of **learning theory**, which argues that organisms learn how to reduce aversive states of arousal, innately triggered by certain internal and external stimuli. This learning theory of motivation is similar to that of Freud in that both theories postulate that goal-directed behaviours are learned on the organism's discovery that their performance releases innately generated sources of **energy**. Although the theories differ in their emphasis on the importance of learning in the development of particular motives, they all stress the salience of physiological and biological constraints. They claim implicitly that these biological factors have been selected for through evolution because they are adaptive, so human, as well as animal, motivations are rooted in biology. The problem has been to show how motives are so rooted. This is difficult for motives such as hunger, thirst and sex, which have clear biological bases. It is much harder for motives like the need for self-assertion or acquisition, whose innate bases (if any) are unknown.

McDougall's instinct theory fell into disrepute, not only because of the growth of behaviourism, but also because many felt his view was circular – if humans seek a certain group of goals, they invent a new instinct. His approach has been partially rehabilitated by ethologists such as Tinbergen (1951). It was noted that animals often show stereotyped behaviours (known as **specific action patterns**) when highly specific stimuli (known as **innate releasing mechanisms**) are present. The behaviours appear in the stimuli's presence without previous learning, although they may not be present at birth and can be modified by later experiences. Ethologists have elucidated within this framework many complex sequences of reproductive, parental and aggressive behaviours for fish, birds, insects and, to a lesser extent, mammals. Intricate behaviour patterns have been analysed into hierarchically arranged stimulus-response components, which allow a sufficiently flexible relationship between the searching **appetitive** stages and the final **consummatory** stage of instinctive behaviours. Although **imprinting** has been one of the more influential of ethological ideas, mammalian behaviour has proved less amenable to analysis because of the much greater role of learning.

Nevertheless, many goal-related mammalian activities, including eating, drinking, mothering, mating and aggression, can be influenced by stimulating or lesioning brainstem structures, such as the hypothalamus and midbrain. Hormonal modulation of these structures was also found to affect these behaviours. Early work seemed compatible with the claim that specific brainstem systems controlled specific kinds of motivated behaviour. For example, electrical stimulation of one hypothalamic site may lead an animal to eat voraciously whereas stimulation of another site may cause it to mate or show aggression. Combined behavioural and physiological analyses have led some people to claim, for example, that mammalian aggression is controlled by several independent instinctual systems (see Moyer, 1971). The relative significance of brainstem and neocortical structures in mediating motivated activities has prompted the view that the activities are based on an unlearnt template; i.e., mammals, including man, tend to behave in certain ways regardless of their learning experiences.

Learning theorists, dominated by Hull, have, in contrast to the ethologists, stressed the role of learning in motivation and minimized that of innate, biological factors. They postulated that arousal states, known as **drives**, are innately triggered by certain conditions. Drives have two basic features: they are **aversive** states which energize behaviour in a nonspecific fashion; and each drive is also supposed to be associated with a **discriminable** stimulus state.

Organisms learn by trial and error that certain goal behaviours lead to reduction of specific drive states. These behaviours are 'stamped in' by the reinforcing effects of drive reduction and are triggered by the appropriate discriminable drive stimulus. Thus eating is excited by hunger, but mating follows sexual arousal because the two drives are sensorily discriminable. Individual differences in motivated behaviour can be explained by this learning process, and the dominance of different drives at different times is explained by the fact that the arousing conditions for drives are only present intermittently. It is worth noting that alcoholism and drug addiction can be construed as artificial drives because prolonged absence of the drug causes an acutely uncomfortable aroused state which can only be relieved by the appropriate agent.

According to the **drive-reduction theory of motivation**, drives are activated by two kinds of physiological conditions or needs. Drives such as hunger and thirst are homeostatic whereas those for sex and aggression are nonhomeostatic. **Homeostasis** is the process whereby the body maintains a constant internal environment so that it can function optimally. Efficient functioning requires that many physiological states are kept within narrow limits. The states include body temperature, oxygen and carbon-dioxide levels, cellular water balance and mineral levels, and the cellular supplies of glucose. Small deviations from the optimum are corrected by reflex mechanisms, which are not under voluntary control. Sweating and shivering are examples of the reflex control of temperature. Larger deviations from the optimum are meant to cause an activated drive state, which energizes all the behaviour of the organism and sets in train the motivated behaviour, which will restore the appropriate physiological state to its optimal value and thus also reduce the drive state. The periodic dominance of hunger and thirst is clearly related to the regular disturbances of the body's water and energy balances.

Sexual and aggressive behaviours, on the other hand, cannot be controlled via the maintenance of hypothetical homeostatic balances. Learning theorists postulated that the drives for these activities were stimulated by both internal and external factors. For example, sexual arousal is triggered both by sex hormones, such as testosterone circulating in the blood, and suitable external stimuli, for example attractive conspecifics of the opposite sex. The hormonal levels themselves are partly under the control of an autonomous genetic programme and partly under that of complex seasonal factors, such as day-length. They do not remain at a constant level. For this reason, external stimuli produce different levels of sex drive depending on the organism's age, the season and the phase of the sexual cycle. However engendered, the presence of a sexual or aggressive drive causes organisms to seek the means for their reduction – a process which involves learning. The theory therefore embodies the notion of catharsis, whereby sexual behaviour reduces sexual arousal and aggression reduces aggressive arousal.

Both homeostatically and nonhomeostatically based drives are innate in the sense that their physiologically triggered arousal does not require learning. Hullian theory, however, was faced with the problem of explaining the origins of many more abstract motivations, such as needs for self-fulfilment, beauty, glory and knowledge. The theory claimed that these were learned, or **secondary drives**. Miller and Dollard (1941) argued that they were acquired through a process of classical conditioning. If a neutral stimulus is repeatedly paired with the presence of a drive, they proposed that eventually it came to elicit a similar drive state which the organism would work to reduce, presumably by removing itself from the conditioned drive stimulus. The best-known example of this process, and the only one to have been studied in any detail, is conditioned fear. Miller and Dollard have claimed that pairing a neutral stimulus with a painful one causes the neutral stimulus to elicit fear from which an organism attempts to escape.

Another major extension to the learning theory account of motivation has been the introduction of the concept of **incentive motivation** (see Hill, 1963). In its original form, the only role for rewards allowed by the theory was drive reduction, which merely acted to 'stamp in' certain goal-directed behaviours. Later, however, it was accepted that rewards (and punishments) could influence motivated activities more directly. The anticipation of rewards or punishments (incentive motivation) was added to the nonspecific arousing effects of the drive state to produce an even higher degree of behavioural excitation. Like the drive state, the incentive motivation also was linked with a distinctive sensory state which the organism could learn to associate with the goal-directed responses. It was thought that incentive motivation, like secondary drives, came to be associated with the primary drives by classical conditioning. Learning theorists introduced the notion to explain why subjects worked harder for bigger rewards, or became more active when stimuli were paired with frustration, but its effect was to bring the counterintuitive theory more in line with common sense rationalism – the theory came to seem more like a mechanistic underpinning than a denial of the rationalist account.

Nevertheless, today the learning theory view of goal-directed activities is seen as both naive and inadequate. Its chief deficiency perhaps lies in the concept of drive reduction. This concept required that activities or stimuli are rewarding because they reduce drives. Always counterintuitive, it became blatantly so following the discovery that electrical stimulation, particularly in the hypothalamus and brainstem, can direct behaviour more potently than many natural rewards (see Olds and Fobes, 1981, for a review). Rats have been found to press levers to get such stimulation for thousands of presses, until they are too exhausted to continue. Brain stimulation can not only reward in an essentially nonsatiating way (contrary to the drive-reduction view of reward), but it has often been found to increase the level of arousal shown by the stimulated animal. Drive reduction should, of course, decrease such nonspecific activation. Since most researchers now believe that these self-stimulation effects involve the excitation of the neural circuits which cause natural rewards, it seems that rewards are either not directly drive-reducing or that they may be either drive-reducing or drive-increasing. Most likely, their effect on behaviour has nothing to do with reducing drives.

The idea that humans and animals naturally try to decrease their level of arousal by engaging in a range of goal-directed activities also has great difficulties in encompassing a set of characteristic mammalian behaviours which for convenience might be described as being motivated by curiosity. These behaviours include play activity, stimulus-seeking activities and drives to engage in activities which seem to act as their own reward. The centrality of curiosity in humans can scarcely be exaggerated. Even in non-human primates it is easy to demonstrate its primacy. For example, Harlow (see Hill, 1963) has shown that monkeys will repeatedly unopen a clasp device without any other rewards, and it has also been shown that when monkeys are kept in dull, closed cages they will work to open a window so that they can see what is happening outside. Rats have been shown to be willing to work for the opportunity of exploring a novel maze. Although there is some evidence that curiosity behaviours become more intense the longer they have been prevented, they do not appear to satiate in the way that drive-reduction theory requires. For example it has been observed that rats explore a second maze with undiminished enthusiasm even though they have just circumnavigated another one. The impression that many curiosity behaviours actually increase nonspecific arousal is compatible with sensory and perceptual deprivation studies in humans, which show that low levels of stimulation severely disturb perception, thought and attention.

Berlyne (1960) and others have tried to accommodate curiosity within a modified drive theory by arguing that organisms seek an optimal level of arousal at which they function most efficiently. They engage in de-arousing activities when under the influence of traditional drives but switch to arousal-generating behaviours when their level of activation becomes suboptimal. Although animals do sometimes work to increase their arousal level, this theory as a general perspective on motivation is desperately *ad hoc*. The fact that curiosity behaviours can be elicited by the effects of boredom does not mean they always are. Clearly, they usually occur 'spontaneously' with no evidence of prior low-arousal levels. Furthermore, the basic form of many curiosity behaviours seems to arise innately, with little evidence of learning, and indeed the conceptual arsenal of ethologists is better equipped to explain their specific forms. Learning theorists' attempts to account for all motivated behaviour in terms of a single process of nonspecific arousal, like the hedonist's attempt to do the same with 'pleasure' and 'pain', are doomed to fail. Goal-directed behaviour is controlled not by one or two processes, but probably by the excitation of many independent ones. Arousal influences such behaviours, but not in a monolithic fashion. Even eating often occurs without the influence of deprivation-induced hunger. Perhaps the main contribution of drive theory has been to stress that much motivated behaviour is energized in a way not seen with less emotional activity.

Emotion is considered in the next chapter but it is worth pointing out here that there is a close and interlocking relationship between motivated behaviour and emotions. There is no clear distinction between the drive states such as hunger and sexual arousal, and emotions such as fear and joy. The reduction or elicitation of particular emotional states may become the goal of motivated activity. More generally, many goal-directed activities are coloured by the presence of particular emotions, which have arousing effects as well as being pleasant or unpleasant. This means that cognitive and motor efficiency is appreciably affected by emotional arousal so as usually to increase the chances of attaining the selected goal.

Social psychologists do not believe that ethological and learning theory notions adequately explain the origins of most human motivations. Although they admit that innate, biological processes play a vestigial role in the development of these motivations, they regard learning within very broad structural constraints as the guiding force in goal-directed activity. Sociobiologists who extrapolate ethological ideas to humans are criticized as exaggerating the importance of innate, biological factors, and depreciating the salience of learning. It is indeed with the 'socially directed' motivations that most confusion and controversy abounds with respect to the relative contribution of innate and learning factors. The complaint against drive theories, on the other hand, is that they take too narrow a view of the learning processes involved. In addition to classical conditioning, social psychologists emphasize the role of more complex kinds of social learning. For example, they argue that many goal-directed activities are acquired through vicarious or imitation learning. Children model their behaviour on that of high-status adults, so they may become aggressive or sporty because that is what their models are like. The stress on cognitive processes in learning is also apparent in the social psychologists' interpretation of the outcome of goal-directed behaviours. These are seen, not only as having their direct rewarding or punishing effects, but also as causing a self-evaluative reaction. This depends on whether the behaviours conform to the individual's standards, standards which emerge from the play of complex social pressures. Thus, an individual may enjoy bullying, but think poorly of himself for acting in this way, and consequently may desist from doing so. It should be noted that personality can largely be characterized by the goals which an individual typically seeks and by his manner of pursuing them. (See also pages 662–5.)

Cognitive processes, greatly stressed by social psychologists, have been shown to mediate even the motivating effects of innate biological conditions, such as deprivation states. For example, when subjects undergo prolonged water or food deprivation without an adequate incentive being provided by the experimenter, they report feeling less hungry or thirsty, and eat and drink less in compensation than do subjects whose deprivation is based on more satisfactory incentives. This is an instance of cognitive dissonance which is considered more fully on pages 424-5. Cognitions have also been shown to mediate other phenomena supposedly explained by learning theory accounts of motivation. Thus **anxiety** has usually been found to improve the learning of simple tasks and impair that of complex ones. Learning theorists usually construed anxiety as a drive, which increased the dominance of prepotent responses. High anxiety was thought to impair complex learning as this comprised the essential elicitation of many weak responses. It has been shown, however, that the usual interaction between anxiety and task complexity can be abolished by giving subjects misleading feedback about their success. Subjects doing easy tasks were given the impression that they were failing, whereas those doing difficult ones were misled into believing they were doing very well. It was found that high-anxiety subjects learned the hard tasks faster than low-anxiety subjects whereas the latter subjects were better at easy tasks. The effect of anxiety seems to depend on subjects' cognitions about their success. These and similar cognitively mediated motivational phenomena are reviewed by Heckhausen and Weiner (1980).

Traditional motivational theories have tried to explain how the standard goals come to direct behaviour. They have been less successful in showing in detail how goal-directed behaviour operates. This task requires an explanation of how the goal representation then directs behaviour. The one serious try at this – by the learning theorists – was jejune and implausible. Future attempts will rely heavily on the theories of **cybernetics** and **artificial intelligence** (see Miller *et al.*, 1960). A key desideratum for any theory such as this is the ability to predict how goals are selected and conflicts resolved. Little work on these lines has been done but there are some interesting ethological observations of conflict situations. Conflict-bound animals are often reported to engage in **displacement activities** unrelated to the conflicting drives (for example, hunger and fear), but stimulated by some previously less noticed feature in the environment (for example, preening initiated by itchy feathers or fur). Displacement activities are usually engaged in vigorously, which suggests that the 'irrelevant' arousals now energize them.

Maslow (1970) has made another attempt to predict which motivations are likely to control behaviour at any time. Within the framework of **humanistic psychology** he arranged motives in a hierarchical scheme. At the base of the hierarchy were placed the innate biological drives and at the apex was placed the abstract need for **self-actualization**. In between was an ascending order of increasingly complex drives, ranging from safety needs through affiliative ones, to those associated with esteem, knowledge and beauty. Maslow argued that the higher needs only assumed importance for an individual when the lower ones were at least partially fulfilled. In general, a starving man cares little for safety and nothing for self-actualization. The idea is clearly plausible but is too sketchy to constitute a proper theory of goal selection. For example, even the above generalization has its limitation. Under some conditions, motivations high on the hierarchy are so strong that they may outweigh those lower on the hierarchy. An extreme case is provided by the hunger striker whose ideals lead to denial of his more 'basic' urge to eat (see Box 13.2).

The intricate history of thinking about motivation has now been outlined, and to gain a more exact knowledge of goal-directed behaviours the individual motivational systems will now be reviewed more fully. The biologically based drives will be considered before the more complex social drives, which many believe are shaped mainly by learning. Sleep will be discussed first for two reasons. First, there is an interesting puzzle about whether it is a homeostatically based drive. Second, the sleep-wake cycle is associated with marked fluctuations in nonspecific arousal. Studying the cycle may therefore tell us much about the effects of arousal on cognition and about its likely role in motivated behaviour.

Sleep and arousal

All animals sleep. They show periods of relative immobility in which their responsiveness to external events is markedly reduced.

This immobile, unresponsivity of sleep tends to occur at species-specific times of day and in species-typical places, such as in caves or burrows, or up trees. The interval before sleep is accompanied by what might be called appetitive sleep behaviour, which becomes more intense if sleep is artificially prevented. Animals will, for example, search for appropriate sleep sites and, on finding them, adopt suitable sleeping postures. In humans, this presleep phase is accompanied by subjective feelings of tiredness and drowsiness in which the level of arousal falls appreciably. If sleep is prevented, such feelings become so strong that they are almost impossible to resist, so that even people powerfully motivated to be awake will experience microsleeps. Sleep therefore has the feature of a primary drive, like hunger and sex. Periodically, it becomes a goal which dominates behaviour, and whereas its satisfaction reduces the drive's dominance, its deprivation tends to increase it. Unlike the other primary drives, however, the sleep need is reflected in decreased and not raised levels of arousal and its fulfilment seems to be associated with a further reduction in arousal. For this reason, sleep is a serious exception to the view that organisms seek a single optimum level of nonspecific arousal.

The recurring need for episodes of sleep, universal in the animal kingdom, has suggested to many that the state restores one or more homeostatic balances. If this is so, it has been argued, then depriving organisms of sleep should prevent restoration of these balances, so that behaviour should be disturbed increasingly and in specific ways. Although deprivation does have some effects on behaviour and mental functioning, interpreting these effects involves a consideration of the complexity of sleep, and of the distinction between sleep mechanisms and functions.

Since the Second World War the physiology of mammalian sleep has been intensively studied. This work has revealed that sleep consists of two rather different states. One is known as **quiet sleep** (QS) and the other as **active sleep** (AS). QS usually initiates a sleep sequence but is followed by AS. The two then alternate in a cycle (the **ultradian rhythm**) which has a species-typical length, throughout the sleep period. Generally speaking, smaller mammals with higher metabolic rates have shorter ultradian rhythms. In humans, the rhythm has roughly a ninety-minute period, but it changes in the course of a night, with QS predominant early and AS predominant

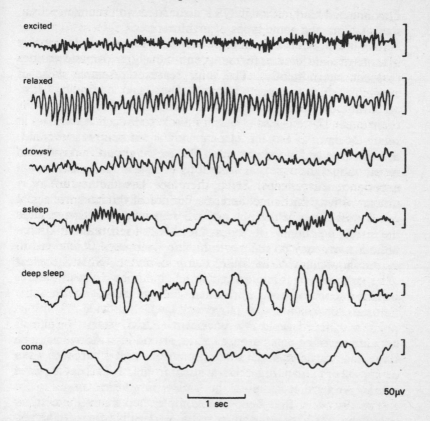

Figure 7.1 Typical EEG records for a normal person passing from arousal through sleep and into coma. (From Jasper, in Penfield and Jasper, 1954)

late in the sleep sequence. As the name implies, human QS involves a general decrease in bodily activities and autonomic processes. For example, heart rate is slowed down. As the state deepens, the periodic electrical activity, recorded from the neocortex and other parts of the brain, slows down and increases in amplitude (see Figure 7.1). Deep QS is characterized by large delta waves with a frequency of one or two cycles per second. Mental activity does occur in this state but only of a vague, disconnected kind, although QS is associated with somnambulism, sleep-talking and some types of nightmare.

In contrast, AS is a much more labile state, which is describable in terms of **tonic** features (present continuously) and **phasic** features (present intermittently). The tonic features resemble those of active wakefulness in some respects. They include fairly fast, low-amplitude electrical activity, which can be recorded from many brain sites. There is also a loss of muscle tone so that the body is relatively limp, and an increase in many autonomic measures such as heart rate and blood pressure. These changes are accompanied by puzzling signs of sexual arousal (erections in males and genital engorgement in females), and by dreaming. **Dreaming** is not simply mental activity but is a coherent sequence of thoughts, reflecting one or more plots, which is associated with vivid visual imagery and has strong emotional overtones. This kind of self-referential symbolic activity may be unique to humans although subhuman primates show many of the other components of AS. It is unclear whether dreaming is intermittent in AS, but known phasic features include fluctuations in heart rate and blood pressure, twitches of the limbs and coordinated eye movements, which provide AS with its popular name of **rapid eye movement** (REM) sleep. Despite its appearance of being an aroused state, attention in AS seems to be directed inwards, as under some circumstances it is harder to wake an animal or human from this state than from QS. This finding gives rise to yet another name for the state – **paradoxical sleep**.

The discovery that sleep was complex led many theorists to postulate that each substate may be responsible for specific **restorative functions**, and that in humans there may be further functions for dreaming. If sleep does serve such functions, then the restorative needs of different mammals must differ considerably because whereas some species (the bottle-nosed dolphin) hardly seem to sleep at all, others (including the brown bat and the opossum) sleep for nineteen or more hours a day. Although variables such as body size, brain size, metabolic rate and even longevity have been related to total sleep time, to the period of the ultradian rhythm and to the relative proportions of QS to AS, sleep measures are also powerfully influenced by the kind of ecological niche which a species has occupied. Thus, although QS has been negatively correlated with a species' body size, AS is less, the greater the danger to which a species is exposed. Species exposed to predation, who cannot find safe sleep sites and must spend much of each day searching for and consuming essential energy and water supplies, sleep very little. This group is typified by herd animals. Predatory species who sleep in safe places like trees and can satisfy their food and water needs quickly sleep for the majority of the day. Lions are typical of this group. Restorative theories of sleep must accommodate these observations.

In 1949, Moruzzi and Magoun showed that a diffuse structure which projected through the floor of the midbrain was very important in maintaining arousal and controlling the sleep-wake cycle. It was found that stimulating this structure awoke sleeping animals, and made awake ones more alert. Conversely, large lesions of this structure, called the midbrain reticular formation, made animals go into comas from which it was hard to arouse them. These effects were not found by stimulating or lesioning the pathways which carried specific sensory information to the neocortex. This was interesting because anatomical work showed that these pathways fed their information into the reticular formation in such a way as to lose the specific significance of the information but such that the more information was fed in, the greater was the reticular formation's excitation. Other work showed that the reticular formation projected to the neocortex and other forebrain systems, diffusely rather than in a point-to-point fashion, so as to determine the background level of excitability of these systems in a nonspecific fashion. It seemed that the midbrain reticular formation must be the neural mechanism of general arousal and that sleep occurred when its level of activity fell below a critical level. This implied that sleep was a passive process which began when sensory stimulation was minimized.

The passive view of sleep generation soon faced difficulties. First, it needed to be extended to allow for the presence of pathways running back from the cortex to the reticular formation. It was suggested therefore that levels of thinking as well as sensory input must decline for sleep to begin. Second, and more fundamentally, the passive view conflicted with the behaviours usual in the presleep period and with subjective feelings of drowsiness. Third, it was shown that there were structures in the reticular formation, lying lower in the core of the brainstem than the midbrain, which actively produced sleep by inhibiting the midbrain arousal system. Jouvet (1967) identified the raphe nucleus at the level of the pons as critical in initiating QS. Lesions to it caused severe insomnia in cats, and naturally occurring lesions seem to have the same effect in humans. Jouvet also claimed that a small structure known as the locus coeruleus is critical in controlling AS. Although evidence now shows that there are other brainstem and forebrain systems which play a role in triggering sleep, and that the importance of the structures identified by Jouvet has been exaggerated, there is no doubt that sleep arises when the midbrain arousal system becomes inactive. The appearance of AS, however, depends on a more complex modulation of the midbrain arousal system. This is because AS is a unique kind of aroused state (see Carlson, 1985, for a detailed discussion of these issues).

The structures which inhibit the midbrain arousal system presumably become active when the need for sleep develops. This need shows a **circadian rhythm** which can continue to run even in the absence of entraining events, such as the daily cycle of light and dark. These events help set the onset of sleep to a particular time of day, and without them the sleep-wake cycle runs freely in humans with a period of more than twenty-four hours, so that sleep onset shifts around the clock. It is believed that the autonomous rhythm is maintained by the suprachiasmatic nucleus of the hypothalamus. Messages from this nucleus probably influence structures like the raphe nucleus. Hibernation, which also continues periodically in the absence of seasonal entraining events, must be triggered by a system autonomously showing a circannual rhythm. There are, however, many more specific stimuli which increase the need for sleep. They include excessive warmth, the digestion of large meals, sexual activity and repetitive monotonous stimuli, such as flashing lights or regular loud sounds. Some of these effects may be mediated by the nucleus of the solitary tract which lies in the medulla. Stimulation of this nucleus produces sleep-like electrical activity, which is known to inhibit the midbrain reticular formation. It is also thought to be activated by repetitive, tactile stimuli (such as those used to lull a baby to sleep) and by stimuli from the digestive tract (which would be most intense following a large meal). Thermal stimuli may influence the need for sleep via the preoptic nucleus of the hypothalamus (see Carlson, 1985, for a discussion).

One popular view of sleep as a restorative state is that it dissipates toxic substances which have accumulated during wakefulness. Isolation of such substances, if they existed, would be difficult, because it is known that the sleep-wake cycle is influenced not only by neurotransmitters, such as serotonin and noradrenaline, but also by small polypeptides which are borne in the blood and cerebrospinal fluid. These agents are likely to concentrate as the need for sleep grows. The need should also increase as toxic substances accumulate. Thus the distinction between agents related to function as opposed to mechanism is hard to demonstrate. It is partly for this reason that the effects on **sleep deprivation** have been studied. Unfortunately, these face not dissimilar problems. Humans and animals have been deprived of all sleep, or of AS or the deeper part of QS, and the effects on cognition examined. Early research suggested that people totally deprived of sleep hallucinate and may even become psychotic. It is now clear, however, that this is unusual and that the only obvious effect of deprivation is greater sleepiness and a tendency to show moderate increases of recovery sleep. Sleepiness during deprivation is greatest at night, and QS is compensated prior to AS in the rebound stage of recovery. Furthermore, selective deprivation of these sleep stages leads to selective rebound effects. Even 264 hours of remaining awake did not noticeably disturb the cognitive and emotional functions of an American teenager called Randy Gardner (Gulevich *et al.*, 1966). After a recovery night with fifteen hours of sleep he then slept normally. Even the rare cases of hallucination and personality change are very likely nonspecific effects of frustrating a very strong drive. Similar effects have been reported following the frustration of other strong drives such as hunger (Murray, 1965). Total sleep deprivation does not seem to prevent vital restorative functions. Its effects are rather those of frustrating a powerful drive. Generally, only performances requiring prolonged attention suffer.

Despite these negative results, restorative roles for QS and AS have been claimed. Oswald (1974) has proposed that QS restores bodily processes which have deteriorated during the day, whereas AS restores brain processes, partially through stimulating neural protein synthesis. The empirical basis for these claims is controversial. For example, daytime exercise has, under some conditions, been found to increase QS, and the deeper stages of QS are specifically correlated with the release of growth hormone which is thought to facilitate cellular restoration. Protein synthesis in the brain has been reported to increase in AS, and time spent in this sleep stage has been found to increase during recovery from brain damage or following intensive learning experiences. It has indeed become popular to argue that AS plays a critical role in the stabilization of certain kinds of memory, particularly those with emotional significance or which involve 'unprepared' learning. Not only do these kinds of learning lead to increases in AS, but their retention may be disturbed when learning is followed by a period of AS deprivation. If such a function exists, it may involve a stimulation of consolidation processes. This hypothesis applies to animals and humans, but it has an extension concerning dreaming which may be unique to humans. Unlike Freud's suggestion that dreams express unconscious wishes in a disguised form, this hypothesis asserts that dreams integrate recent experiences into the pool of well-established memories. This **cross-indexing hypothesis** is an interesting speculation, but has little direct support. Dreams do incorporate new experiences in the fabric of their plots to a certain extent, and this rehearsal may help integrate such experiences. Most likely, however, any such effects are insignificant and dreams are probably best conceived as **low-grade mental activity** similar to that found in individuals who are drunk.

More recently, sleep has been seen as serving an **immobilizing function**, which may enable energy to be conserved and protect an animal from environmental dangers. Meddis (1979) has argued that sleep is an instinctive system which ensures that animals remain immobilized for prolonged periods. This immobilization may have many adaptive functions, depending on the species, but none of these functions need be the restoration of a homeostatic balance disturbed during wakefulness. Sleep duration in a species will depend on how long an animal need stay awake to fulfil its vital biological needs and also on whether sleep increases or decreases predatory and natural hazards. The existence of two stages of sleep poses a problem for this theory. For example, it has been argued that whereas most AS is nonessential as its intensity depends on time of day, not on the length of previous wakefulness, QS is obligatory because its duration depends to a much greater degree on the length of the preceding period of wakefulness.

Meddis has argued, however, that AS evolved before QS in reptiles which do not maintain a constant core temperature. In AS thermoregulation seems to break down and this would cause a physiological crisis if the state were to be prolonged in mammals, which are homeothermic (do keep a steady core temperature). The evolution of QS enabled mammals to maintain homeothermy while being immobilized for long periods. In most animals AS does not exceed more than a quarter of total sleep time. Evidence for Meddis's suggestion is scanty, but it is interesting that, relative to QS, the features of AS are more apparent in primitive mammals and neonates (maturation is often said to recapitulate evolution). Indeed, neonatal humans and other mammals not only sleep in a polyphasic fashion much longer than adults, but also show disproportionately large amounts of AS. For a while after birth AS decreases and QS increases, despite the decline in total sleep time, and in humans, sleep slowly becomes confined to a single long period. It is assumed, but unproved, that the adult pattern emerges with the minimal influence of learning.

Sleep is a state which absorbs a third of our lives, and is initiated by a drive which eventually becomes irresistible. This distinguishes it from other motivations which require some degree of active striving to achieve their goals. It is also distinct in that its functions remain a partial mystery. The adaptive value of being immobile in a safe place is minimal for modern man and no restorative functions of sleep have been unequivocally identified. Nevertheless, the urge to sleep can only be defied by humans at the cost of increasing sleepiness and discomfort, which are signs of the drive's intensification. Meddis (1979) has suggested that if this 'sleep instinct' could be suppressed there might be no harmful effects. There are indeed some nonsomniacs who happily sleep for an hour or less a night for many years, perhaps because of some active disturbance of their brainstem sleep mechanisms. They should be distinguished from insomniacs, who, despite a strong urge to sleep, cannot easily do so. Insomnia has many causes, but one common aggravating factor is the arousal generated by trying excessively hard to fall asleep.

There are other kinds of sleep disorder. These include disorders of excessive sleep, of which a striking example is narcolepsy. This disorder is associated with daytime sleepiness, in which the individual atypically goes straight into AS (normal sleep begins with QS). The episode may be triggered by emotional excitement, and the components of AS may appear in fragmented form so that the victim may experience hallucinations, cataplexy or sleep paralysis. Oswald (1974) refers to a narcoleptic woman who was disadvantaged at poker because whenever she had a good hand the excitement led to the loss of muscle tone typical in AS, and her jaw dropped. In some people nocturnal AS may also be a particularly hazardous state in which respiratory and cardiovascular functions fluctuate wildly and sometimes fail altogether. Even QS is associated with damaging behaviours such as head-banging and bruxism (in which the teeth are ground with great force). Finally, sleep can be disrupted by disturbances in the sleep-waking circadian rhythm, as, for example, in the 'jet-lag' syndrome. The nature of these pathologies reveals sleep to be a state as complex as waking rather than a simple condition of passivity.

Sleep deprivation leads to reduced levels of arousal, so along with other factors which influence this variable, e.g., white noise and personality, it is used as a means of examining the effects of arousal on performance. These effects are conveniently summarized by the **Yerkes-Dodson 'law'** which states that as arousal increases, cognitive performance improves up to a peak and then declines. This peak is reached sooner, the more complex is the task. High levels of arousal increase the vigour with which responses, particularly dominant ones, are performed, but when success depends on co-ordinating several responses there may be disruption. Although everyone accepts that the Yerkes-Dodson law summarizes a body of received wisdom, there is much uncertainty about what arousal actually is. The process is supposedly affected by sleep deprivation, fever, drugs, noise, the interest in stimuli and by personality. Its intensity is supposed to be indexed by autonomic nervous system activity, as measured by heart rate and skin resistance, and by the nature of the brain's electrical activity. It is unclear, however, what these measures reflect. Worse, they do not always covary when excitation is increased, which has led some to suggest that there are several kinds of arousal. The problem will be resolved only when one or more brain processes can be identified which influence most types of cognitive activity in the way Yerkes and Dodson described.

Homeostatic drives

HUNGER

Like sleep, the activities of eating and drinking play dominant roles in human and animal lives. It is commonly supposed that we eat and drink when hungry and thirsty; that what we eat and drink are the foods and liquids which best satisfy our hunger and thirst; and that hunger and thirst arise from the disturbance of certain homeostatic imbalances. The partial truths underlying these suppositions will be expanded in this section. They are, however, only partial truths. Hunger and thirst are not the only spurs to eating and drinking. These activities are also initiated through **habits** and by the pleasant effects of ingesting certain foods and drinks, and are facilitated by the sight of others eating and drinking. Drinking and, even more, eating are, then, behaviours only partly under the control of their physiological imbalances.

Animals and, to a lesser extent, humans can maintain constant body weights over long periods of time. Le Magnen (1971) has shown that rats, given free access to food, eat regular meals but that the size of these meals is not a simple function of the time since the previous one. On the other hand, meal size determines how long an animal will wait before its next meal – the larger the meal, the longer the delay. These observations are important because they show that the factors which control the onset of eating must differ from those which control its cessation. This conclusion is supported by the finding that a blood transfusion from a donor rat which has just eaten does not inhibit the eating of a recipient. Inhibition is only found when the blood is removed long after the donor has stopped eating (Davis *et al.*, 1969). Meal size depends little on physiological need and depends much more on factors like variety and palatability of food. Weight constancy is maintained by spacing meals rather than varying their size. In humans, this control is diminished by the fact that meals are habitually eaten at regular intervals. When meal sizes are great because food is highly palatable there may be long-term overeating with consequent obesity.

To understand food regulation it is necessary to know (1) what processes are being homeostatically controlled, (2) where the receptors which measure these processes are and where they send their information, (3) how this information is integrated in the brain to initiate eating, and (4) what factors cause eating to stop at the end of a meal. The answers to these problems are complex – eating is under multiple controls which are still poorly understood. Before considering the problems in more detail, it is worth sketching the consensus view of a decade ago – a view now undergoing revision. It was thought that weight was controlled by the regulation of some aspect of glucose metabolism – perhaps the rate of glucose uptake by the body's cells. It was also speculated that the level of this regulation might be influenced by a similar control of lipid (fat) and amino acid (constituents of proteins) metabolism. Glucose metabolism was thought to be monitored by receptors in the **hypothalamus**, which integrated the relevant information with the help of limbic system influences. The **lateral hypothalamic nucleus** (LH) was supposed to activate hunger and hence eating. Its destruction led animals to starve themselves to death unless they were supported artificially, and electrical stimulation of this nucleus led animals not only to eat, but to eat as if hungry – for example, they would work or endure shocks in order to obtain food. They would also eat if already gorged. Another structure, the **ventromedial nucleus of the hypothalamus** (VMH), appeared to be a satiety centre which inhibited eating at the end of meals. Electrical stimulations of the VMH blocked eating in hungry animals and its destruction led to **hyperphagia** (overeating) and obesity. Many believed that obesity and **anorexia** (undereating or self-starvation) in humans are caused by malfunctions of these two nuclei or their connections.

For convenience, the nutritional state of the body can be divided into the **absorptive phase**, when energy and nutrients are being absorbed through the intestine, any excess being stored as fat, and the **fasting phase** when energy has to be drawn from the liver and adipose tissues because the gut is empty. The fasting phase causes hunger and leads to eating. It is probable that the mechanisms controlling these phases trigger hunger and satiety. The key difference between the phases lies in the metabolism of glucose. In absorption, uptake of glucose by the cells is stimulated by insulin release, whereas in fasting glucagon, growth hormone and adrenaline are released to maintain blood glucose levels and the liver is stimulated to convert glycogen into glucose. There are neurons in the hypothalamus which are sensitive to glucose metabolism (they actually monitor the metabolic rate) but they seem to control the release of adrenaline and not hunger. Hunger feelings (and satiety) are activated by monitors of metabolic rate in the liver. Small injections of glucose into the liver's blood supply inhibit hunger, but this effect is itself blocked if the vagus nerve is severed (Novin *et al.*, 1974). This nerve sends the signals of the liver receptors to the brain. Conversely, injections of substances into the portal system of the liver, blocking glucose metabolism there,cause an immediate increase in eating of over 200 per cent (Novin *et al.*, 1973). It has also been shown that sugars which do not cross the blood-brain barrier into the brain inhibit hunger. These sugars stimulate the liver receptors.

When too many calories are consumed for the body's needs they are converted to fat (unless they are burnt off by specialized brown fat cells). Fat reserves are used during periods of fasting. It seems plausible that the level of these reserves may be monitored and regulated over long periods of time. Although there is a poor relationship between fat metabolism and the short-term control of eating, there is evidence that fat levels are controlled in the long term. Liebelt and his colleagues (1973) have shown that fat tissue transplanted into recipient mice withers away, unless some of their fat tissue had previously been removed. Mice with VMH lesions also accepted fat transplants when they were gaining weight. These findings are consistent with the observation that animals forced to overeat and accumulate fat subsequently reduce their food intake until they return to their initial weight. Fat-reserve regulation through the control of hunger probably involves hormonal mechanisms but very little is known about these. Ignorance is even greater about the possibility that some aspect of amino acid metabolism regulates food intake. There is evidence, however, that the long-term intake of amino acids is controlled.

The last point warrants emphasis. Animals and humans regulate more than their energy balance (and hence body weight). Amino acid, vitamin and mineral intakes are also controlled. The intake of sodium salts seems to have a strong innate basis. Rats, deficient in this salt following adrenal removal, show a marked preference for sodium within fifteen seconds of exposure (Nachman, 1962). This preference is also shown for lithium salts, which rats cannot discriminate from sodium salts, even though ingesting lithium makes them ill. Other kinds of regulation seem to depend on the learning mechanisms described in Chapter 5, in which if a diet lacks some vital ingredient or contains a poison, an animal, after becoming ill, will shift its diet until it finds one which abolishes the feelings of illness. It then stays with the new diet.

If long-term regulation of ingestion and the initiation of eating are controlled by learning and the monitoring of glucose and lipid metabolism then control of short-term satiation of meals is differently controlled. The early stages of eating palatable food actually stimulate appetite – the peanut effect. Even rats, given the same food but in four differently tasting forms, will eat much more. Feedback from the mouth, related to taste and smell, does, however, inhibit food intake. Cabanac (1971) has observed in humans that the subjective appreciation of a food's pleasantness declines as the individual becomes satiated. This decrease in how rewarding a food is, seems to be specific to each taste. If new foods are introduced, they may still taste very pleasant and be eaten. Satiety is also triggered by sensory feedback from the gut. This includes feedback from a distended stomach, and chemical information from the stomach as well. Stomach contractions, by contrast, have been associated with hunger. These sensations are not critical since people with stomachs removed still experience hunger and satiety. Satiety is also signalled shortly after eating when food enters the duodenum. The signals may involve neural signals to the brain and release of the hormone enterogastrone – but no one is sure. Finally, as well as by receptor mechanisms in the mouth, stomach and duodenum, satiety may also be signalled by a specially rapid system in the liver. The combined influence of these mechanisms determines meal size.

Recent work has challenged the view that the VMH integrates this information to cause satiety. Although VMH lesions cause obesity, the disorder has two stages. A dynamic stage of weight increase is followed by a static phase in which weight is maintained at a much higher level. Early research showed that VMH-lesioned animals are very sensitive to food taste, but recent work makes it unlikely that this is related to their overeating. For example, cutting the vagus nerve from the liver in VMH-lesioned animals abolishes their hyperphagia but not their finickiness about food. VMH stimulation is aversive so it is hard to know whether it specifically causes satiety rather than simply unpleasant feelings. More seriously, lesions restricted to the VMH do not cause hyperphagia whereas damage to the ventral noradrenergic bundle, which passes by the nucleus, does. These nerves may be sending satiety information to other brain regions. Friedman and Stricker (1976) have argued that large VMH lesions, which damage the ventral noradrenergic bundle as well, may cause hyperphagia because they alter metabolism and put the body into a continuous absorptive phase. Fat is created even in what should be the fasting phase, therefore eating occurs to satisfy tissue needs and not because a satiety mechanism is damaged.

Similar problems affect the interpretation of LH lesions. Interestingly, animals recover from the **aphagia** and **adipsia** (respectively, loss of eating and drinking) which such damage causes, if they are kept alive artificially. Teitelbaum (1971) has suggested that stages of recovery of regulation resemble the development of infantile motivational systems, progressing from reflex to homeostatic controls. This process seems to require increasing cortical participation. Recent research has led many to conclude that it is damage to the nigrostriatal bundle (and perhaps also the trigeminal nerve), which passes near the LH, and not the nucleus itself, that causes aphagia and adipsia. All of these lesions seem to produce a diminished responsiveness to stimuli in the environment and what seems to be a reduction of arousability. These findings can be related to the interesting observation that even satiated rats can be induced to eat by a mild pinch of the tail (see Robbins, 1978). It has also been shown that rats with LH or nigrostriatal bundle lesions will eat so as to regain their preoperative weights if tail-pinching is continued long enough.

It is possible that mild tail-pinching or LH stimulation cause eating because they enhance animals' responsiveness to many different stimuli by raising the general level of arousal. The process need not be aversive: it may be partly mediated through the nigrostriatal bundle. The traditional view of hypothalamic stimulation has been that there are specific neural circuits controlling each drive behaviour – hunger, thirst, sex, etc. This may well be the case, but it has been claimed that both LH stimulation and tail-pinching lead to eating as a secondary effect of nonspecific activation.

Electrical stimulation causes drinking, gnawing and hoarding as well as eating. The response appears to be motivated rather than automatic, but depends on the goal-objects initially present during stimulation. Once a behaviour has been established then an animal tends to stick with it. Very similar effects are found following tail-pinching. The phenomena seem to fit with the learning theory notion of a general drive energizing behaviours, which are selected through stimulus conditions. They also resemble displacement in which the arousal from conflicting drives energizes another behaviour elicited by local stimuli present at the time.

Eating induced by tail-pinching is blocked by agents that inhibit the action of neurons in the nigrostriatal system which use dopamine as a neurotransmitter (Antelman *et al.*, 1975). Displacement behaviours are similarly affected when the antidopamine blockade is confined to a related system known as the mesolimbic dopamine system (Robbins and Koob, 1980). This treatment did not disturb deprivation-induced drinking. Both the nigrostriatal and mesolimbic systems, then, use dopamine as a neurotransmitter and seem to control motivated behaviours, such as eating, in slightly different ways by eliciting nonspecific activation, which makes individuals more sensitive to external stimuli.

In humans, weight regulation breaks down in obesity and the disorder of anorexia nervosa. The latter is very common in teenage girls and may sometimes lead to their starving themselves to death. Are these disorders of the homeostatic mechanisms themselves, or are they instances where either the rewarding effects of food override the controls or other drives dominate eating behaviour? Even rats initially consume great amounts of tasty but non-nutritive saccharin, and there is no doubt that if meals are consumed regularly from habit, taste factors can partly inhibit satiety. But do these people differ in the way they react to stimuli relevant to eating as has been claimed? Obese people are reported to respond much more to taste than normal-weight people. They overeat pleasant foods but undereat bland or slightly unpleasant foods. The obese are also supposed to be less sensitive to internal cues provided by hunger feelings. Thus, they are easily fooled into eating long before their usual mealtimes when given clocks which run fast (Schachter and Gross, 1968). Also, they eat far more after viewing amazing or sexually arousing films than after watching boring ones, presumably because these arousal states are for them so similar to hunger (White, 1977). Further direct evidence shows the obese to be insensitive to stomach contractions. Interesting as these observations are, it appears that many of these effects are also seen in normal-weight people who are dieting. As most obese people are dieting, and the effects are not seen in the hyperobese who may not be, these effects may be those apparent in the chronically hungry. The issues are unresolved, but there is evidence that the obese may have a higher steady point for body fat, related to the number of adipocytes (fat cells) they develop in a sensitive period after birth. It may also be that they lack the brown fat cells, which in normal-weight people burn off excess calories.

Anorexia nervosa is even less well understood. It appears to involve a vicious circle of effects. Teenage girls, in whom it is most common, may start dieting possibly as an indirect means of avoiding adult responsibilities by preventing their bodies undergoing the changes of puberty. At this stage their appetites may be normal, although there may be some reduction because of the stress of menarche. Later, however, their hormonal control may be disturbed and their **oestrogen function** become abnormal. This has a direct effect in reducing appetite. It should also be noted that, quite independently, prolonged starvation does not increase hunger but eventually diminishes it along with arousal and sex drive. These partially supported speculations therefore suggest that hunger drive is disturbed in anorexia due to a complex interaction of drive conflict and the biological factor of **hormone imbalance**.

THIRST

Water intake must be regulated more tightly than food intake as it is only possible to survive a few days without water. Water balance is maintained by drinking and by hormonal mechanisms which conserve water in the body. Loss of water not only causes thirst, it also activates hormonal mechanisms which reduce the rate of loss or minimize its effects. Thus **antidiuretic hormone** (ADH) is released into the bloodstream from the posterior pituitary and acts on the kidneys so that urine is concentrated by the reabsorption of water. When blood volume decreases from water deprivation the kidney itself releases a hormone called renin, which causes the blood vessels to constrict, so minimizing the effects of the loss of blood volume.

The bodily states which elicit thirst are rather better understood than those which elicit hunger. As water deprivation is prolonged it causes two alterations in the distribution of body fluids: a decrease of water volume within cells and a decrease in the volume of water in the extracellular spaces, including the blood vessels. Both these changes independently act as stimuli for thirst. This is shown by hypertonic injections of saline which elicit thirst by reducing intracellular volume, and by injections of colloids into the abdomen which cause thirst by reducing the volume of the extracellular space. Wounded soldiers become thirsty as a result of haemorrhage-induced fluid loss despite the fact that blood does not become more concentrated.

Intracellular fluid volume is a function of osmotic pressure. In osmosis water is withdrawn from cells in an attempt to equalize the concentration of the solutions on either side of the cellular membrane. Although dehydration occurs in all body cells, it seems that there are specialized **osmoreceptors** in parts of the hypothalamus, some of which activate ADH and others of which excite thirst. For example, Johnson and Buggy (1978) showed that lesions of the periventricular region of the hypothalamus block the drinking which normally follows injections of hypertonic saline.

Loss of extracellular fluid is monitored by **baroreceptors** (measuring pressure) in the walls of veins and by a kidney mechanism which monitors blood flow. Both sets of receptors can activate drinking: for example, animals without kidneys still show hypovolemic thirst. When the kidney mechanism is excited, the renin released into the bloodstream is converted into angiotensin I by an enzyme called angiotensinogen, found in blood proteins. Angiotensin I is converted to angiotensin II when it passes in the blood through the lungs. This hormone then stimulates the periventricular region of the hypothalamus so that drinking is very rapidly elicited. It is unknown how the baroreceptors excite the brain to elicit hypovolemic thirst.

As with hunger, thirst is excited by peripheral stimuli such as a dry mouth. These peripheral changes are probably secondary to central ones that actually initiate drinking. Thirsty dogs do stop drinking, however, even when the water passes straight out of their oesophaguses via a fistula (Adolph, 1941). Although drinking restarts again in ten minutes, the finding suggests that the mouth and throat somehow monitor water intake so as to inhibit drinking. Unlike overeating, though, there is little problem caused by moderate overdrinking as the fluid can easily be voided in the urine. Furthermore, water is absorbed more rapidly than food, and drinking is inhibited by central changes in many animals. Indeed, dogs seem to depend more on peripheral satiety cues than do many animals – horses treated like Adolph's dogs drink to exhaustion.

Under some circumstances, drinking occurs not in response to thirst but in anticipation of a future need. This particularly applies to drinking in association with meals. The processes of digestion have a dehydrating effect, the degree of which is greater with high-protein than with high-carbohydrate diets. Rats, as well as humans, can adjust their drinking at the time of eating to anticipate accurately this future dehydration. When shifted from a high-carbohydrate to a high-protein diet they initially drink extra water after the meal, but gradually learn to show the appropriate increase before the meal is digested.

Humans often drink far in excess of that required to satisfy thirst and bodily needs. This kind of drinking can be understood in terms of habit, social pressures and facilitation, and the rewarding taste of some beverages.

Rewards and punishments

It is a platitude that humans and animals seek pleasure (or rewards) and try to escape or avoid punishments. It is also clear that anticipated or experienced rewards and punishments may impair the ability of homeostatic drives to regulate key variables or make some nonhomeostatic behaviours unduly dominant. Nevertheless, rewards normally form part of the fabric of regulatory systems and behavioural control. Part of the reason for this has become clearer from research on the **brain's reward systems**.

Brain stimulation at some sites is believed to mimic specific rewards, like those obtained from eating, drinking and copulation. For example, it has been shown that single neurons in the hypothalamus, which are excited by specific natural rewards such as the taste of glucose or water, are also excited by rewarding brain stimulation at certain sites. Interestingly, it seems that the degree of reward obtained by stimulation of these sites is actually modulated by the appropriate drive. Thus **lateral hypothalamic self-stimulation** is considerably faster in hungry rats although that at other sites may be unaffected. Similarly, Cagguila (1970) has shown that male rats decreased their self-stimulation rates for electrodes in the posterior hypothalamus following castration. Their lateral hypothalamic self-stimulation was unaffected. These observations provide the neural counterparts to Cabanac's (1971) claim that foods taste less pleasant as satiation approaches. Although brain stimulation at many sites seems to elicit specific rewards and is modulated by drive state, that at other sites is not so modulated and seems to excite a more general pleasurable state. Self-stimulating humans have reported sexual feelings but more often they experience a diffuse state of pleasure.

The evidence is strong, then, that neurons which mediate natural rewards have their effects modulated by other neurons which mediate drive states such as hunger and thirst. Although these two neural groups are often superimposed, they can usually be differentiated because, for example, they have different stimulation thresholds. Rewarding effects and drives may cease to be well correlated when organisms are exposed to strong, artificial rewards, such as those provided by alcohol and other drugs. Addictive behaviours are probably only minimally maintained by the unpleasant and arousing effects of drug withdrawal. They are much more strongly influenced by the general pleasure states caused by taking the drugs – states which are little affected by any natural drives. One of the most plausible accounts of the origin of individual differences in susceptibility to **addictions** like alcoholism is that some people are physiologically constituted so as to find drug-taking more rewarding and less punishing than the majority. Quite generally, the sensitivity of people's reward and punishment systems probably differs; this has been related to personality differences and is discussed in Chapter 13. The role of **contextual factors** should not be neglected, however.Addictions are habits and are strongest in those circumstances in which they were acquired.

If motivated behaviours are to be properly controlled then it is important to learn which stimuli are rewarding or punishing, or lead to reward or punishment. There is evidence that the **amygdala** in the temporal lobe limbic system and the **prefrontal cortex** are involved in such learning and that they influence activity in hypothalamic reward systems. Both sites can support self-stimulation, and neurons in both can be excited by hypothalamic self-stimulation. The amygdala seems to help form stimulus-reward and stimulus-punishment associations. Thus, Fuster and Uyeda (1971) found amygdala neurons which responded differently to signals for reward and punishment. The differential responding to the signals ceased when the associations were extinguished. Following amygdala lesions, humans and animals act as if they no longer know and can no longer learn what the rewarding or punishing associations of stimuli are. Lesioned monkeys eat inedible objects like faeces, no longer fear humans, do not show learned aversions and attempt to copulate with inappropriate objects such as members of other species (Klüver and Bucy, 1939). In contrast to the amygdala, parts of prefrontal cortex seem to be important in extinguishing associations of stimuli to reward and punishment. Frontal lesions often cause pathological persistence of behaviours which are no longer appropriate. This perseveration could indicate that stimuli retain their originally learnt reward or punishment associations even though these should now have been extinguished. Phobias and obsessional-compulsive disorders show unusual persistence of reward and punishment associations and may be related to abnormal frontal functions.

Frontal lesions, particularly of the orbitofrontal cortex, have another interesting effect. They often reduce the intensity of unpleasant emotions like anxiety, and also decrease the emotional response to pain. Patients with **frontal lobotomies** frequently report that they still feel pain but that it doesn't bother them, and similarly lesioned monkeys show a deficit in learning to avoid punishment (Tanaka, 1973). Pain is a complex process which has distinct sensory and motivational-emotional components. It can be elicited not only by noxious peripheral stimulation but also by central stimulation of certain regions of the brainstem and thalamus. It is likely that central stimulation sometimes causes the arousal of aversive states independent of pain, which organisms will also try and avoid. These states may include the discomforts associated with fatigue, sensory deprivation, extremes of temperature or the accumulation of waste products in the body. The aversive, motivating effects of pain seem to be modulated by several systems in the brain. The frontal mechanisms may have an important role in hypnotic analgesia and a lesser one in pain reduction through acupuncture. Acupuncture may also act by stimulating a brainstem system which seems to work in part through the release of naturally occurring opiates (the opioids) known as **enkephalins** and **endorphins**. These substances are released by the brain and the pituitary and, by modulating neural activity, reduce the motivational and aversive impact of **pain**, as well as having many other actions (Basbaum *et al.*, 1976). Their action is antagonized by the drug naloxone which also reduces the pain-reducing actions of hypnosis and acupuncture. Naloxone also antagonizes the effects of morphine and heroin. The pleasant effects of these drugs probably depend on their ability to excite brain receptors designed for the opioids.

Opioids are released in circumstances, such as during pregnancy, where the aversiveness of extreme pain serves no useful function. It seems possible that central brain mechanisms, such as the frontal cortex and the opioid systems, modulate the awareness of pain, so that its motivating effects are greatest in those circumstances where it is most essential to escape or avoid more serious damage or danger. The importance of pain as a motivator of escape is dramatically illustrated by those unfortunate individuals who have congenital absence of pain. They may die of complications from severe arthritis brought on by a failure to adjust body positions periodically because they are not aware of the warning signals of pain which a normal person would be receiving. Even when pain must be escaped, there is some modulation of it by brain systems. For example, there is evidence that a wide range of stresses reduce pain sensitivity, probably via a nonopioid system (Bodner *et al.*, 1977). These mechanisms are of limited efficiency, however, and much research is being directed towards finding means of activating them more readily.

Nonhomeostatic drives

SEX AND REPRODUCTIVE BEHAVIOURS

Reproductive behaviours involve many activities in addition to copulation. In most species, copulation is preceded and accompanied by territorial and aggressive behaviours, and is accompanied and followed by parental behaviours. These behaviours restore no homeostatic balances but have evolved because their concerted effect is the successful propagation of the species. Reproductive behaviours are nearly always **sexually dimorphic**, with males and females differing in their mode of copulatory behaviour, the nature of their preferred partners and their characteristic territorial, aggressive and parental activities. In the higher primates, including humans, these differences are shown in the adoption of different **sex roles**, which involve many social behaviours only distantly related to reproduction. There is also evidence for cognitive style as well as emotional differences, with males evincing greater visuospatial skills in contrast to females' superior verbal abilities. Individuals also vary greatly in their levels of sexual interest and their preferred types of sexual activities and partners. Learning, particularly in humans and other primates, is very important in the development of these motivated behaviours, but hormonal factors also play a significant role in the growth and expression of reproductive behaviours, and these will be considered first.

The sex hormones are largely manufactured in the gonads and are steroids with cholesterol as their common precursor. Cholesterol is initially converted into **progesterone**, which is found predominantly in females at ovulation and during pregnancy. Progesterone is convertible into **testosterone**, which is produced mainly in the male's testes, and also into several other predominantly male hormones, known as **androgens**. Finally, testosterone is convertible into oestradiol, which is one of the female homones known as **oestrogens**.

At conception, female mammals differ from males in possessing two sex chromosomes as opposed to the male's XY combination. The embryo contains a primitive **bipotential gonad**. An XX chro-

mosome pair causes this gonad to develop into an ovary whereas
an XY combination leads it to develop into a testis. This testis
releases testosterone in the embryo and its action during a critical
period, which is species-dependent, causes the basically female
form of the embryo to develop the penis and scrotal sack of a male.
Without testosterone, the labia and vagina of the female form.

Testosterone also acts on the brain of the developing embryo.
All embryos contain neural pathways for both male and female
patterns of sexual behaviour. Testosterone sensitizes the male
pathways so that male sexual behaviour dominates in adulthood.
Without testosterone the female pathways predominate. A part of
these pathways and a locus of testosterone action seems to be in
the hypothalamus. Studies in rats, mice and guinea pigs have
shown that it is possible to masculinize females by testosterone
injections given at the appropriate early stage of development, and
to feminize males by castrating them at the same early stage before
their testes can influence brain differentiation.

In primate adult females, ovulation is controlled by the menstrual cycle and in subprimates it is controlled by the closely similar
oestrous cycle. These cycles themselves are controlled by complex
interactions between the gonadotrophins of the anterior pituitary
and the ovarian hormones. Oestrogen release is stimulated by the
pituitary luteinizing hormone, and oestrogen and progesterone
levels peak around ovulation and thereafter decline until
luteinizing hormone initiates the next cycle. This cycle is controlled from the hypothalamus, and in subprimates is 'switched off' by
the action of testosterone in males during the critical period. In
primates this does not seem to occur. For example, Goy and Resko
(1972) were able to masculinize the external genitalia and also the
sexual and aggressive behaviours of genetically female rhesus
monkeys, by injecting their pregnant mother with testosterone.
These masculinized females were, however, able to menstruate
and to conceive. Testosterone may not be the only hormone which
affects the development of sexual behaviour. Progesterone is
found in relatively high amounts in foetal monkeys and baby rats
and it has been suggested that it acts as an antiandrogen, counteracting the masculinizing effects of testosterone. Stevens and-
Goldstein (1978) have even reported that baby male rats treated
with progesterone show feminized behaviour in adulthood.

Sex hormones also affect the development of other behaviours related to reproduction. For example, Goy (1966) reported that the female young of rhesus monkey mothers, treated with testosterone during pregnancy, showed more rough-and-tumble play and initiated play more than normal female young. Prenatal androgen excess cannot be produced experimentally in humans but is found either when mothers are treated with synthetic sex hormones to prevent miscarriage or in the adrenogenital syndrome. In this syndrome, an abnormality of the adrenal glands causes the production of excessive levels of androgens. Nowadays, girls with these hormonal problems are usually given genital reconstruction surgery at birth and are given continuous hormone therapy where necessary. Like Goy's monkeys, these girls tend to show male play patterns and have masculine interests. They also show a reduced interest in rehearsing traditional female roles. There is tentative evidence that the girls show increases in aggression, which are associated with their tomboyish outlook. Increases in general intelligence have been reported as well, but these may be caused by a subtle intellectual selection factor which operates in families with the adrenogenital syndrome since prenatal treatment with synthetic sex hormones does not have this effect (see Ehrhardt and Meyer-Bahlburg, 1981, for a discussion).

Despite the above changes, girls affected prenatally with excess androgens adopt a normal gender identity, i.e., they see themselves

---

BOX 7.1
Psychological sex differences in humans and animals

Apart from differences in overt sexual behaviours, it has been claimed men and women differ psychologically in other ways. Men and boys are reported to be more aggressive, dominant, competitive and active, and less anxious and nurturant than women and girls. Equally, men are reported to show superior visuopatial and mathematical abilities whereas women show superior verbal abilities. The rise of the women's movement has been associated less with a challenge to these claims than with a depreciation of their sociopolitical significance. In turn, this depreciation has tended to be linked with the view that any psychological sex differences are results of the ways in which boys and girls are brought up in our culture, rather than because of genetically transmitted biological factors.

The role of such biological factors in human sexual differentiation is currently poorly understood (see Hines, 1982, for a discussion). In other mammals and birds, however, evidence is now strong that **sex hormones** (whose activities depend on genetic control) released around the time of birth influence the development of specific brain regions, which control dimorphic emotional and cognitive behaviours. For example, in zebra finches only males develop full songs. This ability seems to depend on the release of the male hormone testosterone first in the newly hatched state and later in adulthood. The early testosterone activity causes an increase in the number and size of certain forebrain neurons. These neurons are known to mediate singing in zebra finches. Female zebra finches given testosterone treatments at hatching and in adulthood develop male-type singing (see Konshi and Gurney, 1982).

The evidence for humans is much weaker. There is, however, evidence that the brain controls **verbal** and **spatial functions** differently in men and women. For example, in men, left-hemisphere lesions selectively impair verbal functions and right-hemisphere lesions impair spatial functions. In women, right-hemisphere lesions have little effect on either kind of function, whereas left-hemisphere lesions impair both kinds of function to the same degree that they are impaired by the appropriate lesion in men (Inglis *et al.*, 1982). These results suggest that functions are differently lateralized in women. It seems plausible that this pattern of differences may be partly caused by sex hormones released in early life, influencing the way in which specific neuronal groups develop. Certainly in rats the early release of sex hormones seems to affect lateralization. It has been shown that in males a part of the right hemisphere's cortex is thicker than the mirror-image region on the left, whereas in females this pattern is reversed. Since even in rats the right hemisphere may be specialized for spatial tasks, it is striking that the male pattern of hemisphere anatomy is found in females who have their ovaries removed at birth (see Denenberg, 1981, and Diamond *et al.*, 1981).

as women and do not become transexuals, and they do not show an increased level of homosexual interests. Money and Ehrhardt (1972) have argued that **gender identity** depends much more on the role assigned during upbringing than on biological factors. Genetic girls with prenatal hormonal problems have been reared successfully as girls or boys – hormonal therapy being given where required to ensure normal growth of secondary sexual characteristics. Imperato-McGinley and his colleagues (1974) have, however, described a group of male pseudohermaphrodites in Central America, who appear to be, and are raised as girls until puberty, when the causal androgen deficit is largely corrected and a phallus appears, together with male secondary sexual characteristics. The children then adjust normally to being boys and men. This remarkable phenomenon does not necessarily reveal a key role for hormonal influences in the growth of gender identity. The effects of rearing may be reversible, especially in an easy-going tropical culture.

Although it is fashionable to regard homosexuality, and sexual orientation in general, as consequences of factors in upbringing (such as the relative dominance of parents), their origins are largely unknown. There is, however, some evidence concerning biological influences. Male and female homosexuals tend to show patterns of **neuroendocrine regulation** which are intermediate between their own and the opposite sex. It is uncertain, however, whether these changes reflect causes or are effects. It has been suggested that prenatal stress inhibits androgen production in foetal males so that they are partially feminized. Ward (1972) has shown that male rats so treated showed less male, and more female sexual behaviour in adulthood. This is not the same thing as sexual orientation in humans, however, and there is only weak evidence that the male children of stressful pregnancies become homosexual. It is perhaps significant that lesions of the medial temporal lobes (including the amygdala) can cause their victims to become homosexual in orientation.

Mammalian sexual behaviour is very variable and cyclical except in humans. In **seasonal breeders** such as the red deer, the female only conceives during a short period each year and the male will show very high sexual activity only at this time when his androgen levels peak. In nonseasonal breeders, the male's androgen levels remain fairly steady throughout the year and the frequency of mating depends more on the state of the oestrous cycle in subprimates and of the menstrual cycle in primates. Androgens appear important for the male sex drive in all mammals, including man. Castration causes a decline in sexual interest although how long this takes varies enormously from animal to animal, and also between species. This may depend on factors like age and experience, but is poorly understood. It is clear anyway that testosterone treatments restore sex drive.

Three factors are important in determining sex drive in females (Beach, 1976). Female rats only allow males to copulate with them during oestrus, when they are ovulating under the influence of high progesterone and oestrogen levels. This **receptive phase** is abolished by ovariectomy, but the presence of these hormones is sufficient for copulation since female rats, like other subprimates, are essentially passive. Female sex drive in primates is indirectly influenced by their **attractiveness**. During oestrus, primate females may mate with many males, who seem to be attracted to the 'right' females by scents, emanating from their vaginas. The scents are known as **pheromones** and are produced by the interaction of oestrogen and bacteria in the vaginal mucosa. How far sex pheromones affect human sexuality is a matter of controversy. The third factor is known as **proceptivity**. In primate females, including humans, sex drive does not decline after ovariectomy, but does do so after the adrenal glands are removed. Herbert (1974) found that monkeys without ovaries and adrenals showed no return of sexual interest following progesterone and oestrogen therapy. Their sex drive was restored, however, by small injections of testosterone. Unlike subprimates, primate females actively initiate sexual encounters. This proclivity, controlled perhaps by adrenal androgens, shows copulation to be partially freed from procreation, so that it can play a key role in maintaining group cohesion. Such a suggestion is supported by the occurrence of orgasms not only in human females but also in the females of other primates. Subprimate females are probably not so rewarded.

The greater social role of sexuality in primates is consistent with claims that learning is critical for sexual behaviour in this group. It is also interesting that male monkeys use penile erections as threat displays, and studies show that electrical stimulation of parts of the limbic system causes such responses in rebound to initial fear (Maclean *et al.*, 1963). Humans, also, commonly use symbolic sexual displays as threats or insults. Learning may be less important in subprimate sexuality. Male rats mate relatively normally in adulthood even when they have been raised in social isolation. Much of their sexual behaviour seems to be integrated by the hypothalamus. Thus mating in male rats can be elicited by applying electrical stimulation or testosterone to the preoptic nucleus of the hypothalamus. Lesions of this structure abolish sexual behaviour and the effect is not reversed by testosterone treatment. Female sexual behaviour in rats is inhibited by the preoptic region and is excited by another, neighbouring nucleus. Sex hormones probably act on these systems which are also probably influenced to a greater extent by limbic system and neocortical activity, reflecting learning factors. Also, in primates sexual satiety is probably largely dependent on the inhibition of hypothalamic excitation following orgasm.

The studies of Harlow and his colleagues (Harlow, 1973) have shown that monkeys reared in isolation show abnormal sexuality. Although isolated males show the rudimentary mechanics of sex, they are incapable of copulating with receptive females. Isolated females tend actively to repulse the advances of experienced males. The emergence of normal sexual behaviour depends, not only on hormonal influences, but also on two other processes. The first is the development of basic sexual responses such as pelvic thrusting, which are acquired by monkeys in the course of preadolescent play and are later refined. The second process involves formation of affectional bonds between the sexes. These are acquired through early interactions with the mother and with peers, and provide the basis of trust essential for sexual encounters.

Human sexual behaviour is even more dependent on learning than is that of other primates. Not only do the mechanics of sexual activity have to be learned, but sexual practices differ widely in different societies and are clearly strongly affected by cultural influences. Sexual behaviours are so variable that it is tempting to argue that innate biological factors are insignificant in determining the form of human sexuality. This conclusion is premature and contrary to some of the evidence already cited; nevertheless hormonal and innate mechanisms have their main effect on sexuality by determining levels of sexual arousal and the intensity of orgasm and other sexual rewards. The means of achieving orgasm is learned, as are many of the stimuli which cause sexual arousal. The temporal lobes may be important in the classical conditioning which enables previously neutral stimuli to become sexually arousing. Temporal lobe epileptics, whose temporal lobes are believed to be 'overactive', have been reported to develop fetishisms for peculiar objects such as safety pins. Such fetishisms perhaps arise by the chance association of the fetish object with sexual arousal.

The relative importance of innate and learning factors arises again in the case of **maternal behaviour**. In female rats the drive to look after their young is so strong that females will endure levels of pain to reach their young which they would not tolerate to reach food or water when hungry or thirsty. Virgin female rats, presented with another rat's pups for around a week, will begin to show mothering behaviours without any previous experience. If they are given blood plasma injections from a mothering rat, they begin to show the behaviours in less than a day (Tertel and Rosenblatt, 1968). The behaviour is elicited by the smell and sight of the pups, but is greatly sensitized by hormonal activities. These activities probably include the sequential release of oestrogen, progesterone and prolactin (the hormone which stimulates milk secretion). These hormones no doubt sensitize hypothalamic systems integrating maternal behaviours. These have been partially identified and differ from the systems controlling female sexuality. Thus some hypothalamic lesions block maternal but not female sexual behaviour.

If these 'innately programmed' behavioural tendencies exist in primates, they can clearly be overridden by learning. Thus female monkeys raised with cloth or wire surrogates fail to show maternal behaviours when they first become mothers, although they become more effective with subsequent offspring. Similar influences might be inferred in humans, given the number of parents who neglect, abuse or even kill their children, especially as such parents have often been badly treated by their own parents (Helfer and Kempe, 1968). Anecdotal evidence nevertheless suggests that human maternal feelings are primed by hormones such as prolactin, and by the presence of babies. Maternal and sexual urges may both be aroused by stimuli, which are either innately activating or for which there is a biological predisposition to associate them with arousal through a process of rapid learning. In humans and primates, the behaviours to which these arousals lead may be largely learned on the basis of their rewarding and punishing consequences.

AGGRESSION

In humans, aggression is usually understood as behaviour which is intended to harm another person, either physically or verbally. The term is also used in an extended sense to describe any actions which are performed with persistence and energy. Some psychoanalytic and ethological theorists have speculated that behaviours which are aggressive in the strict and extended senses are related by a common source of energy. This view is unsupported, however. Many theorists have also drawn a distinction between **hostile aggression**, where the sole aim is to harm another, and **instrumental aggression**, where this harm is merely a means to another end. A soldier's aggression may often be of this latter kind since its purpose may be to avoid punishment or to save his country. The distinction depends on the interpretation of intentions, and in practice this is very hard to make, even in humans. In animals it can only be done indirectly, so it has proved difficult to show whether hostile and instrumental aggression rest on different mechanisms. The supposition has generally been that hostile aggression is an instinct or drive, largely determined by innate biological factors, whereas instrumental aggression involves the learning of responses because they are rewarding or have been seen to be performed by influential models.

Ethological conceptions of aggression, which stress its innate, biological origins, have been widely circulated in the past fifteen years. A sophisticated strand of this influence is represented by the work of Moyer (1971). He has drawn tentative distinctions between various kinds of aggression, including predatory, intermale, fear-induced, irritable, territorial, defensive, maternal and instrumental. In his view, all of these forms of aggression (except perhaps instrumental) involve basically unlearnt and stereotyped behaviours, elicited by specific stimuli and controlled by distinct, if overlapping, neural systems in the hypothalamus and limbic system. The sensitivity of these systems to external stimuli is affected by hormonal influences, such as the level of testosterone in the blood. Individual differences in aggression are mainly caused by innate variations in the sensitivity of these systems. The sensitivity of an individual's aggression systems will also vary over time depending on the level of hormonal influences. On Moyer's view, these forms of aggression might be modified, and aggression appear in new circumstances, when it was learnt that performance of the relevant behaviours was rewarding or avoided punishment. This would be instrumental aggression.

Moyer's ideas represent a programme rather than a confident set of conclusions. They are, however, quite well supported. For example, **stereotyped** aggressive behaviours differ considerably. Intermale aggression in stags involves clashing antlers whereas antipredator aggression involves kicking with the front hooves. In cats, predatory attack not only differs from defensive aggression behaviourally – it involves quiet stalking, in contrast to the behavioural and emotional excitement of defensive aggression – but it is elicited by stimulation of more lateral hypothalamic sites than is defensive aggression (Egger and Flynn, 1963). More medial stimulation produces a rage reaction in a cat which may well attack the experimenter but will ignore a rat near to it. Location of other kinds of aggression is still in its rudimentary stages, but Moyer believes that the amygdala may be important in controlling predatory, fear-induced and irritable aggression. Damage to the amygdala has, for example, been found to reduce fear-induced aggression in many mammals, including man, but some evidence suggests that damage to parts of it may increase irritable aggression. Stimulation of the human amygdala has been reported to produce violent attacks of rage, and similar attacks in some temporal lobe epileptics are believed to be caused by overactivity of this nucleus. In contrast, electrical stimulation of the septum inhibits certain kinds of aggression. This has been demonstrated most dramatically by Delgado (1969), by stopping a bull in mid-charge by radio-controlled stimulation of its brain.

It has already been indicated in the last section that androgens, present during an early critical period, sensitize certain systems mediating sexual and aggressive behaviours. Hormones also affect the sensitivity of these systems in adulthood. Androgen reduction following castration is known to decrease intermale aggression in many mammals and has been used as an extreme measure to abolish sexual violence in humans. Circulating oestrogens appear to act like antiandrogens, and their artificial administration has been shown to decrease aggression in animals and humans. As well as hormonal levels, other body states like hypoglycaemia (low levels of blood glucose) seem to sensitize some kinds of aggression (irritable aggression in the case of hypoglycaemia).

Aggression in subhuman mammals can undoubtedly be controlled to a considerable extent by hormonal manipulation, chemical and electrical stimulation and certain brain lesions. It has been fashionable to try and control extreme cases of human violence by similar means. This psychosurgical approach is often applied to individuals who have no known neurological abnormalities, such as epilepsy. Lesions of the amygdala or frontal lobes frequently do lead to reductions of violence, but the operations are irreversible and cause many other poorly understood but disturbing effects on cognition and behaviour. Equally important, much human aggression is probably learnt and only weakly controlled by the systems delineated by Moyer. Psychosurgery may help reduce violent attacks of rage, occurring in disturbed individuals, but is likely to be far less successful in controlling the 'cool', learned aggression, epitomized by war-like behaviour, which is far more destructive.

Ethological studies have been valuable in highlighting the variety of aggressive systems and the wide range of circumstances which initiate such behaviours. They have also drawn attention to the adaptive significance of behaviours which, *prima facie*, are destructive and maladaptive. Aggression has evolved to serve many social and individual functions. Thus, **territorial aggression** ensures that a species is distributed so as not to overtax available resources; **maternal aggression** protects the young; **irritable aggression** helps the individual to remove frustrations; and **intermale aggression**, particularly in primates, enables dominance hierarchies to be formed, which stabilize transactions between individuals so that maintenance and reproductive behaviours can be performed more efficiently. Even so, these benefits are obtained at a cost. Despite evidence that many aggressive displays in animals are **ritualized**, comprising more threat than outright violence and involving submissive signals which inhibit killing, animals of the same species do kill each other in nature. Goodall (1978) has described warfare between two colonies of chimpanzees which ended in the killing of every male in one of the groups. In some situations, therefore, inhibitory signals may be no more effective in animals than they appear to be in humans.

Ethological studies do imply that aggression can be reduced by removing the conditions which are believed to initiate it. For example, overcrowding increases aggression as it multiplies the frustrations attendant on the greater competition for food and other basic resources. Rational demographic policies might, then, be effective means of reducing human aggression. This idea would not have been accepted by Freud who believed that aggression or self-destruction were the only effective means of discharging the energy of the death instinct which built up spontaneously over time. Although Freud allowed that some of this energy may be discharged in 'symbolic' forms of aggression, his view of aggression as a spontaneous energy source led him to undervalue social engineering as a method of control. Both Freud and the ethologists have tended to see aggressive behaviours as drive-reducing, and rewarding in their own right. Social learning theorists, on the other hand, have laid more stress on the incidental rewarding or punishing effect of aggressive behaviours in human societies.

According to Bandura (1977), people become aggressive because they have learned by experience, observation and/or imitation that it pays (see Figure 7.2). For example, he argues that frustration does not innately lead to aggression but will do so if the individual has learned that this kind of behaviour is reinforcing.

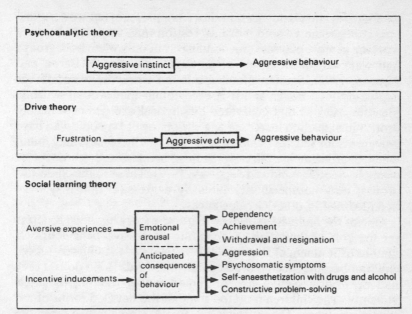

Figure 7.2 Schematic comparison of psychoanalytic, frustration and social learning theories of aggression. The social learning theory allows for much more varied responses to the provoking stimuli.

Humans can learn this, in principle, not only by being repeatedly reinforced for acting aggressively, but also by observing that others are so reinforced and then imitating them. Alternatively, an individual may learn that other responses to frustration are more rewarding. Thus, when frustrated he may withdraw from the situation, or try even harder to solve it rationally, rationalize what's happened, anaesthetize himself with alcohol or adopt some combination of these responses. Frustration is an appropriate example for social learning theory because many ethologists and Dollard and his colleagues (1939) have regarded it as a drive state which innately releases aggressive behaviour. The truth may be that humans do show an innate tendency to follow frustration with aggressive acts, but this tendency is greatly modifiable through learning.

Humans also learn to show aggression in many other situations where frustration is not present. For example, subjects working in a hot, stuffy room showed more aggression than controls who were working in more pleasant surroundings, but only when both groups had watched the activities of an aggressive model (Baron and Lawton, 1972). Similar effects are found when the discomfort is caused by loud noise, and it is even found that arousal which is pleasant, such as that generated by physical exercise or watching erotic films, leads to increased aggression towards people who have been previous sources of annoyance. But this increase is only found when aggression has already been expressed and learned (for example, see Zillmann and Sapolsky, 1977). These studies show that arousal may nonspecifically intensify aggression that may have been learned in other circumstances.

One of the hallmarks of social learning theory has been its stress on the role of **imitation** in acquiring aggressive behaviours. A famous experiment of Bandura's (1973) showed that nursery school children became much more aggressive towards Bobo dolls if they had previously seen a live or filmed model treating the dolls violently. The children imitated some of the detailed forms of the model's violence. These effects are greatly strengthened when the imitator is reinforced for his behaviour. Aggression can have many consequences: the victims may concede, ignore the attacker or even counterattack, and external agents may modify these consequences. In this context, it is possible that the greater physical aggression shown by human males is partly a result of their being more rewarded for this behaviour than are physically weaker females. It has been argued that females show more verbal aggression because their possibly greater verbal skills mean that these behaviours are more effective than physical violence.

It is still a matter of controversy whether watching **film and television violence** influences aggressive behaviour to any great extent (Kaplan and Singer, 1976, for example, versus Parke *et al.*, 1977). Although several studies have shown a correlation between the amount of television-viewing and level of interpersonal aggression, it has proved difficult to determine whether this is cause or effect. Nevertheless, one study by Eron and his colleagues (1972) found that in American boys, the amount of television violence viewed at the age of nine predicted aggressiveness ten years later, and the investigators claimed to have controlled statistically for the level of aggression at the younger age. In addition to imitation, there seem to be several plausible mechanisms which could produce such effects. First, watching violence increases arousal which is known to intensify aggression. Second, watching violence reduces negative emotional reactions to its consequences. This desensitization may make people readier to engage in acts of aggression because their unpleasant effects are greatly decreased. More generally, watching acts of aggression has been shown to weaken the restraints on such behaviour afforded by guilt and fear of retaliation or disapproval. Third, watching programmes in which conflicts are resolved by physical violence may have a widespread effect on an individual's attitude towards the place of violence in society. For example, Gerbner and Gross (1976) have reported that 'heavy' television viewers are more distrustful, overestimate the risk of criminal violence, and buy more locks, dogs and guns to protect themselves (the viewers were American).

Those who deny that saturation viewing of mass-media violence is harmful often argue that watching violence is cathartic, i.e., it releases pent-up aggression. This hypothesis is implausible, however, in the light of studies which show that the actual performance of aggressive acts is far from cathartic, contrary to the views of Freud and some ethologists. For example, adults become more, not less punitive when given repeated opportunities to shock an unretaliating victim (Buss, 1966). Furthermore, Loew (1967) has shown that angry subjects also become more vicious with repeated attacks. Aggression is more likely to cease because it is punished or because some distracting interest is created.

Aggression has many forms, controlled by partially independent systems, and in humans these have been so overlaid with learning as to be hard to identify. War, the most devastating expression of human aggression, is a complex social activity. Its origins are not to be sought in overactive amygdalas, but in the nature of the abstract goals which leaders seek for their countries, and in the motivating forces of loyalty and obedience. These sources of war indicate that many human actions involve the pursuit of abstract goals and that their fulfilment often depends on the existence of social needs such as loyalty and obedience.

Cognitive and social motives

Although the way in which cognitive and abstract goals are acquired is poorly understood, it has been claimed that humans experience a general need to reduce dissonance between conflicting beliefs, or conflicting beliefs and actions. This view, known as **cognitive dissonance theory** (Festinger, 1957), in some ways resembles the learning theory account of hunger. It is suggested that whenever people are aware that they have inconsistent beliefs or are acting contrary to their beliefs an uncomfortable state of cognitive dissonance is produced, motivating its subjects to alter their beliefs or actions so they are once more consistent.

The theory does not specify whether dissonance is a learnt state of arousal – it can plausibly be argued that individuals come to experience it because they learn that inconsistent beliefs have punishing effects. On the other hand, the roots of dissonance and dissonance reduction may lie in the ill-understood, but initially innate urges of curiosity, universal among mammals. This heterogeneous group of 'drives' may sometimes be activated by boredom resulting from sensory, perceptual or social deprivation. However, curiosity and exploratory behaviour are also excited by novelty, surprise or incongruity. Normal display of this group of activities seems to require that the limbic system, particularly the hippocampus, is intact. Perhaps these structures detect novelty in conjunction with the neocortex, and then activate exploratory behaviours. Berlyne (1954) found that 'epistemic curiosity', as he called it, increased in people who received surprising answers to questions about animal behaviour. When their curiosity was aroused by surprise, subjects remembered more and expressed more interest in what they were learning. Surprise, uncertainty and inconsistency relating to knowledge seem, then, to stimulate an urge to reorder the problematic material so that it makes sense to the knower. Although learning no doubt plays an important role in the development of this urge, such learning probably elaborates an innate tendency universal in mammals.

Dissonance theory is a weak one but makes one kind of interesting prediction. The less someone is compelled to act contrary to their beliefs, then the greater should be their experienced dissonance. They will therefore be more likely to modify their beliefs.

This prediction is supported. For example, Festinger and Carlsmith (1959) found that students who were paid only one dollar, as against twenty, for performing a boring task were more willing to tell the next subjects how interesting the task had been. It has also been found that children who obey a mild request not to play with a toy are more likely to come to see it as unattractive than children who obey under threat of severe punishment. (See also Chapter 11.)

If dissonance reduction is one of the processes which leads to the formation of new cognitive or abstract goals then a gamut of unspecified social influences must be even more important. In humans, the dependent period of infancy is greatly prolonged. Not only does its prolongation allow humans to acquire sophisticated cognitive structures and aims, through the auspices of the probably innate tendencies to show playfulness, inventiveness and curiosity, but also it makes them very dependent on other humans. Cognitive learning occurs in a context of social dependency and the cognitive aims which emerge in adulthood are likely to be strongly influenced by the views of those with whom an individual interacts most and on whom he is most dependent. It is interesting that humans and other 'cultural' primates seem to show affiliative needs from a very early age. This is apparent in the smiling response made by babies to human faces in the first five months of life. Such affiliative tendencies are probably innate. Mammals, like many bird species, may also develop early social preferences through an imprinting-like process. For example, monkeys who receive extensive early exposure to a human, prior to social isolation, later seek the human in preference to their own species. Early affiliative experiences therefore strongly influence later patterns of social dependency.

Early experiences influence, not only an individual's choice of persons with whom to form friendships or from whom to seek aid and sympathy, but also the intensity of the need for such people. Sears, Maccoby and Levin (1957) found that it was those children whose rearing involved both the satisfaction of their physical needs and frustration of them, who showed most dependence on adults when in school. Less frustrated children, who had been fed on demand and weaned gradually, showed less need in stressful circumstances to seek succour from adults. The experimenters argued that frustrated children learned that if they persisted in showing dependent behaviours then their frustrations would eventually be removed. It is striking that affiliative and dependent needs are particularly aroused by frustrating and anxiety-provoking circumstances. For example, Schachter (1959) has reported that when subjects are forced to wait before taking part in a study which is made to seem threatening, they show a strong preference to wait in groups rather than alone. This preference is weaker when no threat is perceived and is reduced in later-born children as compared to first-born or only children. It is suggested that first-born and only children receive more pressures, frustrations and attention than later-born, which gives rise to stronger affiliative needs when threatened.

Early experience of helplessness and frustration, combined with the rewards offered by larger, stronger people, may help partially to explain why people are so vulnerable to the pressures exerted by authority, even when these pressures are not backed by the threat of punitive sanctions. The tendency towards **blind obedience** is dramatically illustrated in the work of Milgram (1974). In Milgram's studies subjects were asked to deliver a series of increasingly strong shocks to another subject every time the latter made an error in a learning task. The learner, who was actually a confederate of the experimenter, was strapped to a chair in an adjacent room, and had been instructed to make many errors and also to show signs of growing distress as the severity of the shocks was supposedly increased. If the experimental subjects expressed uncertainty the experimenter merely said, 'Please go on', or gave similar instructions.

Sixty-five per cent of the subjects continued to obey instructions up to the maximum level of shock, which would have been fatal if really delivered. All subjects continued to give shocks up to 300 volts when the stooges were becoming vociferous in their distress. These results surprised professionals and lay people alike because they showed how readily individuals will continue to pursue goals, which a minimum of thought would indicate to be wrong, merely because they are asked to do so by persons in authority.

Many researchers believe that early life experiences also help shape what are often referred to as the **ego-integrative motives**. These motives involve reference to the self and include aims connected with morality, religion and aesthetics – aims whose pursuit is regulated by factors such as self-perception and self-esteem. The need for **achievement** has been one of the most studied of these motives. This need may be defined as the urge to achieve something of value, which satisfies criteria for excellence. The level of this motivation in an individual has often been assessed indirectly by examining the extent to which imaginative stories, written by the individual, contain themes related to achievement. People who show a high need for achievement on this measure have been found to do better on anagram and other tasks than less motivated individuals (see McClelland, 1955). Many studies have indicated that high achievement motivation arises in children who are forced to think and act independently from an early age. Such children have mothers who make demands for achievement at an earlier age than less motivated children (Winterbottom, 1953). There is some evidence that people low on achievement motivation may have been exposed early to lack of success and have a stronger fear of failure. Atkinson (1953) has reported that whereas students with high achievement motivation remember tasks they have been unable to complete better than completed tasks, students with low measured achievement motivation show the opposite pattern of memory.

Culture strongly influences rearing practices and shapes the strength of the need for achievement. It has been claimed, for example, that American Indian societies, which value achievement, place great stress on inculcating independence during childhood. Attempts have been made to use literary references to achievement in historical societies in order to measure the prevalent level of achievement motivation during different periods so that these could be correlated with the society's productivity and other indices of success. This has been done for ancient Greece, England between 1550 and 1800, and America over the past 180 years. The studies revealed a good correlation between measures of success and achievement motivation. Clearly, there must be a complex interaction between societal success and achievement motivation (see Wiggins *et al.*, 1971).

McClelland and his colleagues showed that need for achievement could be activated in American students in situations which emphasize competition and social acceptability. Once again, this illustrates the importance of social conditions in exciting specific needs. Social factors in childhood not only provide the bases for the acquisition of complex human motives; the social conditions present on a given occasion may also selectively stimulate an acquired motive. It has been argued by Freud (1938) that even the need to believe in and worship a god is derived from the child's early relationships to its father and the resolution of the Oedipus complex. No doubt this is wrong in detail. Nevertheless, it remains plausible that early experience of powerful, authority figures may help shape the need for religious beliefs together with the impetuses provided by fear of various kinds and the curiosity-derived urge to find meaning in the structure of events. However derived, religious needs are representative of complex human motives in that they involve the pursuit of long-term goals and are more importunate at some times than they are at others.

Conflict and goal selection

When many goals, both short- and long-term, vie with each other, an individual is often unable to select one, and suffers the frustration of conflict. Such a conflict arises frequently when a goal involves both desirable and unpleasant features. An approach-avoidance conflict results. An interesting feature of this kind of conflict is that as the goal is approached, the desire to avoid its negative features increases at a faster rate than the desire to approach its positive features. Individuals faced with conflict often behave in ways which may be maladaptive. They may show aggression, or if the conflict is unresolved and prolonged they may develop the apathy of learned helplessness, perhaps also regressing to immature modes of behaviour. Depth psychologists have also identified ways in which individuals cope with conflict by distorting reality. These **defence mechanisms** include the conscious denial of undesirable aspects of the conflict; the unconscious repression of painful, but relevant memories; the manufacture of excuses for behaviour, known as rationalization; the denial of a motive by the expression of its opposite, known as reaction formation; and intellectualization or distancing oneself from the conflict. There is reasonable evidence that these largely unconscious mechanisms operate when humans are faced with difficult conflicts of motive (see Chapter 13 for a further discussion).

Defence mechanisms provide temporary respite from the emotionally threatening consequences of conflict, but hinder the eventually adaptive solution of such situations. There is as yet no clear theory about decisions which are made between different goals. Some preliminary points can be made, however. A large number of activities and states are either rewarding or punishing to humans and animals. The development of these rewarding and punishing qualities depends on both innate biological and learning factors. At any time, only some of these goals will influence the decision-making system. The selected action will be directed towards one or more of these goals. The goals which influence the decision-maker do so because certain stimulus conditions bias perception, memory and cognition. They 'grab' attention, as is illustrated by the way hungry people report seeing food-related objects more often, when looking at ambiguous stimuli. The stimuli which bias attention and often increase nonspecific arousal may be caused by internal needs (lacks or disturbances in physiological functions), external events (such as the sight of a book of interest), or they may involve external stimuli, reaction to which is sensitized by internal factors (as when the presence of sex hormones sensitizes reaction to the sight of an attractive conspecific). In humans, 'motives' may also be aroused indirectly when stimuli associatively trigger a train of thought (the book reminds you of a girl . . .). These arousing and biasing stimuli may acquire their arousing powers without learning, and in subprimate mammals their biasing and even action-eliciting powers may also be innate. In humans, however, learning is invariably involved in creating or modifying their biasing and action-eliciting powers. These stimuli also often produce emotional arousal, which further colours the manner and nature of ensuing behaviour, as will be discussed in the next chapter.

If the thought of a goal has gained access to the decision-maker, whether or not it is selected probably depends on its perceived attractiveness and the perceived probability of obtaining it. The former will depend on innate factors and past experience but will not remain constant over time. The perception is influenced, for example, by internal states such as hunger and hormonal levels. Learning may also alter a goal's attractiveness. If completely unlearnt goal-directed behaviours exist in some animals, then initially, at least, these cannot be regulated by representations of the features of goal objects. However, all motivated behaviour which requires learning must partly depend on such representations. Learning forms the essential basis for any estimates of the probability of achieving a goal. The complexity of these computations will involve neocortical systems, so primates and humans will show far more sophisticated decision-making behaviours than will subprimates. In humans, behaviour may be regulated so that several short- and long-term behaviours may be pursued in tandem. The achievement of a goal, in addition to being rewarding or punishing, may temporarily reduce the attention-seizing powers of that particular goal. This need not be so in the short term, however, as the goal activities may be self-excitatory, or, in pathological cases such as obsession, it may not even be true in the long term.

Little is known about how decisions are computed and then carried out when they have been made. This is really the problem of **voluntary behaviour**, interest in which has revived since the publication of the seminal *Plans and the Structure of Behavior* by Miller, Galanter and Pribram (1960). These scientists lay stress on the way in which action plans are organized hierarchically so that achievement of the overall goal can be divided into several levels of subgoals, some of which will be under automatic, unconscious control. The coordination of such plans seems to depend critically on controlling systems in the frontal cortex. More recently, Reason (1979) has argued that voluntary actions are initiated by a mental representation of the movements necessary to achieve a goal and are modulated by comparator mechanisms, which identify whether goals and subgoals have been achieved. These processes depend on learning. The problem is, at what point does the representation of the goal and the means to its achievement become strong enough in attention to trigger an action?

Further reading

Introduction and historical background

For the heroic, a massive and comprehensive review of all aspects of motivation is provided by:

COFER, C.N. and APPLEY, M.H. (1964) *Motivation: Theory and Research*. New York: Wiley.

For a clear and brief account of the learning theory of motivation see:

HILL, W.F. (1963) *Learning*. London: Methuen.

A lucid exposition of ethological thinking about motivation with copious examples is provided by:

TINBERGEN, N. (1951) *The Study of Instinct*. London: Oxford University Press.

A controversial application of ethological notions to human social behaviour is illustrated by:

WILSON, E. (1975) *Sociobiology: the New Synthesis*. Cambridge, Mass.: Harvard University Press.

Sleep and arousal

The best short introduction is:

MEDDIS, R. (1979) The evolution and function of sleep. In D.A. Oakley and H.C. Plotkin, eds., *Brain, Behaviour and Evolution*. London: Methuen.

The following gives a recent, comprehensive overview of the field:

MAYES, A.R., ed. (1983) *Sleep Mechanisms and Functions in Humans and Animals: an Evolutionary Perspective*. Wokingham: Van Nostrand.

Many useful articles can be found in the journal *Sleep* and there are many review and research books on the subject. Coverage of recent thinking about possible functional roles of sleep in memory is provided by:

FISHBEIN, W. (1981) *Sleep, Dreams and Memory*. Lancaster: MTP Press.

A good treatment of sleep disorders is offered in:

MENDELSON, W.B., GILLIN, J.G. and WYATT, R.J. (1977) *Human Sleep and its Disorders*. New York: Plenum.

A comprehensive treatment of the mental concomitants of sleep is provided by:

ARKIN, A.M., ANTROBUS, J.S. and ELLMAN, S.J. (1978) *The Mind in Sleep: Psychology and Psychophysiology*. Hillsdale, NJ: Erlbaum.

The clearest discussion of the physiological mechanisms controlling sleep is given in Chapter 9 of:

CARLSON, N.R. (1985) *Physiology of Behaviour*. Third edition. London: Allyn and Bacon.

Homeostatic drives

A comprehensive and influential overview of current thinking about hunger is given by:

NOVIN, D., WYRWICKA, W. and BRAY, G.A. (1976) *Hunger: Basic Mechanisms and Clinical Implications*. New York: Raven Press.

A similar, if rather more physiological treatment of hunger is given by:

EPSTEIN, A.N., KISSILEFF, H.R. and STELLAR, E. (1973) *The Neuropsychology of Thirst: New Findings and Advances in Concepts*. Washington, DC: V.H. Winston.

Many good physiological psychology textbooks treat these topics and an excellent example is provided again by Carlson, *op. cit.*, Chapters 12 and 13.

Rewards and punishments

A lucid, fascinating and short introduction to recent work on the physiology of reward is given by:

ROLLS, E.T. (1975) *The Brain and Reward*. Oxford: Pergamon.

An interesting and comprehensive introduction to the psychology and physiology of pain is given by:

MELZACK, R. (1973) *The Puzzle of Pain*. Harmondsworth: Penguin.

A more advanced recent review of the area is provided by:

OLDS, M.E. and FOBES, J.L. (1981) The central basis of motivation: intracranial self-stimulation studies. *Annual Review of Psychology*, **32**, 523–74.

Nonhomeostatic drives

There are several excellent recent reviews of sexual behaviour. These include:

BERMANT, G. and DAVIDSON, J.M. (1974) *Biological Bases of Sexual Behavior*. New York: Harper and Row.

This focuses on animal research, whereas an emphasis on human sexual development is offered by:

MONEY, J. and EHRHARDT, A.A. (1972) *Man and Woman, Girl and Boy*. Baltimore: Johns Hopkins University Press.

A good example of the ethological approach to aggression is offered by:

MOYER, K.E. (1971) *The Physiology of Hostility*. Chicago: Markham.

Further discussion of these ideas and their possible relevance for humans is found in the book by Wilson, *op cit*. For a different approach see:

BANDURA, A.L. (1973) *Aggression: a Social Learning Analysis*. Englewood Cliffs, NJ: Prentice-Hall.
MONTAGU, A., ed. (1978) *Learning Non-Aggression: the Experience of Non-Literate Societies*. New York: Oxford University Press.

Cognitive and social motives

An approach to human motivation which stresses cognitive factors is provided by:

JUNG, J. (1978) *Understanding Human Motivation: a Cognitive Approach*. New York: Macmillan.

Cofer and Appley, *op. cit.*, contains useful reviews of the development of social, ego-integrative and cognitive motivations.

Conflict and goal selection

An interesting and theoretical treatment of decision-making in practice is given by:

JANIS, I.L. and MANN, L. (1977) *Decision Making: a Psychological Analysis of Conflict, Choice and Commitment*. New York: The Free Press.

8. Emotion

Box

Figures

8. Emotion

The nature of emotions

The term **emotion** is peculiarly difficult to define, yet we all use the term and know to what, in our own experience, it relates. Others use the same language to describe their own responses to events, and we can readily assume that they, too, are experiencing emotions. When we try to describe these emotional experiences, 'feeling' is a commonly used term. We could attempt to base a definition of emotion on this, by saying that emotion is the feeling aspect of mental life, as distinct from **cognition** (thinking) and **volition** (willing). Yet it is becoming clear that, just as cognition involves feeling, so emotion involves cognitive processes.

Feeling is certainly one aspect or component of human emotion (the **experiential** component), but two other components must be recognized, namely the **physiological** (the bodily changes that occur in emotional circumstances), and the **behavioural** (the instrumental and/or expressive acts that are performed in such circumstances). The roles, interactions and relative importance of these components are the central problems in the study of the emotions, and also form the basis of the many and diverse theories that have been proposed. Different theories have stressed different components, even to the extent of denying the importance or existence of another. The behaviourists, for example, rejected not only the distinction between different emotions, but also considered experiential aspects to be mere 'collateral products' of our genetic and environmental history. Emotion was said to consist of a state of strength (physiological arousal) that energizes behaviour in a direction determined by stimulus properties (see Skinner, 1938).

Activation theorists (Duffy, 1962) also rejected the notion of emotions, seeing 'emotional states' merely as extremes on a dimension of activation or arousal. However, Duffy did allow for the effects of external stimuli to be mediated by expectancies and goal orientation, a possibility excluded by the behaviourists. Cerebral theories have been based on a search for cerebral structures that mediate emotional behaviour. Generally, they have used techniques of brain stimulation or ablation, mostly in infrahuman species, and have looked at the effects of these on certain types of behaviour labelled 'emotional'. Often, workers in this area have paid little attention to emotional experience. We shall return to brain mechanisms on pages 472–7.

Most theories, however, do not adopt such an extreme attitude but attempt to account for the role which each of the three components plays in the total reaction we call emotion. In the next section we shall consider four of the most influential theories in more detail. In the remainder of this section we look briefly at attempts to understand the general nature of the emotions, through attempts at classification.

Attempts to classify the emotions long predate the emergence of psychology as a scientific discipline, but we start our brief review with Wundt, who, in 1896, suggested that emotional experience could be described by combinations of three dimensions: pleasantness-unpleasantness, calm-excitement and relaxation-tension. Schlosberg (1941) returned to this type of dimensional analysis of emotion, deriving three similar dimensions (pleasantness-unpleasantness, acceptance-rejection and, later, sleep-tension) from an analysis of subjects' ratings of a series of photographs of posed facial expressions. Schlosberg and his colleague Woodworth revived the study of facial expression as a method of investigating the nature of emotion, and we shall have more to say about this on pages 461–71. It was later shown that the last two of Schlosberg's dimensions are correlated, suggesting that they are not separate dimensions of emotional expression. Osgood (1966) used live emotional expressions and derived three dimensions (pleasantness, activation and control) which correspond to the dimensions of his **semantic differential** scale (evaluation, activity and potency), which has been widely used in many areas of research in psychology.

A different approach to classification that has been adopted by a number of theorists is to propose that certain emotions are fundamental (or primary, or basic), and that others are mixtures or blends of these. Earlier lists seem not to have had any firm empirical or theoretical basis, but more recent ones have been derived either from evolutionary considerations or from the study of facial expressions. Plutchik (1980) proposed eight primary emotions (see Figure 8.1), each of which is a patterned bodily reaction corresponding to one of eight underlying, adaptive biological processes common to all living organisms. Thus, *acceptance* corresponds to *incorporation* (of food and water), *anger* to *destruction* (of a barrier to satisfaction), and *sorrow* to *deprivation*. As is shown in Figure 8.1 the emotions are considered to fall along a single, circular dimension, with adjacent emotions being most similar, and opposite ones having contrasting qualities.

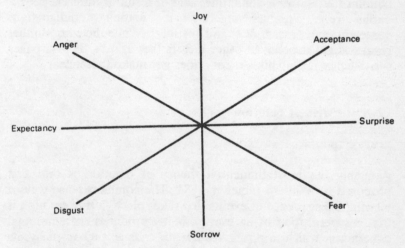

Figure 8.1 Plutchik's circular ordering of eight primary emotions.

Primary emotions combine, according to Plutchik, in a way similar to additive colour mixture, to produce secondary emotions. On the basis of studies in which, for example, subjects were asked to name what they thought were the primary components of numerous nonprimary emotions, Plutchik presented a list of equations representing the make-up of the secondary emotions. For example, pride=anger+joy; love=joy+accceptance; hate=anger +surprise; guilt=joy+fear; and shame=fear+disgust. The simplicity of this idea is one of its main weaknesses. If anger and surprise together form hate, we could never experience the two primaries together, as they would be replaced by hate (just as mixing red and green lights produces yellow in which the components cannot be discerned). The extent to which emotions can be expressed and experienced simultaneously has only very recently become the subject of investigation, but it seems likely that, at least under some circumstances, the apparently simultaneous experience of two emotions may in fact result from the rapid alternation of those emotions. The empirical base of Plutchik's proposal is also suspect. Certain secondary emotions are described as the result of more than one combination of primaries (e.g., guilt is also said to be sorrow+fear), and, conversely, the same combination of primaries is sometimes said to result in different secondaries (e.g., disgust+anger=scorn, loathing, indignation, contempt, hate, resentment and hostility). While the emotion that results might depend on other factors (see Izard's theory, pages 446–8 below), Plutchik's theory does not make these clear.

Four theories of emotion

JAMES'S THEORY

Arguably the most influential theory of emotion is that first proposed by William James in 1884. The common sense way of viewing the sequence of events that takes place during emotion is that the perception of an event directly produces the emotional experience, which in turn gives rise to, or is accompanied by, its bodily expression. James's key proposal was to change this sequence: 'The bodily changes follow directly the perception of the exciting fact, and our feeling of the same changes as they occur *is* the emotion. We feel sorry *because* we cry; angry *because* we strike; afraid *because* we tremble.' Thus, each discernible emotion is the result of the perception of a distinct pattern of bodily responses, including autonomic and behavioural changes.

Most of the evidence James used to support his theory would not be acceptable to modern psychologists. For example, we are invited introspectively to divest an imagined emotion of its bodily

BOX 8.1
Fundamental and blended facial expressions

Ekman (see Ekman *et al.*, 1972) recognizes six primary emotions (surprise, fear, disgust, anger, happiness and sadness), defined by research demonstrating universality in their expression on the face (see pages 462–4). Ekman and Friesen (1975) have used photographs of models following instructions to produce particular facial muscle movements, to analyse the components of emotional expressions and to demonstrate the significance of 'partial' expressions (that is, for example, an expression involving only the mouth, or only the brows), and of combinations of partial expressions (using composite photographs). The face is divided into three areas that are capable of independent movement (brow/forehead, eyes/lids/root of nose, and lower face). Given that each area is capable of a number of different movements, a large number of possible combinations can be produced.

In contrast to Plutchik, Ekman and Friesen argue that more than one emotion can occur simultaneously, and will be reflected in the facial expression. Indeed, some expressions, such as neutral surprise, probably occur only fleetingly in isolation, but are usually blended with, and become replaced by, an emotion such as fear or happiness. Sometimes the blends of emotions referred to by Ekman and Friesen may lead to a new, nonprimary emotion. It is instructive (and fun) to use cartoon representations of the more obvious facial movements to see if some of the equations presented by Plutchik on the basis of introspection hold also for combinations of facial expressions. For example, does the combination of anger brow and joy mouth give an appearance of pride? Figure 8.2 represents some of the chief facial expression features, and also shows some combinations to start your own experimentation. Remember that only a few possibilities are shown in this figure, and even these are highly stylized, so that your observations will be illustrative rather than conclusive.

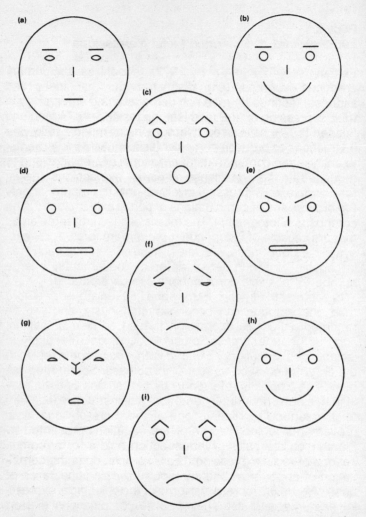

Figure 8.2 Pure and blended facial expressions: (a) neutral, (b) happy, (c) surprised, (d) afraid, (e) angry, (f) sad, (g) disgusted, (h) angry brow and eyes, happy mouth, (i) surprised brow and eyes, sad mouth.

accompaniments. Most people doing this, James states, will verify that what is left is a cold, neutral state of 'intellectual perception', and those who do not, have not understood what was asked of them! Clearly this is an unsatisfactory form of evidence. The fact that we cannot imagine experiencing, say, fear without the accompanying physiological changes tells us merely that the emotion and the feelings are closely associated, not that emotion depends on those feelings. Other evidence is anecdotal. James wrote, for example, of how imagining the symptoms of an emotion can lead to the emotion itself: 'Not to speak of coarser examples, a mother's imagination of the caresses she bestows on her child may arouse a spasm of maternal longing.' However, imagining the symptoms of an emotion is likely to involve imagining the stimulus as well. In the example, the caresses must be caresses of the child.

James did suggest more empirical tests of his theory, such as proposing that the voluntary arousal of the symptoms of an emotion ought to produce the emotion itself. He admitted that this was difficult to test, since many of the manifestations are in organs over which we have no voluntary control. He argued, however, that, within limits, experience fully corroborates the proposal, for example giving way to feelings of anger or grief increases these emotions. Furthermore, we can counter undesirable tendencies in ourselves by performing the actions of contrary dispositions: 'Smooth the brow, brighten the eye, contract the dorsal rather than the ventral aspect of the frame, and speak in a major key . . . and your heart must gradually thaw.' Again, however, it might be that one can only perform these opposite actions when the undesirable emotion is already waning.

This suggestion of James's has reappeared in more recent times in three forms. First, **biofeedback** could provide a way of producing control over involuntary physiological changes (see pages 455–6). Second, the notion that we can remove undesirable emotion by arousing incompatible responses formed the original theoretical basis for **systematic desensitization** (Wolpe, 1958). Third, control of the expression of emotion should control its intensity (see pages 467–9 below).

The crucial test of the theory, which James admitted would be hard to obtain, would be to examine the emotional experience of individuals with complete anaesthesia, yet without motor or intellectual impairment. He referred to three patients who might meet these requirements, but since he did not see them himself, and none was examined with the aim of establishing the quality of his emotional life, the fact that two of them exhibited at least some emotional behaviour (no mention of emotion was made in the third case) is not good evidence for the theory, as James himself admitted. We shall return to the possibility of testing the theory from this direction on page 449. Although he had earlier criticized the theory, it was Cannon's (1927) critique that was, until quite recently, considered devastating. He stated five objections. First, *total separation of the viscera from the CNS does not alter emotional behaviour*. This conclusion was based on his own work, removing the sympathetic nervous system of cats, and an experiment by Sherrington (1900) involving the transection of the spinal cord and vagus nerves of dogs. In both studies, the transmission of afferent impulses to the brain was interrupted, yet the animals were reported to show apparently normal emotional reactions. As we have already noted, however, the appearance of emotional behaviour does not necessarily imply the experience of emotion, and in James's theory emotional behaviour has to occur *before* emotional experience, so these results are actually irrelevant.

Secondly, *the same visceral changes occur in very different emotional states and in nonemotional states*. Cannon believed that his own work and that of others demonstrated this to be so. Thirdly, *the viscera are relatively insensitive structures*. Cannon claimed that we are almost totally unaware of visceral and circulatory activity. Fourthly, *visceral changes are too slow to be a source of emotional feeling*. Fifthly, *artificial induction of the visceral changes typical of strong emotions does not produce them*. Injection of adrenaline into humans does not, Cannon claimed, produce emotions.

In later sections of this chapter we shall consider more recent evidence suggesting that Cannon's critique does not have the force with which it was long credited, either as a demonstration that autonomic activity has no role to play in the production of emotion, or as a 'disproof' of James's theory.

SCHACHTER'S TWO-FACTOR THEORY

Schachter's (1964) view of the role of physiological arousal in emotion is diametrically opposed to that of James. According to Schachter, the same state of arousal could underlie all emotions. The occurrence of some form of arousal gives rise to a cognitive search for an explanation of the arousal. If a nonemotional explanation is available (for example, exercise), no emotion is experienced. If no such explanation is available the individual searches the context in which the arousal has been produced (most importantly, the social context) until he or she is able to label the arousal as a particular emotion. Thus, the same state of arousal could be labelled (and experienced) as emotions as diverse as joy and fury. Emotion is seen to result only when the two factors of physiological arousal and an emotional context that is used as a label for the arousal are both present. Emotion is not experienced when either arousal or an emotionally labelled cognition is absent.

The chief support claimed by Schachter for his theory is an experiment (Schachter and Singer, 1962) which we shall consider, along with attempted replications, on pages 456–8. Although, as we shall discover, the empirical support is scant, the theory has been widely accepted, and has influenced research in a number of areas. For example, Schachter (1971) applied this view of the labelling of arousal to obesity and to crime. Other extensions of this work will be considered in later sections.

LAZARUS'S COGNITIVE THEORY

Lazarus and his coworkers (e.g., Lazarus *et al.*, 1970) regard emotion as, most importantly, a cognitive function, the result of **appraisal** of environmental events. The pattern of behavioural, physiological and subjective components that occurs under certain circumstances is definitive of emotion. Every stimulus is appraised and classed as either threatening or nonthreatening, and is then subject to a continuing process of **reappraisal**. In this way, our emotional reactions constantly change with reappraisal of changing stimulus conditions. Stimuli appraised as nonthreatening, and reappraised benignly, give rise to positive emotional states, the particular emotion experienced depending on the other circumstances, such as the removal of threat (elation), the existence of a sense of security (euphoria), or a sense of belonging, warmth and identity (love). Stimuli appraised as threatening may lead to direct action (such as attack, avoidance or inaction) together with the subjective and physiological components characteristic of anger, fear and depression respectively. If direct action is impossible, threatening stimuli may be reappraised as benign, by way of **coping strategies** that may be either realistic (a recognition that a stimulus is not, despite first appearances, dangerous), or distorting (such as denial, e.g., refusing to recognize a real danger).

Lazarus, then, sees cognition as important not simply for providing an emotional label for arousal, as does Schachter, but, as appraisal, as the central mechanism of emotional arousal. Physiological arousal only occurs as a consequence of certain types of appraisal. Emotions are, in principle, differentiable by the identification of specific patterns of cognitive, physiological and behavioural patterns. One important feature of Lazarus's approach is that cultural factors are seen as important by affecting our perception of social relationships and emotional stimuli, and by influencing our expression of emotion, sometimes through ritualized behaviour, such as is shown in cultural differences in mourning and grieving. Lazarus's theory remains poorly developed, and has very little empirical support. Only in the area of response to stress has research derived from the theory been conducted, and we shall consider this on pages 484–5.

IZARD'S DIFFERENTIAL EMOTIONS THEORY

Izard (1977) has set out to provide a much more general and formal theory than those discussed so far. He considers the emotions to be the primary motivational system for human beings, and is therefore concerned to understand not simply their nature, but their importance in every aspect of life, in pathological as well as 'normal' states, and in development.

Izard proposes a slightly different set of three components of emotions, the **neurophysiological**, which is activity in the sensory cortex and the limbic system (see pages 472–3), **neuromuscular** (chiefly facial expressive behaviour), and **phenomenological**. Autonomic arousal is viewed by Izard as a consequence, not a determinant of emotions. Many emotions involve autonomic-visceral-glandular processes as auxiliary systems, often important in amplifying and sustaining the emotion. The sequence of events that occurs during the activation of an emotion is as follows. An internal or external event is perceived and causes changes in neural activity in the sensory cortex and the limbic system. Impulses from these regions pass to the hypothalamus which determines what facial expression will be produced, and from there to the facial muscles by way of the motor cortex. Afferent impulses from receptors associated with the facial muscles pass (probably via the posterior hypothalamus) to the sensory cortex. The subjective experience of emotion arises from this sensory feedback. We shall discuss this last-mentioned aspect of this theory in detail on pages 467–9.

Izard proposed ten (later, eleven) fundamental emotions that constitute one of three types of **affect**, the others being **drives/bodily feelings** (for example, hunger, fatigue, sex) and **affective-cognitive structures**, which are relatively stable associations between an emotion or drive and certain cognitive processes, such as ideas and beliefs. More persistent and pervasive affective-cognitive structures may be viewed as personality traits. For example, a child who receives attention and rewards for assertiveness may come to take a great deal of interest in him- or herself, and develop feelings of superiority over others, associated with the emotion of contempt, and with other emotions being aroused by 'suitable' events (e.g., enjoyment from gaining something at another's expense). This would be an affective-cognitive structure of egotism. Other examples are introversion-extraversion, scepticism and vigour. Emotions other than the fundamentals are viewed as interactions, often complex, of affects, and Izard and his colleagues have particularly investigated the states with clinical significance, using a variety of methods, notably the Differential Emotions Scale, a self-report instrument on which subjects rate the degree to which a number of adjectives (three for each fundamental) apply to their feelings during a particular period of interest. Using the DES, depression has been shown to be an interaction of distress and variable combinations of anger, disgust, contempt, fear, guilt and shyness, together with other affective factors. Anxiety involves fear as the dominant emotion, together with one or more of distress, shame, guilt, anger and interest.

The eleven fundamental emotions that Izard lists (those mentioned above plus enjoyment and surprise) are each assumed to have a specific innately determined neural substrate, and a characteristic facial expression or neuromuscular-expressive pattern, feedback from which is the chief determinant of the quality of the felt emotion. The chief empirical basis for the identification of these as fundamental emotions is, according to Izard, research on the universality of the facial expression of emotions. We shall consider this evidence in more detail on pages 462–4, simply noting at this point three of the weaknesses of this method as a way of identifying fundamental emotions. First, the most emotion categories used in any of the research cited by Izard is eight. Guilt and shyness have not been studied in this way, so that the empirical basis for identifying these is unclear. Secondly, no 'nonfundamental' emotions have been studied in this way, so the possibility that other emotions may be cross-culturally recognizable cannot be excluded. Thirdly, although contempt is considered a distinct fundamental emotion, in Izard's study of facial expression it was considered a more intense form of disgust, so no evidence is available of its separate recognizability.

Although the notion of fundamental emotions is a very attractive one, it does seem that their nature and identity needs re-examining. This should not be read as a criticism of the contribution Izard has made to our understanding of emotion. His theoretical and empirical work have done much to extend our understanding of the complexity of emotions in everyday life, of the interaction of emotions with other personality and motivational systems and with socialization processes, and of their importance in human development and in perceptual and cognitive function.

Physiological arousal and emotion

The theories discussed in the preceding section illustrate that there are certain key questions about the nature of emotion. In this section we look at one of these, namely, what is the role of physiological arousal in emotion? James gave it an important role in differentiating emotions, but Schachter argued that, while physiological arousal is a prerequisite for an emotion to occur, the nature of the arousal is immaterial. Both Lazarus and Izard see arousal as a component of the emotional response, not a cause of it. We look now at the evidence concerning this question.

STUDIES OF SENSORY DYSFUNCTION

Dana (1921) discussed the case of a patient with a spinal cord lesion at the fourth cervical level who showed grief, joy, displeasure and affection, despite having no sympathetic function and extremely limited muscular function. He also discussed a number of other conditions in which pathological disruption of sensory input left emotional experience apparently intact.

Hohmann (1966) interviewed twenty-five patients with lesions at different levels of the spinal cord. If emotional experience depends on experienced arousal then patients with higher lesions, eliminating more afferent input, should experience less strong emotions. For fear, anger and sex, patients reported decreases in feelings since injury, with apparently greater decrements for those with higher lesions. For grief, however, only those with highest lesions showed any decrease, while all patients reported *increases* in sentiment.

There seems to be some evidence here, at least for fear, anger and sex, that emotional intensity depends on the availability of afferent information. However, consideration of some of the statements made by patients about their experiences implies a different conclusion. 'Seems like I get thinking mad, not shaking mad', 'It's a mental kind of anger', 'I don't really feel afraid, not all tense and shaky, with that hollow feeling in my stomach like I used to'. Such statements refer specifically to the absence of visceral components; the patients seem still to be experiencing emotion. A further difficulty with this approach is that afferent impulses are carried in the parasympathetic nervous system, entering the CNS at the sacral and cranial levels. The latter will have been disrupted in none of these patients, while the former will in all. Neither does this research allow us to distinguish between the effects of general autonomic feedback and differentiated arousal patterns, to which we turn next.

ADRENALINE AND NORADRENALINE SECRETION IN FEAR AND ANGER

Cannon interpreted James's theory as implying that every discriminable emotion is accompanied by a different pattern of visceral responses. However, Cannon overlooked two fundamental matters. First, James did not restrict the elements of physiological patterns to visceral responses, but gave a lot of weight to expressive behaviour. We shall look at the role of emotional expression on pages 467–9. Second, we are all aware of physiological changes in ourselves or others that accompany specific emotions. These include blushing with embarrassment, blanching with fear and going purple with rage, as well as such internal sensations as nausea in fear and disgust, 'butterflies' in nervousness, and the 'lump in the throat' of sadness.

A number of attempts have been made to provide more formal evidence of the physiological differentiation of emotions, starting with observations made by Wolf and Wolff (1947) on a patient with a gastric fistula, allowing observation of his gastric mucosa. When the patient was depressed, anxious or feeling overwhelmed, there was a decrease in secretion and motility, but these increased when he was angry or resentful. These observations have since been confirmed on other fistulous patients.

Subsequently, more systematic investigations of this question were undertaken. Ax (1953) recorded a number of physiological functions in the laboratory while inducing fear and anger in his subjects with staged incidents. Seven out of fourteen measures differentiated between these two states, fear being accompanied by increased heart rate, skin conductance level (SCL), muscle action potential frequency and respiration rate; anger by increased diastolic blood pressure, frequency of spontaneous SC responses, and action potential size. He suggested that the fear pattern corresponded to the action of **adrenaline** (A), and the anger pattern to that of **noradrenaline** (NA). Schachter (1957) added a painful stimulus to Ax's, and concluded that pain led to an NA-like response pattern, fear to an A-like pattern, and anger to a mixed pattern. Closer examination of Schachter's results, however, reveals that this last pattern is mixed only in the sense that some subjects gave an A response, others an NA pattern. It is possible that, since the anger manipulation always followed fear, some subjects were still experiencing the effects of the fearful manipulation.

Elmadjian *et al.* (1957) measured the urinary excretion of A and NA in various psychiatric and nonpsychiatric groups. Professional ice-hockey players, in a sport entailing considerable aggressive activity, showed increases in both NA (sixfold) and A (threefold) excretion. Two players who were excluded from the game, and were spectators, showed little or no increase in NA, but a marked increase in A-excretion. On the basis of these and other results, Elmadjian concluded that 'Active, aggressive emotional displays are related to increased excretion of norepinephrine [NA], with or without increased secretion of epinephrine [A], whereas tense, anxious but passive displays are related to increased excretion of epinephrine with normal excretion of norepinephrine.'

A series of experiments by Frankenhaeuser and her colleagues provides further evidence (see Frankenhaeuser, 1975). In one study subjects attended four sessions, in the first three of which they were given increasing control over receiving electric shocks (the fourth session was a relaxation period). A-excretion decreased over the sessions, whereas NA was slightly elevated but showed no tendency to decrease. Frankenhaeuser suggested that it is not anxiety as such that is accompanied by increased A-excretion, but conditions of novelty, anticipation and unpredictability.

PHYSIOLOGICAL PATTERNING IN OTHER EMOTIONS

Sternbach (1962) showed eight-year-old children the film *Bambi*, and measured a variety of physiological functions. Changes occurring during scenes which each child judged the saddest, 'scariest', happiest, and funniest were assessed. Little consistency was observed in responses to scariest and funniest scenes, but the saddest were characterized by a decrease in eye-blinks and an increase in skin resistance. The happiest scene was accompanied by a slowing of gastric contraction rate. The response pattern during the sad part of the film was tentatively interpreted as an inhibition of sympathetic activity, and that in the happy scene as possibly reflecting a decrease in parasympathetic activity.

Averill (1969) attempted to induce sadness in adult subjects by showing them film of the assassination of President Kennedy, and produced a sympathetic response pattern. While this contrasts with Sternbach's results, one would not expect a simple or uniform response to Averill's stimulus material. Averill (1968) has reviewed the psychophysiology of grief, and concluded that it has no single distinct pattern since it passes through different stages and is accompanied by other emotions such as anger, guilt and anxiety. Despair is often described as a sympathetic response, while weeping is parasympathetic (Sternbach's children may have blinked less in the sad scenes as their eyes filled with tears). Weeping, however, is frequently absent in abject grief.

Evidence for differential physiological patterning in other emotions is sparse. There are, however, reasons why it would be difficult to demonstrate such specificity as might exist. First, there is the difficulty of inducing pure emotions under laboratory conditions – a difficulty that applies in all areas of research into emotion. Second is the possibility of **individual response specificity**, the tendency of individuals to have a characteristic pattern of responding independently of the nature of the stimulus. Third, it is possible that any physiological differences that do exist are not detected by the techniques used, either because the techniques are too coarse for what may well be subtle differences, or because the wrong physiological functions are monitored.

OTHER ENDOCRINE SYSTEMS

Mason (1975) has argued that the endocrine systems should be considered as intimately interdependent, so that we should consider patterns of secretory change instead of concentrating on single endocrine responses. The initial results of this type of approach broadly confirmed Cannon's view that emotional arousal is accompanied by physiological preparation for activity. Monkeys were subjected over seventy-two hours to sessions of a conditioned avoidance procedure (in which the animal has to learn to press a lever to avoid receiving electric shocks). During this period, increases were found in those hormones that promote energy mobilization (**catabolism**) or preparedness for exertion (such as adrenaline, noradrenaline and thyroxine and the adrenal-cortical hormones), while those that promote restoration or energy storage (**anabolism** – insulin, testosterone, oestrone) decreased. After the end of the period, secretion of anabolic hormones increased while the secretion of catabolic hormones declined slowly. Very similar patterns were observed in monkeys in response to other stressors, such as physical restraint.

The usual endocrine reaction to stressful situations is that just described. However, Mason refers to instances where the stressor changed and a different pattern emerged. A female hospital patient made angry by having her anticipated release from hospital postponed showed an increase in corticosteroid secretion, *and* in the gonadal hormones androsterone and oestradiol, which in 'standard' stressful circumstances decrease. Similar observations have been made in an army recruit subjected to humiliation, and in other cases.

Mazur and Lamb (1980) have shown that relationships between status change and testosterone secretion known to occur in monkeys also occur in humans. Men who won tennis matches for a 100-dollar prize showed an increase in testosterone production compared to losers, except for one pair who won only narrowly. Winning the same prize in a lottery produced no such increase. Testosterone secretion also rose one to two days after student subjects were ceremonially awarded their MD degrees. That these changes are related to a feeling of achievement (or pride, status change) is supported by the finding that testosterone secretion was closely paralleled by self-reports of elation.

A commonly cited example of the supposed influence of hormones on emotion is the occurrence of **premenstrual tension**. It is popularly supposed that the irritability experienced at this time by some women is caused by increased secretion of oestrogens. However, the time of maximal oestrogen production is mid-cycle, with progesterone peaking some eight days before menstruation. Moreover, recent work has cast doubt on the generality and validity of reported menstrual-cycle-related mood changes. Ruble (1977), for example, showed that women in the mid-menstrual stage who believed they were premenstrual provided reports of more symptoms than those who knew their true position in the cycle. Lahmeyer *et al.* (1982) point out the unreliability of the methods used to measure mood, and sometimes position in cycle, in earlier studies. Using carefully constructed questionnaires and accurate assessments of cycle, they found that only water-retention symptoms were reliably elevated in the premenstrual phase. However, they used only eleven subjects, and their data show a premenstrual anxiety peak which might have been reliable with a larger sample. Nevertheless, it seems safe to conclude that a large part of the premenstrual syndrome is due to socially mediated expectations.

CATECHOLAMINE INFUSION

Cannon supported his fifth objection to James's theory by citing the results of early studies of the effect of the injection of catecholamines into human subjects, who only reported a real emotion if they were predisposed to experience it, for example by prior discussion of bereavement. In the most widely cited of such studies Marañon (1924) reported that his subjects reported 'as-if' emotions, for example, 'I feel as if afraid', 'as if awaiting a great joy', or 'as if I were going to weep without knowing why'. This is described as a clear separation of the 'peripheral phenomena of vegetative emotion and the psychical emotion proper'. Yet both Cannon and Marañon ignore the fact that these subjects are describing *particular* 'as-if' emotions – their feelings are not a generalized excitement. What is missing in these reports, but present in the rarer cases of real emotion mentioned above, is the perception of an eliciting stimulus. In a later study, Frankenhaeuser and colleagues (1961) caution that their subjects appeared 'very reluctant to admit any severe emotional changes, and seemed to attempt to ignore their symptoms as far as possible' (p. 185).

What remains to be established is why these subjects reported a range of emotions. The most frequently reported emotion is anxiety, and Breggin (1964), in his review of these studies, attributes these to either the association of the physical symptoms produced by catecholamines with those experienced in previous anxiety states, or to the experimental situation itself producing anxiety, exacerbated by the catecholamine-induced arousal. The evidence reviewed on pages 450–1 above, however, would lead us to suppose that adrenaline infusion *per se* might produce anxiety. Breggin's second suggestion would also account for the other emotions that have been reported, with the subject's prevailing mood or emotional response to remembered events or the inter-action with the experimenter being increased by arousal. The idea that arousal serves as a modulator of emotional intensity rather than as a determinant of emotional quality will be considered further on pages 456–61.

PHYSIOLOGICAL SELF-CONTROL AND EMOTION

Another way of looking at Cannon's fifth objection to James's theory is to change a person's physiological state by methods of self-control, rather than with pharmacological agents. Relaxation methods for the control of anxiety have been in use for some considerable time. Ancient meditation techniques are methods of achieving relaxation, and the method of progressive muscular relaxation used by Wolpe (1958) in his behaviour therapy technique of systematic desensitization, for example, is based on the method of Jacobson (1938). More recent work has used the technique of **biofeedback** to modify autonomic responses and to assess the effect of this on emotional state or responses to emotionally toned stimuli. Biofeedback is a procedure in which information about physiologi-cal activity is made available to a person by being detected at the body surface and then, after appropriate signal conditioning, dis-played to the person, usually in visual or auditory form. People are able to use this information to learn to control functions that are normally considered not to be under voluntary control, and which normally provide little or no feedback available to consciousness. Most often, and mainly because of potential therapeutic impli-cations, the direction in which subjects have been trained to control their physiological functions is in the direction of decreasing arousal.

Sirota and colleagues (1974) trained subjects either to increase or to decrease heart rate (hr) while anticipating receiving electric shocks. The effects of changing hr depended on whether the subjects were rated as 'cardiac aware' or 'unaware' on questionnaire measures of awareness of physiological response to stress. Cardiac aware subjects who increased hr reported much more pain than similar decrease subjects. For cardiac unaware subjects the differ-ence was reversed, but much smaller. Similar results have been obtained with increases and decreases of hr on pain produced by cold pressor tests (the hand plunged into ice-cold water); hr decreases have been shown to reduce public-speaking anxiety, fear of snakes and of spiders.

We need to be cautious in interpreting such results as indicating that changes in physiological functions produce emotional changes. First, the processes involved in biofeedback learning are far from clear. In particular, we cannot assume that the learning is a direct, unmediated visceral learning. It is possible, some would say probable, that control over physiological processes is achieved *secondarily* to direct control over mental states (for example, by the use of imagery). Second, as each of these research groups has realized, a factor such as perception of, or belief in, the ability to control their own reactions might have the emotion-modifying effect. Gatchel *et al.* (1979), for example, compared groups given real and false biofeedback, and a systematic desensitization group, in the reduction of speech anxiety. The false feedback group showed as much reduction in self-reported and observer-rated anxiety as the other two groups. It was also discovered that only the real biofeedback group produced decreases in hr, showing that behavioural, subjective and physiological components of anxiety do not always covary. Thus, cognitive factors, as well as arousal, are important in the maintenance and control of anxiety. In the following sections we look further at the interaction of cognition and arousal in emotion.

Cognition and arousal

TESTS OF TWO-FACTOR THEORY

Since Schachter's theory separates the two factors of arousal and a cognitive search for a label, one can readily envisage an experimental test of the theory. It would be necessary to manipulate independently arousal and the available cognitions in such a way that the subject was unaware that arousal was being manipulated (thereby causing a cognitive search), while providing an emotionally toned label that does not itself produce arousal. Schachter and Singer (1962) attempted to do just this in an experiment that has become one of the most widely cited in psychology. Arousal was manipulated by injecting some subjects with adrenaline, others with a placebo. They were then subjected to a situational manipulation intended to provide a label of either euphoria or anger, by means of the behaviour of a confederate of the experimenters who was ostensibly waiting to take part in the same experiment. The confederate acted either in a euphoric manner (hula-hooping, playing with scrap paper) or became angry at an insulting questionnaire he and the real subject were both completing.

Subjects' arousal was measured by the change in pulse rate from before to after the situational manipulation. Their emotional state was assessed both behaviourally, by observers rating the degree to which they joined in with the confederate's behaviour, and by self-report scales. Schachter and Singer concluded from the results that subjects were 'readily manipulable into the disparate feeling states of anger and euphoria', a conclusion that has been widely quoted, despite the fact that the mean self-reports of all experimental groups were on the happy side of neutral! So Schachter's theory is not supported by his own experiment. Yet we should not discard the theory on this basis alone, since the study has numerous flaws (see, for example, Manstead and Wagner, 1981). Most importantly, Schachter and Singer failed to manipulate arousal and cognition *independently*. Injections (of drug or placebo) are not likely to be affectively neutral, nor would the effects of adrenaline be experienced without affective colour, particularly by subjects who were misinformed or kept ignorant of the changes that would follow the injection. The situational manipulations seem to do rather more than provide a label. The subject was invited to join in with the bizarre behaviour of the confederate in the euphoria condition, and completed an insulting questionnaire in the other. Manstead (1979), and other workers, have conducted role-playing replications of all or part of the experiment. Subjects in these studies report a variety of different emotions that might be elicited by the manipulations, and it is concluded that the two manipulations were not sufficiently distinct and unambiguous to provide a test of the two-factor theory.

More recently there have been attempts to improve on the design of the original experiment. These, however, suffer from some of the same difficulties, as well as introducing new ones (such as the use of 'posthypnotic amnesia' as a way of preventing awareness of the real source of arousal). In the best of these studies, Erdmann and Janke (1978) induced arousal by asking subjects to test four ways of administering a drug which they would be asked to take at a later stage. They were told that each was an inert substance, but one in fact contained the stimulant ephedrine. While this is an improvement over other methods, their situational manipulations are not. In anger and happiness conditions subjects were asked insulting or complimentary questions, respectively, about performance on an intelligence test. In an anxiety condition they were told they were to be given electric shocks, before receiving three shocks. In a neutral condition they read, and answered questions on, a description of nature. The first three of these would certainly be expected to provide more than merely a label for the emotions concerned.

Attempts to test the theory directly, then, have provided it with little support, although this could be due to inadequacies of the attempts. Despite this, Schachter's view of the roles of arousal and cognitive factors in the experience of emotion has been widely accepted. In the following sections we look briefly at some research that has been influenced by this approach.

FALSE AUTONOMIC FEEDBACK

Valins (1966) proposed what is effectively an extension of two-factor theory. He suggested that information concerning, or belief in, the occurrence of physiological arousal is enough to cause a search for the source of that arousal. In his classic study to investigate this proposal, Valins asked male college students to view a series of photographic slides of semi-nude women. The subjects were wired up with dummy electrodes and heard prerecorded sounds that were described as either their own pulse or as extraneous sounds. For half the subjects in each group the rate of sounds increased during presentation of half the slides, for the others it decreased. After the slide presentation, subjects were asked to provide ratings of the attractiveness of the women portrayed. As expected, subjects who were told the sounds were of their pulses rated the change slides as more attractive than no-change slides. This **Valins effect**, as it has become known, did not occur for subjects told the sounds were extraneous, who showed a small reversed effect. What was less expected was that 'pulse-rate' subjects also rated 'decrease' slides more attractive, although this effect was less than half that for 'increase' subjects. The Valins effect, but not the effect obtained with apparent decreases in hr, has been replicated several times.

Valins suggested that the basis for the effect was that the apparent change in arousal caused subjects to search the slide for attributes that might have caused the reaction, and that search process might have led to the discovery of more positive attributes, an idea that has found some empirical support. Alternatively, Parkinson and Manstead (1981) have suggested that it might be mediated by differences in attention produced by the changing sound. They supported this by demonstrating in an experiment of their own that the effect occurred only when subjects were instructed to attend to the sounds, and did not depend on the meaning assigned to them. It seems likely that the effects of false autonomic feedback actually have nothing to tell us about the role of arousal cognitions in the experience of emotion.

MISATTRIBUTION OF AROUSAL

In the attempts to test the two-factor theory that we considered on pages 456–8, arousal was manipulated by artificial means. Another way to look at the role of arousal in emotion is to examine the effects of persuading a person experiencing arousal that it has been caused by some other agent. Two-factor theory would predict that subjects who misattribute their arousal in this way will experience less emotion than those who correctly attribute it to emotion-inducing circumstances.

Nisbett and Schachter (1966) gave subjects a pill, actually a placebo, telling them it would produce side-effects that were either those that would result from electric shocks, or were irrelevant to shock. Half the subjects in each group were told they would receive extremely painful shocks (high-fear condition), the others mild and easily tolerable shocks (low-fear). Those subjects able to attribute their reactions to the pill reported pain and tolerance thresholds higher than those unable to make this attribution. They also reported the last shock to be less painful. However, these differences only occurred for low-fear subjects. It was concluded that misattributing arousal to a nonemotional source decreases the effects of an emotionally toned stimulus, providing that the person is not too strongly aroused emotionally.

Many subsequent studies have demonstrated that misattribution of arousal can alter responses to stimuli. More recently, however, a number of workers have failed to obtain misattribution effects. Furthermore, Calvert-Boyanowsky and Leventhal (1975) have criticized the methods of this research. Most experiments have not used a manipulation check, that is, subjects nave not been asked after the experiment about their understanding of the procedure, which leaves open the possibility of demand characteristics producing the results. In most studies, only subjects in misattribution conditions have been given a list of symptoms. Subjects not given an accurate list might well be made more agitated by experiencing the 'wrong' symptoms, and these authors provide evidence that this is so. Thus, the results of the research considered in this section might reflect a direct calming effect of preparatory warning of symptoms rather than their misattribution.

EXCITATION TRANSFER

Zillmann (1978) has argued that if arousal is not attributed to the stimuli that actually produced it, it is available to energize the response to a subsequent stimulus. This view can be tested using experimental paradigms that depend on inducing arousal of which a subject is not aware. One way of doing this is to plot the course of recovery following exercise-induced arousal. Most people report that they have returned to pre-exercise levels of arousal some time before physiological indices have fully recovered. This provides three recovery phases in which the effects of arousal may be studied. First, a phase of subjective and physiological arousal; second, physiological arousal with no subjective arousal; and third, complete recovery. Traditional views might predict that responses to emotionally toned stimulation will be enhanced by arousal most in phase one, next in phase two, and not at all in phase three. Excitation transfer theory predicts that enhancement of subsequent responses will only occur in phase two, since only then is there residual excitation that is free for transfer by being attributed to the new stimulus. In phase one, the arousal will be correctly attributed to exercise, and will not affect other responses. Using this paradigm, Zillmann and his coworkers showed that sexual arousal ratings of erotic films were increased only when viewed in phase two. This and similar paradigms have also been reported to show the intensification of anger and aggressive behaviour after exercise and sexual arousal, and that disgust can facilitate musical enjoyment and humour appreciation.

Zillmann (1982) has argued that the potentiation of aggressive behaviour that is a well-documented consequence of the viewing of violent materials (e.g., television), at least among children, is a consequence of the arousal-producing fast pace of such materials, rather than of the violence itself. A number of pieces of evidence support this view, for example, the extent to which high-action cartoons increase the incidence of aggressive behaviour in pre-school children is independent of the amount of violence the cartoons contain. It is possible that this is an example of the excitation transfer phenomenon. However, some recent work has cast doubt on Zillmann's model. Some attempts to replicate the phenomena reported by Zillmann have failed, and it seems likely that arousal alone cannot account for all the results in the research in this area. For example, in some studies it has been found that aggressive responses are not enhanced when additional arousal originates in an incompatible (hedonically opposite) state (e.g., erotic stimulation). Such results have been explained by incompatibility hypotheses, and by distraction hypotheses, the former stating that it is not easy to return to a former state after incompatible stimulation, the latter that the intervening stimulation distracts attention from the original state.

Facial expression and emotion

EVOLUTION OF EMOTIONAL EXPRESSION

One view of emotions that gives them a clear functional role is that originating with Darwin, most clearly in his book *The Expression of the Emotions in Man and Animals* (1872). Darwin was concerned to establish the continuity of behaviour, as well as of structure, from 'lower' animals to humans. He saw emotionally expressive behaviour as good evidence for this continuity, basing his conclusions on evidence from a number of sources: animals in zoos, observations by himself and explorers and missionaries, including those on preliterate human groups. A considerable amount of similarity could be observed in emotional behaviour at different phylogenetic levels, and these behaviours could be interpreted as fulfilling roles with survival value. For example, one of the most general patterns serves to make the animal appear larger, and thereby more frightening. This can be seen in the erection of body hair in mammals (and of feathers in birds). Toads and frogs can take in air and expand enormously. Some reptiles similarly expand throat pouches or frills, or erect dorsal crests. A parallel pattern in humans involves the 'throwing-out' of the chest, standing more erect, thrusting the head forward, and, often, piloerection.

Displays of this type have vocal as well as bodily components, and, as we move up the phylogenetic scale, may include facial expressions. In vertebrates below the mammals, the facial muscles are largely devoted to opening and closing the eyes and mouth. Primates, particularly humans, have an extremely complex and well-innervated facial musculature, capable of extremely fine gradations of patterns of response. Ethological studies of the circumstances surrounding primate facial expressions, the reactions of other animals to them, and subsequent behaviour, confirm that facial expressions are, or form part of displays, that is, they are a form of social communication (see Chapter 10).

Darwin concluded that some facial expressions are innate, and based this on four types of evidence: (i) some expressions appear to be identical in different human racial and cultural groups; (ii) some appear in the same form in infants and adults; (iii) some are shown in the same way by those born blind and the sighted; and (iv) similar expressions appear in lower animals, particularly primates. In succeeding sections we shall consider further evidence for and against the conclusion that emotional expressions are innate.

UNIVERSALITY OF EMOTIONAL EXPRESSION

Darwin cited numerous instances of the same facial expressions being used in different cultures to convey the same emotion. Thus, frowning was reported as a sign of puzzlement among Australian Aborigines, Malays, 'Hindoos', African 'Kafirs', and South American Guaranis, as well as in Western cultures. A similarly apparent universal expression is that of grief, and Darwin called the muscles involved in it the 'grief muscles'. Anger and rage were said to be expressed in more variable ways, although numerous groups show similar patterns. Little further empirical work was undertaken on this matter until the second half of this century.

Ekman and colleagues (1969) showed thirty photographs judged to represent 'pure expressions' of what they and other authors considered to be primary or basic emotions (happiness, surprise, fear, anger, disgust, sadness) to adults in the USA, Brazil, Japan and preliterate societies in New Guinea and Borneo. All photographs were of Caucasians. Each observer was asked to choose the emotion label (translated) that named each expression. Subjects from the literate societies showed agreements of up to 90 per cent, levels of agreement that have been replicated. Preliterate cultures showed greater variability, ranging from 92 per cent agreement on happiness to 38 per cent for surprise and 31 per cent for disgust, all better than would be expected by chance. The authors concluded that the results support Darwin's suggestion.

A number of criticisms can be made of this study, including the possibility that the small numbers of observers used in the preliterate groups might have had considerable experience of Westerners, including viewing movies. In a further study, Ekman and Friesen (1971) studied a larger number of adults and children in New Guinea who had seen no films, and had very little contact with Westerners. Subjects performed the simpler task of identifying the picture (of three presented together) that depicted the expression of the person in a story they had just been read. Much higher agreement was obtained, with 68 per cent for surprise, and 83 per cent for disgust. Similar results have been obtained with adults from Malaya and Selangor judging Caucasian facial expressions.

It is possible to conclude from studies such as these that there is a high degree of universality in the expression of emotions. Results that show lower universality might reflect the effects of learning and cultural factors that would modify expressions in three ways: (i) through culture-specific differences in the conditions that elicit emotions; (ii) by differences in the consequences of displaying emotions; and (iii) by 'display rules' that specify when a particular individual may or may not express a particular emotion. It must also be noted that viewing still photographs is a highly artificial situation. Much emotional communication is contained in *changes* of expression, and what have been called **micromomentary expressions** that are unlikely to be caught by the camera. Furthermore, most of these studies have used posed expressions, and these are likely to differ considerably from naturally occurring ones. Finally, we should note, as does Ekman, that the demonstration of universality does not necessarily imply innateness. Similar patterns of expression in different cultures could arise from any source that is constant for humans, and although inheritance is a likely source, common environmental influences cannot be ruled out.

EMOTIONAL EXPRESSION IN INFANCY

Little systematic investigation of expression in infancy was conducted until Watson's (1919) experimental study of the effects of various types of stimuli, including dropping, loud sounds, restraint, tickling, shaking, rocking, stroking an erogenous zone, and various odours. Watson concluded that very young infants showed three differentiated patterns of expression, which he tentatively likened to **fear**, **rage** and **love**, although, in characteristically behaviourist manner, he preferred to call them patterns X, Y and Z. The precise forms of these patterns, however, were not clearly described. Later attempts to repeat Watson's findings were largely unsuccessful.

In 1932 Bridges produced a description of emotional development based on observation of the behaviour of infants at the Montreal Foundling and Baby Hospital. This description was for a long time the most influential view of emotional development. Bridges concluded that infants in the first month or so exhibited only an undifferentiated **general excitement**, with **distress** emerging as a response to painful stimuli at about three to four weeks. This is followed at three to four months by **anger**, at five to six months by **disgust**, and at seven to eight months by **fear**. **Jealousy** is seen from about fifteen to eighteen months. Positive states start to develop somewhat later, with **positive delight** (as distinct from mere absence of distress) at about two months, **elation** at eight to nine months,

affection at nine to ten months, and **joy** not until the second half of the second year. Despite the widespread influence that this scheme has had, it is based on observations of infants in an institutional environment by one observer.

Some support for Bridges's view that, at birth, infant emotion is undifferentiated has come from the research of Emde and colleagues (1976) on the origins and development of a limited number of particular emotional expressions. **Crying**, which is, of course, present at birth, occurs in response to hunger, pain and other discomfort, but also occurs in the absence of identifiable stimuli, when it is called **fussiness**. This shows a characteristic pattern of development, being virtually unaffected by styles of mothering and other environmental influences, increasing to a peak at about one month, and virtually disappearing by six months. Emde and his colleagues argue that fussiness is an innately determined behaviour, which serves the adaptive function of increasing the proximity and attention of parents.

Emde *et al.* observed that smiling in young infants occurs in two forms. **Endogenous smiling** appears in REM sleep (associated with dreaming in adults) at birth, and gradually decreases in frequency, to disappear at about six months. **Exogenous smiling** appears after the first month in response to various stimuli, such as rocking and mild stimulation. From about six to eight weeks, it is best elicited by the sight of a human face, and after three to four months best by the mother's face. Fraiberg (1971) demonstrated that this same developmental course occurs in blind-born children, except that exogenous smiling becomes responsive to the mother's voice and touch, not to her face. This evidence supports Darwin's contention that children born blind show emotions in the same way as sighted children. A number of other studies have shown this to be true of a range of expressions.

Oster (1978) has recently undertaken a detailed investigation of the development of emotional expression. She avoids problems arising from having adults label infant emotional expressions, which has been the chief method in other research, by the use of the Facial Action Coding System (FACS), which is based on the identification from videotapes of movements in facial muscles. She has demonstrated that the majority of facial movements of which adults are capable can occur immediately after birth. Furthermore, these movements occur in integrated patterns that not only would be described as emotional in adults, but are observed in social exchanges. For example, alternating smiling and **brow-knitting** can be recorded in newborn infants watching the face of a person leaning over them. This puts the origin of social smiling at birth rather than after one month, as Emde's group concluded.

The potential of FACS for the analysis of facial expression is well illustrated in the case of brow-knitting, or **frowning**. This has usually been considered an expression of negative affect, an interpretation that is consistent with the traditional view that emotion in early infancy is restricted to a single dimension from quiescence to distress. In this view alternating smiling and frowning is difficult to interpret. Oster has shown that brow-knitting which occurs in alternation with smiling is qualitatively different to that occurring before crying, an undoubted sign of distress. She has conjectured that brow-knitting represents the operation of cognitive effort to 'make sense of' the environment. This is a notion borrowed from Darwin, who observed that in adults frowning occurs 'whenever the mind is intent on some subject and encounters some difficulty'.

Emotional expression and emotional experience play an important role in the development of the infant. It is becoming widely recognized that infants exert an enormous control over parents, not only in the general sense of changing lifestyles, status and so on, but on an interpersonal level. Crying, for example, elicits a variety of behaviours in the caregivers, such as attention, holding, patting, speech, imitation, mutual visual regard, and rocking, as well as attempts to remove the source of distress. As Saarni (1978) has said, 'The functional value of expressive displays available immediately after birth is, in fact, to modify others' behavior in such a way that the infant's probability of survival is increased' (p. 366).

One result of these interactions is the formation of **attachments** between infant and caregivers. Bowlby (1969) has reviewed earlier work on the formation of such attachments or **affectional bonds**, and is the best-known exponent of a view of development known as attachment theory. The expressive displays just described, **attachment behaviour**, are genetically programmed, and lead to the formation of attachment between the infant and his or her primary caregiver. While it is easy to see how and why the infant forms an affectional bond with the caregiver, attachment theory is much less clear about how the mother becomes attached to the infant. It is assumed that this, too, is genetically based, and it has been speculated that hormonal changes during and immediately after pregnancy serve to dispose the mother to become attached to her infant. However, there is little direct evidence for this, and more recent work suggests that environmental factors are important.

Ainsworth (1980) has looked at attachment behaviour in abusing families, and concluded that child abuse is likely to be related to anomalies in the development of attachment. The fact that crying is a behaviour particularly likely to stimulate acts of physical violence in an abusing parent, despite its more usual function, testifies to this view. Abusing parents have been found to have had anxiety-provoking experiences with their attachments to their own parents (threats of separation, real separation), and to be generally less responsive to their children's emotional communications. There is, however, also evidence that abuse might be provoked by the abused child. Certainly, it is often the case that only one child in a family is abused. Furthermore, separation from the infant at birth, as happens frequently with premature babies, is known to be a predisposing factor, indicating that mother-infant interaction in the first days of life is of particular importance (see also Chapter 12).

THE FACIAL FEEDBACK HYPOTHESIS

As we have seen, Darwin, James and, more recently, theorists such as Izard, have given to feedback from the facial muscles an important role in the generation of emotional experience. We cannot really specify one hypothesis by the title **facial feedback hypothesis**, since it is possible to hold that facial feedback is a sufficient cause of emotional experience, a necessary component of it, or a modifier of it. It is also possible to identify at least two routes through which activity in the facial muscles could influence emotion. Izard, who holds a sufficient cause view, maintains that it is sensory feedback from the muscles themselves that produces emotional experience. However, it is also possible that an **efference copy** of the motor commands to the facial muscles determines or influences emotional experience. As we shall see, these differences cause complications for attempts to test facial feedback hypotheses.

Two distinct experimental paradigms have been used in attempts to test the facial feedback hypothesis. In one, subjects are asked to maintain a particular facial expression while being exposed to emotion-inducing manipulations. As an example, Laird (1974), in the first attempt to test directly the hypothesis, showed subjects two types of pictorial stimuli – children playing or Ku Klux Klan members. Subjects were asked to contract or relax certain facial muscles until (without being explicitly instructed to frown or smile) these facial expressions were produced. Analysis of their ratings of their affective reactions to the slides showed that, while slide type had the greatest effect on their reactions, this was modified by facial expression, so that feelings of pleasure were enhanced by smiling, but reduced by frowning, and conversely for reactions of displeasure. These results support one of the weaker versions of the facial feedback hypothesis.

In the other paradigm subjects are asked to accentuate or suppress a naturally occurring expression. Lanzetta and colleagues (1976) conducted a series of experiments in which subjects were administered electric shocks under conditions of no instructions, instructions to pose an expression of intense pain, or not to show any expression. It was found that posing intense shock produced greater, and posing no shock lower, ratings of the intensity of pain than in no-pose conditions. These effects were greater for more intense shocks. More recent research has produced contradictory evidence. Kraut (1982) has shown that subjects posing the expression of smelling pleasant odours consistently, but weakly, rated odours as more pleasant than those posing unpleasant odours, or reacting spontaneously. This effect did not occur with the most unpleasant substances. McCaul and colleagues (1982), in contrast, showed no influence of posed facial expression (afraid, calm or normal) on otherwise unstimulated reports of level of anxiety, nor of posed afraid, happy and calm expressions on rated loudness of bursts of noise.

A number of difficulties in the interpretation of results of both of these paradigms are apparent. First, emotional self-reports are likely to be highly susceptible to influence by demand characteristics. Some studies have attempted to assess such influences. For example, in the experiments of Lanzetta and his colleagues, subjects were instructed that the aim of the facial expression manipulation was to influence the detectability of emotion by observers later viewing videotapes. This would, perhaps, not lead subjects to suspect that their feelings might be expected to change.

A second difficulty is that it is not necessary for the influence of facial muscle activity to be mediated by actual muscular contraction. It is possible that voluntary posing of either no expression or a different expression does not stop the registration of an efference copy of the natural motor commands, even though these do not noticeably affect the muscles, and that, as noted earlier, this efference copy could be the basis of the emotional experience. The more recent work that has failed to find an effect has, of course, not tested such a version of the hypothesis. Furthermore, it is likely that posed or voluntary emotional expressions use different neural pathways to natural ones, and that it is impossible to perfectly match a natural expression without experiencing the emotion, so that these paradigms are not good tests of the hypothesis.

Another difficulty is that it might be the *effort* involved in posing no emotion or an inappropriate one that reduces the impact of emotional stimuli. Tourangeau and Ellsworth (1979) incorporated a nonemotional facial expression (one eye closed, lips pursed, cheeks puffed out) together with an unmanipulated expression and expressions of fear and sadness (produced by instructions to contract particular muscles) in an experiment in which subjects viewed one of three films – frightening, saddening or neutral. Subjects' self-reports of emotional response to the films were not affected by any of the facial expression conditions, except that there was a tendency for subjects viewing the neutral films to produce self-reports consistent with their facial expression. In view of these difficulties, it seems that the facial feedback hypothesis is not empirically testable by psychological methods.

NONVERBAL EXPRESSIVENESS AND PHYSIOLOGICAL RESPONDING

Some of these difficulties of interpretation apply also to studies that have assessed the relationship between expressiveness and physiological responding in the same individual. It could be argued that if people hide their emotions by not allowing them to show facially, they should not only experience less strong emotion but should show less pronounced physiological responding to emotional stimuli. Much research, including some already discussed above, has confirmed this relation. Tourangeau and Ellsworth (1979) showed, however, that an increase in skin conductance responding accompanied their nonemotional expression, as well as their other posed expressions, and that these increases were not related to emotional self-reports. It might be that the correlation usually found between facial expression and physiological response depends on the effort involved in posing a facial expression. McCaul and colleagues (1982), however, concluded that a more likely cause was the amount of movement involved in posing, since they found no correlation between heart rate and subjects' ratings of the effort involved, but positive correlations between heart rate and observers' ratings of amount of movement.

It has also been suggested that the facial feedback hypothesis predicts that individual differences in emotional expressiveness should be directly related to differences in physiological responding. However, the hypothesis does not necessarily make predictions about individual differences. It relates, essentially, to the prediction of (variations in) the emotional experiences of an individual. One could argue that the full range of emotional experience is available to each of us, and the quality and intensity of the experience at any time is determined by the facial expression in relation to the individual's range of emotional expressions. Thus, we do not have to assume that persons who are more limited in their spontaneous emotional displays are necessarily limited in their emotional experiences.

Nevertheless, a number of authors (see the review by Buck, 1980) have attempted to test the facial feedback hypothesis by correlating emotional expressiveness (as indexed by the accuracy of judgements of the individual's expression) with SCL (skin conductance level). These studies have invariably found an *inverse* relation between the two measures. While we would argue that this does not have any necessary relevance to the hypothesis under consideration, it is a very interesting result for theories of emotion. Why do those individuals who readily express their emotions respond less readily at a physiological level? We might argue that this results from differences in socialization, in that people differ in the extent to which they are allowed or encouraged to express emotion. The

suppression of expression might involve the exertion of some sort of effort, which would be reflected in SCL changes. The result would be that those who are able to hide their feelings do so at the cost of physiological arousal.

If this suggestion is correct then we can identify groups who should demonstrate differences in expressiveness and autonomic lability. In our society, for example, the traditional male role is one that involves the suppression of the expression of most emotions. Women, on the other hand, are 'allowed' to express emotions more freely. Buck and his colleagues (see, for example, Buck *et al.*, 1974) have produced good evidence that there is, indeed, a female advantage in sending emotional information nonverbally. (We should note that there is also considerable evidence for a female advantage in decoding such messages, see Hall, 1978.) Further-more, men have a tendency to produce larger SCL changes than women in these experiments. If this male/female difference is a consequence of differential restrictions on emotional expression by boys and girls, the sex differences should not be present in young children. Buck (1975) has investigated this possibility in children aged between four and six years. The ability of student judges to read children's facial expressions is inversely related to the child's age for boys but not for girls. This clearly supports the notion that over this age range boys are learning to hide their emotions to a greater extent than are girls.

Cutting across this sex difference is a personality difference. **Externalizers** are expressive individuals, while **internalizers** are individuals who show little emotion externally, but are found to be physiologically reactive. The externalizer-internalizer dimension is closely related to the extraversion-introversion dimension, with extraverts tending to be externalizers. This relation could be attributed to the less ready socialization that has been suggested for extraverts, coupled with either a greater physiological arousability for the same stimulus for introverts, or the effects of the effort to pose a nonemotional response on the part of introverts, or both of these factors.

Central mechanisms in emotion

BRAIN MECHANISMS AND EMOTIONAL BEHAVIOUR

Early in the present century it was shown that experimental destruction of the neocortex of dogs produces 'sham rage', so called because the rage-like behaviour is not directed at the eliciting stimulus. Such observations suggest that the cortex normally provides an inhibitory influence on subcortical structures that organize emotional behaviour. Further studies with lesions demonstrated that deep-lying regions of the temporal lobe, including the **limbic system**, have a role in emotional behaviour. Animals with temporal lobe lesions become docile, and show neither the fear nor the aggression to humans shown by unoperated animals.

Papez (1937), using a combination of methods including post mortem studies of the brains of humans who had suffered emotional disorders, and of rabid dogs, proposed that the limbic system includes a set of interconnected pathways and centres (later called the **Papez circuit**). According to Papez the physiological expression of emotion is controlled by the hypothalamus, with emotional behaviour and feelings resulting from activity in a circuit including the hypothalamus, the mamillary bodies, the anterior thalamus and the cingulate gyrus. Since that time considerable research has been conducted using lesions in the Papez circuit in attempts to elucidate its functions. Much of this work has implicated parts of the circuit in the control of aggressive behaviour. To take two examples, Downer (1962) divided the corpus callosum and optic chiasma of a monkey, so that information from each eye projected only to the same side of the cortex, and then removed the right amygdala. After the animal had recovered it was noted that it behaved normally (with aggressive and fearful behaviour) when approached from the left, but was docile when approached from the right. Rosvold and his colleagues (1954) removed the amygdala from the dominant monkey in a social group. On its return to the colony it showed a rapid fall in its position in the hierarchy.

The hypothalamus also has an important role in the control of aggressive behaviour. Early work by Bard (1928) showed that the sham rage produced in cats by removal of the cortex largely disappears if the hypothalamus is also removed. Conversely, stimulation of the hypothalamus produces attack behaviour. Later research has shown that stimulation or lesions of different parts of the amygdala may have either facilitatory or inhibitory effects on aggression, suggesting a controlling or moderating role for the amygdala and an integrative role for the hypothalamus. Stimulation of two adjacent points in the hypothalamus of cats produces quite different response patterns – one consisting of rage and attack, and the other of quiet predation.

Lesions of another part of the limbic system having connections with the hypothalamus, the **septum**, also produces aggressive behaviour. More interestingly, perhaps, Olds and Milner (1954) demonstrated that rats would learn to press a bar when the only reward they received was a burst of electrical stimulation to the septal area via indwelling electrodes. Stimulation of the same region in conscious humans results in reports of pleasure or warmth. Subsequent work with this self-stimulation technique has attempted to delineate the neural mechanisms involved in this behaviour. It seems likely that the mechanisms involved in self-stimulation are involved also in mediating the effects of other reinforcements (such as food, water, social stimulation). It is also possible that the same mechanisms are involved in the production of emotional states. We look next at research that has attempted to relate these behavioural studies of animals to the emotional experiences of humans.

MONOAMINE SYSTEMS

In the early 1960s a number of writers noted that certain drugs that affect human mood also have effects on the activity of brain systems using catecholamine neurotransmitters. For instance, hypertensive patients treated with reserpine, a drug that depletes the three monoamines – NA, dopamine and serotonin – frequently developed depression. Amphetamines, and the major groups of antidepressant drugs, the monoamine oxidase inhibitors and the tricyclic antidepressants, all act to increase the amount of NA at adrenergic nerve endings, and all elevate mood.

On this basis the **catecholamine hypothesis** of affective disorders was proposed: 'Some, if not all, depressions are associated with an absolute or relative deficiency of catecholamines, particularly norepinephrine, at functionally important adrenergic receptor sites in the brain. Elation conversely may be associated with an excess of such amines' (Schildkraut, 1965, p. 509).

Three further sources of evidence potentially support the role of these neurochemicals in affective disorders, namely post mortem analysis of the brains of those who have died during depressive illnesses, and the analysis of the neurochemicals and their metabolites in the cerebrospinal fluid and the urine. The results of all three types of investigation have been inconsistent; in each case some workers have found lowered levels of these substances, while others have not. A number of reasons for this confused picture may be identified. In the case of post mortem studies, most of the brains were from suicides, and it is not clear whether or not they are representative of depressives in general, or whether cognitive activity preceding suicide might have affected neurochemical activity. In all cases, it is necessary to consider recent and past history of medication. The most intriguing possibility is that there may be biochemically distinct subgroups of depressive illness, each involving dysfunction of one or more transmitter. Although some of these may have symptomatic differences – for example, patients with bipolar depression seem to show decreased urinary excretion of NA metabolites, whereas unipolar and reactive depressives do not – it is likely that much of the confusion in the research data results from an inability to distinguish clinically distinct disease entities.

One of the more recent neurochemical theories of depression (Anisman and Zacharko, 1982) attributes it to neurochemical changes resulting from stress. Under normal circumstances, neurochemical synthesis is balanced by utilization, re-uptake by the neuron, and breakdown by enzymes. Brief stress leads to increased synthesis and utilization and to a build-up of transmitter levels that result in heightened arousal. Controllable stress leads to a re-establishment of balance by enhanced enzyme activity, while uncontrollable stress causes utilization rates to exceed synthesis, resulting in a depletion of chemical levels. The result in the last case is depression. These changes may occur in one or more of the neurochemical systems, or may involve changes in sensitivity of postsynaptic receptors rather than in rates of synthesis. This latter suggestion fits better with the time-scale of the action of antidepressant drugs, which normally require repeated doses to have their effect, whereas their effect on transmitter availability is rapid.

Unfortunately, just as there is little incontrovertible evidence to link neurochemical levels with affective disorders, so there is little direct evidence that stress acts to precipitate depression. The links between stress, depression and neurochemical function are correlational, and tell us little about causation. There is now evidence that neurochemicals act in a rather more general fashion on the brain, and recent research has paid attention to the actions of **endorphins**, which are naturally occurring, morphine-like substances that appear to have a role in the response to painful stimuli. But it must be recognized that one role, perhaps the more important one, of these substances is to act as transmitters of information across synapses. At the moment, we cannot determine whether the chemical changes result from changes in the activity in neural pathways, or whether changes in neural activity follow from biochemical changes. An indication that it would be more fruitful to look at neural mechanisms rather than biochemical concentrations comes from a consideration of Parkinson's disease. This is confidently attributed to a disorder of a dopamine system, and responds well to treatment with L-DOPA, a precursor of dopamine. Yet depression is not an essential aspect of this disease, nor does depression respond well to attempts at treatment with L-DOPA. If a general biochemical disorder was involved, we would expect a general clinical picture.

Information about brain mechanisms that might subserve affective states has been obtained from studies of the effects of brain lesions on certain types of behaviour in animals. Comparing the effects of such studies with the effects of drugs that affect brain neurochemistry allows the identification, at least tentatively, of the neural pathways involved and their possible relation to affective states in humans. Much research has led to the postulation of three systems based on the catecholamines NA and dopamine, and on serotonin (or 5-HT). The catecholamine systems seem to mediate the effects of rewards; the serotonin system, those of punishment. The systems are interconnected, so that punishment might cause a serotonin system to inhibit a reward system, so that, for example, cessation of punishment results in a rebound reinforcement effect, causing the learning of behaviour that preceded the offset of punishment.

Gray (1982) has used a similar approach to investigate the neuropsychology of anxiety. He postulates a **behavioural inhibition system** (BIS) that mediates the behavioural changes resulting from three types of stimulation: punishment, frustrative nonreward (the failure to be received of an expected reward), and novel situations. In normal laboratory animals each of these leads to three general behavioural changes: ongoing responses are inhibited, the level of arousal increases, and there is increased attention to the environment. Drugs which, in humans, alleviate anxiety (benzodiazepines, barbiturates and alcohol) block or reduce the occurrence of these types of behaviour in animals, and are thought to act on the BIS. These effects are distinct from the sedative and muscle-relaxing effects of the drugs; under some conditions they can involve increased motor activity.

Gray postulates that many of the functions of the BIS are subserved by neural circuits in the septo-hippocampal system (SHS) and the Papez circuit. He proposes that the function of these systems is, generally, to compare actual and expected stimuli. When the two match, they operate in 'checking mode', having no control over behaviour. When a mismatch is detected or a stimulus is aversive, the SHS switches to 'control mode', and activates two of the classes of behaviour mentioned above, inhibition of behaviour and increased attention. Various nuclei in the SHS and Papez circuit are given particular roles in this scheme. Of particular interest here is a gate mechanism that has been shown physiologically to occur between the **dentate gyrus** and **area CA3** of the hippocampus. This acts to control the influence of incoming information, screening out unimportant signals. The gate is controlled by noradrenergic and serotonergic pathways, inputs from which 'open' the gate. Anti-anxiety drugs are said to act by reducing these inputs, thereby closing the gate so that the system treats fewer inputs as important.

Aside from changes in emphasis and the necessity to speculate beyond the data, these views are generally consistent with others we have considered. The chief advantage of this type of approach is that it recognizes that neurochemicals do not act in isolation from neural pathways. However, we must not allow advances on this front to blind us to the importance of social and cognitive causes of emotional experience and disorders. It may be that neural or even biochemical dysfunction is important in some pathological states, and certainly alterations in brain chemistry can be used therapeutically. These mechanisms, however, *mediate* our responses to environmental events, even in pathological states; they do not necessarily *determine* those responses.

The effects of emotion on cognition and health

MOOD AND COGNITION

In other parts of this chapter we have examined the role played by cognitive factors in the generation of emotion. We look now at the converse of this: how does emotion influence cognitive processes? Two converging lines of research stemming from social psychology and from cognitive psychology have contributed to our knowledge of this influence.

The first of these originated with work in the 1970s demonstrating, not surprisingly, that positive affective states have a facilitating effect on social interaction, particularly on helping others and on interpersonal attraction. Of more interest than these observations themselves is to try to understand why the effects occur. It was suggested by Isen and her coworkers (see Clark and Isen, 1982) that positive mood might operate on social behaviour by influencing the decision-making process that determines whether or not to engage in a social act. These workers have gone on to investigate the influence of mood on cognitive processes that contribute to decision-making.

One way in which a mood might influence decision-making would be to make a person more likely to reduce the load on working memory by reducing the complexity of decisions which could be achieved, by adopting the simplest strategy, by considering fewer alternatives, or by doing little or no checking of information, hypotheses and tentative conclusions. Thus, we might expect a happy person to act more quickly and to adopt the simplest and most obvious strategy. Isen's group has started a series of studies aimed at testing predictions made from the general hypothesis about working memory. For example, it has been shown that inducing positive mood by providing refreshments to subjects increases the proportion who adopt an incorrect, yet easy and intuitively correct-seeming solution to a problem, in preference to the more taxing correct solution. In another study, subjects were given information about six fictitious cars and were asked to decide which they might buy. Positive mood subjects took less time than control subjects and were more likely to ignore some of the information.

The tendency of positive mood subjects to adopt the first solution that occurs to them is modified if they are given immediate feedback on a task and allowed to continue. A good example of this is a study using the classic candle task devised in 1945 by Duncker as a demonstration of **functional fixedness**. Subjects are given a candle, a box of drawing pins and a book of matches, and are instructed to attach the candle to the wall in such a way that it will burn without dripping wax on to the floor. In this study, 75 per cent of subjects who had been shown a comedy film were successful, compared with 20 per cent who saw a control film, and 13 per cent who saw no film. Under these conditions, the positive mood subjects had a lot of ideas and tried them rapidly, until most of them solved the problem (by realizing that a drawing-pin box could be used as part of the solution, not simply as a container for the pins, if it was pinned to the wall as a platform for the candle). In contrast, control subjects tended not to be so active and to continue with an ineffective attempt. Here, positive mood not only speeds up reaction but increases the flow of ideas and the person's responsiveness to feedback. Yet the general process seems to be the same as in other cases: positive mood subjects are being impulsive, in the sense that they immediately try the first, and here successive, solutions without checking procedures in the decision-making process.

This suggests that people in a positive mood might be more prone to take risks in decision-making. This could occur because positive affect makes people more optimistic, and there is considerable evidence that in such states people make more positive judgements of relatively ambiguous stimuli, such as consumer products and facial expressions, which might reflect this optimism. However, whether or not people will be more likely to make risky decisions when happy depends on the level of risk and the possible consequences. In particular, people are *less* likely to take risks if the risk might threaten their maintenance of a positive mood. In social interaction, people in a positive mood will be more readily helpful to others because, it is suggested, they act more spontaneously, without assessing any risk that might be involved.

The second line of research has been concerned chiefly with the effects of mood on memory, thinking and judgement, the general effect being that moods facilitate the processing of information that has a congruent emotional tone (Bower and Cohen, 1982). In these experiments, emotional states of happiness, sadness or anger have been induced, usually with the aid of hypnotic suggestion. In one such study happy and sad subjects read a story involving a happy man and a sad man, and the following day, in a neutral mood, were able to recall more information about the character whose mood was congruent with their own when they had read the story. In addition to this mood-congruity effect at information storage, Bower and his colleagues have also demonstrated that mood influences the ease with which memories are accessed. People in a particular mood can best recall items stored when they were in the same mood. This selective process (or 'emotion-state-dependent memory') can be demonstrated, for example, in the recall of childhood memories, as well as in more formal experiments in which subjects learn two word-lists, one while happy, the other while sad, later attempting to recall both lists when in one of the two moods. Recall is better for lists learned in the same mood as the subjects are in during the recall period, and is worse than under control conditions when recall is of lists learned in a different mood. Similar results have been obtained by workers using methods of inducing moods other than hypnosis.

The explanation proposed by Bower for these effects is to assume that human memory can be thought of as an associative network of semantic concepts and schemata (the **semantic network theory**). An event is represented in memory by a cluster of **descriptive propositions**, which are the units of thought. Each concept is represented by a **node**, which may be activated to varying degrees. When the activation of a node exceeds a certain threshold the concept it represents enters consciousness. Nodes are connected by associative linkages, allowing the activation of one node as a consequence of the activation of an associated node. The process of learning is that of establishing, and increasing the strength of these associative linkages. It is further proposed that each emotion has a specific node or unit in memory, and that this node collects together, by associative links, the many behaviours, verbal labels, cognitive acts and events that occur in association with that emotion. When the emotion node is activated it will in turn increase the activation of associated nodes, though not necessarily above threshold. Thus, stimuli that were encoded or learned while a person was in a particular mood will be primed for recall whenever the subject is in the same mood, and can be recalled by relatively weaker cues. If conflicting emotion nodes are mutually inhibitory, this accounts for the poorer performance for recall of items learned in a contrasting mood, as their activation will be decreased, requiring a stronger stimulus for recall.

The semantic network theory can be applied to the results described earlier in the context of social interaction. Indeed, Clark and Isen (1982) have proposed a similar explanation. It can also be extended to cover such phenomena as, for example, the tendency of verbal free-associations to a neutral stimulus word to reflect the person's prevailing mood, the tendency for ambiguous or unclear stimuli to be perceived in accordance with a person's mood, and the finding that people's estimates of the probabilities that particular events would happen in the future were affected by their mood, in such a way that positive events were estimated to be more likely and negative events less likely by happy people (and the converse by depressed people). This theory is, then, a powerful one, linking as it does the effects of mood on a wide range of cognitive and social processes.

STRESS AND ILLNESS

We have mentioned stress in earlier sections of this chapter. Now we look more closely at the effects of stress on human health. Like emotion, stress is a difficult term to define, but for our purposes we shall use the term **stress** to refer to the adverse psychological and physiological effects of a wide variety of physical, pharmacological and psychosocial stimuli (**stressors**).

The notion that stress is a state associated with strain on the mechanisms that control the internal environment can be traced back to Cannon's notion of an emergency reaction involving general sympathetic arousal. Selye (1950) shifted the emphasis to the adrenal cortex in his **general adaptation syndrome** (GAS) which he conceived of as a nonspecific physiological response to demands placed on the organism, and involving three main stages. The **alarm reaction** involves SNS activation and adrenal discharge, and is a stage of decreased resistance to further stress. If the stressor is too severe for adaptive mechanisms, death can ensue. Otherwise, the operation of these processes leads to the stage of **resistance**, which will, however, be overcome by continued application of the stressor, leading to the stage of **exhaustion**, when the body again has decreased resistance to further stressors as the adaptive processes fail. The responses of the alarm reaction reappear, and death may ensue.

Continued operation of the adaptive responses leads to the **diseases of adaptation**, but Selye envisaged the GAS as a component of all physical illnesses. While this last point presaged current views of the role of stress in illness, Selye's concentration on physiological responses paid insufficient attention to psychological factors as mediators and modifiers of the stress reaction. As an example, surgical procedures do not normally produce the GAS in otherwise fit patients, whereas they would almost certainly do so if conducted without anaesthetic. There is also reason to doubt whether the GAS is a feature of all illnesses, and we have already reviewed evidence that different stressors can produce different patterns of physiological change.

More recent approaches to stress have placed greater emphasis on psychological factors. Kagan and Levi (1975), for example, emphasize **life-events** as an important aetiological factor in physical illness. An enormous amount of research effort has taken place following the identification of this factor. Holmes and Rahe (1967) introduced the Schedule of Recent-life Experiences (SRE), which is a checklist of forty-three life-events and associated relative impacts on the individual. These were based on the judged amount of readjustment required for each factor. This has since been widely used in prospective and retrospective studies, but there is considerable disagreement about its usefulness, even from those who feel life-events are important (see Birley and Connolly, 1976).

Some researchers report low reliability of SRE scores, while others have obtained very poor predictions of morbidity. The finding, among others, that only neurosis is reliably predicted by high SRE scores has led to the suspicion that the schedule is too crude, and may say more about the individual's personality than about real events.

Nevertheless, there is indisputable evidence that particular life-events can predispose to illness. Bereavement is a potent stressor that has received much recent attention. Bowlby (1980) mentions several studies showing that 'almost always health suffers'. Apart from the obvious emotional reactions, there is a threefold increase in hospital admissions. The nonpsychiatric condition with the largest increase is osteoarthritis. Mortality is also increased, largely from cardiac and cerebrovascular disease (especially coronary thrombosis). In one study (Rees and Lutkins, 1967), the mortality rate in the first year after death of a relative was seven times that in a nonbereaved group. As would be expected, the greatest increase was among spouses, and among those whose relatives died suddenly. This last finding is typical of those showing that a period of warning before bereavement allows the individual better to adjust to it.

One group of illnesses that does *not* show a marked increase after bereavement is the so-called 'psychosomatic diseases'. The field of **psychosomatic medicine** is today as much concerned with establishing the social and psychological factors that help determine susceptibility to and recovery from illness in general (see Eiser, 1982). This is not to say that research does not continue into specific diseases that are thought to have a greater dependence on stress than others, such as peptic ulcers, heart disease and essential hypertension.

There is evidence that those who develop particular symptoms are especially responsive in the system involved. For example, ulcer patients differ from others in the amount of gastric activity they evidence (for example, Walker and Sandman, 1977). There is also evidence that persons who suffer coronary thrombosis have a particular personality: 'Type A' (Friedman and Rosenman, 1959). The Type A person is characterized by extremes of competitiveness, a strong sense of time urgency, and hostility, and shows greater SNS responses to stress than others (see, for example,

Lovallo and Pishkin, 1980). Most research on psychosomatic illness has been retrospective, making it difficult to decide whether physiological or psychological changes in the individual precede or result from stress and pathological changes. This is true of most of the research on Type A behaviour, and is especially true in the case of essential hypertension. Although blood pressure increases follow even mild stressors, and despite the widely held view that stress, especially when accompanied by an inability to express hostility towards others, will predispose people to develop hypertension, there is very little research actually demonstrating such links (see Chapter 13 for a further discussion of this issue).

Psychosocial and emotional factors have also recently been considered in relation to the aetiology and course of various types of cancer. Owing to the long time taken for many cancers to become clinically apparent, research, especially prospective research, is particularly difficult in these cases. A fifteen- to twenty-year prospective follow-up of a group of medical students, however, showed that those who later developed cancers were more likely to have reported a lack of closeness, as children, to their parents. This feature was also noted in those hospitalized for mental illness, or who committed suicide, but was not reported by those who became hypertensive or developed heart disease. Other research has shown that malignant melanoma patients showing high psychological distress, and breast cancer patients with high levels of hostility tend to live longer than sufferers without these characteristics. The apparent contradiction between these findings may be resolved by recognizing that the emotional change in the latter groups was most likely a result of having the disease.

Recognizing that factors such as these might be important in disease processes does not, of course, of itself necessarily contribute to the prevention or treatment of the diseases. It is not clear at the moment, for example, whether or not the Type A person can be changed, nor if changing his or her behaviour, or teaching people not to conceal anger, would have the effect of lowering their chances of later developing the disease. It must also be recognized that these factors are only contributors in the multifactorial causation of disease. Relatively few Type A persons develop heart disease and others also develop the disease, just as not all smokers and some nonsmokers develop lung cancer.

It is of great interest to consider the possible mechanisms by which stress contributes to illness, and the psychological factors that might protect individuals from such adverse effects. We have already looked briefly at hormonal and central effects of stress in this and earlier sections. One route that we have not yet considered is that stress might influence disease processes and susceptibility by effects on the immune system. There is now considerable evidence that social factors such as isolation and crowding, as well as such physical stressors as restraint, noise and electric shock, increase the susceptibility of laboratory animals to infectious diseases. Furthermore, there is some evidence that stressors reduce the rejection of transplanted tissues in animals. Together, these facts suggest that stress involves suppression of the immune system, and direct measures of antibody responses have now demonstrated that this does occur. There is also evidence that the immune system is susceptible to influence by learning. How the immune system is influenced remains unclear. In part, it could be a result of hormonal changes, as it is known that several circulating hormones, particularly the adrenal corticosteroids, suppress the immune system. Recent research showing that lesions in the anterior hypothalamus can protect animals against normally lethal anaphylactic shock suggests hypothalamic control of the effects, perhaps via circulating hormones.

Clearly, stressors affect people in different ways, and a number of factors have been identified that modify these effects. These can be classed as **person factors** (including personality, personal resources such as motivation, beliefs, attitudes, past history, sociodemographic factors, genetic factors, and nongenetic biological factors such as physical condition); **environmental factors** (social supports, physical environment, social climate, cultural factors, and major stressors such as bereavement and economic upheaval); and **process factors** (cognitive appraisal of an event, and coping strategies used to react to or to negate the effects of an event). These last two are those incorporated in Lazarus's theory of emotion (see pages 445–6).

Lazarus and his colleagues (see Lazarus *et al.*, 1970) have demonstrated the role of appraisal in modifying the effects of stressors. In one study subjects were shown a stressful film (an Australian Aborigine subincision ritual, involving the cutting with a stone knife of the penis and scrotum of boys). Different soundtracks were added, intended to promote **intellectualization** (a detached, unemotional, anthropological commentary), **denial and reaction formation** (a commentary claiming the operation was not painful, and that the victims found the occasion a joyous one), or **trauma** (emphasizing the painfulness of the procedure). A fourth group of subjects saw the film without a soundtrack. Measures of heart rate and skin conductance showed that subjects responded with physiological indications of stress when viewing the operation scenes. Compared with the silent group, the trauma group showed greater response, and the other two groups showed a smaller response. These results show not only that appraisal can modify the physiological effects of stressors, but also that appraisal processes can be influenced by other sources of information.

Other evidence shows that the unprompted adoption of different coping strategies affects people's subjective and physiological response to various stressors, including laboratory-induced and chronic pain. It is also becoming apparent that people differ in coping style; that is, individuals adopt characteristic strategies for attempting to cope with stressors, and these are more or less effective for avoiding stress. A number of researchers are currently investigating **repression** as a response to stressors, and it is possible that this is related to the differential expressiveness of cancer victims noted earlier. Now that the importance of these factors in illness has been established, further research is clearly necessary to unravel genetic and learned, and personal and environmental contributions to the aetiology of disease.

Further reading

The nature of emotions and theories of emotion

Good general discussions are provided by:

SCHERER, K.R. and EKMAN, P., eds. (1984) *Approaches to Emotion*. Hillsdale, NJ: Erlbaum.

PLUTCHIK, R. (1980) *Emotion: a Psychoevolutionary Synthesis*. New York: Harper and Row.

Physiological arousal and emotion

The evidence for and against the physiological differentiability of emotions is discussed in the following (especially Chapters 7 and 8):

KEMPER, T.D. (1978) *A Social Interactional Theory of Emotions*. New York: Wiley.

Work on catecholamine assays is discussed in:

FRANKENHAEUSER, F. (1975) Experimental approaches to the study of catecholamines and emotion. In L. Levi, ed., *Emotions: Their Parameters and Measurement*. New York: Raven Press.

Almost all the available work on catecholamine infusion is reviewed in:

BREGGIN, P.R. (1964) The psychophysiology of anxiety, with a review of the literature concerning adrenaline. *Journal of Nervous and Mental Disease*, **139**, 558–68.

Biofeedback is discussed in:

YATES, A.J. (1980) *Biofeedback and the Modification of Behavior*. New York: Plenum.

Cognition and arousal

Schachter and Singer's experiments are discussed in detail by Kemper, *op. cit.*, and by:

MANSTEAD, A.S.R. and WAGNER, H.L. (1981) Arousal, cognition and emotion: an appraisal of two-factor theory. *Current Psychological Reviews*, **1**, 35–54.

For a comprehensive review of research on false autonomic feedback see:

LIEBHART, E.H. (1979) Information search and attribution: cognitive processes mediating the effect of false autonomic feedback. *European Journal of Social Psychology*, **9**, 19–37.

Misattribution and excitation transfer are reviewed by:

ZILLMANN, D. (1978) Attribution and misattribution of excitatory reactions. In J.H. Harvey, W. Ickes and R.F. Kidd, eds., *New Directions in Attribution Research*, Volume 2. Hillsdale, NJ: Erlbaum.

Zillmann also describes excitation transfer theory in the following book, which contains a number of other chapters relevant to the psychophysiology of emotion:

CACIOPPO, J.T. and PETTY, R.E., eds. (1983) *Social Psychophysiology: a Sourcebook*. New York: Guilford Press.

Facial expression and emotion

Plutchik, *op. cit.*, Chapters 7 and 8, discusses emotional expression from the evolutionary and comparative standpoints. The question of the universality of facial expressions is discussed in:

EKMAN, P., ed. (1972) *Darwin and Facial Expression: a Century of Research in Review*. New York: Academic Press.

A survey of studies of the development of emotion is provided in this collection of papers:

LEWIS, M. and ROSENBLUM, L.A., eds. (1978) *The Development of Affect*. New York: Plenum.

Bowlby provides an outline of attachment theory, and applies it to separation and bereavement:

BOWLBY, J. (1980) *Attachment and Loss*, Volume 3, *Loss: Sadness and Depression*. London: Hogarth Press.

For a comprehensive discussion of the area of nonverbal communication, see:

BUCK, R. (1983) *Emotion and Nonverbal Behavior: the Communication of Affect*. New York: Guilford Press.

Central mechanisms in emotion

The following two reviews survey the evidence supporting a catecholamine disorder explanation of affective illness (the first book also has other chapters of interest):

SCHILDKRAUT, J.J. (1978) The current status of the catecholamine hypothesis of affective disorders. In M.A. Lipton, A. DiMassio and K.F. Killan, eds., *Psychopharmacology: a Generation of Research in Progress*. New York: Raven Press.

ANISMAN, H. and ZACHARKO, R.M. (1982) Depression: the predisposing influence of stress. *Behavioral and Brain Sciences*, **5**, 89–137.

An account of research and theory relating anxiety to neural mechanisms is provided in:

GRAY, J.A. (1982) *The Neuropsychology of Anxiety: an Enquiry into the Functions of the Septal-hippocampal System*. Oxford: Oxford University Press.

The effects of emotion on cognition and health

The relation between emotion and cognition is the subject of the following collection of papers:

CLARK, M.S. and FISKE, S.T., eds. (1982) *Affect and Cognition*. Hillsdale, NJ: Erlbaum.

The following volume provides another analysis of the same area, with the emphasis on theory and on developmental studies.

IZARD C.E., KAGAN, J. and ZAJONC, R.B., eds. (1984) *Emotions, Cognition, and Behavior*. New York: Cambridge University Press.

The concept of stress is discussed by:

COX, T. (1978) *Stress*. London: Macmillan.

A discussion of psychosomatics is provided by:

CHRISTIE, M.J. and MELLETT, P.G. (1981) *Foundations of Psychosomatics*. London: Wiley.

A broad view of stress and health, bringing together reports from several discussion panels, is in:

ELLIOTT, G.R. and EISDORFER, C., eds. (1982) *Stress and Human Health*. New York: Springer.

The following work provides a more detailed view of the role of emotion in illness:

TEMOSHOK, L., VAN DYKE, C. and ZEGANS, L.S. (1983) *Emotions in Health and Illness*. New York: Grune and Stratton.

9. Thought and Language

Cultural determinants of language and thought 554

Boxes

Figures

Tables

9. Thought and Language

Introduction

THE NATURE OF THOUGHT

For thousands of years, thought, along with language, has been deemed to be man's highest and crowning achievement, distinguishing man from all other animal species. In attempting to understand the *nature* of thought, however, we are immediately confronted with a fundamental problem, namely, 'Are there any human mental activities which we would *not* class, in some form or other, as "thought"?' In other words, is there a unique set of processes in which we engage when thinking but not when, for example, attending, perceiving or memorizing?

Part of the answer to this puzzle depends, of course, on how 'thought' is defined. In an influential book Craik (1943) argued that the major function of thought is to create a model of reality through the use of internal symbols in much the same way that, in a formal fashion, a scientist may formulate a theory to account for the results of a particular set of experiments: he generates a hypothesis which he feels might explain or interpret certain kinds of experimental information available to him. This 'model' of the part of reality which is of interest to him can then be used, at least if the hypothesis is well specified, to predict possible new events, and will lead to certain kinds of further experimental activities. Craik argued that the defining characteristic of thought is this ability to predict events based upon some kind of internal mental model of the external world.

Now such a view of thought would apply equally well to descriptions of memory and perception, since in some sense all our rational mental activities involve the formulation of hypotheses and the making of inferences based upon them. For example, if you are trying to remember where you left your keys, the struggle to recall may obviously involve complex mental activity, requiring the reconstruction of where you might have been and generating likely hypotheses as to where, in general, keys may be left. Thus, while operations such as judgement, speculation, hypothesis generation and hypothesis testing and so on are all characteristic of thought, they are equally characteristic of other mental activities. In reality we do not perceive, remember and think as separate, unrelated and independent processes: perceiving and remembering are, at least in part, instances of problem-solving or rational thought as applied to particular classes of problems. The demarcation of psychology textbooks (including this one) into various 'topics' (perception, memory etc.) reflects a convenient didactic practice which should not obscure the fact that similar mental operations may well be involved in all cases.

There have been various attempts to classify thinking, and such typologies at least serve to give us the flavour of the dish even if the recipe does not always lead to productive science. Turner (1977), drawing on Bartlett (1958), distinguished five types of thinking: everyday; artistic; logical and mathematical; explanatory; productive. **Everyday thinking** is depicted as the somewhat formless activity that characterizes social situations when group consensus is more important than empirical evidence. Logical analysis is suspended in favour of social harmony. However loose this form of thought, it has the advantage of requiring minimal amounts of cognitive effort. It may also throw up ideas which can later be subjected to more rigorous analysis.

Artistic thinking lays great stress on the imagination and the ability to make the sort of intuitive leaps that lead to innovation in areas such as music, art and literature. This is not to say that such thinking is without structure since artistic composition is seldom totally improvisatory.

Logical and mathematical thinking is the highly analytic rigorous thinking typical of those engaged in formal logic. Piaget believed that the higher levels of thinking that children eventually attain can be described in terms of logicomathematical systems known as groups. He has tried to show, with limited success, that the patterns of thought used by children to discover principles such as that of conservation (see Box 9.2) correspond to mathematical groups (see pages 513–14).

Closely allied to logical thinking is **explanatory thinking**. This is the **hypothetico-deductive thinking** which is said to characterize scientific method in which hypotheses are proposed to explain phenomena, experiments are subsequently designed to test the hypothesis and conclusions are deduced on the basis of the test. Whether science is actually carried out in such a clear-cut manner is a matter of some dispute (e.g., Tweney, Doherty and Mynatt, 1980) but it can be regarded as an ideal towards which science strives.

Finally there is the category that Wertheimer, a pioneer of the study of reasoning, called **productive thinking**. This refers to the sort of insightful thought that goes beyond deduction to inference. It frequently requires that the problem-solver goes beyond his or her initial conceptualization and restructures the problem to reach a solution. Such thinking, sometimes termed **lateral thinking**, has been popularized in a series of books by De Bono (e.g., 1977).

In such a complex area, any typology is only one of a number that are possible. Piaget, as we shall see, has one based on age. A more popular tendency in cognitive psychology is to conflate the categories to produce the dichotomies that abound in behavioural science. Examples are **concrete versus abstract, convergent/ divergent, intuitive/analytic** and **explicit/implicit**.

THE NATURE OF LANGUAGE

On being asked to describe the nature of a car, one of four possible positions could be adopted. First, **comparatively**, we may contrast cars with other forms of transport, saying, for example, that cars are different from bicycles in that the former are self propelling while the latter are not. Second, **structurally**, a car may be described as having four wheels, an internal combustion engine connected to a gear box, etc. This blueprint of a car is thus a structural description of it. Third, and more **functionally** speaking, we may simply describe a car as a form of transport to get us from point A to point B. Fourth, **procedurally**, we may describe the way in which the vehicle is actually assembled, i.e., those processes which tend to be involved in making cars from blueprints (casting, welding etc.).

Such alternative ways of thinking about a form of transport are equally applicable to attempts to identify the nature of language. For example, Hockett (1960), in attempting to describe the unique characteristics of human languages, has listed several criteria which he believes distinguishes them from other forms of animal communication. These criteria include the facility of being able to refer **arbitrarily** to things in the world; to refer to things which are remote in time and space; and to combine symbols together to form **new meanings**. Hockett's **design features** of human language have been of some interest of late since they have provided a yardstick by which attempts to train chimpanzees to use a language can be evaluated (see pages 500–3).

Human languages principally make use of two levels of **structure**, **the word** and **the sentence**. The concepts for which a community has words is to some extent arbitrary, and words, in all probability, are learned individually. While the sentences that people use are also arbitrary (they can refer to anything), they simply could not be learned individually. Practically every sentence is unique and children could not learn how to produce and understand sentences by memorizing the sentences that they hear. For this reason it has been assumed that children in the course of 'language acquisition' are building some kind of grammatical machine in their minds. Thus **grammar** is simply a set of rules for producing acceptable sentences; these rules are not acquired consciously nor, once learned, are they available to introspection. This implicit syntactical knowledge that we possess, enabling us to produce acceptable sentences and to reject improper ones (such as 'they haved gone away' or 'they gone away have'), is called our linguistic **competence**. The language that we actually produce in speech, which may have various errors due to particular forms of cognitive failures, has been termed our linguistic **performance**.

Through the manifestation of language in speech we are able to express our thoughts and ideas to others and, equally, as listeners, we can attempt to reconstruct their thoughts or feelings. This **functional description** of language (it tells us what language might do) involves the content of what is said in a given utterance (the words and their relationships through the syntax expressing the ideas) and the intention of the speaker. Thus to ask a particular question phrases an area of ignorance to a listener but also implies an expectation upon the part of the speaker that he will receive some reply; to hear someone say, 'It's hot in here', is easy enough to understand as an English sentence, but whether the speaker's intention is merely to 'assert' or to seek reassurance for opening a window can only be made clear by nonlinguistic contextual factors (see Chapter 10 for an expansion of this argument).

The characteristics, structure and function of language do not, as already hinted, reveal the psychological processes by which sentences are spoken and understood; they do not tell us how our linguistic performance comes about. Thus, for example, we might be able to give a structural description of a particular sentence in terms of subject, verb, object etc., and to suggest what the intention was behind the utterance, but this description does not tell us what cognitive activities the speaker or the listener might have carried out while saying or understanding it. If we have a **plan** for a sentence, for example, there are several different processes which could 'fill in' the words in the sentence frame: they may be selected in a random order, in a sequential order, or in a 'structured' order (e.g., nouns first, then verbs). The construction of sentences from plans requires a set of cognitive procedures, and much psychological research in psycholinguistics has been concerned with developing descriptions of these language-related mental processes.

LANGUAGE AND THOUGHT

People the world over share identical types of processing capacities and, on the whole, have similar personal and social needs. Groups of speaking individuals need, for example, to refer to objects and actions in their environment, and thus certain kinds of linguistic units are reflections of the basic human need to communicate experience. The languages that we have may differ in their precise form, but the requirement to refer to objects is common to all languages; this communality among different languages, reflecting common human desires, aspirations and anxieties, has been called **linguistic universality**.

Of course particular cultures may to some extent differ in their needs through various accidents of environment and, consequently, the kinds of things for which people have words may differ from one linguistic community to another. For example, distinguishing various forms of rice may be relatively unimportant in Western technological cultures but may be much more important in other societies where rice is a staple diet. The number of rice-related terms may therefore be greater in the latter community than in the former. These linguistic differences, which are a direct reflection of cultural differences, have been termed **linguistic relativity**.

Rather than words' merely reflecting patterns of thought and interest within a given society (as common sense might argue), at its most extreme form the notion of linguistic relativity has led to the view that patterns of thought are actually shaped by the words a society has agreed to use. The linguist Whorf has been the most influential exponent of this particular idea, and Miller (1981) has recently expressed this speculation in a most elegant way:

> People who live in very different societies live in different worlds, not merely the same world with different labels attached to things. People cut up nature and think about it as they do, Whorf said, not because those categories and concepts are necessarily given in the same form to all men, but because all men are willing parties to an agreement to cut it up and think about it that way. Such an agreement is obligatory throughout the speech community and is codified in the patterns of that language. People in different cultures think differently, he said, because they are parties to different agreements. (pp. 98–9)

According to Whorf (1956), thought and language are not independent processes with the latter ultimately being the overt manifestation of the former, but our thinking about the world is only possible through the ways in which we reflect it in language. People who have a relatively extended or relatively restricted vocabulary obviously talk about things differently but, in addition, according to Whorf, they may actually *perceive* things differently.

The relationship between thought and language is not a problem which has been confined to the speculations of linguistics. We can examine their relationships empirically by various means, but especially by investigations of thinking processes in people whose linguistic ability is poor as a consequence of genetic, accidental or social conditions (see pages 547–56).

Biological basis of thought and language

THE EVOLUTION OF INTELLIGENCE AND LANGUAGE

In vertebrate evolution there appears to be a general increase in the size and complexity of the brain relative to the spinal cord, and it is generally assumed that this increase, especially in the cerebral cortex of mammals, is directly related to intelligence where this is defined in terms of increased complexity and modifiability of behaviour.

Speculations about the origins of language are manifold, but, given a threefold increase in brain volume from our hominid ancestors, one influential view has been that as a result of this increase in brain size, man's increasing intelligence reached such a level that language was simply *invented*. In other words, the human facility for language may not be a happy consequence of a single, or a series of, mutant gene or genes, but rather that, in our prehistory, we invented natural languages to talk to each other in much the same way that we have recently invented computer languages to talk to microprocessors.

While it is unlikely that the dramatic increase in brain size of the hominids during the evolution of homo sapiens has nothing to do with the ability to act intelligently or with making possible linguistic communication, changes in the *organization* of the brain of early ancestors of man may have been of even more importance. Control of speech production and comprehension in modern right-handed man is undertaken by the left hemisphere of the brain. Further, in adults, the organization of the left hemisphere is such that particular parts of it control quite specific aspects of linguistic functions. Our current understanding of the organization of language skills within the left hemisphere has come from investigations of the linguistic performance of aphasic patients (those people who have partially lost their ability to use language through brain damage).

BOX 9.1
Language and the brain

Figure 9.1 shows the parts of the left hemisphere of the brain which, when damaged, lead to difficulties in speech production and comprehension. These two areas have been called **Broca's area** and **Wernicke's area** respectively, after the neurologists who first reported an association between particular linguistic deficits and specific regions of the brain. Broca's aphasics speak in short phrase lengths, use few function words (such as prepositions), but have relatively good comprehension of language. Wernicke's aphasics, on the other hand, have very poor comprehension of language and, although their spontaneous speech is fluent and not agrammatic, it lacks 'content' words (nouns and verbs). Both these types of patient have difficulty in repeating back exactly what someone else has said, but a further group of aphasics, called **conduction aphasics**, may have no obvious speech production or comprehension deficits and may *only* have a deficit in repetition.

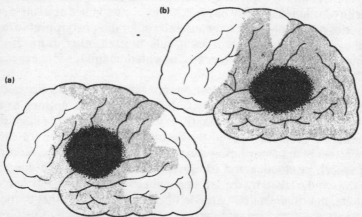

Figure 9.1 (a) Broca's area, (b) Wernicke's area. Based on the average of 13/14 aphasic patients. (After Kertesz, Lesk and McCabe, 1977)

Although right-hemisphere lesions may cause problems with speech intonation, they do not produce *linguistic* deficits in right-handed people. This does not mean that the right hemisphere has no linguistic skills, however, since studies of **split-brain** patients have shown that while stimuli mediated by the right hemisphere cannot be overtly *named*, the right hemisphere nevertheless shows good levels of comprehension of single words (see Zaidel, 1976; 1977). However, the right hemisphere is relatively poor at comprehension of sentences, and this suggests the right hemisphere possesses little syntactic ability, or, since sentences involve a number of words in sequence, the absence of a speech-related short-term memory in this hemisphere. In any event, the absence of obvious linguistic impairment after right damage suggests that, whatever language-related skills it may possess, it may simply duplicate some aspects of left-hemisphere functions. (See pages 125–6.)

In short, damage to the frontal cortex may lead to difficulties largely in the realm of speech production, while damage to the temporal cortex may cause problems with language comprehension (see Box 9.1).

Language abilities in adults are not therefore diffusely 'spread' throughout the left hemisphere but particular functions appear to be localized in specific regions of it. This fairly complex organization of linguistic functions, not to mention the presence of rather specialized auditory and vocal apparatus, is unlikely to have resulted from a single genetic mutation. Rather, it is probably the result of a gradual series of adaptations: linguistic processes must have evolved. Accordingly, we might well expect that there must have been intermediate forms of communication between hominids, but since there are no remnants of behaviour in the fossil record, what these might have been like will forever remain obscure. However, given this evolutionary perspective, some clues as to the possible percursors of modern languages might be obtained by studying communication in nonhuman animals.

LANGUAGE, THOUGHT AND COMMUNICATION IN ANIMALS

Although we think of human languages primarily in terms of their expression in speech, a language need not necessarily rely on the oral-aural vehicle as its medium. Messages can be conveyed from one person to another in almost any form so long as it is agreed between individuals what specific signs stand for and how they are to be combined.

In spite of the fact that it has recently been reported that some monkeys make several different vocal calls which appear to apply to particular predators (Seyfarth *et al.*, 1980), attempts to train a chimpanzee called Viki to speak human languages were largely unsuccessful – the chimp had a three-word vocabulary after extensive practice (see Hayes, 1951). However, it must not be concluded from this that chimps cannot express themselves in a language or understand one, since, if the animals' limited vocal apparatus is bypassed using some other form of expression, substantial linguistic abilities might be laid bare.

In recent years there have been several attempts to teach primates languages based upon **gestural communication**. In particular, great apes have been given the opportunity to acquire a sign language used by deaf people and the most famous of these is a chimp called Washoe (Gardner and Gardner, 1975). Washoe has been trained to make and respond to many individual gestural signs (the equivalent of individual spoken words) used by deaf people. The critical issue is whether Washoe *knows* that the signs that she uses refer to objects, actions and situations or does she merely *behave* in particular ways when specific stimuli are presented? In other words, does she employ words in the same way that humans do or does she behave merely in the manner of a superior circus animal who can perform various tricks on demand?

To the extent that Washoe (and other primate linguists) *generalize* from specific situations to other different but related ones, it has been argued that she extracts critical features of stimuli in order to form concepts and that these concepts are capable of being expressed in a symbolic (gestural) way. Further, it is claimed that the errors of generalization made by these chimps are similar to those made by young human children in the process of acquiring their native language. In short, it is argued that Washoe does not merely make fixed responses to fixed stimuli in the way that a dog does when it sits upon command, but, like humans, she makes arbitrary responses which are based upon symbolic representations of objects and situations.

In addition to the ability to use 'words' (through gesture), it is also contended that chimpanzees can use the other kind of structure employed by human languages, i.e., the use of syntactical rules to create sentences.

The original excitement engendered by these early reports of chimpanzee linguists is now becoming more critical. Apart from apes, many animals, including pigeons, dogs and horses, show generalization of responses to related stimuli and Terrace (e.g., Terrace *et al.*, 1979) has argued that the *simplest* explanation of the chimps' ability to use individual visual symbols is not that the function of these symbols is to identify things or to convey information but rather, since the animals are given food upon successful execution of a sign, that their function is to satisfy a demand that the ape uses the symbol to obtain some reward. While Terrace's argument about individual signs relies upon an appeal to parsimony, he argues that there is actually little *evidence*, first, that chimps can create sentences or, second, that they behave in such a way that an observer might believe that they take part in conversations.

At the level of grammar, Terrace (Terrace *et al.*, 1979) has shown that during a period when a chimpanzee (called Nim) doubled its 'vocabulary', there was little change in the length of his multisign utterances (his 'sentences') and, further, what three-sign utterances there were did not elaborate or qualify two-sign utterances in the way that the utterances of young children do. At the level of **discourse**, Terrace suggests that human conversations are rather like a game with participants taking turns to move a topic along; children soon become aware of this **turn-taking** in talking to others and act accordingly. Children's communication with adults can be classified as either **imitations** of adult speech (the child's utterance contains all the words of the adult's and nothing else) or **expansions** of adult conversation (the infant says some of the words used by the adult and some new ones). As children get older, the proportion of their utterances which are expansions of adult speech increases but no such trend has been noted over time for Nim. Indeed, in contrast to children, the bulk of Nim's communications with his trainer are imitative. Furthermore, Nim shows little sign of turn-taking in his 'conversations' with his trainer and, at least in comparison with very young children's conversations, frequently interrupts the utterances of the teacher.

Terrace therefore argues that although the sequences of signs produced by apes may sometimes superficially resemble the early speech of children there is as yet no unequivocal evidence that they have acquired the syntactic, semantic and conversational aspects of human languages.

Clearly it is now the case that the early convictions that apes could learn and use human-like languages are being called into question. An alternative way of thinking about the prerequisites of human languages is to ask if primates are actually intelligent enough to use language. Several comparisons have been made between the abilities of chimps and young children on tests of conceptual and other 'high-level' abilities. For example, Hayes and Nissen (1971) examined the performance of Viki on the ability to discriminate animate from inanimate objects, male from female people and complete versus incomplete pictures. The chimpanzee performed at about the same level as a three-and-a-half-year-old child on tasks such as these and also on other tasks involving rule learning. As Cohen (1977) puts it: 'There is plenty of evidence that primates possess many of the components of thinking such as memory, some forms of abstraction, concepts, the ability to learn and apply rules and to make judgements', and some of these components in apes may be comparable in level to those observed in young children who are at stages of development where relatively complex, if error-prone, linguistic skills are manifest. Conceivably, therefore, primates may have the necessary intellectual abilities to acquire languages.

However, the mechanisms by which adult apes carry out these complex activities may be different from the ways in which young humans execute them, in the same way that Terrace has argued that the 'linguistic' processes of chimpanzees and humans, although superficially similar, may actually be quite unrelated. Further, even if the mature apes mediate various tasks in cognitive ways similar to those of young children, it would not necessarily follow that primates have the requisite level of thinking processes to support linguistic communication: the *kinds* of intelligence which apes and humans have in common may not be appropriate for the mediation of language. Human beings may have special apparatus which equips them for language learning.

A LANGUAGE ACQUISITION DEVICE: BIOLOGICAL PERSPECTIVES

The functional differences between the two hemispheres in human adults are manifold and it is pertinent to ask at what point in time these differences become manifest. Are they present at birth or do they, as a result of natural (maturational) or nurtural factors, emerge as children grow up? In particular we might ask this question about the **lateralization** of linguistic functions (for most people) in the left hemisphere.

In adults a part of Wernicke's area has been found to be larger in size than the equivalent area in the right hemisphere and it has been speculated that this asymmetry may reflect the complex linguistic processes mediated by the left hemisphere. This anatomical asymmetry is present at birth and may therefore indicate that lateralization of linguistic functions is also present at birth. On the other hand, the relationship between anatomical and functional asymmetries is unclear and, further, although such asymmetries are not observed in various monkeys, they are found in chimps, gorillas and orang-utans in whom the evidence for linguistic facility is equivocal. We cannot currently be confident, therefore, as to how these anatomical asymmetries should be interpreted (see Springer and Deutsch, 1981, for references).

Some evidence for the existence of hemisphere specialization at birth comes from evoked potential studies (see Chapter 2). It has been shown that the magnitude of the electrical response of the brain elicited by speech sounds are of greater amplitude in the left hemisphere than in the right. Conversely, nonspeech sounds (such as a piano chord) produce greater evoked potentials in the right hemisphere. These effects are noted not only in adults but also, some claim (but controversially), in neonates. Clearly the baby does not *know* it is being played speech or music but it does appear to possess specific structures localized within the two hemispheres which might mediate such experiences throughout the rest of life (see Springer and Deutsch, 1981, for references).

Occasionally an operation called hemispherectomy is carried out where the whole of one hemisphere of the brain is removed. Removal of the left hemisphere early in life does *not* lead to profound linguistic impairments; on the contrary, on casual acquaintance such children when ten or so years old may not show any obvious language problems. This might be taken to suggest that lateralization of aspects of cognitive function is not present early in life but develops over time, and that initially both hemispheres are predisposed to mediate linguistic processes. However, it has recently been shown that children who have had their left hemisphere removed at birth do show, when formally tested, deficits in linguistic skill – especially in syntactical ability (Dennis and Whitaker, 1976). Thus, despite the brain's power to reorganize itself after damage to specific regions, this reorganization may be relatively restricted, and the absence of critical left-hemisphere structures may impede the acquisition of syntactic and perhaps other subtle linguistic skills.

Even if for most people aspects of language function are controlled from birth onwards by the left hemisphere, this does not mean that linguistic experience has no effect upon the extent of that control. Deaf people and people from impoverished linguistic backgrounds show reduced evidence of lateralization of language-related abilities in comparison to appropriate controls (see Springer and Deutsch, 1981). Indeed, a recent report about a tragic girl called Genie, who had suffered extreme linguistic deprivation from twenty months to thirteen and a half years, showed that she had *right*-hemisphere specialization for her woefully impaired language in spite of being unambiguously right-handed (Curtiss, 1977).

In all probability human infants come equipped with left-hemisphere systems which are specialized for the processing of linguistic information but the extent to which this left-hemisphere control subsequently becomes dominant will depend upon the quantity and quality of the linguistic input that it receives.

Concept development

A very influential approach to our understanding of the nature of **representation**, particularly in terms of what it is that has to be explained, is the **cognitive developmental approach**. This approach has a number of distinctive features, many of which derive from its foremost exponent, the Swiss genetic epistemologist Jean Piaget (1896–1980).

First, as the name implies, there is a belief that an effective way of discovering the nature and properties of complex phenomena such as thought, memory and language – in short, intelligence – is to study the **development** of these systems from their earliest appearance. The course of this development, and this is the *second* feature, proceeds by way of a series of **qualitative changes**, often referred to as **stages**. Cognitive development is not seen as a steady accretion of skills but as a series of rather sudden 'leaps'. Although one stage grows out of another and might be considered a reconstruction of earlier knowledge, the result is very much a new way of looking at the world. Stages are thus marked by a variety of common properties as revealed in, say, problem-solving, which differ qualitatively from earlier and later stages. A final property of stages is that they appear in an **invariant order**. The speed with which individuals pass through stages may vary but not the order.

A third feature of the cognitive developmental approach is that the child is seen as an **active contributor** to his or her cognitive growth, the very antithesis of a reinforcement model with its emphasis on reward and punishment and the shaping of a rather passive organism. The action-based, child-centred focus of this approach cannot be stressed too much and has led to such systems sometimes being termed **constructivist theories**. A fourth, related property of theories of this tradition is that they are **interactionist**. Despite the importance given to the child's own actions, these theories are not nativist in conception. Growth is considered to be dependent on the reciprocal interaction of persons and their environments. Development is a transactional process relying on feedback, thus the child influences the parents who influence the child who further affects the parents' reactions and so on.

Fifth, and last, change in the cognitive developmental approach is accounted for by a **conflict model**. All organisms capable of adapting to their environments are said to have a built-in propensity to achieve **equilibrium** within themselves and with their environments. This necessarily entails continually resolving problems and conflicts that arise because of a mismatch between how one is conceptualizing the world and how it actually is. Internal conflicts can also arise as, for instance, when one's understanding of a problem or body of knowledge is incomplete.

Following this outline of the principal features of cognitive developmental theory some additional points about Piaget's influential approach need to be made. First, we should be clear about Piaget's position on intelligence and the nature-nurture controversy. His view is an unorthodox one, namely that there are two sorts of heredity, specific and general. **Specific heredity** determines our physical structure including the way in which we perceive the world. For example, the make-up of the human eye limits us to seeing certain wavelengths. **General heredity**, in contrast, enables us to overcome the limitations of specific heredity. It refers to an inherited mode of intellectual functioning, that is, a particular way of interacting with the environment. This means that intelligence is seen as evolving in the course of development, ultimately allowing us to conceptualize what wavelengths outside the visual spectrum are like and, in all sorts of ways, speculate about things beyond our immediate sensory experience. The significant point about general heredity is that because it is inherited, and not acquired, this mode of functioning (the way development occurs) remains constant throughout life.

Piaget's early training was in biology and this was primarily responsible for him seeing development as a process of **adaptation** depending on the twin components of **assimilation** and **accommodation**. New knowledge is acquired by assimilating novel information to existing structures – that is, making sense of it according to the knowledge one has already – and at the same time accommodating to the demands of the new experience. In this way existing structures are modified. An example may help. Much, if not all, of the material in this book will be new to you. But you are able to make sense of it by calling on your existing knowledge in the general area of the biological and social sciences as well as your personal experience of human behaviour. At the same time, because there are new concepts and terms to be acquired, you must make concessions to them and adapt some of your existing structures in order to advance your knowledge base.

Having said this, has Piaget explained cognitive development or merely offered a description of what might happen? Perhaps it is fair to say that he is attempting an explanation as much as information-processing theorists have explained similar phenomena (see page 318). An associated issue is that of motivation which is seen as an **intrinsic drive** to achieve cognitive competence. This is expressed in terms of the mastery of particular systems such as number, space and time which are endeavouring to attain a state of equilibrium such that our understanding of these concepts is internally consistent. Since it is virtually impossible to achieve a state of total mastery in any cognitive domain, the system never reaches equilibrium but remains instead in the state of **equilibration**. This is Piaget's motivational term signifying the active desire of higher organisms to adapt to their environment and is not unlike other cybernetic notions of self-regulating systems dependent on feedback.

STAGES OF CONCEPT DEVELOPMENT

There are four main stages in the development of thought: sensorimotor, preoperational, concrete operations and formal operations. There are also dozens of intermediate stages related to particular concepts such as space, causality, chance, and even dreams and morality. Although a child may be referred to as being in, say, the preoperational stage of thinking, strictly speaking the area of conceptual behaviour under consideration should be specified since the child may be at different stages in different tasks.

Sensorimotor intelligence. Piaget has been instrumental in making psychologists reconsider the significance of infancy as a period of human development. Rather in the way workers in the field of language development came to see that the period before speech was relevant to an understanding of language acquisition, so Piaget has demonstrated that thought has its roots in the sensorimotor patterns of nonthinking infants. The sensorimotor stage is of interest as the period in which the highest level of intelligence possible without symbolic processes is achieved. But for Piaget it is much more than this since he believes that the structures used by the child in dealing with the world during this period are subsequently internalized to become covert actions in the mind, which he calls **operations**. An evaluation of this claim requires that one follows through the course of a particular concept, such as the **object concept**, to see how representation at one stage grows out of the earlier stage.

The object concept refers to the discovery that infants are not equipped at birth with the capacity to believe in the existence of objects independent of their perceptual *contact* with objects. Thus, if a six-month-old child is playing with a toy brick and that brick is covered with a cloth or inverted cup, the child will react as though the object no longer exists; that is, no attempt will be made to retrieve the brick. Only at about eight months does the child demonstrate representation of the object independent of its being in view so that a hidden toy can be regained. But even with this accomplishment the child is very far from having a mature conception of objects. For instance, if an object is hidden at point A on a number of occasions, the child will have no difficulty in retrieving it, certainly by twelve months of age. But if, subsequently, the object is hidden at point B, making no attempt to disguise the fact from the subject, the infant will continue to search at point A however obvious the actual location of the object (see Figure 9.2). Even when this knowledge is established, the child can still be fooled by **invisible displacements**. An object taken from the child and concealed in the closed fist which then moves to the adult's pocket will puzzle the fifteen-month-old child. If the hand is removed from the pocket without the object, the child cannot make the inference that the object must therefore be in the pocket. It takes between eighteen months and two years to master these various transformations so that we can say that the child has constructed the concept of the object.

This rudimentary account of one of Piaget's most fascinating discoveries (Piaget, 1954) ignores the large amount of work that enriches the original description (e.g., Bower, 1982). We now know that the manner in which objects disappear critically affects the infant's response and that the object concept is not simply about disappearing objects but their spatial and temporal relationship to

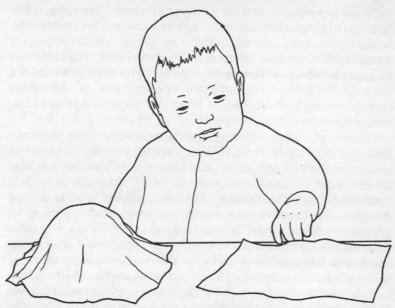

Figure 9.2 The child who has not achieved stage IV of Piaget's object concept thinks that an object that has been hidden at one point on a number of occasions will always be found there. Even though the object is large and the child has seen it hidden in the new location, he will still go to the old hiding place and show surprise at not finding the object.

context in general (see Chapter 3). Moreover, it is important to be clear that for Piaget an understanding of intelligence cannot be gained from simply looking at maturational components and environmental influences since the mind of the child itself mediates both these factors and directly affects the process of development.

Preoperational thought. The ability to represent an object or event which is not present depends on the existence of signifiers or symbols, and this, of course, is what this chapter is about. But rather than confining representation to thought and language, Piaget prefers a broader notion which he terms the **semiotic function.** This comprises imagery, symbolic play, drawing and gesture as well as language. The semiotic function starts to emerge towards the end of the sensorimotor period during the second year; forms such as **role-playing** and **pretending** are early examples. (The function of play is considered in Chapter 12.) Later comes **drawing**, which Piaget sees as a particularly good medium to investigate spatial skills and which has received fresh attention in recent years (e.g., Goodnow, 1977; Freeman, 1980). The mental **image**, for Piaget, is not a simple copy of perception but based on internalized imitation and therefore rooted in action, a claim that has some neurological support. Finally there is language which has the enormous advantage of being a social system allowing the communication of ideas. Nevertheless, because **language** is only one particular form of the semiotic function, and because it is also developmentally later and more complex than the individual symbols, it follows that thought precedes language. For this reason Piaget has always been an ardent opponent of the determinist position on language and thought (see Sinclair, 1969, for a vigorous defence of the Piagetian position). At the same time Piaget recognizes that language profoundly transforms thought by allowing more advanced conceptualization and more mobile abstraction.

Being able to think gives an organism clear advantages over one that cannot, which means that the preoperational child has this advantage over the sensorimotor infant. It is less easy to state succinctly what these advantages are, however. The critical gain is that thought can now be detached from action. This gives the organism *speed* in representing a long series of actions, *liberation* from the immediate situation and allows *simultaneous* representation of related elements. An analogy often used is that the preoperational child thinks like a cine film in contrast with the slide projector of the sensorimotor child.

During the preoperational period – from about two years until the early school years – the child's thought progresses from initial verbal schemes which, although primitive, permit the child to categorize the world on the basis of functional and perceptual attributes, through 'preconcepts' to a mode of conceptual thinking which, though superficially resembling that of the adult, does in fact contain limitations and contradictions. 'Preconcepts' can be seen in the child's early language which expresses notions which 'remain midway between the generality of the concept and the individuality of the elements composing it' (Piaget, 1950). Only when the child has conceptual structures that can handle the

BOX 9.2
The conservation problem

Adults are often surprised to learn that young children believe that the amount of orange juice in a glass changes when poured into a vessel of different proportions, and that the number of objects alters if they are moved closer together or further apart. The ability to recognize that quantities remain the same in spite of irrelevant transformations is the essence of the conservation problem. It was Piaget who demonstrated that the principle of **invariance** has a developmental history. The phenomenon has been investigated for such concepts as mass, number, length, area, weight and volume. It has its roots in object permanence, the first indication the child shows of conservation despite perceptual information to the contrary.

Conservation has been studied more widely than any other Piagetian discovery. This is probably because the behaviour is so dramatic, because it is easy to administer and because it has such important implications for reasoning and therefore education. The basic procedure is straightforward. Taking conservation of continuous amount as an example, the experimenter first establishes with the child that two balls of plasticine are equal in amount and then changes one of the balls by flattening it into a pancake shape or by dividing it into a number of smaller balls. The child is then asked if there is the same amount of plasticine in the ball as in the pancake or whether there is more in one than the other.

The preoperational child reveals himself to be a non-conserver by saying that the pancake has more in it than the ball and will point to extended area to justify his judgement. A conserver needs to judge the pieces as equivalent in *amount* and offer appropriate logical justifications. This latter requirement is essential for Piaget as is the child's ability to withstand challenges to her response. The whole point about conservation is that the child moves from a condition where her judgement is swayed by perceptual factors such as centration (see Figure 9.3) to logical considerations independent of the transformation. The operational child *knows* that changing the shape of the plasticine does not affect amount as long as nothing is added or subtracted, and offers logical arguments in support involving compensation, identity or reversibility (Piaget, 1952).

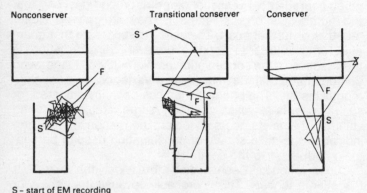

S – start of EM recording
F – finish of EM recording

Figure 9.3 The eye-movement scan paths of three subjects during a conservation-of-liquid task, showing the perceptual centring of the nonconserving child and the decentration of the conserver. (After O'Bryan and Boersma, 1971)

Although the conservation problem has been replicated on countless occasions, controversy surrounds the explanation for success and failure. Explanations in terms of attention, memory, language and social factors have been proposed and it is clear that the precise circumstances in which the task is administered affects performance. McGarrigle and Donaldson (1974), for instance, showed that the usual procedure directs the child's attention to the irrelevant transformation giving rise to the erroneous assumption that the experimenter *intends* a question about the length of a row of counters rather than number. When steps are taken to remove these misleading cues, performance improves significantly.

While the many hundreds of conservation studies generated by Piaget's work have clarified the nature of the problem and the skills needed to solve it, there is no reason to doubt Piaget's claim that the conceptual competence of the child as 'measured' by Piagetian structures changes radically between four and seven years and that this change can be studied very effectively using the conservation problem.

relations *all* and *some* does a mature system of classes become available.

Despite the advantage of the semiotic function, the pre-operational child is handicapped by a lack of flexibility in thought, by a tendency to focus on **states** rather than **transformations** and by **egocentrism** (See Chapter 10). These limitations are demonstrated in tasks such as **conservation** (see Box 9.2).

Concrete operations. During the primary school years the child becomes 'operational'. Operations are mental actions which have properties derived from Piaget's use of logico-mathematical models in understanding cognitive structures. These properties include reversibility, composition, associativity, identity, tautology and iteration (see Ginsberg and Opper, 1979, for a discussion). The advantage of operations is that the child has logical processes and is no longer at the mercy of his perceptions; he is **decentred**. This accounts for success in conservation (Box 9.2) and the ability to understand the relation between classes and nested hierarchies. In gaining ideas about number, for instance, the child comes to realize that the cardinal number, 7, depends on the operation of grouping seven objects together, while 7 as an ordinal number means that it must be seen as one in a sequence of natural numbers between 6 and 8. The child must know where to place it and why, and what its relation is to other numbers.

Piaget's faith in the relevance of certain logico-mathematical structures such as groups and lattices to represent human thought is by no means widely shared. They may be considered useful insofar as they model the actual organization and process of cognition in middle and later childhood. They constitute ideal patterns which the living operational systems in the subject closely approximate. They may be said to give us a useful image of how the cognizer might be organized just as models of artificial intelligence attempt to do (see page 521).

Formal operations. In this final stage abstract thought emerges with complete decentring and **reversibility**. The subject can be guided by the form of an argument or situation and ignore the content if so wished. Unlike the concrete operational child, she is not confined to the concrete or real, she may consider hypotheses that may or may not be true, that is, hypothetico-deductive reasoning. It has been suggested that adolescents' taste for theorizing and criticizing is largely due to their new-found ability for seeing that the way things are is not inevitable – things could be different (and better).

Experimental work at this stage requires subjects to carry out scientific investigations (or solve purely verbal problems), seeing to what extent they are able to hold some variables constant while varying others, and observing whether or not they can do this in a systematic manner, testing and discarding hypotheses when neces-

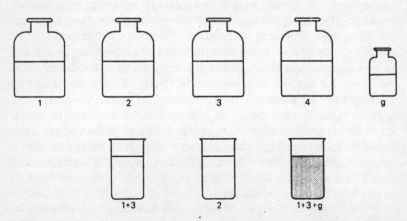

Figure 9.4 Materials for experiment on combinatory operation. (After Inhelder and Piaget, 1958)

sary. Take, for example, the task illustrated in Figure 9.4. The subject sees four flasks, all with a similar amount of colourless liquid. Each flask, in fact, contains a different chemical solution. A fifth flask contains an indicator. The subject is then shown two glasses which also hold colourless solutions. The indicator is added to both glasses, one of which turns yellow. The subject's task is to reproduce the colour using all or any of the five flasks. What is interesting, of course, is not so much obtaining the correct answer (which could happen by chance) as the method employed. It is the extent to which the child demonstrates the properties of formal operational thinking that interests the Genevan investigators. Do the children operate like young scientists or is it unsystematic trial and error?

EVALUATING PIAGET'S THEORY

In this brief overview of Piaget's theory little critical comment has been included. This is not because the theory is without fault but because there are dangers in damning a theory before it has been assimilated. The danger is particularly acute in this case since Piaget's theory is complex, difficult and alien to the mainstream of Anglo-American empiricist psychology. Indeed, there are undoubtedly those who would welcome any excuse to 'leave Piaget out of the reckoning'. This would be a grave mistake for at least two reasons. First, Piaget has provided an unrivalled account of the growth of children's thinking in fascinating detail using ingenious experimentation in a wide variety of domains; that is, the empirical work *is* important in itself. Second, Piaget's is the only attempt to provide a description of the whole intellectual system as it unfolds. It is a psychological theory on the grand scale that provides a powerful and effective counterargument to the behaviourist vision of child development by focusing on the constructive nature of cognitive growth and on the consistency of behaviour when interpreted through underlying structures.

For this reason piecemeal refutations of particular Piagetian experiments need not cast doubt on the wider theory and may, in fact, have little to say about Piaget's account of cognitive growth. Critiques which evoke respect are those based on a profound acquaintance with the theory, and examples which warrant serious consideration are Bryant (1974), Donaldson (1978) and Flavell (1977). Undoubtedly Piaget has underestimated the role of context and content on performance, and the significance of the linguistic and social dimension has also been undervalued (see Chapter 10). It is important that these shortcomings are recognized and, if possible, remedied. In the meantime one can confidently encourage newcomers to psychology to acquaint themselves with Piaget's theory. It will not be time wasted.

THE SOVIET VIEW

Another European psychologist celebrated for his work with children is the Russian Lev Vygotsky (1896–1934). His best-known work, *Thought and Language*, is full of sharp insights and challenging ideas, if thin on empirical data. His description of conceptual growth is closely related to Piaget's, both theorists giving a central role to the child herself as an active rather than reactive agent. They shared an interest in the development of scientific concepts and both charted concept development as taking place on roughly the same time-scale, true concepts (or operations) not appearing until about thirteen years. Both also emphasized cognitive development as an adaptive process and employed similar methods of careful observation of naturalistic performance, drawing inferences about underlying thought processes.

The similarities between these major figures tend to be ignored in contemporary accounts in favour of the differences. The main difference is that Vygotsky gave language and, indeed, culture, a central role in the development of thought. For this reason he has also been influential in education via American disciples such as Bruner and Cole. Vygotsky saw the child's habit of talking to himself as a vital component of intellectual planning and growth. For him it was language that was eventually internalized to become thought, rather than the actions preferred by Piaget.

Vygotsky's best-known pupil is Alexander Luria who has made a major contribution to our understanding of brain function. Luria also demonstrated the **regulative function** of language in cognition in a series of fascinating studies (Luria, 1961). He traced the child's facility in regulating her actions through language in a simple task requiring a variable motor response to different coloured lights. The findings, which have not gone unchallenged (Miller *et al.*, 1970), are that speech by an adult can initially serve as an instigator but not inhibitor of action. Later the child will inhibit a response when asked to, but it is not until about five years that the child is able to tell herself out loud what to do and what not to do. Eventually the action can be undertaken without overt language when, it is assumed, speech has been internalized to become thought. As a theory of thought this is undoubtedly too simplistic, even granting the inadequate account given here. Cognitive capacities apart from language are also developing in this period, and all are affecting the child's ability to respond to instructions (see Flavell, 1977).

Vygotsky once defined intelligence as the ability to benefit from instruction, and his ideas about the role of culture in thinking have become increasingly influential in the area known as **social cognition**. In *Mind and Society* the **zone of proximal development** is introduced; this refers to the additional ability a child can show when given help on a problem. Traditional methods of testing intelligence leave the testee to solve puzzles and answer questions unaided. Vygotsky's argument, which deserves a more extended treatment, is that we are reared as dependent members of a culture and that knowledge is garnered with the active assistance of concerned members of the culture, notably parents and teachers. It makes sense, therefore, to examine the additional capacity a child can show when given the normal prompting of an adult in tasks testing intellect.

The contemporary importance of Vygotsky's contribution is not so much his rather 'heavy' linguistic determinism but the attention he has drawn to social factors in the working of the mind. Along with another theorist of the 1930s, G. H. Mead, he is exerting considerable influence on developmental and educational psychologists of the present time (see, for example, Cole and Scribner, 1974; Light, 1979).

THOUGHT AS CONCEPT FORMATION

Concepts are the very stuff of thought. They allow us to think in terms of categories, such as 'books', rather than any particular book. A concept depends on a process of abstraction, therefore, in which the common properties of a class are determined as making up the underlying concept. 'Book' is in fact a complex concept despite books' ubiquity. For instance, they consist of printed matter, but then so do newspapers. They have stiff, heavy covers but paperbacks do not, and yet they are undoubtedly books. In formal terms the criteria are difficult to pinpoint and for this reason concept attainment tasks have generally used special test material in which variables like size, number, colour and goemetric form can be operationally defined. The subject may be given a sorting or matching task during which time the concept must be derived. The assumption underpinning these types of experiments is that the common element or elements *are* the concept.

Work of this nature (e.g., Bourne, 1966; Kendler and Kendler, 1962) has been criticized on a number of counts. One danger is that of trying to define concept too explicitly. Concepts, like other aspects of thought, resist being pinned down. They are fuzzy, loose assemblies rather than sharp, tight entities. For this reason the nearest we can probably get to them is to talk of **prototypes** or typical exemplars rather than exhaustive definitions. The concept 'dog', for instance, might bring to mind a terrier but not an Irish wolf hound. Terrier, or something like it, would be the prototype for the concept. This approach to the study of thought has yielded some promising research (e.g., Rosch, 1973).

Another criticism of the concept formation approach is that these tasks tell us nothing about the way in which we acquire and manipulate concepts in everyday life. This partly relates to the explicit/implicit distinction. Many psychological experiments have a problem-solving character to them in which the subject calls on his deductive powers to try to discover the solution that is there to be found. But there is evidence to suggest that we do not naturally acquire concepts in this way. The studies described in Box 9.3 show how the content or context of the task makes a considerable difference to performance despite the formal demands being the same. There are really two points involved here. Much of our conceptual thinking is not acquired by the logical processes investigated in concept attainment tasks. As Wason and Johnson-Laird (1977) put it, it is acquired either 'willy-nilly', that is, implicitly, or by verbal definition. Accordingly, and this is the second point, implicitly acquired associations are aroused by materials used in tasks. These can work to the advantage of the subject, as in Johnson-Laird and Legrenzi's task (see Box 9.3), or they can impede propositional thinking which demands attention to the form of the argument rather than the content.

BOX 9.3
Reasoning

The above diagram represents one side of four cards each of which has a letter on one side and a figure on the other. You are given the following information: if a card has a vowel on one side, then it has an even number on the other side. Your task is to say which of the cards needs to be turned over to find out whether the information is accurate. The most common answers to this problem tend to be 'A and 4' or 'only A', and both are wrong. The right answer is 'A and 7' since if odd numbers and vowels were to co-occur then the information would be false but otherwise it would be true.

In a series of studies investigating this sort of problem, Wason and Johnson-Laird (e.g., 1970) have found that even highly intelligent subjects have problems with this task, very few getting the answer right spontaneously. One reason for errors is the illegitimate assumption that if vowels imply even numbers then even numbers imply vowels. But this proposition is not contained in the rule. Such problems are the staple diet of logicians, and these research findings would seem to show that we do not reason logically despite the claims of theories such as Piaget's.

Wason and Johnson-Laird have also presented their problem in a different guise (see Johnson-Laird *et al.,* 1972). On this occasion the subjects were asked to imagine they were postal workers engaged in letter-sorting and to determine whether or not the following rule had been violated: if a letter is sealed then it has a 5p stamp on it.

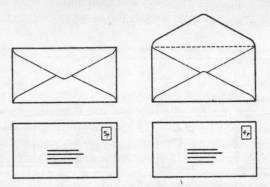

The subjects, when presented with the problem as illustrated, were asked to say which envelopes had to be turned over to ascertain the validity of the rule. In this situation twenty-two out of twenty-four subjects made the correct selection while in the 'control' task, which corresponded to the original abstract problem, only seven of twenty-four subjects was correct. What is going on? Since both tasks are tapping the same logical structure, it seems that introducing an element of realism into the task improves performance dramatically. The subjects' everyday experience is apparently relevant to problem-solving, a point since conceded by Piaget (1972).

It is not only that relating a problem to concrete experience greatly enhances performance, but that even test-sophisticated subjects find it difficult to treat propositions in logical tasks in a formal manner since logical validity has no intrinsic utility in real life. Experience, therefore, is an ever-present intruder in the laboratory, causing subjects to change, reject, overlook or even insert premises which do not correspond to the premises given. One explanation for the facilitating effect which 'realistic' problems seem to have on performance is that we can use what Tversky and Kahneman (1973) called **availability heuristics** based on learned associations which serve to cue the subjects' response. While these heuristics are adaptive in everyday situations, they can lead to error in formal tasks. (See Pollard, 1982, for a recent discussion of this issue; and page 639 below.)

Thus many tasks which purport to measure thinking capacity are stacked against the subject because they impose a method of thinking which may be both alien and inappropriate. At the same time it is impossible to eliminate the knowledge and modes of thinking which the subject brings to the task and which inevitably affect performance. This might not matter if our aim were only to investigate logical thinking, but those operating in this field have made broader claims than this. Nevertheless, it is widely held that because thought aspires to an abstract hypothetico-deductive form, since this is the final stage of Piaget's theory of intellectual development and it is the mode that has been responsible for most scientific advance, the focus is fully justified. (Ironically, Piaget, when asked how much of his time was spent in the formal operational mode of thinking, replied that it was 'for only a small part of the day – the rest of the time I am dealing with empirical trial and error' [Tanner and Inhelder, 1960, p. 126].) To some extent this is the view of Neisser (1976b) who, while being a leading critic of the orthodox approach which he says 'can only treat intellectual life as a series of puzzles, not as a sustained encounter with reality' (Neisser, 1976b, p. 144), nevertheless concludes that the enormity of the task may make it 'prudent to settle for the lesser problem'.

COGNITIVE DEVELOPMENT AND ARTIFICIAL INTELLIGENCE

The essential feature of the artificial intelligence (AI) approach to thought and language is that it uses computer programs to investigate the thought processes and knowledge structures used by intelligent information-processing systems whether they be human or machine. AI has captured the imagination of many cognitive psychologists because it seems to provide a means of formalizing the powerful concepts employed in theories of cognition, just as, in an earlier era, psychologists attempted to formulate the laws of learning in mathematical models (see Chapter 5).

Like Chomsky's theory of transformational grammar (see page 524), AI uses a **generative system** in which it is possible to create infinite power from a finite set of rules. A number of features of AI made it particularly attractive to Piaget. Though he, personally, never worked with such models, others have, and we will briefly mention two pieces of work. Before doing this, it will be useful to examine the appeal of AI for Piaget.

Piaget saw AI as providing the formalism for which he was always searching and he recognized that programs were closer to the structuralism which he espoused than the mathematical models which he had employed. AI models possess the active self-regulating properties of Piagetian structures which can 'construct, analyse, compare, select and otherwise manipulate varied information in increasingly adequate (equilibrated) ways' (Boden, 1979, p. 134). Computers tend to imply counting but it is, on the contrary, the qualitative rather than quantitative features of programs that are significant, for it is these that allow the flexible integration and transformation of information that is denied strictly quantitative procedures (see Boden, 1977, for a comprehensive account of this area).

One especially imaginative use of Piagetian theory in an AI context is the work of Papert (1980). In a specially created environment at the Massachusetts Institute of Technology in Boston, Papert has been teaching young children how to program robots which he calls 'turtles'. The turtles will draw pictures in response to the child's instructions – any mistakes it makes are due, of course, to the 'bugs' or errors in the programs. The special programming language, LOGO, which Papert has developed, allows the children to acquire mathematical concepts as a result of the self-correcting procedures which they use in their work with the turtle. Papert sees this as conforming to the essential features of Piaget's equilibration model with its emphasis on autonomy rather than the more imposed procedures favoured by some theories of instruction.

Work by Young (1976) has concentrated on one particular Piagetian operation, namely **seriation**. According to Piaget, the ability to order objects in terms of size, length, weight or whatever develops by way of a series of stages. By breaking the task down into its components and writing programs to specify these procedures, Young has demonstrated that his programs not only correspond to the strategies that children use but cast doubt on the stage-related account offered by Piaget. Young's procedures are, in essence, condition-action pairs in which a decision is first made as to what is the next step in the sequence and then the action appropriate to the achievement of that step is specified. The importance of Young's approach is not so much his refutation of Piaget's account (which is controversial and enters the competence-performance debate) but rather the advantages it offers in terms of clarifying the subsystems at work within the overall operation.

Language development

DO WE LEARN LANGUAGE?

The nature-nurture controversy has been prominent in the study of language development. There is a common sense view which tells us that children *learn* language from those around them. The child raised in Wigan speaks English with a Lancashire dialect and not French with a Marseilles dialect. A more sophisticated learning account would point to the role of constructs like association, imitation and reinforcement. When a child pairs a particular sound, 'ball', with a small, round object that can be bounced or rolled across the floor, he has learned, by **association**, the meaning of the word ball. Being able to produce the sound 'ball' depends on the process of **imitation** – the child copies what he hears others say. Progress in language depends on **reinforcement**; parents reward their children ('Clever girl, that's right') for appropriate utterances, encouraging them to string words together to form sentences.

This common sense view of language is epitomized in both the title and content of B. F. Skinner's book *Verbal Behavior*, published in 1957. The principles that account for (laboratory) animal learning were believed also to explain language acquisition. Skinner's position received a devastating attack at the hands of the linguist Noam Chomsky in a review of Skinner's book which proved to be one of the rallying cries for the cognitive, and ultimately rationalist, revolution in psychology. Chomsky showed how a theory restricted to habits and associations was inadequate to explain the acquisition of a system as complex as language, such that by the age of five, sentences never previously heard before can be generated.

Before explaining why the learning theory account of language came to be rejected, it is important to understand the fundamentally new direction which Chomsky gave to the study of language development. As a linguist he was interested in the structure of language, particularly the collection of rules which enable us to speak a language grammatically. This he characterized as **competence** in a language. In contrast, behaviourists such as Skinner restrict their concern to language as it is used – the level of **performance**. Linguistic competence refers to the ability of the language-user to apply the rules of his language in order to associate sounds and meanings. Psycholinguists have tended to study competence – the knowledge a person needs to speak a language adequately – while basing their studies on inferences from performance – the language that you and I speak which may fall a long way short of competence.

Chomsky's concern with underlying structure is not unlike Piaget's in his approach to thought and, like Piaget's theory, the conceptualization had some basis in empirical observation. This caused Chomsky to postulate two levels of structure: **surface structure**, the arrangements of words as they actually appear in speech; and **deep structure**, a more fundamental form (reflecting competence) from which surface forms could be derived. To take a simple example, 'Romeo loves Juliet' is a deep structure from which the following surface forms can be derived: 'Juliet is loved by Romeo', 'It is Juliet that Romeo loves', 'Does Romeo love Juliet?' and so on. Rather than believing that the child acquires these surface forms one at a time, it is more parsimonious to assume, argues Chomsky, that they first acquire the deep structure and subsequently discover rules for turning this into the various spoken types. These rules Chomsky calls **transformational rules**, and **transformational grammar** provides a system of rules which will *generate* sentences to show that each sentence has a deep and surface structure and to show the relationship between the two. Deep structure is said to be primary and to determine meaning. It is said to be something that all languages have in common, that is, a language **universal**. If such a universal did not exist, it is argued, we would be unable to translate languages from one to another. What differs between languages are the generative rules, which are also the features that the child, and indeed the psychologist who is studying child language, needs to discover. Thus much research in the 1960s was directed to ascertaining the substance and reality of transformational grammar, albeit with mixed success (see Greene, 1972, for a review).

THE PSYCHOLINGUISTIC APPROACH

Whatever the ultimate fate of transformational grammar and the competence-performance distinction, Chomsky's influence on the psychology of language will remain. This is not only because of his effective refutation of the behaviourist position and the rationalist alternative he offered (see below) but because he was primarily responsible for getting psychologists to consider child language from the point of view of the linguist. Chomsky's impact was timely since psychologists interested in language development had begun to show impatience with the normative studies (emphasizing milestones such as vocabulary growth) that had predominated hitherto and turned to asking questions about underlying knowledge.

If the linguist can be said to have *a* point of view, it is to describe languages in formal terms as **rule-governed systems**. When encountering exotic languages for the first time the linguist aims to write a grammar of the unknown language by collecting as large a corpus of the speech as possible, which means spending much time with speakers of the novel tongue and an interpreter. This is precisely the approach taken in a group of pioneering studies in the 1960s (Braine, 1963; Miller and Ervin, 1964; Brown and Fraser, 1963) when child language was viewed as a system in its own right rather than as an inferior version of adult language. The studies quoted are characterized by very small samples of subjects but very large corpora of data, collected longitudinally in the child's own home. From this data, with the help of the 'interpreter' (parent), the researcher determines the extent to which child language is a rule-governed system (see Box 9.4).

This research confirmed that language is not simply a question of acquiring words, or even sentences. Learning a vocabulary is only part of language acquisition – it is much more about acquiring a rule system which makes it possible to generate an infinite variety of sentences, many never heard before. In Brown's words, language learning is best described as a creative process. As in Piaget's theory, the child is given an active, constructive role. But to say that the child acquires construction rules, e.g., where to put the subject and object in relation to the verb, or how to form a question, is not to say the child does this explicitly. The young language learner cannot tell you the rules he or she uses, and neither, for the most part, can parents.

Although contemporary work cautions us to be much less confident about the role of parents in the business of language acquisition (see Chapter 10), there is general agreement that the child appears to extract from speech a set of construction rules rather than being explicitly taught them. The evidence for this is in the errors children produce which result in forms they have never heard adults produce. Thus, 'mans' (or 'mens') will be formed from the rule which states that to obtain the plural, add an 's' to the singular. As we know, this works for most words but not all. The example with which parents will be most familiar involves the past tense of verbs. The regular rule is to take the base form and add '-ed', as in 'wished' and 'jumped'. Young children, however, not unreasonably extend this rule to produce anomalies like 'comed', 'goed' and 'hurted'.

How, therefore, do children progress in their language? The limited evidence available (Brown, 1973) suggests that parents do not act as correcting agents in this matter (but see Robinson, 1981, for an alternative view). The disappearance of forms like 'sheeps' and 'hitted' seems to be due to children working out for themselves that new rules are required – presumably they are ready cognitively to take on more complexity – and they gradually recognize that these forms do not appear in the language they hear.

Parents *will* act as correcting agents when their children make semantic errors, as when they call a pear an apple, but it appears that they unconsciously translate sentences like 'Why the car won't go?' to 'Why won't the car go?' Brown (1973) also reports that experiments which provide the appropriate forms when the child makes grammatical errors are unsuccessful in eliciting a change in performance. In line with other evidence concerning **expansions** (children cannot be made to produce three-word utterances when they are at the two-word stage), it seems that children will only produce the new forms spontaneously. Parents' intuitions in this matter, therefore – if that is what they are – are adaptive.

A LANGUAGE ACQUISITION DEVICE: DEVELOPMENTAL PERSPECTIVES

If learning theory accounts of language acquisition are inadequate, what do psycholinguists offer as an alternative? There are three options available. One is a strongly **nativist** account proposed by Chomsky and taken up by McNeill and Lenneberg. A second possibility has been dubbed the **cognition hypothesis**, which essentially argues that language grows out of existing sensorimotor knowledge. The third account we might call the **functionalist** position which claims that language arises from a need to communicate and that early forms can be explained in terms of parent-child interaction. Although this third option has been very influential we will not take it up here since it forms part of the next chapter. It should be stressed, however, that although we distinguished three positions for the purposes of exposition, they are not necessarily mutually exclusive. Bruner (1975b) and Bates (1976), for instance, who are associated with the functionalist/pragmatic school, have considerable sympathy with the cognition perspective and have drawn attention to the sorts of cognitive precursors that are implicated in language development.

The nativist platform has two planks. One is the biological argument propounded by Lenneberg (1967) and resting on empirical work with animal populations as well as normal and handicapped children (see pages 497–504, above). The basic claim is that language is a species-specific capacity which follows its own natural history. The child can avail him or herself of that capacity as long as the environment provides a minimum of stimulation and opportunity and that development takes place during the **critical period** (before puberty) after which acquisition becomes progressively more difficult. The evidence for this claim comes from various quarters. Lenneberg looked at development in many societies, and with deaf and hearing mothers with normal children, and consistently found a strong correlation between motor milestones, such as sitting, standing, reaching, running etc., and language milestones such as babbling, one word, two words and so on (see Table 9.1). This correlation was far higher than that between language and age, a correlation lacking altogether for retarded children, for whom the high correlation between language and motor development is nevertheless also present. These findings suggest an important maturation component, and together with other evidence from twin studies and that related to brain function caused Lenneberg to conclude that language acquisition should be seen as much more like learning to walk than, say, learning to read.

More recent work on cerebral function and case studies like that of Genie (see page 555) require us to modify some of Lenneberg's claims (see Elliot, 1981, for a concise overview). Moreover, even an accurate account of the biological basis of language, should it ever be realized, can never be the whole story as far as our understanding of the growth and use of language is concerned. For that we need to consider also the cognitive and functional positions. But first, the other plank of the nativist platform.

The belief (Chomsky, 1965) that our species possesses an inbuilt **language acquisition device** (LAD) was offered as the only possible explanation of three 'facts' about language development. First, infants appear able to attend to speech elements rather than all the other noises in their environment. How do they do it? Second, the child acquires a highly complex system, which language assuredly is, in something less than four years, at a time when other intellectual accomplishments are relatively limited. How do the children become mature language-users by the time they start school? Third, how, out of the mass of speech they hear, much of it ungrammatical and imperfect, are children able to abstract enough to start speaking themselves? (See Box 10.1.)

What LAD might look like has been given most attention by McNeill (1970). Starting from Chomsky's transformational grammar, he has tried to show that syntactic development cannot be explained by learning theory principles such as association and reinforcement, let alone by random events. It fits better with

Table 9.1 Correlation of motor and language development

Age (years)	Motor milestones	Language milestones
0.5	Sits using hands for support; unilateral reaching	Cooing sounds change to babbling by introduction of consonantal sounds
1	Stands; walks when held by one hand	Syllabic reduplication; signs of understanding some words; applies some sounds regularly to signify persons or objects, that is, the first words
1.5	Prehension and release fully developed; gait propulsive; creeps downstairs backwards	Repertoire of 3 to 50 words not joined in phrases; trains of sounds and intonation patterns resembling discourse; good progress in understanding
2	Runs (with falls); walks stairs with one foot forward only	More than 50 words; two-word phrases most common; more interest in verbal communication; no more babbling
2.5	Jumps with both feet; stands on one foot for 1 second; builds tower of six cubes	Every day new words; utterances of three and more words; seems to understand almost everything said to him; still many grammatical deviations
3	Tiptoes 3 yards (2.7 metres); walks stairs with alternating feet; jumps 0.9 metre	Vocabulary of some 1000 words; about 80 per cent intelligibility; grammar of utterances close approximation to colloquial adult; syntactic mistakes fewer in variety, systematic, predictable
4.5	Jumps over rope; hops on one foot; walks on line	Language well established; grammatical anomalies restricted either to unusual constructions or to the more literate aspects of discourse

(From E.H. Lenneberg, On explaining language, *Science*, **164** [1969]) notions such as deep and surface structure and the rules that enable the speaker to get from one to another, permitting certain combinations and outlawing others. Allied to this are various grammatical intuitions we appear to have which enable us to generate (and recognize) grammatical utterances. A famous illustration of this is these two sentences:

> Colourless green ideas sleep furiously
> Furiously sleep green ideas colourless

Chomsky argues that although both these word sequences are meaningless and novel, we recognize the first as grammatical and the second as a jumble. This implicit knowledge of orderly English is postulated to be part of LAD.

Further support for the nativist position is supplied by the notion of **universals**. This is the claim that all languages (at least, that minority that have been studied) develop in basically similar ways. All languages, for example, seem to have basic distinctions such as subject and predicate, modifier and noun, verb and object. Having said that, it is difficult to see where this argument takes us. Are we to believe the child is innately equipped with the ability to distinguish verbs and objects? This idea is less fanciful than it sounds if we turn from focusing exclusively on language to looking at the broader knowledge structure of which language is a part. In doing this we move to a consideration of the cognition hypothesis.

BOX 9.4
Two types of child grammar

Although Chomsky's transformational grammar influenced investigators of child language in the early 1960s, there were at the time no prescribed procedures for obtaining generative grammars. Accordingly **distributional analysis**, an earlier technique based on the frequency of occurrence of words in child speech, was used. It was found that in two-word utterances, words fell into two groups. One group used terms such as 'more' and 'see' and occurred in either first or second position but rarely in both (e.g., 'more milk'; 'Daddy see'). Braine (1963) called this group of words **pivots** while the other group came to be known as the **open** class of words. The examples given below are from Braine's original corpus.

PIVOT   all gone, bye bye, big, more, pretty, my, see, night
            night, hi
·OPEN   boy, sock, boat, fan, milk, plane, shoe, vitamins, hot,
            Mummy, Daddy

In adult language these two classes closely correspond to function and content words, and Brown and colleagues, working at the same time as Braine, called his similar categories 'functors' and 'contentives'. A third team, Miller and Ervin, described their types as 'operators' and 'non-operators'. **Pivot grammars**, as the generic term came to be known, allowed three syntactic arrangements: pivot+open; open+pivot; open+open. It was the dominant account of child grammar in the 1960s.

Subsequently many limitations were exposed in pivot grammar (see Brown, 1973, for a detailed argument), chiefly to do with the failure to take account of underlying intentions (see text). The pivot grammar was too restricted a system to handle the richness that became apparent, even in two-word utterances, once context and meaning were incorporated. This ultimately led to a series of new grammars offered by workers such as Bloom, Schlesinger and Bowerman. These are often called **semantic relations grammars** and Brown offers a typical example drawn, in part, from the contributions of the above investigators.

Apart from the range of meanings covered by two-word utterances, the examples also illustrate that small children, like the senders of telegrams, are extremely economical in their speech. **Telegraphic speech**, as Brown called it, is notable for the absence of function words like articles, prepositions and conjunctions.

Table 9.2 **The first sentences in child speech**

Structural meaning	Form	Example
1. Nomination	that+N	that book
2. Notice	hi+N	hi belt
3. Recurrence	more+N	
	'nother+N	more milk
4. Nonexistence	allgone+N	
	no more+N	allgone rattle
5. Attributive	Adj+N	big train
6. Possessive	N+N	mommy lunch
7. Locative	N+N	sweater chair
8. Locative	V+N	walk street
9. Agent-action	N+V	Eve read
10. Agent-object	N+N	mommy sock
11. Action-object	V+N	put book
12. Conjunction	N+N	umbrella boot

(Adapted from R. Brown, *Psycholinguistics*. New York: Free Press, 1970, p. 220)

Although semantic relations grammar is a great advance on pivot grammar, it is not without critics. By no means all utterances can be accounted for by the system and even in Brown's original work, the number of utterances specified varied from 30 to 80 per cent. Workers in other languages have reported lower levels than Brown. One factor that seems to be accounting for these anomalies is the *prevalence* of the function words which Brown claimed were relatively infrequent. These are not easily accommodated by current versions of semantic relations grammars. However, no one has, as yet, produced an alternative to rival Brown's scheme – which has doubtless something to do with grammar-writing being unfashionable.

THE COGNITION HYPOTHESIS

The term cognition hypothesis, as applied to language development, was first used by Cromer (1974), who referred to it as the proposal that 'we are able to understand and productively to use particular linguistic structures only when our cognitive abilities enable us to do so' (Cromer, 1974, p. 246). This proposal stemmed from attempts to answer questions about the emergence of language and the recognition that speech did not appear out of a vacuum. The child who produces his first words has usually been developing in perceptual, cognitive and social terms for at least twelve months. The cognition hypothesis seeks to give weight to this fact by pointing to the cognitive accomplishments of the child before language starts. This has been done in general terms by Bruner (1975) and Macnamara (1972) and, more specifically (Brown, 1973), by tying sensorimotor schemas, as identified by Piaget, to particular linguistic constructions.

Schlesinger (1971), for example, traced language back to early cognitive development and said that LAD was unnecessary since early syntactics was essentially early semantics which, in turn, was early cognition. That is to say, we first get the sequence: agent (e.g., the child) – action (e.g., eats) – receiver of action (e.g., apple). Only later does it make sense to talk about subject – verb – object. Workers such as Brown (1973) have reported that an agent-action rule fits their data better than the usual transformational grammar categories. And Sinclair (1969), the leading Piagetian researcher into language acquisition, has said that sequences like agent-action are what would be predicted from patterns of sensorimotor intelligence (action schemas) in Piaget's theory.

The outcome of this is that while we may retain the ideas of deep structure and transformation, they are no longer the esoteric preserve of linguistics. They now have their roots in cognition. The source of deep structure is the logical structure of early thought, and transformations are ways of ordering, lexicalizing and expressing those thoughts.

To illustrate why a purely linguistic analysis is inadequate, consider the example of 'possession'. If we wanted to know if the child at the two-word stage had the possessive form in his repertoire, we would look for examples of apostrophe 's' in his speech, e.g. 'Jane's doll'. But we would not find them. Would this therefore mean that the child did not have this feature as yet? Both Bloom (1970) and Brown have shown that this is not the case. If utterances are examined in conjunction with their environmental and linguistic context (the so-called **method of rich interpretation**), then we see that the child will use utterances like 'Jane cup' and 'Jane chair' and be referring to possession.

The method of rich interpretation has opened up a field of research in language development which allows us to make judgements about children's probable semantic intentions. Although this procedure is not without difficulties (Brown, 1973), it has not only led to a more sophisticated account of syntactic growth (see Box 9.4), but has also been influential in the study of communication development (see Chapter 10).

How does the cognition hypothesis affect the status of LAD? One view is that of Bruner and Sherwood (1981) who claim that the cognitive processes available to the child prior to language are the foundation upon which language acquisition is constructed. These are given shape and direction by the child's own referential requirements and communication objectives together with the caregiver's desire to share the world of meaning with her child. This approach to language development will be taken up in the next chapter. For the moment we should note that it changes LAD's gender: LAD becomes what Bruner calls a Language Acquisition System (LAS) which involves not only cognitive precursors but a vital social and, indeed, teaching component.

An alternative viewpoint is that of Slobin. He was in the vanguard of the cognition hypothesis, offering a series of operating principles which children use in acquiring language, based on careful analysis of almost all the cross-linguistic data available at the time (Slobin, 1973). Examples of **information-processing devices** which have obvious utility are 'pay attention to the ends of words' and 'pay attention to the order of words'.

More recently Slobin (1979) has expressed doubts about the status of the cognition hypothesis. He concedes that a study of prelinguistic behaviour indicates the importance of structures of attention in adult-child interaction, giving rise to data on *functions* of language, such as referring and requesting, but not the *forms*. Slobin's contention is that once grammar appears (word order, inflections, etc.), 'a new sequence of development is set in motion . . . which occupies the several years *after* the achievement of sensorimotor intelligence'. Structure begins to be important once the child reaches the two-word stage, when we observe skills that are not simply transferred to the linguistic context. As Slobin (1979, p. 7) puts it:

> Perceptual skills of segmentation, combination, order and stress are involved, along with attention to foreground and background, agent and patient. But these skills are called into play in language-specific ways. This is what the transition to *language* is about. Linguistic expression requires a new organization of sensorimotor capacities. Language is not a direct mapping of thought or experience.

Slobin, in arguing for a return to an examination of language itself in order to discover *how* the structure is acquired, signals a new direction in the brief but tortuous history of developmental psycholinguistics.

BOX 9.5
Words and meaning

Words and meaning are clearly related but the direction of the relation is less clear. Common sense tells us that we hear or read sentences and put meanings to them. Macnamara (1972) queried this view by saying that rather than language being a clue to meaning, meaning is a clue to language. He made this claim in the context of language acquisition, implying that the child has a world of meanings before words are produced or even understood. The infant has been categorizing the environment and discovering, for instance, that cups are entities that hold liquid and may be drunk from, may be stood on saucers (but not the other way round) and have certain tactile and visual properties. Macnamara's argument essentially is that infants rely on contextual information and whatever conceptual knowledge they have obtained to determine, independent of language, the meaning which a speaker intends to convey to them. They then work out the relationship between meaning and language.

There is evidence to substantiate this claim. Clark (1973) looked at children's comprehension of the prepositions *in, on* and *under*. The children were asked to place small objects such as a toy mouse in, on or under larger objects such as boxes and tables. The pattern of performance showed that two-year-olds were operating according to **nonlinguistic rules** so that they would always place the smaller object *in* the larger object, whatever the instruction, if it was a container. If the large object was not a container but had a supporting surface then the small object was placed *on* it, again regardless of instruction. Even more dramatic than the language data were the results of a modelling task. When the children were asked simply to imitate an action carried out by the experimenter — for example, an object placed *beside* a glass or *under* a table — the children respectively placed the objects *in* the glass and *on* the table. Even in the absence of language, context is exerting a powerful influence on comprehension. Furthermore this finding is not confined to very young children. Donaldson and her colleagues (Donaldson, 1978) have shown that relational terms like *more* and *less*, *same* and *different*, and *all* and *some* are assigned meanings, well into the school years, that do not correspond to adult intentions.

Allied to the experimental work on function words are the well-known naturalistic studies which show that semantic development of concrete nouns proceeds by way of over-extensions. Many a mother has been embarrassed by her child referring to strange adult males as 'Daddy', and the early use of 'dog' to refer to all four-legged creatures is ubiquitous. An example familiar to one of the authors is a two-year-old who used the word 'bah' to refer initially to 'bath' and then generalized this quite quickly to water (in the sink), swimming pool, sea, pictures of water and, ultimately, the colour blue on a label. These sorts of observations tell us something about the criteria on which children assign meaning and, incidentally, create concepts.

Current research shows that the development of word meaning is an even more complex process than was thought. Extracting meaning from words involves a complex interplay between not only language and physical context but also features of the wider discourse, shared and unshared presuppositions and the relationship between the participants involved (see Chapter 10). While we can agree that meaning is in the final analysis a matter of interpretation and negotiation, we would be unwise to conclude that the meanings which children give to words correspond to adult convention. Recent research is important, however, in charting the manner in which the significance of various contextual, social and linguistic factors changes with age (see Carey, 1982, for a well-researched review). It is perhaps safe to say that with maturity the relationship between meaning and language that Macnamara identified reverses, but since, in practice, the two aspects are so complementary, making any claims for primacy is a risky enterprise.

Intelligence: individual differences in thinking skills

CONCEPTIONS OF INTELLIGENCE

Variations between individuals' abilities to think rationally and logically have traditionally been studied by assessing intellectual skills through tests of intelligence. That there are differences in the quality of thinking – efficient thought being equated with intelligence, and sloppy thinking with its absence – is intuitively incontrovertible. Unfortunately, however, there has been little, if any, formal agreement by psychologists about how intelligence or intelligent behaviour should be characterized, and Table 9.3 illustrates some of the variety of ways in which the term intelligence has been defined.

Definitions such as these raise two problems. First, some of them

Table 9.3 **The variety of ways in which psychologists have defined the term 'intelligence'.** (After Pyle, 1979)

Binet:	to judge well, to comprehend well, to reason well.
Spearman:	general intelligence which involves mainly the education of relations and correlates.
Terman:	the capacity to form concepts and to grasp their significance.
Vernon:	all-round thinking capacity or mental efficiency.
Burt:	innate, general, cognitive ability.
Heim:	intelligent activity consists in grasping the essentials in a situation and responding appropriately to them.
Wechsler:	the aggregate or global capacity of the individual to act purposefully, to think rationally and to deal effectively with the environment.
Piaget:	adaptation to the physical and social environment.

may simply be wrong; for example, level of thinking abilities need not be innately determined. Second, all are certainly so obscure and vague that it is difficult to see in which ways they could be directly translated into some observable technique that might evaluate the intelligence of a given person; in other words, there is a large gap between hypothesis and experiment. In addition to these two difficulties, conceptions of what constitutes intelligent behaviour are almost certainly culturally biased. For example, in Western intelligence tests the ability to 'abstract' is highly valued. Assessment of this skill typically involves 'categorization' tests including sorting numerous different objects into conceptual categories. However, an African tribe called the Kpelle, when asked to put together twenty objects, five taken from each of four categories such as food and tools, tended to sort into ten groups of two. Furthermore, the type of grouping and the reasons given would be termed extremely concrete, e.g., 'The knife goes with the orange because it cuts it.' In commenting upon this type of work Glick (1975) has noted that occasionally the Kpelle volunteered 'that a wise man would do things in the way this was done'. When the frustrated tester eventually asked, 'How would a fool do it?' he was given back the groupings in four categories exactly as was initially expected. It would be untrue to say that the Kpelle cannot work with abstractions (or that they are unintelligent). Rather their conceptions of intelligent behaviour are different from ours and, in contrast to schooled people, the Kpelle do take the particular situation far more into account: indeed the origin of the different approaches to such Western puzzles has been specifically attributed to the characteristics of formal schooling which are, of course, absent in the Kpelle (see Scribner and Cole, 1973).

TESTS AND MODELS OF INTELLIGENCE

In Western culture, given the vagueness of the definitions of intelligence, **intelligence tests** have been devised which are based initially upon the *intuitions* of researchers about the nature of intelligence and do not stem directly from formal, precise definitions of what constitutes 'good thinking'. Such tests are usually engineered to span a range of abilities which, *prima facie*, might be thought to involve separate cognitive skills. Thus there may be tests of ability to visualize geometric patterns in different orientations, tests of the ability to perceive detail in pictures, assessment of the skills involved in comprehending the meaning and relationships of words, measures of arithmetical facility and possibly tests of logical reasoning ability.

In constructing a specific test many items of a particular type (e.g., all arithmetical ones) are initially included according to the researchers' presuppositions about what is appropriate, and these items are then given to a large group of people. Those that everyone passes or those that everyone fails are then discarded as being undiscriminating: the items which are left can then be graded in difficulty in terms of the percentage of people who succeeded in solving the particular puzzle. A set of such items can then be put together which, with suitable selection, should straddle the ability range of the whole of the relevant population. Scores on the test when administered subsequently can then be evaluated by relating performance to the previously obtained criterion group by finding what percentage of all people might be expected to get at least the score of the person concerned; in other words, a person can be graded in relation to his peers in terms of what proportion of them would get the same or better score. This procedure, in a somewhat more sophisticated form, forms the basis of all intelligence assessment and is the source of the famous **intelligence quotient**, or IQ.

Armed with these tests, an empirical approach to intelligence is possible: actual performance can be analysed and models of intelligence can be suggested on the outcomes of these analyses. Such an approach was pioneered by Spearman in 1927. In looking at the results of people's performance on a wide range of tests, Spearman noted that however different two tests might superficially appear to be (e.g., a test of vocabulary and a test of mentally manipulating geometric forms) scores of the two tests tended nevertheless to be correlated. In other words, if a person scored well on one test he would also tend to score well on the other; equally, if someone scored poorly on the first test he would in all probability obtain a low score on the second. Spearman's statistical analysis of the intercorrelations among many tests (called **factor analysis**) led him to the conclusion that because all the tests were positively correlated they must all involve in part the same cognitive process. This process Spearman called **general intelligence** since it was common to all tests however superficially different, and this general factor which comes out of correlational analyses is sometimes termed simply 'g'. Since tests do not *equally* correlate with each other, not all tests measure 'g' to the same extent – tests therefore measure 'g' to a greater or lesser degree but also measure a specific ability which may be unique to that particular test. Spearman argued that an individual's performance on a given test will depend upon a general factor of intelligence together with a more specific factor associated with that test, and thus his theory has been termed a **two-factor theory** of intelligence.

Subsequently, Cattell (1971) has suggested that 'g' might be split into what he terms 'fluid' general intelligence, which is the biologically determined aspect of intellectual functioning that allows the solution of totally new problems, and 'crystallized' intelligence, which represents the concepts, skills and strategies that we have acquired throughout life. Crystallized abilities are therefore determined by the interaction of fluid intelligence and environment and culture.

Unfortunately the factor analysis technique is one which allows

BOX 9.6
An intelligence test: the WAIS

A widely used intelligence test for adults is the Wechsler Adult Intelligence Scale (WAIS); there is also a similar version for children called the WISC (Wechsler Intelligence Scale for Children). The test is divided into two parts, one assessing verbal and related abilities and the other measuring nonverbal skills (or 'performance' abilities, as they are sometimes called). Within each of these two parts there is a set of subtests which assess particular aspects of verbal and nonverbal factors:

Verbal Scales (1) Information – measures general knowledge. (2) Comprehension – tests the ability to use knowledge in practical settings (e.g., 'What would you do if lost in a large, strange town?'). (3) Arithmetic. (4) Similarities – measures conceptual and analogical reasoning (e.g., 'In what ways are a book and a TV alike?'). (5) Digit span – examines short-term memory by requiring people to repeat back short strings of digits in the same order as presented or in reverse order. (6) Vocabulary – the person is given a word and asked to say what it means.
   None of the verbal tests are timed.

Performance Scales (1) Picture completion – assesses visual efficiency and visual memory by asking people to spot missing items in drawings. (2) Picture arrangement – measures sequential understanding by requiring subjects to arrange a series of pictures to tell a story. (3) Block design – tests the ability to perceive and analyse patterns by asking individuals to copy pictures using multicoloured blocks. (4) Object assembly – a series of jigsaw puzzles requiring the ability to relate parts to wholes. (5) Digit symbol – assesses the ability to memorize and order abstract visual patterns.
   All of these are timed.

Each subtest gives a 'scale' score which relates a given

individual's performance on the particular subtest to the score of the criterion group, and each set of these subtest scores can be combined together to give a 'Verbal IQ' and a 'Performance IQ'. Finally, these two IQs can be combined together to yield an overall IQ.

considerable scope for variability among researchers as to how it is to be applied to a given set of data. Accordingly it may not be surprising to discover that some workers have argued that the mind is made up of separate, equally important special skills *without* a general intellectual component – so-called **multifactor theories** of intelligence. Estimates of these special skills have ranged from seven (the seven 'primary mental abilities', as Thurstone has called them) to Guilford's estimate of one hundred and twenty. Thurstone's seven primary mental abilities involve spatial, numerical, perceptual, word meaning, word fluency, memory and reasoning skills. Guilford's theory of a hundred and twenty separate abilities is based upon the notion that human functioning can be organized around three aspects, involving five kinds of cognitive operations, four kinds of 'contents' (or material with which to deal) and six types of 'products' of the results of applying operations to contents.

Because of the wide range of factors suggested by the various researchers, Block and Dworkin (1974), among others, have questioned the relevance of factor analysis in providing an understanding of intelligent thought. Although Vernon (1979) has recently attempted to argue that the differences between the various factor analytic models are more apparent than real, it remains the case that 'factors' are the arbitrary names given by researchers to the results of statistical analyses. Merely to label a factor in one way or another is not necessarily to advance our understanding of the nature of intelligence; what is needed is a description in detail of what constitutes effective thought and what *processes* are involved in creating, reasoning about and solving problems (see Sternberg, 1980; and pages 227–30, above).

INTELLIGENT THINKING AND COGNITIVE PSYCHOLOGY

Aware of the difficulties mentioned above, some psychologists have attempted to relate scores on intelligence tests – particularly 'verbal' intelligence – to performance on tasks which have been designed by cognitive psychologists to **fractionate** the processes involved in a particular mental activity. In other words, these researchers are trying to root notions of intelligence in the rather more explicit views of human performance given by information-processing theories.

Thus, for example, cognitive psychologists have found that when people are asked to say whether two visually presented letters share a common name or not (e.g., Aa or Bc), they take longer than when simply requested to judge whether or not the two letters are physically identical (e.g., AA or CD). From the point of view of cognitive psychology, the difference in time involved in these two tasks might tell us that the former was executed *after* the latter (since the first took longer to carry out) or, more simply, that the 'name' task is more complex than the 'physical' task. If, however, the interest is in what causes variability between individuals, the differences in time taken to carry out the two tasks might be taken as an index of how well people can retrieve linguistic information, and thus might be expected partially to underlie their verbal intellectual abilities. In fact correlations between psychometric measures (scores on traditional IQ tests) and indices of performance derived from information-processing theories are invariably small (see Hunt, 1980). Very occasionally, large correlations have been reported, but these have resulted from the inclusion of extreme groups of people such as mental retardates (see Nettlebeck, 1982); the problems of assessing relationships between two variables (such as IQ and speed) when two or more groups of people are included, is illustrated in Figure 9.5.

Although the approach of examining individual differences in thought in the context of information-processing models is an attractive one in principle, it is still in its very early stages. Irrespective of whether or not the various parts of these models correlate with traditional intelligence measures, it remains to be seen whether the actual processes postulated by cognitive psychologists

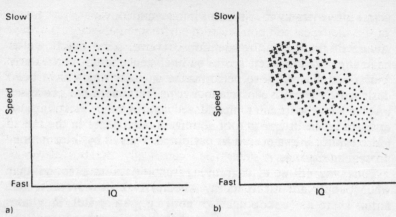

a)   b)

Figure 9.5 (a) shows hypothetical data collected from a homogenous group of people illustrating a genuine relationship between IQ and speed of processing. Each dot represents the scores of one person. (b) shows hypothetical data which illustrate information derived from normal people (shown as dots again) and retarded people (shown in the Figure as small crosses). Within both groups of people little relationship between IQ and speed is evident. However, if the fact that we are dealing with two different groups of people is ignored and the data shown in (b) are taken as a whole, then it might appear (spuriously) that there is a strong relationship between IQ and speed of mental processing.

are of such a degree of specificity that they are capable of pinpointing the ways in which people differ from each other.

THE DEVELOPMENT AND DECLINE OF INTELLIGENCE

Adult intelligence cannot be determined solely by **environmental factors** operating during infancy. If it were, we could expose lumps of ancient inert rock to stimulating environments and subsequently observe budding Cambrian Newtons and Einsteins. There must be some inborn, **genetically determined** and possibly unique component in human beings which enables them to take advantage of what environments have to offer. The ability to act and think intelligently is therefore part of being human. Whether the difference between people's intelligence (as assessed by intelligence tests) is due largely to variations in the amount, capacity or extent of this biological component, with environmental factors playing a quite subsidiary part, or whether, conversely, the genetic determinant of our intelligence is relatively trivial and its expression in behaviour is largely governed by the kind of culture in which we are raised, are questions which cannot be answered from the armchair.

There are two main empirical techniques for investigating the roots of efficient thinking. First, relationships between the IQs of various **kinship groups** can be examined. Thus, it has been argued that if intelligence is determined genetically, the IQs of monozygotic twins (those twins resulting from the splitting of one ovum and who share identical genetic make-up) might be more alike than dizygotic twins (who occur after two eggs are fertilized by two sperms and whose genetic background is thus no more alike than ordinary siblings); in turn dizygotic twins might be expected to be more alike in intelligence than cousins, and so on. Unfortunately, extant kinship data appear rather variable, due to differences in the particular tests employed on the one hand, and test unreliability on the other (see Vernon, 1979). However, even if satisfactory data were available on the relationships between measures of intelligence among several different kinship groups and even if these data fitted a genetic model of the origins of intelligence, it is not clear that an environmental explanation of the roots of thought would have to be discounted since the rank ordering of similarities of IQ among kinship groups that is predicted by an environmental view of the factors determining intelligence will be precisely the same as that expected by views propounding an innate component in ultimate intellectual facility. Thus, for example, it is likely that monozygotic twins will be reared in far more similar ways than will ordinary siblings born several years apart – the IQs of the former may thus be expected to be more similar than those of the latter, given an environmental as well as a genetic view of the origins of scores on tests. (A study of monozygotic twins reared apart might solve this problem since they would have identical heredity but differing environments; separated twins, however, tend to go to members of the same family or are selectively placed by adoption agencies so that their cultural backgrounds are, to all intents and purposes, very similar.)

The other strategy for investigating the **heritability** or otherwise of IQ is through the examination of the intelligence of adopted children. In a sophisticated design Scarr and Weinberg (1977) have found that two adopted children (with genes therefore unrelated both to each other and to the foster parents) growing up in the same household had IQs which were about as similar as the IQs of two natural children brought up together. Such results would tend to support environmental determinants of intelligence since it might be expected that the adopted children would tend to show more IQ variability than the natural ones if thinking skills were genetically linked.

Until recent times it has been fashionable to argue that genetic influences are predominant in determining level and quality of child and adult thought. While the evidence for such a view now seems quite untenable and the actual balance of the contributions of culture and heredity to our intelligence are, quite simply, unknown, nevertheless some aspects of our ability to think must be determined innately in order that we may actually benefit from experience. It still remains a major task for psychology to determine what this factor is and, probably more important (because we can manipulate them), what environmental and educational influences are conducive to the efficient development of cognitive processes in general. (See also pages 77–80.)

Studies on changes in human performance, and in thinking in particular, during the years from maturity to retirement and old age also involve two approaches. First, cross-sectionally, we might compare at a given moment in time groups of young, middle-aged and old people. Second, longitudinally, we might follow up a group of individuals who were young at the start of the study right through to old age. Both of these approaches have problems. **Cross-sectional studies** are problematical because differences between age groups in some aspect of performance may not simply reflect their age difference: the groups may differ in other ways such as educational opportunity, attitudes and motivation, which may subtract from or interact with their performance upon specific tasks. Quite apart from their time-consuming nature, **longitudinal studies** pose interpretative problems since people may become practised as a result of repeated testing upon the same types of skills; further, the sample may become distorted as the group ages, because only those people who do well in the various assessments will tend to carry on in the investigation. Not surprisingly, therefore, a comparison of cross-sectional and longitudinal investigations of intellectual functioning across the adult life-span reveals that the former technique shows far greater loss of function than the latter. Some measures, however, even on cross-sectional testing, do not show any deterioration with age and may even show improvement (vocabulary is such a measure).

The *extent* of the deterioration of intelligence in old age is unclear, but it is almost certainly not simply an artefact of cultural differences (or other non-age-related factors) between the young and the old since animal work has revealed that monkeys and apes also show drops in performance as they age and, further, there are demonstrable variations in the brains of the young and the elderly. Intriguingly, however, it has recently been suggested that the decline that is manifest with advancing years may not reflect a progressive impairment throughout the period of life after maturity but may only occur when people are within five or so years of their death (the dramatically named **terminal drop hypothesis**). The apparent continuous decline manifest across large samples of individuals (whether assessed cross-sectionally or longitudinally) from our middle years to our eighties might therefore simply reflect the fact that more and more people are coming within five years of their death as the higher average age of the samples increases.

The relationship between language and thought

INTRODUCTION

Language and thought may be related in three possible ways. First, at one extreme, language may make thought possible: without language, it might be argued, there could be no thought. Second, and at another extreme, language and thought may be quite separate activities, the former being simply the socially acceptable way of communicating the latter. Third, and not surprisingly, between these two extremes, thought and language may be separate processes to some extent but, in certain situations, language may structure our thinking in significant ways.

The *independence* of some cognitive activities from language has been demonstrated by the examination of people's use of colour names. The English language has eleven basic colour words such as 'red', 'green' and so on. Words such as these are defined as 'basic' since they are short and used frequently; nonbasic colour terms (such as magnolia) are long and rarely used. Brown and Lenneberg (1954) have shown that English-speaking people find it easier to remember basic colours in comparison to nonbasic colours, raising the question as to whether this is because native English speakers have more readily available words for the former colours and can thus 'encode' their experiences more easily. In other words, it may be that our language is determining our cognitive abilities – in this case, determining our memory.

To clarify this point, Heider (1972) has looked at memory for colours in the Dani, a tribe in New Guinea. Unlike English, the Dani language has only two basic colour terms. Do the Dani perceive (and thus remember) fewer colours than the English? Heider has shown that this is not the case. The colours which are best remembered by native English speakers (which, of course, tend to be those which have 'basic' colour names) are also those which are best perceived and remembered by the Dani, even though they have no words for them. In other words, focal colours are probably processed (perhaps in a special way) by all people, irrespective of the range of their linguistic terminology for colours. The colour terms that people actually employ will depend upon historical, social and cultural factors but the terms themselves do not determine their perception and responses to colour. Focal colours are perceptually salient whether we have names for them or not and our 'thought' about colours is not structured by our language.

Although it is almost certainly wrong to assume (as Whorf did) that language determines our thought processes, it would be equally wrong to assume that language has no influence upon cognition and that language and thought are totally separate processes. In memorizing shapes, for example, labelling a visually presented ambiguous figure in one way rather than another will bias its subsequent reproduction in the direction of the object named by the label. In such situations what is stored in memory may be an accurate, undistorted 'visual' description of what was seen (a 'visual' code) and a linguistic interpretation of what the shape reminded the subject of (a label or 'verbal' code). Such linguistic interactions with nonlinguistic processes are ubiquitous, and recently Loftus and Palmer (1974) have shown similar effects in eye-witness testimony, while Glucksberg and Weisberg (1966) have reported related phenomena in the field of problem-solving.

If language and thought are neither one and the same thing nor entirely separate processes, just how extensive is the influence of language upon thinking? One obvious way in which this question can be answered is, following Cohen (1977), through an examination of the thinking capacities and limitations of those people who, for one reason or another, lack extensive linguistic facility.

THINKING WITH IMPAIRED LANGUAGE

Effects of brain damage: aphasia. A widely used measure of intellectual functioning after organic brain damage is the WAIS (see Box 9.6). If brain damage is widespread (as it may be in progressive dementing illnesses such as Alzheimer's disease) there may be, over time, corresponding deterioration in *all* the WAIS subtests. However, with more focal lesions (i.e., damage confined to small areas of the brain) deficits in the ability to think rationally and logically (as indexed by the various WAIS subtests) are not widespread but can be confined to one or two areas. McFie (1975) has recently charted the gross regions of the brain which, when

Table 9.4 **WAIS subtests reflecting impairments with localized lesions.** (After McFie, 1975)

Site of lesion	WAIS test showing greatest deficit
Left frontal	Digit span
Left temporal	Similarities
Left parietal	Arithmetic, digit span, block designs
Right frontal	Picture arrangement
Right temporal	Picture arrangement
Right parietal	Block designs, object assembly, picture arrangement

damaged, manifest greatest deficits on the WAIS subtests. These relationships are shown in Table 9.4.

Crudely, WAIS subtests assessing **visuospatial abilities** appear to be impaired after right-hemisphere damage while **linguistic abilities** seem to be compromised after left-hemisphere lesions. Accordingly, linguistic skills may be significantly impaired *without* a corresponding reduction in nonverbal abilities, and conversely, linguistic skills may remain largely intact while activities requiring nonverbal cognitive processes may be grossly disturbed. It is interesting to note, however, that there are clear sex differences in the degree of this 'lateralization' of visuospatially based and linguistically based thought processes. Lesion studies (as well as evidence for hemispheric asymmetries from studies of dichotic listening and visual half-field performance) all tend to show that the separation of linguistic and nonlinguistic processes in the left and right hemispheres respectively is more marked in men that it is in women (see Inglis and Lawson, 1981). This sex difference could be genetically linked or could arise from environmental factors shaping cognitive styles and thus, consequentially, affecting the organization of the brain (see Chapter 7).

Another, related way of looking at the link between language and thought is to examine the extent to which impairment in linguistic comprehension after brain damage is directly linked to deficits in performance in nonverbal tasks. The outcome of such studies is unequivocal: while aphasic patients as a whole tend *not* to perform entirely normally on nonverbal tasks, the extent of their impairment on these tests is quite unrelated to the severity of their linguistic deficits (e.g., Basso *et al.*, 1973). In other words, while language must play some role in the mediation of some nonverbal activities (since aphasics' performance on such tasks is not normal), it cannot completely determine them (since the extent of nonverbal deficit is unrelated to the extent of linguistic deficit).

In addition to the more logical skills involved in visuospatial tasks, artistic abilities can also be relatively well preserved in the face of marked aphasic deficits. In a recent review of musicians rendered aphasic after left-hemisphere damage, Gardner (1982) has concluded that, in spite of their marked linguistic impairments, these musicians retained their capacity and their desire to take part in musical activities. In contrast, right-hemisphere lesions (sparing the left hemisphere and thus leaving language abilities intact) lead to deficits in aspects of musical appreciation involving tonal memory and sensitivity to timbre and intensity.

Although formal, experimental assessment of musical ability and creativity is difficult, study of these brain-damaged people suggests that artistic endeavours can proceed, at least in part, even with substantially impaired language; conversely, previously excellent artistic talent can be diminished while the ability to communicate and think in language remains at a very high level. Our ability to think in words is dissociable from our ability to think musically.

Language and nonverbal skills in the deaf. The significance of the deaf in the study of the relationship between language and thought has been recognized for some time, for reasons that are quite simple. If thinking involves language then people who are born deaf and thus never hear and never acquire language should be incapable of thought as we know it. Of course the deaf person will necessarily be impaired on any test of verbal functioning, but how might deaf people fare on tests *not* obviously requiring linguistic analyses for their success? In very many studies this issue has been addressed through an examination of deaf and hearing people's abilities on the 'performance' (nonverbal) scales of intelligence tests where such tests are used as convenient nonlanguage measures of the thought processes involved in deduction, reasoning and concept formation.

Vernon (1967; 1968) has summarized much of this work, from which it is apparent that the range of performance on such tests among those with profound hearing loss is as great as among those with normal hearing and, furthermore, the mean scores of some deaf individuals in these nonverbal tests are comparable with their normal controls. Although it would be a mistake to assume that the deaf are necessarily dumb   given that there are degrees of deafness, it is not surprising that there are corresponding associated degrees of linguistic abilities – there is, nevertheless, little correlation between the degree of deafness (which should in turn be systematically related to quality of linguistic skills) and performance on nonverbal tests.

Furth (1966) has been the clearest exponent of the view that intellectual functioning in the deaf is inferior only on tasks which, in normal people, are largely mediated by language. However, some studies do show that deaf people may sometimes perform less well than hearing controls on tests not obviously involving language. This may well mean that at least some linguistic intervention occurs in normal people even when the task they are executing is ostensibly nonlinguistic. On the other hand, Vernon (1968) has suggested that the etiologies of profound deafness (such as maternal rubella) may be responsible in some deaf people for *other* neurological impairments which might result in impaired performance on tasks related to nonverbal intelligence. That is, as Vernon summarizes it, 'The relationship, if any, between mental retardation and deafness is not causal but is due to the common etiology which brought about the deafness and the retardation.' This view receives some support from the observation that, on the whole, congenitally deaf children outperform other children whose deafness has been acquired peri- or postnatally. In short, it may be that the deaf are a heterogeneous group and that the degree of deafness alone (and its corresponding relation to linguistic facility) may not therefore be the only factor in determining some deaf individuals' level and pattern of thinking. However, the fact that at least *some* profoundly deaf people show levels of nonverbal thinking abilities comparable to those of hearing controls strongly suggests that some mental activities can proceed efficiently without the need for natural language.

An intriguing series of reports reviewed by Conrad (1979) suggests that genetically deaf children born to deaf parents may be *more* intelligent than hearing children and are certainly more intelligent than genetically deaf infants whose parents have normal hearing. Noting that bilingual hearing children, carefully matched to monolingual hearing controls, are more advanced in both nonverbal as well as verbal intelligence (see Lambert, 1977), Conrad has speculated that the reason for the very good performance of the genetically deaf child of deaf parents is that the child is actually being exposed to two forms of language: sign language with its parents in the home, together with a predominantly oral mode of communication at school. In other words, such deaf children may effectively be bilingual in the sense of possessing a more or less efficient sign language and, in addition, some command of natural oral English. It may be that the differences between this group of children and other deaf groups are present *before* the acquisition of their second language; equally, however, it may be that their better performance is a direct consequence of learning two languages.

Schizophrenic language. The characteristics of schizophrenic patients' speech have frequently been documented. Two major factors in such talk distinguish it from normal. First, in the process of imparting information there is a poverty of speech content, such that it conveys little information, is vague, frequently repetitive and stereotyped. Second, in response to questions, schizophrenics' answers are often oblique, tangential or simply irrelevant, although the response is related to the question in some way (for example, when asked for today's date the patient might reply, 'I was born on 11 November 1944').

The scrambled nature of schizophrenic speech (it has been termed a 'word salad') has been taken to reflect an underlying disorder in formal thought. While this may well be true, some circularity of argument frequently crops up in discussions of schizophrenic thought and language since it is claimed on the one hand that incoherent speech reveals disordered thought, and on the other that impaired thought processes are reflected in speech anomalies.

Interestingly, however, although lowered intelligence is associated with schizophrenia, there is little divergence of performance on verbal and nonverbal measures. This might well be taken to suggest that intellectual and linguistic functions are closely related, or that the latter determines the former. However, schizophrenia may well result from disorders of a variety of neurochemical systems (e.g., van Praag, 1977) and extensive cognitive impairments may not necessarily reflect the critical role of language in thought but rather indicate that the etiology of schizophrenia may be such as to impair simultaneously many independent cognitive processes.

As far as schizophrenic language itself is concerned, Rochester and Martin (1979), noting that normal people improve their memory for words if the words are presented in strings which progressively approximate to proper English sentences, have reviewed similar work on word and sentence memory in schizophrenics and have concluded that they are able to take the same advantage of those syntactical constraints in sentences that improve perception and memory in nonpsychotic individuals. Accordingly, sensitivity to syntactic structure may well be left intact in schizophrenics, and the difficulties that they find in speech comprehension and the anomalous nàture of their utterances are unlikely to arise from a syntactic impairment but probably have their source at a deeper, semantic level. (See also pages 727–32.)

CULTURAL DETERMINANTS OF LANGUAGE AND THOUGHT

In addition to the profound linguistic disturbances which arise through structural anomalies in the central or peripheral nervous systems, it is also of relevance to consider the effects of linguistic 'deficiencies' on nonverbal thought when such language impoverishment is induced by social conditions.

In a series of reports, Bernstein (e.g., 1971) has argued that the language of working-class boys is characterized by short sentences with few subordinate clauses. He has termed this kind of speech a **restricted code**, contrasting it with the longer, more complex and more contentful **elaborated code** of the middle classes. Thus, it is argued, the speech samples of working-class children reflect disadvantages in cognition which result from the cultural environments in which they were raised. Much of this kind of work has been criticized, however, since it is known that some 'impoverished' speech, for example black American English, is not a substandard form of middle American English but is an interverbally consistent, rule-governed dialect which is merely different from, but in its own way as complex as, 'standard' English (Labov, 1969). Nevertheless, it is interesting to note that children from lower socioeconomic classes tend to have higher nonverbal IQ scores than verbal ones, and this might well indicate that the form of language affects performance on verbal scales of intelligence tests but does not so markedly affect nonverbal measures; some independence of language and thinking skills might therefore be inferred. On the other hand, the disparity between verbal and nonverbal measures in working-class children could conceivably reflect the fact that the test (and usually the tester) reflects a mode of language not shared by the testee: verbal and nonverbal measures may well coincide in working-class children (but *diverge* in middle-class ones) if the former assessments could in some way be based upon tests which reflect working-class children's language use (see Chapter 10).

Although the equivalence of dialects is widely accepted by linguists in academic circles, the differences between them still lead to disadvantages for children not brought up in middle-class homes. As Edwards (1979b) has put it, 'The form of language . . . [demonstrates] the difference between cognition and social problems. It is one thing to recognize that language varieties and dialects are of equal communicative validity for their users; it is quite another to assume that dissemination of this fact will rapidly remove social barriers among languages, dialects and accents.' In this connection Edwards has shown that when tape-recordings of children from differing socioeconomic backgrounds (all of whom read from the same passage) were played to judges who were asked to rate the child on seventeen different scales, the working-class children were rated less favourably than the middle-class ones on all seventeen scales. Since these scales involved the judges in rating such factors as 'enthusiasm' and 'happiness' as well as 'intelligence', it appears that the way in which something is said is probably as influential as the content in making an impression upon others.

Implicit in the work quoted above is the assumption that in some way the circumstances of childhood might affect our thinking abilities. Whatever these cultural effects may be – and it is clear that their direct effects upon cognition are uncertain – their magnitude might be expected to be trivial in comparison with the effects upon language and thought of practically total isolation from society. Children who suffer the vicissitudes of **extreme social deprivation** in early life are, fortunately, extremely rare. Occasionally such infants are discovered, however, and recently a girl (given the pseudonym Genie) who was locked in a room with minimal contact with people for several years after birth has been the subject of extensive analyses of her linguistic and cognitive abilities (see Curtiss, 1977). Over the years that Genie has been studied, it has been observed that she is learning the English language from mere exposure although, interestingly, her language comprehension and production are not progressing in the same way or at the rate of normal (younger) children acquiring their first language during the early years of life. For example, in contrast to normal children who begin to ask questions almost as soon as they utter their first words, Genie had not asked a question during the five or so years after her discovery. Normal patterns and speed of language acquisition therefore may conceivably depend upon extensive exposure to language during an early critical period: language acquisition may be possible after puberty but it may not then follow normal routes and, speculatively, may never reach normal levels.

On a variety of nonverbal tests Genie performed at least as well as might be expected for her age, and occasionally outperformed expected adult levels. These tests typically were those which required a 'wholistic' or Gestalt strategy for their solution. But Genie did not perform well on those nonverbal tests which required a more analytical approach. Curtiss has suggested that Genie's right hemisphere is mediating her thinking, since this hemisphere is assumed to process visuospatial information in a wholistic way while the left hemisphere is claimed to process the information in a more piecemeal fashion. Whatever the merits of describing Genie as a right-hemisphere thinker, she clearly performs some complex nonverbal tasks at least as successfully as might be expected for her age even though her linguistic abilities fall well short of the skills of normal children of equivalent age.

Further reading

Biological basis of thought and language

A seminal source for the work and ideas on evolution, brain size and intelligence is:

JERISON, H.J. (1973) *Evolution of the Brain and Intelligence*. New York: Academic Press.

Also worth examining are the relevant chapters in:

OAKLEY, D.A. and PLOTKIN, H.C. (1979) *Brain, Behaviour and Evolution*. London: Methuen.

A good positive account of primate language use is given in:

LINDEN, E. (1976) *Apes, Men and Language*. Second edition. Harmondsworth: Penguin.

For the negative view, see Terrace's review of Premack's *Intelligence in Apes and Man*:

TERRACE, H.S. (1979) Is problem-solving language? *Journal of the Experimental Analysis of Behavior*, **31**, 161–75.

A particularly useful source for the biological determinants of language (especially Chapters 7 and 8) is:

SPRINGER, S.P. and DEUTSCH, G. (1985) *Left Brain, Right Brain*. Revised edition. Oxford: Freeman.

Concept development

There are two ways of discovering Piaget's theory: through reading the original works or by relying on someone else's interpretation. The latter is more painless since it is generally agreed that Piaget makes difficult reading. From a wide range, the first book listed below is recommended as a reliable primer; the second is the one which introduced Piaget to many English-speaking psychologists, and it remains a model of its kind:

GINSBERG, H. and OPPER, S. (1979) *Piaget's Theory of Intellectual Development: an Introduction*. Englewood Cliffs, NJ: Prentice-Hall.
FLAVELL, J.H. (1963) *The Developmental Psychology of Jean Piaget*. Princeton, NJ: Van Nostrand.

If you prefer the undiluted version, the following is intended as an introduction to the theory:

PIAGET, J. and INHELDER, B. (1969) *The Psychology of the Child*. London: Routledge and Kegan Paul.

To get the flavour of Piaget, however, read one of his early books such as:

PIAGET, J. (1952) *The Origin of Intelligence in the Child*. London: Routledge and Kegan Paul.

The following book represents a middle way by linking extracts from Piaget's work with explanatory commentary:

GRUBER, H. and VONECHE, J., eds. (1977) *The Essential Piaget: an Interpretive Reference and Guide*. London: Routledge and Kegan Paul.

Critiques of Piaget are also plentiful. Two of the best have the additional merit of being short:

BODEN, M. (1979) *Piaget*. London: Fontana Paperbacks.

DONALDSON, M. (1978) *Children's Minds*. London: Fontana Paperbacks.

Social cognition has been informed by the seminal work of Mead and Vygotsky:

MEAD, G.H. (1934) *Mind, Self and Society*. Chicago: University of Chicago Press.

VYGOTSKY, L.S. (1962) *Thought and Language*. Cambridge, Mass.: MIT Press.

VYGOTSKY, L.S. (1978) *Mind in Society*. Cambridge, Mass.: Harvard University Press.

The next book looks at the role of culture by incorporating a cross-cultural perspective:

COLE, M. and SCRIBNER, S. (1974) *Culture and Thought: a Psychological Introduction*. New York: Wiley.

The relevance of some of the orthodox approaches to the study of thinking is taken up in this book of readings:

WASON, P. C. and JOHNSON-LAIRD, P. N., eds. (1977) *Thinking: Readings in Cognitive Science*. Cambridge: Cambridge University Press.

A more polemical but very readable view is that of:

NEISSER, U. (1976) *Cognition and Reality*. San Francisco: Freeman.

Language development

The following two books are good guides to work in language development. The first sets out the basic issues in a very readable manner; the second is a more comprehensive volume:

DE VILLIERS, P. and DE VILLIERS, J. (1979) *Early Language*. Fontana Paperbacks.

DE VILLIERS, P. and DE VILLIERS, J. (1978) *Language Acquisition*. Cambridge, Mass.: Harvard University Press.

At a more advanced level, the first of the next two books provides a good British perspective, while the second is for those who want the nitty-gritty of syntactic growth:

ELLIOT, A.J. (1981) *Child Language*. Cambridge: Cambridge University Press.

BROWN, R. (1973) *A First Language: the Early Stages*. London: Allen and Unwin.

The broader field of psycholinguistics is authoritatively reviewed in:

SLOBIN, D.I. (1979) *Psycholinguistics*. Glenview, Ill.: Scott Foresman.

Two books by the British linguist, John Lyons, deserve mention, being valuable introductions to important topics:

LYONS, J. (1977) *Chomsky*. Second edition. London: Fontana Paperbacks.
LYONS, J. (1981) *Language, Meaning and Context*. London: Fontana Paperbacks.

A carefully selected book of readings in this area is:

LEE, V., ed. (1979) *Language Development*. London: Croom Helm.

(More readings on language are given at the end of Chapter 10 below.)

Intelligence: individual differences in thinking skills

An excellent general introduction to traditional approaches to the study of intelligence is:

PYLE, D.W. (1979) *Intelligence*. London: Routledge and Kegan Paul.

A book which is also useful, and includes contributions on cross-cultural studies of intelligence, is:

RESNICK, L.B., ed. (1976) *The Nature of Intelligence*. New York: Wiley.

A clear account (especially Chapter 1) of test construction, standardization, validation and reliability is in:

JENSEN, A.R. (1981) *Straight Talk about Mental Tests*. London: Methuen.

The next book gives a lucid account (especially Part I) of the various factorial approaches to intelligence:

VERNON, P.E. (1979) *Intelligence: Heredity and Environment*. San Francisco: Freeman.

The linkage of cognitive psychology and psychometrics is a relatively new area of research, but a good source of references is:

STERNBERG, R.J. (1985) *Human Abilities*. New York: Freeman.

The environmental or genetic origins of intelligence is currently a polemical issue. The best source is:

EYSENCK, H.J. *v.* KAMIN, L. (1981) *Intelligence: the Battle for Mind.* London: Pan.

The possible demise of intellectual abilities in old age is well discussed in:

SCHAIE, K.W. (1979) The primary mental abilities in adulthood: an exploration in the development of psychometric intelligence. In P.B. Baltes and O.G. Brim, eds., *Life Span Development and Behavior*, Volume 2. New York: Academic Press.

The relationship between language and thought

The following book will repay reading for its general discussion on the nature of language and thinking:

MILLER, G.A. (1981) *Language and Speech*. Oxford: Freeman.

Springer and Deutsch, *op. cit.*, especially Chapter 6, is a useful source of references for hemisphere differences related to sex.

A classical, clinical review of intellectual functioning in aphasia is:

ZANGWILL, O. (1964) Intelligence in aphasia. In A.V.S. de Reuck and N. O'Connor, eds., *Disorders of Language*. London: Churchill.

The best source for work on deaf individuals is:

CONRAD, R. (1979) *The Deaf School Child*. New York: Harper and Row.

The following book on schizophrenic language is worth reading in full:

ROCHESTER, S. and MARTIN, J.R. (1979) *Crazy Talk: a Study of the Discourse of Schizophrenic Speakers*. New York: Plenum.

10. Communication

10. Communication

Introduction

Whenever two or more individuals are together communication is taking place. Even in total silence and the complete absence of overt nonverbal signals information is being transmitted and we infer something from the other's behaviour. In social situations, therefore, it is impossible not to communicate. In Chapter 12 we will focus on the interpersonal processes that govern the human as a social being, but here we continue the account begun in Chapter 9. There we examined the nature of language as a formal system that plays a central part in human cognition and interacts in a still little understood manner with thought. We also charted the course of language acquisition, with particular emphasis on the methods and discoveries of psycholinguistics. What received relatively little attention, however, was the role that language plays as a system for the transmission of meaning – of ideas, feelings, likes and dislikes, attitudes and beliefs, aspirations and worries; in short, language as communication.

We are not confined to language, of course, in our communication with one another, and we will consider the role of nonverbal communication both allied and unallied with language. Nor is communication restricted to vocalization. Apart from the sign languages discussed in the previous chapter, in the majority of cultures there is a graphic means of imparting information. Many humans, but probably less than half the world's population, learn to read and write, and we will consider the psychological significance of this form of expression and indicate what is known about the development of these skills.

One of the most significant developments in the past decade has been the re-emergence of a psychology of language which sees the enterprise as a dynamic human activity which has its origins in the earliest exchanges between infants and parents.

Evolution

Historically, accounts of the origins of communication have taken an evolutionary rather than an ontogenetic line. However, as one anthropologist has put it, 'To know how human speech emerged as something distinct from a system of calls – the assorted grunts, barks, screams and hoots typical of nonhuman primates – demands nothing less than a step-by-step reconstruction of the evolutionary process, and for that the evidence is still lacking' (Pfeiffer, 1970, p. 392).

Studies of animal communication systems have included insects, birds and aquatic mammals as well as nonhuman primates. Despite the sophistication of these systems no one has convincingly demonstrated that they have the properties of a language as defined, for instance, by Hockett (1960). Specifically, animals do not use a symbol system or code in which the message stands for something else (but see the discussion of 'talking' chimpanzees in Chapter 9). They do not appear to have the ability to displace their messages in time or space from what the messages stand for – rather they are tied to the immediate sensory environment. Finally, nonhuman communicative systems lack the generative power of human speech. People are able to produce and comprehend complex utterances including ones never heard before. Normally we operate within a grammatical structure but we can move outside it if we wish. The scope, flexibility and power of human verbal communication seem to place it in a category apart from the communicative patterns of other species. As we pointed out in Chapter 9, those studies which have taught chimpanzees signalling systems appear to have no counterpart in the wild. It has been suggested, in fact, that the study of nonhuman primate communicative systems is more revealing about affective than cognitive functions: 'The more that is known about the communication systems of nonhuman primates the more obvious it is that these systems have little relationship with human language, but much with the ways human beings express emotion through gesture, facial expression and tone of voice' (Lancaster, 1968).

The development of communication

ORIGINS

Although it is fascinating to speculate about the evolution of language and its diversity of form (see Pfeiffer, 1970, for a stimulating argument), we have gained most from the study of communication in the developing human species. It is now recognized that if we want a theory of communication development we begin not with the first word but with the earliest interactions between parent and child. The human infant may be limited in its range of communicative functions, and there are difficulties in knowing when to credit it with intention, but limitation should not be mistaken for total absence. Eye contact and direction of gaze, head movements, facial expressions – especially the smile – and primitive vocalizations such as the cry are all in the young infant's repertoire. These are the cues or signals that a mother looks for in order to engage in communication with her child. But it is essentially because communication is a social activity that we can be confident about using the word 'communication' to describe much of the behaviour that makes up the infant's waking life with its parents.

In this social dialogue the parent is the senior partner in every respect. First of all she (the parent) brings a richer and more mature repertoire of signals, one of which is speech itself. Secondly, she recognizes, whether consciously or not, the limitations of the junior partner and therefore provides a disproportionate contribution to the interaction; disproportionate, that is, in relation to what prevails in dialogues between peers. This behaviour has been referred to as **scaffolding** and is also aptly described as 'holding up both ends of the dialogue', a role that adults continue to play to varying degrees as language is acquired. A third aspect of the caregiver's role, related to the previous point, is their sensitivity to the infant's need both for stimulation and the opportunity to respond. Effective dialogue fulfils this need since it involves **turn-taking**, which in mature conversation becomes speaking and listening. Work by clinicians, such as Stern (1977), shows that mothers vary in their ability to establish a dialogue with their infant. Synchrony requires not bombarding the child with excessive amounts of stimulation and recognizing when the immature organism is ready to make his contribution to the interaction. It seems to demand that the caregiver accommodates to the child's rhythm in a 'dance', and like all dances the goal is mutual satisfaction or **reciprocity**.

Such a relationship has obvious adaptive significance in the growth of emotional bonds between infant and caregivers, and this process will be examined in Chapter 12. Its significance for communication, and as a precursor to language, is not only that it marks the beginnings of a process that plays an enormous part in human affairs but that it is central to the notion of what it is to be human. The argument, briefly put, is that humans are social from birth and their development and ultimate nature can only be understood by studying them in such a context. The child's own awareness of what it is to be human depends on the significant adults in its life treating its behaviour *as though* it were human. This means, for example, imputing the child with intentions which may well not exist. It is claimed, however, that the child comes to have intention and recognize the significance of its actions and of other people through being treated as a purposeful individual from the outset.

Workers from traditions as diverse as linguistics, biology and psychoanalysis are agreed that there is an important change in infant awareness round about the age of ten months. Before this time the child acts as though there is a world of objects and a world of people but that the two are unconnected. The infant will play with objects or with people but is unable to employ objects in games with people. The significance of the new acquisition for the growth of communication has been noted by Bates (1976). When an infant can make requests of an adult by employing gestures in relation to objects, it is reasonable to infer the existence of intentional behaviour. Adults will invest meaning in an infant's point in the direction of a cup and hand the child the object or provide the appropriate label 'cup' or do both. Thus, while the first nine months – the stage of **primary intersubjectivity** – sees much communication between infant and caregiver, it is the appearance of **secondary intersubjectivity** that marks the beginnings of a truly intentional contribution by the child to the social dialogue (see Trevarthen and Hubley, 1978). Soon after, the infant starts to produce systematic vocalizations – if not yet words – and Bates has argued that we can trace these back as precursors to language.

BOX 10.1
How parents talk to children

'Would you like a biscuit?'
'Mummy give John bicky?'

An obvious but neglected fact that has received attention in recent years is that parents, adults and, as we shall see, even older children, have a special way of talking to young children. We have no difficulty in telling which of the questions at the top of this page was directed at an infant. If we had actually heard the utterances we would be even more certain. Parents speak more slowly, in shorter, simpler sentences, in a higher pitch and with exaggerated stress patterns to babies. No special experience seems to be necessary; adults who are not parents show the same capacities as do children as young as four years when talking to toddlers (Shatz and Gelman, 1973). We also tend to do this with foreigners if their command of the language is limited, though we usually refrain from including nursery forms like 'doggie' and 'horsie', let alone 'bow-wow' or 'gee-gee'. Interestingly, other **baby-talk** forms like 'tummy' and 'Mummy' frequently survive into language between adults. And it has been suggested that the language between lovers bears some resemblance to baby talk.

As Brown (1977) points out, the **expressive features** of baby talk serve to enhance the emotional bond in families and capture the child's attention. 'Choo-choo' has more force than 'train' in this respect. The purpose of simplifying and clarifying the language we provide for those acquiring the medium is to facilitate comprehension and to aid the learning process or, more controversially, the teaching function.

Apart from its intrinsic interest, the main reason for focusing on the way parents talk to their children is to establish if the content of parental speech has any direct effects on children's language. Up to now the evidence is equivocal, but one myth has been dispelled. The idea put forward to support an innate language acquisition device, that children learn from a degraded speech environment that is ungrammatical, full of false starts, interruptions and so on, receives no support from these studies (Snow and Ferguson, 1977). Instead it seems more plausible that parents plan their utterances to make it easier for the child to acquire both meaning and grammar. Obtaining evidence to support this claim, however, has proved difficult.

Ideally one wants to show that there is a clear correlation between input and the forms used by children. Schaerlaekens (1973) looked at the language development of triplets who shared an identical language environment. She found that the grammars of the children at the two-word stage differed considerably in terms of structure used and rate of development. It appears from this study that children are constructing different grammars from the same input, if we are right in assuming the input is the same. Two other studies have shown that the intelligibility of mother's speech does correlate with advanced performance (Cross, 1978), and that yes/no questions (e.g., 'Have you washed your hands?') are correlated with the number of auxiliaries in the child's speech (Newport *et al.*, 1977). This is in line with other evidence showing a tendency to attend to the beginnings of utterances. These two positive findings must be set against the many measures of parent and child speech which failed to show any significant correlation. The general conclusion from the three studies cited is that the child's role appears to be more critical than the input *per se* in deriving structure, but this must be a cautious conclusion since this area is currently attracting much interest (see Lieven, 1982, for a stimulating review).

Longitudinal studies of communication growth by Bruner and his colleagues have demonstrated the importance of regular routines which Bruner calls **formats**. These range from nursery games like 'round and round the garden' and 'peek-a-boo' to joint-action enterprises like 'give and take' and 'build and bash'. Later come rituals like 'book reading' where the emphasis is not on reading but on **reference**, that is, giving things names. The primary significance of formats is as vehicles for teaching the rules of dialogue such as turn-taking and role-shifting. As the child begins to produce words, so the mother's teaching role is increasingly one of slotting in labels to a 'dialogue' that has already been in existence since the relationship began. Thus, by the time the child is actually using words he has a history of communication that has lasted at least twelve months. What is more, there are good grounds for thinking that language maps on to the existing framework, though the extent to which that framework actually accounts for the future course of language development is a matter of controversy (see Bruner, 1975a, for an eloquent account of the **pragmatic** viewpoint; and also page 534 above).

THE COMMUNICATION PROCESS

We may regard the communication process as involving speakers, listeners and messages within a particular context. The speaker's role is to construct messages and the listener's job is to interpret them. The context will play a large part in the process. Defined broadly it can include the relationship between the participants in the dialogue, the situation in which they find themselves and their topic of discourse. We will briefly consider these contextual factors and then examine the way psychologists have studied the communication process.

The relationships between individuals engaged in conversation can vary on a great many dimensions including age, sex, familiarity, status and occupation. One of the most important factors will be the knowledge that the speaker believes the listener to have. Assuming a particular topic, what can be taken for granted, what must there be some doubt about and what can be confidently assigned to the realm of ignorance? An effective speaker constructs messages with such considerations in mind. A simplified example may help to show how the inferential aspect of the speaker's task interacts with the specific topic and situation at hand. The scene is the hall of a house in which two of the occupants, Mr Brown and his son Tom, are hanging a picture. Mr Brown says, 'I'm going to need my gimlet', whereupon Tom leaves the scene, returning shortly with a gimlet. Mr Brown's response is, 'No, not that one, the blue one.'

Note first of all the linguistic sophistication of Tom. He perceives the intention behind the declarative statement, 'I'm going to need my gimlet', namely an indirect request for Tom to fetch the said tool. The familiarity between the participants ensures that polite forms and explicit requests are unnecessary. It is also unnecessary for Brown to explain what a gimlet is or to indicate its location: Tom knows it is in the tool cupboard in the kitchen. The shared knowledge between these participants does not prevent the communication being unsuccessful, however. In making his request, the speaker forgot he had more than one gimlet. On arriving at the cupboard Tom was faced with a choice between the blue-handled and the thicker green-handled gimlet.

Such an exchange involves **referential communication**, that is, messages that are meant to inform or, literally, to refer to a particular thing or referent. Most communication is of this nature, although language can also serve other functions in fields as diverse as poetry, prayer and propaganda. The referential function of language has received a considerable amount of research attention because it can be regarded as primary both in terms of its ubiquity and because it underlies other complex functions. It is also the form that has priority developmentally. Finally, as has been indicated, it lends itself to an examination of the communication process.

EXPERIMENTAL STUDIES

Two main paradigms have been used in the investigation of the communication process. In one the speaker describes one of a series of items for the listener to identify on the basis of the verbal message. This is the referential communication approach already mentioned and it enables the investigator to focus on speaker, listener and task variables. The other main paradigm is that developed by Bales in the investigation of **communication networks**. This work, which examines the manner in which communication in groups functions in terms of problem-solving efficiency and member satisfaction, will be discussed in Chapter 12.

Adult performance
Referential communication studies with adults indicate that even if adults are not always able to produce messages that unambiguously identify a unique referent, they are able to modify their descriptions

in response to listener feedback. They show themselves to be aware of the listener's perspective and to recognize the interactive nature of effective communication.

One aspect of mature communication that has been noted in experimental situations is that it does not follow a principle of **minimum redundancy**. The example given by Olson (see Table 10.1) illustrates this and also makes some important points about the nature of message construction. From this example we note that although the referent is the same in each case, the message changes according to the context in which the referent appears. As Olson puts it, we specify referents in terms of the competing alternatives. In the earlier example of Mr Brown and Tom it was necessary to specify *which* gimlet was required because there was a competing alternative, namely the green-handled one. Competing alternatives can, of course, be inferred as well as concretely present. Tom's father did not have to specify the location of the gimlet because he realized that this knowledge was already available to the listener.

Table 10.1 **The relation of an utterance to an intended referent.** (Adapted from Olson, 1970)

	Event	Alternative	Utterance
Case 1	○	●	. . . the white one
Case 2	○	□	. . . the round one
Case 3	○	●□	. . . the round, white one

Returning to Olson's paradigm case, it is also evident that messages do not exhaust the potential attributes of any referent. Apart from critical features of size and colour, there are properties such as form, texture, background, hue etc. which add no information in terms of denoting the selected item. In a test of Olson's model, Freedle (1972) found that adults, like children, do not restrict themselves exclusively to reporting defining attributes. In a series of trials they will tend to report all the dimensions on which the referent array varies. There would appear to be two reasons for this. First, it requires less mental effort to report all three attributes – say, big red circle – rather than go through a comparison process that would reveal that the message 'big circle' would identify the referent. Second, redundancy is often useful to the listener in providing more information than is strictly necessary since allowances are made for lapses in the listener's attention.

Children's performance

Some of the earliest studies of referential communication in children were done by Piaget (1926/1959). He found that children below the age of seven were extremely deficient in providing what he called **adapted information**. When asked to recount a story they had heard or explain the working of an instrument such as a fountain pen, which had been explained to them, they took little account of the needs of the listener. They did not structure their stories or explanations coherently nor did they appear to keep in mind the extent of the listener's ignorance. For this reason Piaget characterized young children's speech as being predominantly **egocentric** rather than social.

Piaget's theory of cognitive egocentrism has been influential in depicting the preoperational child as one who is unable to take the perspective of another. This affects abilities which depend on role-taking, such as empathy, moral judgement and communication. The sort of evidence on which Piaget based his idea of egocentrism was tasks or situations which required the ability to predict or infer the view (literal or metaphorical) of another. For instance, does the child realize that an object, such as a car, varies in appearance according to the particular perspective that one has of it? Piaget found that young children were able to pick out pictures that represented their own viewpoint but not those which showed what others saw, viewing from a different angle. The same deficiency is revealed in conceptual terms. Jane could tell that she had a sister named Susan but answer 'No' to the enquiry, 'Does Susan have a sister?' To Swiss children the French were seen as foreigners but they did not see themselves as foreigners to the French.

Despite this sort of evidence, Piaget's theory of egocentrism is untenable on a number of counts. First, the tasks: in many instances Piaget chose to use a procedure which was excessively demanding. Prime examples are the tasks used in the early referential communication studies. Not only were the stories long, with little internal consistency, the instruments they had to explain were ones to tax the ingenuity of much older children. Studies which have employed simpler problems (e.g., Light, 1979) or broken down the original tasks into component skills to ensure that children understood the response that was required of them (Hughes, 1978) have achieved considerably more success.

More fundamentally, egocentrism has been used as a global term to explain children's failure to adapt to the needs of others in the areas indicated. The evidence from studies which have sought to isolate the variables involved in behaviour that Piaget would label egocentric reveals a more complex picture. It will be appropriate to examine communication in this vein.

EGOCENTRISM AS A CAUSE OF COMMUNICATION FAILURE

Egocentrism means perceiving the world from the standpoint of self coupled with a basic inability to take account of another's point of view. This seems to imply a serious handicap to communication. One way of testing the assertion is to show that young children construct messages which are uninformative to others but meaningful to themselves. It has, in fact, been shown that communication which is publicly uninformative is also privately uninformative (Asher, 1976), suggesting that the critical skills are those needed to identify a particular object or event with language.

No one would deny that being aware of the listener's perspective is a necessary part of communication but egocentrism is too diffuse a concept to serve as an explanation of even the communication process, let alone the wider field. It is not only a shift from self to others that is required but the ability to discriminate among others and take account of differences in age, sex, knowledge and so on. As Flavell (1977) has pointed out, learning about the needs and characteristics of people is a lifelong task and there is a real sense in which we have continually to resist the egocentric claims that are made on us, at any age, in order to relate successfully to other people.

As far as other factors are concerned, we know that changes in vocabulary, attention, memory and thinking enhance communicative efficiency (Shatz, 1978). Most important of all is the capacity to sustain an effective dialogue. This requires the ability to switch speaker and listener roles constantly, to monitor the effects of one's messages and modify them according to feedback received from the listener. The listener must recognize inadequate communication and signal the fact. Listeners who expect speakers to do all the work cannot complain if they fail to understand what is meant. Speakers who believe that communication is like a game of twenty questions, in which they answer 'Yes' or 'No' while being interrogated by their audience, must not be surprised if the audience loses interest. Adequate communication is, in short, a **dynamic interactive process**.

Nonverbal communication

INTRODUCTION

While the study of language and verbal communication is a research field that has expanded with remarkable rapidity during the last two decades, there has also been a considerable upsurge of interest in nonverbal communication. The term 'nonverbal communication' is used to denote any communication that occurs between two or more persons through nonverbal channels. These channels are surprisingly numerous when considered one by one. There are nonverbal channels involving the movement or attitude of parts of the body, for example gaze direction, facial expression, body posture and hand gestures. The study of body movements is sometimes referred to as **kinesics**, a term used by American anthropologist Ray Birdwhistell to describe the science of body movements that he has tried to develop. A second major group of nonverbal channels involves the physical distance between persons, ranging from the distance between persons in face-to-face interaction to the organization of physical space within and between buildings. The study of the way in which people unconsciously structure the space between them is generally known as **proxemics**, a term coined by another American anthropologist, Edward T. Hall. A third important group of nonverbal channels includes all the nonverbal aspects of utterances, such as their speed, loudness, pitch, fluency, pause distribution, and so on. These vocal, but nonverbal, cues are often collectively described as **paralanguage**.

Nonverbal *behaviour* should be distinguished from nonverbal *communication*. Some nonverbal behaviours, such as changes in voice pitch during attempted deception, may be unselfconsciously enacted by an individual, and may go unnoticed by those with whom the individual interacts. Here we cannot speak of nonverbal communication because no communication as such has occurred via this nonverbal channel. Other nonverbal behaviours, such as gaze patterns, may also be unselfconsciously enacted by the individual in the course of social interaction, but may be noticed by those with whom he or she interacts. To the extent that the others – consciously or unconsciously – attach meanings to the individual's gaze patterns, we can say that nonverbal communication has taken place, despite the fact that there was no communicative intent on the part of the individual. Someone who speaks with a level gaze may be thought (rightly or wrongly) to be telling the truth, while another who speaks with a shifting gaze pattern may be thought (again, rightly or wrongly) to be lying. Still other nonverbal behaviours, such as certain hand-arm gestures, may be quite deliberately enacted by one individual and specifically directed at another or others who are left in no doubt about the nature of the message being conveyed. Thus, when one person shakes a fist at another, it is clear to all who see the gesture that the first person is angry with the second person.

Rather than attempting to provide what would inevitably be a very superficial overview of the extensive research literature on nonverbal communication, we shall here limit ourselves to the examination of two channels of nonverbal communication – **gaze** and **facial expression**. Indeed, there are good reasons for considering these two channels rather than any of the others mentioned above. First, there are grounds for thinking that these two channels are of particular significance: gaze patterns are intimately related to the acquisition of information through vision, and vision is (as we have seen in Chapter 3) the most important of the various senses; and there is evidence that the face is more highly attended and typically more informative than other nonverbal channels. A second, presumably related, reason for focusing on these two channels is that there is rather more research on gaze and facial expression than on other nonverbal channels. A third reason is that in one respect they provide an interesting contrast: whereas gaze patterns tend to be heavily influenced by situational and cultural factors, facial expressions are to some degree independent of these factors.

GAZE

Much of the extensive research on gaze has been directed at uncovering the relationship between gaze and ongoing social behaviour. For example, the relationship between speech and gaze has received much experimental attention. Kendon (1967), studying two-person interactions, found that the pattern of an individual's looking behaviour while speaking was quite different from that found when the same individual was listening. Kendon began by noting how gaze direction changes when an individual begins and ends a long utterance (i.e., one that lasts for five seconds or more). Figure 10.1 shows the frequency of other-directed gaze during the three seconds leading up to the end of person A's utterance and the three seconds immediately following the beginning of person B's utterance. There is a clear tendency for a speaker to look away when beginning a long utterance, and to look at the other as the end of the utterance approaches. Commenting on these findings, Kendon observed that 'insofar as looking away at the beginning of an utterance, and looking back as it ends, are regular occurrences, these changes in direction of gaze can come to function as signals . . .' (p. 33).

Specifically, Kendon proposed that the speaker's gaze direction may mark 'points of significant change' in his or her behaviour, and may be exploited by the speaker to regulate the listener's behaviour. By looking away at the beginning of an utterance, the speaker may help to forestall any response from the listener; and by looking at the listener as the utterance comes to an end, the speaker may be 'offering the floor' to the listener. To test this latter proposal, Kendon examined the latencies between utterances where the speaker did look at the listener as the utterance ended and those where the speaker did not do so. Consistent with this proposal, Kendon found that of those utterances which ended with an extended look, only 29 per cent were followed by either no response or a delayed response from the listener; while of those that

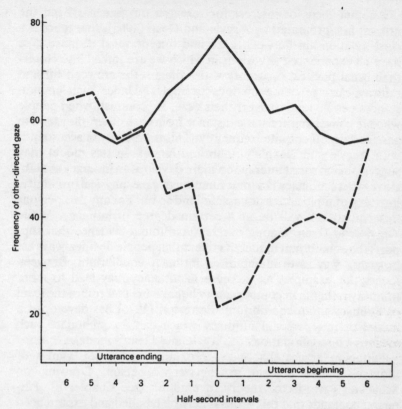

Figure 10.1 Direction of gaze at beginning and end of long utterances. The graph shows the frequency of other-directed gazes in the half-second intervals just before and just after beginning (broken line) or ending (solid line) a long utterance. (After Kendon, 1967)

ended without the speaker gazing at the listener, 71 per cent were followed by either no response or a delayed response. Such findings strongly suggest that a speaker's gaze patterns help to indicate when an utterance is coming to an end, thereby facilitating the process of turn-taking in conversations. It should be noted, however, that Kendon's findings on the gaze-speech relationship have been challenged by other researchers (e.g., Levine and Sutton-Smith, 1973).

Another focus of interest for research on gaze has been the notion, first promoted by Argyle and Dean (1965), that there is a close relationship between gaze and **interpersonal distance**. We have all experienced situations in which we are forced into closer-than-usual physical proximity with others – the crowded lift and railway carriage being obvious examples. Under such circumstances people tend to avert their gaze. By contrast, when people who are conversing are some distance from each other, they tend to gaze at each other quite frequently. This is precisely in accordance with Argyle and Dean's equilibrium model. In this model they suggest that in social interaction there develops an **intimacy equilibrium**, where intimacy is a joint function of gaze, physical proximity, intimacy of topic under discussion, and so on. For any two persons this equilibrium will be at a certain degree of intimacy. While Argyle and Dean, among others, have found evidence that supports the equilibrium model, it is clear that people do not always act in such a way as to maintain an intimacy equilibrium. Between lovers, for example, an increase in intimacy may lead to more intimacy rather than compensatory behaviours that return the level of intimacy to an equilibrium. Patterson (1976) has developed a model of interpersonal intimacy which can accommodate such everyday disconfirmations of Argyle and Dean's model.

Patterson argues that gaze, proximity and other signals of intimacy create arousal in the target person. Drawing on Schachter's two-factor theory of emotion (see Chapter 8), Patterson contends that this arousal may be labelled and experienced either positively or negatively, depending upon contextual factors. How the target person reacts to signals of greater intimacy from another individual will depend on the nature of the resulting emotional state. If the latter is positive, then the target person will, according to Patterson, respond by reciprocating signals of intimacy. If the emotional state is negative, as indeed was the case among Argyle and Dean's subjects when they were exposed to increased gaze, then the target person will respond in such a way as to maintain the intimacy equilibrium.

So far we have been concerned primarily with the messages conveyed by person A's gaze patterns to person B. But what of the factors determining person A's gaze patterns? Why does person A gaze at person B at all? One obvious answer to this type of question is that by looking at B's face, A gains information about B's general attitude to A and reaction to A's utterances. One important component of this information is B's gaze direction. Thus, if B spends much of the encounter looking away from A, A might well infer that B's attention is not focused on the present interaction. A second important component of the information acquired by gazing at B is B's facial expression. The type and extent of the information that can be gleaned from facial expressions is considered below. Before moving on, however, it has to be added that most of the research on gaze has been conducted in Western cultures, and that there is some reason to be cautious about the extent to which the findings can be straightforwardly generalized to other cultures. Watson (1972) argues, for example, that while too much gaze is considered insulting, threatening and disrespectful by Africans, Asians and Indians, too little gaze is seen to be insincere by Arabs and South Americans. Clearly, gaze may communicate different messages in different cultural contexts.

FACIAL EXPRESSION

As was seen in Chapter 8, there is by now good reason to believe that there is cross-cultural universality in the facial expression of some emotional states. One major finding emerging from the research on the universality of facial expressions is that members of different cultures show the same facial expression when experiencing the same emotion – unless culture-specific display rules interfere. If there is a stable link between the experience of certain emotional states and the facial expressions that accompany these states, it seems probable that observers will be accurate in inferring how an individual feels, given only that person's facial expression. Indeed, this is the other major finding of the cross-cultural research: regardless of culture, observers tend to label at least some facial expressions of emotion in the same way. This clearly implies that by gazing at B's face, A can acquire information about B's current emotional state.

However, there is one limitation that applies to nearly all of this cross-cultural research, and this is that the facial expressions presented to observers tend not to be spontaneous concomitants of genuine emotional experiences. Rather, they are typically still photographs of expressions posed by persons who have been instructed to display a particular emotion, or to move certain facial muscles. It seems possible that posed expressions of emotion will be exaggerated in some respect and will therefore be easier to recognize than spontaneous, naturally occurring facial expressions. There is, indeed, experimental evidence to support this supposition (Zuckerman *et al.*, 1976). It is therefore likely that studies of the nonverbal communication of emotion via posed facial expressions overestimate the extent of this communication as it occurs in everyday interactions. Fortunately the development of relatively low-cost, closed-circuit television and videorecording systems has enabled recent research in this field to study spontaneous facial expressions, i.e., facial expressions that are exhibited when the individual is unaware that he or she is being observed or videotaped.

Studies of the nonverbal communication of emotion via spontaneous facial expressions typically proceed by exposing one group of subjects (**senders**) to emotionally laden stimuli – usually photographic slides or films – and covertly videotaping their facial expressions as they watch these stimuli. Another group of subjects (**receivers**) is subsequently shown the videotaped expressions indicating the sender's emotional state and/or the kinds of stimuli the sender was viewing during particular videotape sequences. One version of such a procedure is known as the slide-viewing paradigm, and was developed by Buck and his colleagues from R. E. Miller's studies of nonverbal communication in rhesus monkeys. Miller first taught two monkeys to press a bar when a light came on, either to obtain food or to avoid shock. The animals were then paired such that the sender could see the light but not press the bar, while the receiver could press the bar but not see the light. This receiver monkey was instead provided with the televised image of the face and head of the sender monkey who was actually in another room. Thus, the receiver had to judge when to press the bar on the basis of the sender's facial expressions. Miller and his associates (e.g., Miller *et al.*, 1967) found that normal rhesus monkeys could perform this task with ease, thereby suggesting an effective level of nonverbal communication via facial expressions.

Buck's variant of Miller's procedure employs colour slides as the emotional stimuli, and humans as senders and receivers. The senders are shown a series of twenty-five slides which fall into one of five categories: sexual, scenic, pleasant, unpleasant and unusual. Having seen each slide, the sender rates the strength and pleasantness of the emotion evoked by the slide. The receiver's task is to judge which category the slide being watched belongs to, and to rate the strength and pleasantness of the sender's emotional experience. Three measures of nonverbal communication of emotion are used: (1) the percentage of slides correctly categorized; (2) the correlation between sender's and receiver's strength ratings; and (3) the correlation between sender's and' receiver's pleasantness ratings. Buck and his colleagues (Buck *et al.*, 1972, 1974) found that both the first and last of these measures were greater than would be expected by chance. In other words, significant communication accuracy was occurring. However, it is also clear from this and other research that there are sizeable individual differences both in nonverbal sending accuracy – the tendency to emit communicative facial expressions – and in nonverbal receiving ability – the ability to decode accurately others' facial expressions.

One of the most reliable findings regarding individual differences in this field is that females are on average better than males in nonverbal receiving ability (Hall, 1978). There is also some evidence that females are on average better than males in nonverbal sending accuracy (Buck *et al.*, 1974). The finding that females are superior to males in decoding others' facial expressions is consistent with the commonly held view that women are more interpersonally sensitive than men, but why this should be the case is by no means clear. It may be that females learn to be more interested in others' emotional states and are consequently more practised and motivated in the art of decoding facial expressions. It has also been suggested that it may have been functional for women to develop a sensitivity to facial expressions in others, since this would enable them to anticipate others' behaviours (e.g., outbursts of violence) which men would be better able to cope with by physical retaliation or intervention. At any rate, it seems very likely that female superiority in nonverbal receiving ability is a consequence of sex-role learning. The same would appear to be true of the female advantage in nonverbal sending accuracy, for Buck's

(1975, 1977) studies of preschool children (aged four to six) have found little sign of a sex difference in sending accuracy, and also a tendency for boys (but not girls) to become less facially communicative as they grow older.

Despite the growing body of evidence that emotional states can be communicated via facial expressions, the information value of the face as a channel of communication relative to other channels should not be overstated. In a recent study by DePaulo and her colleagues (1982), receivers' judgements of senders' messages were compared across a number of communication channels. The senders were describing people they knew, and they sometimes did this truthfully (for example, by honestly describing someone they liked), while at other times they did this deceptively (for example, by pretending to like someone they disliked). The receivers' task was to rate these person descriptions on a number of dimensions, such as deceptiveness, tension and ambivalence. It was found that when receivers had access to verbal cues (whether these were provided via written transcript, audio tape, or full audiovisual record), their ratings of truthful messages differed much more sharply from their ratings of deceptive messages than was the case when the available cues were purely nonverbal. Particularly where judgements of deceptiveness are concerned, it seems that verbal cues are more informative than nonverbal cues.

Styles of communication

A number of variables can be examined under the heading 'styles', including subcultural differences such as accent and dialect, as well as age, sex and class differences. Our focus is determined by the direction of research, much of which has been guided by a concern for the extent to which limitations in communicative competence affect a child's ability to utilize the education system. Latterly this concern has been turned on its head so that education is examined (and generally found wanting) in regard to the manner in which it meets the requirements of different sections of society.

We will consider two questions which fairly reflect the major theoretical issues. First, what are the significant subcultural (including class) differences in patterns or styles of communication? Second, to the extent that such differences exist, are there particular socialization factors that account for them? Two names – one British, one American – dominate this field. Basil Bernstein is an English sociologist who has been working for some twenty-five years on the relation between language use, social class and education. The sociolinguist William Labov has been conducting similar work in the United States with special emphasis on the language of black Americans.

Bernstein's position

Data on language use among working-class and middle-class youths was obtained by recording discussions on the topic of capital punishment. The working-class boys were found to use shorter words, more personal pronouns and longer phrases. In contrast, the middle-class children produced more pauses and greater variety in their speech – factors which may be causally related. The main differences, found also in a follow-up by Lawton (1968), concerned the contextually bound nature of the working-class speech. Called **restricted speech** by Bernstein, it was effective in communication only so long as the listener shared the background knowledge. Lawton (1968) found that the middle-class children with the less context-dependent **elaborated code** were more adept at switching from a restricted to an elaborated code if the topic demanded it. For example, a move from discussing the day's events in school with a classmate to expounding one's views on, say, honesty to the head teacher.

There are obvious educational implications to these findings, and the debate has been a heated one. One of Bernstein's claims is that an elaborated code is necessary to the sort of theory-building in which the scientist indulges, since theories are all about universals. The restricted code is tied rather to individual experience, which might hamper formal argument. This issue is taken up in the next section when considering the function of the printed word in the development of modes of thought. Before examining Labov's alternative position, one other feature of Bernstein's work is of interest. This concerns communication style and the family. Bernstein claims to have married his speech codes to types of interaction within families. The **positional** family is one where the child's place in the hierarchy is stressed, which, in linguistic terms, leads to a proliferation of imperatives and assertions about what is, and what is not, permitted. In such families a restricted code predominates. The **personal** family, on the other hand, is seen to value the child as an individual and to deal with conflict situations with explanations (which use the elaborated code) rather than prescriptions. Whether families that conform to these stereotypes exist is another matter and the evidence is only partially supportive. It is worth noting, however, that the effectiveness of personal-type rearing styles – called by Aronfreed (1976) the **induction technique** – on the development of empathy and altruism has generally been supported.

Labov's critique

The work of Bernstein and his colleagues has been interpreted as meaning that working-class children are deficient in verbal skills and that this in turn requires remedial programmes in schools to make good the deficit. (Bernstein himself claims not to subscribe to this view – see Edwards, 1979a, for a balanced account.)

The research which has been used more than any other to rebut the **deficit theory** is that of Labov (1973). As Edwards (1979a) has noted, 'It is no overstatement to say that this article is the single most powerful assault upon the environmentalist position on disadvantage in general, and upon verbal deprivation in particular' (p. 55). Labov's article contains a critique of Bernstein and an important guide to methodology but its major contribution is the linguistic analysis of black American English. This demonstrates conclusively that it is in no sense a substandard form but is a rule-governed system with all the complexity and richness of the standard form. It requires the child to learn the grammar of such forms as the double negative – 'He don't know nothing'; the omission of the possessive 's' – 'You got John book'; and the deletion of the copula when it contracts in standard English – 'He wild tonight'.

A consensus is being reached that the notion of certain groups of children, defined by social class or ethnic minority, being deficient or substandard in language is a myth and a dangerous myth at that. What is agreed is that there are differences in the language styles that individuals use, not simply between groups but within groups. As Labov points out, there is no such thing as a single-style speaker and it is vital for research to recognize that it is the context that determines the style employed. Assuming that we wish to develop theories about the most natural style or vernacular that a person uses, we must take steps to ensure that methods achieve such samples of speech. At the same time it is recognized that some groups will find experiences such as school difficult because the vernacular is different from that used and, frequently, valued in the school. It is how such a *difference* should be addressed that constitutes the focus of contemporary debates (e.g., Davies, 1977) on education and communicative styles, an issue to which science is unlikely to provide an answer.

The printed word

Communication of a more specialized kind is taking place while the writer of this chapter puts the words on the page. Just as the speaker presupposes a listener, so the writer assumes a reader. The graphic mode, however, does not have the dynamic quality of the oral medium. The burden is placed very squarely on the writer to have the reader's needs in mind while putting his or her ideas in print. On the face of it this seems an impossible task since every reader's needs are different. Yet, if the prospect is daunting, it does not stop thousands of individuals speaking with many millions through the medium of the printed word. Into this category we can also place much of the output of the broadcasting media where the needs of the audience have to be inferred without the means of reciprocal feedback.

How does the process work? Paradoxically, many people believe they can communicate better on paper than they can in speech. This does not mean that such individuals believe that intentions concerning the enjoyment of a meal are better put in writing rather than saying 'Please pass the salt'. (Such behaviour would probably qualify as a *disorder* of communication.) The advantages of the printed word are threefold. A much larger audience can be reached; an enduring record is created; the expression of abstract ideas, especially, is facilitated. The first two claims are self-evident but the third is more polemical and it is to this that we now turn.

There is a story, probably apocryphal, that as an undergraduate the Oxford philosopher, A. J. Ayer, wrote only two words on his tripos paper: 'Viva me.' Whether the story is true or not, only an exceptional person would prefer to be judged on the basis of a spoken rather than written performance when the assessment relates to complex abstract ideas. Putting the account in writing allows us to make tangible our thoughts and, arguably, facilitates the organization of our thinking. It certainly gives us more time and the resulting transcript is likely to be more coherent, and therefore comprehensible, than the spoken account. The drawback, of course, is that it is a passive form of communication – you cannot ask questions of a book. This is, in fact, only a half-truth. Psychologists who have studied the learning process point out the importance of taking an active approach to study. Thus books (and lectures) should be approached in a critical frame of mind in which questions are asked about the material, and answers sought from elsewhere when necessary.

Learning to read and write is a significant acquisition for children. Apart from the obvious increased opportunity it provides for gaining knowledge, there is something about the enduring written word which assists cognitive growth. The argument, put forward persuasively by Olson (1977) and Donaldson (1978), is that the written word, because of its permanent and relatively context-free form, allows a focus on language itself. The significance of this is that the literal meaning of propositions, and the arguments that follow from them, can start to be attended rather than the intentions behind utterances which children grasp early because of their sensitivity to nonverbal context.

If this is a key to the development of what Piaget would call operational thinking (Donaldson prefers the term **disembedded thinking**) then there is clearly a case for a considerable research effort on the role of reading and writing in cognition. It could be, for instance, that although reading is the necessary first step in this process, it has a limited effect because it is essentially a passive process. Writing, however, is an active affair, assuming it is something more than mere transcription. Olson has referred to the importance of imagination in enabling the child to move from the world of stimulus-bound 'concrete' statements to that of logical arguments where imagined states of affairs may be important. Imagination in the creative, rather than fantasy sense is certainly involved in writing.

Moreover, there is probably an interaction between reading and writing as well as between these processes and thinking. Evidence suggests that a plateau is reached at the reading age of nine or ten and that many individuals do not go beyond this – a fact which may explain the popularity of newspapers which demand no more than a reading age of ten. It would be informative to know what carries children beyond the plateau and what responsibility can be afforded to the act of writing.

Many societies, of course, have only an oral tradition; and those with a graphic tradition vary in their writing systems, some (e.g., the alphabetical) being much more powerful than others (e.g., pictorial) (see Haas, 1976). Language is learned as an oral phenomenon and depends on an acoustic process and a communicative system which is intimately dependent on context, as we have indicated in this chapter. But approaches such as Chomsky's to the study of language, which we briefly outlined in Chapter 9, are based on language as a written form. As such they may be fundamentally misconceived as accounts of language development. (See Olson and Torrance, 1983, for an expansion of this argument.) Whatever the merits of this position, it is becoming increasingly clear that the movement from utterance to text, in which a reliance on memory (and the speech forms that facilitate it) is replaced by a focus on logical or formal analysis, marks a major transition in cognitive as well as communicative growth.

Disorders of communication

Disorders of communication may arise through a variety of causes. We have already discussed in Chapter 9 two of the major varieties, namely aphasia, brought about by brain damage, and the developmental disorders associated with either hearing loss or language deprivation. In this section we shall confine our attention to problems of written communication, particularly the area that has generated much research – reading.

As in any learning task, people vary in the speed with which they acquire the information or skill involved in reading. We do not regard someone who learns to read slowly as having a disorder, any more than the individual who acquires knowledge of arithmetic more slowly than others. This is because we know that rate of acquisition is affected by inbuilt individual differences as well as environmental factors such as mode of teaching. The person who is slow to read may be quick to pick up other facilities involving, say, motor and spatial skills. We reserve the term 'disorder' for a pattern of performance that falls clearly outside the normal range for that ability. The word 'normal', however, is a minefield in psychology (see Chapter 13) and we need to be clear what we mean.

The most obvious case of 'disorder' is following brain injury when various intellectual capacities, such as reading and writing, may be impaired. Such a person, having been a fluent reader before the brain damage, may legitimately be said to have **acquired dyslexia** if obvious reading difficulties are displayed. It may be, of course, that this person suffers other language-based debilities such as aphasia and agraphia. So-called **developmental dyslexia** is much less easy to determine. A useful definition of such dyslexia is: 'a disorder of children who, despite conventional classroom experience, fail to attain the language skills of reading, writing and spelling commensurate with their intellectual abilities' (Critchley, 1970, p. 11). (See page 75.)

Our understanding of this disorder owes much to the work of educationalists and clinicians (e.g., Critchley, 1970). In the space available we will concentrate on the contribution of experimental psychologists, many of whom have worked within an information-processing framework. They have looked for an explanation of poor reading in terms of the processing systems that are involved in the activity. As was pointed out in Chapter 3, reading involves more than the eyes. Since the printed word is a representation of something that can be articulated, and since spoken language precedes reading developmentally, it is evident that there must be a relationship between the spoken word and reading. Furthermore, the educational process encourages novice readers to read aloud since this is the main way in which teachers and parents can evaluate progress. In line with this is the fact that deaf children rarely learn to read well (Conrad, 1977).

One approach to research on the cause of dyslexia has looked for deficiencies in the visual-auditory intermodal integration system that we have suggested is involved. Vellutino and his associates (see Vellutino, 1979), working with nine- to eleven-year-old children, found that in a task which required the subjects to match forms, both visual (geometric forms) and verbal (nonsense words), there was a significant difference between good and bad readers in the visual-verbal task but not in the visual-visual task. This suggests that an ability to deal simultaneously with visual and verbal information is important in learning to read. Workers who have looked separately at the auditory and the visual processing systems of poor readers have uncovered some significant impairments. It has been found, for instance, that dyslexics have trouble perceiving speech sounds, but if they are artificially slowed down (e.g. 'b' from 50 msec to 100 msec) the perceptual problem disappears.

Table 10.2 **The ability of normal readers and dyslexic children to recognize and describe two stimuli presented close in time**. The figures refer to the time needed between stimuli before recognition and description are possible. At times lower than these, the two forms are seen as one, that is, as a cross inside a square.

STIMULI:	$+ \ \square$	
	RECOGNIZE	KNOW (SAY/DRAW)
NORMALS	100 msec	180
DYSLEXICS	140	320

There are comparable problems in the visual modality. Table 10.2 shows that dyslexics take longer both to recognize the existence of two discrete figures and also to describe what they have seen. This suggests that one of the dyslexic's difficulties is a perseverating and interfering trace at the earliest stages of processing. This shows itself as a **masking problem** in the reading process and gives rise to the sort of errors which dyslexics typically show in pronouncing ordinary words (see Table 10.3).

As Farnham-Diggory (1978) argues, if these children were saying what they saw then we might conclude: 'dyslexic children . . . pick up letters from a line of print at a rate that is incompatible with their processing rate. Once the printed features move inside, they may move through buffers, synthesizers, or working memory, just

Table 10.3 **Misreadings by dyslexic children.** (Adapted from Farnham-Diggory and Gregg, 1975)

Test words (exposed for 2 sec)	What the reader said
bracket	broket
conceal	concol
kerosene	konsen
screw	scree
alternate	alfoonite
definite	defynit
estimate	extermate
majesty	marijest
solution	slotion
uncomfortable	icomfort

slowly enough to be clobbered by the next incoming unit' (p. 129). She goes on to argue that if this is true, it should lead to a new teaching method in which one letter or orthographic unit at a time is displayed on a screen sequentially at a speed to suit the individual child.

A substantial amount of evidence has accumulated showing that a **memory deficit** is contributing to the poor reader's problem. The normal serial position curve showing primacy and recency effects in a serial learning task with poor recall in the middle of the list (see Chapter 6) is not manifested by poor readers. Spring and Capps (1974), for instance, found that poor readers showed a **recency effect** comparable with that of normal readers in a recall task using digits. Buffered short-term memory seemed unimpaired. The **primacy effect**, relating to the early items in the list and dependent on rehearsal, was present for the normal readers but not for the dyslexics. Since eye movements were recorded during the task, it was also shown that poor performance was correlated with **non-serial scanning**, a feature common to many of the dyslexics but virtually nonexistent in the good readers. There is other evidence (e.g., Corkin, 1974) to show that deficiencies in serial ordering (clearly a prerequisite for reading) is present in dyslexics but Spring and Capps favour a different explanation. In another study they showed that poor readers were significantly slower than normals at naming nonverbal stimuli including digits, colours and pictures. This naming lag, they argue, leaves the poor reader little time for rehearsal, demonstrated by a significant relationship between naming speed and effective scanning strategy.

The relationship between the visual and auditory modalities which, we have argued, is central to the reading process, crops up again in the debate over the role of short-term memory in reading deficits. In an experiment which required ten-year-old children to recall sequences of digits presented either orally or visually, Farnham-Diggory and Gregg (1975) found that differences between good and poor readers were most dramatic if first and last trials were compared. All the children showed a decrement in performance as a function of trials so that they were getting many fewer items correct at the end of the sessions, almost certainly as a result of fatigue. But for the normal readers, when they switched modalities, performance returned to the level shown at the start of the earlier block of trials. Thus memory fatigue disappears when a new modality is introduced, regardless of direction: aural-visual or visual-aural. After ten trials there is also a similar decrement in the number of items recalled in the second modality. The dyslexic children showed no such recovery following a switch in modality. Indeed, in the switch from auditory to visual mode there is a further drop in performance from that realized at the end of the auditory block of trials. Thus, arguments about the role of short-term memory in dyslexia need to take account of both **modality** and **practice/fatigue effects**.

Farnham-Diggory and Gregg also studied what they called **memory scanning** with the same population of subjects. This was closer to the demands of reading in that subjects were presented with a sequence of letters and asked questions about which letters came first, last or in the middle. Again the material was presented in the two modalities and speed of response was the dependent variable. The results, summarized in Figure 10.1, show that over trials, while the good readers' performance in both modalities was more or less constant over time, there was a marked discrepancy among the poor readers. Their ability to scan auditory elements in working memory deteriorated over time while performance in the visual mode notably improved. The authors concluded: 'Auditory-visual scanning synchrony may be critical to the efficient flow of the reading process. If, as seems to be the case for poor readers, auditory retrieval gradually lags relative to visual retrieval, a devas-

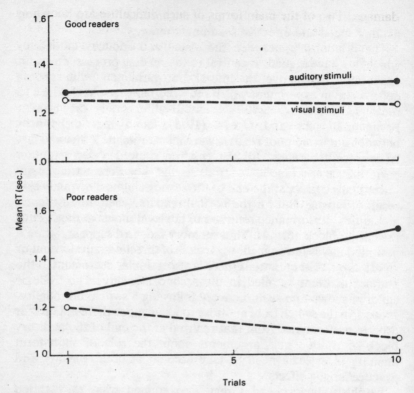

Figure 10.2 Synchrony and asynchrony in the reaction time for memory scanning of good and poor readers. (Adapted from Farnham-Diggory and Gregg, 1975)

tating type of asynchrony could result: Attention to a visual particle would move on before the auditory associate could be retrieved' (Farnham-Diggory and Gregg, 1975, p. 295).

This brief review of dyslexia as a disorder of child development is enough to demonstrate that the problem does not seem to have a single underlying cause. A variety of cognitive deficits seem to be associated, and it remains to be determined whether this heterogeneity gives rise to the same basic disorder or whether we are actually dealing with a **group of disorders**. A similar problem arises with acquired dyslexia – the reading difficulties that follow brain damage. Two of the main forms of such difficulties are known as surface and deep dyslexia. **Surface dyslexia** was first labelled by Marshall and Newcombe (1973) and has recently been described by Coltheart and his associates (1983).

Surface dyslexia is distinguished by problems with reading irregular (but not regular) words such as 'bear' and 'broad' which will tend to be regularized into 'beer' and 'brode'. There is also a tendency to confuse homophones, that is, words which sound the same but have different spellings and meanings, such as 'saw' and 'soar'. A further characteristic is to regularize spelling so that a word like 'search' becomes 'surch'.

Deep dyslexia has been described by Shallice and Warrington (1980). Among the key defining features they mention are:

1. Difficulty in using phonological information in reading, giving rise to problems in reading nonsense words.

2. The critical role of part of speech on reading performance, nouns being read most easily, followed by adjectives and verbs and, finally, function words, which are most difficult.

3. The effect of imageability on performance. This may be related to the second point (above) since nouns, e.g. 'dog', tend to have high imageability while function words, e.g. 'with', are low in imageability. The effect can also be demonstrated within one word-class, however, since there are a plethora of abstract low-imageable nouns.

Coltheart and his colleagues (1983) report case studies of a developmental and an acquired dyslexic who both showed features characteristic of surface dyslexia. The view that this means acquired and developmental dyslexia have common roots has been put forward by Jorm (1979) and challenged by Baddeley and his colleagues (1982). They examined the claim with respect to the first and third features of deep dyslexics described above. Their study used only developmental dyslexics and suitable controls, and compared their performances with data collected by other workers (notably Patterson and Marcel, 1977) who used patients with deep dyslexia as subjects. Baddeley and his associates' first study required subjects to pick out real words from easily pronounceable nonwords, the nonwords being of two kinds: homophonic (e.g., stane, frute) and nonhomophonic (e.g., dake, selt). The results showed that dyslexics were slower and less accurate than controls of the same reading age, but that the same pattern of difficulty emerged for the two groups. There was a 'consistent tendency for homophonic nonwords to lead to slower and less accurate decisions, indicating the use of phonological coding in both groups' (Baddeley *et al.*, 1982, p. 191). This was not true of Patterson and Marcel's acquired dyslexics.

A second study required the children simply to read through a list of words, some of which were pronounceable but not meaningful (e.g., dake). Again, the dyslexic children showed a significantly poorer performance in terms of reading time and error rate than the controls, which included children with the same reading age but three years younger chronologically. Nevertheless, the authors note that the pattern of performance is not qualitatively different from that of younger children with a similar reading age and that any difference 'is far from dramatic in comparison with the disproportionate difficulty in reading nonwords displayed by deep dyslexic patients' (p. 193).

The final study looked at the effects of imageability on reading accuracy. It was found that low-imageability words gave rise to significantly more errors but that the dyslexic group did not differ in this respect from the reading age controls. The authors argue that although this performance is comparable to that of the acquired dyslexics, because the phenomenon seems to be true also of young normal readers it does not argue for a common basis for deep and developmental dyslexia.

Although Baddeley and his colleagues come down firmly on the side of those who dispute the claim for a common basis in deep and acquired dyslexia, they are careful not to rule out the possibility that the same components of reading are defective in both cases and that subsequent histories (such as phonological training in the case of the children, or a more devastating impairment in the case of the patients) may account for the differences. There would seem to be something to be gained, therefore, from further studies comparing developmental and acquired dyslexia.

Further reading

General

An enticing, well-written but somewhat out-of-date introduction to this field is:

MILLER, G.A., ed. (1973) *Communication, Language and Meaning.* New York: Basic Books.

The development of communication

A good discussion of the issues involved in functional explanations of language development is provided by:

ELLIOT, A.J. (1981) *Child Language.* Cambridge: Cambridge University Press.

More advanced accounts can be found in the chapters by Shatz, and Bates and McWhinney (1982) in:

WANNER, E. and GLEITMAN, L., eds. (1982) *Language Acquisition: the State of the Art.* Cambridge: Cambridge University Press.

Brown's introduction is particularly worth reading in this collection of papers concerned with the verbal input to children:

SNOW, C.E. and FERGUSON, C.A., eds. (1977) *Talking to Children: Language Input and Acquisition.* Cambridge: Cambridge University Press.

A book which still repays reading as an introduction to the field of child communication is:

PIAGET, J. (1926/1959) *The Language and Thought of the Child.* London: Routledge and Kegan Paul.

A guide to current methodology and issues as well as empirical findings is available in:

LLOYD, P. and BEVERIDGE, M. (1981) *Information and Meaning in Child Communication.* London: Academic Press.

A good short review of work in referential communication can be found in:

ASHER, S. (1978) Referential communication. In G. Whitehurst and B. Zimmerman, eds., *The Functions of Language and Cognition.* New York: Academic Press.

The authoritative source book is:

DICKSON, W.P., ed. (1981) *Children's Oral Communication Skills*. New York: Academic Press.

Nonverbal communication

A systemic overview of research on nonverbal communication is provided in:

HARPER, R.G., WIENS, A.N. and MATARAZZO, J.D. (1978) *Nonverbal Communication: the State of the Art*. New York: Wiley.

A useful book that deals specifically with gaze is:

ARGYLE, M. and COOK, M. (1976) *Gaze and Mutual Gaze*. Cambridge: Cambridge University Press.

Some of the more important recent research on individual differences in nonverbal communication is reviewed in the following book (the chapters on sex differences by Hall and by Rosenthal and DePaulo are recommended, together with Buck's chapter on the relationship between facial expressiveness and physiological responding):

ROSENTHAL, R., ed. (1979) *Skill in Nonverbal Communication: Individual Differences*. Cambridge, Mass.: Oelgeschlager, Gunn and Hain.

Some stimulating chapters on nonverbal behaviour and sex differences are collected in:

MAYO, C. and HENLEY, N.M. (1981) *Gender and Nonverbal Behavior*. New York: Springer-Verlag.

Styles of communication

Bernstein's views are set out at length in the three volumes of:

BERNSTEIN, B. (1971–5) *Class, Codes and Control*. London: Routledge and Kegan Paul.

Labov's position can be found in:

LABOV, W. (1976) *Language in the Inner City*. Pittsburgh: University of Pennsylvania Press.

A clear and balanced introduction to the area of language and disadvantage is provided by:

EDWARDS, J.R. (1979) *Language and Disadvantage*. London: Edward Arnold.

The printed word

A rash of books has appeared in recent years on the acquisition of reading and writing and their impact on cognitive development. An authoritative work is:

SCRIBNER, S. and COLE, M. (1981) *The Psychology of Literacy*. Cambridge, Mass.: Harvard University Press.

Worth reading is Olson's provocative account of the role of the printed word in cognition:

OLSON, D. (1977) From utterance to text: the bias of language in speech and writing. *Harvard Education Review*, **47**, 257–82.

Also recommended are:

MARTLEW, M., ed. (1983) *The Psychology of Written Language: a Developmental Approach*. Chichester: Wiley.
PERERA, K. (1984) *Children's Writing and Reading*. Oxford: Blackwell.

Disorders of communication

A readable, short introduction to dyslexia as a developmental disorder is:

FARNHAM-DIGGORY, S. (1978) *Learning Disabilities*. London: Fontana Paperbacks.

A more detailed treatment can be found in:

MILES, T.R. (1981) *Understanding Dyslexia*. London: Hodder and Stoughton.

A good review of work on acquired dyslexia is provided by:

PATTERSON, K.E. (1981) Neuropsychological approaches to the study of reading. *British Journal of Psychology*, **72**, 151–74.

The following is a good source book for work in this area:

COLTHEART, M., PATTERSON, K.E. and MARSHALL, J.C., eds. (1980) *Deep Dyslexia*. London: Routledge and Kegan Paul.

(General references on reading can be found at the end of Chapter 3 above.)

11. Attitudes and Person Perception: Aspects of Social Cognition

11. Attitudes and Person Perception: Aspects of Social Cognition

Introduction

In this chapter we shall be concerned with how, in the course of everyday life, we think about and orient ourselves towards the social world around us. We shall therefore be focusing on *internal* structures and processes rather than external behaviour, on social cognition rather than social interaction.

The term **social cognition** warrants some comment: how does social cognition differ from the 'nonsocial' cognitive processes, such as attention, learning, memory, thinking and language, which have been discussed in preceding chapters? This question can be answered on two levels. On one level, it can with some justification be asserted that the distinction between social and nonsocial cognition is a false one, in that cognition is intrinsically social. The knowledge of the world that we acquire in the course of development is socially transmitted and is profoundly influenced by the cultural and social circumstances of our lives. There is a real sense, then, in which all cognition is social.

On another level, however, there is some value in drawing a distinction between social and nonsocial cognition. This is well captured by Forgas (1981, p. 174):

Social cognition differs from nonsocial cognition in at least two crucial respects: First, inferences, attributions and extrapolations lie at the heart of social cognition since the information to be dealt with is usually not directly and unambiguously 'given', but has to be discerned from indirect cues . . . Second, social cognition is always modulated by affective reactions . . . [It] ought to be obvious that there is something fundamentally different in the way that we think about object categories such as furniture, animals, motor cars or fruits . . . and social categories such as persons . . . stereotypes . . . or interaction episodes. Feelings, moods, emotions and preferences lie at the heart of thinking about these latter domains.

These two crucial features of social cognition, namely that it is primarily inferential in nature and that it is profoundly coloured by the individual's preferences and evaluations, are central themes of the present chapter.

The notion that social cognition involves preferences and evaluations is strongly reflected in social psychological research on **attitudes**, for attitude is a term that is generally used to refer to an individual's relatively enduring positive or negative feelings about someone or something. In the present chapter we shall begin our analysis of attitudes by considering more closely what the term 'attitude' means and what holding an attitude towards someone or something involves. Then we shall examine some ways of measuring attitudes, and some of the key factors determining the formation and development of attitudes. Next we shall address the question of attitude change, by discussing in some detail two different lines of research on this issue. This section on attitudes will finish with an examination of the relationship between the attitudes we hold and the way we behave.

The notion that social cognition involves inferences, attributions and extrapolations is clearly reflected in social psychological research on **person perception**. The psychological qualities of other persons (for example their personalities, wishes, feelings and attitudes) are not manifested unambiguously in the way they behave. Rather, these qualities have to be inferred from their behaviour. The means by which we make these inferences is the focus of theory and research on the **attribution process**, and our analysis of person perception in the latter half of this chapter is concerned with attribution theory and research. This section will begin by examining two theoretical models of the attribution process and will continue by considering **self-attribution**, that is, the means by which we make inferences about *our own* psychological qualities. Then we shall examine the extent to which the inferences actually made by adults conform to the logical models proposed by attribution theorists. This section on person perception will finish by considering an increasingly popular approach to explaining and understanding how we make social inferences, which argues that we employ **heuristics**, or rules of thumb, rather than following the comparatively sophisticated models proposed by attribution theorists.

Thus the two main sections of this chapter reflect the two distinguishing qualities of social cognition identified by Forgas (1981). Having established this much, we should now consider how attitude research relates to person perception research. In the present chapter, attitudes and person perception are considered in discrete sections. If both attitudes and person perception are fundamentally involved in social cognition, how valid is it to treat them separately? It must be acknowledged that this separate consideration of attitudes and person perception is principally a reflection of the way in which research in these two fields has developed. Attitude research is arguably as old as social psychology itself, and much of the research dealt with in the present chapter was conducted in the 1950s and 1960s. By contrast, the attributional approach to person perception considered in this chapter did not really take off until the early 1970s. As well as this chronological difference between these two lines of research, they focus on different facets of social cognition. Attitude research focuses on the evaluative aspects of social cognition, while person perception research focuses on the information-processing aspects of social cognition. It is clear that a rounded picture of social cognition must include both a model of how information about the social environment is processed by the individual and an account of how the individual's preferences and evaluations influence and are influenced by this information-processing. As yet, social psychologists have not developed such an integrated view of social cognition, so we have to content ourselves for the time being with the more partial perspectives afforded by considering attitude and person perception research separately.

The final point to be made by way of introduction concerns the relationship between social cognition and social behaviour. Earlier it was stated that the emphasis of this chapter will be on social cognition rather than social behaviour. However, we cannot completely overlook social behaviour in the present context, because it is obvious that the way we perceive and think about our social environment is intimately related to our interactions with other people. Clearly, social cognition reflects our experiences of social behaviour; but it also actively influences our behaviour towards others, and thereby helps to shape the 'reality' that confronts us in everyday life. Perhaps the best way to illustrate this point is by reference to the phenomenon of the **self-fulfilling prophecy**. This term was coined by Merton (1957) in order to describe the way in which a perceiver can cause another person to behave in such a way as to confirm the perceiver's expectations. As Merton puts it, 'The self-fulfilling prophecy is, in the beginning, a *false* definition of the situation evoking a new behaviour which makes the originally false conception come *true*. The specious validity of the self-fulfilling prophecy perpetuates a reign of error. For the prophet will cite the actual course of events as proof that he was right from the very beginning' (1957, p. 423). As we shall see towards the end of this chapter, there is experimental evidence supporting this notion that our expectations of others can bias our interactions with those persons in such a way that they conform to our expectations.

Attitudes

THE PROBLEM OF DEFINITION

In the first edition of the *Handbook of Social Psychology*, Allport (1935) noted that, 'The concept of attitude is probably the most distinctive and indispensable concept in contemporary American social psychology', and he went on to remark that, 'In fact several writers . . . *define* social psychology as the scientific study of attitudes' (p. 798). While no present-day social psychologists would accept such a definition of their field, none would seriously dispute the central status of attitudes in social psychological theory and research.

Before examining research on attitudes and attitude change, we should consider what is meant by the term attitude in the context of social psychological theory and research. The definitions of attitude that have been proposed are remarkably numerous and diverse (cf. Campbell, 1963; Greenwald, 1968). Furthermore, the ways in which researchers have measured attitudes are also highly diverse

(Fishbein and Ajzen, 1972). Fortunately, some consensus among social psychologists has emerged in recent years, enabling us to cut through the jungle of partly conflicting definitions and measurement procedures. At a rather general level, most social psychologists would agree that an attitude is a 'learned predisposition to respond in a consistently favourable or unfavourable manner with respect to a given object', as Fishbein and Ajzen (1975, p. 6) have observed. However, this definition still leaves some key questions unanswered. How, for example, can one distinguish between attitudes, on the one hand, and concepts such as beliefs and values, on the other? Are the latter not learned predispositions to respond in a consistently favourable or unfavourable manner with respect to a given object? To see whether these three concepts can be distinguished analytically, we shall consider the meanings of beliefs and values before returning to the definition of attitudes.

Beliefs represent the knowledge or information one has about the environment. As Fishbein and Ajzen (1975, p. 12) put it, 'a belief links an object to some attribute . . . For example, the belief "Russia is a totalitarian state" links the object "Russia" to the attribute "totalitarian state". Another belief may link "using birth-control pills" (the object) to "preventing pregnancy" (the attribute).' In other words, beliefs concern the relationships between objects and attributes. They are distinguished from attitudes by the fact that they do not in themselves express evaluation. Returning to Fishbein and Ajzen's examples, the belief that 'using birth-control pills prevents pregnancy' does not in itself reveal whether the individual who adheres to this belief thinks that the prevention of pregnancy is good or bad. Attitudes, by contrast, are thought by most social psychologists to involve an evaluative component.

Values are less easily distinguished from attitudes, but can be regarded as premises or assumptions from which attitudes are derived. For example, Bem (1970) asks us to consider an individual who has a positive attitude to the accumulation of personal wealth, and who is asked *why* he has this attitude. He might reply that being wealthy would enable him to retire. Asked why he wants to retire, he might reply that retirement would enable him to study music. Asked why he wants to study music, he might reply that being able to play a musical instrument would enable him to attain self-fulfilment. It would probably make little sense to the man if you asked *why* he wanted to attain self-fulfilment, for he would probably regard this as self-evidently desirable, an end in itself rather than a means to an end; in short, a value. Values are intimately related to attitudes, for attitudes are widely assumed to involve a strong evaluative component. Thus one is likely to have a favourable attitude towards anything that promotes the achievement of one's values, and an unfavourable attitude towards anything that blocks the achievement of one's values.

Thus the key characteristic distinguishing attitudes from beliefs is their evaluative nature, i.e., their reflection of the degree of negative or positive affect felt by an individual towards the attitude object. Although there are some theorists who would balk at this definition of attitude *simply* in terms of affect or evaluation, as we shall see, most investigators would accept that this evaluative quality is the quintessential feature of attitudes.

ATTITUDINAL COMPONENTS

What does an attitude consist of? Are there identifiable **components** of attitudes, and if so, do these components relate to each other in characteristic ways? A widely held view of the internal structure of attitudes is the **three-component view**, which distinguishes between affective, cognitive and conative (or behavioural) components. Such a view is represented schematically in Figure 11.1. This figure implies that an individual's responses to an object are mediated by his or her attitude to that object, and that three classes of response can be distingushed: **affective responses** (autonomic responses, self-reports of affect); **cognitive responses** (perceptual responses, self-reports of belief); and **behavioural responses** (overt behaviours, self-reports of behaviour or behavioural intentions). Each class of response corresponds to one component of attitude.

One issue arising from this conception of attitudinal components is the degree to which the three components are related. Most advocates of the three-component view of attitudes assume that the three components are highly interrelated, such that positive feel-

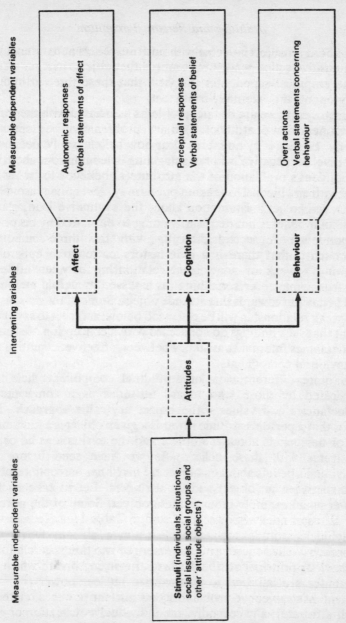

Figure 11.1 Schematic conception of attitudes. (After Rosenberg and Hovland, 1960)

ings about an object co-occur with positive beliefs about the object and positive action-tendencies towards that object. Indeed, there is some empirical support for the view that these three attitudinal components are internally consistent.

However, there are distinct problems associated with the three-component view of attitudes. Two such problems will be mentioned briefly. First, it is by no means clear how beliefs can be defined as 'positive' or 'negative' without smuggling in assumptions about the respondent's evaluation of the attribute(s) believed to be associated with an object. These assumptions may *seem* quite reasonable, but a researcher's assumption about the evaluative loading of a particular belief is not necessarily going to be shared by his or her respondents. A second difficulty with the three-component approach is that there is a long history of research apparently showing a weak or nonexistent relationship between attitudes towards someone or something (as assessed by verbal measures) and behaviour towards that attitude object. Some of the reasons for this weak relationship will be discussed below; suffice it to say at this point that such findings do not accord with a conception of attitude that assumes internal consistency between affective, cognitive and behavioural components.

A quite different view of attitudinal components has been advocated by those who regard attitudes as a composite of expectancies and values – the **expectancy-value approach**. This holds that a person's attitude towards a given object is a function of his or her beliefs about the object and the evaluations he or she associates with these beliefs. As we have seen before, an individual's beliefs about an object are his or her perceptions of the links between an object and its attributes. Let us take nuclear power as an example of an attitude object. Some of the possible attributes of nuclear power are listed in Table 11.1. To assess an individual's attitudes towards nuclear power, an expectancy-value approach would require a measurement of two things in relation to each of its principal attributes: first, the strength with which the attributes are believed to characterize nuclear power (i.e., the individual's subjective probability that nuclear power is related to each attribute); and secondly, the individual's evaluation of each attribute. Some hypothetical belief strength and evaluation scores are shown in Table 11.1. Fishbein suggests that belief strength and evaluation should be assessed on scales which run from -3 to $+3$, with endpoints labelled 'unlikely' and 'likely' in the case of belief strength, and 'bad' and 'good' in the case of evaluation. An individual's attitude towards nuclear power is defined as the sum of the products of the belief strength and evaluation scores. Summing the products of the belief strength and evaluation scores of the hypothetical individual represented in Table 11.1 shows that the subject's overall attitude to nuclear power is moderately negative.

Table 11.1 **Hypothetical data reflecting an individual's attitude towards nuclear power**

NUCLEAR POWER	Belief strength	Evalua-tion	Product
1. is a source of low-cost electricity	+1	+3	+3
2. is hazardous to the environment	+3	-3	-9
3. is helpful to the national economy	+2	+2	+4
4. is a source of weapons-grade plutonium	+1	-3	-3
5. frees the country from dependence on oil supplies	+2	+1	+2
			sum $= -3$

The major difference between the expectancy-value model of attitudinal components and the three-component view discussed above relates to the assumptions made about consistency between components. As we saw earlier, the three-component view tends to assume that there is consistency between the affective, cognitive and conative components. Expectancy-value theorists do not assume that evaluations (affect) and beliefs (cognition) are positively related. Furthermore, behavioural tendencies towards the attitude object are not seen as an integral component of the individual's attitude, so there is no explicit assumption that an individual's behaviour towards an object will be consistent with his or her attitude to that object.

ATTITUDE MEASUREMENT

We shall not attempt here to provide a detailed treatment of the issues and methods involved in attitude measurement. Comprehensive overviews of measurement techniques and problems in this field can be found elsewhere (see Further reading at the end of this chapter). Instead, our aim will be to provide a brief account of the most commonly employed formal procedure for measuring attitudes in social psychology, which is known as **Likert scaling**, and then to contrast this method with an alternative but related technique.

The first step in constructing a Likert scale to measure attitudes is to collect a large pool of items known as **attitude statements**. These are statements of opinion, belief, intentions and so on, relating to the attitude object. Imagine, for example, that one is interested in measuring attitudes to trade unions. In constructing a Likert scale to measure such attitudes, one would begin by collecting many attitude statements about the pros and cons of trade unions. Some relevant statements might be: 'Trade unions play an important role in making working conditions safer and healthier'; 'Workers should never be compelled to join a trade union as a condition of their employment'; 'The improvement in the standard of living of workers in this country has been chiefly due to trade unions'; and 'The government should do more to regulate the activities of trade unions'. Having assembled a large set of such statements, taking some care to achieve an approximate balance between those that are favourable and those that are unfavourable to the attitude object, the investigator administers these statements to a sample of persons who are representative of the target population. These persons are asked to indicate their agreement/disagreement with each statement in terms of the following five-point scale:

1	2	3	4	5
agree strongly	agree	undecided	disagree	disagree strongly

Responses are scored from one to five in such a way that agreement with favourable statements and disagreement with unfavourable statements result in a higher score. An index of each individual's attitude can then be derived by summing his or her scores across all the statements. The higher the total score, the more favourable the individual's attitude. It is at this stage that the investigator can select those statements to be used in the final attitude measurement instrument. This selection is achieved by means of **item analysis**, i.e., examination of how well the respondents' scores on an individual statement correlate with their total scores. By selecting the twenty or so items which correlate most highly with the total score, the investigator ends up with a set of statements that is **internally consistent**. This set of statements can then be administered to the target population for them to indicate their agreement/disagreement with each item. The scoring of responses is achieved in the same manner as that described above, and each individual's attitude score is found by summing his or her responses to the statements. If twenty statements were included in the final measure, then attitude scores could range from twenty (most unfavourable attitude score possible) to one hundred (most favourable attitude score possible).

It is worth considering briefly the relationship between Likert scaling and the measurement procedure implicit in Fishbein's (1963) expectancy-value approach to attitudes. Fishbein's approach calls for two types of measure to be taken: a measure of **belief strength**, reflecting subjective probabilty of relation between object and attribute; and a measure of **evaluation**, reflecting perceived 'goodness' and 'badness' of each attribute. In effect, the Likert scaling procedure for attitude measurement taps strength of belief concerning the relationship between an object (e.g., the trade unions) and attributes (e.g., improvement in the standard of living of workers in this country). Thus strong agreement with the statement, 'The improvement in the standard of living of workers in this country has been chiefly due to trade unions', reflects in effect a strong belief in the relation between object and attribute. In this sense, the Likert scaling procedure measures belief strength on a five-point scale. The evaluation of each attribute is assessed by defining each statement as favourable or unfavourable to the attitude object, which determines whether an 'agree strongly' response will be scored as one or five. Thus the chief difference between the Fishbein measurement approach and the Likert scaling method is that the latter technique only allows for two categories of attribute evaluation (favourable or unfavourable) and makes assumptions about the evaluative weightings of each opinion statement for *all* respondents, whereas Fishbein's approach allows attribute evaluation to vary across several (typically seven) categories and uses empirically derived evaluative weightings of each attribute for *each* respondent.

ATTITUDE FORMATION AND DEVELOPMENT

Given that attitude theorists generally agree that attitudes are *learned*, what learning processes might be involved in attitude formation? Some researchers have examined the applicability of the principle of classical conditioning (see Chapter 5) to attitude formation. The idea here is that feelings of positive or negative affect can be directly conditioned to a stimulus through classical conditioning, and thereafter provide the basis for the individual's evaluation of that stimulus.

Some of the earliest experiments claiming to show evidence of classical conditioning of attitudes (e.g., Staats and Staats, 1958) have been criticized by Page (e.g., 1969) and others, on the grounds that the subjects in such studies may not only have been aware of the repeated pairings of neutral, conditioned stimuli (CS) and emotionally loaded, unconditioned stimuli (UCS), but may also have correctly guessed that the experimenter expected the evaluations of the CS to be negative or positive as a result of being paired with the UCS. If the nationality 'Swedish', for example, was consistently paired with pleasant words (e.g., gift, happy), while the nationality 'Dutch' was consistently paired with unpleasant words (e.g., litter, failure), and subjects are subsequently asked to rate the pleasantness of these and other nationalities, it is likely that some subjects, at least, would guess that the experimenter expected evaluations of 'Swedish' to be more positive and evaluations of 'Dutch' to be more negative than evaluations of other nationalities. Subjects may be inclined to behave in accordance with their perceptions of the experimenter's expectations. Indeed, Page (1969) found that this 'classical conditioning' effect was *only* evident among subjects who were aware of the experimenter's hypothesis.

Later studies have attempted to reduce the likelihood that subjects will correctly guess the hypothesis under test. For example, Zanna, Kiesler and Pilkonis (1970) ran what appeared to be two unrelated studies, each conducted by a different experimenter. In the first study, subjects received electric shocks, ostensibly so that their physiological reactions could be monitored. One of two words ('light' or 'dark') signalled shock onset, while the other word signalled shock offset, thereby pairing one with an inherently negative event and the other with an inherently positive event. In the second study, attitudes to various words were assessed, including *light* and *dark*, words related to these two (e.g., *white* and *black*), and unrelated (control) words. As predicted, words that had signalled shock onset and words related to this shock-onset signal were evaluated more negatively than control words; similarly, words that had signalled shock offset and words related to this shock-offset signal were evaluated more positively than control words.

It is not easy to see how Zanna and his associates' findings could be explained in terms other than the classical conditioning of attitudes. Thus it seems that under certain circumstances attitudes can be formed by a classical conditioning process. However, conditioning processes are only likely to be involved in attitude formation when the attitude object is unfamiliar or neutral. As Petty and Cacioppo (1981) have noted, 'As people learn more about a stimulus . . . their thoughts about it become increasingly more important determinants of their attitude toward it' (p. 56). Thus when we meet people we gain information that influences our beliefs about them. We discover their political preferences, for example, and from this **descriptive belief** about political preferences we may well infer other beliefs (**inferential beliefs**) about their attitudes to (say) nationalization, or law and order, or immigration. Depending on how we evaluate these attributes (certain political preferences, certain attitudes to nationalization, and so on), we form an attitude to the individual that is more favourable or less favourable. Thus beliefs about the relations between an attitude object and its attributes will result in attitude formation, to the extent that the attributes are positively or negatively evaluated by the perceiver. Although conditioning processes may be involved in the formation of attitudes towards novel or neutral stimuli, it is likely that attitude formation is typically mediated by a greater degree of information-processing.

ATTITUDE CHANGE

In this section we shall examine two types of process which have the potential to change attitudes, each of which has been the subject of a considerable body of experimental research. The two processes concerned are (1) engaging in counter-attitudinal behaviour, and (2) exposure to persuasive communications.

Counter-attitudinal behaviour

The attitudinal consequences of engaging in counter-attitudinal behaviour have been studied intensively within the framework of **cognitive dissonance theory**. This theory, first proposed by Festinger (1957), is perhaps the best known among a group of theories which deal with the effects of inconsistencies between beliefs, attitudes and behaviours. What these **cognitive consistency theories** have in common is an assumption that such inconsistency is a source of tension and/or discomfort, and that the individual will therefore prefer where possible to reduce or eliminate the inconsistency. Cognitive dissonance theory itself is concerned with consistencies and inconsistencies between cognitions, which are defined by Festinger (1957) as 'the things a person knows about himself, about his behavior, and about his surroundings' (p.9). Thus the knowledge that one smokes cigarettes would be a cognition, as would the knowledge that smoking causes disease. The relationship between any two cognitions is one of three types: dissonant, consonant or irrelevant. The relationship is said to be **dissonant** if the obverse of one cognition would follow from the other cognition. 'To state it a bit more formally,' writes Festinger (1957), 'x and y are dissonant if not-x follows from y' (p. 13). Thus knowledge that 'I smoke' is dissonant with knowledge that 'smoking causes disease'. The relationship between two cognitions is said to be **consonant** if either one does follow from the other. Thus knowledge that 'smoking helps one to relax' is consonant with knowledge that 'I smoke'. Where two cognitions carry no implications for each other, the relationship between them is said to be **irrelevant**. Thus knowledge that 'I drink alcohol' is irrelevant to knowledge that 'smoking causes disease'.

The awareness of a dissonant relationship between two cognitions is thought to give rise to cognitive dissonance, a psychologically uncomfortable state, the existence of which will motivate the individual to reduce the amount of dissonance being experienced. There are two characteristics of cognitions which have a bearing on the amount of dissonance experienced. First, cognitions vary in their **importance to the individual**. Other things being equal, the amount of dissonance experienced increases with the importance of the cognitions involved. A second characteristic of cognitions is that they vary in their **resistance to change**. Cognitions based on objective reality (e.g., knowledge that 'I publicly advocated the return of the death penalty') are more resistant to change than cognitions with a more subjective basis (e.g., knowledge that 'I don't believe that the return of the death penalty would have any deterrent value'). The more resistant cognitions are to change, the more difficult it will be to eliminate dissonance experienced as a result of awareness of a dissonant relationship between them.

An instructive way of thinking about how dissonance is aroused and resolved is provided by the following equation:

$$\text{Amount of dissonance associated with cognition } k = \frac{\text{Sum of cognitions dissonant with } k, \text{ weighted by importance}}{\text{Sum of cognitions consonant with } k, \text{ weighted by importance}}$$

Let us return to the smoking example to see how this equation applies to the case of a heavy smoker. If we wanted to establish the amount of dissonance associated with this individual's cognition that she smokes, we would need to establish which of this person's cognitions are dissonant with her knowledge that she smokes, and how important to her each of these cognitions is; and which of her cognitions are consonant with her knowledge that she smokes, along with the importance to her of each of these cognitions. Cognitions **dissonant** with the knowledge that she smokes might include: smoking damages one's health; smoking is expensive; some of my friends find smoking offensive; and so on. Cognitions **consonant** with the knowledge that she smokes might include: smoking helps me to relax; smoking is a physically pleasurable activity; smoking keeps my weight down; and so on. Of course, not every smoker will have each of these cognitions, and the importance of each dissonant and consonant cognition is likely to vary to some extent from one smoker to the next. Nevertheless, there are likely to be several dissonant and consonant cognitions involved, and what is apparent from the above equation is that the amount of dissonance associated with cognition k ('I know that I smoke') can be reduced by any change which produces a reduction in the overall ratio of dissonant elements to consonant elements. The perceived importance of dissonant cognitions can be reduced; the perceived importance of consonant cognitions can be enhanced; dissonant cognitions can be removed from awareness, through repression; and new consonant cognitions can be added.

Experimental research aimed at testing predictions derived from dissonance theory was a major preoccupation of social psychologists during the 1960s, with the result that there are many more lines of research than can possibly be reviewed here. Instead, we shall describe some of the research concerned with just one of the many and diverse phenomena studied by dissonance theorists. The phenomenon we shall examine is attitude change resulting from engaging in counter-attitudinal behaviour, sometimes (but rather misleadingly) referred to as 'forced compliance'.

In a so-called **forced compliance situation**, an individual is induced to engage in behaviour that is inconsistent with his or her attitudes. For example, a teenage boy might be induced by the unanimous smoking behaviour of his friends to smoke a cigarette, even though he regards smoking to be a dangerous and unpleasant activity. Is there any possibility that the boy's engagement in this counter-attitudinal behaviour will result in a change in his attitude to smoking? According to dissonance theory, there is. Engaging in behaviour which runs counter to important beliefs and attitudes should give rise to cognitive dissonance, due to the inconsistency between cognitions about beliefs or attitudes ('I know that I believe smoking to be a dangerous and unpleasant activity') and cognitions about behaviour ('I know that I have just smoked a cigarette'). The only additional condition which needs to be satisfied in order for the dissonance to be aroused is that there should be no features of the setting in which the cigarette was smoked which could justify that action. In other words, the boy should not be able to justify having smoked a cigarette by thinking that he had been *forced* to smoke, or by the knowledge that in smoking the cigarette he was winning a sizeable sum of money as a result of a bet. Given that there is no compelling justification for the smoking behaviour, and that cognitive dissonance is experienced as a result of this action being counter-attitudinal, how could the boy reduce the amount of dissonance he experiences? There is little he can do about the cognition concerning his behaviour: he cannot change the fact that he smoked a cigarette. It is likely, therefore, that some aspect of the cognitive elements that are dissonant with this behavioural cognition will be changed. For example, the boy might reason that smoking one cigarette does not constitute addiction, and that without such addiction there is no damage to health. Or he might change his attitude towards smoking, either by beginning to doubt whether it is as vile a habit as he has been led to believe, or by regarding it as a pleasurable (if dangerous) activity.

Festinger and Carlsmith's (1959) experiment was the first direct test of the attitudinal consequences of 'forced compliance'. These investigators recruited male students to participate in a study of 'measures of performance'. Each subject performed two boring and repetitive tasks while the experimenter appeared to measure their performance. After the second task, the experimenter explained that the purpose of the study was to compare task performance under two conditions; one of these was the condition the subject had been in, while the other involved an assistant of the experimenter posing as someone who has just participated in the experiment and telling the next subject, as he waited to participate in the study, that the experiment was 'interesting and enjoyable . . . fun . . . intriguing . . . exciting', with a view to seeing how the resulting positive expectation influenced his performance. Subjects were now split into three groups, one control and two experimental. Control subjects were simply directed to another room in order to answer some questions in a survey allegedly unrelated to the experiment. Experimental subjects were told that the experimenter's assistant was not available today and that a fresh subject was already waiting to participate in the study. The experimenter then proposed that the subject should take on the assistant's role, and tell the waiting 'new' subject that the experimental tasks were interesting and enjoyable. In one experimental condition subjects were offered a one-dollar payment for performing this role, while subjects in the other experimental condition were offered twenty dollars. Subjects in these two conditions were then introduced to the new subject (who was in fact an assistant of the experimenter) and they told her that the tasks she was going to work on were interesting and enjoyable. Experimental subjects were then asked the same questions as part of an 'unrelated' survey that control subjects were asked.

In the course of the survey interview, subjects were asked, 'Were the tasks interesting and enjoyable?' and answered this question by making a rating on an eleven-point scale. Subjects in the one-dollar condition rated the tasks more positively on this measure than did subjects in the twenty-dollar condition, whose ratings did not differ significantly from those of control subjects. This pattern of findings supports the prediction made by Festinger and Carlsmith on the basis of dissonance theory, and suggests that under certain conditions size of incentive is related inversely to amount of attitude change.

Why is this finding consistent with dissonance theory? Subjects in the two experimental groups engaged in counter-attitudinal behaviour in telling the 'waiting subject' that the tasks she was about to perform were interesting and enjoyable, when these subjects knew from their own experience that the tasks were boring and monotonous. Awareness of the inconsistency between these cognitions should, in the absence of any cognitions consonant with the behaviour, create cognitive dissonance. However, the payment offered to the subject for acting as the 'experimenter's assistant' is clearly consonant with the behaviour. The amount of the payment can be seen as equivalent to the *importance* of this consonant element, such that knowledge that one has been paid twenty dollars to engage in the counter-attitudinal behaviour is sufficient justification for having performed it. The lesser importance of the one-dollar payment as a consonant element results in knowledge of this payment being *insufficient justification* for performing the counter-attitudinal behaviour. Subjects in the one-dollar group should therefore have experienced more cognitive dissonance than their counterparts in the twenty-dollar group. An obvious way of reducing this dissonance would have been to change one's attitude to the experimental tasks. If they are now seen as moderately enjoyable, then the behaviour of telling the next subject that the tasks are interesting and enjoyable is no longer counter-attitudinal, and dissonance is thereby reduced. This, according to dissonance theorists, is what occurs in the course of a 'forced compliance' experiment. As the size of incentive for engaging in counter-attitudinal behaviour (or the amount of punishment for *not* doing so) increases, so too does the individual's perceived justification for performing this behaviour. Larger incentives therefore serve to reduce the amount of dissonance experienced and (since attitude change should vary directly with amount of dissonance) the amount of attitude change.

Festinger and Carlsmith's (1959) experiment was the first of many studies of the attitudinal consequences of engaging in counter-attitudinal behaviour. There has been much controversy about the precise conditions under which the size of incentive offered for performing such behaviour is related inversely to the amount of attitude change. Without wishing to suggest that this debate has been fully resolved, we can summarize research on 'forced compliance' by stating that the inverse relationship between incentive size and attitude change is found most reliably when (a) subjects feel that they have *voluntarily* engaged in or committed themselves to the counter-attitudinal behaviour, and (b) subjects believe that *important (typically aversive) consequences* will arise as a result of performing the behaviour (Collins and Hoyt, 1972).

Persuasive communications

In contrast to the research on the effects of counter-attitudinal behaviour, attitude change research concerned with persuasive communications has not been dominated by theoretical concerns. The pioneering work on persuasive communications was conducted by Hovland and his colleagues in the Yale Communication and Attitude Change Program in the 1950s. Rather than developing a formal theory of attitude change, the Yale researchers adopted a more pragmatic approach which can be characterized as a **message-learning approach** (Petty and Cacioppo, 1981). The basic idea of this approach is that in order for a persuasive communication (e.g., a political speech or an advertisement) to be effective (i.e., to result in attitude change), the message contained in the communication must be *learned*, such that it is remembered. This retention of the message is thought to depend upon prior mediating processes, such as **attention** to the message and **comprehension** of its content. As Hovland and Janis (1959) put it, 'attention and comprehension determine what the recipient will *learn* concerning the content of the communicator's message; other processes, involving changes in motivation, are assumed to determine whether or not he will accept or adopt what he learns' (p. 5.) In other words, learning a message is necessary but not sufficient for attitude change to occur; in addition, the individual must *accept* the learned message.

The Yale programme is best described as investigating *who* says *what* to *whom* and with *what effect* (see Smith *et al.*, 1946). Thus the research examined how attitude change, which was the usual index of an effect, is influenced by variations in attributes of the **source** of the message (who), the **message** itself (what), and the **audience** (whom). In what follows we shall confine ourselves to reviewing a representative study of the effects of varying one attribute within each of these three groups of factors.

Beginning with research on the impact of **source** attributes, one such attribute that was studied intensively was **communicator-credibility**, i.e., the overall 'believability' of the source. Kelman and Hovland (1953) had their subjects listen to a message which advocated more lenient treatment of juvenile offenders. The ostensible source of the message was either a prestigious juvenile court judge or a man who had recently been arrested on a drug-peddling charge. When subjects' attitudes towards the advocated position were assessed immediately after the communication, it was found that the high-credibility (judge) source was more persuasive than the low-credibility (alleged drug-peddler) source. This in itself is hardly surprising. Of greater interest are the findings obtained when subjects' attitudes were reassessed three weeks later. Prior to this reassessment, half the subjects in each credibility condition were reminded of the identity and characteristics of the source, whereas the other half simply completed the attitudinal measure. Where there was no reminder about the source, there was a significant *decrease* in persuasiveness in the high-credibility condition and a small (nonsignificant) *increase* in persuasiveness in the low-credibility condition. Where there was a reminder about the source, however, the impact of source-credibility on attitudes to the advocated position was maintained. How can this pattern of findings be explained?

Hovland and his associates argued that the connection between the arguments and conclusion of a message is remembered longer than the connection between a 'cue' such as communicator-credibility and the conclusion of a message. In other words, cues – whether they cause the recipient to accept or reject the message – tend to become dissociated from the message conclusion over time. Kelman and Hovland's results can therefore be seen as reflecting a dissociation of the message conclusion from its source, at least in the high-credibility condition. To summarize, communicator-credibility is likely to be maximally influential immediately following the communication. As time progresses, the impact of this source cue is likely to diminish in the absence of any reminder about the source.

Turning now to the impact of varying attributes of the **message** itself, a major concern of researchers has been to examine the effectiveness of messages which arouse fear in recipients. How effective are high-fear appeals, such as television advertisements which depict horrifying traffic accidents in an attempt to persuade viewers to avoid drinking and driving? Firm conclusions on this issue are difficult, given the presence of contradictory findings from early studies, but recent research suggests that fear appeals *are* effective when the perceived efficacy of the recommended preventive measures is high, and when the perceived probability of a noxious event occurring in the absence of the recommended measures is also high. Rogers and Mewborn (1976) manipulated these two variables in the context of a study of the effectiveness of antismoking communications on the intentions of smokers to quit smoking. The probability of smokers contracting lung cancer was described in these communications as either high or relatively low. Independently of this manipulation, the efficacy of the recommended preventive measures was also varied so that it was high or low. As shown in Figure 11.2, the perceived efficacy of the recommended measures only had an impact on intentions to adopt these measures where the probability of lung cancer occurring was said to be high. When this probability was high, the message which stressed the efficacy of the advocated measures resulted in much stronger intentions to adopt these measures. This suggests that messages which arouse fear in the recipients by arguing that a threatening state of affairs will occur without preventive measures

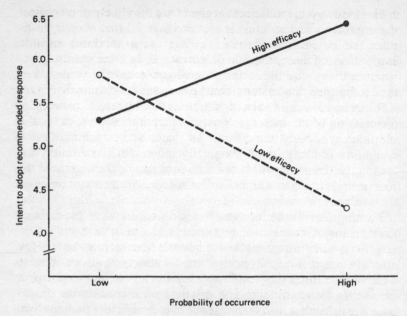

Figure 11.2 Interaction effect of probability of occurrence and efficacy of coping response on intent to stop smoking. (After Rogers and Mewborn, 1976)

being taken will only be influential to the extent that the recommended preventive measures are seen by the recipient as effective.

The Yale researchers recognized that variations in the attributes of **message recipients** might well have a bearing on the effectiveness of a message. However, early research produced a confusing picture. With respect to intelligence, for example, it was sometimes found that this was related to greater persuasibility, and sometimes with less persuasibility. McGuire (1968) helped to clarify thinking in this area, by pointing out that an attribute such as intelligence or self-esteem probably has contrasting effects on message **reception** (including attention, comprehension and retention) and **yielding**. Intelligent receivers are likely to be better than their less intelligent counterparts at comprehending and remembering a message, which should *enhance* message reception and, thereby, attitude change. However, intelligent receivers are also likely to be critical of a message and (perhaps) more confident of their existing attitudes, which should *diminish* yielding and, therefore, attitude change. If McGuire's reasoning is correct, then the relationship between receiver attributes, such as intelligence and self-esteem, and persuasibility should be something approaching that shown in Figure 11.3. Since the probability of accepting the advocated message is assumed to be a joint function of reception and yielding, the relationship between the receiver attribute and persuasibility will be determined by the combined curves relating reception and yielding to the attribute. If the attribute has opposing effects on these mediating processes, as McGuire suggests, then the attribute-persuasibility relationship is likely to be curvilinear, as shown in the figure. Evidence consistent with McGuire's model comes from Nisbett and Gordon's (1967) study of self-esteem and persuasibility. They measured their subjects' self-esteem and one week later gave them a number of statements about health which were either simple, unsubstantiated statements or were statements plus supporting documentation. The unsubstantiated statements should have been easy to comprehend but not especially likely to produce

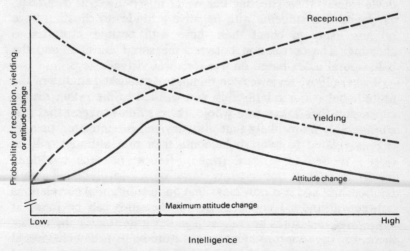

Figure 11.3 Curvilinear relationship between intelligence and attitude change as a function of intelligence having opposite effects on the two mediators, reception and yielding.

yielding; the substantiated statements were more difficult to comprehend but contained more reasons for yielding. It was found that subjects with medium self-esteem changed their attitudes most when the statements were unsubstantiated, whereas high-self-esteem subjects displayed most attitude change when the statements were more complex.

THE ATTITUDE-BEHAVIOUR RELATIONSHIP

One of the main reasons for the tremendous interest in attitudes displayed by social psychologists is the assumption that attitudes have a causal impact on behaviour. However, the validity of this assumption has been questioned by many researchers over the years. Typically, such researchers obtained a measure of subjects' attitudes towards an issue or an ethnic group and a measure of the same subjects' behaviour in relation to the issue or towards members of the ethnic group in question. Corey (1937), for example, measured his students' attitudes towards cheating and subsequently measured (with some ingenuity – and deviousness!) their cheating behaviour in scoring their own tests. He found that students with negative attitudes to cheating were no less likely to cheat than those with positive attitudes to cheating. The correlation between measured attitudes and the behavioural index based on five tests was virtually zero.

Wicker (1969) reviewed the findings of published studies of the attitude-behaviour relationship and was led to the rather dismal conclusion that 'taken as a whole, these studies suggest that it is considerably more likely that attitudes will be unrelated or only slightly related to overt behaviours than that attitudes will be close˙ related to actions' (p. 65). Recent research has done much to relieve this gloomy view of the attitude-behaviour relationship, and it is now clear that quite substantial correlations between attitudinal and behavioural measures can be found if *appropriate* measures are taken. The key criterion for the assessment of the appropriateness of attitudinal and behavioural measures is **correspondence**. In other words, the attitudinal measure must correspond to the behavioural measure before sizeable correlations between the two can reasonably be anticipated. In what respects should the two measures correspond?

Ajzen and Fishbein (1977) have pointed out that attitudes and behaviours consist of four different elements: the **action** involved (e.g., smoking, drinking), the **target** at which the action is directed (e.g., cigarettes in general, specific brands), the **context** in which the action is performed (e.g., own home, party, pub), and the **time** at which the action is performed (e.g., today, this month, this year). A study by Davidson and Jaccard (1979) is particularly instructive about the need for correspondence between attitudinal and behavioural measures. These investigators examined the relationship between the attitudes of married women to using oral contraceptives and having children, and whether or not these women used oral contraceptives or gave birth to a child during the subsequent two years. The attitudinal measures employed varied with respect to their correspondence with the two behavioural measures, and it was found that the attitude-behaviour relationship increased in strength as the degree of correspondence increased. For example, when *attitudes towards birth control* were correlated with the actual use of oral contraceptives during the two-year period, there was virtually no relationship ($r = .08$). When *attitudes towards oral contraceptives* were measured, the attitude-behaviour relationship increased substantially ($r = .32$), reflecting the target correspondence. When *attitudes towards using oral contraceptives* were assessed the attitude-behaviour relationship was even stronger ($r = .53$), reflecting target and action correspondence. When *attitudes towards using oral contraceptives during the next two years* were assessed, the attitude-behaviour relationship was stronger still ($r = .57$), reflecting target, action and time correspondence.

Another factor which has been shown to moderate the attitude-behaviour relationship is the degree to which the attitude involved is based on direct behavioural experience. Imagine, for example, that we are interested in the relationship between an individual's attitude towards tennis and that person's subsequent tennis-playing behaviour. If the individual has actually played tennis prior to the attitudinal assessment, we might expect the measured attitude to be more predictive of subsequent tennis-playing than if the individual has simply watched others playing tennis. Fazio and Zanna (1981) have reported a number of studies in which experimental support was found for the notion that attitudes based on direct experience have greater predictive utility than those based on indirect experience. In one such study the relationship between students' attitudes towards participating in psychology experiments and their willingness to commit themselves to such participation in the future was examined as a function of the number of experiments in which the students had already participated. The students were all taking a course in social psychology, so had a comparable and quite extensive amount of *indirect* experience of psychology experiments and what participation in them would entail. They differed, however, in the amount of *direct* experience of participation they had. As predicted, those with little direct experience showed a negligible attitude-behaviour correlation ($r = .03$) while those with moderate direct experience displayed a stronger correlation ($r = .36$), and those with a large amount of direct experience had the highest correlation ($r = .42$). One fairly straightforward reason why attitudes based on direct experience are more predictive of behaviour is that direct experience provides the individual with more information about the attitude object, enabling clearer and more confident evaluation of the object. Another, less obvious reason suggested by Fazio and Zanna (1981) is that direct experience may lead to the formation of an attitude which is more readily accessed from memory than an attitude based on indirect experience: greater accessibility shôuld result in the same attitudinal information being considered when reporting one's attitude verbally as when behaving towards the object.

Person perception

Our interactions with others can evoke in us some of the strongest feelings we shall ever experience, ranging from intense happiness and satisfaction to equally intense misery and disappointment. Partly because of this powerful capacity of other people to involve us in such positive or negative experiences, we are keenly interested in our fellow human beings. A large proportion of our lives is spent in trying to understand, influence and win the approval of others.

Given that other people are such significant elements of our social environment, it is hardly surprising to find that a key branch of research in social cognition is concerned with person perception. Before considering examples of theory and research in this area, let us consider the different processes involved in person perception. A good idea of the variety and complexity of these processes is provided by Schneider, Hastorf and Ellsworth (1979), who identify six such processes:

1. **Attention.** The 'inputs' to this process are the physical appearance of the person in question, the context in which they behave, and the stream of their behaviour. In attending to these inputs, an observer will *select* certain of their features and will *categorize* the target person's appearance and behaviour. After observing someone's behaviour at a party, for example, we will have categorized that individual's appearance (tall, fair, well dressed) and behaviour (talking, laughing, dancing).

2. **Snap judgement.** This is a direct inference from an individual's appearance and/or behaviour which involves little or no cognitive effort. This may be one's immediate affective reaction to an individual (i.e., attraction or repulsion), or stereotypic judgements made on the basis of the categorized appearance or behaviour (e.g., the stereotyped judgement that people who talk, laugh and dance at parties are 'extraverts').

3. **Attribution.** In contrast to snap judgements, attributions are more reflective inferences which involve a greater investment of cognitive effort. Let us assume that our tall, fair, well-dressed party-goer, who up to now has been talking, laughing and dancing, becomes engaged in an argument. As an observer, one may well be interested in knowing what caused this switch in behaviour. *Why* is the individual arguing? The answer to such a question is an *attribution*, and one may see the individual's argumentative behaviour as having been caused primarily by *external* factors (e.g., another's provocation) or as having been caused primarily by *internal* factors (e.g., the individual's own argumentative disposition). The implicit rules or principles which shape attributions of causality for events observed in our social environment have been the focus of much research in recent years, and we shall consider these in greater detail below.

4. **Trait implication**. As we have just seen, one possible inference from the attribution process is that the individual has a certain *trait* or *disposition* (e.g., 'argumentative'). Furthermore, such an inference might have been made as a snap judgement, as with the prior example of the stereotypic judgement that persons who engage in certain categories of behaviour at parties are 'extraverts'. The inference that an individual possesses a certain trait opens the way for trait implication. The 'knowledge' that a person possesses one trait may well imply to us, as perceivers, that he or she also possesses one or more other traits, for we have implicit theories about the co-occurrence of personality traits.

5. **Impression formation**. Given that an individual is thought to possess a group of personality traits (e.g., sincere, modest, reliable, serious), what kind of global impression of this person do we form? The impression formation process particularly concerns how we *organize* a person's characteristics in such a way as to form a coherent impression. Some characteristics are given more weight than others in this process; in particular, there is a tendency for characteristics presented or inferred earlier in time to exert more influence on the global impression formed than characteristics which appear subsequently – the 'primacy effect'.

6. **Prediction of future behaviour**. The acquisition of knowledge about other persons should permit the perceiver to make predictions about how a given target will behave in future situations. This is perhaps the least studied of the person perception processes, although many theorists tend to assume that other person perception processes are motivated, at least sometimes, by the need or desire to predict the other persons' future behaviour.

The six person perception processes just summarized *can* be regarded as forming a sequence, but Schneider and his colleagues (1979) caution against viewing this sequence as either linear or inevitable: 'In other words, perceivers need not go through all the sequences – they may stop at any point, and they may backtrack or skip steps' (p. 17). In what follows we shall concern ourselves with just one of these six processes: the attribution process.

THE ATTRIBUTION PROCESS

As we have seen already, attributions are inferences about *why* some event in our social environment occurred. The 'attribution process' is the term given by social psychologists to the inferential processes linking the event in question to an attribution. There are several models of the attribution process, each of which attempts to spell out the implicit rules and principles according to which underlying causes are attributed to perceived events. Although there are many similarities between the different models of the attribution process, there are also some important differences. In what follows, however, we shall confine ourselves to a discussion of one theorist's contributions to our understanding of the attribution process, and the interested reader is advised to consult the Further reading at the end of this chapter, with a view to comparing and contrasting the different attribution models.

The most influential contributions to our understanding of the attribution process are those made by Kelley (1967, 1972, 1973). Kelley's theoretical statements involve two attribution models, the covariation model and the causal schemata model, and we shall now consider those models in turn. The **covariation model** has at its heart the principle of covariation, which states that 'An effect is attributed to one of its possible causes with which, over time, it covaries' (Kelley, 1967, p. 108). What this amounts to is an assumption that perceivers make causal attributions as if they were analysing patterns of data by means of a statistical technique known as analysis of variance, or ANOVA. (For this reason the covariation model is sometimes referred to as the ANOVA model.) Analysis of variance indicates whether one or more independent variables exert a significant effect on a dependent variable; for example, does the amount of alcohol consumed and/or the number of hours since last resting exert a significant effect on driving ability? In terms of the attribution process, the 'dependent variable' is the behaviour we are seeking to explain, such as the argumentative behaviour of the party-goer, referred to earlier. What are the 'independent variables'? In other words, what are the 'possible causes' alluded to by Kelley in his statement of the covariation principle? Kelley argues that there are three important kinds of cause in relation to social behaviour: persons, entities and contexts.

Thus social behaviour can vary as a function of who is behaving (i.e., **persons**). Are *all* the people who are at the party becoming argumentative, just *some* of the people, or *only* the target person? Social behaviour can also vary as a function of whom or what the behaviour is directed towards (i.e., **entities**). Does the target person behave in an argumentative fashion towards *all* others around her, just *some* of them, or *only one* particular other? Finally, social behaviour can vary as a function of when and where the behaviour occurs (i.e., **contexts**). Does the target person behave argumentatively in *all* settings, just *some* of them, or *only* at parties?

The extent to which the behaviour we are seeking to explain covaries with each of these three classes of possible cause provides the perceiver with useful information. **Consensus** information is provided by the extent to which the target behaviour generalizes across or is shared by different persons. If *all* persons at the party are argumentative, consensus is said to be high; if *only* the target person is arguing, consensus is said to be low. **Distinctiveness** information is provided by the extent to which the target behaviour is specific to a particular stimulus. If the target person is argumentative towards *all* persons at the party, distinctiveness is said to be low; if she is arguing only with *one* other person, distinctiveness is said to be high. Finally, **consistency** information is provided by the extent to which the target person's behaviour is stable across time and place. If the behaviour does not vary with context, consistency is said to be high; if it varies markedly across contexts, consistency is said to be low. What effects do combinations of consensus, distinctiveness and consistency information have on the nature of causal attributions? Kelley's reasoning on this point is summarized in Table 11.2. It can be seen that Kelley's model holds that, in order for a target behaviour to be attributed to the actor (i.e., a **person attribution**), both consensus and distinctiveness should be low, but consistency should be high. Thus if the argumentative party-goer is the only person arguing (low consensus), appears to be arguing with everybody (low distinctiveness), and also has a known record of striking up arguments in a variety of contexts (high consistency), a perceiver should, according to Kelley's model, see the cause of her argumentative behaviour as residing within her (e.g., 'She likes to pick arguments, that's the kind of person she is'). Any pattern of information including high consensus (and particularly the one shown in Table 11.2) should, according to the model, result in a **stimulus attribution**. If nearly all the party-goers are arguing, and the focus of their arguments appears to be one individual and most people are known to argue with this individual in a variety of contexts, then the target person's argumentative behaviour should be attributed to the one individual who is the focus of all the arguments. Finally, any pattern of information including low consistency (and particularly the one shown in Table 11.2) should, according to Kelley, result in a **circumstance attribution**. If our party-goer is known not to be argumentative in other contexts, then we should explain her behaviour in terms of some feature of the party context (e.g., the fact that she has drunk a lot of alcohol).

Table 11.2 **The relationship between information patterns and three kinds of causal attribution.** (Adapted from Table 1 in Orvis, Cunningham and Kelley, 1975)

Attribution to:	Type of Information		
	Consensus	Distinctiveness	Consistency
Person	Low	Low	High
Stimulus	High	High	High
Circumstance	Low	High	Low

To summarize, Kelley's covariation model of the attribution process treats the perceiver as if he or she were a highly *rational* processor of social information. Indeed, there is some evidence that when perceivers are supplied (in written form) with patterns of information corresponding to those shown in Table 11.2, they do make the types of attribution predicted by Kelley's model (see McArthur, 1972). However, Kelley (1973) recognizes that the perceiver's rationality may sometimes break down: 'The assumption is that the man in the street, the naive psychologist, uses a naive version of the method used in science. Undoubtedly, his naive version is a poor replica of the scientific one – incomplete, subject to bias, ready to proceed on incomplete evidence, and so on' (p. 109). This is a point to which we shall return later.

There is another sense in which the attribution process implied by the covariation model must be regarded as 'idealized'. This arises from the fact that it assumes that perceivers are in possession of large amounts of information, derived from multiple observations, before they make a causal attribution. It is intuitively obvious that perceivers nevertheless *do* make causal attributions without having the time and/or motivation required to make multiple observations. Kelley has recognized this point and his **causal schemata model** was developed with the specific aim of explaining how causal attribution proceeds in the absence of the full set of observations required by the covariation model.

Causal schemata embody an individual's knowledge of the causal structure of his or her environment. More specifically, any particular causal schema is 'a conception of the manner in which two or more causal factors interact in relation to a [given] effect' (Kelley, 1972, p. 2). Such conceptions are derived from direct experience of cause-effect relationships and from what others have taught us about such relationships. According to Kelley (1972), they enable the perceiver to make 'economical and fast attributional analysis, by providing a framework within which bits and pieces of relevant information can be fitted in order to draw reasonably good causal inferences' (p. 2). Let us now turn to some concrete examples to see how causal schemata might operate.

Experience tells us that some of the behaviours that we observe in our social environment can occur for any of several reasons. For example, the behaviour of a celebrity who extols the virtues of a product in a television commercial might be caused by his or her respect for the product in question *or* by the fee that he or she receives for appearing in the commercial. *Either* cause is *sufficient* to produce the observed behaviour, i.e., there are *multiple sufficient causes*. This knowledge is a causal schema, one which Kelley calls the multiple sufficient causes schema. Use of this schema helps us to make rapid attributions because knowledge about one of the sufficient causes automatically carries implications for the role played by the other sufficient cause. For example, in the case of the TV commercial, it is reasonable to assume that the celebrity is receiving a fat fee for his or her appearance, and this in itself is a sufficient cause of the behaviour. We therefore *discount* the other cause: we do not infer that the celebrity's behaviour is a function of respect for the advertised product. This kind of causal reasoning reflects the operation of what Kelley (1973) calls the **discounting principle**: 'The role of a given cause in producing a given effect is discounted if other plausible causes are also present' (p. 113).

The causal reasoning implicit in the multiple sufficient causes schema can be contrasted with that implicit in another schema described by Kelley, which he calls the multiple necessary causes schema. The classic example of a behavioural effect requiring multiple necessary causes is the achievement of a task known to be very difficult, such as obtaining a first-class honours degree. Such achievements depend upon the joint presence of two causal factors: ability and effort. If we observe the achievement, then we will confidently infer the presence of both causes, since their joint presence is necessary for the effect to occur. If the effect does not occur, i.e., the task is not achieved, then either or both of the necessary causes may have been absent – we cannot make a confident inference, other than the inference that at least one of the causes was absent.

Kelley (1972) has described a number of other causal schemata, along with their inferential implications, and has speculated upon the conditions under which each schema is elicited. Relatively little empirical work has been conducted in connection with the causal schemata model of the attribution process. Some of the work that has been conducted has examined the **development** of causal schemata. For example, Smith (1975) has shown that while nine-year-olds are consistent in their use of the discounting principle, six-year-olds are inconsistent, and kindergarten children show virtually no evidence of using discounting. This is not wholly surprising, given the complexity of the multiple sufficient causes schema. It requires the child to take account of two (or more) causes in making attributions, and to understand that either (or any) of these is sufficient to produce the behaviour in question.

SELF-ATTRIBUTION

The attributional approach to self-understanding holds that there are important similarities between the way in which we perceive and think about ourselves and the way in which we perceive and think about others. In explaining one's own behaviour to oneself, in other words, one may be drawing on and processing information about causality in much the same way as attribution theorists such as Kelley suggest we do when explaining other people's behaviour.

A major proponent of this attributional, information-processing approach to self-understanding is Bem (1967, 1972). It is interesting to note that his **self-perception theory** was originally developed in an attempt to explain the results of 'dissonance-type' experiments, such as the Festinger and Carlsmith study discussed earlier, in terms owing nothing to cognitive dissonance theory. Bem's prime objection to dissonance theory is that it invokes the operation of internal, unobservable (and therefore entirely hypothetical) motivational processes, in the shape of dissonance arousal and dissonance reduction. Bem argues that we can explain the results of any dissonance experiment without recourse to such hypothetical processes.

Bem's reanalysis of dissonance-type experiments begins by examining how we know what our attitudes and other internal states (such as emotions) are. He argues that the internal cues which might be used in making self-descriptive statements are often weak, ambiguous and uninterpretable. Where this is the case, and an individual is asked to express an attitude or to describe his or her feelings, simple introspection will not provide the individual with an unambiguous basis for an answer. In these situations, Bem suggests, the individual's self-descriptive statements are based – partly, at least – on inferences from his or her own overt behaviour and the context in which that behaviour occurred. Clearly, there are some interesting parallels between Bem's self-perception theory and Schachter's (1964) two-factor theory of emotion, which was discussed in Chapter 8. Both theorists argue that the labelling of an internal state is not exclusively determined by processes occurring *within* the individual; rather, the individual makes use of information about his or her own behaviour and the context in which that behaviour takes place.

An important feature of the rationale of self-perception theory is Bem's contention that when internal cues are ambiguous and uninterpretable, the individual stands in much the same relation to his or her internal states as does an observer. Just as an observer infers our internal states from our overt behaviour, so too does the individual. This point can be illustrated by drawing on one of Bem's own examples. Imagine a man who is asked, 'Do you like brown bread?' He replies, 'I guess I do, I seem to eat a lot of it.' If the man made use of his behaviour towards brown bread in providing his attitude statement, as his answer implies, then anyone who knows that man well – such as his wife – should be in just as good a position to describe his attitude to brown bread, for they have access to the same information from which his own attitude statement was inferred. Thus, 'Does your husband like brown bread?' can be answered, 'I guess he does, he seems to eat a lot of it.'

How, then, does self-perception theory account for the results of dissonance experiments such as the Festinger and Carlsmith (1959) study? Bem asks us to consider first an outside observer who hears the subject making favourable statements about the experimental tasks to the next participant in the study, and who knows the subject was paid to do this. What inference would this observer make about the subject's attitude to the tasks? If the payment involved was small (one dollar), the observer can rule out financial incentive as a cause of the positive statement, and infer that the subject's attitude is consistent with the view expressed in the statement. If, however, the payment was large (twenty dollars), the observer can infer little or nothing about the subject's attitude because the financial incentive appears to be a sufficient cause of the behaviour. Bem goes on to argue that the subjects in the original study behaved just like these hypothetical observers. When asked their attitude towards the tasks, they review their behaviour (making a positive statement about the tasks) and the context in which it occurred (low or high financial incentive). The one-dollar subjects infer that, in the absence of a strong incentive, their positive statement must reflect their attitude, and therefore infer that they like the tasks. The twenty-dollar subjects, on the other hand, discard their behaviour as a guide to their attitude, because the high incentive is a sufficient cause of that behaviour. They therefore express similar attitudes to the tasks as the control subjects, i.e., somewhat negative. By arguing that the attitude statements of Festinger and Carlsmith's subjects are self-attributions made on the basis of their own behaviour and contextual constraints, Bem is able to account for their findings without recourse to the concept of dissonance.

This is not the appropriate place in which to review the history of the theoretical dispute between self-perception theory and cognitive dissonance theory. Many researchers (e.g., Fazio, Zanna and Cooper, 1977) are now agreed that the two theories differ with respect to the domains to which they are most appropriate. As West and Wicklund (1980) put it, 'Dissonance theory applies readily when the person holds an extreme attitude or is in an extreme state such as thirst and then carries out a behavior that is contrary to that attitude or state. Self-perception theory generally provides the best account of attitude effects and other self-description effects when the person does not have a strong attitude' (pp. 112–13). With respect to the link between self-perception theory and the attribution process as it applies to the perception of *others*, it is worth noting that the self-perception analysis of the Festinger and Carlsmith study implicitly involves the use of Kelley's multiple sufficient causes schema: *either* a high incentive *or* a positive attitude is sufficient to cause the positive statement about the tasks, such that when one of these causes (high incentive) is known to be present, the role of the other is discounted; in the absence of the high incentive, however, a positive attitude is inferred to be present.

BIAS IN THE ATTRIBUTION PROCESS

According to the normative models proposed by attribution theorists such as Kelley, information about social causality is processed in a systematic and semi-scientific fashion, albeit with the occasional hiccup induced by factors such as the personal needs of the perceiver. However, from the beginnings of empirical research on the attribution process, there has been a steady accumulation of evidence that individuals do not conform to these normative models when making causal attributions. Departure from the normative models of 'rational attribution' proposed by attribution theorists is typically regarded as evidence of **attributional bias**, although Schneider and associates (1979) have pointed out that this way of diagnosing the presence of such bias is problematic. As they put it, 'Obviously if a given perceiver's judgements do not match those predicted by a particular theory, we know that at least one is incorrect. But it is by no means clear which one' (p. 225). Setting this problem to one side, let us now examine some of the evidence that people arrive at biased causal inferences. We cannot do justice here to the extensive literature on various facets of attributional bias. We shall confine ourselves to discussing evidence of *one* bias, the underutilization of consensus information, with a view to bringing out some of the general issues involved in this field.

The various attribution models differ from each other in several respects, but they do share the assumption that the degree to which a behaviour is shared or popular (i.e., high in consensus) is highly informative about the causal role played by impersonal forces in determining the behaviour. The greater the consensus in behaviour, the more we should ascribe causality to impersonal factors rather than factors internal to the actor. Yet Nisbett and Borgida (1975) found evidence for their view that consensus information is often ignored by perceivers in making causal attributions. For example, they gave subjects in one study written accounts of an experiment on helping behaviour in which one individual is heard (over an intercom) having what appears to be an epileptic seizure, and those listening have to decide whether to go to his aid. Some of Nisbett and Borgida's subjects were then given accurate information about the results of the helping study, namely that most of those who witnessed the seizure helped only after a long delay or did not help at all. Other subjects did not receive this information. Of course the information given or withheld is consensus information, in that it shows the extent to which nonhelping behaviour was common to those who witnessed the seizure. All of Nisbett and Borgida's subjects were then asked to make attributions about the behaviour of one of the witnesses, who never helped. Was his behaviour caused by situational factors or personality factors? Possession of consensus information should have led subjects to attribute this individual's behaviour more to situational causes. However, subjects who received consensus information did not differ significantly in their attributions from subjects who were not given the information.

Subsequent research on the utilization of consensus information suggests that Nisbett and Borgida's view that perceivers may *ignore* consensus information is an overstatement. Nevertheless, the fact remains that consensus information is often *underutilized*. Why should this be the case? One explanation favoured by Nisbett and his colleagues concerns the **vividness** of consensus information. Consensus information, they argue, particularly as it has been manipulated by researchers in experiments, is pallid and abstract by comparison with the 'competing' information about the actor or the stimulus. It tends to be presented in the form of statistics such as percentages or in tables of data. Either way, the information lacks vividness, and is consequently given insufficient weight by the perceiver. To test these ideas, Borgida and Nisbett (1977) conducted a study in which the vividness of information was manipulated. Students who were choosing psychology courses were given information about how these courses were evaluated by those who had taken them. One group was given statistical information, in the form of the mean ratings of several courses made by a large group of students. The other group heard a small panel of students discussing and rating the courses. It was found that course choices were influenced more strongly by the panel discussion than by the statistical summary derived from many more students.

The notion that perceivers attach greater inferential weight to vivid information than to pallid information has a close parallel in the well-established finding that **attentionally salient information** receives disproportionate weighting in subsequent attributions. In the typical study of salience effects, subjects are asked to observe a social episode involving interaction between a small group of individuals, and their attention is manipulated such that one member of the group receives more attention than do the others. The salience of this one individual is achieved by making him or her especially prominent in the observer's visual field, or by having him or her possess some attention-grabbing attribute, such as unusual clothing. McArthur's (1981) review of these studies shows that these salient individuals are subsequently rated differently from other group members: they are better remembered, they are judged to have played a greater causal role in the social interaction, and their attributes are rated in more extreme terms.

The underutilization of pallid information and the disproportionate weighting given to salient information are by no means isolated examples of perceivers' tendencies to depart from the normative standards of inference prescribed by attribution theorists. Research on attribution processes during the last decade has increasingly focused on errors and biases in the attributional process (see Ross, 1977, for a review). Initially researchers were concerned to identify the conditions under which rational processing of social information occurs, but more recently leading theorists have been led to question whether there are any circumstances in which unbiased processing is guaranteed. As Taylor and Thompson (1982) put it, 'Biases, oversights, and shortcuts appear to be intrinsic to the cognitive system rather than introduced into the process by extraneous, interfering affective commitments or needs' (p. 155). This move away from the notion that perceivers are essentially naive scientists who process social information rationally but are occasionally led astray, towards the notion that perceivers are essentially nonscientific in their processing of social information has undoubtedly been accelerated by developments in cognitive psychology. In particular, the work of Kahneman and Tversky (e.g., 1973) on decision-making and probability estimation has been highly influential in leading social psychologists to question the naive scientist model of social information-processing.

COGNITIVE HEURISTICS

According to Kahneman and Tversky people depend on a small number of heuristics when solving inferential tasks under conditions of uncertainty. Of course, the inferential tasks involved in social perception are typically characterized by a degree of uncertainty, either because we do not have at our disposal all the information that would be necessary for us to be certain, or because the information relevant to a particular judgement is too complex and voluminous to be utilized properly. Under such conditions, it is suggested, we arrive at judgements by employing cognitive heuristics, or rules of thumb.

Of the heuristics discussed by Kahneman and Tversky, the one which is most relevant to causal attribution is the **availability heuristic**: 'A person is said to employ the availability heuristic whenever he estimates frequency or probability by the ease with which instances or associations come to mind' (Tversky and Kahneman, 1973, p. 208). In playing a bridge hand, for example, an individual may need to judge the frequency with which cards from a certain suit have been played in previous hands. This judgement may be made (by the casual bridge-player, at least) according to the ease with which instances of such cards being played come to mind. This rule of thumb avoids the need to engage in the more exhaustive procedure of recalling each and every instance of cards of the suit in question being played and then calculating how many cards of that suit remain. It is important to note that the use of availability in estimating frequencies or likelihoods will often produce reasonably accurate, unbiased judgements, since events that are more frequent *are* typically recalled more readily. As Nisbett and Ross (1980) put it, 'To the extent that availability is actually associated with objective frequency, the availability heuristic can be a useful tool of judgment' (p. 19). It necessarily follows, however, that when events differ in their availability due to factors *unconnected* with frequency, use of the availability heuristic will result in biased judgements.

How might the availability heuristic be involved in causal attributions? The disproportionate weighting of vivid and salient information in arriving at causal attributions (discussed above) would seem to reflect a tendency for perceivers to attribute more causality to potential causes that are high in availability. It may well be that individuals involved in social interaction who are attentionally salient to onlookers are seen to be disproportionately potent causal agents because they are disproportionately *available* to the onlookers. If this were the case, then one would expect to find evidence that salience effects are mediated by differential recall of salient and nonsalient causal information. Recent research has indeed found evidence that recall mediates the impact of salient stimuli on attributions, although the nature of the mediation is complex (Fiske *et al.*, 1982).

THE IMPACT OF SOCIAL COGNITION ON SOCIAL INTERACTION

At the beginning of this chapter it was noted that the impressions we form of other people can operate as self-fulfilling prophecies, in that our behaviour tends to elicit from them evidence that confirms our original impressions. Evidence of the tendency for our impressions of others to be self-fulfilling comes from a famous (but controversial) study by Rosenthal and Jacobson (1968), who led elementary school teachers to expect rapid growth of intellectual ability in certain children. These children had ostensibly been identified by means of a psychological test measuring potential for 'intellectual blooming', but were in fact chosen on a random basis by the investigators. It would appear that the teachers' expectancies led them to behave towards these children in such a way as to elicit intellectual growth, for when the children's IQs were measured at the end of the school year the supposed 'bloomers' showed significantly larger mean increases than their classmates.

Further evidence of the self-fulfilling prophecy comes from a laboratory study by Snyder, Tanke and Berscheid (1977). Male subjects were asked to converse via an intercom with a female partner whom they had not met and could not see. They were led to believe that this female was either physically attractive or unattractive. The investigators audiotaped the female's side of the conversation and played the recordings to another group of males, who were asked to make ratings of the speaker. These ratings differed according to whether the original male conversant believed the female to be attractive or unattractive. Female partners who were believed to be attractive by the original males were subsequently judged more positively than females who were believed to be unattractive. Thus it would appear that the original male subjects' belief that they were talking to an attractive woman led them to converse in a manner which induced her to speak in a way that was perceived by others to be attractive. Once again, an *impression* of another person has influenced *behaviour* towards that person in such a way as to elicit responses which confirm the original impression.

The serious implications of the self-fulfilling prophecy for everyday social interactions should be evident. For example, there is a widespread feeling among black and immigrant communities that potential employers discriminate against them when they apply for jobs. Research by Word, Zanna and Cooper (1973) shows how subtle this discrimination can be. They had white subjects take the role of job interviewer, and carefully trained black and white confederates to serve as job applicants. This training ensured that there were no objective differences in the behaviour of black and white applicants. It was found, however, that the interviewers behaved differently towards the two groups of applicants: for example, white applicants were interviewed for longer and received more eye contact. In a second stage of this study, interviewers were trained to behave differently towards two groups of white applicants, the differences matching precisely those found in the interviewers' behaviour towards white and black job applicants in the first stage. Those who were treated by the interviewer in the same fashion as black applicants had previously been treated were rated by independent judges to have performed worse than those who were treated in the same way as white applicants had previously been treated. This pattern of results suggests that interviewers behave towards black applicants in such a way as to elicit a poor interview performance from them. While the bulk of the theory and research on social cognition discussed in the present chapter treats perceptions of others as inferences made on the basis of their behaviour, the research on self-fulfilling prophecies serves to remind us that these inferences are not passive. Once formed, they can shape the course of future interaction and thereby influence the behavioural evidence on which subsequent inferences are based.

Further reading

Attitudes

An excellent introduction to theory and research on attitudes and attitude change is provided by:

PETTY, R.E. and CACIOPPO, J.T. (1981) *Attitudes and Persuasion: Classic and Contemporary Approaches*. Dubuque, Iowa: William C. Brown.

The following is a classic synthesis of the pre-1969 literature on attitudes and is still well worth reading:

McGUIRE, W.J. (1969) The nature of attitudes and attitude change. In G. Lindzey and E. Aronson, eds., *Handbook of Social Psychology*, Volume 3. Reading, Mass.: Addison-Wesley.

The following is an in-depth treatment of the various techniques that are available for measuring attitudes:

DAWES, R.M. (1972) *Fundamentals of Attitude Measurement*. New York: Wiley.

The next book is a clear and concise presentation of the authors' 'theory of reasoned action' – an attempt to spell out how attitudes, beliefs and other factors combine to determine behaviour – together with some examples of how the theory has been applied to practical problems. This is recommended reading for anyone who has to rely on questionnaire responses in order to predict subsequent behaviour:

AJZEN, L. and FISHBEIN, M. (1980) *Understanding Attitudes and Predicting Social Behavior*. Englewood Cliffs, NJ: Prentice-Hall.

Person perception

The following is highly recommended as an introductory text that does justice to the complexity of the person perception process while also being lucid and readable:

SCHNEIDER, D.J., HASTORF, A.H. and ELLSWORTH, P.C. (1979) *Person Perception*. Second edition. Reading, Mass.: Addison-Wesley.

The following is an edited volume that shows the diversity of topics (including close relationships and depression) that have been analysed in attributional terms:

HARVEY, J.H. and WEARY, G., eds. (1985) *Attribution: Basic Issues and Applications*. New York: Academic Press.

A recent analysis of bias in the attribution process that draws on the notion of heuristics is provided in:

ROSS, L. and ANDERSON, C.A. (1982) Shortcomings in the attribution process: on the origins and maintenance of erroneous social assessments. In D. Kahneman, P. Slovic and A. Tversky, eds., *Judgment under Uncertainty: Heuristics and Biases*. Cambridge: Cambridge University Press.

The following is the original statement of self-perception theory, and is relevant to the material on attitudes as well as to that on person perception:

BEM, D.J. (1972) Self-perception theory. In L. Berkowitz, ed., *Advances in Experimental Social Psychology*, Volume 6. New York: Academic Press.

A reasonably comprehensive review of work on how attributional inference develops in children is provided in:

RUBLE, D. and RHOLES, W.S. (1981) The development of children's perceptions and attributions about their social world. In J.H. Harvey, W.J. Ickes and R.F. Kidd, eds., *New Directions in Attribution Research*, Volume 3. Hillsdale, NJ: Erlbaum.

The following is a lively and readable analysis of the impact of cognitive heuristics and schemata on social judgements:

NISBETT, R.E. and Ross, L. (1980) *Human Inference: Strategies and Shortcomings of Social Judgment*. Englewood Cliffs, NJ: Prentice-Hall.

A good overview of research on self-fulfilling prophecies and placebo effects can be found in the following:

JONES, R.A. (1977) *Self-fulfilling Prophecies: Social, Psychological and Physiological Effects of Expectancies*. Hillsdale, NJ: Erlbaum.

Social cognition

An admirably clear and up-to-date introduction to much of the research on social cognition can be found in:

FISKE, S.T. and TAYLOR, S.E. (1984) *Social Cognition*. Reading, Mass.: Addison-Wesley.

12. Interpersonal Processes and Intergroup Relations

12. Interpersonal Processes and Intergroup Relations

Introduction

From the first relationship between mother and child onwards, other people are important sources of satisfaction to the individual. Previous chapters have examined how individuals communicate with each other (Chapter 10) and how they think about and evaluate their social environment (Chapter 11). The present chapter will focus more directly on interpersonal relations, and in particular on the psychological and behavioural consequences of social interaction within and between social groups. We shall begin by examining the origins of interpersonal relations, comparing social interaction between humans with social interaction that occurs in other species. We shall then consider the development of interpersonal relations in children, taking in the roles played by parents, family and peers. The section that follows will deal with different aspects of intragroup processes: the influence that can be exerted on individuals by the mere physical presence of other people; how groups are formed and how they develop; the impact of group pressure on individual behaviour; the way in which a group responds to the presence of 'deviant' opinions or behaviours in its midst; and how and why decisions made by groups differ from those made by individuals. In the final section of this chapter we shall turn to relations *between* social groups, seeking to understand the psychological bases of social conflict.

The origins of interpersonal relations

A key question to be considered in connection with human social interaction is why it is that we have such a strongly social orientation. Of course, humans are by no means unique in being social animals, and this fact has led some to argue that studying the social behaviour of other species should shed light on human social behaviour. However, in comparing the social behaviour of one species with that of another, we need to be aware of some fundamental qualitative differences between behaviours which might all appear at first sight to be instances of social behaviour.

Annett (1976) has distinguished between three types of social interaction among members of a given species. First, there are interactions in which the individual seeks contact or proximity with *any* conspecifics. Second, there are interactions limited to a particular *subgroup* of conspecifics. Third, there are interactions between *individual* conspecifics. These three types of social interaction can be seen as progressing from a rather limited to a much more complex level of social behaviour.

The first type of interaction is only 'social' in a very restricted sense. Here individual members congregate instinctively and in doing so may satisfy a nonsocial need, such as thirst. This kind of behaviour can be observed in some insect species. The second type of social interaction, with *groups* of conspecifics, is found in several species. Rats and mice, for example, are species in which individuals do not recognize each other as individuals, but do recognize from smell cues whether a given animal belongs to *their* group (Eibl-Eibesfeldt, 1970). Because there are no individualized acquaintanceships within such social groups, there can be no dominance hierarchy of group members. The benefits of this type of social interaction are still mainly nonsocial, in that by virtue of cooperative interaction the group occupies a territory containing physical resources, such as food and water, and defends this territory against intruders.

The third type of social interaction, with individual conspecifics, involves the capacity to recognize individuals, resulting in fairly consistent behaviour towards a given individual across different contexts. The capacity to recognize individuals can be inferred from the presence of **pair-bonding** and/or **dominance hierarchies**. For a pair-bond to become established the partners have to be able to recognize each other. Dominance hierarchies develop when group members learn from a series of conflicts which individuals are superior and inferior to themselves, and then behave appropriately towards the dominant and subordinate individuals.

This third level of social interaction clearly involves a kind of social behaviour that is qualitatively different from the other two. The group still facilitates the satisfaction of biological needs, such as hunger and thirst, but the means by which these needs are satisfied involve a much stronger social component. In species displaying this type of social interaction, for example primates, the young are often highly dependent on adults for food and defence against predators for a relatively long period. The existence of pair-bonds between adults naturally facilitates the process of caring for and training the young. The survival of group members depends to some extent on the ability of the group to keep intragroup conflict to a minimum and to cooperate in defending the group against predators. The existence of a dominance hierarchy naturally helps to control intragroup aggression, and cooperation between group members is facilitated by playful interactions between the young and by reciprocal grooming in adults. Thus a fairly complex pattern of social interactions functions in such a way as to enhance the chances of survival of individual group members. It is not clear, however, whether this social behaviour is simply a means to an end or whether it becomes an end in itself. In other words, the richness and complexity of social behaviour within certain species does not *of itself* constitute grounds for inferring that these animals interact with each other simply because they want to interact.

Evidence that bears rather more directly on this question of whether or not nonhuman species have innate social needs comes from a well-known study by Harlow (1959). While others had supposed that the dependence of infant primates on their mothers results from associating the mother with the satisfaction of biological needs, especially hunger, Harlow showed that young rhesus monkeys preferred to cling to a soft, cloth-covered surrogate mother, rather than a wire surrogate mother – even when milk was supplied via the wire 'mother'. When both 'mothers' were cloth-covered, the monkeys preferred the lactating surrogate. This pattern of findings suggests that young rhesus monkeys have a basic need for bodily contact, and that their dependence on their mothers reflects this 'social' need, as well as biological needs.

How does this brief analysis of social behaviour in nonhuman species help us in considering the origins of human interpersonal relations? It is clear that there is a rough correspondence between the structural complexity of an organism and the complexity of social behaviour found in that species of organism. Simple organisms engage in a minimal type of social behaviour, the purpose of which is to enable or enhance the satisfaction of individual biological needs. Complex organisms engage in a rich pattern of social interaction, one effect of which is to facilitate the satisfaction of biological needs and to enhance the chances of individual and group survival, but which may also either reflect an inbuilt need for social contact or come to have inherent reward value. Although we can quite easily make conceptual distinctions between biological needs and social needs, in reality there is a complex interplay between these two types of motivation. In lower species, social behaviour tends to be a direct reflection of biological needs. As one proceeds up the phylogenetic ladder, so the patterns of social interaction found become less obviously a simple product of biological needs, and correspondingly more likely to be reflections of social needs. This analysis is consistent with, but not directly supportive of, the view that humans are innately social beings. To evaluate this view further, we shall now look at social behaviour in human infants.

The development of interpersonal relations

Very young babies are responsive to human beings, in that they **smile** at them and apparently enjoy being handled by them. Fantz (1961) found that babies as young as two weeks old spent longer looking at a lifesize cartoon face than at stimuli of similar shape and complexity that did not depict faces. While this finding does not preclude the possibility that babies *learn* to prefer face-like stimuli to other stimuli, it does seem unlikely that learning is solely responsible for the existence of this preference at such an early age.

Nevertheless, there are considerable difficulties involved in disentangling the influences of learned and innate behaviours in this area. This much can be seen by carefully considering Ahrens's (1954) observation that six-week-old babies smile in response to face-like stimuli. Ahrens considered that smiling is a 'social' response in that it is elicited by face-like stimuli, the eyes being especially important in stimulating the smile at six weeks; progressively more facial details are required to elicit the response at later ages. However, later research (e.g., Zelazo and Komer, 1971) has shown that smiling is elicited in young babies by *familiar* objects, whether these are social or not. Furthermore, the human face is very likely to be the most familiar object that young babies encounter, due to the perceptual constraints that make it especially likely that the infant will focus on his or her mother's face during feeding (Stern, 1977).

Although experience does seem to play a role in shaping the infant's smiling response to another human face, it nevertheless seems to be the case that the face in general and the eyes in particular are prepotent in eliciting a smile. Because adults tend to find the infant's smile attractive, it in turn tends to elicit gazing from caregivers, and so these patterns of smiling in the infant and gazing in the adult tend to be mutually rewarding. The interactive quality of infant-mother gazing patterns has been shown clearly by Stern (1974). He found that when mothers played with three-month-old babies the mother tended to gaze at the child for fairly long periods, while the baby looked at the mother, then away, then back again. In other words, it is the child who establishes and breaks off contact with the mother, rather than the other way round. The mother appears to produce what Stern calls 'supernormal' stimuli – she leans toward the baby, speaks in a particularly clear voice, gestures in a slow and deliberate fashion, and employs exaggerated facial expressions. Stern's findings show that while the mother steadily provides this intensive stimulation for the infant, the child alternates between attending and not attending to it. Stern believes that this alternation has a regularity which may be the manifestation of a biological 'given' that the infant brings to the interaction, and he has suggested that the regularities in the patterning of mother-infant gazing are similar to those found in adult verbal exchanges.

Whatever inferences concerning innateness of behaviour are drawn from these findings, it is clear that the patterns of gazing observed by Stern and others reveal a high degree of **synchronization** and **reciprocity** in the exchanges between adult and child. If the human infant is to some degree predisposed to respond to social stimuli and through such responses elicits further social stimulation, what consequences do these exchanges between child and caregiver have for the quality of their relationship? A much studied and somewhat controversial concept used to describe the quality of the relationship between a child and the caregiver is that of **attachment**.

ATTACHMENT

The precise onset of attachment behaviour, that is, behaviour in which proximity to particular individuals is sought, remains uncertain. There are increasing reasons to believe, however, that babies are born with a set of structures that predispose them to engage actively with responsive conspecifics (see Chapter 10, pages 565–9). Schaffer (1977, p. 105) has described three steps in attachment formation:

1. The infant's initial attraction to other human beings that makes him prefer them to inanimate features of the environment.
2. His learning to distinguish among different human beings so that he can recognise his mother as familiar, and strangers as unfamiliar.
3. His ability, finally, to form a lasting, emotionally meaningful bond with certain specific individuals whose company he actively seeks and whose attention he craves, though he rejects the company and attention of other, strange individuals.

Thus, even granting inbuilt capacities, the development of bonds is a process that extends over many months. (But note a contrasting view from some American paediatricians [Klaus and Kennell, 1976] who claim that the first twenty-four hours are critical to the bonding process.) Bonding requires the capacity to recognize attachment figures, which means differentiating them from others, and to retain a memory of those who provide emotional security so that brief separations can be endured. The evidence allowing us to conclude that attachment is the foundation on which toleration of separation as well as exploration of the unfamiliar (the very antithesis of attachment) is built, derives largely from the pioneering studies of Ainsworth and her colleagues (e.g., Ainsworth, 1979). Using a measure called **strange situation**, they have observed one-year-olds in a sequence of settings: (1) with mother and stranger in an unfamiliar setting **(preseparation)**; (2) without mother and with an unfamiliar adult in an unfamiliar setting **(separation)**; (3) with mother in unfamiliar setting **(reunion)**.

They found that securely attached children used mother as a **secure base** from which to explore in the preseparation period. In the separation stage exploration diminished and distress was likely. On reunion these infants sought contact with, or proximity to, their mothers. Such infants were contrasted with those who, on the basis of earlier home observations, had been categorized as having anxious attachments. While it is an oversimplification simply to contrast the secure with the insecure, since Ainsworth's research has identified eight patterns of attachment, it is worth noting that less secure infants showed anxiety during the preseparation period and were inclined to exhibit extreme behaviours (intense distress or rarely crying) during separation. On reunion the intensely distressed infants were ambivalent towards their mothers, showing **approach-avoidance behaviour**, while those who had not cried avoided their mothers.

What distinguishes the mothers of securely attached infants from those of anxious infants? Ainsworth recognizes that attachment is a dual process and that some children are constitutionally difficult. Nevertheless, she believes that maternal behaviour is the main determining factor and that successful relationships arise when mothers are responsive and sensitive to the baby's signals. Such behaviour is most clearly revealed outside normal caretaking duties when attachment figures are playing with their infants. For this reason studies of kibbutzim children indicate that ties with parents remain stronger than with metepelets even though more time may be spent with these daytime caretakers.

The study of attachment involves a number of problems of design and interpretation. In using separation situations as measures of attachment we must control for the effects of strangers as well as unfamiliar surroundings. Strangers are not an homogeneous group and may therefore vary in their effects. The infant's history of previous separations will be relevant as will the sensitivity with which the mother handles the parting. Interactions between such factors and child's age, sex, birth order and number of attachment figures continue to receive investigation. Even more important is the need constantly to be aware that the infant we are studying is both an active participant and an organizer of experience. Perhaps the main goal of the infant, as Dunn (1977) has suggested, is to strive to maintain a harmonious balance between the need for a loving relationship and the desire to go beyond it in discovering the world beyond.

PEER RELATIONS

Our understanding of the growth of interpersonal processes is hampered by the lack of longitudinal data in this area. The information that we have indicates important links between attachment and later peer relations as well as intellectual development. Ainsworth reports that securely attached infants develop cooperative and sympathetic relationships with peers and show persistence and curiosity in both play and problem-solving. In contrast, those whose bonds have been less secure show aggression and are easily frustrated. They tend to score less well on language and other developmental tests. Rutter (1978) has pinpointed difficulties in making relationships with other children as one of the most reliable indicators of current or subsequent mental disorder or delinquency.

In assessing the significance of peer relations it is important to keep in mind that these extend beyond the preschool nursery, the focus of much work on children's play and social interaction. Apart from the fact that such relations continue into the school years and beyond, many children do not attend a nursery, or only go part time. Peer relations mainly develop in two spheres – the home and the neighbourhood. The family, which includes those who come into the home as well as siblings, will be discussed below. Neighbourhoods vary in their opportunities for peer relations, but the majority of urban children, particularly, form their closest friendships with children in the immediate locality, such relationships being fostered by self-help playgroups. Few parts of Great Britain can be considered isolated and most rural communities offer similar opportunities for children to meet playmates.

The significance of peer relations will be illustrated by focusing on two important topics. One, play, is an activity that has almost acquired the status of a process through its role in many theories of child development. The other, friendship, is preeminently a peer-related accomplishment, and one which is receiving increasing attention from psychologists.

Play

There is a voluminous literature on play in human and nonhuman primates. Yet, although everyone knows what play is, it is a term that eludes precise definition. Garvey (1977) lists a number of the properties of play, which seems a sensible approach to definition. The principal elements are pleasure and exuberance, spontaneity, absence of extrinsic goals, and active engagement. A further aspect concerns the relationship between play and nonplay activities. Bruner (1972), among others, has emphasized the importance of play as an arena for trying out cognitive and social strategies where the consequences have none of the seriousness of nonplay situations.

This latter feature has given rise to some confusion. Piagetian theory portrays the child as an active discoverer of knowledge through play. Hutt (1966) prefers to make a distinction between *exploration*, in which the properties of new objects (or events) are learned, and *play*, which is typically what ensues once the process of discovery is complete. Whether one sees these as distinct entities or two ends of a continuum is largely a matter of theoretical preference.

Play is such a large part of the young child's world that the growth of interpersonal processes can be viewed entirely through the window of play. Thus friendship, empathy and role-taking skills are acquired largely through the medium of play. Play offers children their most fruitful opportunities for enacting their knowledge as well as their desires in creative and fantasy situations. For the student of child development it is a fertile ground for learning about 'children's concepts of social rules and obligations, their understanding of the physical environment, and their knowledge of language structure' (Garvey, 1977, p. 118).

We think of play as being synonymous with childhood, but it is not restricted to that period of life. We encounter problems of definition, however, if we see adult leisure activities as play. Adult sports or games usually have extrinsic goals and are seldom spontaneous. Moreover, *in extremis*, they can bring nations into war – which was the outcome of a disputed result in a 1970s soccer World Cup eliminator between Honduras and El Salvador. But although they fall outside Garvey's properties of play, there is surely a real sense in which bridge and bowls, darts and golf, and swimming and dancing represent the adult at play. And it is biologically adaptive for species that have an extended period of dependency to retain an interest in and love of play. As we know, normal human development requires that adult caregivers engage in a sensitive relationship with their children, a principal component of which is play.

Friendship

Friendships are a highly significant feature of most people's lives and for some individuals they are more influential than the family. Even where family ties are strong, friends serve to broaden and deepen the individual personality by providing a new range of interests as well as a challenge to be met in terms of maintaining relationships where no blood ties exist. Because such relationships are a powerful feature of childhood, it is not surprising that most of the work in this area has been done by developmental psychologists.

There are two effective ways of studying how friendships arise and are maintained. One method is to ask children about their friendships; the other is to watch interactions between friends and compare them with those between strangers. Studies that have used the former procedure are focusing on what children *think* about relationships, and such study is part of the burgeoning field of social cognition. Not surprisingly, research shows that children's cognitions about friendship become increasingly complex with age. A change in the concept of friendship is not as easy to identify as are, say, changes in vocabulary and expression. As an individual's knowledge increases, does the *process* of friendship change? The research of workers like Selman (1976) and Damon (1977) suggests it does.

There seem to be three important developments in the growth of social understanding. First, the ability to take the perspective of another, **role-taking**, is a critical component of communication skill (as we saw in Chapter 10), so it is not surprising to learn that this is important in friendship. A second factor is the ability to see people not merely as physical entities but also as **psychological beings**, an ability that has a developmental history. Thirdly, there is a movement from seeing friendship as momentary encounters serving a hedonistic function to a conception in which friendships are seen as **valuable enduring relationships**.

The cognitive approach appears to neglect the contributions of the various **agents of socialization** such as parents. But, as Rubin (1980, p. 41) says, 'Most developmental psychologists believe that the principal architect of social understanding is not the child's culture but the child himself.' This position, sometimes called the **constructivist approach**, after Piaget, is one in which 'children work out for themselves what social relationships are all about on the basis of their actual encounters with others' (Rubin, 1980, p. 45).

The advantage of a **naturalistic observational approach** is that information about the nature of friendship does not get filtered through adult questionnaires or protocols. Children are not being asked to interpret questions and articulate answers – they have simply to be themselves.

Observational studies have their own limitations but these are recognized in a carefully conducted study by Gottman and Parkhurst (1980). They tape-recorded thirteen children at free play in their own homes with both best friends and strangers. The age range was from three to six years and same-sex pairs (both sexes) and different-sex pairs were represented. A number of relevant social processes were identified as being important in forming friendly acquaintanceships. These are best illustrated by describing the theory of friendship development which the authors offer.

First of all, the children must engage in conversation, which is usually initiated by the host child. With young children this is most successful if it is here-and-now, activity-based talk – 'Do you want to play with my garage?' and if both partners answer one another's questions. If friendship is to develop, children must establish similarities in such things as possessions and play activities. Once common ground is achieved they can tolerate, and even welcome, differences of attitude and action. (Such a pattern has also been noted among marriage partners.)

Even among friends there is a **power** dimension and the possibility of disagreements. Friends recognize that the child on home ground has certain rights and that guests must comply with requests, particularly to polite suggestions by the host. A robust finding concerned the role of **fantasy**, which not only exemplified the successful relationships, in that extended fantasies of both the domestic (playing shops) and adventure (monsters) types were typical among close friends, but also frequently served to resolve conflict. Fantasies themselves, of course, can *create* conflict and fear, and Gottman and Parkhurst noted the manner in which established friends would skilfully invoke empathy and support to dissipate fear and distress.

A further observation worth noting arose from the authors' comparison of the younger (under five) and older children. The young child's philosophy seemed to be to try to make friends with strangers. If the attempt proved unsuccessful, so be it. The older children appeared to have learned that strangers are to be approached differently from friends. They were more cautious, and restricted conversation to more neutral topics, eschewing fantasy, for instance. This finding led the authors to speculate that the need for close friendship is at its zenith in the preschool years. It may therefore be that they 'are more competent at [friendship] . . . than older children and adults' (p. 24) and that we have, accordingly, something to learn from them.

THE FAMILY

The growth of interpersonal processes not only has its beginnings and basis in the family (in Western and many other cultures) but is governed by this fact in contexts beyond the home. Thus, patterns of work and play and ways of coping with anxiety and conflict have their roots in the family situation.

Despite this almost self-evident fact, research and theory in this area tends to restrict itself to the role of the *mother* and her influence on social and emotional development. Many theorists might argue that 'mother' is shorthand for family. But even in the unlikely event of the father's role in childrearing being exactly comparable to the mother's, the relationship *between* parents, as well as factors such as **birth order** and **sibling rivalry**, has been shown to exert considerable influence. In short, the family can seldom be regarded as a unitary factor but must rather be seen as a complex of interacting variables.

Childrearing styles

Two major problems confront those who wish to prescribe an ideal style of childrearing for parents seeking advice. First, in no area is the belief that we are each individuals more relevant than in this one. Not only do children vary in their susceptibility to patterns of rearing but parents themselves have a psychological history that will make it difficult, if not impossible, for them to fit into roles they find alien. If this were not enough, the other major problem is that styles of childrearing are extremely sensitive to changes in society's circumstances and values. A community that regards the mother's place as being in the home will engender attitudes different from those propagated by one that encourages women to pursue careers as well as family life. A contemporary and related concern is the changing role of fathers in societies where women's rights are achieving greater expression. Does research carried out in the 1950s and 1960s have anything to tell us in the 1980s?

The answer is that various parental styles have been identified and their consequences for child development charted. To the extent that it is possible to characterize parents as permissive or restrictive, warm or hostile, consistent or inconsistent, and anxious or relaxed, then certain effects tend to follow. The dimension that has received most attention is **restrictive/permissive**. At the restrictive end of the continuum is a figure who sets firm guidelines for behaviour, punishing infringements of the code and discouraging self-expression in the form of personal desires and autonomous goals. The archetypal permissive parent offers little or nothing in the way of a code of conduct and is indulgent towards expressions of personal wishes even if these should impose on the rights of others.

Research has shown (Baumrind, 1967) that neither of these types is satisfactory and, when allied to inconsistency and/or hostility, can be positively destructive. The child of restrictive parents may appear polite and obedient on the surface but this often veils bitter resentment which can show itself as violence in other circumstances, notably when interacting with less dominant individuals, such as younger children. The permissively reared child, in contrast, will often be uninhibited in displays of aggression and, if permissive parents are also inconsistent, emotional disturbance and delinquency may well result. Such an outcome is often based on a mistaken, even romantic, view, according to Baumrind, in which children are seen as dominated by egotistic and impulsive forces. The authoritarian seeks to constrain such 'primitive' tendencies while the permissive parent sees them as natural, healthy traits to be given full rein. In reality there is good reason to believe that children require consistent models with which to identify at a time when their powers of reasoning are largely undeveloped. Most experts are agreed that an optimal approach requires the sort of secure foundation described in our discussion of attachment. Rules of conduct should be fairly and consistently maintained in a style that allows children to participate in decisions that affect their welfare.

Birth order

In Britain in the 1970s the average family contained 2.25 children, and large families are now an exception rather than the rule. In such a situation it might seem of little value to consider the effect of birth order. However, children with siblings are considerably more common than only children and the latter can be regarded as special cases of first borns. A variety of research (reviewed by Zajonc and Markus, 1975) has shown that **first borns** tend to be ambitious, conservative, principled and successful. They are also more sensitive, anxious and dependent than later borns. Such patterns of behaviour are attributed to their having had the exclusive attention of parents who themselves are inexperienced (and therefore anxious) in the business of childrearing.

In families with more than two children it is reasonable to talk of **last borns**. They bear some resemblance to first borns in receiving a disproportionate amount of attention (from siblings as well as parents), and 'spoiling' can result. They tend to mature less quickly than first borns and to suffer from a lack of responsibility. Such a pattern may lead to enduring feelings of inferiority.

Middle children are characterized as being subject to a lack of attention, and having self-perceptions which are low in ability and achievement. They often seek success in nonacademic pursuits and sometimes court unconventional life styles and ideas. Such children are usually popular with their peers for their easy-going and gentle approach to life.

In drawing general conclusions such as these, we risk not doing full justice to a complex issue. Nothing has been said, for instance, about **sex differences**. Second borns who are a different sex from the first borns will be treated more like first borns. Furthermore, every reader will know of more than one exception to the outlines we have provided. Nevertheless, the consistency of the literature is impressive, and further research into the relations between siblings as well as the effects of birth order seems fully warranted.

Fathers

All children necessarily have fathers as well as mothers and yet the psychological literature on child development might sometimes cause you to question this truism. We have already referred to the growth of paternal consciousness in recent times and it is now established, if not universally accepted, that childrearing is not a role unique to women. What effects do differing styles of father-hood have on interpersonal growth?

Before tackling this question a note on method is in order. Many of the studies in this field have investigated the effects of father absence in comparison with intact families. Such research has not always controlled for the effects that father absence might have on the mother in terms of emotional and financial insecurity. Such effects, in themselves, may have significant influences on the children.

Lamb (1979) argues that fathers have a primary role in developing sex roles. In most households fathers spend less time than mothers with the children and their major activity with the children is play. Almost by default the mother comes to be seen as the caretaker figure. Hence traditional sex roles are modelled by the parents. Studies (see Parke, 1981) show that fathers are 'primarily responsible for the initiating of . . . sex-differentiating treatment since it is they who begin to pay special attention to their sons and apparently withdraw from their daughters' (Lamb, 1979, p. 939). The child's response is typically to develop preferences for the same-sex parent which, Lamb argues, 'may be one of the major factors in the acquisition of gender identity' (p. 939).

It is, of course, a broad and sometimes dangerous oversimplification to see parents simply as sex role models rather than as a general socializing influence. But Lamb argues that it is only when gender **identity** is secure – that is, the child has confident views of the self as either male or female – that atypical gender **roles** can be accepted by both child and parent as valuable to healthy growth.

MORALITY

One view about morality is that it is a subjective matter and therefore not susceptible to scientific study. This is a powerful objection but it has not prevented psychologists examining the topic. This is due to two reasons. First, it can be shown that children's ideas about right and wrong do change with age, and therefore there is a phenomenon to describe and explain. Second, moral issues are central to most people's lives and so it is not surprising that we should look to psychologists to throw some light on them.

There are three chief approaches to moral development, each focusing on a different psychological level. These are: psycho-analytic theory, which deals with feelings through notions such as **conscience**; social learning theory, which is concerned with behaviour or **conduct**; and cognitive theory, which is interested in **moral judgements** and ideas. We shall consider each of them briefly.

The main contribution of Freud's psychoanalytic theory (see Chapter 13) in this area is the account given of conscience development. For Freud, conscience is the superego which seems to fulfil a number of needs. It makes us feel ashamed when we are morally inadequate and guilty when we transgress the moral code. On the more positive side it gives us resistance to temptation and makes us feel self-esteem when we are virtuous. **Guilt**, therefore, is the mainspring of morality in Freudian theory. Guilt arises when we fall below the standards we set ourselves, though it should be recognized that, in some cases, the standards set are unrealistically high. For Freud, conscience develops through the years of parental dependency. Children incorporate their parents' standards through the little understood process of **identification**.

Most theories agree that some form of **internalization** must take place for a conscience to develop, otherwise satisfactory behaviour would always be contingent on the presence of overt rewards and punishments. Some theories, such as that of Eysenck (see page 296), characterize the conscience as a **conditioned anxiety response** based on the fear of punishment, but this seems an unduly narrow conception. It leaves out the role of other forms of learning, such as imitation, and it assumes the subject does not *think* about situations involving moral decisions or actions. Furthermore, it predicts that the strongest moral consciences will result from the most severe punishment, when the reverse is, in fact, true.

As we saw in the section on childrearing, parental styles differ and they have an impact on moral development. A landmark study by Sears, Maccoby and Levin (1957) found that the antecedents of a well-developed conscience boiled down to three factors: the use of temporary love-withdrawal, rather than physical punishment, by parents who have a warm relationship with their children; the use of reasoning in connection with discipline; consistency in attitudes and behaviour, and high mutual esteem and trust in the family. These findings may seem obvious to the reader but, unfortunately, there is plenty of evidence that 'psychological' methods of discipline are not universally acknowledged, let alone practised.

We stated earlier that children's ideas about right and wrong change with age. Piaget (1932) showed this in a series of studies which involved watching children play a rule-governed game such as marbles and asking them questions about stories which contained moral transgressions. The story might contrast John, who had stolen six bread rolls for his friend who was starving, with Roger who had taken one roll because he wanted it. Piaget's main findings, which have been widely replicated, were as follows. First, young children differ from older children in that they judge an act to be bad in terms of its physical consequences rather than the intention behind it. Thus John would be judged naughtier because he stole more rolls. Second, young children seem unaware of relativism in issues of moral judgement – they do not admit of any diversity of views about right and wrong. Third, they regard an act as bad because it will be punished, not because it breaks a rule or harms others. Finally, young children do not use the idea of **reciprocity** – the realization that if I do something to you, you will probably do it to me in return – as a reason for consideration for others.

Piaget's two stages of **moral realism** (where moral rules are external, rooted in authority and insensitively applied) giving way to the **morality of cooperation** (where another's view is taken into account and the role of human relationships in deriving moral rules is recognized) conform to his theory of cognitive development (see Chapter 9) and have been extended by Kohlberg (e.g., 1976). There is not enough space here to present Kohlberg's elaborate theory but his cognitive developmental approach has been influential in this area because it offers a possible way of finding underlying consistency in behaviour which seems to change with each situation (see Box 13.1). At the same time there is, of course, more to morality than judgements about the actions of others, and recent work (Gerson and Damon, 1978; Weston and Turiel, 1980) is trying to add a behavioural dimension while accepting the value of the cognitive framework.

Intragroup processes

EFFECTS OF THE MERE PRESENCE OF OTHERS

Before we consider how membership of social groups influences thoughts, feelings and actions, we should be aware that **the mere physical presence** of other persons can have an influence on these variables, whether or not these other persons are fellow group members. One type of mere presence effect is known as **social facilitation**. This is a generic term used to describe *all* effects (detrimental as well as beneficial) on task performance that are due to performing the task in front of others. After many years of rather inconclusive findings on this issue, Zajonc (1965) proposed an elegant answer to the question of whether the presence of others enhances or inhibits task performance. Zajonc argued that the type of effect produced depends on the type of task being performed. If the task is simple or well learned, such that *correct* responses are likely to be dominant, then an audience *enhances* task performance, according to Zajonc; but if the task is complex or poorly learned, such that *incorrect* responses are likely to be dominant, then an audience inhibits task performance. Thus the general effect of an audience is to enhance the likelihood of dominant responses being emitted. In explaining *why* audience presence should have this effect, Zajonc drew on Hull-Spence learning theory, which holds that any increase in drive (which corresponds very roughly to arousal) enhances the probability of dominant responses being emitted. Thus the full argument is that the mere presence of others increases drive and thereby enhances the performance of simple, well learned tasks and inhibits the performance of complex, poorly learned tasks. Today this drive theory explanation is still conventionally regarded as the best available account of social facilitation phenomena (Geen and Gange, 1977); however, the research findings are by no means wholly consistent with Zajonc's theory (Glaser, 1982), and other, rather more cognitive explanations have been suggested (e.g., Sanders, 1981).

GROUP FORMATION, STRUCTURE AND DEVELOPMENT

How does membership of and participation in social groups such as families, friendship groups and work groups, influence the way we think, feel and behave? The study of **group processes** involves the identification of those properties of social groups that are psychologically significant, and the examination of how these properties influence individual group members.

The first question that must be tackled is a definitional one: what is meant by the term **social group**? How does a social group differ from a mere aggregation of individuals? Shaw (1976) has surveyed psychologists' many attempts at a definition. One approach has been to argue that the defining characteristic of a group is that its members share **common motivations or goals**. The idea here is that individuals join a social group in the hope or belief that by doing so they will fulfil some need. A rather different approach is adopted by those who choose to stress the **organizational properties** of social groups. For example, group members tend to have certain roles and statuses, with the result that relations between group members tend to be more structured than is the case with individuals drawn together on a random basis. Yet another approach is taken by those who emphasize the **interdependence** of group members, by which is meant that a social group consists of a number of individuals who are interdependent in the sense that something that affects one person also affects the others.

Each of these attempts to identify the quintessential feature of a social group seems to focus on an important characteristic, but each could probably be refuted by citing an example of a social group that does not possess the proposed defining quality. Shaw's solution to this definitional issue is to adopt a more comprehensive approach. He stresses the significance of the **social interaction** between group members, arguing that they communicate with each other on a frequent and regular basis, and that this interaction tends to be face-to-face rather than indirect. Because this approach stresses the quality of sustained interaction between group members, it subsumes the other approaches to defining a social group. Sustained face-to-face interaction seems to require both common motivations and a degree of organization of relations between group members; furthermore, a degree of interdependence between group members seems to be a likely consequence of sustained face-to-face interaction.

Earlier in this chapter we saw that human beings are for a number of reasons highly predisposed to seek out and respond to social stimulation. The fact that the main characteristic distinguishing groups from mere aggregations is sustained interaction between group members therefore goes a long way towards explaining why individuals form or join social groups. Groups help to satisfy the individual's basic need to affiliate with others. However, we can also ask whether this need to affiliate varies across situations. If individuals were especially inclined to seek out the company of others under particular conditions, then social groups would be more likely to be formed under these conditions.

Relevant to this question is a well-known experiment conducted by Schachter (1959). In this study female students were recruited to participate in an experiment ostensibly being conducted by the university's department of neurology. The experimenter explained that participation involved receiving electric shocks, and these shocks were described either as painful (high-fear condition) or as very mild (low-fear condition). Subjects were then told that they would have to wait while the experimental apparatus was set up, and were given the choice of waiting alone or with other women. In the high-fear condition 63 per cent of subjects elected to wait with others, while in the low-fear condition only 33 per cent chose to do so. In a follow-up study employing the same general procedure, high-fear subjects were either given the option of waiting alone or with other women taking part in the experiment, or given the option of waiting alone or with other women who were supposedly going to 'see a professor'. Schachter found that when subjects had the option of waiting with fellow-subjects, 60 per cent chose to wait with others, but that when subjects had the option of waiting with students who were not taking part in the experiment, none chose to wait with others.

In explaining these findings, Schachter argued that the enhancement of affiliative tendencies in threatening circumstances reflects a need to engage in **social comparison**, i.e., to compare one's own behaviour with that of others, with the aim of assessing whether or not one's response to the threatening circumstances is appropriate. If a subject felt aroused and disturbed at the prospect of receiving painful electric shocks, then some of her concern may have been about the appropriateness of such reactions. By choosing to wait with fellow-subjects, the subject could see how they were reacting and evaluate the appropriateness of her own reactions by comparing them with those of her fellows. Subsequent research has shown that this need to engage in social comparison does play a causal role in the **fear-affiliation relationship**, as Schachter argued, although other factors may also mediate this relationship (see Cottrell and Epley, 1977).

Schachter's research on the fear-affiliation relationship indicates that individuals are especially inclined to seek out the company of certain other individuals in threatening circumstances. However, choosing to wait in the company of others, rather than alone, is a long way from being part of a social group. Why and how would a few students who have elected to wait together become a social group in the sense defined above? Much the same point can be made about individuals who join together or are brought together to perform some task or to achieve a certain goal. Why and how would such individuals become a social group? The answers to these questions are to be found in studies of how the structural properties of social groups emerge as three or more individuals interact together over time. Let us now examine two lines of research relevant to this issue, the first concerned with the emergence of social norms and the second with the emergence of roles and the development of communication patterns.

The emergence of norms

One of the classic studies in social psychology is Sherif's (1935) demonstration of how norms emerge in social groups. Sherif made creative use of an optical illusion known as the **autokinetic phenomenon**, the illusory perception of movement that occurs when an individual is asked to observe a single small point of light in an otherwise completely dark room. The light *appears* to move, although it is in fact quite stationary. Because the movement seen is purely illusory, and because there is no frame of reference for judging how far the light 'moves', individuals tend to differ in their estimates of the amount of movement they perceive. Sherif was interested to see how knowledge of others' estimates would influence individual judgements. To do this, he ran two conditions: one in which subjects first made their judgements individually, and then in a group context; and another in which this sequence was reversed. He found that with the first sequence, subjects in the group sessions modified their previously established individual estimates in such a way that the estimates of group members converged over trials; and that with the second sequence the judgemental norm on which subjects converged in the group context tended to carry over into the individual sessions.

In the highly ambiguous context of the autokinetic phenomenon, therefore, individuals clearly make use of others' judgements when making their own. Sherif argued that his findings show the operation in a social context of a general psychological phenomenon, namely the tendency for our experience of the world to be organized around and modified by **frames of reference**. Thus the growing uniformity of judgements in the group sessions resulted from the frame of reference that group members' estimates provided for each other. The consensus that emerged was a **group norm**. Although Sherif's experiments show how judgemental norms emerge when individuals are asked to make judgements about ambiguous *physical* phenomena, there is no reason for assuming that this process is any different when individuals are making judgements about *social* phenomena, such as political parties, racial groups or social policies. Particularly where these phenomena are ambiguous and complex, individuals will tend to look to each other's opinions and to use these as frames of reference.

The strength of group norms, as reflected in their power to influence the attitudes and behaviours of individual group members, will clearly be maximal where no objective basis for assessing the correctness of an opinion or a behaviour exists. The strength of group norms also varies to a large extent with the real or imagined sanctions that will, or may, be invoked when norms are violated. As we shall see below, such can be the individual's dependence on the group that in some cases an apparent group norm exerts considerable influence on the individual even when there is less ambiguity about the task being performed.

The emergence of roles and communication patterns
Apart from norms, the other key aspects of group structure that emerge as a social group develops are roles and communication patterns. A large and well-known programme of research that is informative about the emergence of these structural properties was conducted by Bales and his colleagues (Bales, 1970). A distinctive methodological feature of this research was its use of a category scoring system for coding verbal interactions in small group settings. This scoring system is known as **interaction process analysis**, or simply IPA, and it involves the use of trained observers who code each behavioural act that occurs within a group into one of twelve categories, shown in Table 12.1. It can be seen that there are four basic categories – *positive reactions*, *attempted answers*, *questions*, and *negative reactions* – each divided into three subcategories.

Bales's research strategy largely consisted of assembling small *ad hoc groups* in a laboratory setting and scoring their verbal interactions by means of the IPA. These groups would meet for a number of sessions, thereby enabling the researchers to chart the development of communication patterns within each group. Using evidence from the IPA system, Bales and Slater (1955) found quite marked differences between the communications made by the two most talkative members in social groups. One person, who was likely to score highly in the 'attempted answers' category,

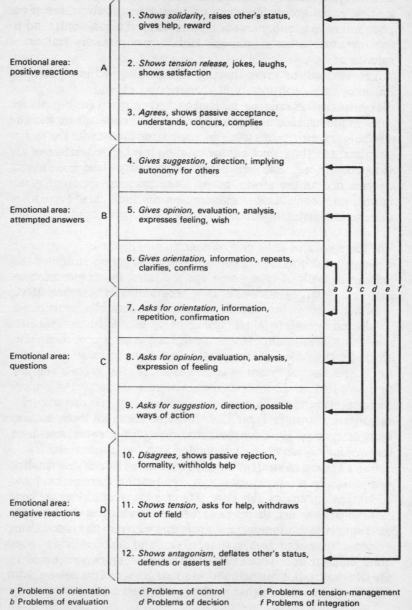

Emotional area: positive reactions	A	1. *Shows solidarity*, raises other's status, gives help, reward
		2. *Shows tension release*, jokes, laughs, shows satisfaction
		3. *Agrees*, shows passive acceptance, understands, concurs, complies
Emotional area: attempted answers	B	4. *Gives suggestion*, direction, implying autonomy for others
		5. *Gives opinion*, evaluation, analysis, expresses feeling, wish
		6. *Gives orientation*, information, repeats, clarifies, confirms
Emotional area: questions	C	7. *Asks for orientation*, information, repetition, confirmation
		8. *Asks for opinion*, evaluation, analysis, expression of feeling
		9. *Asks for suggestion*, direction, possible ways of action
Emotional area: negative reactions	D	10. *Disagrees*, shows passive rejection, formality, withholds help
		11. *Shows tension*, asks for help, withdraws out of field
		12. *Shows antagonism*, deflates other's status, defends or asserts self

a Problems of orientation   *c* Problems of control   *e* Problems of tension-management
b Problems of evaluation   *d* Problems of decision   *f* Problems of integration

Table 12.1 The system of categories used in interaction process analysis.

tended to be seen by others as the group leader. This individual seemed to be oriented towards achieving the group's goals. The other talkative group member typically scored highly in the 'positive reactions' category, tending to be warm, friendly and emotionally supportive towards other group members. This person's major role seemed to be the maintenance of good interpersonal relations with the group.

To explain this **two-role leadership** that emerged in their social groups Bales and Slater suggested that the first of these individuals, the 'task leader', is a source of tension and potential focus for resentment by the group, because of the goal-directed nature of his or her behaviour. The need for a **socioemotional leader** therefore arises, and a somewhat less active but better liked group member assumes this responsibility. Thus the leadership of the group comes to be centred around two different but complementary roles, one being the 'task specialist' and the other the 'socioemotional specialist'. Later research has tended to support this theory of leadership role differentiation, although it should be noted that the extent of role differentiation is likely to increase with the unrewardingness of the group's task (see Secord and Backman, 1964, p. 359).

A very different approach to the study of communication patterns in small groups is represented by research on **communication networks**. In this type of research the experimenter *imposes* a communication structure, or 'network', on the group, thereby limiting the free exchange of information. Some of the many different networks that have been employed in research on five-person groups are shown in Figure 12.1. The circles represent individual group members, and the lines represent channels of communication between the members.

One of the earliest studies using the communication network procedure was conducted by Leavitt (1951). He compared the wheel, chain, Y and circle networks (see Figure 12.1) to see how they influenced the emergence of leaders. The groups were given a fairly simply task to perform; after fifteen trials on this task, group members were asked whether their group had a leader, and if so who the leader was. The results showed that persons occupying the *central* positions in the wheel, Y and chain networks were nominated more often than were other members. Furthermore, in groups operating with the circle network, where there is no central position, no one was more likely than any other to be perceived as the group leader. So the person who occupies the *central* position in a communication network has a high probability of emerging as group leader – a finding that has been replicated in several subsequent studies.

Communication network studies such as Leavitt's provide a useful contrast to Bales's research on communication in small groups. Bales's studies highlight the fact that communication patterns *reflect* the emerging group structure, with the two leaders talking more than their fellow group members but at the same time making different kinds of communications from one another. The communication network studies serve as a reminder that where the channels of communication are to some degree imposed on the

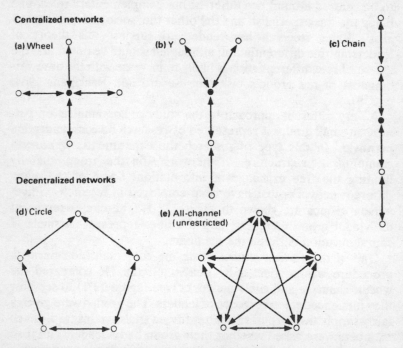

Figure 12.1 Communication networks used in laboratory studies (five-member groups). The darkened circle indicates the central position in diagrams (a), (b) and (c).

group – as indeed they often are in organizational settings – communication patterns may partly *determine* the kind of group structure that emerges.

GROUP PRESSURE

We noted above that the impact of group norms on individuals' attitudes, opinions and behaviours is maximal (a) under ambiguous circumstances, where the responses of other group members provide a frame of reference for the individual's responses; and (b) where the ability of other group members to sanction the individual for violation of norms is high. Such is the power of the group, however, that conformity to group norms may occur in relatively unambiguous contexts, and where the ability of other group members to sanction the individual is confined to psychological sanctions (such as social rejection), and is in any case more imagined than real.

As Kiesler and Kiesler (1969) have pointed out, the motivating force behind conformity in such circumstances is **group pressure**, which they define as 'a psychological force operating upon the individual to fulfil others' expectations . . . including especially those expectations of others relating to . . . behaviours specified or implied by the "norms" of the group' (p. 31). There is no doubt that individuals do, under certain conditions, yield to group pressure. What is of interest, from a psychological perspective, is to identify the conditions under which such yielding occurs, and then to draw some inferences about *why* it occurs.

The classic experimental demonstration of the effects of group pressure was conducted by Asch (1952). Where Sherif had used a highly ambiguous judgemental task, Asch used a task in which the correct response was obvious – in the absence of group pressure. This task involved judging the lengths of lines. Figure 12.2 shows an example of the type of stimulus material employed. The subjects' task is to assess which of the three comparison lines (A, B or C) is the same length as the standard line, and then to call out its associated letter. In the first of Asch's experiments on this topic, subjects were given twelve trials of this judgement task. Subjects were tested in groups of eight, and simply called out their judgements in turn. Seven of these eight persons were in fact confederates of the experimenter, and had been instructed to answer incorrectly, but unanimously, on seven of the twelve trials. So the majority verdict on these 'critical' trials was patently incorrect, but it was also unanimous. The order in which the eight individuals announced their judgements was subtly rigged so that the one naive subject was last or second to last to respond. Asch was interested to see whether naive subjects would yield to group pressure, by going along with the majority on the critical trials, or would stick to the evidence of their own eyes.

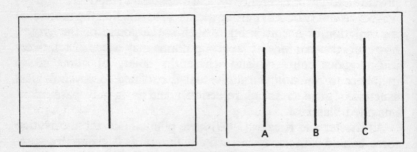

Figure 12.2 Example of material used by Asch to study group pressure.

Confronted with this conflict, only one-fifth of Asch's subjects were completely error-free in their judgements. However, of the total number of judgements made on the seven critical trials, the majority (67 per cent) were correct. The remaining 33 per cent were errors identical to the false majority verdict. Asch also ran a control condition, in which subjects made their judgements privately, in writing. Here errors were only 7.4 per cent of the total judgements. So although the majority of the responses of subjects exposed to group pressure were correct, there was a much greater tendency for subjects to make judgemental errors than was the case under control conditions. Moreover, all the errors that were made corresponded to the false majority judgement.

Asch conducted a number of further studies, all of which followed the same basic procedure. For example, he studied the effect of varying the **size of the unanimous majority**. He found, predictably enough, that pitting a naive subject against *one* confederate who gave false judgements on critical trials produced minimal conformity. However, some yielding to the majority verdict was found when there were two confederates, and the incidence of this yielding rose quite markedly when the size of the majority was increased to three persons. However, Asch found that increasing the majority size beyond three did not produce any significant increase in the amount of yielding. Although other researchers (e.g., Rosenberg, 1961) also found that yielding levels off at majority size three, subsequent research has tended to find that yielding increases steadily as the majority size increases up to seven (e.g., Gerard, Wilhelmy and Connelley, 1968).

Asch also studied the consequences of varying the **unanimity of the majority** judgement on critical trials. He found that when the naive subject was given a 'partner' in the form of a confederate who made correct judgements throughout the experiment, and whose judgement preceded that of the naive subject, the influence of the false majority was markedly weakened. Here, only 13 per cent of the total number of critical judgements conformed to the majority error. In a further variation Asch pitted a *naive majority* against *one* confederate who answered incorrectly on critical trials. The reactions of the naive majority are described by Asch (1952, p. 479) as follows: 'At the outset they greeted the estimates of the lone dissenter with incredulity. On later trials there were smiles and impromptu comments. As the experiment progressed, contagious, and in some instances uncontrolled, laughter swept [through] the group.' However, when the number of confederates was increased to the point where they became a substantial minority within the larger group (i.e., nine out of twenty), the reactions of the naive subjects were quite different. The ridicule and derision heaped on the sole dissenter in the previous study were replaced by a more serious attempt to account for the judgemental discrepancy in terms of fairly objective factors, such as optical ability or misunderstanding of instructions.

The general conclusion to be drawn from Asch's findings is that unanimity of judgement is crucial to the impact of group pressure, at least in this experimental context. Two or more individuals unanimously providing *correct* judgements validate each other, and enables them to stand out against the influence of the incorrect majority. When one individual is pitted against a unanimous majority of three or more persons a substantial degree of conformity occurs.

Asch's research is helpful in identifying the conditions that promote conformity to group norms. A further issue of considerable interest is *why* individuals tend to conform to group norms in these circumstances. Deutsch and Gerard (1955) proposed that two distinct processes are responsible for the yielding observed in Asch's experiments, namely **normative social influence** and **informational social influence**. By the term 'normative social influence' Deutsch and Gerard mean the tendency of individuals to conform to their perceptions of other people's expectations in order to be socially accepted (or to avoid being socially rejected) by these others. By 'informational social influence' Deutsch and Gerard mean the tendency of individuals to conform to what other people think or do because these people are seen as sources of evidence about reality, so their thoughts and actions cannot be ignored in assessing the validity or correctness of one's own thoughts and actions. If six or seven of your peers report that line C is the same length as the standard line, whereas it seems to you that line B is the correct answer, who is more likely to be right: you or they? Unless you have some reason for doubting either their competence or their motives, the sheer unanimity of your peers' judgements will tend to make you doubt your own judgement.

To test the operation of these two theoretically distinct processes of social influence, Deutsch and Gerard conducted a number of studies based on the Asch procedure, each incorporating a key modification. In one condition subjects were told that theirs was one of several groups participating in the study, and that the five groups making the fewest errors would win a prize. Responding independently of the false majority under such circumstances carried the risk of being responsible for the group's failure to win a prize. This should have enhanced the impact of normative social influence, and indeed Deutsch and Gerard found that subjects did make more conforming errors here than in a standard Asch-type face-to-face condition. In another condition subjects' responses were not identifiable as *theirs*. This should have minimized the role of normative social influence, and indeed Deutsch and Gerard found that subjects made *fewer* conforming errors here than in the face-to-face condition. However, subjects in the anonymous condition still made *some* conforming errors, indicating that informational social influence also plays a part in producing conformity in the Asch situation.

It might be objected that these demonstrations and explorations of yielding to group pressure have limited validity, because they involve *verbal* conformity (being influenced in calling out a judgement) rather than *action* conformity (being influenced in executing some action), and because the *consequences* of yielding to the majority are not of great moment. Both of these objections are addressed in a study by Milgram (1964). This is one of a well-known series of studies of **destructive obedience**, i.e., the tendency of individuals to obey an authority's commands to administer what appear to be severe electric shocks to a protesting victim (see Chapter 7). Milgram was concerned to see whether the unanimous suggestions of two persons who appeared to be fellow-subjects (and therefore had no particular *authority* over the subject) could induce individuals to deliver severe shocks to a protesting victim. He found that exposure to group pressure, in the form of unanimous majority suggestions, influenced subjects to inflict shocks of much higher levels than those chosen in the absence of such pressure.

REACTIONS TO OPINION DEVIANCE IN SMALL GROUPS

In the studies of conformity conducted by Asch, Deutsch and Gerard, Milgram, and many others, the strategy employed by the investigators was to create a small group with an initial divergence of judgement or opinion, with a view to seeing how this divergence is resolved. Usually, the divergence is such that most group members hold one position, while a minority – often only one person – holds the other. The focus of interest in such research is on how the minority behaves: does the lone minority member go along with the unanimous majority or not? However, there is another, less heavily researched, aspect of opinion divergence in small groups: how do the *majority* members react to this opinion deviance?

Perhaps the best known study of majority reaction to opinion deviance was conducted by Schachter (1951). In this study subjects were recruited to participate in discussion groups. Each group contained between five and seven naive subjects and three confederates. One of these three (the **mode**) agreed with the modal group opinion throughout the discussion. Another (the **slider**) began the discussion by adopting a very deviant position, but in the course of the discussion came to agree with the modal opinion. The third (the **deviate**) maintained a highly deviant position throughout the discussion. Following the discussion, subjects had to complete a questionnaire indicating how attractive they found each of the other group members, and then had to nominate group members for jobs of varying attractiveness.

Schachter found that the deviate was disliked by the subjects more than either the mode or the slider, who were not significantly different in this respect. Moreover, there was a marked tendency for the deviate to be overnominated for less attractive jobs and undernominated for more attractive jobs. Schachter also kept a record of the number of communications addressed to the three confederates during the group discussion. It was found that the deviate received approximately four times as many communications as the slider, and seven times as many as the mode.

Taken together, Schachter's findings indicate that there are pressures towards opinion uniformity in social groups, that opinion deviates are disliked and to some extent socially rejected, and that communication is used to achieve group uniformity. On the basis of these findings, it is difficult to see how a deviant individual or minority in a group could exercise influence over the majority. Yet it is clearly the case that deviant individuals and minorities *can* influence a majority and persuade it to move from an entrenched position. All innovations, be they social, political or technical, originate in individuals or minorities, and yet some of these innovations eventually gain widespread acceptance. Psychoanalytic theory is a case in point: Freud's ideas were initially rejected and reviled by the vast majority of his medical and scientific colleagues, yet psychoanalysis gained a secure foothold in psychology.

The occurrence of minority influence seems puzzling in the light of the preceding discussion of norms, group pressure and deviate rejection, because majority influence over minorities is explained in terms of the **dependence** of the minority on the majority. In the case of informational social influence, the minority is conceptualized as dependent on the majority for information about social or physical reality. In the case of normative social influence, the minority is conceptualized as dependent on the majority for social acceptance and approval. Minorities appear to have neither the numbers nor the resources to exercise normative or informational social influence. The experimental research on minority influence shows that several factors have an impact on the extent of minority influence, the most important of which are the **consistency** and **extremity** of the minority position. The evidence suggests that minority influence is maximized when minority members consistently uphold their position. For example, Moscovici and his colleagues (1969) had six-person groups judging the colour of blue slides that varied in brightness. In one condition two confederates deviated from the group consensus by judging *all* slides to be 'green'. This consistent minority influenced the naive subjects to give more green judgements than were given under control conditions. When the investigators later ran an inconsistent minority condition, in which the two confederates judged only two-thirds of the slides to be 'green', no minority influence was observed. The evidence also suggests that minority influence is greater when the minority position is moderately, rather than extremely, deviant. In a study similar to the one just described, Nemeth and her colleagues (1974) had pairs of confederates deviating from the colour judgements of four naive subjects exposed to blue slides. In the moderate deviance condition the confederates consistently judged the slides to be 'green-blue', while in the extreme deviance condition they judged all slides to be 'green'. The moderate deviants were rather more influential than their extreme counterparts.

Summarizing the reasons for the effectiveness of minority influence under certain conditions, Moscovici and Nemeth (1974) argue that the key factor is the minority's **behavioural style**. By behaving consistently rather than inconsistently, and in a moderate rather than an extreme fashion, a minority leads others to attribute to its members qualities such as conviction, autonomy and competence. The behavioural style that makes a minority effective is one 'that leads to perceptions that they (i.e. minority members) have a position, that they believe in it, that they will maintain it even in the face of disapproval and criticism . . . . By such means, they illustrate certainty that makes the majority question its position, and offer stability towards which a majority can move' (Moscovici and Nemeth, 1974, p. 248).

GROUP DECISION-MAKING

As we have seen in the preceding sections, research on group processes during the years leading up to 1960 was strongly oriented towards the study of conformity. Experiments such as those by Sherif, Asch and Schachter encouraged researchers to associate social interaction in group settings with the tendency of group members to conform to perceived norms. If we now consider group decision-making from such a perspective, we would clearly expect groups to make less extreme, more moderate decisions than individuals. Presumably differences of opinion within a group are resolved in favour of the majority, so that 'deviant' or extreme views would have little impact on the group decision.

Given this climate of thought, one can see why social psychologists were surprised and intrigued by the results of a study conducted by Stoner (1961). He set out to test the then widely held belief that groups make more conservative decisions than individuals. Stoner's decision-making task involved a series of twelve 'choice dilemmas', each of which described a hypothetical situation in which a central figure is confronted by the need to choose between a safe but dull alternative, and an alternative that is much more attractive but also much riskier. For example, one dilemma involved a mediocre chessplayer who is participating in a tournament; he has to choose between making a very risky move which, if it worked, would enable him to beat a higher ranked player, and making a safer, more conventional move. The subject's task is to imagine that he or she is advising the central figure in each of these choice dilemmas, and then to indicate the lowest probability of success (expressed in odds) that he or she would require before advising the central figure to choose the risky alternative. Thus, if the subject indicated that he or she would advocate the risky alternative, even if there were only a three-in-ten chance of its being successful, this would be a fairly risky decision. If, on the other hand, the subject indicated that the risky option should only be adopted if there were a nine-in-ten chance of success, this would be a much more cautious decision.

Stoner's experimental procedure had three phases. First, four or five subjects made individual decisions on each of the twelve choice dilemmas. Second, these subjects were told to discuss each dilemma as a group and to reach a consensus decision. Finally, the subjects were asked to make individual decisions once again. Stoner compared the average of the individuals' prediscussion decisions with the group decision, and with the average of their postdiscussion decisions, and found that both the group decision and the average of postdiscussion decisions were riskier than the average of prediscussion decisions. Thus Stoner's groups made riskier decisions than had their individual members. Moreover, this so-called **risky shift** induced by the group process carried over into the individuals' postdiscussion decisions.

Stoner's findings stimulated much further research and a lively controversy over the causes of the risky shift. This research effort, spurred on no doubt by the apparent relevance of this phenomenon to decision-making by cabinets, juries, boards of directors and so on, rapidly established that the shift to risk is a reliable outcome of Stoner's experimental procedure. It also became apparent that the crucial feature of the group phase of this procedure was the group *discussion*, and not the group *decision*, since variations in which each dilemma was discussed without the need to reach a decision also induced shifts to risk. A turning point in this research came when, rather belatedly, it was discovered that different choice dilemmas produced different kinds of shift. In fact two of the original twelve dilemmas typically produced *cautious* shifts. It has subsequently become apparent that the whole concept of risky shift and all the explanations that were proposed to account for the *riskiness* of group decisions are based on a misconception arising from the composition of the original set of twelve choice dilemmas. It turns out that the best predictor of the *direction* of a group discussion induced shift is the **inherent riskiness** of the issue under discussion. Choice dilemmas which produce average prediscussion decisions displaced towards the risky end of the risk-caution continuum typically induce group shifts to risk. On the other hand, dilemmas which produce average prediscussion decisions displaced towards the cautious end of this dimension typically induce group shifts to caution. Indeed, the relationship between average prediscussion decisions and size of group shift is strong and linear. In other words, *group discussion acts to enhance the initially dominant point of view within a group*.

Recent research on group decision-making has studied group-induced shifts to risk or caution within the framework of research on **group polarization**. This is a term coined by Moscovici and Zavalloni (1969) to describe their finding that groups, on average, become more extreme in their responses following group discussion, where these responses had nothing to do with risk or caution. Polarization simply means movement towards that pole or end of the scale or dimension which is already preferred, and is illustrated in Figure 12.3. So it seems that the shifts to risk and caution found by researchers studying group decision-making are part of a more general phenomenon, group polarization. But what is it about group discussion that produces group polarization? The evidence suggests that the explanation of group polarization resides in two complementary theoretical approaches.

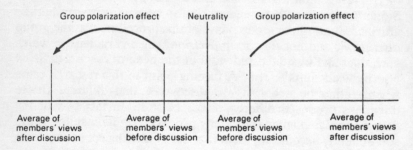

Figure 12.3 Group polarization effects. Following group discussion, members often shift toward positions more extreme than the ones they held initially, but in the same general direction.

The **informational influence approach** holds that when a group of people discusses an issue, there will naturally be a predominance of arguments presented in favour of the viewpoint initially favoured by group members as individuals. It is likely that some of these arguments will be **novel** to some group members, i.e., arguments that they did not think of when making their individual decisions; and that other arguments will strike some group members as particularly **cogent**. To the extent that the arguments aired in favour of the initially preferred viewpoint are novel and cogent, they are likely to persuade group members, and will therefore serve to shift the group as a whole in a more extreme direction.

The **social comparison approach** holds that people are motivated to perceive and present themselves favourably, relative to others, and that finding out the average decision of other group members in the course of the discussion elicits a tendency for the individual to deviate from this norm, by shifting his or her own view in the socially desirable direction. When individuals confront an issue for the first time, their response to it is likely to be a compromise between an ideal, fairly extreme response, and what they assume to be the group norm, which is seen as much more moderate. The group discussion may then reveal that the norm is closer to their ideal than they had imagined, thereby encouraging them to shift their responses closer to the more extreme ideal.

Evidence exists to support both of these theoretical approaches (see Myers, 1982). It follows that whenever the circumstances of group decision-making permit or encourage the presentation of novel and cogent arguments in group discussion, or foster the desires of individual group members to present and perceive themselves in a desirable light relative to their peers, the outcome of group discussion will be polarization. On the other hand, where the circumstances of group decision-making do not offer scope for the presentation of persuasive arguments, and the issues being decided do not carry evaluative implications for the self-perceptions of the decision-makers, then group discussion is unlikely to result in polarization.

A rather extreme instance of group decision-making conditions which do *not* produce polarization effects is the **groupthink** phenomenon described by Janis (1982). In studying some of the decisions made by key policy-making groups in the highest echelons of various USA administrations, Janis has developed a theory that under certain conditions such groups are liable to make poor decisions, *at least partly* for social psychological reasons. Specifically, Janis argues that certain antecedent conditions promote groupthink, which is his term for the undermining of critical and independent thought within a group that results from strong pressures within the group for **uniformity of opinion**. Having analysed high- and low-quality decisions made by policy-making groups, Janis believes that groupthink is more likely to arise when the decision-making group is *highly cohesive*; is *insular* (i.e., is relatively cut off from other groups and individuals); *lacks methodical procedures* for searching out and appraising information; has a *leader who is directive* rather than receptive; and is under *stress* to arrive at a decision. Each of these conditions is likely to strengthen pressures towards uniformity of opinion, and to decrease the willingness of each group member to voice his or her private reservations about any consensus that shows signs of emerging. When several of these conditions obtain, the group begins to lose touch with reality and has the potential to make spectacularly disastrous decisions. One of the low-quality decisions analysed by Janis has been called a 'perfect failure'; it was the decision made by the United States administration to invade Cuba in 1961.

An especially interesting feature of groupthink is the tendency for the group to perceive itself in favourable terms and its rival or opponent groups in very unfavourable terms. One of the symptoms of groupthink, according to Janis, is an 'illusion of invulnerability', a belief on the part of the group that it cannot fail. Another symptom is a 'belief in the inherent morality of the group', a belief that it can do no wrong. A third symptom is that the group develops negative stereotypes of rival or opposing groups, i.e., it ascribes to almost all members of such groups negative qualities such as weakness or stupidity. These contrasting perceptions of one's own group as right and good and of rival groups as wrong and bad are particularly interesting because they are pervasive features of interactions *between* social groups, as we shall see in the following section.

Intergroup relations

Tension and conflict between social groups are familiar features of social existence. Several attempts have been made to explain prejudiced attitudes and discriminatory behaviour in terms of attributes and processes of *individuals* who hold prejudiced attitudes and/or behave in a discriminatory way. Many of these individualistic theories have their intellectual roots in Freud's views about intergroup behaviour, which are encapsulated in his belief that: 'It is always possible to bind together a considerable number of people in love, so long as there are other people left over to receive the manifestations of their aggressiveness' (Freud, 1930, p. 114). Explanations of prejudice derived from Freud's thinking share the general assumption that hostile attitudes and behaviours of people towards outgroups are ways of resolving individual emotional problems in an intergroup setting. Only relatively recently has this individualistic account of prejudice and discrimination been seriously challenged. The critics accept that the individualistic approach may help to explain some individual cases of prejudice and discrimination, but they argue that it is ultimately a much too narrow approach to be able to provide an understanding of **general social conflict**. As Tajfel (1978) has argued, explanations of intergroup conflict in terms of individual motivations fail because in most instances of such conflict, persons do *not* deal with each other as individuals; rather they behave primarily as members of social groups: 'When in conditions of racial discrimination people find it difficult to obtain accommodation or employment, it is not because they are ugly or handsome, short or tall, smiling or unsmiling, but because they are black' (Tajfel, 1978, p. 27–8).

A similar point was made by Sherif (1967), who was the first social psychologist to study intergroup hostility in an explicitly intergroup context. He held that 'Whenever individuals belonging to one group interact, collectively or individually, with another group or its members in terms of their group identification, we have an instance of intergroup behaviour' (p. 12). Sherif wanted to study how hostility between social groups develops as a consequence of the relations between those groups. He therefore tested the effects of modifying relations between social groups, in a series of now classic field experiments. The three studies were carried out in 1949, 1953 and 1954, using as subjects boys aged between eleven and twelve who were staying at summer camps in the USA. Between them, these studies involved four stages in the development and modification of intergroup relations. In the first stage (**spontaneous friendship formation**) all activities were pursued by the boys in one large group, and friendships between individuals developed in the normal way. In the second stage (**group formation**) the boys were divided into two groups in such a way that the majority of friendship pairs now found themselves in different groups. All camp-wide activities now ceased. The two groups had separate activities and sleeping quarters. In the third stage (**intergroup conflict**), the two groups were placed in competition with each other. Sporting encounters and camp chores were used to award points to the group performing more adequately. These points were to be totalled as part of a tournament and the winning group was to receive a prize. In the last study of this series, Sherif included a fourth stage (**intergroup cooperation**) in which the two groups encountered desirable goals which could only be achieved by cooperative action between the groups.

The consequences of these systematic modifications of intergroup relations were quite dramatic. During the third stage there was a marked deterioration in intergroup relations:

> The tournament started in a spirit of good sportsmanship. But as it progressed good feeling soon evaporated. The members of each group began to call their rivals 'stinkers', 'sneaks' and 'cheaters'. They refused to have anything more to do with individuals in the opposing group. The boys in the 1949 camp turned against buddies whom they had chosen as 'best friends' when they first arrived at the camp. A large proportion of the boys in each group gave negative ratings to all the boys in the other. The rival groups made threatening posters and planned raids, collecting secret hordes of green apples for ammunition. In the Robber's Cave (1954) camp the Eagles [one group], after a defeat in a tournament game, burned a banner left behind by the Rattlers [the other group]; the next morning the Rattlers seized the Eagles' flag when they arrived on the athletic field. From that time on name-calling scuffles and raids were the rule of the day. (Sherif, 1967, p. 82)

Such overt intergroup hostility was diminished during the fourth stage, when superordinate goals were introduced. By design rather than accident, the camp's water supply was interrupted, and on another occasion a food truck broke down. In each case the two groups worked together to overcome the problem. As Sherif notes,

> These joint efforts did not immediately dispel hostility . . . But gradually the series of cooperative acts reduced friction and conflict . . . The boys stopped shoving in the meal line. They no longer called each other names, and sat together at the table. New friendships developed between individuals in the two groups. (pp. 89–90)

On the basis of these findings, Sherif developed a disarmingly simple theory of intergroup relations, which proposes that **competitive goals** cause intergroup conflict, and that **superordinate goals** give rise to intergroup cooperation. Competitive goals are defined as goals that one group attains at the expense of the other. Superordinate goals are defined as goals which are compelling for both groups, but which neither can achieve without the cooperation of the other. More specifically, Sherif argued that the conflict engendered by competitive goals is accompanied by: (1) unfavourable attitudes and images of the outgroup; (2) increased in-group solidarity; and (3) overevaluation of ingroup products and performances, and underevaluation of those of the outgroup.

As Turner (1981) points out, Sherif's is a *functional* theory of intergroup behaviour. It implies that functional interdependence between groups for the achievement of their goals leads directly either to competitive interaction and consequent antagonism (where the interdependence is negative), or to cooperative interaction and consequent cohesion (where the interdependence is positive). There is little doubt that Sherif's predictions about the consequences of competitive and cooperative interaction are correct, but subsequent research questions the importance of functional interdependence. As Turner (1981) comments, the major difficulty with the functional theory 'is that ingroup-outgroup membership sometimes seems to cause intergroup differentiation when there is neither cooperative interaction within nor competitive interaction between groups' (p. 75).

Particularly important in this context is the research of Tajfel and his colleagues on the minimal conditions required for intergroup discrimination to occur. Tajfel's research is founded on the assumption that **social categorization** is sufficient to induce bias in favour of the ingroup and discrimination against the outgroup. From this perspective, any categorization rule that provides a basis for classifying persons as belonging to one social group rather than another is sufficient to produce divergence in attitudes and behaviour towards the two groups, even in the absence of intergroup competition. While Sherif holds that the sufficient condition for intergroup discrimination is the *existence of two groups competing for goals that only one group can attain*, Tajfel argues in effect that the sufficient condition for intergroup discrimination is the *existence of two groups*.

Support for Tajfel's argument comes from a number of studies, one of the earliest being that reported by Tajfel and his associates (1971). These investigators tested whether simply classifying individuals into two groups would lead to intergroup discrimination. However, these were no ordinary social groups. As Tajfel (1981) has explained, the aim of this study 'was to establish minimal conditions in which an individual will, in his behaviour, distinguish an ingroup from an outgroup' (p. 268). To create **minimal groups** the experimenters divided the subjects into two groups on the basis of criteria assumed to be quite unimportant to the subjects. In the study under discussion the male school student subjects were shown pairs of slides depicting paintings by artists (Klee and Kandinsky) of whom they had not heard, and had to express a preference for one in each pair. They were then split into a 'Klee' group and a 'Kandinsky' group, supposedly on the basis of their preferences, although in reality the allocations were random. Each subject was informed which group he was in, but he did not know anything about the group membership of any other subject. He was then asked to make decisions about the monetary rewards to be received by two other subjects, about whom he knew nothing other than their group membership. The basic finding from this study was that when deciding the rewards to be received by anonymous ingroup members and anonymous outgroup members, subjects discriminated in favour of their own group and against the outgroup.

This study also revealed an important feature of the strategy that subjects followed in making their decisions. When subjects could choose between maximizing their own group's profit and maximizing the *difference* in profit between ingroup and outgroup, it was the latter strategy that prevailed. Even if maximizing the profit differential between ingroup and outgroup meant that one's own group would receive less total profit, subjects generally favoured this strategy. Differentiation of outcomes rather than profit maximization seems to be the goal of intergroup discrimination in this type of situation.

So the mere identification of anonymous others as belonging to the same or a different group can result in intergroup discrimination – what is known as the **minimal intergroup discrimination effect**. Two kinds of explanation for this effect need to be considered. The first of these focuses on the **categorization process**. Tajfel (1969) proposed that the imposition of categories or classes upon an objectively continuous stimulus dimension results in the perceptual accentuation of within-class similarities and between-class differences. Thus if you take eight lines which differ in length by a constant ratio and present them one by one to subjects who have to judge the length of each line, you can test (as did Tajfel and Wilkes, 1963) the consequences of imposing a classification on these lines by drawing a large letter 'A' above each of the four shorter lines, and a large letter 'B' above each of the four longer lines. Subjects who make their judgements under these conditions were found to accentuate length differences between class A and class B, and to accentuate length similarities within class A and class B, by comparison with subjects who made their judgements under control conditions. Doise (1978) argued that the operation of this process in a social context causes intergroup discrimination: the imposition of social categories upon individuals leads those individuals to perceive themselves and others in terms of group memberships, and therefore to see themselves as similar to ingroup members and different from outgroup members. This perceptual differentiation leads to differentiation in attitudes and behaviour towards ingroup and outgroup.

The second type of explanation for the minimal intergroup discrimination effect centres on social identity and social comparison. Tajfel and Turner (1979) proposed that mere social categorization motivates individuals to compare themselves with others for the purposes of self-evaluation. They assume (a) that individuals desire positive self-evaluation; (b) that in a social context the evaluation of one's own group contributes to self-evaluation; and (c) that evaluation of one's ingroup is made by comparing it with a relevant outgroup. These assumptions lead them to conclude that individuals are motivated to establish positively valued differences between ingroup and outgroup. Intergroup discrimination is therefore treated as a means by which individuals enhance their self-evaluations, which are in turn boosted by perceiving the ingroup as different from and superior to the outgroup.

There is evidence to support both of these explanations of the discriminatory consequences of social categorization. As Turner (1981, p. 82) suggests,

> The simplest solution is to assume that the categorization and social comparison processes are complementary . . . . The categorization process produces the perceptual accentuation of intragroup similarities and intergroup differences and thus makes salient or perceptually prominent the criterial or relevant aspects of ingroup-outgroup membership. . . . The social comparison process . . . motivates the competitive enhancement of criterial differences between the groups . . . to achieve positive distinctiveness.

In the minimal intergroup experiments conducted by Tajfel and his colleagues these 'criterial differences' were, of necessity, monetary rewards, since this was the only dimension on which ingroup and outgroup could be differentiated. In everyday life, however, there is a rich and varied set of dimensions along which such differentiation can be achieved. Examined from the perspective of a minority or 'inferior' social group, the social identity of such groups can be enhanced by, for example, positively reevaluating *existing* group characteristics. The positive reevaluation of blackness ('Black is beautiful') and the reassertion of positive status for minority languages (e.g., French in Canada) are instances of this approach to the achievement of positive distinctiveness. Another approach is to create *new* attributes which establish such distinctiveness. The 'rebirth' of a minority language such as Welsh is an example of this. If 'inferior' groups are thus motivated to seek out positively valued distinctiveness from other social groups, what hope is there of diminishing intergroup conflict?

Having acknowledged that there are no easy solutions to this urgent issue, Tajfel (1981, p. 343) suggests:

It may be useful to see in each intergroup situation whether and how it might be possible for each group to achieve, preserve or defend its vital interests, or the interests which are perceived as vital, in such a way that the self-respect of other groups is not adversely affected at the same time. We must hope that the increasing complexity and interweaving of conflicts between groups will lead to a progressive rejection of simple 'all-or-none' solutions, of the crude divisions of mankind into 'us' and 'them'. To achieve this we need less hindsight and more planning. There is no doubt that the planning must involve two crucial areas of human endeavour: education and social change which must be achieved through genuinely effective legislative, political, social and economic programmes.

Further reading

The origins and development of interpersonal relations

The following book provides an excellent introduction to the origins of interpersonal relations:

STERN, D. (1977) *The First Relationship*. London: Fontana Paperbacks.

(Other pertinent references are given in the Further reading to Chapter 10 above.)

Good, short introductions to the development of interpersonal relations are:

DUNN, I. (1977) *Distress and Comfort*. London: Fontana Paperbacks.
SCHAFFER, H.R. (1977) *Mothering*. London: Fontana Paperbacks.

And a variety of perspectives and issues are presented in:

SCHAFFER, H.R., ed. (1977) *Studies in Mother-Infant Interaction*. London: Academic Press.

The serious student should consult the three-volume landmark work by Bowlby which is informed by a lifetime of clinical experience as well as theoretical insights:

BOWLBY, J. (1969, 1973, 1980) *Attachment and Loss*. Harmondsworth: Penguin.

A good source book on play is:

BRUNER, J.S., JOLLY, A. and SYLVA, S. (1976) *Play*. Harmondsworth: Penguin.

Those interested in contemporary issues in this area are referred to:

SMITH, P.K. (1982) Does play matter? Functional and evolutionary aspects of animal and human play. *Behavioral and Brain Sciences*, 5, 139–84.

A good, short introduction to friendship is:

RUBIN, Z. (1980) *Children's Friendships*. London: Fontana Paperbacks.

The field more generally is reviewed in:

FOOT, H., CHAPMAN, A.J. and SMITH, J.R., eds. (1980) *Friendship and Social Relations in Children*. Chichester: Wiley.

Sibling relationships, birth order and the family are all included in the following well-researched and sensitive study:

DUNN, J. and KENDRICK, C. (1982) *Siblings*. London: Grant McIntyre.

The controversial area of childrearing styles is addressed in the volumes arising from the Newsons' longitudinal study, e.g.:

NEWSON, J. and NEWSON, E. (1976) *Seven Years Old in the Home Environment*. London: Allen and Unwin.

And see:

RAPOPORT, R.N., FOGARTY, M.P. and RAPOPORT, R. (1982) *Families in Britain*. London: Routledge and Kegan Paul.

The best source book on moral development is:

LICKONA, T., ed. (1976) *Moral Development and Behavior: Theory, Research and Social Issues*. New York: Holt, Rinehart and Winston.

The next book should also be read:

TURIEL, E. (1983) *The Development of Social Knowledge: Morality and Convention*. Cambridge: Cambridge University Press.

Intragroup processes

The following is an excellent introductory text on group processes (Chapters 1, 3, 5, 7, 9, 12 and 13 are relevant to the issues discussed in this chapter, but the rest of the book is well worth consulting):

FORSYTH, D.R. (1983) *An Introduction to Group Dynamics*. Monterey, Calif.: Brooks/Cole.

An interesting compendium of chapters dealing with research on social influence in group settings is the following (the chapters on social facilitation by Geen and Zajonc, and the chapter by Levine on reactions to opinion deviancy in small groups are recommended):

PAULUS, P.B., ed. (1980) *Psychology of Group Influence*. Hillsdale, NJ: Erlbaum.

The following is a concise account of some of Asch's classic studies of conformity in social groups:

ASCH, S.E. (1955) Opinions and social pressure. *Scientific American*, **193** (5), 31–5.

Next is a very lucid account of Milgram's notorious obedience experiments, together with his rather speculative explanation for his findings:

MILGRAM, S. (1974) *Obedience to Authority*. London: Tavistock.

Research on minority influence is clearly discussed in the following chapter:

MOSCOVICI, S. and NEMETH, C. (1974) Social influence II: minority influence. In C. Nemeth, ed., *Social Psychology: Classic and Contemporary Integrations*. Chicago: Rand McNally.

The topic of minority influence is dealt with at greater length and rather more provocatively in:

MOSCOVICI, S. (1976). *Social Influence and Social Change*. London: Academic Press.

The following chapter is a very readable overview of theory and research on group polarization:

MYERS, D.G. (1982) Polarizing effects of social interaction. In H. Brandstätter, J. Davis and G. Stocker-Kreichgauer, eds., *Group Decision Processes*. London: Academic Press.

Fascinating applications of the groupthink concept to US foreign policy decisions can be found in the following book, of which the second edition includes a groupthink analysis of the Watergate episode:

JANIS, I.L. (1982) *Victims of Groupthink*. Second edition. Boston: Houghton-Mifflin.

Intergroup relations

Research on intergroup discrimination and other aspects of intergroup relations is reviewed in the following book (Chapters 1, 2, 3 and 7 are especially relevant to the issues discussed here):

TURNER, J.C. and GILES, H. (1981) *Intergroup Behaviour*. Oxford: Basil Blackwell.

The following edited volume reviews work on the *contact hypothesis*, the idea that intergroup hostility and prejudice can be reduced by increasing the frequency and intensity of contact between social groups that are normally socially segregated:

MILLER, N. and BREWER, M.B. (1984). *Groups in Contact: the Psychology of Desegregation*. New York: Academic Press.

13. Personality

Figures

Table

13. Personality

Introduction

'Of all areas of psychology, the study of personality is the most important.' This bold statement made by Fontana (1982) would be disputed by many psychologists but there are good grounds for making it. It is through the study of personality that we understand one another and also ourselves. In our relationships with others it is the personality that largely governs how we react towards people, how we choose our friends, the activities we engage in, the conclusions we reach about people. But we also spend much of our time contemplating ourselves. In making assessments about our personal goals and about people with whom we might have successful relationships, we need to know the kind of person we are, which means, essentially, what sort of personality we have.

But there are problems with this viewpoint and they arise whenever attempts are made to define complex notions like personality. The above approach is in danger of defining personality as such a broad, all-embracing phenomenon, equivalent to the person him- or herself, that it is tantamount to saying that personality is identical to psychology – the study of all human behaviour and mental life. In this view personality is not an aspect of psychology – it *is* psychology. This position is reflected in the manner in which theory has developed in this field. Many of the grand theories in psychology are by figures we generally see as making contributions to the study of personality such as Freud, Jung, Erikson, Rogers, Murray, Kelly, Cattell and Allport. Indeed, Murray talked of 'personology' as though it were a science in itself.

A quite different approach to personality is to see it, in common with behaviour such as memory and language, as a property of people that can be measured in order to find out how much of it we possess. This is an approach, as we have seen, that some take towards complex human capacities such as intelligence and attitudes. More usually the claim is that we can measure how individuals compare with one another on a scale that purports to measure personality but, in fact, tends to pick out one or two aspects of personality, such as whether we are outgoing or reserved, and ignores many others. This is a **peripheral** view of personality, often called the **trait** approach, and we shall consider its influence, which has been considerable, in this chapter.

A third way of regarding personality is to say that it uniquely identifies the person and that it may be possible to obtain a personality profile for each individual that does some justice to the complexity of the whole person. This perspective sees personality as the essence of the person – that which makes someone uniquely identifiable from others. At the same time, in practice, we should expect a great deal of overlap in profiles of a large sample of individuals, thus giving us insight into *types* of personality.

THEORY CONSTRUCTION

In this book we have looked at the processes that constitute the parts of active human beings. It is fitting, therefore, that we conclude with a chapter that sees the person as an overall whole. It would be somehow logical if that viewpoint literally comprised the sum total of the processes we have examined in some composite and integrated whole. Would that it were possible! The reasons why it is beyond the scope of this book (or of any work of which we are aware) are many, including the problems of equating empirical evidence from techniques and from sources not obviously compatible. Our attempts at integration within the various chapters represent the summit of our achievements and we are aware that this is far from perfect.

But, even if it were possible to produce a composite person from the various accounts of constituent processes, it is unlikely that the outcome would be much like anyone with whom we would be prepared to sit down and dine. The reason for this is partly captured in the dictum that the whole is greater than the sum of the parts. A person is somehow more than the sum total of his or her memory, emotions, attitudes and thoughts although clearly, if we knew all these we would know a great deal about someone. It is the way in which the parts go together and are organized and affected by societal factors that has something to do with the ineffable nature of personality. But there is also the role of what **depth theorists** call the unconscious in our make-up. While this concept is anything but uncontroversial, any consideration of personality cannot fail to note the contribution of figures like Sigmund Freud. We shall therefore start this chapter with a brief discussion of how personality theorists differ in their approach to the subject, before going on to describe some of the more important insights offered. If the emphasis tends towards the holistic and phenomenological end of the spectrum, this is justified as a counterweight to the empirical approach which predominates elsewhere in the book. Such an approach also represents the most substantial addition to what we have learned already in this book about people.

Many of the most notable contributors to personality theory do not have an orthodox psychology background. A major input has come from **clinicians** of various schools. Theory is not always based on empirical tests of hypotheses, but constructed from clinical experience and rational thought. Nor is **intuitive knowledge** disparaged in the study of personality, since what we believe and feel about other people is an important guide to our estimation of their personality. In a recent book on personality, Hampson (1982) devotes two out of ten chapters to what she calls the **lay perspective**. At the same time, in formal theory construction, intuitive knowledge should be only a first approximation, to be replaced by empirically based assertions when they become available. The problem in personality, as in other complex behaviours, is that empirical evidence falls a long way short of the models provided by rational analysis and the intuitions of sensitive therapists.

Theoretical approaches

PSYCHOANALYTIC THEORY

Sigmund Freud is the founder and principal exponent of psychoanalytic theory and one of the most significant figures in twentieth-century thought. It is obviously impossible to provide more than the bare bones of his theory, let alone consider the contributions of other major figures in the psychoanalytic tradition such as Jung, Adler and Erikson. We will try to compensate for any distortion that may result by giving a considered guide to further reading in the field at the end of the chapter.

Freud's is a **tripartite theory** consisting of two great and competing forces and a third, mediating component which attempts to keep the peace between the warring factions. The first force is made up of instinctive drives such as hunger, thirst and the sexual urge. Named the **id**, this is conceived as both a life-preserving force and pursuer of pleasure. It is in a constant state of tension and seeks perpetually to reduce this tension by having its needs satisfied. The pleasure principle was the aspect of the id that most interested Freud since he felt it was sexual energy (**libido**) that gave rise to most conflict with the other great force, which is **society**.

The individual and society have different aims. The former is self-centred and avaricious, demanding immediate satisfaction. Society stands for the corporate good and as such punishes those who transgress its rules. Freud saw society as the source of punishment and guilt which all individuals suffer. Because society is more powerful than the individual, the selfish impulses of the id must be controlled. The agents of society with which a growing individual is most in contact are parents, who are said to play a special role in inhibiting the id's excesses. They create within us what Freud called a **superego** which replaces the threat or need of actual punishment by guilt at the consequences of antisocial behaviour. No very satisfactory account of the development of the superego has been provided but it is thought to depend on a process of **identification** with parents and an eventual internalization of the standards which they uphold.

Between the id, our hedonistic impulses, and the superego, our learned morality and inhibitions, lies a third factor, the **ego**. This is the mediating force which tries to maintain some sort of balance between the internal driving force and the external controlling force. Freud saw it as representing the **reality principle**, and successful living involves keeping this well in view. Indeed, the Freudian view of life is the constant attempt to maximize instinctual gratification while minimizing punishment and guilt. The only way this can be achieved is through the **defence mechanisms** which, ideally, stay within bounds of the reality principle.

Defence mechanisms. Defences are ways of keeping unwelcome thoughts and actions hidden from others and ourselves while at the same time trying to give them some outlet. If they have no outlet the build-up of energy in the system, or tension, becomes unbearable, leading to a release of undiluted id. Examples of defence mechanisms include projection, denial, reaction formation, regression and rationalization. **Projection** is the attribution of unacceptable impulses in oneself on to others. Thus, criticizing someone else for promiscuous behaviour may result from repressing similar urges in oneself. **Denial** is the ego warding off reality by altering perception and, in some cases, appearance. This could, unkindly, be called the Hemingway syndrome in which one is unwilling to give way gracefully to declining sexual and physical powers, and through one's appearance and activities prolong a youthful image. **Reaction formation** is where the feelings in the conscious are the opposite of those in the unconscious. Love becomes hate, and prudery and moralizing are the reaction formations to sexuality. **Regression** is another way of dealing with anxiety whereby the individual resorts to earlier modes of behaviour to avoid conflict. Sometimes both partners in a relationship will regress, as in Osborne's *Look Back in Anger* or Albee's *Who's Afraid of Virginia Woolf?* As in all defences, the responses are basically inappropriate to solve the problems encountered but they are the best the ego can do in the circumstances. **Rationalization** is the well-known defence in which the person fails to recognize the real, instinctual significance of his or her thoughts and actions and substitutes a fictitious reason which puts the self in a better light.

Freud's account of the role played by *unconscious* motives and drives in human behaviour is possibly his major contribution in psychology. Defences function to maintain a conspiracy of silence about these unconscious motives. Not merely are we unaware of what is being repressed but we are also unaware of the mechanisms we use to ensure the repression. The reason for this is that if we were able to get behind our defences they would not be effective in insulating us from guilt. Defences are therefore a way of lying to oneself as well as to others.

What, then, is the role of psychoanalysis? Is it not to irradicate these irrational defences and replace them with a healthy realism and a true understanding of what motivates one's behaviour? This, emphatically, was not Freud's view. Defences are considered a necessary and inevitable part of living. Should they break down, they must be reinstated. At the same time defences vary in the extent to which they distort reality. The aim is to keep as close to reality as possible while always seeking to gratify the instincts. This is the meaning of Freud's phrase, 'Where id was, there ego shall be'. The goal of psychoanalysis, therefore, is to replace defences which heavily distort truth, such as projection, with those which give less distortion. **Sublimation** is an example of a successful defence mechanism. Sexual possession can be sublimated in friendship, intellectual curiosity and creativity. Sublimation for the anal character (see below) is said to reveal itself in activities such as painting and pottery.

Methodology. We shall return to the issue of defences, and we shall look at the developmental aspects of Freud's theory in the next section, but before leaving the subject we must remedy an omission. This concerns the data base on which Freud constructed his theory. In order to appreciate this we must refer again to the role the unconscious plays in his theory. The psychoanalyst's task is to elicit the unconscious but because of the effective censoring job done by repression, underlying motives are extremely difficult to uncover. The methods which Freud found most effective were **free association** and **dream analysis**, often used in conjunction. In free association the subject says whatever comes into his or her head in response to a word or dream event presented by the analyst. The patient's cooperation in this enterprise is essential since honesty and candour are prerequisites.

Dream interpretation, Freud's 'royal road to the unconscious', cannot be explained in a couple of sentences. You will need to consult *The Interpretation of Dreams*, which Freud regarded as his most significant book. The justification for using dreams as material is that, for Freud, they represented **wish fulfilments**. Furthermore, the censoring mechanisms of the mind are more relaxed in sleep and so dreams are the best way of uncovering our unconscious desires. Even so, repression is by no means absent and accordingly dreams are often in disguised and symbolic forms. A related phenomenon is also said to occur in waking life. In *The Psychopathology of Everyday Life* Freud calls attention to parapraxes, erroneous actions, slips of the tongue and forgetful behaviour which reflect underlying intent.

These, then, are the data on which classical psychoanalysts build their interpretations of personality and, ultimately, a theory. The key word here, of course, is *interpretation*. Since psychoanalysis is a quest for meaning, its significance ultimately is for the individual. If the theory makes sense of events in your life which were hitherto a mystery then the interpretation may be said to be valid. But as a theory in the formal scientific sense it is more problematic (see below).

TRAIT THEORY

Underlying the trait approach is the assumption that individuals can be characterized on the basis of a limited number of attributes which manifest themselves whatever the place or the time. The goal of the personality theorist is to locate and measure these attributes or traits. This approach asserts that personality structure is something we all have in common, lying along dimensions like **extraversion/introversion** or **field dependence/independence**, but also gives room for individual differences which are represented by the particular combination of trait scores an individual obtains.

We shall illustrate this approach with the theory of one of its most notable proponents, H.J. Eysenck, who uses the technique of factor analysis to establish relevant traits. This first requires the assembly of a personality questionnaire or test which is done in much the same way as the intelligence tests described in Chapter 9. The basic idea of factor analysis is to discover which test items correlate highly with one another while correlating little, or not at all, with others. The resulting item clusters are then examined to see what they have in common. In Eysenck's case two underlying factors (later three) are said to account for the clustering profile obtained: introversion-extraversion (borrowed from Jung) and neuroticism-stability. Figure 13.1 shows how these orthogonal dimensions relate to a variety of traits as well as to the classic Greek

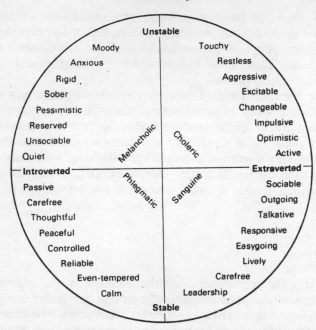

Figure 13.1 Eysenck's two-dimensional classification of personality. (From Eysenck and Rachman, 1965)

humours: phlegmatic, melancholic, choleric and sanguine.

An individual who gave affirmative answers to questions like 'Do you often feel "just miserable" for no good reason at all?' and 'Do you often feel disgruntled?' would score at the neuroticism end of that dimension. Those who give positive answers to questions such as 'Do you like to have many social engagements?' would tend towards the extraversion end of that dimension. The typical profiles that these types present are familiar. The **extravert** is sociable, impulsive and enjoys new experiences while the **introvert** is quiet, serious and prefers solitary activities. The **neurotic** is contrasted with his opposite number on this dimension by having sleep problems, tension and interpersonal difficulties. An important tenet of the theory is that the two major dimensions are independent. This means that similarities between two types classed as neurotic and introvert – e.g., unsociable and withdrawn – are said to have different roots. Healthy introverts *choose* to be alone – they are not afraid of social contact – while neurotics are shy through fear of other people.

Biological Basis. Eysenck has attempted to provide some physiological basis to personality. In the case of introversion/extraversion the related physiological substrate is thought to be the **reticular activating system** which determines arousal level (see Chapter 2). Extraverts are characterized by a low arousal level which is why they seek out stimulation. Conversely, introverts are already over-aroused and therefore avoid additional stimulation. The other dimension, neuroticism, is linked with the autonomic nervous system since it is known that anxiety is associated with ANS activity.

If these links exist they ought to have implications for psychological performance. We would expect introverts, with their higher arousal level, to do better at vigilance tasks, and this is indeed the case (Harkins and Green, 1975). Similarly, we might expect extraverts to cope better with physical extremes such as pain and to welcome risky enterprises, and there is evidence to support this prediction. The relation between Eysenck's dimensions and learning has been a particularly fruitful area of research and we shall take up this issue in a later section.

Trait theory of the factor analytic type would seem, by its objective approach, to score heavily over psychoanalytic theory. However, we should not overlook the shortcomings of multitrait theories. For a supposedly objective technique it contains a large element of subjective judgement in how many factors to rotate, the method of rotation and the inspection of high-loading items where bias may be difficult to exclude. A much more serious criticism of trait theory is that the claimed consistency in an individual's personality is illusory. Far from behaving as trait theory would predict, individuals may be dependable in some situations and irresponsible in others, aggressive in some circumstances and passive in others. This criticism, based on a review of results using the tests favoured by trait theorists, is, essentially, the heredity-environment debate in another form and is taken up in Box 13.1.

BOX 13.1
Personality: who you are or where you are?

The fundamental tenet underlying personality theories as diverse as those of Freud and Eysenck – that personality is a stable, enduring phenomenon – has been seriously questioned. After reviewing the evidence, Mischel (1968) came to the conclusion that rather than consistency, people's behaviour was marked by diversity depending on the situation in which they found themselves.

Mischel's special target for attack was trait theory. Much of his argument hinges on the series of studies carried out by Hartshorne and May (1928) who studied children's honesty in a variety of settings: home, school; alone, with peers; classroom tests, athletic events. The most startling finding was the lack of consistency in the children's behaviour such that honesty in one situation, say the classroom, was not correlated with honesty in, say, the home. This led Hartshorne and May to conclude that honesty is a function of situation and not an invariant personality trait.

The strength of **situationism**, as Mischel's position came to be called, is that it confirms everyday observation as well as experimental evidence. People, whoever they are, behave differently according to whether they are in court, at a party or at a funeral. Furthermore, the situation – for example, being a member of a jury in court – will give more clues as to how the person is likely to behave than traits derived from a personality test. The social learning theory of personality which Mischel offers does not ignore individual differences. It recognizes that factors such as age, sex, occupation and economic circumstances, as well as differences in ability, are important determinants of behaviour. But, it claims, their influence is felt in the situations which individuals encounter. And it is situations which determine real behaviour.

Nevertheless, while we acknowledge that situations can profoundly affect the way that we behave, there is an important sense in which we are identifiably the same person no matter what the situation. The noisy extravert may be more subdued in church than at a party but close observation will reveal differences in behaviour between the extravert and the introvert in the same situations. It is easy to overstate the situationist case. The aura of a courtroom may affect how participants such as witnesses and jurors behave but it does not follow that the individual's personality is neither influencing his or her behaviour as a witness nor how the interaction with counsel or magistrate might be conducted. Furthermore, the pantomime that takes place in court may be as nothing to the discussion which ensues in the jury room where individual personalities are likely to be much more influential.

More formally, Bowers (1973) has pointed out that the experimental method favoured by social learning theories is specifically designed to investigate behavioural change (dependent variable) as a function of situation (independent variable) rather than to examine behavioural stability. If a scientific method does not allow a proposition – for example, that behaviour is situation dependent – to be falsified, then by Popper's (1959) criterion the method is no longer scientific. Bowers goes on to argue that seeing behaviour as either situation or trait is simplistic since most behaviour is a consequence of an interaction between the two. Though this is scarcely an earth-shattering conclusion – both Levin and Piaget were advocating such a position in the 1930s and Hebb and Anastasi restated the case in the 1950s – the notion has been seized upon (e.g., Pervin and Lewis, 1978). It seems that psychologists have continually to learn the lesson that no behaviour is possible except through an interaction between a person and an environment. Thus general traits such as anxiety are of limited value since a person may be very anxious in social situations but quite unafraid in the face of physical danger. If we are prepared to qualify traits in this way, using a person by situation interaction, some measure of stability in personality can be maintained. The problem which arises, however, is at what point do we stop qualifying the trait? The more accurately predictive we wish to be about a particular individual, or even a small subgroup of individuals, the more hedged around with qualifications our taxonomy will become (see Cronbach, 1975, for further discussion of this issue).

To conclude on a more positive note, it is fair to say that our understanding of personality has advanced by taking account of the situationist critique – people are not static, they change according to where and with whom they find themselves. But Mischel overstated his case and eventually was obliged to account for individual differences. He did this by turning his model into a **cognitive social learning theory** (Mischel, 1973) which maintains that individuals approach situations in characteristic cognitive styles as a result of past learning experiences. These determine the meaning that will be given to situations. Whether one subscribes to Mischel's position or to the more traditional trait account, the lesson that has been learned is that there is a reciprocal effect between people and situations (which include other people) which any worthwhile theory of personality must incorporate.

FULFILMENT THEORY

There is a group of theories which takes a **phenomenological approach** to personality and sees healthy growth as the expression of a great force within each individual. Unlike Freud's id, this great force (if left unchecked) is not destructive but **self-fulfilling**. Rather than aiming at conformity to avoid conflict with society, as in Freud's theory, these theories do not advocate such a compromise. The aim is to transcend society so that an existence based on imaginative, spontaneous, self-reliant individuality is achieved during which opportunities to discover new things about oneself are welcomed.

The notion and role of *self* assumes considerable significance in such theories and we shall take as our exemplar the **client-centred approach** of Carl Rogers, who can be regarded as the founder of this school and a considerable influence on the broader horizon of psychology.

Rogers is often credited with putting a human face on psychology, not only because of his particular theory, but also because of his philosophy of science. In a celebrated debate with the behaviourist B.F. Skinner, Rogers spelled out his creed (see Miller and Buckhout, 1973). Although he recognizes objectivity as the prerequisite of science, he believes that the emphasis on laboratory instrumentation can deflect the psychologist from the need 'to observe acutely, to think carefully and creatively' (Rogers, 1959, p. 189). In personality research, phenomenological subjective experience is at the centre of Rogers's approach, captured in this definition of the theory's goal in this area: 'the persistent, disciplined effort to make sense and order out of the phenomena of subjective experience' (ibid, p. 188).

Rogers's theory has three components – the **organism**, the **phenomenal field** and the **self**. The organism has both biological and Gestalt aspects. As an organized, integrated whole, the organism is best fitted both for enhancement and survival.

The phenomenological approach in psychology maintains that behaviour is influenced not only by present and past experiences but by the personal meanings which each individual attaches to those experiences. The concern is thus with a person's perception of reality, not with reality itself. The significance of this for Rogers is that the person's own internal frame of reference is the best vantage point for understanding his or her behaviour. The phenomenal field, therefore, is the sum total of an individual's experience, some of which will be unconscious.

The concept of self is by no means limited to fulfilment models of personality, as we shall see when we discuss cognitive approaches. For Rogers, self is defined as 'the organized, consistent conceptual Gestalt composed of characteristics of the "I" or "me" and the perceptions of the relationships of the "I" or "me" to others and to various aspects of life, together with the value attached to these perceptions' (ibid, p. 200). The self is 'created' by the child's own experiences and also by the reactions of others towards the self, the obvious influences being parents and other significant figures in the child's world. In the process of personality growth, the self is important not simply as a passive frame of reference but also as an active controlling and integrative force. The importance of this idea for Rogers can be appreciated by the fact that of the nineteen propositions that constitute the formal statement of his theory (Rogers, 1951), no fewer than twelve of them concern the self. Self has the motivating force reminiscent of Piaget's notion of 'equilibration' and, like that construct, is considered to be intrinsic to the organism and always seeking consistency (see Chapter 9). Experiences which are not congruent with the self may be blocked or distorted and this can give rise to maladjustment. The individual should always be attempting to integrate this new information to produce a more rounded or fulfilled personality (again akin to Piaget's characterization of how cognitive structures change).

Precise evaluation of Rogers's theory is not possible. Its popularity has as much to do with clinical application as with empirical evidence. The client-centred approach to therapy is intended to create a climate in which the client (the preferred name for patient) gains greater self-awareness, ultimately leading to a more realistic assessment of oneself and one's relationships. Practitioners of this approach have no 'bag of tricks' such as might be employed by a psychoanalyst or even a trait theorist, and it is imprudent to pass judgement on the method without taking steps to examine and perhaps try out the procedures involved (see Burns, 1979). Empirical research has been of the type that measures the effect of therapy on personal stability. The measures have been of performance using the Q technique (Stevenson, 1953), a test which requires the subject to indicate the degree to which each of a set of statements is characteristic of him or herself. Findings reveal a greater discrepancy between actual and ideal selves among a 'clinical' population compared with controls and a significant reduction of this difference following client-centred therapy.

But perhaps the more interesting conclusion to be drawn about fulfilment theory concerns its comparison with other depth approaches to personality, such as that of Freud. Rogers does not share Freud's view that defences are a necessary part of successful living. The idea of transcending rather than conforming to society, of being yourself, of self-actualizing (Maslow, 1970) is appealing to many and underlies many fringe humanist movements especially in the United States. This is not to lay at Rogers's door the excesses of

BOX 13.2
Fulfilment as self-actualization: Maslow's humanistic perspective

The self-fulfilment model of personality achieves its most optimistic expression in the theory of Maslow, who sees the person as made up of two complementary sets of forces. One ensures the individual's *survival* by satisfying basic physical needs such as hunger, and the other, known as **self-actualization**, is the push towards realizing one's potentialities, notably in the intellectual and creative sphere. Although these sets of needs are considered to be equally important, the survival functions are regarded as prior to the other needs if only because the pursuit of the higher planes of happiness is possible only if physiological needs are satisfied.

Figure 13.2 illustrates the nature of the **need system** described by Maslow, which can be considered hierarchical on a number of 'dimensions'. Higher needs are regarded as: (1) a later evolutionary development – we share the need for food with, for example, slugs, but not the need for self-esteem; (2) ontogenetically later – the child is dominated by the need for physical satisfaction and security, it is only later in life that an interest in autonomous and self-fulfilling activities emerges; (3) less imperative for survival; (4) dependent on experience rather than inborn.

After the basic needs of physical survival and safety, Maslow places the need for belongingness and love, the need for intimate relationships which may be satisfied by family or friends. The next highest group of needs are covered by the term 'esteem'. This is a need for self-respect as well as the esteem of others. There are echoes here of Rogers's *self* and Erikson's *ego*. At the summit of the hierarchy is the need for self-actualization. This is the most celebrated aspect of Maslow's scheme. He defines it as 'man's desire for self-fulfilment, namely, to the tendency for him to become actualized in what he is potentially . . . to

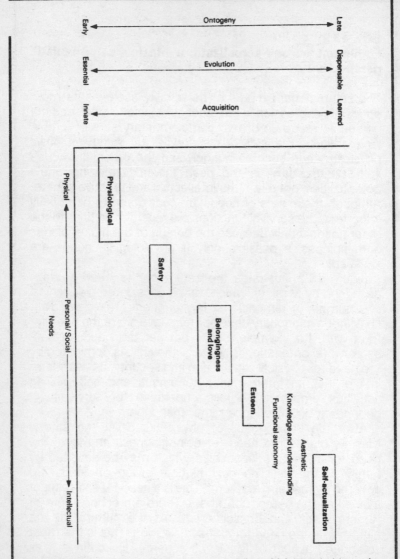

Figure 13.2 A diagrammatic representation of Maslow's hierarchy of needs.

become more and more what one idiosyncratically is, to become everything that one is capable of becoming' (Maslow, 1970, p. 46).

Because much of the popular interest in the theory has been directed at those whom Maslow picked out as self-actualizers, e.g. Albert Einstein, William James and Aldous Huxley, it is sometimes overlooked that Maslow did not see self-actualization as the preserve of the famous. He recognized that at this final level the role of individual differences would be at their greatest. Thus, self-actualization might be achieved through parenthood, athletic feats, art or science. The common thread is that the 'clear emergence of these needs rests upon some prior satisfaction of the physiological, safety, love and esteem needs' (ibid, p. 47), an assumption challenged by Maddi (1976).

CHARACTERISTICS OF SELF–ACTUALIZERS

So that you might recognize a self-actualizer when you come across one, we list below the fifteen properties that Maslow (1970) derived from his study (much of it taken from secondhand sources) of fifty-one self-actualizers, using college students as controls.

1. More efficient perception of reality and more comfortable relations with it.
2. Acceptance (self, others, nature).
3. Spontaneity, simplicity, naturalness.
4. Problem-centred (rather than self-centred).
5. The quality of detachment, the need for privacy.
6. Autonomy, independence of culture and environment, will, active agents.
7. Continued freshness of appreciation.
8. The mystic experience.
9. *Gemeinschaftsgefuhl* (empathy, a genuine feeling for others).
10. Profound interpersonal relations.
11. The democratic character structure.
12. Discrimination between means and ends, between good and evil.

13. Philosophical, unhostile sense of humour.
14. Creativeness.
15. Resistance to enculturation (normative influences); the transcendence of any particular culture.

the wilder fringes of these movements but to set the theory and its influence in a wider cultural context.

COGNITIVE THEORIES

At first sight it may seem odd to talk of cognitive theories of personality since personality is often equated with **affect** and thus contrasted with the cognitive. When we think of personality we have in mind emotions and feelings, attitudes and aspirations, and we reflect that our everyday experiences indicate no necessary correlation between intellectual capacities and personality. People whom we might regard as very clever may be given to almost childish displays of temper or selfishness. On the other hand, there are those apparently lacking intellectual achievements who yet appear outstanding in emotional stability, integrity and ability to support and counsel others. This contrast is useful and it accurately mirrors the emphasis in most theories of personality. At the same time, as soon as we begin to take account of others and their views of us and engage in the process of **self-understanding**, we are using our cognitive faculties. This is recognized in the currently expanding field of social cognition (see Chapter 11) and is also true of some specific approaches to personality.

By far the most important of these is that of George Kelly, the originator of **personal construct theory**. The earlier theories we have considered have focused on the specific content of personality (e.g., traits) and inherent forces such as the id. In personal construct theory the emphasis is on compatibility between various aspects of personality or elements of content. These elements, uniquely held by each individual, are the cognitive constructs about the world and about the self. These constructs form a complex network which we use in making decisions about behaviour. In its emphasis on self-determination the theory has affinity with Rogers's system, but the approach is more avowedly cognitive, regarding human beings as problem-solvers who use rational principles to predict and categorize behavioural events whether perpetrated by others or themselves. The objective of this problem-solving approach is to eliminate inconsistency which gives rise to an uncomfortable state of tension and anxiety. This is achieved not by erecting defences but by being prepared to modify the network if existing constructs fail to predict accurately the occurrences observed.

The repertory test. A clearer idea of the basis of Kelly's theory can be gained by considering the data-gathering procedure. The role construct repertory test (REP test) rests on Kelly's contention that constructs are created through the process of categorizing certain events as similar and then contrasting them with other events which are considered different. Allied to this is the idea that constructs are dichotomous in nature, for example weak-strong and kind-cruel. It should be said that this simple notion is abstracted from a complex account in Kelly (1955) involving eleven corollaries. In practice, it means that the subject or client initially provides names of people who are influential or important to her or him. Examples would be parents, spouses, friends, teachers and employers. The names are elicited through a series of questions and then permutated into various groups of three. The client is then asked to say how two of the three people are alike while at the same time being different from the third. This process produces a construct with two poles, the likeness providing one pole, say hardworking, and the opposite, lazy, making up the other pole of the construct. Using this procedure, a description of an individual's personal constructs, including the number, range and manner in which significant individuals enter the system, is obtained. When used in the popular grid version of the test, it is possible to subject the results to factor, or cluster, analysis (see Bannister and Mair, 1968).

The expanding influence of cognitive psychology has encouraged interest in George Kelly, but his emphasis on the phenomenological and subjective is not to everyone's taste. Like Rogers, Kelly and his followers draw attention to the way in which psychological research is conducted. In their view it is impossible to ignore the subject's thoughts and feelings while participating in psychological experiments If the conception of the person is one of a thinking, creative being capable of predicting the future and changing constructions on the basis of events then this has far-reaching implications for research methodology (see Fransella, 1980).

Kelly's theory predates the cognitive revolution in psychology (see Chapter 1), and theorists have only recently begun to make use of the ideas thrown up by work on memory and thinking. Rosch's notion of **prototypicality** (see Chapter 9) has been taken up by Cantor and Mischel (1979) who believe that the concept can be applied to people as well as objects. The notion comes close to the stereotype, such as we might hold for a professor or a soldier, and allows economy in information-processing connected with people. Research indicates that such prototypes do have biasing effects on memory and 'influence the ease with which informations about . . . [a] character can be encoded, retrieved and elaborated' (Cantor and Mischel, 1979, p. 204).

Origins and growth of personality

When considering the origins of personality, the most productive approach has been in terms of **temperament**. This is partly because parents report marked differences in their children's temperament from the earliest days, and partly because there has been a major empirical study of temperament. The American paediatricians Alexander Thomas and Stella Chess (1977) have conducted a longitudinal study of 136 infants from twelve weeks through to adolescence, focusing specifically on temperament. Using interview and observational data, detailed profiles were obtained and nine components of temperament isolated. These included such features as activity levels, degree of distractability, attention span, rhythm of bodily function and quality of mood (e.g., cheerful/irritable).

Three general types of temperament accounted for 65 per cent of the sample. The majority (40 per cent) they called **easy children** who were characterized by a friendly disposition, regularity of bodily functions and a positive approach to new situations. In infancy these children quickly established regular feeding and sleeping schedules and subsequently adapted to new routines and foods and, in later childhood, to school without fuss.

A much smaller number of children (10 per cent) were labelled **difficult**. They were irregular in bodily functions, intense in their reactions and tended to withdraw in the face of new situations. Any frustration might produce tantrums and in general they required considerable tolerance on the part of their parents.

The third type of temperament was shown by a group called **slow-to-warm-up**. They had a low activity level, somewhat negative mood and were reluctant to take on new experiences but, given time, would adapt. They comprised 15 per cent of the sample.

Membership of these three groups has been found to remain remarkably constant. The study found the children followed virtually the same pattern at twelve years as they had at twelve weeks. For instance, 70 per cent of the 'difficult' group had developed behaviour problems by adolescence compared with only 18 per cent of the 'easy' children. The implication that temperament is a stable and innate commodity is given further support by the finding that no significant differences emerged in the rearing styles or environments of the three groups. We also know that identical twins are much more similar in temperament than are fraternal twins. Another line of evidence is found in cross-cultural studies. Freedman (1979) observed striking differences in temperament between Caucasian and Chinese infants, the latter being far more adaptable and amenable than the more fretful Caucasian children. Since relevant environmental variables were closely controlled and the study was conducted at the age of forty-eight hours, the possibility of a socialization explanation is unlikely.

This conclusion does not mean that environment has no impact on temperament. Thomas and Chess found that difficult and slow-to-warm-up children were much more likely to learn to cope successfully with their temperaments given patient and consistent parenting. Confrontation methods were unlikely to succeed, leading to stubbornness rather than cooperation. Assuming sympathetic childrearing styles, the advantage which the 'easy' children continue to possess is their flexibility in the face of new situations. The important lesson that the researchers draw from this large-scale study is the need for harmony between the child's own characteristics and his or her environment. This is more likely to take place if parents, teachers and others who come into regular contact with children take steps to determine temperament and adapt the environment accordingly.

FREUD'S PSYCHOSEXUAL THEORY

Any consideration of personality growth must acknowledge Freud's contribution. His theory of psychosexual development may be unique in providing a major thesis on psychological growth without any significant study of children (*pace* Little Hans). His **stage-dependent** account, emphasizing the successive role of oral, anal and genital influences on personality growth, is known well beyond the confines of psychology. Rather than attempt an inadequate potted account, we refer the reader to sources in Further Reading and here concentrate on the implications of psychosexual theory.

Freud's claim is that the sexual urge is not restricted to life after puberty but is the key to understanding the human psyche from birth onwards. The infant's focus on parts of its own body for the purpose of sexual stimulation helps to explain not only child behaviour but also adult personality. Essentially the link is with the *regime* in which the child's interest in his or her own body was practised. Depending on parental attitudes, the personality could be arrested or significantly affected at any of the stages of psychosexual development. This has led to obsessive interest in issues such as breast versus bottle feeding (oral stage) and toilet training (anal stage). (See Kline, 1981, for a review of the empirical evidence.)

As we saw earlier in this chapter, Freud believes that we make use of defences to cope with the insistent demands of the id. **Oral fixations** arising from sudden weaning or indulgent demand-feeding are said to give rise to personality characteristics such as garrulity, dependency and optimism. The **anal stage**, with its emphasis on retention and expulsion, is responsible for traits such as parsimony, orderliness and materialism. These are defences against the desire either to retain or smear the faeces.

As well as the fascinating but controversial links between psychosexual stages and adult personality, Freud charted the route by which the mature personality emerges. After the oral and anal stages comes the **phallic stage** in which, for a boy, rivalry with the father for the affections of the mother assumes major proportions. The male child at this stage (four to six years) is said to resemble Oedipus, but reality does not allow the possession of the mother nor the vanquishing of the father. The associated guilt and sexual longing is relieved by the process of **identification** in which the boy strives to become like his father. This process is responsible for the acquisition of the sex role and, inasmuch as it is generalized to the attitudes and standards of both parents, leads ultimately to the formation of the superego or internalized conscience.

EVALUATION

The psychosexual theory has received considerable criticism. It has been argued that the emphasis on sexuality arises out of the moral climate of the early part of this century. Freud found it necessary to shake people out of their highly restricted view of sexuality. In doing so he may have exaggerated the role of sexuality and directed us away from the other important concerns of contemporary life. Other psychoanalytic theorists, such as Erikson, have preferred to use terms like pleasure-seeking and self-fulfilment in preference to the sexual motive, and in so doing have gained a wider audience.

Freud himself was unhappy with the **Oedipal complex** as an explanation for the development of sex roles and the superego in females. Accordingly, the notion of the **Electra complex**, incorporating penis envy, was offered as an alternative process for girls, but it has not endeared itself to many. The major problem is how to fit this theory into the rest of psychology. It does not easily lend itself to the hypothetico-deductive method, although Kline (1981) disputes this often-stated view.

In a careful review of more than a thousand studies, Kline concluded that Freud's ideas were generally subject to empirical test and that the theory did not stand or fall as a whole. Parts could be accepted while other parts must either be rejected or have judgement suspended pending further evidence. Kline's review, and also that of Fisher and Greenberg (1977), allows us to make a number of reasonably firm concluding statements.

(1) Work of trait theorists such as Cattell supports Freud's tripartite division of personality.

(2) The personality traits corresponding to oral and anal characters have been found but there is no evidence to link them with psychosexual stages.

(3) Although the existence of defence mechanisms has been powerfully supported, the stronger claim that all behaviour is defensive is in doubt. There seem to be some people who do not distort reality unduly.

(4) The idea that dreams represent wish fulfilment has not been verified, but that they are replete with significant sexual and psychological content is not in doubt.

(5) Psychoanalysis as therapy is difficult to evaluate and unequivocal evidence is awaited.

Many academic psychologists and academic courses in psychology are content to remain in ignorance of Freud, without, perhaps, realizing that his ideas permeate psychology nonetheless, for example, identification and repression. However, Freudian theory and the academic science of psychology will probably remain out of wedlock, leaving individuals to discover for themselves the insights which Freud can give into personality and personal relationships.

The mature personality

Maturity is a difficult concept with which to deal in psychology. In other parts of the animal kingdom it seems relatively straightforward – a member of a species is mature once it is fully grown and (possibly) engaged in successful reproductive behaviour. The signs of maturity are external, such as size of antlers and colour of plumage. But in human behaviour it is unwise to give the assignation 'mature' to someone solely on the basis of external appearance. A person may have stopped growing and attained the external appearance of an adult; they may have taken on extensive family and occupational responsibilities. But these features, in themselves, tell us nothing about that person's psychological maturity. It may be that there are many situations in which such an individual behaves immaturely. The problem, then, is to char-

Table 13.1 Erikson's eight stages of psychosocial development. (The 'basic virtues' were defined by Erikson as the 'lasting outcome of the favourable ratios' for each stage.)

Stage	Age period	Bipolar crisis		Basic virtue	Freudian stage
		Favourable outcome *v.* Avoided outcome			
1	Early infancy	Basic trust *v.* Mistrust		Hope	Oral
2	Later infancy	Autonomy *v.* Shame and doubt		Willpower	Anal
3	Early childhood	Initiative *v.* Guilt		Purpose	Phallic
4	Middle childhood	Industry *v.* Inferiority		Competence	Latency
5	Adolescence	Identity *v.* Role confusion		Fidelity	
6	Early adulthood	Intimacy *v.* Isolation		Love	
7	Middle adulthood	Generativity *v.* Stagnation		Care	
8	Late adulthood	Ego integrity *v.* Despair		Wisdom	

acterize psychological maturity. The major contributions in this important area have come from personality theorists, notably Erikson, Rogers and Kelly.

Erik Erikson, who was trained in Vienna – the birthplace of psychoanalysis – between the wars, established his own approach to personality once he emigrated to the United States. He expanded Freud's theory of psychosexual development into adolescence and adulthood and switched the emphasis from the sexual to the interpersonal. Erikson's eight **psychosocial stages**, summarized in Table 13.1, cover the entire life span. Erikson's view of maturity is that we must overcome a number of **crises** in order to achieve maturity.

The childhood stages correspond to those of Freud in temporal terms but the focus is more on tasks accomplished than on coping with the bodily fixations aroused by the pleasure principle. Thus **trust** is the first accomplishment, which reveals itself in the capacity to use the familiar adult as a secure basis from which to explore and later to tolerate brief absences of the parent. In the second stage Erikson recognizes the need for **autonomy**. But if the child is regularly punished for demonstrating independence of action, the feeling will tend to be one of shame and doubt rather than a sense of self-esteem and achievement.

In early childhood the child begins to build on her autonomy by showing **initiative** and planfulness in activities. The negative side of this stage is guilt engendered by the feeling that not all one's desires, such as covetousness and aggression, are acceptable. In the second half of primary school initiative is harnessed as **industry**. The emphasis shifts to productivity, and the use of skills acquired in the home and school to get things done becomes paramount. Failure at this stage leads to feelings of inadequacy which can persist unless remedied. It is also a time when social relations become more important inasmuch as getting things done frequently requires the cooperation of others.

Adolescence. Erikson's theory has become particularly prominent in accounts of adolescence, partly, no doubt, because he introduces stages which have no parallel in Freud's theory. Adolescence is seen as the period in which young people begin to seek the answer to the question, 'Who am I?' This is not to say that self-identity does not exist before adolescence (see Chapter 3) but that the various concepts of the self that have existed up until this point begin to coalesce into the kind of person one is and will become. Nor does the theory argue that personality growth is complete by adolescence; the point rather is that in adolescence the fluid personality of the child will give way to the firmer, more stable personality of adulthood. But, in achieving this consistency, the young person must use the opportunity of adolescence, when legal and social accountability are still in the process of being established, to sort out the role confusion that is present. Thus, in attempting to resolve the 'Who am I?' question, we may 'overidentify' with figures as diverse as teachers and pop stars, friends and literary characters.

This experimentation with roles is regarded as a necessary feature of the **identity crisis**, and much has been written about the importance of the peer group in allowing freedom in these matters. The cognitive changes that take place around puberty, described in Chapter 9, clearly contribute both to arousing the identity crisis and to its resolution. Reflection on hitherto unconsidered abstract issues, such as justice, truth and beauty, will lead an individual to examine values and objectives which formerly might have been taken for granted. This can lead to idealism and also bitterness at the apparent or real cynicism of the adult world. Subsequently, in arriving at decisions about life goals, powerful analytic properties of formal operational thinking can be usefully employed.

Adulthood. The latter stages of Erikson's developmental model focus on interpersonal relationships, self-fulfilment in parenthood and career, and a final sense of contentment in late adulthood. Erikson has emphasized the role of love rather than sex in the capacity to establish an intimate relationship with another. That is to say, **intimacy** and commitment are necessary before sex can become a truly fulfilling and social experience. Intimacy comes about most often through relationships with the opposite sex during which, through the other's eyes, a clearer idea of the self emerges. A failure to fuse one's identity with that of another, it is said, will lead to isolation which can prove destructive.

The notion of **generativity** is used by Erikson to express the need which mature individuals feel to establish and guide the next generation. This does not necessarily imply parenthood since one can make a contribution in other ways: in the community, in one's career. Failure to achieve this end leads to stagnation, Erikson argues.

It will be apparent by now that Erikson's theory is an attempt to see personality growth in terms of the steady expansion or integration of the whole person or ego, the emphasis being on social rather than biological factors. The successful culmination of this process is the final stage of **ego integrity**, defined by Erikson as 'the acceptance of one's one and only life cycle as something that had to be and that, by necessity, permitted of no substitutions' (Erikson, 1965). Where this feeling of acceptance and contentment is lacking and resentment about missed opportunities or misfortune holds sway, then despair and fear of death are common preoccupations. Furthermore, there is a link between ego integrity and the first psychosocial stage, since Erikson claims that trust will evolve as long as the elder generation have the integrity not to fear death.

Has this ideal picture anything to do with reality? Does anyone achieve the integrated personality described by Erikson? The first thing to say is that although Erikson's theory has been put to empirical test and acquired some support (see Further reading) it is, like all psychoanalytic theories, a difficult system to subject to rigorous test. Its greatest use has been as a source of explanatory concepts, notably in the areas of adolescence and ageing. But an inability to surmount Erikson's stages in a positive manner does not inevitably mean failure in life. Successful people in business and public life, for example, may show **role confusion** – an inability to develop self-identity which may cause personality problems. One of Erikson's messages is that the mature personality cannot be judged simply on the basis of material success. It shows itself more reliably in subtler areas such as personal relationships, degree of self-insight and a unifying philosophy of life.

The deviant personality

PROBLEMS OF DEFINITION

As soon as we consider the abnormal in human behaviour we are faced with the question, 'What is abnormal?' Perhaps we regard it as deviant to steal, to lie and to cheat, but who of us can claim never to have done those things? Some degree of deviancy seems to be the norm. Belson (1975) obtained self-reports from a random sample of 1445 secondary schoolboys in London, nearly all of whom admitted to some form of prosecutable offence. Other studies have reported figures as high as 99 per cent confessing to undetected offences. Does this mean that the person we label criminal is unfortunate in getting caught or is there a category of person we can consider a criminal personality? We shall tackle this question shortly after considering the pathological personality in its wider sense.

Although we have difficulty finding the nondeviant individuals when violation of the law is our criterion, there is surely less of a problem when we consider mental illness. A simple rule of thumb might be that people who are under treatment from a psychiatrist are suffering from personality disorder. But if we learn that 20 per cent of the female population consult a psychiatrist at some time in their lives, while the figure is nearer 40 per cent for those who visit their family doctor for treatment of depression, stress and other anxiety states, then disorders of personality assume proportions we can scarcely regard as abnormal. When so many are exhibiting behaviours we regard as abnormal our definitions of the norm become very shaky.

Our confidence about what is abnormal is undermined still further if we give credence to the position advocated by Szasz. In a celebrated article, 'The myth of mental illness', Szasz (1960) claimed that there are no absolute criteria for mental illness, and that society chooses whom it will categorize as insane because of an unwillingness to tolerate minority groups or behaviours. There is a sense in which Szasz is undoubtedly right. The most dramatic example is, perhaps, the Soviet Union where some who have openly criticized totalitarian ideology have been certified insane and committed to psychiatric hospitals. But if we look at our own history we see that although we now provide more humane treatment to the mentally ill than in earlier times, we are less willing to absorb, or at least contain, the disordered mind, such as the so-called senile and the alcoholic, within the community. There are also a sufficient number of documented cases of individuals incarcerated in mental institutions for nothing more than profound deafness to make us question our definitions of morbidity when it

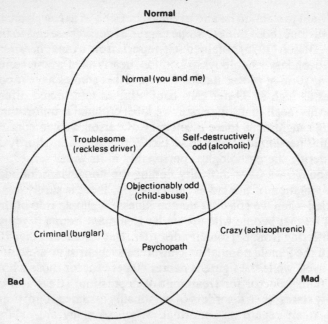

Figure 13.3 The three labels, bad, mad and normal, and their areas of overlap. (After Stone, 1975)

comes to mental health. These problems of definition are summarized in Figure 13.3.

MENTAL ILLNESS

In any discussion of madness, the crucial issues are those of **cause** and **treatment**. Mental illness, like most physical illness, can be regarded as having organic causes. An example of an illness is general paresis, a disorder giving rise to a general decline in physical and psychological functions. If left untreated, delusions will give way to paralysis and eventually death. Research has shown that this is due to a syphilitic infection which can be cured with penicillin. Unfortunately, very few mental illnesses lend themselves to such a clear diagnosis. Even with disorders such as senile dementia and alcoholism, which are associated with atrophy or damage to cortical structures, the role of nonorganic factors cannot be ruled out. What drives a person to drink? Is it part of his or her constitutional make up, or have there been predisposing environmental factors such as financial ruin or marital discord? We often find, when we look at personality disorders, a complex interplay of organic and psychogenic factors, many of which can only be guessed at. Having said that, evidence is beginning to accumulate about the aetiology of some **psychoses**.

Schizophrenia. We have space to consider only one of the psychoses in any detail and schizophrenia is an appropriate choice not only because it provides one of the dramatic examples of the loss of contact with reality but also because it illustrates the ways in which psychologists gather and interpret data about personality disorders. It is also true that schizophrenics fill something like half the beds in psychiatric hospitals.

The extract of dialogue between a doctor and thirty-two-year-old female patient, reproduced below, portrays important symptoms of the illness.

Doctor: When did you come here?
Patient: 1416, you remember, doctor . . .
Doctor: Do you know why you are here?
Patient: Well, in 1951 I changed into two men. President Truman was judge at my trial. I was convicted and hung.
Doctor: Can you tell me the name of this place?
Patient: I have not been a drinker for sixteen years. I am taking a mental rest after a 'carter' assignment or 'quill'. You know, a 'penwrap'. I had contracts with Warner Brothers Studios and Eugene broke phonograph records but Mike protested. . . . I am made of flesh and blood – see, doctor (pulling up her dress).
(Coleman, 1976, pp. 280–1)

This patient appears to have some of the classic schizophrenic symptoms of disordered thought and attention and there are signs of language difficulties – the so-called 'word salad'. Individuals who have recovered from the illness have mentioned the breakdown of the **attentional mechanism**. Experimental studies, too, show that selective attention is severely impaired (McGhie and Chapman, 1961). Unrelated events become connected, and perceptions which are normally filtered out assume considerable dimensions. Loosely speaking, we might say that the patient in the above extract is in a world very different from our own. The answers are not always unrelated to the questions, yet the patient has problems in maintaining any sort of coherent theme.

The schizophrenic frequently withdraws into a private world of **delusions** and **hallucinations**. The delusions often involve paranoid fears of persecution: strangers seen talking are plotting against the patient and sometimes the whole is wrapped up in a perceived conspiracy in which family and friends as well as strangers are involved. A common hallucination is voices (in the absence of actual sensory stimulation) which may be subscribed to God or the devil. Peter Sutcliffe, the Yorkshire Ripper and convicted mass murderer, claimed to have heard voices which ordered him to embark on his terrible orgy of killing, and these were, undoubtedly, a major factor in the psychiatric diagnosis of schizophrenia. There is some evidence (McGuigan, 1966) that hallucinations arise from an inability to distinguish between one's own memory images and external perceptual experiences. In other words, the voices are the subject's own and the process may be akin, in an extreme form, to Freud's concept of projection.

Schizophrenia also manifests itself in **emotion** and **behaviour**. Initially the schizophrenic may be emotionally oversensitive, the slightest disagreement triggering a strong outburst, but with time the emotions become blunted. In some cases feelings are present but situation and emotion seem uncoordinated so that tragedy provokes laughter and neutral events produce rage. The best known behavioural disorders are the **catatonic stupor**, where the patient may remain immobile for hours in a strange posture, and **catatonic excitement** which is short-lived but often frenzied and violent. Less extreme but more common are the grimaces and repetitive movements that accompany some varieties of the illness.

As the last sentence implies, schizophrenia is probably not a single illness. However, the classic quartet described by Bleuler (1911/1950) – hebephrenic, catatonic, paranoid and simple (see Stafford-Clark and Smith, 1979, for a description) – is not altogether satisfactory. An alternative classification talks of **reactive schizo-**

phrenia, where the symptoms arise suddenly as a reaction to a major personal catastrophe, and **process schizophrenia**, where the onset is gradual, without any obvious precipitating factor. (The distinction is similar to that between 'endogenous' and 'reactive' in depression.) Surveys indicate that reactive schizophrenia responds to treatment much better than the chronic illness.

In trying to impose order on this plethora of symptoms, most experts conclude that the primary deficit is cognitive and that the disturbances to language and thought give rise to symptoms such as delusions and hallucinations and, more controversially, to social withdrawal and emotional disturbance. The question then becomes, is the illness due to organic or functional causes? Much of the evidence which bears on this question is circumstantial rather than directly causal but the picture which emerges suggests a genetic basis to the illness.

Some assert that mental illness is a creation of advanced industrialized societies. In the case of schizophrenia data exist from such diverse cultures as Eskimo, Yoruba (W. Africa), Sweden and Canada, indicating that the incidence of the illness is roughly similar. This implies that environmental factors such as childrearing practices probably do not account for the illness. But, at the same time, there is demographic evidence to show that the incidence of schizophrenia is associated with the poorest members of society and the slum, inner-city areas which they inhabit (Kohn, 1968).

The evidence for an **heredity factor** in schizophrenia comes from studies of twins. The probability of an identical twin who is schizophrenic having a twin who is also schizophrenic is 0.44 compared with a concordance rate of only 9 per cent if the twins are fraternal (Rosenthal, 1970). There is also firm evidence to show that children born to schizophrenic mothers are more likely than matched controls to become schizophrenic themselves, even though raised by foster parents.

The most powerful organic evidence would be a demonstration that a certain centre or malfunction in the nervous system accounted for the disorder. One theory is that a disorder of the **neurotransmitters** gives rise to an excessive build-up of a biochemical agent which is known to affect attentional states (Carlson, 1977). Dopamine, one of the catecholamines (see page 91), which has an arousing function in the brain, is a likely candidate since it is known that the group of drugs called phenothiazines, which have been notably successful with schizophrenia, act by blocking dopamine at the synapse. Furthermore, the administration of substances which enhance dopamine activity (e.g. amphetamines) has been shown to produce extreme symptoms in hitherto mild schizophrenics and to induce schizophrenic behaviour in normal people.

Despite the apparently strong evidence to support an organic explanation for schizophrenia, there is an influential view which states that schizophrenia is something inflicted on individuals by societies and not an inherent disorder of the individual. There are two points to note here. The first is that the existence of a neurological defect may tell us why someone is behaving in a certain way but not what gave rise to that condition. Excess of dopamine is an explanation at one level, but if the condition was brought about by a particular set of family circumstances then it is these we must address for a true understanding of the disease. This brings us to the second point – made by Laing (1967), among others – that madness is a label put on some people by society. Laing himself seems to feel that schizophrenia should be seen as a form of mental rebirth, and the community support that he advocates is designed to help sufferers through the process. Critics point out that Laing's patients have been predominantly reactive schizophrenics for whom there is a high rate of spontaneous recovery.

To sum up, schizophrenia is an example of a severe psychosis

BOX 13.3
Defining insanity: a question of labelling?

A particularly dramatic demonstration of madness being in the eye of the beholder is provided by Rosenhan (1973). He arranged to have himself and seven other normal persons admitted as patients to psychiatric hospitals across the United States. The same symptoms were always reported, namely the hearing of voices saying 'empty', 'hollow' or 'thud'. Apart from pseudonyms and in some cases misrepresentation of occupation, the pseudopatients made no attempt to change their life histories and current circumstances. All the subjects were admitted, and all but one were diagnosed as schizophrenic.

Once in hospital the patients behaved completely normally and reported that the voices had disappeared. Despite this, no deception was detected (except by other patients), and their behaviour, including the note-taking which they carried out as part of the study, was interpreted in line with the original diagnosis. This labelling greatly affected the patients' experience. They felt depersonalized, powerless and cut off from the medical staff with whom their average daily contact was less than seven minutes.

The participants in the study had agreed that they would try to get discharged without outside help, by convincing the staff they were sane but without admitting the original deception. This proved no easy matter: it took in one case fifty-two days. The diagnosis on discharge was 'schizophrenia in remission' and the validity of the original diagnosis was never questioned.

On the face of it this is strong support for **labelling theory** since the psychiatrist is apparently unable to detect the difference between the sane and the insane, pinning his diagnosis to a self-inflicted symptom. But the psychiatrist can only interpret that which is presented, namely auditory hallucinations. The idea that they are part of an elaborate deception simply does not occur to the medical personnel. The decision to admit the patients for observation seems a reasonable one. It is also understandable that subsequent acts are interpreted in the light of the diagnosis. The staff cannot simply ignore the information – complaining of hearing voices – with which their patient came to them.

There is cause for concern in Rosenhan's study, however. It supports the complaints of genuine patients about the unenlightened conditions prevalent in many mental hospitals and paints a vivid picture of the depersonalization process experienced. It also argues that there may be merit in regarding diagnostic labels as provisional, pending additional information.

which manifests itself primarily as a cognitive disorder. The underlying pathology seems to be organic, a biochemical defect being the most likely factor on current evidence. More remote causes include a heredity predisposition exacerbated by environmental stresses associated with the conditions of poverty and inner city living.

Other varieties of mental illness. Schizophrenia is only one example of one branch of personality disorder – the psychoses. We have said nothing about **affective disorders** such as manic-depressive psychosis where the dominant disturbance is one of **mood**. Nor have we examined the **neuroses** whose primary symptoms are **anxiety**, or defences that try to ward off anxiety. Because neuroses are generally considered to have a psychogenic rather than organic pathology, they often come to the attention of practising clinical psychologists who might employ varieties of psychotherapy in the treatment of phobias, obsessions and compulsions and other anxiety states (see Epilogue).

Still another group of disorders are those known as **psychosomatic**, such as **hypertension** and **emotional stress**. This is where stress induced by an environmental event, such as an overdemanding occupation or personal difficulties, is sufficient to produce a physical symptom such as high blood pressure which, in turn, may lead to a heart condition.

Assuming the stress we are under is sufficient to give rise to a physiological disorder, what determines whether the symptom is a peptic ulcer or high blood pressure? According to one theory – the **weak link hypothesis** – the body gives way at its most vulnerable point which will itself be determined by pre-existing genetic susceptibility. Thus, a susceptibility to respiratory troubles, which tends to run in families, will tend to give rise to an asthmatic rather than duodenal condition in response to sustained stress.

An alternative theory proposes that individuals differ in their predominant emotions and these will determine the physical organ which is affected. The evidence for this view is based on clinical accounts. Thus, those with high blood pressure feel threatened: they would like to show hostility but keep it bottled up. This creates a state of hypertension since the autonomic nervous system is in a perpetual state of readiness for combat which does not take place. Ulcer patients, in contrast, are outwardly strong but have a suppressed desire to be loved and taken care of. This frustrated dependency shows itself in gastric secretions (the psychoanalytic link between dependency and hunger satisfaction?) which, if sufficient, can produce an ulcer. A realistic position is that both explanations play a role and both therefore need to be examined to understand the toll exacted by stress on a particular individual.

THE CRIMINAL PERSONALITY

A number of difficulties arise in the study of the criminal personality. We have already noted that it is by no means straightforward to determine what is deviant or criminal in terms of behaviour. Even behaviour as extreme as infanticide may be condoned in certain societies. Nevertheless, despite the impact of cultural relativism, we do recognize that while few of us are innocent of any criminal behaviour, it is a small minority who practise crime as a trade – the hardened criminals. If we take, therefore, the criminal as a *person*, rather than considering criminal behaviour, we must first dispose of two other problems.

As mentioned in the introduction to this section, those convicted of crime are but a small proportion of those confessing to crime. Since studies of the criminal personality will inevitably resort to the criminal population, we should be cautious about extrapolating from theories derived from studies of those who get caught. Ideally, such studies should be complemented by research with self-confessed offenders. A second problem is that the condition of the person we study may arise as a result of the prison or conviction experience rather than anything inherent in the personality. There is no obvious solution to this objection but since most workers believe that personality must be enduring rather than short-term to be worthy of the name, they have been prepared to disregard the problem.

Eysenck's theory. As we saw in Box 5.2, Eysenck claims to have established a link between certain profiles on his tests and the criminal personality. He found that offenders scored highly on extraversion, neuroticism and psychoticism. This conforms to Eysenck's further finding that extraverts take longer than introverts to condition. Since, for Eysenck, conscience is a conditioned anxiety response, this accounts for the link between extraversion, absence of conscience (or psychopathy), and criminality. Eysenck's theory has been elaborated by Gray. He found that introverts only conditioned better than extraverts when punishment was involved. When a reward system was in operation, extraverts conditioned better. This led Gray (1972) to propose a more sophisticated notion of conditioning and personality in which relations between events are involved and not merely the automatic process which conditioning theory usually implies.

Eysenck's position has not gone unchallenged. In her review of the evidence Hampson (1982) concludes that although there is some support for criminals being highly neurotic, the neurotic extravert tag is not supported. Indeed, the search for any personality trait or dimension such as intelligence or moral reasoning which will differentiate criminals from non-criminals has been singularly unsuccessful.

Social labelling theory. This failure to find any inherent personality defect is no surprise to those who advocate a sociological theory of criminality. For such theorists (e.g. Goffman) criminality does not reside in the individual; it is a label put on a certain sector of society, partly with a view to maintaining the existing social order. It is demonstrable that a disproportionate number of lower class and ethnic minorities figure in the official criminal statistics. Bennet (1979), in a study of police procedure, found that significantly more middle-class than working-class children were let off with a caution and thus avoided court appearance. Bennet absolves the police of any culpability in this behaviour, putting it down to the inferior social skills of the working-class children rather than police prejudice.

There are two strands to social labelling theory. One is the **conspiracy element** which states that those in power use the deviant sector in society to provide a constant example of what is acceptable and unacceptable in public behaviour. The media are an important factor in this process, public hangings and floggings having ceased (in this country at least).

The second strand refers to the society-bestowed label being taken up by the offender through the process of **role identification** such that the victim begins to adopt a criminal identity and the associated lifestyle. Although there is some experimental evidence (Snyder and Swann, 1978) to show the power which assigned labels can have on behaviour, everyday experience suggests it is not a simple matter of cause and effect. If it were, then every individual convicted of a criminal offence would be embarked on a career of crime.

Criminal thinking patterns. The key to this dilemma, Hampson argues, may be in the self-perceptions which are at work, and in this vein she describes the intriguing work of Yochelson and Samenow (1976) who, from clinical interviews and tests with some 240 hard-core male criminals over a period of twelve years, have identified what they call criminal thinking patterns. These refer to emotions and attitudes as well as cognitive processes. Yochelson and Samenow see the criminal as totally immersed in criminality, in the way that the alcoholic is in alcohol.

In brief, the criminal personality that emerges from the work of Yochelson and Samenow is of someone with enormous energy reserves and a need for continual excitement. He is aggressively masculine and constantly fearful of 'put-downs'. Machismo is maintained by physical and sexual prowess, money and possessions. In contrast to the excessive amounts of anger and pride is the sentimentality found in every hardened criminal seen by Yochelson and Samenow. Most obviously this is directed towards the criminal's mother, but also towards helpless groups such as the elderly, the disabled and animals. The somewhat disparate attributes of hard machismo and sentimentality are able to coexist because the two conform to the criminal's self-image of being a good person. In cognitive terms the criminal personality combines a **vivid imagination** with the ability to compartmentalize dissonant information. The vivid imagination allows constant rehearsal of criminal fantasies, preparing him for action when the time comes. The **fragmentation** permits inconsistency between attitudes and behaviours, a feature common to all of us but present on a massive scale in criminals. This allows the criminal to be both sentimental and ruthless, a self-perceived figure of moral rectitude who commits acts of gross immorality. It means that crime can be plotted and executed and the adverse consequences ignored.

Various methodological defects in Yochelson and Samenow's work are listed by Hampson but it remains a notable study in need of testing. It gains some support from biographical material cited by Hampson; and John McVicar, a convicted violent criminal who since his release has made a scholarly and informed study of the criminal personality, appears to agree with the conclusions of Yochelson and Samenow and their proposed method of treatment which amounts to ethical reindoctrination (McVicar, 1979). Finally, it is worth noting that Yochelson and Samenow began their work with a commitment to the social labelling view of criminal behaviour but concluded with the provocative observation that the 'model of the criminal as victim is a subversive myth cultivated by the machinations of the criminal mind and nurtured by the gullibility of social scientists' (cited in Hampson, 1982, p. 271).

Further reading

General

There are countless textbooks in this area but the two recommended, one British, one American, are more than simply compilations of theories and facts. They take a clear, undoctrinaire line on the subject and make a contribution to the literature as well as to our understanding of this complex area:

HAMPSON, S.E. (1982) *The Construction of Personality*. London: Methuen.

MADDI, S.R. (1976) *Personality Theories: a Comparative Analysis*. Homewood, Ill.: Dorsey Press.

Theoretical approaches

Psychoanalytic theory
There is no substitute for an acquaintance with Freud's own writings, and the complete works, in translation, are now available in paperback as *The Pelican Freud Library*, Penguin Books. An abridged edition of the classic

biography of Freud is also available in paperback and serves to introduce the theory as well as the man:

JONES, E. (1964) *The Life and Work of Sigmund Freud*. Harmondsworth: Penguin.

A definitive and readable account of defence mechanisms can be found in the book by Freud's daughter:

FREUD, A. (1966) *The Ego and the Mechanisms of Defence*. London: Hogarth Press.

As well as in Maddi, *op. cit.*, an introduction to Freud and the other psychoanalytic theorists (Adler, Jung, etc.) can be found in:

BROWN, J.A.C. (1961) *Freud and the Post-Freudians*. Harmondsworth: Penguin.

The discipline has been rendered a valuable service by Paul Kline who exhaustively reviews the empirical evidence in an attempt to provide an objective evaluation of the theory:

KLINE, P. (1981) *Fact and Fantasy in Freudian Theory*. London: Methuen.

Trait theory
A concise and lively introduction to the psychometric approach is provided by:

KLINE, P. (1983) *Personality: Measurement and Theory*. London: Hutchinson.

For those who want the 'horse's mouth':

EYSENCK, H.J. and EYSENCK, S.B.G. (1969) *Personality Structure and Measurement*. London: Routledge and Kegan Paul.

The situationism debate is reviewed in Hampson, *op. cit.*, and the articles by Mischel and Bowers in the 1973 volume of *Psychological Review* are worth reading. A forthright defence of trait theory can be found in:

EYSENCK, M.W. and EYSENCK, H.J. (1980) Mischel and the concept of personality. *British Journal of Psychology*, **71**, 71–83.

Fulfilment theory
Maddi, *op. cit.*, provides a good account of fulfilment theories; and the best summary of the leading figure's theory is his own:

ROGERS, C.R. (1959) A theory of therapy, personality and interpersonal relationships as developed in the client-centered framework. In

S. Koch, ed., *Psychology: a Study of Science*, Volume 3. New York: McGraw-Hill.

The celebrated debate between Skinner and Rogers (reproduced in the book listed below) provides a very readable way of confronting the issue of determinism and free will in human behaviour as well as giving a good insight into Rogers's standpoint.

MILLER, G.A. and BUCKHOUT, R. (1973) *Psychology: the Science of Mental Life*. New York: Harper and Row.

For those seeking further enlightenment on self-actualization and the humanist perspective, the following is recommended:

MASLOW, A.H. (1970) *Motivation and Personality*. New York: Harper and Row.

Burns's book is worth buying for the cartoon on the front cover, alone, but it also represents a valuable review and source book for this important notion:

BURNS, R.B. (1974) *The Self Concept*. London: Longman.

Cognitive theories

Don Bannister is the leading British advocate of personal construct theory and his writings are invariably stimulating. An authoritative introduction to Kelly's theory is:

BANNISTER, D. and MAIR, J.M.M. (1968) *The Evaluation of Personal Constructs*. London: Academic Press.

A briefer account is:

BANNISTER, D. and FRANSELLA, F. (1980) *Inquiring Man*. Harmondsworth: Penguin.

The current impact of cognition on personality is to be found most notably in the area known as social cognition which was presented in Chapter 11 above. The significance of Rosch's influential prototype theory is considered in:

CANTOR, N. and MISCHEL, W. (1979) Prototypes in person perception. In L. Berkowitz, ed., *Advances in Experimental Social Psychology*, Volume 12. New York: Academic Press.

Origins and growth of personality

A detailed exposition of Freud's psychosexual theory can be found in:

FREUD, S. (1977) *The Pelican Freud Library*, Volume 7, *On Sexuality*. Harmondsworth: Penguin.

Other reading relevant to this section can be found in the Further Reading for Chapter 12 above.

A sensitive account of the significance of temperament, drawing on the work of Thomas and Chess, is:

DUNN, J. (1979) Individual differences in temperament. In M. Rutter, ed., *The Scientific Foundations of Developmental Psychiatry*. London: Heinemann.

Two neglected (companion) works which have the rare distinction of charting personality growth from birth to adolescence using careful observational, psychometric and clinical measures are:

ESCALONA, S. (1968, 1973) *The Roots of Individuality*. London: Tavistock.

MURPHY, L.B. and MORIARTY, A.E. (1976) *Vulnerability, Coping and Growth*. New Haven: Yale University Press.

The mature personality

Erikson's major work should be consulted for an appreciation of the breadth of his theory and the evidence upon which it is based:

ERIKSON, E. (1965) *Childhood and Society*. Harmondsworth, Penguin.

References to empirical tests of Erikson's theory are available in Maddi, *op. cit*. A multitude of perspectives on adolescence can be found in the following source book:

ADELSON, J. ed. (1980) *Handbook of Adolescent Psychology*. New York: Wiley.

The Freudian view that adolescence is a period of storm and stress is challenged by the following large-scale normative study:

RUTTER, M., GRAHAM, P., CHADWICK, O and YULE, W. (1976) Adolescent turmoil: fact of fiction? *Journal of Child Psychology and Psychiatry*, **17**, 35–56.

As well as providing a very readable British perspective in an area dominated by American workers, the following book has the merit of including at the end of each chapter extracts from interviews with a sample of adolescents.

COLEMAN, J.C. (1980) *The Nature of Adolescence*. London: Methuen.

Little has been said about the life-span approach to psychology but it is becoming increasingly influential, particularly on the continent of Europe.

Such work will, hopefully, tell us more about the under-researched area of the mature personality.

BALTES, P. and SCHAIE, K.W., eds. (1973) *Life-span Developmental Psychology: Personality and Socialisation*. New York: Academic Press.

The deviant personality

A reliable textbook which includes good case studies is:

BARCLAY, M. (1977) *Abnormal Psychology*. New York: Holt, Rinehart and Winston.

A good orthodox (British) medical text is:

STAFFORD-CLARK, D. and SMITH, A. (1979) *Psychiatry for Students*. London: Unwin.

A recent and entertaining presentation of Szasz's position (in conversation with Jonathan Miller) can be found in:

MILLER, J., ed. (1983) *States of Mind*. London: BBC Publications.

For those with strong stomachs, a frank account of the experience of mental illness (and a critique of the treatment given) by a contemporary experimental psychologist:

SUTHERLAND, S. (1977) *Breakdown*. London: Paladin.

An original approach to psychotic illness is available in:

LAING, R.D. (1960) *The Divided Self*. London: Tavistock.

Hampson, *op. cit.*, provides a well rounded chapter on the criminal personality. Eysenck's position is set out in detail in:

EYSENCK, H.J. (1977) *Crime and Personality*. London: Paladin.

An eloquent example of the sociologist's (labelling theory) approach to deviance is:

GOFFMAN, E. (1968) *Asylums*. Harmondsworth: Penguin.

Epilogue

A note on applying psychology

The integrated approach that we have tried to follow in this book breaks down when we look at the area of applied psychology. Indeed, by even considering an 'area' rather than a process or property of people we are departing from our avowed intention. This is not to say that an integrated approach to applied psychology is impossible, but it is rarely encountered. The reality seems to be that there are many applied psychologies, each tackling their own special problems and frequently using their own specialist techniques. In this Epilogue, therefore, we will confine our attention to the relationship between pure and applied psychology, and to the related issue of ecological validity.

Although a pat definition of applied psychology is impossible, because of the multiplicity that exists, it is nevertheless possible to differentiate *two* clear types of applied pschology. One we might call the psychology of the practitioner, into which category would go clinical, educational, occupational and consumer psychologists, and indeed anyone who has gained a specialist postgraduate qualification enabling him or her to practise a particular branch of the subject. Such individuals are usually employed by large public bodies such as the National Health Service, the Civil Service, local authorities and certain private companies (e.g., advertising agencies).

The duties of such practitioners are sometimes enshrined in statute or at least contained within a code of practice. Thus, educational psychologists are required to determine the special educational need of any child referred to the school psychological service. This need may arise from a specific impairment, such as deafness, or a more general disability such as slow learning or maladjustment. The educational psychologist, in common with most practitioners, seldom functions independently. He or she will liaise with teachers, social workers, clinicians of various sorts, and civil servants. As well as carrying out assessments and recommending placements, the educational psychologist offers advice and treatment programmes to schools. Because of heavy caseloads, educational psychologists have little time to engage in work outside the remedial sphere. But their training well qualifies them to collaborate with schools in mainstream activities such as drawing up curricula, examination techniques and teaching methods and educational objectives. If resources allowed, there would surely be a case for considering the appointment of an educational psychologist to every school, although members of the teaching profession might need convincing of the wisdom of this suggestion.

The other broad division of applied psychology is that practised by researchers who direct their efforts to 'problems that come fairly directly from real-life situations' (Warr, 1978). This work can be carried on from any institutions where facilities for research are available. It may be full-time or part-time and by academics or practitioners. Clinical psychologists, for instance, might carry out research as part of their job, but it will usually be the case that such research is fitted in when other commitments allow. One could make the same point about teachers in higher education for whom research is a major activity but not a full-time one. It is only in a few specially designated research units financed by the research councils or government departments that a full-time programme of research devoted to 'real world' problems is pursued.

Although the specialist units may be few in number, their influence on the development of psychology has been considerable. In the United Kingdom, for example, the Medical Research Council Applied Psychology Unit (APU) at Cambridge has been a fertile ground for ideas as well as practical solutions. APU figures such as Craik and Bartlett, who started the unit, and their successors as directors, Broadbent and Baddeley, are known not so much for their applied work as for their theoretical contributions in the area of memory, attention, vigilance and human skills. At the same time the APU at Cambridge has been responsible for advising on practical problems such as the design of the postal code and decimal coinage. Much of Broadbent's theoretical work (1958, 1971) has grown out of practical problems such as how noxious stimulation, e.g. noise, affects the ability to make decisions or attend to a task.

The applied tradition has always been strong in psychology, often encouraged by the need to make a contribution to national causes. Rapid advances in theory, and empirical discovery in areas such as attention, were a consequence of the recruitment of psychologists to the war effort. Real problems such as the ergonomic design of control panels in pilots' cockpits and optimal systems for radar operators focus and perhaps accelerate the efforts of researchers. This has led some to claim that all psychological research should be applied. If, for a moment, we accept this debatable claim, the implications for research are by no means clear since it does not follow that *one* method of research is desirable. Just as there are a number of applied psychologies, so there are a variety of ways of investigating applied issues.

The APU at Cambridge has carried out much of its most successful work by simulating the applied problem in the laboratory, to look, for instance, at the effects of stress on performance. This will usually mean studying the work situation in advance to ensure that the appropriate variables are being considered in the laboratory. Having done that, work of a controlled experimental nature can be conducted, unfettered, in laboratory conditions.

A different approach has been followed by another major applied psychology unit at Sheffield, although traditional experimental methods are also used there. This group has been pioneers in **action research** – that is, research which takes place in the working environment in conjunction with the workforce concerned. This means that participant observation rather than the detached procedures used by ethologists is employed. So, when the process of industrial bargaining was being investigated, Warr (1978) chose to become a member of a trade union negotiating team, which meant he attended and contributed to all meetings over a period of several months. In this way firsthand experience was gained of the procedure that unions and management used to determine matters of common concern, namely, wages, manning levels, working conditions, production targets and so on.

A picture of applied psychology should be starting to emerge. In general, it is distinguished by the population studied – real people with real problems; by the research setting – society's institutions and places of work: schools, hospitals, factories and prisons; and by the goal of the research effort – to find a solution to a practical problem or, at least, gain more understanding of that problem.

We must now return to the claim that applied psychology, however practised, is the preferred model for research in the subject. To evalute this claim we must examine the relationship between pure and applied psychology and try to see what value it has and what the problems are.

The relationship between the academic discipline of psychology and the real world to which it might be expected to relate is a vexed one. At first blush this is surprising since, as Kay (1972) argued, the important problems left for the world to solve concern the nature of human beings themselves. Accordingly, the psychologist ought to have a major contribution to make. Yet, this is by no means a universally held view. The difficulty is one that the conscientious reader of this book is bound to have spotted. Human problems may be ubiquitous but, however obvious appear to be the answers, closer examination will almost invariably show that the behaviour is a complex interaction of many variables. This has led to the argument that attempts to provide answers in advance of complete knowledge is a disservice to the public and profession alike: 'Misunderstanding and apprehension amongst the general public must, I think, arise, in part at least, from the readiness of some of our colleagues to make confident public pronouncements of theories, at best unproven, to explain matters of general interest' (Drew, 1973, p. 191).

We are thus faced with a dilemma. A world full of essentially human problems and a science devoted to the analysis of human behaviour ought to be addressing one another constantly and productively. And yet what we find, according to one experienced practitioner, is: 'It is a common experience of applied psychologists that more is expected of them than they can deliver, and the psychologists, in turn, expect their discipline to provide better solutions than it can produce' (Davidson, 1977, p. 273).

Can we get off the horns of this particular dilemma? Davidson's own analysis bears consideration. She argues that the academic course in psychology may not adequately prepare the graduate who wishes to apply the subject. A scientific approach stresses certainty and lawfulness, but the nonpsychologist population does not usually hold a strong belief in the comprehension and predictability of human behaviour. The graduate who goes into the applied field therefore enters a world that does not share his or her value system. Psychologists, by and large, are taken less seriously than, say, chemists, geologists or engineers. This difficulty is exacerbated by the somewhat paradoxical fact that everyone is his or her own psychologist in a way that they are not astronomers or lawyers. Historically, one effect of this has been for psychology to try to ape, excessively, the natural sciences (see Chapter 1). For a long time this led to the psychologist playing safe behind psychometrics or the testing movement.

Davidson sees more hope in some of the newer developments in psychology. Three that she lists are: (1) longitudinal studies which highlight the role of situational variables and dynamic nature of human affairs, not always captured in horizontal, highly structured studies; (2) the recognition of experimenter effects and self-fulfilling prophesies – the realization that psychological studies are the result of one dynamic organism experimenting on another and the inadequacy of the positivist approach to deal with this situation; (3) the appearance of applications, such as behaviour therapy, which see the psychologist change from a passive administrator of tests to an active interventionist.

Such changes bring their own problems, however. The recognition of the true complexity of human affairs has led some to desperate reactions such as a retreat to the laboratory to achieve, if nothing else, scientific respectability. An opposite, but equally desperate reaction is to discard science altogether and rely solely on intuitions since those are what the man or woman in the street uses (Hargreaves, 1979). Davidson counsels less extreme measures. Her plea to the scientific psychologist is threefold. To conduct proper replication before publication since this can save wasted time and possibly embarrassment in the applied arena; to take account of factors which affect ecological validity, such as experimenter effects (see below), in constructing experimental designs; to engage in cooperation, rather than competition, among schools of psychology. An example of the benefits of the latter advice is the way in which the technique of behaviour therapy, derived from learning theory, has been broadened and rendered more efficacious by incorporating a cognitive perspective.

Successful applied psychology requires that there is a system within which pure and applied psychologists, however blurred that distinction, can work productively, deriving mutual benefits. Davidson suggests that the academic research psychologist, comprised of some dedicated research centres but in the main made up of the sort of people who lecture to undergraduates, must remain the backbone of the subject. On the academic will depend the continuing gathering of basic knowledge and theory-building. A second group are those applied psychologists who are paid to work on specific problems. They draw on the knowledge and methods accumulated by the first group and in turn feed back their results to that group indicating to what extent their findings are applicable to the real world. This second group also provides a vital service for the third group – the practitioners. Educational, clinical and occupational psychologists should be able to rely on the second group for the tools of their trade. At the same time they will, as they have always done, be prepared to act in the absence of knowledge and adequate instruments, relying on their professional experience.

Ecological validity

It is not easy to observe contemporary trends in a discipline in which one is engaged but one evident development is the increasing concern for **relevance**, for psychology to say something about behaviour outside the settings in which psychological research is practised.

Psychologists have always been keen to relate their work beyond the confines of the research laboratory, and in the past there have been some dubious extrapolations from organisms such as rats and pigeons to complex behaviour in humans. Psychologists who study learning in animals with a view to explaining complex human behaviour are now a scarce species. But a new worry has materialized. It is now claimed that the study of mental life in artificial situations using contrived tasks tells us little about the cognitive principles that govern intellectual behaviour in everyday life. Leading proponents of this view include Cole (e.g., Cole, Hood and McDermott, 1978), Neisser (1976a) and Bronfenbrenner (1979), and the issue has come to be called one of **ecological validity**.

Cole and his colleagues, in particular, have made the strong claim that findings from laboratory studies cannot be generalized to real-world settings. Their argument is an elaborate one but the main point relates to the ecology of the real world. As Cole and his associates put it, 'The problem environments facing people are multiple . . . [and also] negotiable and organized in the course of interaction.' By this they mean that real problems and decisions, as opposed to those perpetrated by the psychologist, are in fact *created* by individuals in the course of their behaviour with one another and that the problem environment is being constantly altered by the actions of the individuals concerned and, accordingly, the solutions that evolve. For this reason experimental procedures that preclude the dynamic determining features of the real world can never have any relevance for that world. Furthermore it is not only what the environment is, but what has to get done in it, that is important. Cognitive processes like remembering, communicating and decision-making are almost invariably social activities and can only be understood in that context.

The analysis offered by Cole and his associates is not entirely critical. They recognize that modern psychology has provided constructs which are used in ecologically *valid* research. But how is ecologically valid research to be conducted? Cole *et al.* offer a framework that starts with a careful description of the real-world phenomenon that is of interest and then has fluid movement between the 'field' and the controlled situation such that the experimental findings are being constantly monitored and compared with the real-world situation. The problem for Cole is that existing experimental technology cannot provide us with models of everyday cognitive activity. Part of his evidence for this claim is that a search for cognitive principles or strategies uncovered in the 'laboratory', for example the principle of invariance as in conservation studies, is not forthcoming in the real world. This may, of course, be due either to an inadequate laboratory conceptualization or because investigators looking for real-world analogies are looking in the wrong place or have not looked long or carefully enough.

We cannot ignore the critique of Cole and his associates simply because they cannot offer, in turn, an easy 'off-the-peg' method to pursue psychological research. Ultimately it is a criticism that psychology must meet, but prescriptions which require us to abandon all that has gone before are, in the present state of the art, too draconian by far.

Another fervent critic of experimental psychology is Bronfenbrenner. He, too, is concerned that the setting in which research takes place is too constricting. He offers a description of the environment in ecological systems terms, seeing the immediate setting, such as the mother-child dyad, as nested within other systems like the family, community, state and culture (Bronfenbrenner, 1979). He draws attention to the many second-order effects and relations between settings. Thus, what is happening at a parent's place of work may affect the child in school. The course of an adolescent's peer relationships may affect attitudes towards parents which in turn may have knock-on effects throughout the family and the situations in which the family finds itself.

Like Cole, therefore, Bronfenbrenner asks us to abandon unidimensional models for a focus on interactions. An emphasis on manipulation and change is understandable in scientific research but it does not mean that the psychologists themselves must always contrive the changes. Bronfenbrenner points to the many natural changes which take place and which offer excellent opportunities to understand complex environmental effects. Examples abound throughout the life span: home to nursery, nursery to school, junior school to secondary school, school to work, job to job, single living to marriage, childlessness to parenthood and so on. But Bronfenbrenner does not dismiss the laboratory as ecologically invalid. As long as researchers are fully aware of the properties their research environment possesses, especially with regard to the perceptions of the subject, then the laboratory may be as valid as any other setting. It may be, for instance, particularly appropriate for studying the effects of unfamiliar settings on behaviour and, as we have argued above, adjusting to new situations is an important part of behavioural development.

We are able, therefore, to end on an optimistic note. Psychology has undoubtedly advanced a long way, no matter which branch of the discipline you consider. In memory, artificial units such as the nonsense syllable have given way to meaningful units like sentences or even passages of prose. Language studies have forsaken the word for active discourse, and models of the mind have made enormous strides through borrowing from computer science. The golden rule, however, remains one of selecting the task and level of analysis to suit the question being asked. This rule applies to theory and broad approaches in the subject as well as research paradigms. Psychology is still in the business of opening doors, not closing them. In the spirit of this volume the potential of the subject is unlimited if we continue to draw from all the areas of enquiry that inform our understanding of human endeavour.

References

ADAMS, M.J. (1979) Models of word recognition. *Cognitive Psychology*, **11**, 133–76.

ADOLPH, E.F. (1941) The internal environment and behavior: water content. *American Journal of Psychiatry*, **97**, 1365–73.

AHRENS, R. (1954) Beitrag zur Entwicklung des Physiognomie und Mimikerkennes. *Zeitschrift für Experimentelle und Angewandte Psychologie*, **2**, 412–54.

AINSWORTH, M.D.S. (1979) Attachment as related to mother-infant interaction. In J.S. Rosenblatt, R.A. Hinde, C. Beer and M. Busnel, eds., *Advances in the Study of Behavior*, Volume 9. New York: Academic Press.

AINSWORTH, M.D.S. (1980) Attachment and child abuse. In G. Gerbner, C.J. Ross and E. Zigler, eds., *Child Abuse: an Agenda for Action*. Oxford: Oxford University Press.

AJZEN, I. and FISHBEIN, M. (1977) Attitude-behaviour relations: a theoretical analysis and review of empirical research. *Psychological Bulletin*, **84**, 888–918.

ALLPORT, D.A. (1977) On knowing the meaning of words we are unable to report: the effects of visual masking. In S. Dornic, ed., *Attention and Performance*, Volume VI. Hillsdale, NJ: Erlbaum.

ALLPORT, D.A. (1980a) Patterns and actions: cognitive mechanisms are content-specific. In G. Claxton, ed., *Cognitive Psychology: New Directions*. London: Routledge and Kegan Paul.

ALLPORT, D.A. (1980b) Attention and performance. In G. Claxton, ed., *Cognitive Psychology: New Directions*. London: Routledge and Kegan Paul.

ALLPORT, G.W. (1935) Attitudes. In C. Murchison, ed., *Handbook of Social Psychology*, Volume 2. Worcester, Mass.: Clark University Press.

ALPERN, M. (1972) Effect or mechanisms in vision. In J.W. Kling and L.A. Riggs, eds., *Experimental Psychology*. London: Methuen.

ANDERSON, J.R. (1978) Arguments concerning representations for mental imagery. *Psychological Review*, **85**, 249–77.

ANDERSON, J.R. and ROSS, B.H. (1980) Evidence against a semantic-episodic distinction. *Journal of Experimental Psychology: Human Learning and Memory*, **6**, 441–66.

ANISMAN, H. and ZACHARKO, R.M. (1982) Depression: the predisposing influence of stress. *Behavioral and Brain Sciences*, **5**, 89–137.

ANNETT, M. (1976) *Evolution, Genetics and Social Behaviour*. Milton Keynes: Open University Press.

ANTELMAN, S.M., SZECHTMAN, H., CHIN, P. and FISHER, A.D. (1975) Tail pinch-induced eating, gnawing and licking behavior in rats: dependence on the nigrostriatal dopamine system. *Brain Research*, **99**, 319–77.

APPELLE, S. (1972) Perception and discrimination as a function of stimulus orientation: the oblique effect in man and animals. *Psychological Bulletin*, **78**, 266–78.

ARGYLE, M. and DEAN, J. (1965) Eye contact, distance and affiliation. *Sociometry*, **28**, 289–304.

ARONFREED, J. (1976) Moral development from the standpoint of a general psychological theory. In T. Lickona, ed., *Moral Development and Behavior*. New York: Holt, Rinehart and Winston.

ASCH, S. (1952) *Social Psychology*. Englewood Cliffs, NJ: Prentice-Hall.

ASHER, S.R. (1976) Children's ability to appraise their own and another person's communication performance. *Developmental Psychology*, **12**, 24–32.

ATKINSON, J.W. (1953) The achievement motive and recall of interrupted and completed tasks. *Journal of Experimental Psychology*, **46**, 381–90.

ATKINSON, R.C. and SHIFFRIN, R.M. (1968) Human memory: a proposed system and its control processes. In K.W. Spence and J.T. Spence, eds., *The Psychology of Learning and Motivation: Advances in Research and Theory*, Volume 2. New York: Academic Press.

ATKINSON, R.C. and SHIFFRIN, R.M. (1971) The control of short-term memory. *Scientific American*, **225**, 82–90.

AVERILL, J.R. (1968) Grief: its nature and significance. *Psychological Bulletin*, **70**, 721–48.

AVERILL, J.R. (1969) Autonomic response patterns during sadness and mirth. *Psychophysiology*, **5**, 399–414.

AX, A.F. (1953) The physiological differentiation of fear and anger in humans. *Psychosomatic Medicine*, **15**, 433–42.

BADDELEY, A.D. (1966a) Short-term memory for word sequences as a function of acoustic, semantic and formal similarity. *Quarterly Journal of Experimental Psychology*, **18**, 362–5.

BADDELEY, A.D. (1966b) The influence of acoustic and semantic similarity on long-term memory for word sequences. *Quarterly Journal of Experimental Psychology*, **18**, 302–9.

BADDELEY, A.D. (1976) *The Psychology of Memory*. London: Harper and Row.

BADDELEY, A.D. (1982) Domains of recollection, *Psychological Review*,

89, 708–29.

BADDELEY, A.D. (1983) *Your Memory: A User's Guide*. Harmondsworth: Penguin.

BADDELEY, A.D., ELLIS, N.C., MILES, T.R. and LEWIS, V.J. (1982) Developmental and acquired dyslexia: a comparison. *Cognition*, **11**, 185–99.

BADDELEY, A.D. and HITCH, G. (1974) Working memory. In G.H. Bower, ed., *The Psychology of Learning and Motivation*, Volume 8. New York: Academic Press.

BALES, R.F. (1970) *Personality and Interpersonal Behavior*. New York: Holt, Rinehart and Winston.

BALES, R.F. and SLATER, P.E. (1955) Role-differentiation in small decision-making groups. In T. Parsons, R.F. Bales *et al.*, eds., *Family, Socialization and Interaction Process*. New York: Free Press.

BANDURA, A.L. (1977) *Social Learning Theory*. Englewood Cliffs, NJ: Prentice-Hall.

BANNISTER, D. and MAIR, J.M.M. (1968) *The Evaluation of Personal Constructs*. London: Academic Press.

BARBER, T.X. and DE MOOR, W. (1972) A theory of hypnotic induction procedures. *American Journal of Clinical Hypnosis*, **15**, 112–35.

BARCLAY, J.R., BRANSFORD, J.D., FRANKS, J.J., McCARRELL, N.S. and NITSCH, K. (1974) Comprehension and semantic flexibility. *Journal of Verbal Learning and Verbal Behavior*, **13**, 471–81.

BARD, P.A. (1928) A diencephalic mechanism for the expression of rage with special reference to the sympathetic nervous system. *American Journal of Physiology*, **84**, 490–515.

BARON, R.A. and LAWTON, S.F. (1972) Environmental influences on aggression: the facilitation of modelling effects by high ambient temperatures. *Psychonomic Science*, **26**, 80–2.

BARTLETT, F.C. (1932) *Remembering*. Cambridge: Cambridge University Press.

BARTLETT, F.C. (1958) *Thinking: an Experimental and Social Study*. London: Allen and Unwin.

BASBAUM, A.I., CLANLON, C.H. and FIELDS, H.L. (1976) Opiate and stimulus-produced analgesia. functional anatomy of medullospinal pathways. *Proceedings of the National Academy of Science*, **73**, 4685–8.

BASSO, A., DERENZI, E. and FAGLIONI, P. (1973) Neuropsychological evidence for the existence of cerebral areas critical to the performance of intelligence tasks. *Brain*, **96**, 715–28.

BATES, E. (1976) *Language and Context: the Acquisition of Pragmatics*. New York: Academic Press.

BATESON, P.P.G. and CHANTREY, D.F. (1972) Retardation of discrimination learning in monkeys and chicks previously exposed to both stimuli. *Nature*, **237**, 173–4.

BAUMRIND, D. (1967) Child-care practices anteceding three patterns of pre-school behaviour. *Genetic Psychology Monographs*, **75**, 43–88.

BEACH, F.A. (1976) Sexual attractivity, proceptivity and receptivity in female mammals. *Hormones and Behaviour*, **7**, 105–38.

BELMONT, J.M. (1978) Individual differences in memory: the cases of normal and retarded development. In M.M. Gruneberg and P. Morris, eds., *Aspects of Memory*. London: Methuen.

BELOFF, J. (1973) *Psychological Sciences: a Review of Modern Psychology*. London: Crosby Lockwood Staples.

BELSON, W. (1975) *Juvenile Theft: the Causal Factors*. New York: Harper and Row.

BEM, D.J. (1967) Self-perception: an alternative interpretation of cognitive dissonance phenomena. *Psychological Review*, **74**, 183–200.

BEM, D.J. (1970) *Beliefs, Attitudes, and Human Affairs*. Belmont, Calif.: Brooks/Cole.

BEM, D.J. (1972) Self-perception theory. In L. Berkowitz, ed., *Advances in Experimental Social Psychology*, Volume 6. New York: Academic Press.

BENNET, T.(1979) The social distribution of criminal labels: police, 'proaction' or 'reaction'. *British Journal of Criminology*, **19**, 134–45.

BERLYNE, D.E. (1954) An experimental study of human curiosity. *British Journal of Psychology*, **45**, 256–65.

BERLYNE, D.E. (1960) *Conflict, Arousal and Curiosity*. New York: McGraw-Hill.

BERNSTEIN, B.B. (1971) *Class, Codes and Control*. St Albans: Paladin.

BIRLEY, J.T.L. and CONNOLLY, J. (1976) Life events and physical illness. In O.W. Hill, ed., *Modern Trends in Psychosomatic Medicine*, Volume 3. London: Butterworth.

BITTERMAN, M.E. (1965) Phyletic differences in learning. *American Psychologist*, **20**, 396–410.

BLAKE, M.J.F. (1971) Temperature and time of day. In W.P. Colquhoun, ed., *Biological Rhythms and Human Performance*. New York: Academic Press.

BLAKEMORE, C. and CAMPBELL, F.W. (1969) On the existence of neurons in the human visual system selectively sensitive to the orientation and size of retinal images. *Journal of Physiology*, **203**, 237–60.

BLAKEMORE, C. and COOPER, G.F. (1970) Development of the brain depends on the visual environment. *Nature*, **228**, 477–8.

BLAKEMORE, C. and SUTTON, P. (1969) Size adaptation: a new aftereffect. *Science*, **166**, 245–7.

BLEULER, E. (1950) *Dementia Praecox, or the Group of Schizophrenias*. New York: International Universities Press.

BLISS, J.C., CRANE, H.D., MANSFIELD, K. and TOWNSEND, J.T. (1966) Information available in brief tactile presentations. *Perception and Psychophysics*, **1**, 273–83.

BLOCK, N., ed. (1981) *Imagery*. Cambridge, Mass.: MIT Press.

BLOCK, N.J. and DWORKIN, G. (1974) IQ: heritability and inequality. *Philosophy and Public Affairs*, **3**, 331–407.

BLOOM, L. (1970) *Language Development: Form and Function in Emerging Grammars*. Cambridge, Mass.: MIT Press.

BODEN, M. (1977) *Artificial Intelligence and Natural Man*. Brighton: Harvester Press.

BODEN, M. (1979) *Piaget*. London: Fontana Paperbacks.

BODMER, W.F. (1972) Race and IQ: the genetic background. In K. Richardson and D. Spears, eds., *Race, Culture and Intelligence*. Harmondsworth: Penguin.

BODNER, R.J., KELLY, D.D., STEINER, S.S. and GLUSMAN, M. (1977) Stress produced analgesia and morphine produced analgesia: lack of cross tolerance. *Pharmacology, Biochemistry and Behavior*, **8**, 661–6.

BOISBAUDRAN, H.D. DE (1911) *The Training of the Memory in Art*. Translated and edited by L.D. Luard. London: Macmillan.

BOLLES, R.C. and FANSELOW, M.S. (1980) A perceptual-defensive-recuperative model of fear and pain. *Behavioral and Brain Sciences*, **3**, 291–323.

DE BONO, E. (1977) *Lateral Thinking*. Harmondsworth: Penguin.

BORGIDA, E. and NISBETT, R.E. (1977) The differential impact of abstract vs. concrete information on decisions. *Journal of Applied Social Psychology*, **7**, 258–71.

BOURNE, L.E. (1966) *Human Conceptual Behavior*. Boston: Allyn and Bacon.

BOWER, G.H. and COHEN, P.R. (1982) Emotional influences in memory and thinking: data and theory. In M.S. Clark and S.T. Fiske, eds., *Affect and Cognition*. Hillsdale, NJ: Erlbaum.

BOWER, G.H. and KARLIN, M.B. (1974) Depth of processing pictures of faces and recognition memory. *Journal of Experimental Psychology*, **103**, 751–7.

BOWER, T.G.R. (1982) *Development in Infancy*. Second edition. London: Freeman.

BOWER, T.G.R., BROUGHTON, J.M. and MOORE, M.K. (1970) Infant responses to approaching objects: an indicator of response to distal variables. *Perception and Psychophysics*, **9**, 193–6.

BOWERS, K.S. (1973) Situationism in psychology: an analysis and critique. *Psychological Review*, **80**, 307–36.

BOWLBY, J. (1969) *Attachment and Loss*, Volume 1, *Attachment*. London: Hogarth Press.

BOWLBY, J. (1980) *Attachment and Loss*, Volume 3, *Loss: Sadness and Depression*. London: Hogarth Press.

BRADLEY, B.P. and MORRIS, B.J. (1976) *Emotional Factors in Forgetting*. Part II Research Project, Cambridge University Department of Experimental Psychology.

BRADLEY, P., HORN, G. and BATESON, P. (1981) Imprinting: an electron microscope study of chick hyperstriatum ventrale. *Experimental Brain Research*, **41**, 115–20.

BRAINE, M. (1963) On learning the grammatical order of words. *Psychological Review*, **70**, 323–48.

BRANSFORD, J. (1979) *Human Cognition: Learning, Understanding and Remembering*. Belmont, Calif.: Wadsworth.

BREGGIN, P.R. (1964) The psychophysiology of anxiety, with a review of the literature concerning adrenaline. *Journal of Nervous and Mental Disease*, **139**, 558–68.

BREITMEYER, B.G. and GANZ, L. (1976) Implications of sustained and transient channels for theories of visual pattern masking, saccadic suppression, and information processing. *Psychological Review*, **83**, 1–36.

BRELAND, K. and BRELAND, M. (1972) The misbehavior of organisms. In M.E.P. Seligman and J.L. Hager, eds., *Biological Boundaries of Behavior*. New York: Appleton-Century-Crofts.

BRIDGES, K.M.B. (1932) Emotional development in infancy. *Child Development*, **3**, 324–41.

BROADBENT, D.E. (1958) *Perception and Communication*. London: Pergamon.

BROADBENT, D.E. (1971) *Decision and Stress*. London: Academic Press.

BROADBENT, D.E. (1977) Levels, hierarchies and the locus of control. *Quarterly Journal of Experimental Psychology*, **29**, 181–201.

BROADHURST, P.L. (1960) Experiments in psychogenetics. In H.J. Eysenck, ed., *Experiments in Psychology*, Volume 1. London: Routledge and Kegan Paul.

BRONFENBRENNER, U. (1979) *The Ecology of Human Development*. Cambridge, Mass.: Harvard University Press.

BROOKS, L.R. (1968) Spatial and verbal components of the art of recall. *Canadian Journal of Psychology*, **22**, 349–68.

BROWN, J. and MONK, A. (1978) Individual differences in the relation of recognition to recall. In M.M. Gruneberg, P.E. Morris and R.N. Sykes, eds., *Practical Aspects of Memory*. London: Academic Press.

BROWN, R. (1973) *A First Language: the Early Stages*. London: Allen and Unwin.

BROWN, R. (1977) Introduction. In C.E. Snow and C.A. Ferguson, eds., *Talking to Children*. Cambridge: Cambridge University Press.

BROWN, R. and FRASER, C. (1963) The acquisition of syntax. In N. Cofer and B. Musgrave, eds., *Verbal Behavior and Learning: Problems and Processes*. New York: McGraw-Hill.

BROWN, R. and LENNEBERG, E.H. (1954) A study in language and cognition. *Journal of Abnormal and Social Psychology*, **49**, 454–62.

BROWN, R. and McNEILL, D. (1966) The 'tip-of-the-tongue' phenomenon. *Journal of Verbal Learning and Verbal Behavior*, **5**, 325–37.

BRUNER, J.S. (1972) The nature and uses of immaturity. *American Psychologist*, **27**, 687–708.

BRUNER, J.S. (1975a) From communication to language – a psychological perspective. *Cognition*, **3**, 225–87.

BRUNER, J.S. (1975b) The ontogenesis of speech acts. *Journal of Child Language*, **2**, 1–19.

BRUNER, J.S. and SHERWOOD, V. (1981) Thought, language and interaction in infancy. In J. Forgas, ed., *Social Cognition: Perspectives on Everyday Understanding*. London: Academic Press.

BRYANT, P. (1974) *Perception and Understanding in Young Children: an Experimental Approach*. London: Methuen.

BUCK, R.W. (1975) Nonverbal communication of affect in children. *Journal of Personality and Social Psychology*, **31**, 644–53.

BUCK, R.W. (1977) Nonverbal communication of affect in preschool children: relationships with personality and skin conductance. *Journal of Personality and Social Psychology*, **35**, 225–36.

BUCK, R.W. (1980) Nonverbal behavior and the theory of emotion: the facial feedback hypothesis. *Journal of Personality and Social Psychology*, **38**, 811–24.

BUCK, R.W., MILLER, R.E. and CAUL, W.F. (1974) Sex, personality, and physiological variables in the communication of emotion via facial expression. *Journal of Personality and Social Psychology*, **30**, 587–96.

BUCK, R.W., SAVIN, V.J., MILLER, R.E. and CAUL, W.F. (1972) Communication of affect through facial expressions in humans. *Journal of Personality and Social Psychology*, **23**, 362–71.

BURNS, R.B. (1979) *The Self Concept*. London: Longman.

BUSS, A.H. (1966) Instrumentality of aggression, feedback, and frustration as determinants of physical aggression. *Journal of Personality and Social Psychology*, **3**, 153–62.

BYRNE, B. and ARNOLD, L. (1981) Dissociation of the recency effect and immediate memory span: evidence from beginning readers. *British Journal of Psychology*, **72**, 371–6.

CABANAC, M. (1971) The physiological role of pleasure. *Science*, **173**, 1103–7.

CAGGUILA, A.R. (1970) Analysis of the copulation-reward properties of posterior hypothalamic stimulation in male rats. *Journal of Comparative and Physiological Psychology*, **70**, 399–412.

CALEV, A., VENABLES, P.H. and MONK, A.F. (1983) Schizophrenic tendencies and memory deficits in normals. *Personality and Individual Differences*, **4**, 89–94.

CALVERT-BOYANOWSKY, J. and LEVENTHAL, H. (1975) The role of information in attenuating behavioral responses to stress: a reinterpretation of the misattribution phenomenon. *Journal of Personality and Social Psychology*, **32**, 214–21.

CAMPBELL, D.T. (1963) Social attitudes and other acquired behavioral dispositions. In S. Koch, ed., *Psychology: a Study of a Science*, Volume 6. New York: McGraw-Hill.

CAMPBELL, F.W. and KULIKOWSKI, J.J. (1966) Orientational selectivity of the human visual system. *Journal of Physiology*, **187**, 437–45.

CAMPION, J., LATTO, R. and SMITH, Y.M. (1983) Blindsight: extrastiate vision or artefact. *Behavioral and Brain Sciences*.

CANNON, W.B. (1927) The James-Lange theory of emotion: a critical examination and an alternative theory. *American Journal of Psychology*, **39**, 106–24.

CANTOR, N. and MISCHEL, W. (1979) Prototypes in person perception. In L. Berkowitz, ed., *Advances in Experimental Social Psychology*, Volume 12. New York: Academic Press.

CAREY, S. (1982) Semantic development: the state of the art. In E. Wanner and L.R. Gleitman, eds., *Language Acquisition: the State of the Art*. Cambridge: Cambridge University Press.

CARLSON, N.R. (1985) *Physiology of Behavior*. London: Allyn and Bacon.

CARON, A.J., CARON, R.F. and CARLSON, V.R. (1978) Do infants see objects or retinal images? Shape constancy revisited. *Infant Behavior and Development*, **1**, 229–43.

CARPENTER, G. (1975) Mother's face and the newborn. In R. Lewin, ed., *Child Alive*. London: Temple Smith.

CATTELL, A.B. (1971) *Abilities: Their Structure, Growth and Action*. Boston: Houghton Mifflin.

CERMAK, L.S. and CRAIK, F.I. (1979) *Levels of Processing in Human Memory*. Hillsdale, NJ: Erlbaum.

CHERRY, E.C. (1953) Some experiments on the recognition of speech, with one and two ears. *Journal of the Acoustical Society of America*, **25**, 975–9.

CHOMSKY, N. (1965) *Aspects of the Theory of Syntax*. Cambridge, Mass.: MIT Press.

CLARK, E. (1973) Non-linguistic strategies and the acquisition of word meanings. *Cognition*, **2**, 161–82.

CLARK, M.S. and ISEN, A.M. (1982) Toward understanding the relationship between feeling states and social behavior. In A. Hastorf and A.M.

Isen, eds., *Cognitive Social Psychology*. New York: Elsevier.

COHEN, G. (1977) *Psychology of Cognition*. London: Academic Press.

COLE, M., HOOD, L. and McDERMOTT, R.P. (1978) Ecological niche picking: ecological invalidity as an axiom of experimental cognitive psychology. *Laboratory of Comparative Human Cognition Newsletter*, La Jolla, Calif.

COLE, M. and SCRIBNER, S. (1974) *Culture and Thought: a Psychological Introduction*. New York: Wiley.

COLEMAN, J.C. (1976) *Abnormal Psychology and Modern Life*. Glenview, Ill.: Scott, Foresman.

COLLINS, A.M. and QUILLIAN, M.R. (1972) Experiments on semantic memory and language comprehension. In L.W. Gregg, ed., *Cognition in Learning and Memory*. New York: Wiley.

COLLINS, B.E. and HOYT, M.F. (1972) Personal responsibility for consequences: an integration and extension of the 'forced compliance' literature. *Journal of Experimental Social Psychology*, **8**, 558–93.

COLTHEART, M., MASTERSON, J., BYNG, S., PRIOR, M. and RIDDOCH, J. (1983) Surface dyslexia. *Quarterly Journal of Experimental Psychology*, **35A**, 469–95.

CONRAD, R. (1964) Acoustic confusion in immediate memory. *British Journal of Psychology*, **55**, 75–84.

CONRAD, R. (1977) The reading ability of deaf school-leavers. *British Journal of Educational Psychology*, **47**, 138–48.

CONRAD, R. (1979) *The Deaf School Child*. London: Harper and Row.

COOPER, R.M. and ZUBEK, J.P. (1958) Effects of enriched and restricted early environment on the learning ability of 'bright' and 'dull' rats. *Canadian Journal of Psychology*, **12**, 159–60.

COREY, S.M. (1937) Professed attitudes and actual behaviour. *Journal of Educational Psychology*, **28**, 271–80.

CORKINS, S. (1974) Serial-ordering deficits in inferior readers. *Neuropsychologia*, **12**, 347–54.

CORTEEN, R.S. and WOOD, B. (1972) Autonomic responses to shock associated words in an unattended channel. *Journal of Experimental Psychology*, **94**, 308–13.

COTTRELL, N.B. and EPLEY, S.W. (1977) Affiliation, social comparison, and socially mediated stress reduction. In J.M. Suls and R.M. Miller, eds., *Social Comparison Processes*. New York: Wiley.

COWEY, A. (1982) Sensory and non-sensory visual disorders in man and monkey. *Philosophical Transactions of the Royal Society*, London B, **298**, 3–13.

COWEY, A. and WEISKRANTZ, L. (1975) Demonstration of cross-modal matching in rhesus monkeys. *Neuropsychologia*, **13**, 117–20.

CRAIK, F.I.M. and LOCKHART, R.S. (1972) Levels of processing: a framework for memory research. *Journal of Verbal Learning and Verbal Behavior*, **11**, 671–84.

CRAIK, F.I.M. and WATKINS, M.J. (1973) The role of rehearsal in short-term memory. *Journal of Verbal Learning and Verbal Behavior*, **12**, 598–607.

CRAIK, F.I.M. and TULVING, E. (1975) Depth of processing and the retention of words in episodic memory. *Journal of Experimental Psychology: General*, **104**, 268–94.

CRAIK, K.J.W. (1943) *The Nature of Explanation*. Cambridge: Cambridge University Press.

CRAIK, K.J.W. (1966) *The Nature of Psychology*. Cambridge: Cambridge University Press.

CRAWFORD, H.J. (1982) Cognitive processing during hypnosis: much unfinished business. *Research Communications in Psychology, Psychiatry and Behavior*, **7**, 169–79.

CRITCHLEY, M. (1953) *The Parietal Lobes*. London: Edward Arnold.

CRITCHLEY, M. (1970) *The Dyslexic Child*. London: Heinemann.

CROMER, R. (1974) The development of language: the cognition hypothesis. In B. Foss, ed., *New Perspectives in Child Development*. Harmondsworth: Penguin.

CRONBACH, L.J. (1975) Beyond the two disciplines of scientific psychology. *American Psychologist*, **30**, 116–27.

CROSS, T.G. (1978) Mother's speech and its association with rate of linguistic development in young children. In N. Waterson and C. Snow, eds., *The Development of Communication*. Chichester: Wiley.

CROWDER, R.G. (1982a) The demise of short-term memory. *Acta Psychologica*, **50**, 291–323.

CROWDER, R.G. (1982b) General forgetting theory and the locus of amnesia. In L.S. Cermak, ed., *Human Memory and Amnesia*. Hillsdale, NJ: Erlbaum.

CURTISS, S. (1977) *Genie: a Psycholinguistic Study of a Modern-day Wild Child*. New York: Academic Press.

DAMON, W. (1977) *The Social World of the Child*. San Francisco: Jossey-Bass.

DANA, C.L. (1921) The anatomic seat of the emotions: a discussion of the James-Lange theory. *Archives of Neurology and Psychiatry*, **6**, 634.

DARWIN, C. (1872) *The Expression of the Emotions in Man and Animals*. London: Murray.

DAVIDSON, A.R. and JACCARD, J. (1979) Variables that moderate the attitude-behavior relation: results of a longitudinal survey. *Journal of Personality and Social Psychology*, **37**, 1364–76.

DAVIDSON, M. (1977) The scientific-applied debate in psychology: a contribution. *Bulletin of the British Psychological Society*, **30**, 273–8.

DAVIES A., (1977) *Language and Learning in Early Childhood*. London: Heinemann.

DAVIS, J.D., GALLAGHER, R.J., LADOVE, R.F. and TURAUSKY, A.J. (1969) Inhibition of food intake by a humoral factor. *Journal of Comparative and Physiological Psychology*, **67**, 407–14.

DEAN, P. (1982) Visual behavior in monkeys with inferotemporal lesions. In D.J. Ingle, M.A. Goodale and R.J.W. Mansfield, eds., *Analysis of Visual Behavior*. Cambridge, Mass.: MIT Press.

DELGADO, J.M.R. (1969) *Physical Control of the Mind*. New York: Harper and Row.

DEMPSTER, F.N. (1981) Memory span: sources of individual and developmental differences. *Psychological Bulletin*, **89**, 63–100.

DENENBERG, V.H. (1981) Hemispheric laterality in animals and the effects of early experience. *Behavioral and Brain Sciences*, **4**, 1–49.

DENNIS, M. and WHITAKER, H. (1976) Language acquisition following hemidecortication: linguistic superiority of the left over the right hemisphere. *Brain and Language*, **3**, 404–33.

DePAULO, B.M., ROSENTHAL, R., GREEN, C.R. and ROSENKRANTZ, J. (1982) Diagnosing deceptive and mixed messages from verbal and nonverbal cues. *Journal of Experimental Social Psychology*, **18**, 433–46.

DEUTSCH, D. (1970) Tones and numbers: specificity of interference in short-term memory. *Science*, **168**, 1605–6.

DEUTSCH, M. and GERARD, H.B. (1955) A study of normative and informational social influence upon individual judgment. *Journal of Abnormal and Social Psychology*, **51**, 629–36.

DIAMOND, M.C., DOWLING, G.A. and JOHNSON, R.E. (1981) Morphological cerebral cortical asymmetry in male and female rats. *Experimental Neurology*, **71**, 261–8.

DICKINSON, A. (1980) *Contemporary Animal Learning Theory*. Cambridge: Cambridge University Press.

DIEHL, R.L. (1981) Feature detectors for speech: a critical appraisal. *Psychological Bulletin*, **89**, 1–18.

DIXON, N.F. and HENLE, S.H.A. (1980) Without awareness. In M. Jeeves, ed., *Psychology Survey No. 3*. London: Allen and Unwin.

DIXON, N.F. (1981) *Preconscious Processing*. Chichester: Wiley.

DOISE, W. (1978) *Groups and Individuals: Explanations in Social Psychology*. Cambridge: Cambridge University Press.

DOLLARD, J., DOOB, L.W., MILLER, N.E., MOWRER, O.H. and SEARS, R.R. (1939) *Frustration and Aggression*. New Haven: Yale University Press.

DONALDSON, M. (1978) *Children's Minds*. London: Fontana Paperbacks.

DOUGLAS, R.J. (1975) The development of hippocampal function: implications for theory and therapy. In R.L. Isaacson and K.H. Pribram, eds., *The Hippocampus*, Volume 2. New York: Plenum.

DOWNER, J.L. (1962) Interhemispheric integration in the visual system. In V.B. Mountcastle, ed., *Conference of Interhemispheric Relations and Cerebral Dominance*. Baltimore: Johns Hopkins University Press.

DREW, G.C. (1973) On applied psychology in Britain. *Bulletin of the British Psychological Society*, **26**, 191-7.

DUDAI, Y. and QUINN, W.G. (1980) Genes and learning in Drosophila. *Trends in Neurosciences*, **3**, 28-30.

DUFFY, E. (1962) *Activation and Behavior*. New York: Wiley.

DUNKELD, J. and BOWER, T.G.R. (1980) Infant responses to impending optical collision. *Perception*, **9**, 549-54.

DUNN, J. (1977) *Distress and Comfort*. London: Fontana Paperbacks.

DYER, F.H. (1973) The Stroop phenomenon and its use in the study of perceptual, cognitive and response processes. *Memory and Cognition*, **1**, 106-20.

EAGLE, M., WOLITZKY, D.L. and KLEIN, G.S. (1966) Imagery: effect of a concealed figure in a stimulus. *Science*, **151**, 837-9.

EASTERBROOK, J.A. (1959) The effect of emotion on cue utilization and the organization of behaviour. *Psychological Review*, **66**, 183-201.

EDELMAN, R.I. (1972) Vicarious fear induction and avowed autonomic stereotypy. *Behavior Research and Therapy*, **10**, 105-10.

EDWARDS, J.R. (1979a) *Language and Disadvantage*. London: Edward Arnold.

EDWARDS, J.R. (1979b) Judgements and confidence in reactions to disadvantaged speech. In H. Giles and R.N. St Clair, eds., *Language and Social Psychology*. Oxford: Basil Blackwell.

EGGER, M.D. and FLYNN, J.P. (1963) Effect of electrical stimulation of the amygdala on hypothalamically elicited attack behavior in cats. *Journal of Neurophysiology*, **26**, 705-20.

EHRHARDT, A.A. and MEYER-BAHLBURG, H.F.L. (1981) Effects of prenatal sex hormones on gender-related behavior. *Science*, **211**, 1312-18.

EIBL-EIBESFELDT, I. (1970) *Ethology: the Biology of Behavior*. New York: Holt, Rinehart and Winston.

EIKELBOOM, R. and STEWART, J. (1982) Conditioning of drug-induced physiological responses. *Psychological Review*, **89**, 507-28.

EIMAS, P.D. and CORBIT, J.D. (1973) Selective adaptation of linguistic feature detectors. *Cognitive Psychology*, **4**, 99-109.

EIMAS, P.D., SIQUELAND, E.R., JUSCCZYK, P. and VIGORITO, J. (1971) Speech perception in infants. *Science*, **171**, 303-6.

EIMAS, P.D. and TARTTER, V.C. (1979) The development of speech perception. In H.W. Reese and L.P. Lipsitt, eds., *Advances in Child Development and Behavior*, Volume 13. New York: Academic Press.

EISER, J.R., ed. (1982) *Social Psychology and Behavioral Medicine.* Chichester: Wiley.

EKMAN, P. and FRIESEN, W.V. (1971) Constants across cultures in the face and emotion. *Journal of Personality and Social Psychology*, 17, 124–9.

EKMAN, P. and FRIESEN, W.V. (1975) *Unmasking the Face.* Englewood Cliffs, NJ: Prentice-Hall.

EKMAN, P., FRIESEN, W.V. and Ellsworth, P.C. (1972) *Emotion in the Human Face: Guidelines for Research and an Integration of Findings.* New York: Pergamon.

EKMAN, P., SORENSON, E.R. and FRIESEN, W.V. (1969) Pan-cultural elements in facial displays of emotion. *Science*, 164, 86–8.

ELLENBERG, L. and SPERRY, R.W. (1980) Lateralized division of attention in the commissiorotomized and intact brain. *Neuropsychologia*, 18, 411–18.

ELLIOT, A.J. (1981) *Child Language.* Cambridge: Cambridge University Press.

ELMADJIAN, F., HOPE, J.M. and LAMSON, E.T. (1957) Excretion of epinephrine and norepinephrine in various emotional states. *Journal of Clinical Endocrinology*, 17, 608–20.

EMDE, R.N., GAENSBAUER, P. and HARMAN, R.J. (1976) Emotional expression in infancy. *Psychological Issues Monograph*, Volume 37. New York: International Universities Press.

EMLEN, S.T. (1972) Celestial rotation: its importance in the development of migratory orientation. In M.E.P. Seligman and J.L. Hager, eds., *Biological Boundaries of Learning.* New York: Appleton-Century-Crofts.

ENGEN, T. and ROSS, B.M. (1973) Long-term memory of odors with and without verbal descriptions. *Journal of Experimental Psychology*, 99, 222–5.

ERDMANN, G. and JANKE, W. (1978) Interaction between physiological and cognitive determinants of emotions: experimental studies on Schachter's theory of emotions. *Biological Psychology*, 6, 61–74.

ERICSSON, K.A., CHASE, W.G. and FALOON, S. (1980) Acquisition of a memory skill. *Science*, 208, 1181–2.

ERIKSON, E.H. (1965) *Childhood and Society.* Harmondsworth: Penguin.

ERON, L.D., HUESMANN, L.R., LEFTKOWITZ, M.M. and WALDER, L.O. (1972) Does television violence cause aggression? *American Psychologist*, 27, 253–63.

ERWIN, D.E. (1976) Further evidence for two components in visual persistence. *Journal of Experimental Psychology: Human Perception and Performance*, 2, 191–209.

EVARTS, E.V. (1979) Brain mechanisms of movement. *Scientific American*, 241, 146–68.

EYSENCK, H.J. (1977) *Crime and Personality*. St Albans: Paladin.

EYSENCK, H.J. (1979) The conditioning model of neurosis. *Behavioral and Brain Sciences*, **2**, 155–99.

EYSENCK, H.J. (1982) *Personality, Genetics and Behavior: Selected Papers*. New York: Praeger.

EYSENCK, H.J. and EYSENCK, M.W. (1982) *Mindwatching*. London: Michael Joseph.

EYSENCK, H.J. and KAMIN, L. (1981) *Intelligence and the Battle for Mind*. London: Pan.

EYSENCK, H.J. and RACHMAN, S. (1965) *The Causes and Cures of Neuroses*. London: Routledge and Kegan Paul.

EYSENCK, M.W. (1979) Depth, elaboration and distinctiveness. In L.S. Cermak and F.I.M. Craik, eds., *Levels of Processing in Memory*. Hillsdale, NJ: Erlbaum.

EYSENCK, M.W. (1983) Individual differences in memory. In A.R. Mayes, ed., *Memory in Humans and Animals*. Wokingham: Van Nostrand.

EYSENCK, M.W. and EYSENCK, C. (1979) Processing depth, elaboration of encoding, memory stores, and expended processing capacity. *Journal of Experimental Psychology: Human Learning and Memory*, **5**, 472–84.

FANTZ, R.L. (1961) The origins of form perception. *Scientific American*, **204**, 66–72.

FARNHAM-DIGGORY, S. (1978) *Learning Disabilities*. London: Fontana Paperbacks.

FARNHAM-DIGGORY, S. and GREGG, L.W. (1975) Short-term memory function in young readers. *Journal of Experimental Child Psychology*, **19**, 279–98.

FAZIO, R.H. and ZANNA, M.P. (1981) Direct experience and attitude-behavior consistency. In L. Berkowitz, ed., *Advances in Experimental Social Psychology*, Volume 14. New York: Academic Press.

FAZIO, R.H., ZANNA, M.P. and COOPER, J. (1977) Dissonance and self-perception: an integrative view of each theory's proper domain of application. *Journal of Experimental Social Psychology*, **13**, 464–79.

FECHNER, G.T. (1860) *Elemente der Psychophysik*. Leipzig: Bretkopf und Hartel. (Translated by H.E. Adler, D.H. Howes and E.G. Boring. New York: Holt, Rinehart and Winston, 1966.)

FESTINGER, L. (1957) *A Theory of Cognitive Dissonance*. Evanston, Ill.: Row, Peterson.

FESTINGER, L. and CARLSMITH, J.M. (1959) Cognitive consequences of forced compliance. *Journal of Abnormal and Social Psychology*, **58**, 203–10.

FIELD, T.M., WOODSON, R., GREENBERG, R. and COHEN, D. (1982) Discrimination and imitation of facial expressions by neonates. *Science*,

218, 179–81.

FINKE, R.A. and SCHMIDT, M.J. (1978) The quantitative measure of pattern representation in images using orientation-specific color aftereffects. *Perception and Psychophysics*, **23**, 515–20.

FISHBEIN, M. (1963) An investigation of the relationship between beliefs about an object and the attitude toward that object. *Human Relations*, **16**, 233–40.

FISHBEIN, M. and AJZEN, I. (1972) Attitudes and opinions. *Annual Review of Psychology*, **23**, 487–544.

FISHBEIN, M. and AJZEN, I. (1975) *Belief, Attitude, Intention, and Behavior: an Introduction to Theory and Research*. Reading, Mass.: Addison-Wesley.

FISHER, S. and GREENBERG, R. (1977) *The Scientific Credibility of Freud's Theories and Therapy*. New York: Basic Books.

FISKE, S.T., KENNY, D.A. and TAYLOR, S.E. (1982) Structural models for the mediation of salience effects on attribution. *Journal of Experimental Social Psychology*, **18**, 105–27.

FLAVELL, J.H. (1977) *Cognitive Development*. Englewood Cliffs, NJ: Prentice-Hall.

FONTANA, D. (1982) The study of personality. *Education Section Review*, **6** (2), 97–104.

FORGAS, J.P. (1981) Affective and emotional influences on episode representations. In J.P. Forgas, ed., *Social Cognition: Perspectives on Everyday Understanding*. London: Academic Press.

FOSS, D.J. and BLANK, M.A. (1980) Identifying the speech codes. *Cognitive Psychology*, **12**, 1–31.

FRAIBERG, S. (1971) Smiling and stranger reaction in blind infants. In J. Hellmuth, ed., *Exceptional Infant*, Volume 2, *Studies in Abnormalities*. New York: Brunner-Mazel.

FRANKENHAEUSER, F. (1975) Experimental approaches to the study of catecholamines and emotion. In L. Levi, ed., *Emotions: Their Parameters and Measurement*. New York: Raven Press.

FRANKENHAEUSER, M., JARPE, G. and MATELL, G. (1961) Effects of intravenous infusions of adrenaline and noradrenaline on certain psychological and physiological functions. *Acta Physiologica Scandinavica*, **51**, 175–86.

FRANSELLA, F. (1980) Man-as-scientist. In A.J. Chapman and D.M. Jones, eds., *Models of Man*. Leicester: British Psychological Society.

FREEDLE, R. (1972) Language users as fallible information processors: implications for measuring and modeling comprehension. In R. Freedle and J. Carroll, eds., *Language Comprehension and the Acquisition of Knowledge*. Washington, DC: Winston.

FREEDMAN, D.G. (1979) Ethnic differences in babies. *Human Nature*, **2**,

36–43.

FREEMAN, N.H. (1980) *Strategies of Representation in Young Children: Analysis of Spatial Skills and Drawing Processes*. London: Academic Press.

FREUD, S. (1919/1950) *The Interpretation of Dreams*. New York: Random House.

FREUD, S. (1930) *Civilization and its Discontents*. London: Hogarth Press.

FREUD, S. (1938) *Totem and Taboo*. London: Routledge and Kegal Paul.

FREUD, (1954) *The Interpretation of Dreams*. Translated by J. Strachey. London: Allen and Unwin.

FREUD, S. (1975a) *Beyond the Pleasure Principle*. New York: Norton.

FREUD, S. (1975b) *The Psychopathology of Everyday Life*. Harmondsworth: Penguin (The Pelican Freud Library).

FRIEDMAN, M. and ROSENMAN, R.H. (1959) Association of specific overt behavior pattern with blood and cardiovascular findings. *Journal of the American Medical Association*, **169**, 1268.

FRIEDMAN, M.I. and STRICKER, E.M. (1976) The physiological psychology of hunger: a physiological perspective. *Psychological Review*, **83**, 409–31.

FURTH, H.G. (1966) *Thinking without Language*. New York: The Free Press.

FUSTER, J.M. and UYEDA, A.A. (1971) Reactivity of limbic neurons of the monkey to appetitive and aversive signals. *Electroencephalography and Clinical Neurophysiology*, **30**, 281–93.

GALE, A. (1973) The psychophysiology of individual differences: studies of extraversion and the EEG. In P. Kline, ed., *New Approaches to Psychological Measurement*. London: Wiley.

GALLUP, G.G. (1977) Self-recognition in primates. *American Psychologist*, **32**, 329–38.

GALTON, F. (1869) *Hereditary Genius*. London: Macmillan.

GARCIA, J., KIMMELDORF, D.J. and KOELLING, R.A. (1955) Conditioned aversion to saccharin resulting from exposure to gamma radiation. *Science*, **122**, 157–8.

GARCIA, J. and KOELLING, R.A. (1966) Relation of cue to consequence in avoidance learning. *Psychonomic Science*, **4**, 123–4.

GARDNER, J. (1982) Artistry following damage to the human brain. In A.W. Ellis, ed., *Normality and Pathology in Cognitive Functions*. London: Academic Press.

GARDNER, R.A. and GARDNER, B.T. (1975) Evidence for sentence constituents in the early utterances of child and chimpanzee. *Journal of Experimental Psychology: General*, **104**, 244–67.

GARVEY, C. (1977) *Play*. London: Fontana Paperbacks.

GATCHEL, R.J., HATCH, J.P., MAYNARD, A., TURNS, R. and TAUNTON-BLACKWOOD, A. (1979) Comparison of heart rate biofeedback, false biofeedback, and systematic desensitization in reducing speech anxiety: short- and long-term effectiveness. *Journal of Consulting and Clinical Psychology*, **47**, 620–2.

GAZZANIGA, M.S. (1978) Is seeing believing: notes on clinical recovery. In S. Finger, ed., *Recovery from Brain Damage*. New York: Plenum.

GEEN, R.G. and GANGE, J.J. (1977) Drive theory of social facilitation: twelve years of theory and research. *Psychological Bulletin*, **84**, 1267–88.

GEORGE, J.M. (1979) The influence of commitment on recall of consistent and inconsistent information. *Representative Research in Social Psychology*, **9**, 89–102.

GERARD, H.B., WILHELMY, R.A. and CONNELLEY, E.S. (1968) Conformity and group size. *Journal of Personality and Social Psychology*, **8**, 79–82.

GERBNER, G. and GROSS, L. (1976) The scary world of TV's heavy viewer. *Psychology Today*, **9**, 41–5.

GIBBS, M.E. and NG, K.T. (1977) Psychobiology of memory: towards a model of memory formation. *Biobehavioral Reviews*, **1**, 113–36.

GIBSON, E.J. (1969) *Principles of Perceptual Learning and Development*. New York: Appleton-Century-Crofts.

GIBSON, E.J. and WALK, R.D. (1960) The 'visual cliff'. *Scientific American*, **202**, 64–71.

GIBSON, J.J. (1966) *The Senses Considered as Perceptual Systems*. Boston: Houghton Mifflin.

GIBSON, J.J. (1979) *The Ecological Approach to Visual Perception*. Boston: Houghton Mifflin.

GIBSON, J.J., GIBSON, E.J., SMITH, O.W. and FLOCK, H.R. (1959) Motion parallax as a determinant of perceived depth. *Journal of Experimental Psychology*, **58**, 40–53.

GILINSKY, A.S. (1955) The effects of attitude upon the perception of size. *American Journal of Psychology*, **68**, 173–92.

GILLING, D. and BRIGHTWELL, R. (1982) *The Human Brain*. London: Orbis.

GINSBERG, H. and OPPER, S. (1979) *Piaget's Theory of Intellectual Development: an Introduction*. Englewood Cliffs, NJ: Prentice-Hall.

GLANZER, M. and CLARK, E.O. (1979) Cerebral mechanisms of information storage: the problem of memory. In M.S. Gazzaniga, ed., *Handbook of Behavioral Neurobiology*, Volume 2. New York: Plenum.

GLASER, A.N. (1982) Drive theory of social facilitation: a critical reappraisal. *British Journal of Social Psychology*, **21**, 265–82.

GLICK, J. (1975) Cognitive development in cross cultural perspective. In F.D. Horowitz, ed., *Review of Child Development Research*, Volume 4. Chicago: University of Chicago Press.

GLUCKSBERG, S. and KING, L.J. (1967) Motivated forgetting mediated by implicit verbal chaining. *Science*, **158**, 517–19.

GLUCKSBERG, S. and WEISBERG, R.W. (1966) Verbal behavior and problem solving: some effects of labeling in a functional fixedness problem. *Journal of Experimental Psychology*, **71**, 659–64.

GLUSHKO, R.J. (1981) Principles for pronouncing print: the psychology of phonography. In A.M. Lesgold and C.A. Perfetti, eds., *Interactive Processes in Reading*. Hillsdale, NJ: Erlbaum.

GODDARD, G.V. and DOUGLAS, R.M. (1975) Does the engram of kindling model the engram of long-term memory? *Canadian Journal of Neurological Sciences*, **2**, 385–94.

GODDEN, D.R. and BADDELEY, A.D. (1975) Context-dependent memory in two natural environments: on land and underwater. *British Journal of Psychology*, **66**, 325–31.

GODDEN, D.R. and BADDELEY, A.D. (1980) When does context influence recognition memory? *British Journal of Psychology*, **71**, 99–104.

GOLD, P.E. and McGAUGH, J.L. (1975) A single-trace, dual process view of memory storage process. In D. Deutsch and J.A. Deutsch, eds., *Short-term Memory*. New York: Academic Press.

GOODALL, J. (1978) Chimp killings: is it the man in them? *Science News*, **113**, 276.

GOODNOW, J. (1977) *Children's Drawing*. London: Fontana Paperbacks.

GOTTLIEB, G. (1965) Imprinting in relation to parental and species identification by avian neonates. *Journal of Comparative and Physiological Psychology*, **59**, 345–56.

GOTTMAN, J. and PARKHURST, J. (1980) A developmental theory of friendship and acquaintanceship processes. In *Minnesota Symposia in Child Psychology*, Volume 13.

GOY, R.W. (1966) Role of androgens in the establishment and regulation of behavioral sex differences in mammals. *Journal of Animal Science*, **25**, 21–35.

GOY, R.W. and RESKO, J.A. (1972) Gonadal hormones and behavior of normal and pseudohermaphroditic nonhuman female primates. *Recent Progress in Hormone Research*, **28**, 707–32.

GRAY, C.R. and GUMMERMAN, K. (1975) The enigmatic eidetic image: a critical examination of method, data and theories. *Psychological Bulletin*, **82**, 383–407.

GRAY, J.A. (1972) The psychophysiological nature of introversion-extraversion: a modification of Eysenck's theory. In V.D. Neblitsyn and J.A. Gray, eds., *Biological Bases of Individual Behavior*. New York: Academic Press.

GRAY, J.A. (1982) *The Neuropsychology of Anxiety: an Enquiry into the Functions of the Septal-hippocampal System*. Oxford: Oxford University Press.

GREENE, J. (1972) *Psycholinguistics: Chomsky and Psychology.* Harmondsworth: Penguin.

GREENWALD, A.G. (1968) On defining attitude and attitude theory. In A.G. Greenwald, T.C. Brock and T.M. Ostrom, eds., *Psychological Foundations of Attitudes.* New York: Academic Press.

GREENWALD, A.G. (1981) Self and memory. *Psychology of Learning and Motivation*, 15, 201–36.

GRIBBIN, J. and CHERFAS, J. (1982) *The Monkey Puzzle.* London: Bodley Head.

GRIFFIN, D.R. (1976) *The Question of Animal Awareness: Evolutionary Continuity of Mental Experience.* New York: Rockefeller University Press.

GROSS, C.G., ROCHA-MIRANDA, E.E. and BENDER, D.B. (1972) Visual properties of neurons in inferotemporal cortex of the macaque. *Journal of Neurophysiology*, 35, 96–111.

GROSSBERG, S. (1982) Processing of expected and unexpected events during conditioning and attention: a psychophysiological theory. *Psychological Review*, 89, 529–72.

GRUNEBERG, M.M. (1983) Memory processes unique to humans. In A.R. Mayes, ed., *Memory in Humans and Animals.* Wokingham: Van Nostrand.

GRUNEBERG, M.M., MORRIS, P.E. and SYKES, R.N., eds. (1978) *Practical Aspects of Memory.* London: Academic Press.

GUILFORD, J.P. (1982) Cognitive psychology's ambiguities: some suggested remedies. *Psychological Review*, 89, 48–59.

GUITON, P. (1959) Socialization and imprinting in Brown Leghorn chicks. *Animal Behaviour*, 7, 26–34.

GULEVICH, G., DEMENT, W.C. and JOHNSON, L. (1966) Psychiatric and EEG observations on a case of prolonged (264 hours) wakefulness. *Archives of General Psychiatry*, 15, 29–35.

GUR, R.C., PACKER, I.K., HUNGERBUHLER, J.P., REIVICH, M., OBRIST, W.D., AMARNEK, W.S. and SACKEIM, H.A. (1980) Differences in the distribution of gray and white matter in human cerebral hemispheres. *Science*, 207, 1226–8.

GYR, J., WILLEY, R. and HENRY, A. (1979) Motor sensory feedback and geometry of visual space: an attempted replication. *Behavioral and Brain Sciences*, 2, 59–94.

HAAS, W., ed. (1976) *Writing without Letters.* Manchester: Manchester University Press.

HABER, R.N. (1969) Eidetic images. *Scientific American*, 220, 36–44.

HAILMAN, J.P. (1969) How an instinct is learned. *Scientific American*, 221,

98–106.

HALGREN, E., SQUIRES, N.K., WILSON, C.L., ROHRBAUGH, J.W., BABB, T.L. and CRANDALE, P.H. (1980) Endogenous potentials generated in the human hippocampal formation and amygdala by infrequent events. *Science*, 210, 803–5.

HALL, J.A. (1978) Gender effects in decoding nonverbal cues. *Psychological Bulletin*, 85, 845–57.

HAMPSON, S.E. (1982) *The Construction of Personality*. London: Routledge and Kegan Paul.

HANSEL, C.E.M. (1966) *ESP: a Scientific Evaluation*. New York: Scribner.

HARKINS, S. and GREEN, R.G. (1975) Discriminability and criterion differences between extraverts and introverts during vigilance. *Journal of Research in Personality*, 9, 335–40.

HARLOW, H.F. (1959) Love in infant monkeys. *Scientific American*, 200, 68–74.

HARLOW, H.F. (1961) The development of affectional patterns in infant monkeys. In B.M. Foss, ed., *Determinants of Infant Behaviour*, Volume 1. London: Methuen.

HARLOW, H.F. (1973) *Learning to Love*. New York: Ballantine.

HARTSHORNE, H. and MAY, M.A. (1928) *Studies in the Nature of Character*, Volume 1, *Studies in Deceit*. New York: McMillan.

HASHER, L. and ZACKS, R.T. (1979) Automatic and effortful processes in memory. *Journal of Experimental Psychology: General*, 108, 356–88.

HASSETT, J. (1978) *A Primer of Psychophysiology*. San Francisco: Freeman.

HAYES, C. (1951) *The Ape in Our House*. New York: Harper.

HAYES, K.J. and NISSEN, C.H. (1971) Higher mental functions of a home raised chimpanzee. In A.M. Schrier and F. Stollnitz, eds., *Behaviour of Non Human Primates*, Volume 4. London: Academic Press.

HEBB, D.O. (1949) *The Organization of Behavior*. New York: Wiley.

HEBB, D.O. (1980) *Essays on Mind*. Hillsdale, NJ: Erlbaum.

HECKHAUSEN, H. and WEINER, B. (1980) The emergence of a cognitive psychology of motivation. In P.C. Dodwell, ed., *New Horizons in Psychology 2*. Harmondsworth: Penguin.

HEIDER, E.R. (1972) Universals in colour naming and memory. *Journal of Experimental Psychology*, 93, 10–20.

HELFER, R.E. and KEMPE, C.H. (1968) *The Battered Child*. Chicago: University of Chicago Press.

HELLIGE, J.B. and LONGSTRELH, L.E. (1981) Effects of concurrent hemisphere-specific activity on unimanual tapping rate. *Neuropsychologia*, 19, 395–405.

VON HELMHOLTZ, H. (1866) *Physiological Optics*. Translated by J.P.C. Southall. New York: Rochester.

HELSON, H. (1964) *Adaptation Level Theory*. New York: Harper and Row.

HERBERT, J. (1974) Some functions of hormones and the hypothalamus in the sexual activity of primates. *Recent Progress in Brain Research*, Volume 1. New York: Elsevier.

HERBERT, M., SLUCKIN, W. and SLUCKIN, A. (1982) Mother-to-infant bonding. *Journal of Child Psychology and Psychiatry*, 23, 205–21.

HERRMANN, D.J. and NEISSER, U. (1978) An inventory of everyday memory experiences. In M.M. Gruneberg, P.E. Morris and R.N. Sykes, eds., *Practical Aspects of Memory*. London: Academic Press.

HILGARD, E.R. (1977) *Divided Consciousness: Multiple Controls in Human Thought and Action*. New York: Wiley.

HILL, W.F. (1963) *Learning*. London: Methuen.

HILLYARD, S.A., HINK, R.F., SCHWENT, V.L. and PICTON, T.W. (1973) Electrical signs of selective attention in the human brain. *Science*, 182, 177–80.

HINDE, R.A. (1970) *Animal Behaviour: a Synthesis of Ethology and Comparative Psychology*. Second edition. New York: McGraw-Hill.

HINES, M. (1982) Prenatal gonadal hormones and sex differences in human behavior. *Psychological Bulletin*, 92, 56–80.

HITCH, G.J. (1980) Developing the concept of working memory. In G. Claxton, ed., *Cognitive Psychology: New Directions*. London: Routledge and Kegan Paul.

HOCHBERG, J. (1976) Toward a speech-plan eye-movement model of reading. In R.A. Monty and J.W. Senders, eds., *Eye Movements and Psychological Processes*. Hillsdale, NJ: Erlbaum.

HOCKETT, C.F. (1960) The origin of speech. *Scientific American*, 203, 89–96.

HOCKEY, G.R.J. (1978) Attentional selectivity and the problems of replication: a reply to Forster and Grierson. *British Journal of Psychology*, 69, 499–503.

HOHMANN, G.W. (1966) Some effects of spinal cord lesions on experienced emotional feelings. *Psychophysiology*, 3, 143–56.

HOLDING, D.H. (1979) Echoic storage. In N.S. Sutherland, ed., *Tutorial Essays in Psychology: a Guide to Recent Advances*, Volume 2. Hillsdale, NJ: Erlbaum.

HOLMES, T.H. and RAHE, R.H. (1967) The social readjustment rating scale. *Journal of Psychosomatic Research*, 11, 213.

VON HOLST, E. and MITTELSTAEDT, H. (1950) Das Reafferenzprinzip. *Naturwissenschaften*, 37, 464–76. (Translated by R. Martin in *The Behavioural Physiology of Animals and Man*, Volume 1. London: Methuen, 1973.)

HOLWAY, A.H. and BORING, E.G. (1941) Determinants of apparent visual size with distance variant. *American Journal of Psychology*, 54, 21–37.

HONIG, W.K. (1966) *Operant Behavior: Areas of Research and Application.* New York: Appleton-Century-Crofts.

VON HORNBOSTEL, E.M. (1927) The unity of the senses. *Psyche,* 7, 83–9.

HOVLAND, C.I. and JANIS, I.L., eds. (1959) *Personality and Persuasibility.* New Haven: Yale University Press.

HUBEL, D.H. and WIESEL, T.N. (1959) Receptive fields of single neurons in the cat's striate cortex. *Journal of Physiology,* 148, 574–91.

HUGHES, M. (1978) Selecting pictures of another's point of view. *British Journal of Educational Psychology,* 48, 210–19.

HUGHES, T. and GODWIN, F. (1979) *Remains of Elmet.* London: Faber and Faber.

HUMPHREY, N. (1982) Consciousness: a just-so story. *New Scientist,* 95, 474–7.

HUNT, E. (1978) The mechanism of verbal ability. *Psychological Review,* 85, 109–30.

HUNT, E. (1980) Intelligence as an information processing concept. *British Journal of Psychology,* 71, 449–74.

HUNT, R.R. and ELLIOTT, J.M. (1980) The role of non-semantic information in memory: orthographic distinctiveness effects on retention. *Journal of Experimental Psychology: General,* 109, 49–74.

HUNTER, I.M.L. (1957) *Memory: Facts and Fallacies.* Harmondsworth: Penguin.

HUNTER, M., PHILLIPS, C. and RACHMAN, S. (1979) Memory for pain. *Pain,* 6, 35–45.

HUTT, C. (1966) Exploration and play in children. *Symposia of the Zoological Society of London,* 18, 61–81.

IMPERATO-MCGINLEY, J., GUERRERO, L., GAUTIER, T. and PETERSON, R.E. (1974) Steroid 5a-reductase deficiency in man: an inherited form of male pseudohermaphroditism. *Science,* 186, 1213–15.

INGLIS, J. and LAWSON, J.S. (1981) Sex differences in the effects of unilateral brain damage on intelligence. *Science,* 212, 693–5.

INGLIS, J., RUCKMAN, M., LAWSON, J.S., MACLEAN, A.W. and MONGA, T.N. (1982) Sex differences in the cognitive effects of unilateral brain damage. *Cortex,* 18, 257–76.

INHELDER, B. and PIAGET, J. (1958) *The Growth of Logical Thinking: from Childhood to Adolescence.* London: Routledge and Kegan Paul.

ITTELSON, Q.H. (1960) *Visual Space Perception.* New York: Springer-Verlag.

IVERSEN, L.L. (1979) The chemistry of the brain. *Scientific American,* 241, 118–29.

IZARD, C.E. (1977) *Human Emotions.* New York: Plenum.

JACKSON, J.H. (1932) *Selected Writings*, Volume 2. Edited by J. Taylor. London: Hodder and Stoughton.

JACOBSON, E. (1938) *Progressive Relaxation*. Chicago: University of Chicago Press.

JACOBY, L.L. and WITHERSPOON, D. (1982) Remembering without awareness. *Canadian Journal of Psychology*, 36, 300–24.

JAHODA, G. (1969) *The Psychology of Superstition*. Harmondsworth: Penguin.

JAMES, W. (1884) What is an emotion? *Mind*, 9, 188–205.

JAMES, W. (1890) *The Principles of Psychology*. New York: Henry Holt.

JANIS, I.L. (1982) *Victims of Groupthink*. Second edition. Boston: Houghton Mifflin.

JOHN, E.R. (1972) Switchboard versus statistical theories of learning and memory. *Science*, 177, 850–64.

JOHNSON, A.K. and BUGGY, J. (1978) Periventricular preoptic-hypothalamus is vital for thirst and normal water economy. *American Journal of Physiology*, 234, R122–9.

JOHNSON-LAIRD, P., LEGRENZI, P. and SONINO LEGRENZI, M. (1972) Reasoning and a sense of reality. *British Journal of Psychology*, 63, 395–400.

JONES, G.V. (1979) Analysing memory by cuing: intrinsic and extrinsic knowledge. In N.S. Sutherland, ed., *Tutorial Essays in Psychology: a Guide to Recent Advances*, Volume 2. Hillsdale, NJ: Erlbaum.

JORM, A.F. (1979) The cognitive and neurological basis of developmental dyslexia: a theoretical framework and review. *Cognition*, 7, 19–33.

JOUVET, M. (1967) Mechanisms of the states of sleep: a neuropharmacological approach. *Research Publications of the Association for Research in Nervous and Mental Disease*, 45, 86–126.

JOYNSON, R.B. (1974) *Psychology and Common Sense*. London: Routledge and Kegan Paul.

JULESZ, B. (1971) *Foundations of Cyclopian Perception*. Chicago: University of Chicago Press.

KAGAN, A. and LEVI, L. (1975) Health and environment – psychosocial stimuli: a review. In L. Levi, ed., *Society, Stress and Disease*, Volume 2. New York: Oxford University Press.

KAHNEMAN, D. (1973) *Attention and Effort*. Englewood Cliffs, NJ: Prentice-Hall.

KAHNEMAN, D. and TVERSKY, A. (1973) On the psychology of prediction. *Psychological Review*, 80, 237–51.

KANDEL, E.R. (1976) *Cellular Basis of Behavior*. New York: Freeman.

KANDEL, E.R. and SCHWARTZ, J.H. (1982) Molecular biology of learning: modulation of transmitter release. *Science*, 218, 433–43.

KAPLAN, R.M. and SINGER, R.D. (1976) Television violence and viewer aggression: a reexamination of the evidence. *Journal of Social Issues*, **32**, 35–70.

KAY, H. (1972) Psychology today and tomorrow. *Bulletin of the British Psychological Society*, **25**, 177–88.

KEELE, S.W. (1973) *Attention and Human Performance*. Pacific Palisades, Calif.: Goodyear.

KELLEY, H.H. (1967) Attribution theory in social psychology. In D. Levine, ed., *Nebraska Symposium on Motivation*, Volume 15. Lincoln, Nebraska: University of Nebraska Press.

KELLEY, H.H. (1972) Attribution in social interaction. In E.E. Jones, D.E. Kanouse, H.H . Kelley, R.E. Nisbett, S. Valins and B. Weiner, eds., *Attribution: Perceiving the Causes of Behavior*. Morristown, NJ: General Learning Press.

KELLEY, H.H. (1973) The process of causal attribution. *American Psychologist*, **28**, 107–28.

KELLOGG, R.T. (1980) Is conscious attention necessary for long-term storage? *Journal of Experimental Psychology: Human Learning and Memory*, **6**, 379–90.

KELLY, G.A. (1955) *The Psychology of Personal Constructs*. New York: Norton.

KELMAN, H.C. and HOVLAND, C.I. (1953) 'Reinstatement' of the communicator in delayed measurement of opinion change. *Journal of Abnormal and Social Psychology*, **48**, 327–35.

KENDLER, H.H. and KENDLER, T.S. (1962) Vertical and horizontal processes in problem solving. *Psychological Review*, **69**, 1–16.

KENDON, A. (1967) Some functions of gaze direction in social interaction. *Acta Psychologica*, **26**, 22–63.

KERTESZ, A., LESK, D. and McCABE, P. (1977) Isotope localisation of infants in aphasia. *Archives of Neurology*, **34**, 590–601.

KIESLER, C.A. and KEISLER, S.B. (1969) *Conformity*. Reading, Mass.: Addison-Wesley.

KIHLSTROM, J.F. and EVANS, F.J. (1979) *Functional Disorders of Memory*. Hillsdale, NJ: Erlbaum.

KINSBOURNE, M. and COOK, J. (1971) Generalized and lateralized effects of concurrent verbalization on a unimanual skill. *Quarterly Journal of Experimental Psychology*, **23**, 341–5.

KLAUS, M. and KENNELL, J. (1976) *Maternal-infant Bonding*. St Louis: Mosby.

KLINE, P. (1981) *Fact and Fantasy in Freudian Theory*. London: Methuen.

KLÜVER, H. and BUCY, P.C. (1939) Preliminary analysis of functions of the temporal lobes in monkeys. *Archives of Neurology and Psychiatry*, **42**, 979–1000.

KÖHLER, W. (1925) *The Mentality of Apes*. New York: Harcourt Brace

Jovanovich.

KOHN, M.L. (1968) Social class and schizophrenia: a critical review. In D. Rosenthal and S.S. Kety, eds., *The Transmission of Schizophrenia*. London: Pergamon.

KOLATA, G. (1982) Food affects behavior. *Science*, 218, 1209–10.

KOLB, B. and WHISHAW, I.Q. (1980) *Fundamentals of Human Neuropsychology*. San Francisco: Freeman.

KOLERS, P.A. (1963) Some differences between real and apparent movement. *Vision Research*, 3, 191–206.

KOLERS, P.A. (1979) A pattern-recognizing basis of recognition. In L.S. Cermak and F.I.M. Craik, eds., *Levels of Processing in Human Memory*. Hillsdale, NJ: Erlbaum.

KONISHI, M. and GURNEY, M.E. (1982) Sexual differentiation of brain and behavior. *Trends of Neurosciences*, 5, (i), 20–3.

KOSSLYN, S.M. (1981) The medium and the message in mental imagery: a theory. *Psychological Review*, 88, 46–66.

KRAUT, R.E. (1982) Social presence, facial feedback, and emotion. *Journal of Personality and Social Psychology*, 42, 853–63.

KUHN, T.S. (1970) *The Structure of Scientific Revolutions*. Chicago: University of Chicago Press.

KUNST-WILSON, W.R. and ZAJONC, R.B. (1979) Affective discrimination of stimuli that cannot be recognized. *Science*, 207, 557–8.

LABOV, W. (1973) The logic of nonstandard English. In N. Keddie, ed., *Tinker, Tailor . . . the Myth of Cultural Deprivation*.Harmondsworth: Penguin.

LAHMEYER, H.W., MITLER, M. and DELEON JONES, F. (1982) Anxiety and mood fluctuations during the normal menstrual cycle. *Psychosomatic Medicine*, 44, 183–94.

LAING, R.D. (1967) *The Politics of Experience*. Harmondsworth: Penguin.

LAIRD, J. (1974) Self-attribution of emotion: the effects of expressive behavior on the quality of emotional experience. *Journal of Personality and Social Psychology*, 29, 475–86.

LAMB, M.E. (1979) Paternal influences and the father's role. *American Psychologist*, 34, 938–43.

LAMBERT, W.E. (1977) The effects of bilingualism on the individual: cognitive and sociocultural consequences. In P.A. Hornby, ed., *Bilingualism*. New York: Academic Press.

LANCASTER, J.B. (1968) *Primates: Studies in Adaptation and Variability*. New York: Holt, Rinehart and Winston.

LANZETTA, J.T., CARTWRIGHT-SMITH, J. and KLECK, R. (1976) Effects of nonverbal dissimulation on emotional experience and autonomic arousal. *Journal of Personality and Social Psychology*, 33, 354–70.

LASHLEY, K.S. (1929) *Brain Mechanisms and Intelligence*. Chicago: University of Chicago Press.

LAVOND, D.G., McCORMICK, D.A., CLARK, G.A., HOLMES, D.T. and THOMPSON, R.F. (1981) Effects of ipsilateral rostral pontine reticular lesions on retention of classically conditioned nictitating membrane and eyelid responses. *Physiological Psychology*, 9, 335–9.

LAWTON, D. (1968) *Social Class, Language and Education*. London: Routledge and Kegan Paul.

LAZARUS, R.S., AVERILL, J.R. and OPTON, E.M. (1970) Towards a cognitive theory of emotion. In M.B. Arnold, ed., *Feelings and Emotions*. New York: Academic Press.

LEAVITT, H.J. (1951) Some effects of certain communication patterns on group performance. *Journal of Abnormal and Social Psychology*, 46, 38–50.

LEE, D.N. and ARONSON, E. (1974) Visual proprioceptive control of standing in human infants. *Perception and Psychophysics*, 15, 529–32.

LE MAGNEN, J. (1971) Advances in studies on the physiological control and regulation of food intake. In E. Stellar and J.M. Sprague, eds., *Progress in Physiological Psychology*, Volume 4. New York: Academic Press.

LENNEBERG, E.H. (1967) *Biological Foundations of Language*. New York: Wiley.

LEVINE, M. and SUTTON-SMITH, B. (1973) Effects of age, sex and task on visual behaviour during dyadic interaction. *Developmental Psychology*, 9, 400–5.

LEVINE, S. (1960) Stimulation in infancy. *Scientific American*, 202, 81–6.

LEVINE, S. and BROADHURST, P.L. (1963) Genetic and ontogenetic determinants of adult behavior in the rat. *Journal of Comparative and Physiological Psychology*, 56, 423–8.

LEVY, B.A. (1981) Interactive processing during reading. In A.M. Lesgold and C.A. Perfetti, eds., *Interactive Processes in Reading*. New York: Erlbaum.

LEWIS, J.L. (1970) Semantic processing of unattended messages using dichotic listening. *Journal of Experimental Psychology*, 85, 225–8.

LEWIS, M. and BROOKS, J. (1975) Infants' reactions to people. In M. Lewis and L. Rosenblum, eds., *The Origins of Fear*. New York: Wiley.

LIBERMAN, A.M., COOPER, F.S., SHANKWEILER, D.P. and STUDDERT-KENNEDY, M. (1967) Perception of the speech code. *Psychological Review*, 74, 431–61.

LIEBELT, R.A., BORDELON, C.B. and LIEBELT, A.G. (1973) The adipose tissue and food intake. In E. Stellar and J.M. Sprague, eds., *Progress in Physiological Psychology*. New York: Academic Press.

LIEVEN, E.V.M. (1982) Context, process and progress in young children's speech. In M.C. Beveridge, ed., *Children Thinking through Language*.

London: Edward Arnold.

LIGHT, P. (1979) *The Development of Social Sensitivity*. Cambridge: Cambridge University Press.

LOEW, C.A. (1967) Acquisition of a hostile attitude and its relationship to aggressive behavior. *Journal of Personality and Social Psychology*, 5, 335–41.

LOFTUS, E.F. and LOFTUS, G.R. (1980) On the permanence of stored information in the human brain. *American Psychologist*, 35, 409–20.

LOFTUS, E.F. and PALMER, J.C. (1974) Reconstruction of automobile destruction: an example of the interaction between language and memory. *Journal of Verbal Learning and Verbal Behavior*, 13, 585–9.

LOMAS, J. (1980) Competition within the left hemisphere between speaking and unimanual tasks performed without visual guidance. *Neuropsychologia*, 18, 141–9.

LORD, C.G. (1980) Schemas and images as memory aids: two modes of processing social information. *Journal of Personality and Social Psychology*, 38, 257–69.

LORENZ, K. (1937) The companion in the bird's world. *Auk*, 54, 245–73.

LOVALLO, W.R. and PISHKIN, V. (1980) A psychophysiological comparison of Type A and B men exposed to failure and uncontrollable noise. *Psychophysiology*, 17, 29–36.

LOVELESS, N.E. and SANFORD, A.J. (1974) Effects of age on the contingent negative variation and preparatory set in a reaction-time task. *Journal of Gerontology*, 29, 52–63.

LOWE, C.F., HARZEM, P. and BAGSHAW, M. (1978) Species differences in temporal control of behavior, II: human performance. *Journal of the Experimental Analysis of Behavior*, 29, 351–61.

LURIA, A.R. (1961) *Speech and the Regulation of Behaviour*. London: Pergamon.

LURIA, A.R. (1973) *The Working Brain*. Harmondsworth: Penguin.

MACKINTOSH, N.J. (1978) Conditioning. In B.M. Foss, ed., *Psychology Survey No. 1*. London: Allen and Unwin.

MACKWORTH, N.H. and BRUNER, J.S. (1970) How adults and children search and recognize pictures. *Human Development*, 13, 149–77.

MACLEAN, P.D., DUA, S. and DENNISTON, R.H. (1963) Cerebral localization for scratching and seminal discharge. *Archives of Neurology*, 9, 485–97.

MACNAMARA, J. (1972) Cognitive basis of language learning in infants. *Psychological Review*, 79, 1–13.

MADDI, S.R. (1976) *Personality Theories: a Comparative Analysis*. Homewood, Ill.: Dorsey Press.

MAIER, S.F. and SELIGMAN, M.E.P. (1976) Learned helplessness: theory and evidence. *Journal of Experimental Psychology: General*, **105**, 3–46.

MANDLER, G. (1980) Recognizing: the judgement of previous occurrence. *Psychological Review*, **87**, 252–71.

MANNING, A. (1967) *An Introduction to Animal Behaviour*. London: Edward Arnold.

MANSTEAD, A.S.R. (1979) A role-playing replication of Schachter and Singer's (1962) study of the cognitive and physiological determinants of emotional state. *Motivation and Emotion*, **3**, 251–63.

MANSTEAD, A.S.R. and WAGNER, H.L. (1981) Arousal, cognition and emotion: an appraisal of two-factor theory. *Current Psychological Reviews*, **1**, 35–54.

MARAÑON, G. (1924) Contribution à l'étude de l'action émotive de l'adrenaline. *Revue Française d'Endocrinologie*, **2**, 301–25.

MARCEL, A.J. (1983) Conscious and unconscious perception: experiments in visual masking and word recognition. *Cognitive Psychology*, **15**, 197–237.

MARCEL, A. and PATTERSON, K. (1978) Word recognition and production: reciprocity in clinical and normal studies. In J. Requin, ed., *Attention and Performance*, Volume VII. Hillsdale, NJ: Erlbaum.

MARK, R. (1979) Concluding comments. In M.A.B. Brazier, ed., *Brain Mechanisms in Memory and Learning: from the Single Neuron to Man*. New York: Raven Press.

MARLER, P. (1981) Birdsong: the acquisition of a learned motor skill. *Trends in Neurosciences*, **4**, 88–94.

MARR, D.C. (1980) Visual information processing: the structure and creation of visual representations. *Philosophical Transactions of the Royal Society*, London B, **290**, 199–218.

MARR, D.C. (1982) *Vision*. Oxford: Freeman.

MARSHALL, J.C. and FRYER, D.M. (1978) Speak, memory! An introduction to some historic studies of remembering and forgetting. In M.M. Gruneberg and P. Morris, eds., *Aspects of Memory*. London: Methuen.

MARSHALL, J.C. and NEWCOMBE, F. (1973) Patterns of paralexia: a psycholinguistic approach. *Journal of Psycholinguistic Research*, **2**, 175–99.

MASLOW, A.H. (1970) *Motivation and Personality*. New York: Harper and Row.

MASON, J.W. (1975) Emotion as reflected in patterns of endocrine integration. In L. Levi, ed., *Emotions: Their Parameters and Measurement*. New York: Raven Press.

MASSARO, D.W. (1975) *Experimental Psychology and Information Processing*. Chicago: Rand McNally.

MAYES, A.R. (1979) The physiology of fear and anxiety. In W.S. Sluckin, ed., *Fear in Animals and Man*. Wokingham: Van Nostrand.

MAYES, A.R. (1981) The physiology of memory. In G. Underwood and R.

Stevens, eds., *Aspects of Consciousness*, Volume 2. London: Academic Press.

MAYES, A.R. (1983a) The development and course of long-term memory. In A.R. Mayes, ed., *Memory in Animals and Humans*. Wokingham: Van Nostrand.

MAYES, A.R., ed. (1983b) *Memory in Animals and Humans*. Wokingham: Van Nostrand.

MAYES, A.R. (in press) Causes and implications of human organic memory disorders. In R. Stevens, ed., *Aspects of Consciousness*, Volume 4. London: Academic Press.

MAYES, A.R., MEUDELL, P.R. and NEARY, D. (1978) Must amnesia be caused by either encoding or retrieval disorders? In M.M. Gruneberg, P.E. Morris and R.N. Sykes, eds., *Practical Aspects of Memory*. London: Academic Press.

MAZUR, A. and LAMB, T. (1980) Testosterone, status and mood in human males. *Hormones and Behavior*, 14, 236–46.

MCARTHUR, D.J. (1982) Computer vision and perceptual psychology. *Psychological Bulletin*, 92, 283–309.

MCARTHUR, L. (1972) The how and what of why: some determinants and consequences of causal attribution. *Journal of Personality and Social Psychology*, 22, 171–93.

MCARTHUR, L. (1981) What grabs you? The role of attention in impression formation and causal attribution. In E.T. Higgins, C.P. Herman and M.P. Zanna, eds., *Social Cognition: the Ontario Symposium*, Volume 1. Hillsdale, NJ: Erlbaum.

MCCABE, B.J., CIPOLLA-NETO, J., HORN, G. and BATESON, P. (1982) Amnesic effects of bilateral lesions placed in the hyperstriatum ventrale of the chick after imprinting. *Experimental Brain Research*, 48, 13–21.

MCCARLEY, R.W. (1981) Mind-body isomorphism and the study of dreams. In W. Fishbein, ed., *Sleep, Dreams and Memory*. Lancaster: MIT Press.

MCCAUL, K.D., HOLMES, D.S. and SOLOMON, S. (1982) Voluntary expressive changes and emotion. *Journal of Personality and Social Psychology*, 42, 145–52.

MCCLELLAND, D.C., ed. (1955) *Studies in Motivation*. New York: Appleton-Century-Crofts.

MCCLELLAND, J.L. and RUMELHART, D.E. (1981) An interactive activation model of context effects in letter perception. I: an account of basic findings. *Psychological Review*, 88, 375–407.

MCCOLLOUGH, C. (1965) Color adaptation of edge detectors in the human visual system. *Science*, 149, 1115–16.

MCFIE, J. (1975) *Assessment of Organic Intellectual Impairment*. London: Academic Press.

McGarrigle, J. and Donaldson, M. (1974) Conservation accidents. *Cognition*, 3, 341–50.

McGhie, A.A. and Chapman, J. (1961) Disorders of attention and perception in early schizophrenia. *British Journal of Medical Psychology*, 34, 103–16.

McGuigan, F.J. (1966) Covert oral behaviour and auditory hallucinations. *Psychophysiology*, 3, 421–8.

McGuire, W.J. (1968) Personality and susceptibility to social influence. In E.F. Borgatta and W.W. Lambert, eds., *Handbook of Personality Theory and Research*. Chicago: Rand McNally.

McGuire, W.J. (1969) The nature of attitudes and attitude change. In G. Lindzey and E. Aronson, eds., *The Handbook of Social Psychology*, Volume 3. Second edition. Reading, Mass.: Addison-Wesley.

McKay, D.G. (1973) Aspects of the theory of comprehension, memory and attention. *Quarterly Journal of Experimental Psychology*, 25, 22–40.

McLeod, P. (1977) A dual task response modality effect: support for multiprocessor models of attention. *Quarterly Journal of Experimental Psychology*, 29, 651–67.

McNeill, D. (1970) *The Acquisition of Language: the Study of Developmental Psycholinguistics*. New York: Harper and Row.

McVicar, J. (1979) *McVicar by Himself*. London: Arrow.

Meddis, R. (1979) The evolution and function of sleep. In D.A. Oakley and H.C. Plotkin, eds., *Brain, Behaviour and Evolution*. London: Methuen.

Meltzoff, A.N. and Moore, M.K. (1977) Imitation of facial and manual gestures by human neonates. *Science*, 198, 75–8.

Melzack, R. and Wall, P. (1982) *The Challenge of Pain*. Harmondsworth: Penguin.

Merton, R.K. (1957) *Social Theory and Social Structure*. New York: Free Press.

Meudell, P., Mayes, A. and Neary, D. (1980) Orienting task effects on the recognition of humorous pictures in amnesic and normal subjects. *Journal of Clinical Neuropsychology*, 2, 75–88.

Michaels, C.F. and Carello, C. (1981) *Direct Perception*. Englewood Cliffs, NJ: Prentice-Hall.

Michotte, A. (1962) *Causalité, Permanence et Réalité Phénoménales*. Louvain: Publications Universaire.

Milgram, S. (1963) Behavioral study of obedience. *Journal of Abnormal and Social Psychology*, 67, 371–8.

Milgram, S. (1964) Group pressure and action against a person. *Journal of Abnormal and Social Psychology*, 69, 137–43.

Milgram, S. (1974) *Obedience to Authority: an Experimental View*. New York: Harper and Row.

MILLER, G.A. (1956) The magical number seven, plus or minus two: some limits on our capacity for processing information. *Psychological Review*, **63**, 81–97.

MILLER, G.A. (1981) *Language and Speech*. Oxford: Freeman.

MILLER, G.A. and BUCKHOUT, R. (1973) *Psychology: the Science of Mental Life*. New York: Harper and Row.

MILLER, G.A., GALANTER, E. and PRIBRAM, K. (1960) *Plans and the Structure of Behavior*. New York: Holt, Rinehart and Winston.

MILLER, N.E. and DOLLARD, J.C. (1941) *Social Learning and Habituation*. New Haven: Yale University Press.

MILLER, N.E. and DWORKIN, B.R. (1974) Visceral learning: recent difficulties with curarized rats and significant problems for human research. In P.A. Obrist, A.H. Black, J. Brener and L.V. Dicara, eds., *Cardiovascular Psychophysiology: Current Issues in Response Mechanisms, Biofeedback and Methodology*. Chicago: Aldine Press.

MILLER, P.H. and BIGI, L. (1977) Children's understanding of how stimulus dimensions affect performance. *Child Development*, **48**, 1712–15.

MILLER, R.E. (1967) Experimental approaches to the physiological and behavioral concomitants of affective communication in rhesus monkeys. In S.A. Altmann, ed., *Social Communication among Primates*. Chicago: University of Chicago Press.

MILLER, R.E., CAUL, W.F. and MIRSKY, I.A. (1967) Communication of affects between feral and socially isolated monkeys. *Journal of Personality and Social Psychology*, **7**, 231–9.

MILLER, S.A., SHELTON, J. and FLAVELL, J.H. (1970) A test of Luria's hypotheses concerning the development of verbal self-regulation. *Child Development*, **41**, 651–65.

MILLER, W. and ERVIN, S. (1964) The development of grammar in child language. In U. Bellugi and R. Brown, eds., *The Acquisition of Language*. Chicago: University of Chicago Press.

MISCHEL, W. (1968) *Personality and Assessment*. New York: Wiley.

MISCHEL, W. (1973) Toward a cognitive social learning reconceptualization of personality. *Psychological Review*, **80**, 252–83.

MIYADI, D. (1964) Social life of Japanese monkeys. *Science*, **143**, 783–6.

MOLFESE, D.L., FREEMAN, R.B. and PALERMO, D.S. (1975) The ontogeny of brain lateralization for speech and nonspeech stimuli. *Brain and Language*, **2**, 356–68.

MONEY, J. and EHRHARDT, A.A. (1972) *Man and Woman, Girl and Boy*. Baltimore: Johns Hopkins University Press.

MORRIS, P.E. (1978) Models of long-term memory. In M.M. Gruneberg and P.E. Morris, eds., *Aspects of Memory*. London: Methuen.

MORRIS, P.E., GRUNEBERG, M.M., SYKES, R.N. and MERRICK, A. (1981)

Football: knowledge and the acquisition of new results. *British Journal of Psychology*, 72, 479–83.

MORUZZI, G. and MAGOUN, H.W. (1949) Brain stem reticular formation and activation of the EEG. *Electroencephalography and Clinical Neurophysiology*, 1, 455–73.

MOSCOVICI, S., LAGE, E. and NAFFRECHOUX, M. (1969) Influence of a consistent minority on the responses of a majority in a colour perception task. *Sociometry*, 32, 365–80.

MOSCOVICI, S. and NEMETH, C. (1974) Social influence II: minority influence. In C. Nemeth, ed., *Social Psychology: Classic and Contemporary Integrations*. Chicago: Rand McNally.

MOSCOVICI, S. and ZAVALLONI, M. (1969) The group as a polarizer of attitudes. *Journal of Personality and Social Psychology*, 12, 125–35.

MOYER, K.E. (1971) *The Physiology of Hostility*. Chicago: Markham.

MURRAY, E.J. (1965) *Sleep, Dreams and Arousal*. New York: Appleton-Century-Crofts.

MYERS, D.G. (1982) Polarizing effects of social interaction. In H. Brandstätter, J. Davis and G. Stocker-Kreichgauer, eds., *Group Decision Processes*. London: Academic Press.

NACHMAN, M. (1962) Taste preferences for sodium salts by adrenalectomised rats. *Journal of Comparative and Physiological Psychology*, 55, 1124–9.

NEBES, R. (1976) Verbal-pictorial recording in the elderly. *Journal of Gerontology*, 31, 421–7.

NEISSER, U. (1976a) *Cognition and Reality*. San Francisco: Freeman.

NEISSER, U. (1976b) General academic and artificial intelligence. In L.B. Resnick, ed., *The Nature of Intelligence*. Hillsdale, NJ: Erlbaum.

NELSON, T.O. and VINING, S.K. (1978) Effect of semantic versus structural processing on long-term retention. *Journal of Experimental Psychology: Human Learning and Memory*, 4, 198–209.

NEMETH, C., SWEDLUND, M. and KANKI, B. (1974) Patterning of the minority's responses and their influence on the majority. *European Journal of Social Psychology*, 4, 53–64.

NETTLEBECK, T. (1982) Inspection time: an index for intelligence? *Quarterly Journal of Experimental Psychology*, 34A, 299–312.

NEWPORT, E.L., GLEITMAN, H. and GLEITMAN, L.R. (1977) Mother I'd rather do it myself: some effects and non-effects of maternal speech style. In C.E. Snow and C.A. Ferguson, eds., *Talking to Children: Language Input and Acquisition*. Cambridge: Cambridge University Press.

NICKERSON, R.S. (1981) Speech understanding and reading: some differences and similarities. In O.J.L. Tzeng and H. Singer, eds., *Perception of Print*. Hillsdale, NJ: Erlbaum.

NISBETT, R.E. and BORGIDA, E. (1975) Attribution and the psychology of prediction. *Journal of Personality and Social Psychology*, **32**, 932–43.

NISBETT, R.E. and GORDON, A. (1967) Self-esteem and susceptibility to social influence. *Journal of Personality and Social Psychology*, **5**, 268–76.

NISBETT, R.E. and ROSS, L. (1980) *Human Inference: Strategies and Shortcomings of Social Judgment*. Englewood Cliffs, NJ: Prentice-Hall.

NISBETT, R.E. and SCHACHTER, S. (1966) Cognitive manipulation of pain. *Journal of Experimental Social Psychology*, **2**, 227–36.

NISBETT, R.E. and WILSON, T.D. (1977) Telling more than we know: verbal reports on mental processes. *Psychological Review*, **84**, 231–79.

NORMAN, D.A. (1969) Memory while shadowing. *Quarterly Journal of Experimental Psychology*, **21**, 85–94.

NORMAN, D.A. and BOBROW, D.B. (1975) On data-limited and resource-limited processes. *Cognitive Psychology*, **7**, 44–64.

NOTTEBOHM, F. (1982) Laterality, seasons and space govern the learning of a motor skill. *Trends in Neurosciences*, **4**, 104–6.

NOVIN, D., SANDERSON, J.B. and VANDERWEELE, D.A. (1974) The effect of isotonic glucose on eating as a function of feeding and infusion site. *Physiology and Behavior*, **13**, 3–7.

NOVIN, D., VANDERWEELE, D.A. and REZEK, M. (1973) Hepatic-portal 2-deoxy-D-glucose infusion causes eating: evidence for peripheral glucoreceptors. *Science*, **181**, 858–60.

OAKLEY, D.A. (1978) Cerebral cortex and adaptive behaviour. In D.A. Oakley and H.C. Plotkin, eds., *Brain, Behaviour and Evolution*. London: Methuen.

OAKLEY, D.A. (1983) The varieties of memory: a phylogenetic approach. In A.R. Mayes, ed., *Memory in Humans and Animals*. Wokingham: Van Nostrand.

O'BRYAN, K.G. and BOERSMA, F.J. (1971) Eye movements, perceptual activity and conservation development. *Journal of Experimental Child Psychology*, **12**, 157–69.

OLDS, J., DISTERHOFT, J.F., SEGAL, M., KORNBLITH, C.L. and HIRSH, R. (1972) Learning centers of the rat mapped by measuring the latencies of condition unit responses. *Journal of Neuronography Biology*, **35**, 202–19.

OLDS, J. and MILNER, O. (1954) Positive reinforcement produced by electrical stimulation of septal area and other regions of the rat brain. *Journal of Comparative and Physiological Psychology*, **47**, 419–27.

OLDS, M.E. and FOBES, J.L. (1981) The central basis of motivation: intracranial self-stimulation studies. *Annual Review of Psychology*, **32**, 523–74.

OLSON, D. (1970) Language and thought: aspects of a cognitive theory of semantics. *Psychological Review*, **77**, 257–73.

OLSON, D. (1972) Language use for communicating, instructing and thinking. In R. Freedle and J.B. Carroll, eds., *Language Comprehension and the Acquisition of Knowledge*. Washington, DC: Winston.

OLSON, D. (1977) From utterance to text: the bias of language in speech and writing. *Harvard Educational Review*, **47**, 257–82.

OLSON, D. and TORRANCE, N. (1983) Literacy and cognitive development: a conceptual transformation in the early school years. In S. Meadows, ed., *Developing Thinking*. London: Methuen.

ORVIS, B.R., CUNNINGHAM, J.D. and KELLEY, H.H. (1975) A closer examination of causal inference: the roles of consensus, distinctiveness and consistency information. *Journal of Personality and Social Psychology*, **32**, 605–16.

OSGOOD, C.E. (1966) Dimensionality of the semantic space for communication via facial expression. *Scandinavian Journal of Psychology*, **7**, 1–30.

OSTER, H. (1978) Facial expression and affect development. In M. Lewis and L.A. Rosenblum, eds., *The Development of Affect*. New York: Plenum.

OSWALD, I. (1974) *Sleep*. Harmondsworth: Penguin.

PAGE, M.M. (1969) Social psychology of a classical conditioning of attitudes experiment. *Journal of Personality and Social Psychology*, **11**, 177–86.

PAIVIO, A. (1969) Mental imagery in associative learning and memory. *Psychological Review*, **76**, 241–63.

PAIVIO, A. and LINDE, J.T. (1982) Imagery, memory and the brain. *Canadian Journal of Psychology*, **36**, 243–72.

PAPERT, S. (1980) *Mindstorms*. Brighton: Harvester Press.

PAPEZ, J.W. (1937) A proposed mechanism of emotion. *Archives of Neurology and Psychiatry*, **38**, 725–43.

PARKE, R.D. (1981) *Fathering*. London: Fontana Paperbacks.

PARKE, R.D., BERKOWITZ, L., LEYENS, J.P., WEST, S.G. and SEBASTIAN, R.J. (1977) Some effects of violent and non-violent movies on the behavior of juvenile delinquents. In L. Berkowitz, ed., *Advances in Experimental Social Psychology*, Volume 10. New York: Academic Press.

PARKINSON, B. and MANSTEAD, A.S.R. (1981) An examination of the roles played by meaning of feedback and attention to feedback in the Valins effect. *Journal of Personality and Social Psychology*, **38**, 725–43.

PASSINGHAM, R. (1982) Why chimpanzees are not people. *New Scientist*,

96, 288–91.

PATTERSON, K.E. and MARCEL, A.J. (1977) Aphasia, dyslexia and the phonological coding of written words. *Quarterly Journal of Experimental Psychology*, **29**, 307–18.

PATTERSON, M.L. (1976) An arousal model of interpersonal intimacy. *Psychological Review*, **83**, 235–45.

PENFIELD, W. and JASPER, M. (1954) *Epilepsy and the Functional Anatomy of the Human Brain*. Boston: Little, Brown.

PERKY, C.W. (1910) An experimental study of imagination. *American Journal of Psychology*, **21**, 422–52.

PERLOW, M.J., FREED, W.J., HOFFER, B.J., SEIGER, A., OLSON, L. and WYATT, R.J. (1979) Brain grafts reduce motor abnormalities produced by destruction of nigrostriatal dopamine system. *Science*, **204**, 643–5.

PERRETT, D.I., ROLLS, E.T. and CAAN, W. (1982) Visual neurones responsive to faces in the monkey temporal cortex. *Experimental Brain Research*, **47**, 329–42.

PERVIN, L.A. and LEWIS, M., eds. (1978) *Perspectives in Interactional Psychology*. New York: Plenum.

PETTIGREW, J.D. (1978) The locus coeruleus and cortical plasticity. *Trends in Neurosciences*, **1**, 73–4.

PETTY, R.E. and CACIOPPO, J.T. (1981) *Attitudes and Persuasion: Classic and Contemporary Approaches*. Dubuque, Iowa: William C. Brown.

PFEIFFER, J.E. (1970) *The Emergence of Man*. London: Nelson.

PIAGET, J. (1932) *The Moral Judgement of the Child*. London: Routledge and Kegan Paul.

PIAGET, J. (1937) *The Construction of Reality in the Child*. London: Routledge and Kegan Paul.

PIAGET, J. (1950) *The Psychology of Intelligence*. London: Routledge and Kegan Paul.

PIAGET, J. (1952) *The Child's Conception of Number*. London: Routledge and Kegan Paul.

PIAGET, J. (1959) *The Language and Thought of the Child*. London: Routledge and Kegan Paul.

PIAGET, J. (1970) Piaget's theory. In P.H. Mussen, ed., *Carmichael's Handbook of Child Psychology*, Volume 1. New York: Wiley.

PIAGET, J. (1972) Intellectual evolution from adolescence to adulthood. *Human Development*, **15**, 1–21.

PIAGET, J. and INHELDER, B. (1973) *Memory and Intelligence*. New York: Basic Books.

PINCUS, J.H. and TUCKER, G.J. (1974) *Behavioural Neurology*. Oxford: Oxford University Press.

PLUTCHIK, R. (1980) *Emotion: A Psychoevolutionary Synthesis*. New York: Harper and Row.

POLLARD, P. (1982) Human reasoning: some possible effects of availability. *Cognition*, **12**, 65–96.

POPPER, K. (1959) *The Logic of Scientific Discovery*. New York: Basic Books.

POSNER, M.I. and SNYDER, C.R.R. (1975) Attention and cognitive control. In R.L. Solso, ed., *Information Processing and Cognition. The Loyola Symposium*. Hillsdale, NJ: Erlbaum.

VAN PRAAG, H.M. (1977) Significance of biochemical parameters in the diagnosis, treatment and prevention of depressive disorders. *Biological Psychiatry*, **12**, 101–31.

PRIBRAM, K.H. and McGUINNESS, D. (1975) Arousal, activation and effort in the control of attention. *Psychological Review*, **82**, 116–49.

PUTNAM, B. (1979) Hypnosis and distortions in eyewitness memory. *International Journal of Clinical and Experimental Hypnosis*, **27**, 437–48.

PYLE, D.W. (1979) *Intelligence*. London: Routledge and Kegan Paul.

QUINN, W.G. and GOULD, J.L. (1979) Nerves and genes.*Nature*, **278**, 19–23.

RABBITT, P.M.A. (1979) Some experiments and a model for changes in attentional selectivity with old age. In F. Heffmeister and C. Muller, eds., *Brain Function in Old Age*. Berlin: Springer-Verlag.

RABINOWITZ, J.C., CRAIK, F.I.M. and ACKERMAN, B.P. (1982) A processing resource acccunt of age differences in recall. *Canadian Journal of Psychology*, **36**, 325–44.

RACHMAN, S. (1974) *The Meanings of Fear*. Harmondsworth: Penguin.

RATCLIFF, G. and NEWCOMBE, F. (1982) Object recognition: some deductions from the clinical evidence. In A.W. Ellis, ed., *Normality and Pathology in Cognitive Functions*. London: Academic Press.

RAYNER, K. (1981) Eye movements and the perceptual span in reading. In F.J. Pirozzolo and M.C. Whitrock, eds., *Neuropsychological and Cognitive Processes in Reading*. New York: Academic Press.

REASON, J. (1979) Actions not as planned: the price of automatization. In G. Underwood and R. Stevens, eds., *Aspects of Consciousness*, Volume 1, *Psychological Issues*. London: Academic Press.

REES , W.D. and LUTKINS, S.G. (1967) Mortality of bereavement. *British Medical Journal*, **4**, 13.

REYES, R.M., THOMPSON, W.C. and BOWER, G.H. (1980) Judgmental biases resulting from differing availabilities of arguments. *Journal of Personality and Social Psychology*, **39**, 2–12.

ROBBINS, T. (1978) A strange scientific tail. *New Scientist*, **80**, 794–6.

ROBBINS, T.W. and KOOB, G.F. (1980) Selective disruption behaviour by lesions of the mesolimbic dopamine system. *Nature*, **285**, 1–3.

ROBINSON, W.P. (1981) Language development in young children. In D. Fontana, *Psychology for Teachers*. London: BPS and Macmillan.

ROCHESTER, S. and MARTIN, J.R. (1979) *Crazy Talk: a Study of the Discourse of Schizophrenic Speakers*. New York: Plenum.

ROCK, I. and EBENHOLTZ, S. (1962) Stroboscopic movement based on change of phenomenal rather than visual location. *American Journal of Psychology*, **75**, 193–207.

ROGERS, C.R. (1951) *Client Centered Therapy*. Boston: Houghton Mifflin.

ROGERS, C.R. (1959) A theory of therapy, personality and interpersonal relationships as developed in the client-centered framework. In S. Koch, ed., *Psychology: a Study of Science*, Volume 3. New York: McGraw-Hill.

ROGERS, R.W. and MEWBORN, R. (1976) Fear appeals and attitude change: effects of a threat's noxiousness, probability of occurrence, and the efficacy of coping responses. *Journal of Personality and Social Psychology*, **34**, 54–61.

ROSCH, E. (1973) Natural categories. *Cognitive Psychology*, **4**, 328–50.

ROSE, S.P.R., HAMBLEY, J. and HEYWOOD, J. (1976) Neurochemical approaches to developmental plasticity and learning. In M.R. Rosenzweig and E.L. Bennett, eds., *Neural Mechanisms of Learning and Memory*. Cambridge, Mass.: MIT Press.

ROSENBERG, L.A. (1961) Group size, prior experience, and conformity. *Journal of Abnormal and Social Psychology*, **63**, 436–7.

ROSENBERG, M.J. and HOVLAND, C.I. (1960) Cognitive, affective and behavioral components of attitudes. In C.I. Hovland and M.J. Rosenberg, eds., *Attitude Organization and Change*. New Haven: Yale University Press.

ROSENHAN, D.L. (1973) On being sane in insane places. *Science*, **179**, 250–8.

ROSENTHAL, D. (1970) *Genetic Theory and Abnormal Behavior*. New York: McGraw-Hill.

ROSENTHAL, R. (1966) *Experimenter Effects in Behavioral Research*, New York: Appleton-Century-Crofts.

ROSENTHAL, R. and JACOBSON, L.F. (1968) *Pygmalion in the Classroom: Teacher Expectation and Pupils' Intellectual Development*. New York: Holt, Rinehart and Winston.

ROSENZWEIG, M.R. and BENNETT, E.L. (1976) Enriched environments: facts, factors and fantasies. In J.L. McGaugh and L. Petrinovich, eds., *Knowing, Thinking, and Believing*. New York: Plenum.

ROSS, L. (1977) The intuitive psychologist and his shortcomings: distortions in the attribution process. In L. Berkowitz, ed., *Advances in Experimental Social Psychology*, Volume 10. New York: Academic Press.

788   References

ROSVOLD, H.E., MIRSKY, M. and PRIBRAM, K.H. (1954) Influence of amygdalectomy on social behavior in monkeys. *Journal of Comparative and Physiological Psychology*, 47, 173–8.

RUBENSTEIN, H., LEWIS, S.S. and RUBENSTEIN, M.A. (1971) Evidence for phonemic recoding in visual word recognition. *Journal of Verbal Learning and Verbal Behavior*, 10, 645–57.

RUBIN, Z. (1980) *Children's Friendships*. London: Fontana Paperbacks.

RUBLE, D.N. (1977) Premenstrual symptoms: a reinterpretation. *Science*, 197, 291–2.

RUTTER, M. (1978) Early sources of security and competence. In J.S. Bruner and A. Garton, eds., *Human Growth and Development*. Oxford: Oxford University Press.

RYLE, G. (1949) *The Concept of Mind*. London: Hutchinson.

SAARNI, C. (1978) Cognitive and communicative features of emotional experience, or do you show what you think you feel? In M. Lewis and L.A. Rosenblum, eds., *The Development of Affect*. New York: Plenum.

SAKITT, B. (1976) Iconic memory. *Psychological Review*, 83, 257–76.

SANDERS, G.S. (1981) Driven by distraction: an integrative review of social facilitation theory and research. *Journal of Experimental Social Psychology*, 17, 227–51.

SCARR, S. and WEINBERG, R.A. (1977) IQ test performance of black children adopted by white families. *American Psychologist*, 31, 726–39.

SCHACHTER, J. (1957) Pain, fear and anger in hypertensives and normotensives: a psychophysiologic study. *Psychosomatic Medicine*, 19, 17–29.

SCHACHTER, S. (1951) Deviation, rejection, and communication. *Journal of Abnormal and Social Psychology*, 46, 190–207.

SCHACHTER, S. (1959) *The Psychology of Affiliation*. Stanford, Calif.: Stanford University Press.

SCHACHTER, S. (1964) The interaction of cognitive and physiological determinants of emotional state. In L. Berkowitz, ed., *Advances in Experimental Social Psychology*, Volume 1. New York: Academic Press.

SCHACHTER, S. (1971) *Emotion, Obesity, and Crime*. New York: Academic Press.

SCHACHTER, S. and GROSS, L.P. (1968) Manipulated time and eating behavior. *Journal of Personality and Social Psychology*, 10, 98–106.

SCHACHTER, S. and SINGER, J.E. (1962) Cognitive, social and physiological determinants of emotional state. *Psychological Review*, 69, 379–99.

SCHAERLAEKENS, A. (1973) *The Two-word Sentence in Child Language Development*. The Hague: Mouton.

SCHAFFER, H.R. (1977) *Mothering*. London: Fontana Paperbacks.

SCHANK, R.C. and ABELSON, R.P. (1977) *Scripts, Plans, Goals, and Understanding*. Hillsdale, NJ: Erlbaum.

SCHATZMAN, M. (1980) Evocations of unreality. *New Scientist*, **87**, 935–7.

SCHILDKRAUT, J.J. (1965) The catecholamine hypothesis of affective disorders: a review of supporting evidence. *American Journal of Psychiatry*, **122**, 509–22.

SCHLESINGER, I.M. (1971) Production of utterances and language acquisition. In D.I. Slobin, ed., *The Ontogenesis of Grammar*. New York: Academic Press.

SCHLOSBERG, H.S. (1941) A scale for the judgement of facial expression. *Journal of Experimental Psychology*, **29**, 497–510.

SCHNEIDER, D.J., HASTORF, A.H. and ELLSWORTH, P.C. (1979) *Person Perception*. Second edition. Reading, Mass.: Addison-Wesley.

SCHNEIDER, G.E. (1979) Is it really better to have your brain lesion early? A revision of the 'Kennard principle'. *Neuropsychologia*, **17**, 557–83.

SCOTT, J.P. (1958) Critical periods in the development of social behavior in puppies. *Psychosomatic Medicine*, **20**, 42–54.

SCOTT, J.P. (1963) The process of primary socialization in canine and human infants. *Monographs of the Society for Research in Child Development*, **28**, 1–47.

SCRIBNER, S. and COLE, M. (1973) Cognitive consequences of formal and informal education. *Science*, **182**, 553–9.

SEARS, R.R., MACCOBY, E.E. and LEVIN, H. (1957) *Patterns of Child Rearing*. Evanston, Ill.: Row, Peterson.

SECORD, P.F. and BACKMAN, C.W. (1964) *Social Psychology*. New York: McGraw-Hill.

SELIGMAN, M.E.P. and HAGER, J.L., eds. (1972) *Biological Boundaries of Learning*. New York: Appleton-Century-Crofts.

SELMAN, R. (1976) Toward a structural analysis of developing interpersonal relations concepts: research with normal and disturbed preadolescent boys. In A. Pick, ed., *Minnesota Symposia on Child Psychology*, Volume 10. Minneapolis: University of Minnesota Press.

SELYE, H. (1950) *The Physiology and Pathology of Exposure to Stress*. Montreal: Acta.

SENTIS, K.P. and BURNSTEIN, E. (1979) Remembering schema-consistent information: effects of a balance schema on recognition memory. *Journal of Personality and Social Psychology*, **37**, 2200–11.

SEYFARTH, R.M., CHENEY, D.L. and MARLER, P. (1980) Monkey responses to three different alarm calls: evidence of predator clarification and semantic communication. *Science*, **210**, 801–3.

SHALLICE, T. (1982) Specific impairments of planning. *Philosophical Transactions of the Royal Society*, London B, **298**, 199–209.

SHALLICE, T. and EVANS, M.E. (1978) The involvement of the frontal lobes in cognitive estimation. *Cortex*, **14**, 294–303.

SHALLICE, T. and WARRINGTON, E.K. (1977) Auditory-verbal short-term memory impairment and conduction aphasia. *Brain and Language*, 4, 479–91.

SHALLICE, T. and WARRINGTON, E.K. (1980) Single and multiple component central dyslexic syndromes. In M. Coltheart, K.E. Patterson and J.C. Marshall, eds., *Deep Dyslexia*. London: Routledge and Kegan Paul.

SHATZ, M. (1978) The relationship between cognitive processes and the development of communication skills. In B. Keasey, ed., *Nebraska Symposium on Motivation*. Nebraska: University of Nebraska Press.

SHATZ, M. and GELMAN, R. (1973) The development of communication skills: modification in the speech of young children as a function of the listener. *Monographs of the Society for Research in Child Development*, 38, no. 152.

SHAW, M.E. (1976) *Group Dynamics: the Psychology of Small Group Behavior*. Second edition. New York: McGraw-Hill.

SHEPARD, R.N. and METZLER, J. (1971) Mental rotation of three-dimensional objects. *Science*, 171, 701–3.

SHERIF, M. (1935) A study of some social factors in perception. *Archives of Psychology*, 27, no. 187, 1–60.

SHERIF, M. (1967) *Group Conflict and Cooperation*. London: Routledge and Kegan Paul.

SHERRINGTON, C.S. (1900) Experiments on the value of vascular and visceral factors for the genesis of emotion. *Proceedings of the Royal Society*, 66, 390–403.

SHERRINGTON, C.S. (1906) *The Integrative Action of the Nervous System*. London: Constable.

SHULMAN, H.G. (1972) Semantic confusion errors in short-term memory. *Journal of Verbal Learning and Verbal Behavior*, 11, 221–7.

SINCLAIR, H. (1969) Developmental psycholinguistics. In D. Elkind and J.H. Flavell, eds., *Studies in Cognitive Development: Essays in Honor of Jean Piaget*. New York: Oxford University Press.

SIROTA, A., SCHWARTZ, G.E. and SHAPIRO, D. (1974) Voluntary control of human heart rate: effect on reaction to aversive stimulation. *Journal of Abnormal Psychology*, 83, 261–7.

SKINNER, B.F. (1938) *The Behavior of Organisms*. New York: Appleton-Century-Crofts.

SKINNER, B.F. (1957) *Verbal Behavior*. New York: Appleton-Century-Crofts.

SKINNER, B.F. (1971) *Beyond Freedom and Dignity*. New York: Knopf.

SLATER, A., MORISON, V. and ROSE, D. (1982) Visual memory at birth. *British Journal of Psychology*, 73, 519–25.

SLOBIN, D.I. (1973) Cognitive prerequisites for the acquisition of grammar. In C.A. Ferguson and D.I. Slobin, eds., *Studies of Child Language*

Development. New York: Holt, Rinehart and Winston.

SLOBIN, D.I. (1979) Why one can't run a grammatical machine with a sensory motor. Paper given at Biennial Meeting of the Society for Research in Child Development, San Francisco.

SMITH, B.L., LASSWELL, H.D. and CASEY, R.D. (1946) *Propaganda, Communication, and Public Opinion*. Princeton, NJ: Princeton University Press.

SMITH, M.C. (1975) Children's use of the multiple sufficient cause schema in social perception. *Journal of Personality and Social Psychology*, 32, 737–47.

SMITH, S.D., KIMBERLEY, W.J., PENNINGTON, B.F. and LUBS, H.A. (1983) Specific reading disability: identification of an inherited form through linkage analysis. *Science*, 219, 1345–7.

SNOW, C.E. and FERGUSON, C.A., eds. (1977) *Talking to Children: Language Input and Acquisition*. Cambridge: Cambridge University Press.

SNYDER, M. and SWANN, W.B. (1978) Behavioural confirmation in social interaction: from social perception to social reality. *Journal of Experimental Social Psychology*, 14, 148–62.

SNYDER, M., TANKE, E.D. and BERSCHEID, E. (1977) Social perception and interpersonal behavior: on the self-fulfilling nature of social stereotypes. *Journal of Personality and Social Psychology*, 35, 656–66.

SOKOLOV, E.N. (1977) Brain functions: neuronal mechanisms of learning and memory. *Annual Review of Psychology*, 28, 85–112.

SPEARMAN, C. (1904) General intelligence objectively determined and measured. *American Journal of Psychology*, 15, 201–92.

SPEARMAN, C. and JONES, L.L. (1950) *Human Abilities*. London: Macmillan.

SPERLING, G. (1960) The information available in brief visual presentations. *Psychological Monographs*, 74.

SPERLING, G. (1963) A model for visual memory tasks. *Human Factors*, 5, 19–31.

SPERRY, R.W., ZAIDEL, E. and ZAIDEL, D. (1979) Self recognition and social awareness in the deconnected minor hemisphere. *Neuropsychologia*, 17, 153–66.

SPIRO, R.J. (1980) Accommodative reconstruction in prose recall. *Journal of Verbal Learning and Verbal Behavior*, 19, 84–95.

SPRING, C. and CAPPS, C. (1974) Encoding speed, rehearsal and probed recall of dyslexic boys. *Journal of Educational Psychology*, 66, 780–6.

SPRINGER, S.P. and DEUTSCH, G. (1981) *Left Brain, Right Brain*. Oxford: Freeman.

SQUIRE, L.R., COHEN, N.J. and NADEL, L. (in press) The medial temporal region and memory consolidation: a new hypothesis. In H. Weingartner and E. Parker, eds., *Memory Consolidation*. Hillsdale, NJ: Erlbaum.

STAATS, A.W. and STAATS, C.K. (1958) Attitudes established by classical conditioning. *Journal of Abnormal and Social Psychology*, **57**, 37–40.

STAFFORD-CLARK, D. and SMITH, A.C. (1979) *Psychiatry for Students*. London: Allen and Unwin.

STANLEY, G. and HALL, R. (1973) Short-term visual information processing in dyslexics. *Child Development*, **44**, 841–4.

STERIADE, M. (1983) Cellular mechanism of wakefulness and slow-wave sleep. In A. Mayes, ed., *Sleep Mechanisms and Functions in Humans and Animals*. Wokingham: V. Nostrand.

STERN, D. (1974) Mother and infant at play: the dyadic interaction involving facial, vocal and gaze behaviors. In M. Lewis and L. Rosenblum, eds., *The Effect of the Infant on its Caregiver*. New York: Wiley.

STERN, D. (1977) *The First Relationship: Mother and Infant*. London: Fontana Paperbacks.

STERNBACH, R.A. (1962) Assessing differential autonomic patterns in emotions. *Journal of Psychosomatic Research*, **6**, 87–91.

STERNBERG, R.J. (1980) Sketch of a componential subtheory of human intelligence. *Behavioral and Brain Sciences*, **3**, 573–614.

STEVENS, K.N. and HALLE, M. (1967) Remarks on analysis by synthesis and distinctive features. In W. Wathen-Dunn, ed., *Models for the Perception of Speech and Visual Form*. Cambridge, Mass.: MIT Press.

STEVENS, R. and GOLDSTEIN, R. (1978) Effects of neonatal testosterone and progesterone on open-field behaviour in the rat. *Quarterly Journal of Experimental Psychology*, **30**, 157–66.

STEVENS, R. and GOLDSTEIN, R. (1983) Organizational effects of neonatal and pubertal testosterone on sexually differentiated behaviours in the open-field and head-dip apparatus. *Quarterly Journal of Experimental Psychology*, **35B**, 81–92.

STEVENSON, W. (1983) *The Study of Behavior: Q-Technique and its Methodology*. Chicago: Chicago University Press.

STONE, A. (1975) *Mental Health and Law: a System in Transition*. Washington, DC: US Department of Health, Education and Welfare.

STONER, J.A.F. (1961) A comparison of individual and group decisions involving risk. Unpublished doctoral dissertation, MIT, School of Industrial Management.

STROYMEYER, C.F. and PSOTKA, J. (1970) The detailed texture of eidetic images. *Nature*, **225**, 346–9.

SZASZ, T.S. (1960) The myth of mental illness. *American Psychologist*, **15**, 113–18.

TAJFEL, H. (1969) Cognitive aspects of prejudice. *Journal of Social Issues*, **25**, 79–97.

TAJFEL, H. (1978) Interindividual behaviour and intergroup behaviour. In

H. Tajfel, ed., *Differentiation between Social Groups: Studies in the Social Psychology of Intergroup Relations*. London: Academic Press.

TAJFEL, H. (1981) *Human Groups and Social Categories: Studies in Social Psychology*. Cambridge: Cambridge University Press.

TAJFEL, H., BILLIG, M., BUNDY, R.P. and FLAMENT, C. (1971) Social categorization and intergroup behaviour. *European Journal of Social Psychology*, 1, 149–78.

TAJFEL, H. and TURNER, J.C. (1979) An integrative theory of intergroup conflict. In W.G. Austin and S. Worchel, eds., *The Social Psychology of Intergroup Relations*. Monterey, Calif.: Brooks/Cole.

TAJFEL, H. and WILKES, A.L. (1963) Classification and quantitative judgment. *British Journal of Psychology*, 54, 101–14.

TANAKA, D. (1973) Effects of selective prefrontal decortication on escape behavior in the monkey. *Brain Research*, 53, 161–73.

TANNER, J. and INHELDER, B., eds. (1960) *Discussions in Child Development*, Volume 4. London: Tavistock.

TAYLOR, S.E. and THOMPSON, S.C. (1982) Stalking the elusive 'vividness' effect. *Psychological Review*, 89, 155–81.

TEITELBAUM, P. (1971) The encephalization of hunger. In E. Stellar and J.M. Sprague, eds., *Progress in Physiological Psychology*, Volume 4. London: Academic Press.

TERLECKI, L.J., PINEL, J.P.J. and TREIT, D. (1979) Conditioned and unconditioned defensive burrowing in the rat. *Learning and Motivation*, 10, 337–50.

TERRACE, H.S., PETITTO, L.A., SANDERS, R.J. and BEVER, T.G. (1979) Can an ape create a sentence? *Science*, 206, 891–902.

TERTEL, J. and ROSENBLATT, J.S. (1968) Maternal behavior induced by maternal blood plasma injected into virgin rats. *Journal of Comparative and Physiological Psychology*, 65, 479–82.

THOMAS, A. and CHESS, S. (1977) *Temperament and Development*. New York: Brunner-Mazel.

THOMPSON, R. (1982) Evidence that the occipital cortex also functions in place learning in rats. In C. Ajmone-Marsan and H. Matthies, eds., *Neuronal Plasticity and Memory Formation*. New York: Raven Press.

THORPE, W.H. (1972) The comparison of vocal communication in animals and man. In R.A. Hinde, ed., *Non-verbal Communication*. Cambridge: Cambridge University Press.

TIGHE, T.J. and LEATON, R.N. (1976) *Habituation: Perspectives from Child Development, Animal Behavior and Neurophysiology*. Hillsdale, NJ: Erlbaum.

TINBERGEN, N. (1951) *The Study of Instinct*. London: Oxford University Press.

TOURANGEAU, R. and ELLSWORTH, P.C. (1979) The role of facial response in the experience of emotion. *Journal of Personality and Social Psychology*, **37**, 1519–31.

TREISMAN, A. (1960) Contextual cues in selective listening. *Quarterly Journal of Experimental Psychology*, **12**, 242–8.

TREISMAN, A. (1964) Monitoring and storage of irrelevant messages in selective attention. *Journal of Verbal Learning and Verbal Behavior*, **3**, 449–59.

TREISMAN, A. and GELADE, G. (1980) A feature integration theory of attention. *Cognitive Psychology*, **12**, 97–136.

TREISMAN, A. and SCHMIDT, H. (1982) Illusory conjunctions in the perception of objects. *Cognitive Psychology*, **14**, 107–41.

TREVARTHEN, C.B. (1968) Two mechanisms of vision in primates. *Psychologische Forschung*, **31**, 338–48.

TREVARTHEN, C.B. and HUBLEY, P.A. (1978) Secondary intersubjectivity: confidence, confiding and acts of meaning in the first year. In A. Lock, ed., *Action, Gesture and Symbols: the Emergence of Language*. London: Academic Press.

TRYON, R.C. (1940) Genetic differences in maze learning ability in rats. *Thirty-ninth Yearbook of the National Society for Studies in Education*, Part 1, 111–19.

TULVING, E. (1972) Episodic and semantic memory. In E. Tulving and W. Donaldson, eds., *Organization of Memory*. New York: Academic Press.

TULVING, E. (1979) Relation between encoding specificity and levels of processing. In L.S. Cermak and F.I.M. Craik, eds., *Levels of Processing in Human Memory*. Hillsdale, NJ: Erlbaum.

TULVING, E. and MADIGAN, S.A. (1970) Memory and verbal learning. *Annual Review of Psychology*, **21**, 437–84.

TURNER, J. (1977) *Psychology for the Classroom*. London: Methuen.

TURNER, J.C. (1981) Experimental social psychology of intergroup behaviour. In J.C. Turner and H. Giles, eds., *Intergroup Behaviour*. Oxford: Basil Blackwell.

TURNURE, J., BUIUM, N. and THURLOW, M. (1976) The effectiveness of interrogatives for promoting verbal elaboration productivity in young children. *Child Development*, **47**, 851–5.

TVERSKY, A. and KAHNEMAN, D. (1973) Availability: a heuristic for judging frequency and probability. *Cognitive Psychology*, **5**, 207–32.

TVERSKY, B. (1973) Encoding processes in recognition and recall. *Cognitive Psychology*, **5**, 275–87.

TWENEY, R.D., DOHERTY, M.E. and MYNATT, C.R., eds. (1980) *On Scientific Thinking*. New York: Columbia University Press.

TYLER, S.W., HERTEL, P.T., McCALLUM, M.C. and ELLIS, H.C. (1979) Cognitive effort and memory. *Journal of Experimental Psychology: Human Learning and Memory*, **5**, 607–17.

ULLMAN, S. (1980) Against direct perception. *Behavior and Brain Sciences*, **3**, 373–416.

VALINS, S. (1966) Cognitive effects of false heart-rate feedback. *Journal of Personality and Social Psychology*, **4**, 400–8.

VELLUTINO, F.R. (1979) *Theory and Research in Dyslexia*. Cambridge, Mass.: MIT Press.

VENABLES, P.H. (1977) Input dysfunction in schizophrenia. Postscript. In B.A. Maher, ed., *Contributions to the Psychopathology of Schizophrenia*. London: Academic Press.

VERNON, M. (1967) Relationship of language to the thinking process. *Archives of General Psychiatry*, **16**, 325–33.

VERNON, M. (1968) Fifty years of research on the intelligence of deaf and hard of hearing children: a review of literature and discussion of implications. *Journal of the Rehabilitation of the Deaf*, **1**, 1–12.

VERNON, P.E. (1979) *Intelligence: Heredity and Environment*. San Francisco: Freeman.

VURPILLOT, E. (1976) *The Visual World of the Child*. London: Allen and Unwin.

VYGOTSKY, L.S. (1962) *Thought and Language*. Cambridge, Mass.: MIT Press.

WALKER, B.B. and DANDMAN, C.A. (1977) Physiological response patterns in ulcer patients: phasic and tonic components of the electrogastrogram. *Psychophysiology*, **14**, 393–400.

WARD, I. (1972) Prenatal stress feminizes and demasculinizes the behavior of males. *Science*, **175**, 82–4.

WARR, P.B. (1978) *Psychology at Work*. Harmondsworth: Penguin.

WARRINGTON, E.K. (1982) Neuropsychological studies of object recognition. *Philosophical Transactions of the Royal Society*, London B, **298**, 15–33.

WASON, P.C. and JOHNSON-LAIRD, P.N. (1970) A conflict between selecting and evaluating information in an inferential task. *British Journal of Psychology*, **61**, 509–15.

WASON, P.C. and JOHNSON-LAIRD, P.N. (1977) *Thinking: Readings in Cognitive Science*. Cambridge: Cambridge University Press.

WATKINS, M.J. (1978) Theoretical issues. In M.M. Gruneberg and P. Morris, eds., *Aspects of Memory*. London: Methuen.

WATSON, J.B. (1919) *Psychology from the Standpoint of a Behaviorist*. Philadelphia: Lippincott.

WATSON, O. (1972) *Proxemic Behaviour: Cross-cultural Study*. The Hague: Mouton.

WEISKRANTZ, L. (1980) Varieties of residual experience. *Quarterly Journal of Experimental Psychology*, **32**, 365–86.

WEISKRANTZ, L, (1982) Comparative aspects of studies of amnesia. *Philosophical Transactions of the Royal Society*, London B, **298**, 97–109.

WEISKRANTZ, L., WARRINGTON, E.K., SANDERS, M.D. and MARSHALL, J. (1974) Visual capacity in the hemioscopic field following a restricted occipital ablation. *Brain*, **97**, 709–28.

WELLS, M.J. (1958) Factors affecting reactions to Mysis by newly hatched Sepia. *Behaviour*, **13**, 96–111.

WEST, S.G. and WICKLUND, R.A. (1980) *A Primer of Social Psychological Theories*. Monterey, Calif.: Brooks/Cole.

WHITE, B.L. (1971) *Human Infants. Experience and Psychological Development*. Englewood Cliffs, NJ: Prentice-Hall.

WHITE, C. (1977) Unpublished doctoral dissertation, Catholic University, Washington, DC.

WHORF, B.L. (1956) *Language, Thought and Reality: Selected Writings of Benjamin Lee Whorf*. Edited by J.B. Carroll. New York: MIT Press.

WICKELGREN, W.A. (1973) The long and the short of memory. *Psychological Bulletin*, **80**, 425–38.

WICKELGREN, W.A. (1974) Single trace fragility theory of memory dynamics. *Memory and Cognition*, **2**, 775–80.

WICKER, A.W. (1969) Attitudes versus actions: the relationship of verbal and overt behavioural responses to attitude objects. *Journal of Social Issues*, **25**, 41–78.

WIGGINS, T.S., RENNER, K.E., CLORE, G.L. and ROSE, R.J. (1971) *The Psychology of Personality*. London: Addison-Wesley.

WILCOXON, H.C., DRAGOIN, W.B. and KRAL, P.A. (1971) Illness-induced aversions in rat and quail: relative salience of visual and gustatory cues. *Science*, **171**, 826–8.

WILSON, E.O. (1978) *On Human Nature*. Cambridge, Mass: Harvard University Press.

WILSON, R.S., KASZNIAK, A.W., KLAWANS, H.L. and GARRON, D.C. (1980) High speed memory scanning in Parkinsonism. *Cortex*, **16**, 67–72.

WINTERBOTTOM, M. (1953) The sources of achievement motivation in mother's attitudes toward independence training. In D.C. McClelland *et al.*, eds., *The Achievement Motive*. New York: Appleton-Century-Crofts.

WOLF, S. and WOLFF, H.G. (1947) *Human Gastric Function*. New York: Oxford University Press.

WOLPE, J. (1958) *Psychotherapy by Reciprocal Inhibition*. Stanford, Calif.: Stanford University Press.

WORD, C.H., ZANNA, M.P. and COOPER, J. (1974) The non-verbal mediation of self-fulfilling prophecies in interracial interaction. *Journal of Experimental Social Psychology*, **10**, 109–20.

WRIGHT, A. and VLIETSTRA(1975) Development of selective attention: from perceptual explanations to logical search. In L.B. Cohen and P. Salapatek, eds., *Infant Perception: From Sensation to Cognition*. New York: Academic Press.

WUNDT, W. (1916) *Elements of Folk Psychology: Outlines of a Psychological History of the Development of Mankind*. Translated by L. Schaub. London: Allen and Unwin.

YOCHELSON, S. and SAMENOW, S.E. (1976) *The Criminal Personality*. New York: Aronson.

YONAS, A., BECHTOLD, A.G., FRANKEL, D., GORDON, F.R., McROBERTS, G., NORCIA, A. and STERNFELS, S. (1977) Development of sensitivity to information for impending collision. *Perception and Psychophysics*, 21, 97–104.

YONAS, A., PETTERSEN, L. and LOCKMAN, J.C. (1979) Young infants' sensitivity to optical information for collisions. *Canadian Journal of Psychology*, 33, 268–276.

YOUNG, R.M. (1976) *Seriation by Children: an Artificial Intelligence Analysis of a Piagetian Task*. Birkhausen.

YUSSEN, S.R. and LEVY, V.M. (1975) Developmental changes in predicting one's own span of short-term memory. *Journal of Experimental Child Psychology*, 19, 502–8.

ZAIDEL, E. (1976) Auditory vocabulary of the right hemisphere after brain bisection or hemidecortication. *Cortex*, 12, 191–211.

ZAIDEL, E. (1977) Unilateral auditory language comprehension on the Token Test following cerebral commissurotomy and hemispherectomy. *Neuropsychologia*, 15, 1–13.

ZAJONC, R.B. (1965) Social faclitation. *Science*, 149, 269–74.

ZAJONC, R.B. and MARKUS, G.B. (1975) Birth order and intellectual development. *Psychological Review*, 82, 74–88.

ZANNA, M.P., KIESLER, C.A. and PILKONIS, P.A. (1970) Positive and negative attitudinal affect established by classical conditioning. *Journal of Personality and Social Psychology*, 14, 321–8.

ZECHMEISTER, E.B. and NYBERG, S.E. (1982) *Human Memory: an Introduction to Research and Theory*. Monterey, Calif.: Brooks/Cole.

ZELAZO, P.R. and KOMER, M.J. (1971) Infant smiling to nonsocial stimuli and the recognition hypothesis. *Child Development*, 42, 1327–39.

ZIHL, J. (1980) 'Blindsight': improvement of visually guided eye movements by systematic practice in patients with cerebral blindness. *Neuropsychologia*, 18, 71–8.

ZILLMANN, D. (1978) Attribution and misattribution of excitatory reactions. In J.H. Harvey, W. Ickes and R.F. Kidd, eds., *New Directions in*

Attribution Research, Volume 2. Hillsdale, NJ: Erlbaum.

ZILLMANN, D. (1982) Television viewing and arousal. In D. Pearl, L. Bouthilet and J. Lazar, eds., *Television and Behavior: Ten Years of Scientific Progress and Implications for the Eighties*, Volume 2. Washington, DC: US Department of Health and Human Services.

ZILLMANN, D. and SAPOLSKY, B.S. (1977) What mediates the effect of mild erotica on annoyance and hostile behavior in males? *Journal of Personality and Social Psychology*, **35**, 587–96.

ZUCKERMAN, M., HALL, J.A., DEFRANK, R.S. and ROSENTHAL, R. (1976) Encoding and decoding of spontaneous and posed facial expressions. *Journal of Personality and Social Psychology*, **34**, 966–77.

Acknowledgements

Acknowledgement is due to the following authors and publishers for permission to reproduce, or derive, figures and tables in which they hold copyright. (Should appropriate acknowledgement have been omitted in any instance, we apologize, and will correct this in a future edition.)

FIGURES

2.1: B. Kolb and I. Q. Whishaw, and W. H. Freeman Inc. 2.5: W. J. Nauta and M. M. Feirtag, and Scientific American Inc. 4.3: P. McLeod and Academic Press Inc. 4.4: *Neuropsychologia*, 18, J. Zihl, 'Blindsight', copyright ©1980, Pergamon Press Ltd. 5.1: R. N. Shepard and *Science*, 171, copyright © 1971 by the American Association for the Advancement of Science. 6.1: R. C. Atkinson and R. M. Shiffrin, and Scientific American Inc. 6.3: A. D. Baddeley, *The Psychology of Memory*, Basic Books. 9.3: K. O'Bryan and F. Boersma, and Academic Press Inc. 10.1: A. Kendon and North Holland Publishing Co. 10.2: S. Farnham-Diggory and L. Gregg, and Academic Press Inc. 11.2: R. Rogers and R. Mewborn, and the American Psychological Association. 13.1: H. J. Eysenck and S. Rachman, and *Nature*.

TABLES

9.1: E. H. Lenneberg, *Science* and the American Association for the Advancement of Science. 9.2: R. Brown and Free Press, Macmillan. 10.3: S. Farnham-Diggory and L. Gregg, and Academic Press Inc.

Index

Compiled by Alan Pickering